THE PRISON LETTERS OF

NELSON MANDELA

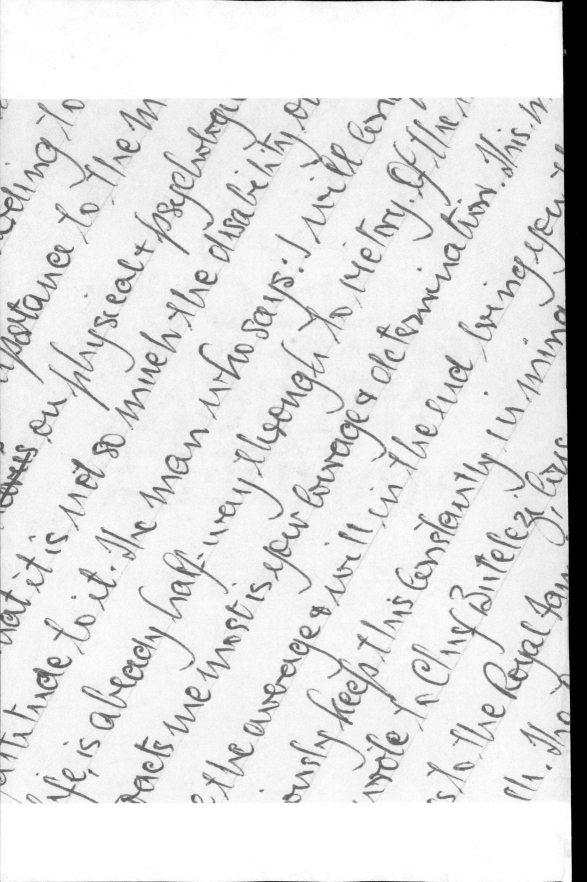

THE PRISON LETTERS OF
NELSON
MANDELA

EDITED BY **SAHM VENTER**
FOREWORD BY **ZAMASWAZI DLAMINI-MANDELA**

LIVERIGHT PUBLISHING CORPORATION
A Division of W. W. Norton & Company
Independent Publishers Since 1923
New York · London

For information about permission to reproduce selections from this book,
write to Permissions, Liveright Publishing Corporation, a division of
W. W. Norton & Company, Inc., 500 Fifth Avenue, New York, NY 10110

For information about special discounts for bulk purchases, please contact
W. W. Norton Special Sales at specialsales@wwnorton.com or 800-233-4830

Manufacturing by LSC Communications, Harrisonburg
Book design by Cameron Gibb
Production manager: Anna Oler

Produced and originated by Blackwell and Ruth Limited
405 IronBank, 150 Karangahape Road, Auckland 1010, New Zealand
www.blackwellandruth.com

ISBN 978-1-63149-117-7

Liveright Publishing Corporation, 500 Fifth Avenue, New York, N.Y. 10110
www.wwnorton.com

W. W. Norton & Company Ltd., 15 Carlisle Street, London W1D 3BS

NELSON MANDELA
FOUNDATION
Living the legacy

www.nelsonmandelafoundation.org

1 2 3 4 5 6 7 8 9 0

CONTENTS

FOREWORD

By the time I was born, my grandfather had already been in prison for seventeen years. In a letter to my grandmother, Winnie Madikizela-Mandela, shortly after his sixty-second birthday, he lists the people that he has received telegrams and cards from, including my Aunt Zindzi, my sister, Zaziwe, and me, and the people he's expecting and hoping to hear from. 'So far I have received not a single one of the multitude that friends have sent from all over the world,' he jokes. 'Nevertheless, it is very comforting to know that so many friends still think of us after so many yrs.' It's one of many examples in this book that shows how communication from the outside world bolstered him through his twenty-seven years in prison, and just how much he yearned for those letters.

During his incarceration, my grandfather wrote many hundreds of letters. The selection that appears in this book intimately acquaints readers not only with Nelson Mandela the political activist and prisoner, but with Nelson Mandela the lawyer, father, husband, uncle and friend, and illustrates how his lengthy incarceration, far away from everyday life, impeded him in carrying out these roles. It revisits a very dark time in South Africa's history where those caught opposing the apartheid government's system to oppress an entire race of people, endured terrible punishments. Through his letters he documents the ongoing persecution of my grandmother and provides insight into what it must have been like for his children, Thembi, Makgatho, Makaziwe, Zenani, and Zindzi, to have an absent father that they could barely communicate with or – this I found unbearable – even visit until they turned sixteen. As much as he tried to parent his children from prison, he couldn't.

What has particularly affected me, especially as a mother, is witnessing through my grandfather's letters what my mother and my Aunt Zindzi went through as children. Often they were left parentless while my grandmother was imprisoned as well, sometimes because of her involvement in anti-apartheid activities but often for being the wife of one of South Africa's most well-known political prisoners.

Most heartrending, is the wistful optimism in many of the letters to my grandmother and his children where my grandfather suggests, 'Perhaps one day we will . . .' and 'One day we shall . . . '. That happily-ever-after day never came for my grandparents, my mom, and my aunts and uncles. The children suffered the most, and ultimately the consequences of forfeiting a stable family life for his ideals was a sacrifice that my grandfather just had to make peace with.

My grandfather always reminded us that we should never forget our past or where we come from. The democratic society that both my grandparents and their comrades fought for was achieved after a lot of suffering and loss of life. This book is a reminder that we could easily go back to that place of hatred, but it also shows that personal resilience can overcome unendurable situations. From day one in prison, my grandfather resolved that he would not break or waver; instead he would insist that he and his fellow prisoners be treated with dignity. In a letter to my grandmother in 1969, he recommends she boosts her spirits by reading psychologist Norman Vincent Peale's 1952 bestseller *The Power of Positive Thinking*. He writes: 'I attach no importance to the metaphysical aspects of his arguments, but I consider his views on physical & psychological issues valuable.

'He makes the basic point that it is not so much the disability one suffers from that matters but one's attitude to it. The man who says: I will conquer this illness & live a happy life, is already halfway through to victory.'

This inspirational outlook sustained my grandfather's unwavering pursuit of justice and an equal society for all South Africans, and is one that I think can be applied to many of life's challenges.

This collection has answered many of the questions that used to baffle me: How did my grandfather survive twenty-seven years in jail? What kept him going? Through his words we can find the answers.

Zamaswazi Dlamini-Mandela

INTRODUCTION

A raft of draconian regulations governing the writing of letters by
South African political prisoners and their random implementation by mean-spirited guards was designed to control the most
precious aspects of a prisoner's soul – their contact with loved ones and
news of the outside world.[1]

After political prisoners were sentenced in court, they were assigned to
the prison where they were supposed to serve their punishment. In Nelson
Mandela's case, his life as a condemned prisoner began in Pretoria Local
Prison after he received a five-year sentence on 7 November 1962 for leaving the country without a passport and inciting workers to strike. Already
a prisoner, he was brought back to court on sabotage charges in 1963, and
on 12 June 1964 he received a lifelong sentence. His wife, Winnie Mandela,
visited him in Pretoria that day, and hours later, without warning, he and six
of the seven comrades sentenced with him were taken from Pretoria for the
long flight in a military aircraft to the notorious prison on Robben Island.
They arrived on a bitterly cold winter morning on 13 June 1964. Unlike
inmates who had committed 'common law' crimes like rape, robbery, and
assault, who were classified as C Grade and sometimes B Grade on arrival,
political prisoners were assigned to D Grade, the lowest possible classification with the least privileges. They were allowed only one visitor every six
months and were entitled to write and receive only one letter of five hundred words every six months. So unpredictable was the process of sending
and receiving letters that six years after he was imprisoned, Mandela met
with his lawyers on Robben Island and listed examples of 'unreasonable
and vexatious behaviour and conduct of the authorities'. He said that the
disruptions to his correspondence, 'indicate a deliberate intention and
policy on the part of the authorities to cut me off and isolate me from all
external contacts, to frustrate and demoralise me, to make me despair and
lose all hope and eventually break me.'[2]

Later on, when the censors tired of counting words, they began accepting letters of a page and a half.[3] Letters to their lawyers and prison authorities did not come from their quota. Saturdays and Sundays were earmarked
for visits, and letters were delivered on a Saturday. Prisoners could give up a

visit in exchange for the receipt of two letters. Initially, both visits and correspondence had to be with 'first degree relatives'. Prisoners were forbidden from mentioning other prisoners in their letters or from writing about prison conditions or anything the authorities may have construed as being 'political'.[4] Every letter went through the Censor's Office on Robben Island, where incoming and outgoing mail was checked.[5] Decades later, Mandela recalled:

> They didn't want you to discuss things other than family matters and especially when they were considered by them to be of a political nature. And that was the reason, that you must confine yourself purely to family matters. And then there was ignorance of language. If you used the word 'war', it doesn't matter what context, they would say, 'Take it out' because they didn't understand the language very well. And war is war; it can't have any other meaning. If you said the 'war of ideas', then you had said something you were not supposed to say.[6]

In his book about the fifteen years he spent as a prisoner on Robben Island, in the same section as Mandela, Eddie Daniels paints a picture of the 'frustration' of arbitrary, incompetent, and 'vindictive' censoring and holding back of letters.[7]

Conditions began to improve slightly from 1967, arguably due to the intervention of Helen Suzman – an opposition member of Parliament to whom Mandela reported 'a reign of terror' on the Island. The International Committee of the Red Cross and the prisoners' own efforts also contributed to these changes. They were then allowed to write and receive one letter every three months and be visited every three months.[8]

A prisoner was supposed to remain in a category of privileges for two years, meaning that after six years D Grade prisoners would be in A Grade, with the most privileges. Mandela, however, remained in D Grade for ten years. We can see from his letters, where he sometimes wrote his grade (the prisoners also referred to this as a 'group'), that he was in B Grade in 1972 and finally received A Grade designation in 1973, allowing the writing and receiving of six letters each month.[9]

Before being upgraded, a prisoner had to have their behaviour assessed by the prison board, which conducted discussions with prisoners that Mandela said were for the purposes of 'victimising' political prisoners.[10]

Despite the relentless censoring by bureaucrats, Nelson Mandela the prisoner became a prolific correspondent. He copied down his letters in notebooks to aid him with rewriting them when the censors refused to send them unless he removed certain paragraphs or when letters went missing in transit. He also liked to keep a record of what he'd said to whom. Jailed from 5 August 1962 until 11 February 1990, he wrote hundreds of letters. Not all of them, however, reached their destination in one piece. Some were censored to the extent that they became unintelligible, others were delayed for no reason, and some were not sent at all. Some he managed to smuggle out in the belongings of prisoners being released.

Prisoners were rarely informed if a letter remained unsent and usually discovered this if a recipient complained of not having received a letter. It is not known, for instance, whether all the letters he wrote to Adelaide Tambo under the guise of various nicknames reached her in London where she was living in exile with her husband, Oliver Tambo, president of the African National Congress (ANC) and Mandela's former law partner. The letters were likely intended for both of them. We do know from fellow prisoner Michael Dingake that Mandela had 'demanded the right to correspond with O. R. Tambo and exchange views on the liberation struggle.'[11]

A father of five young children when he was first taken into prison, Mandela was not allowed to see his children until they were sixteen years old. Letters became a vital tool of his parenting.

In an official letter of complaint to officials twelve years into his imprisonment, Mandela wrote, 'I sometimes wish science could invent miracles and make my daughter get her missing birthday cards and have the pleasure of knowing that her Pa loves her, thinks of her and makes efforts to reach her whenever necessary. It is significant that repeated attempts on her part to reach me and the photos she has sent have disappeared without trace whatsoever.'

The most painful of Mandela's letters is the series of 'Special Letters' in addition to his quota, written after the deaths of his beloved mother, Nosekeni, in 1968, and of his firstborn, his son Thembi, a year later. Forbidden from attending their funerals, he was reduced to consoling his children and other family members in letters through this harrowing time, and writing to thank senior family members for stepping up and ensuring that his mother and son got the send-offs they deserved.

A lawyer by profession, Mandela habitually used the written word to press officials to uphold prisoners' human rights, and on at least two occasions he wrote to officials demanding that they release him and his comrades.

Dingake described Mandela's role in prison from the early 1960s as that of a 'battering ram'.[12] In the face of 'atrocious' conditions, he could not be ignored, 'not only because of his status, but because he would "not let them do it"'.[13] His relentless campaigning for prisoners' rights eventually broke down the resolve of the authorities to have each prisoner raise their complaints individually.[14] Mandela 'defiantly continued to describe general conditions' in his letters to the commissioner of prisons, and the rest of the prisoners began laying personal complaints 'at every opportunity'. It was 'impossible', Dingake writes, for guards to record the 'complaints from every single.one of more than a thousand inmates'.[15] The rule was 'repealed by practice' and individuals or groups from each section in the prison were allowed to speak on behalf of all the prisoners.[16]

During his discussions and in letters to government officials in the late 1980s, Mandela urged for the release of his comrades. See for instance his letters to the commissioner of prisons dated 11 September 1989 (page 545) and 10 October 1989 (page 556). Finally Mandela's efforts bore fruit when the remaining five men sentenced with him to life were freed on 15 October 1989. (Denis Goldberg had been freed in 1985 and Govan Mbeki in 1987.) He walked out of prison less than four months later.

Nelson Mandela has left us a rich archive of letters documenting his twenty-seven years in prison, which echo his anger, his self-control, and his love for family and country.

A NOTE ON THE LETTERS

Nelson Mandela's prison letters are not housed under one roof, and compiling this book has taken almost ten years. These letters have been drawn from various collections: Mandela's prison files held by the National Archives and Records Service of South Africa, the Himan Bernadt Collection, and the collections of Meyer de Waal, Morabo Morojele, Fatima Meer, Michael Dingake, Amina Cachalia, Peter Wellman, and Ray Carter. Letters are also taken from the Donald Card Collection, named for the former security policemen who in 2004 returned to Mandela the hardcover notebooks in which he copied his letters before he handed them in for posting. Both the Himan Bernadt Collection and the Donald Card Collection are held by the Nelson Mandela Foundation. The books were taken from his cell in 1971, and he complains about this in a letter to authorities on 4 April 1971. For a list of where the individual letters are housed, see page 600.

The National Archives and Records Service of South Africa houses by far the majority of Mandela's prison letters. Encased alongside other official paperwork in string-tied bundles assembled in cardboard folders, they fill some fifty-nine boxes. The letters represent the Prisons Department's record of letters he wrote and received. In some cases the originals remain as evidence that they were never sent.

Since most of these letters are copies of the originals, their legibility depends on the way in which they were photocopied, the paper used, and how the ink has faded over time. Some letters are missing words that have been left off the sides during photocopying by prison officials or sliced out of the paper during censoring. In the case of some of the letters, we will never know exactly what Mandela wrote.

Heartbreakingly, a long and loving letter to his youngest daughter, Zindziswa, still neatly folded in its plain white envelope, was found in his prison archives nineteen years after his release from prison. It was accompanied by a note from a prison official who wrote that Mandela was not allowed to send a letter with a Christmas card. Written on 9 December

1979, it is a beautiful reaching out from a father longing for his daughter. She was supposed to have received it in time for her nineteenth birthday from the father she lost when she was a baby of twenty months. Such was the arbitrary and cruel control over correspondence.

The letters in this selection have been reproduced in their entirety apart from in several cases where we have omitted information in the interests of privacy. To avoid repetition, we have also omitted Mandela's address from nearly all of the letters – the book is divided into sections according to the four different prisons and two different hospitals he was housed in.

We have reproduced the text exactly as Mandela wrote it apart from correcting the odd misspelt word or name (of which there are, typically, very few), very occasionally adding or removing punctuation for ease of reading, or removing superscript in numbers that appear in dates. We have retained his various styles of writing dates and his abbreviations. One cannot know precisely why he frequently wrote 'yr' for 'year' and 'chdn' for 'children', but it may have been to keep the letters to the set limit of one and a half pages after prison censors stopped counting the number of words. When discussing books, Mandela usually formatted their titles in quotation marks. In instances where he hasn't, we have formatted these in italics as per standard editorial conventions. Mandela often used square brackets instead of parentheses. However, to avoid confusing his original text with editorial interpolations, we have replaced his square brackets with parentheses unless otherwise noted.

We have retained the underlining that appears under certain words and passages in particular letters. Usually these were made by prison censors suspicious of individuals or events being discussed. Sometimes Mandela underlined passages. We've noted where underlining appears to be the censors' work, where it appears to be Mandela's own, and where it is too hard to tell. Mandela often wrote letters in Afrikaans and isiXhosa, the language he grew up speaking, and we have noted which of these letters have been translated into English for inclusion in this publication. Some letters were also typed by prison officials and we have also noted these instances.

Mandela signed off his letters in various ways depending on who the recipient was. In official correspondence he includes his signature, 'NR Mandela', the 'R' representing his given name, Rolihlahla. In letters to his wife, Winnie Mandela, and certain family members he often signs off as Dalibunga, the name given to him after he underwent the traditional initiation into manhood at the age of sixteen. To others he is Nelson or Nel, the name given to him at his first school by his teacher, Miss Mdingane, according to the custom at the time where African children were given an

English name. To his children he is Tata, 'father' in isiXhosa, and to his grandchildren, he is Khulu, 'granddad' in isiXhosa.

It has not been possible to identify every individual mentioned but, where available, enlightening detail about individuals, locations, and events referred to in the letters has been included in the footnotes. An extensive glossary at the end of the book includes additional information about many of the individuals and events frequently referred to by Mandela.

To avoid readers having to keep track of the host of individuals Mandela refers to, many of whom are often known by more than one name, such as Winnie Mandela, or who are mentioned in letters many years apart, we have treated each letter as its own entity. Therefore, the first time an individual is mentioned in a letter, we have included a footnote explaining who they are despite the same reference appearing in earlier or subsequent letters. We have also applied this approach to the referencing of events and places. Although in some cases this may seem repetitive, we decided it was the most reader-friendly approach, particularly for the reader who chooses to dip in and out of this book which we hope you do, many times.

NELSON MANDELA'S
PRISON NUMBERS

R ather than being identified by name, prisoners were issued with prison numbers by which they were, at first, always referred to and which they had to use in any correspondence. The first part of the number was based on how many prisoners had been admitted to a particular prison that year; the second part of the number listed the year. Nelson Mandela's best-known prison number is 466/64. Years after his release, at a concert in Cape Town launching an HIV awareness campaign using his prison numbers, he said: 'I was supposed to have been reduced to that number.'[17]

Mandela was on Robben Island twice, which meant that he was allocated two different prison numbers for that prison. During his twenty-seven years of incarceration, Mandela was held in four prisons after he was sentenced and was issued with six different prison numbers.

19476/62	Pretoria Local Prison: 7 November 1962–25 May 1963
191/63	Robben Island: 27 May 1963–12 June 1963
11657/63	Pretoria Local Prison: 12 June 1963–12 June 1964
466/64	Robben Island: 13 June 1964–31 March 1982
220/82	Pollsmoor Prison: 31 March 1982–12 August 1988 Tygerberg Hospital: 12 August 1988–31 August 1988 Constantiaberg MediClinic: 31 August 1988–7 December 1988
1335/88	Victor Verster Prison: 7 December 1988–11 February 1990

PRETORIA
LOCAL PRISON

|||||||||||

NOVEMBER 1962–MAY 1963

For just six months in 1962, while on his clandestine tour out of South Africa to African countries and London, UK, Mandela lived the life of a free man when he was not subjected to apartheid rules and could move around as he chose. On Thursday, 11 January 1962 he secretly left South Africa by road for a tour of the newly independent African states. Mandela was asked by the underground structures of his organisation, the African National Congress, or ANC, to speak at a conference of African nations in Ethiopia and also to travel the continent raising funds and support for the fight ahead. Two years earlier, in 1960, the ANC had been outlawed and a year later it had accepted the inevitability of an armed struggle to campaign for equal rights and democracy in South Africa. In the middle of 1961 the organisation had decided to form an armed wing, and Umkhonto weSizwe (Spear of the Nation) was born. Also known as MK for short, it was launched with a series of explosions of strategic targets with the intent to avoid loss of life.

If this known opponent of the apartheid regime had applied for a passport, it would have been refused. Besides, he was wanted by the police for continuing underground the activities of the illegal ANC.

He travelled under the name David Motsamayi, a name he had borrowed from a client at his law firm, and used at least one fake passport. Ethiopia had provided one and, it is said, so did Senegal.

The journey took him to sixteen independent African countries and in two of them, Morocco and Ethiopia, he underwent military training. In between he visited London for ten days where he caught up with old friends and comrades, including Oliver Tambo and his wife Adelaide. Tambo, who later became president of the ANC in 1967 after the death of Chief Albert Luthuli, had joined Mandela on some of his travels in Africa.

Mandela's freedom came to an end one Sunday afternoon on a country road near Howick, a small town in the east of South Africa. It was 5 August 1962. He and fellow anti-apartheid activist and theatre director Cecil Williams were en route by car to Johannesburg. Mandela had been in the area to brief ANC president Chief Albert Luthuli[i] and others about his trip. A meal with friends the day before was to be his last celebration for nearly three decades.

As part of his repertoire of disguises, Mandela would often masquerade

---

i   Chief Albert Luthuli (1898–1967), president-general of the ANC, 1952–67 – see the glossary.

as the chauffeur of a white man. On that day, however, Williams was behind the wheel of his Austin when the driver of a Ford V8 suddenly overtook them and ordered Williams to stop. It was the police. Dressed in a coat and cap and wearing dark glasses, Mandela denied that he was in fact Nelson Mandela and insisted he was David Motsamayi, but they were sure they had their man and so was he. He considered making a run for it but knew that the game, so to speak, was up. Speaking about it just more than thirty years later, Mandela said: 'I was very fit those days, and I could virtually climb any wall. And then I looked at the back, just at the rearview mirror. I saw there were two cars behind, then I felt that no it would be ridiculous for me to try and escape, they'll shoot me. And we stopped.'[18]

The men summarily were arrested and the police drove them back some 9 miles to Pietermaritzburg where Mandela was held overnight, appearing briefly before a local magistrate the next morning. He was driven on to Johannesburg and locked up at the Old Fort Prison, preserved today as a museum within the precinct of the Constitutional Court of South Africa. Over the next ten days Mandela appeared twice in the Johannesburg Magistrates' Court and his case was remanded for trial on 15 October. On Saturday, 13 October he was informed that he would be moved to the city of Pretoria, where, on Monday, 15 October, he appeared in the Old Synagogue, temporarily named a 'special regional court', for his trial. His appearance stunned the public gallery and officials alike. Around his broad shoulders he wore a kaross made of multiple jackal skins sewn together on a large piece of fabric. The rest of his ensemble included a T-shirt, khaki trousers, sandals, and a yellow and green beaded necklace. He wanted to be seen as African in an unequal society.[19]

The lawyer Mandela who, having passed the requisite attorneys' admission examination in 1952, had practised in his own firm for years, defended himself, taking advice from Advocate Bob Hepple,[i] who, ironically, would join him and nine others on trial for sabotage the next year. Mandela employed the tactic of speaking from the dock, which freed him from testifying under cross-examination. In his first speech to the court, on 22 October 1962, he called for the recusal of the magistrate, Mr. W. A. van Helsdingen, saying that as a black man he would not get a fair trial.[20] After hearing his plea, Van Helsdingen refused to step down.

Mandela recalled how on the last day of the trial, 7 November 1962, the prosecutor, Mr. D. J. Bosch, whom he knew from his days as a lawyer, went to the holding cell and apologised to him about having to ask for his conviction. 'He then just embraced me and kissed me on the cheeks, and he

---

i   Bob Hepple (1934–2015), lawyer, academic, and anti-apartheid activist – see the glossary.

says, "Today I didn't want to come to court. For me to come to court to ask for conviction against you is something that upset me." So I thanked him.'[21]

Hepple reluctantly left the room while they spoke, and later wrote: 'When Bosch came out of the cell about five minutes later, I saw tears streaming down his face. I asked Mandela: "What the hell's going on?" He replied: "You won't believe this but he asked me to forgive him." I exclaimed, "Nel, I hope you told him to get stuffed." To my surprise, Mandela responded: "No, I did not. I told him I knew he was just doing his job, and thanked him for his good wishes."'[22]

In his judgment, Van Helsdingen said it was clear that Mandela had been 'the mastermind' behind a strike in May 1961 against South Africa's plans to abandon its membership of the Commonwealth and become a republic.[23]

Mandela made another lengthy speech from the dock after being convicted on both charges, and said: 'Whatever sentence you pass on me, you can rest assured that, when it is completed, I will still be moved by my dislike of race discrimination and will take up again the fight against injustices until they are removed once and for all.'[24]

Van Helsdingen called the case 'distressing and difficult' and declared that Mandela's actions should be 'put down with a strong hand'. It was clear, he maintained, that what Mandela was really doing was trying to 'overthrow the Government'.[25]

At the end of the short trial in which he had mounted no defence apart from his two speeches, Mandela was sentenced to three years' imprisonment on the charge of inciting a strike and to an additional two years' imprisonment for leaving the country without a South African passport. He was forty-four years old.

Immediately after he was sentenced, Mandela had his status changed from that of a prisoner awaiting trial to that of a convict in the same prison. He was held with Robert Mangaliso Sobukwe, a university lecturer and a former ANC colleague who had led a split from the party to found the Pan Africanist Congress (PAC),[26] and several other members of that organisation. Sobukwe and his comrades had been sentenced two years earlier for their involvement in an anti-pass protest in which sixty-nine unarmed demonstrators were shot dead by police. It became known as the Sharpeville Massacre.

The first letter in this collection is one Mandela wrote the day before his conviction and sentencing, to Mr. Louis Blom-Cooper, a British advocate sent by the organisation then known as Amnesty to observe the trial. During the case, Mandela applied a second time for the recusal of the magistrate after Blom-Cooper informed him that he had seen Van Helsdingen driving from the court in the company of the investigating officer. Van Helsdingen again rejected the application, saying only that he 'did not communicate with the two detectives'.[27]

After his release Mandela described Blom-Cooper as 'tremendous', and said of the incident: 'He behaved just like an Englishman, you know, their desire to challenge anything that looks wrong. Whilst I was cross-examining the state witnesses, the magistrate was seen to leave the courthouse with an investigating officer, and Blom-Cooper immediately prepared an affidavit and went to the registrar to sign it before the registrar of the Supreme Court. And he came to me with this affidavit and he says, "Here is an affidavit."'[28]

To the secretary, Amnesty

6.11.62

The Secretary
Amnesty
LONDON

Dear Sir,

We are most grateful to your organisation for sending Mr L Blom Cooper to attend the trial.

His mere presence, as well as the assistance he gave, were a source of tremendous inspiration and encouragement to us.

The fact that he sat next to us furnished yet another proof that honest and upright men, and democratic organisations, throughout the civilised world are on our side in the struggle for a democratic South Africa.

Finally, I must ask you to accept this note as a very firm, warm and hearty handshake from me.

Yours very sincerely,
Nelson

6/11/62   FOR 19

Nelson Mandela
19476/62

The Secretary
Amnesty.
LONDON

Dear Sir,

We are most grateful to your organisation for sending Mr L. Blom-Cooper to attend the trial.

His mere presence, as well as the assistance he gave, were source of tremendous inspiration and encouragement to us.

The fact that he sat next to us furnished yet another proof

Letter to the Secretary of Amnesty, written the day before his conviction and sentencing in November 1962, see opposite.

ROBBEN ISLAND MAXIMUM SECURITY PRISON

||||||||||||

MAY 1963–JUNE 1963

n late May 1963, Mandela was unexpectedly taken from Pretoria to Robben Island with three PAC prisoners.

Crammed in the back of a police van, Mandela and the three others were driven for a day and a half until they reached Cape Town where they boarded a ferry. They arrived on the notorious island on 27 May 1963. It was bleak, brutal, and bitterly cold.

The four men were steered into one cell and made to undress. Each item of clothing was searched by guards and then thrown onto a wet floor. Mandela got into an argument, and one guard moved threateningly towards him. The story Mandela told of the incident became the hallmark of his relationship with the prison authorities going forward. He would not be cowed: 'So I say, "You dare touch me, I will take you to the highest court in this land, and by the time I'm finished with you, you will be as poor as a church mouse." And he stopped. I was not, I was frightened; it was not because I was courageous, but one had to put up a front and so he stopped.'[29]

Less than three weeks later, Mandela was told to pack and was transferred back to Pretoria. He was never given any explanation and later dismissed a notion that it was in relation to the Rivonia Trial because his colleagues were arrested after he'd been transferred – two of them were detained on 24 June 1963 in Soweto and the rest on 11 July 1963.

BACK TO PRETORIA

Mandela found himself back in the Pretoria jail cells in June 1963, and within some weeks discovered that fellow MK operatives Andrew Mlangeni and Elias Motsoaledi had been arrested on their return from a trip to China for military training. One morning Mandela was running up the stairs for his morning meal (at Pretoria he was given the same food as white prisoners and said he looked forward to it) and he saw a group of fellow prisoners he recognised as some of the workers at Liliesleaf Farm, which he and his comrades had used as a hideout. 'That spoiled my whole appetite,' he said.[30]

He describes encountering Thomas Mashifane, who had been the foreman at Liliesleaf Farm, in *Long Walk to Freedom*: 'I greeted him warmly, though I realised that the authorities had undoubtedly led him to my corridor to see if I recognised or acknowledged him. I could not but do otherwise. His presence there could mean only one thing: the authorities had discovered Rivonia.'[31]

Worse was still to come. Once they had completed nearly three months in solitary confinement, Mandela met up with a group of close comrades. 'I was summoned to the prison office where I found Walter [Sisulu]; Govan Mbeki; Ahmed Kathrada; Andrew Mlangeni; Bob Hepple; Raymond Mhlaba, a member of the MK High Command who had recently returned from training in China; Elias Motsoaledi, also a member of MK; Denis Goldberg, an engineer and a member of the Congress of Democrats; Rusty Bernstein, an architect and also a member of the COD; and Jimmy Kantor,[i] an attorney. . . . We were all charged with sabotage, and scheduled to appear in court the next day.'[32]

During this new period while he was awaiting trial, Mandela kept up a steady stream of correspondence to the prison authorities – a habit that was to become a hallmark of his imprisonment.

Mandela and ten of his colleagues, including Bob Hepple, appeared in the Palace of Justice, a court in Pretoria, on 9 October 1963. The others were Walter Sisulu, Govan Mbeki, Ahmed Kathrada, Denis Goldberg, Raymond Mhlaba, Elias Motsoaledi, Andrew Mlangeni, Rusty Bernstein, and James Kantor. The case was remanded until 20 October, and on that day the defence applied to quash the indictment of more than 235 acts of sabotage which it alleged were part of a grand plan of 'violent revolution'.[33] The defence had decided to challenge it because they found it to be 'a shoddy

---

i   For details on all these individuals, see their entries in the glossary.

and imprecise document' which 'made it impossible to discern' what the charges were and who committed them.[34] Lawyer Joel Joffe wrote that the defence team had resolved 'to make it clear from the outset to the court and the prosection that we would not be swayed by the hysteria in the country' and 'we would not abandon any of the normal legal rights'.[35]

On 30 October their application was successful and all the accused, excluding Bob Hepple who had his charges withdrawn and was freed, were immediately rearrested in court and charged with sabotage. Hepple had persuaded the prosecution that he would testify for the Crown as a state witness, but he did not want to testify against people he 'admired and respected',[36] so he and his wife Shirley fled the country.

Back in court, a new indictment was introduced on 12 November. On 25 November the 199 acts of sabotage were reduced to 193, and the defence again applied to have the indictment quashed. Their application was dismissed on 26 November, and the next time the accused appeared in court was 3 December, when all ten pleaded not guilty.

On judgment day, 11 June 1964, Mandela and seven others were convicted. Bernstein was acquitted. Kantor had been acquitted on 4 March.[i]

◇◇◇◇◇◇◇◇

---

i   James Kantor's attorney John Croaker applied for Kantor's discharge 'on the basis that there was no case for him to answer' (Joel Joffe, *The State vs. Nelson Mandela: The Trial that Changed South Africa*, p. 144). Justice de Wet said he did not intend giving his reasons for discharge. On judgment day when Bernstein was acquitted and Mandela and seven others convicted, Justice de Wet said, 'I have very good reasons for the conclusions to which I have come. I don't propose to read these reasons.' (Ibid, p. 244.)

Shortly before they were taken to court to begin the eight-month trial, which became known as the Rivonia Trial, Mandela wrote to the authorities requesting permission to send his wife a birthday telegram. He signed off as 'Dalibunga', the name bestowed upon him after his traditional initiation into manhood. It means 'founder of the Bunga', the traditional ruling body of his home territory of Tran-skei (now part of the Eastern Cape province). To traditionalists, he later wrote in his autobiography Long Walk to Freedom, *this name was more acceptable than his given name of Rolihlahla – 'troublemaker' – or the name Nelson given to him at school as part of the practice of all children being given a 'Christian' name. 'I was proud to hear my new name pronounced,' he said of Dalibunga.*[37]

To the commanding officer, Pretoria Local Prison

[Translated from Afrikaans]

23 September 1963

The Commanding Officer,
The Prison
Pretoria

On the 26th of this month is my wife's birthday.

Please will you be good enough to give me permission to send her the telegram below:[i]

"NOBANDLA MANDELA, 8115 ORLANDO WEST

JOHANNESBURG

MANY HAPPY RETURNS SEE MANY MORE DARLING TONS AND TONS OF LOVE AND A MILLION KISSES DALIBUNGA"

Nelson Mandela, Pretoria

Sincerely
[Signed N R Mandela]
Prisoner No 11657/63

---

i   The text in the telegram is in English.

To the commanding officer, Pretoria Local Prison

8th October, 1963

The Commanding Officer
Pretoria Local Prison

I should be pleased if you would kindly arrange for my eyes to be tested by an eye specialist.

I have used reading glasses since 1945 and the pair I am presently using is apparently worn out. The eyes are sore and, in spite of the treatment prescribed by the Prison Medical Officer, which I have used during the last 3 weeks, the position continues to deteriorate.

The specialist who has previously tested my eyes is DR HANDELS-MAN[i] of Johannesburg and I should be pleased if you would kindly arrange for me to be examined by him again. I might add that the optician from whom I propose to obtain the spectacles, and who has made all my glasses previously, is DR BASMAN, also of Johannesburg. There is naturally the advantage of a discount if I obtain the glasses from him.

I am able and willing to finance the costs of the test and spectacles from my funds in your possession. I might also mention that this application is made on the recommendation of the Prison Medical Officer.

[Signed NRMandela]
Prisoner No. 11657/63

To the commanding officer, Pretoria Local Prison

25th October, 1963

The Commanding Officer
The Prison
PRETORIA

---

i   Dr. Gordon Handelsman was a highly sought-after opthalmologist based in Johannesburg who listed among his many patients the shah of Iran. It is not known whether Mandela was permitted to consult with him.

I refer you to my letter of the 8th instant in which I applied for my eyes to be tested by a specialist.

In the letter aforesaid, I indicated that the application was being made on the recommendation of the Prison Medical Officer. I must add that the condition of my eyes is deteriorating very rapidly and I must ask you to give the matter your urgent attention.

I must further add that I am seriously handicapped in the preparations for the forthcoming trial against me on the 29th instant. The said preparations entail the reading of numerous documents as well as a lot of writing. I find all this trying and dangerous to my health.

Finally, I must ask you to allow me to use my own clothing outfit for the purpose of appearing in court on the 29th instant.

[Signed N R Mandela]
Prisoner no. 11657/63

◇◇◇◇◇◇◇◇

Just as he did the day before he was sentenced in 1962, Mandela wrote another letter of thanks on the day of his conviction for sabotage. It was again to a foreigner who had served as an observer during his trial.

He expressed his gratitude to Mr. Coen Stork, the Dutch ambassador to South Africa, who had attended the Rivonia Trial.

The death sentence was a very real possibility and he and his comrades decided that if it was imposed, they would not appeal.[38]

If he was afraid, he was not showing it. In fact, Mandela observed that as Judge de Wet began to read his judgment, it was he who appeared nervous.[39]

After an eight-month trial the eight men were sentenced to life imprisonment. Mandela had already been in prison for 678 days.

In South Africa then, for political prisoners, 'life' meant exactly that – life. At the age of forty-five he was about to spend the rest of his life in prison.

He only knew the name of the prison that would hold him when he arrived early the next morning.

To Coen Stork, the Dutch ambassador to South Africa

11th June, 1964

Dear Mr Stork,

I am writing to you before the final outcome of this case because, thereafter, it will not be possible for me to do so.

My colleagues and I deeply appreciate the invaluable assistance you have given us. The personal interest you have shown in the case, and the strong support we are receiving from all sections of the Dutch population, give us enormous reserves of strength and courage.

We would like you to know that we regard you as one of our greatest friends, and are sure you will continue to be of assistance to our people in their struggle against racial discrimination.

UNGADINWA NANGOMSO.[i]

Yours very sincerely
[Signed NRMandela]

---

i   'Nangamso' is an isiXhosa word that expresses deep gratitude to a person who has gone beyond the call of duty. Mandela sometimes spelled it nangomso.

Pretoria Prison
Republic of South Africa.
11th June, 1964.

Dear Mr Stork,

I am writing to you before the final outcome of this case because, thereafter, it will not be possible for me to do so.

My colleagues and I deeply appreciate the invaluable assistance you have given us. The personal interest you have shown in the case, and the strong support we are receiving from all sections of the Dutch population, give us enormous reserves of strength and courage.

We would like you to know that we regard you as one of our greatest friends, and are sure you will continue to be of assistance to our people in their struggle against racial discrimination.

UNGADINWA NANGOMSO.

Yours very sincerely
NRMandela

ROBBEN ISLAND
MAXIMUM SECURITY
PRISON

|||||||||||

JUNE 1964–MARCH 1982

Within hours of being sentenced to life imprisonment, Nelson Mandela and six of his comrades were taken from their cells in Pretoria Local Prison, handcuffed, and driven to a nearby military air base. They arrived on Robben Island early the next morning, Saturday, 13 June 1964. Denis Goldberg, the only white accused convicted with them, remained in Pretoria to serve his sentence – apartheid laws decreed that he was forbidden from being incarcerated with black prisoners.

This was Mandela's second time in Robben Island maximum security prison; his few weeks as a prisoner there in mid-1963 had prepared him for the harsh conditions, and he counselled his comrades on the importance of keeping their dignity intact.

Soon after he and three others had arrived his previous time on Robben Island in May 1963, prison guards barked orders for them to walk briskly in twos, herding them like cattle. When they continued walking at the same pace, the guards threatened them. 'Look here, we will kill you here – and your parents, your people, will never know what has happened to you,' Mandela recalled them saying. He and Steve Tefu, a prisoner who belonged to the PAC, then took the lead, maintaining their own pace. 'I was determined that we should put our stamp clearly, right from the first day we must fight because that would determine how we were going to be treated. But if we gave in on the first day, then they would treat us in a very contemptuous manner. So we went to the front and we walked even more steadily. They couldn't do anything, they didn't do anything.'[40]

Conditions on Robben Island were brutal. The prisoners were only allowed to stop doing hard labour fourteen years later in 1978, and until then their existence on the island was stark and cruel, lightened only by their own attitude, as well as visits and letters from family.

In the beginning, the food was barely edible[i] and divvied up according to racist policies. Breakfast for African prisoners was 12 ounces of maize meal porridge and a cup of black coffee, so-called coloured and Indian prisoners got 14 ounces of maize meal porridge with bread and coffee.[41] There were no white prisoners on the island.

'We were like cattle kept on spare rations so as to be lean for the mar-

---

i   In a memorandum to the commissioner of prisons written on Robben Island in January 1970, Mandela writes: 'On numerous occasions since 1964, we have repeatedly stressed that our diet is not adequately nutritional, insufficiently varied and unpalatable.'

ket,' prisoner Indres Naidoo writes. 'Bodies to be kept alive, not human beings with tastes and a pleasure in eating.'[42]

The weather conditions on the island were extreme – 'blistering hot in summer' and in winter 'bitterly cold, raining or drizzling most of the time', recalled former prisoner Mac Maharaj.[43] In the beginning, African prisoners had to wear short pants and sandals year-round, whereas Indian and coloured prisoners were issued with long pants and socks.[i] Prisoners were given a thin jersey on 25 April, which was taken away again on 25 September.[44] There were no beds for the first ten years – prisoners slept on the concrete floor on a sisal mat with three 'flimsy' blankets.[45] It was so cold in winter, they slept fully clothed. For the first ten years, Mandela and his colleagues bathed with cold water.

Throughout the week, prisoners were put to work in the yard, breaking stones with hammers. On the weekends, they were locked in their cells for twenty-three hours a day, unless they had a visitor. At the beginning of 1965, they were set to work digging in the lime quarry.[ii] It was gruelling work, and the glare of the sun on the white limestone seared their eyes. For three years, repeated requests to the prison authorities for dark glasses were rejected. By the time permission was given, the eyesight of many of the prisoners, including Mandela's, had been irreparably damaged.

In 1968, Mandela's mother, Nosekeni, died, and he was refused permission to bury her. The following year, his eldest son, Thembi, was killed in a car accident, and this time his plea to be at the graveside was ignored. He was forced to stand on the sidelines while friends and relatives played his role in the burials. His letters during this period spell out his raw anguish over these tremendous losses.

Around the same time, his beloved wife Winnie was detained by police and spent fourteen months in custody. His letters to her and others about her imprisonment demonstrate his frustration and anguish at not being able to help her or his children during this nightmare.

He kept up a regular correspondence with prison authorities to assert his rights as a prisoner, and even went as far as to demand the release of himself and his comrades or to be treated as political prisoners of war (see his letter to L. Le Grange, the minister of prisons and police, 4 September 1979, page 383).

---

i   In a memorandum to the commissioner of prisons written on Robben Island in January 1970, Mandela writes: 'In May 1967, we were issued with a new outfit which went a long way towards fulfilling the requirements stipulated in the above regulations. But we cannot make maximum use of the improvements because of the standing orders which require us to give up long trousers and jersies in summer and the mechanical manner in which these orders are enforced irrespective of the actual state of the weather conditions.'

ii   In the same memorandum Mandela writes: 'We have been forced to do heavy and uncreative work which sapped our energy and in some cases even adversely affected our health.'

In 1975, on the initiative of his comrades, he began to secretly write his memoirs with the assistance of Walter Sisulu, Ahmed Kathrada, and two other comrades and prisoners, Mac Maharaj and Laloo Chiba. The plan was for the autobiography to be published abroad in time for his sixtieth birthday on 18 July 1978. On his release in late 1976, Maharaj smuggled off the island, hidden within the covers of notebooks, a transcribed version of the manuscript. When part of the original manuscript was discovered buried in a tin near the prison block in 1977, Mandela and his comrades had their study privileges withdrawn from the start of 1978. The manuscript, however, made it to London, but it was not published until 1994 as *Long Walk to Freedom*.

To Frank, Bernadt & Joffe, his attorneys

[Stamp dated 15.6.64 with word in another hand reading 'Special' in Afrikaans][i]

Messrs Frank, Bernadt & Joffe
85 St George's Street
Cape Town

Dear Sirs,

RE STATE V NELSON MANDELA & OTHERS

We should be pleased if you would kindly advise our attorney, Mr Joffe, of Johannesburg that his clients in this matter, with the exception of DENIS GOLDBERG, are now in Robben Island.

There is a possibility that Mr B FISCHER, QC., who led the defence team is now holidaying in the city, and we would be grateful if you would advise him if his whereabouts are known to you.

Yours faithfully
[Signed NRMandela]
NELSON MANDELA

<><><><><><><>

Bram Fischer[ii] was a white Afrikaner advocate who defended Mandela and his colleagues in the Treason Trial of 1956 to 1961[iii] and in the Rivonia Trial. But more than that, he was a comrade and a good friend. He first visited the Rivonia trialists on Robben Island in 1964 to confirm their earlier decision not to appeal their conviction and sentences.

Mandela and some of his colleagues had known Fischer and his wife, Molly, well and had spent many joyful hours at their home in Johannesburg. But on that prison visit when Mandela asked after Molly, Fischer turned and walked away. After he had left the island, a senior prison official told Mandela that she had drowned when their car left the road and plunged into a river. The

---

i   Special letters were not deducted from a prisoner's quota.
ii Bram Fischer, lawyer and political and anti-apartheid activist – see the glossary.
iii The Treason Trial (1956–61) was a result of the apartheid government's attempt to quell the power of the Congress Alliance, a coalition of anti-apartheid organisations. In early-morning raids on 5 December 1956, 156 individuals were arrested and charged with high treason. By the end of the trial in March 1961 all the accused either had the charges withdrawn or, in the case of the last twenty-eight accused (including Mandela), were acquitted.

major gave permission for Mandela to write Fischer a condolence letter. It was
never delivered.

The letter to Fischer is formal, befitting correspondence from a prisoner to
his lawyer – and in this case from a prisoner who was also a lawyer. As prisoners
held a special dispensation to write to their legal advisors, it would have been
preferable not to create the impression that it was a personal letter, which he may
not have had permission to write.

In 1965, Fischer was arrested and tried the next year for furthering the
aims of the Communist Party[i] and conspiring to overthrow the government. He
was sentenced to life imprisonment. While in Pretoria Local Prison he was diag-
nosed with cancer and fell badly in 1974. The authorities finally bowed to public
pressure and released him to his brother's house from which he was forbidden
from moving. He died in 1975 and the Prisons Department had him cremated.
His ashes have never been located.

───────

To Bram Fischer,[53] his comrade and advocate in the Rivonia Trial

2nd August 1964

Dear Mr Fischer,

You will recall that when you visited the Island last time, you discussed with
Major Visser whether it would be permissible for you to arrange for me to
receive the *South African Law Journal*.

I have to date not received the journal and I thought it advisable to
remind you about the matter, should pressure of work have made it difficult
for you to make the arrangements with Juta's & Co.

I have also not received the lecture from Wolsey Hall, London, and the
law books and I would be pleased if you would kindly check up with Mr
Joffe.[ii]

Yours faithfully
[Signed NRMandela]
Prisoner no. 466/64

───────

i   For the South African Communist Party (SACP), see the glossary.
ii   Mandela's attorney, Joel Joffe.

Advocate A Fischer, S.A,.
c/o Innes Chambers,
Corner Von Brandis & Pritchard Sts.
Johannesburg

◇◇◇◇◇◇◇◇

Throughout his imprisonment Mandela perservered with the law studies toward his LLB that he had begun as a young man in 1943. Although he was permitted to practise as an attorney with only a diploma in law, he had set his heart on achieving this goal when he was an activist studying at the University of the Witwatersrand in Johannesburg. He started his three years of legal articles at the firm Witkin, Sidelsky and Eidelman within weeks of enrolling as a student, and a year later he joined the ANC when he helped to found its Youth League. From 1944 he was married to his first wife, Evelyn Mandela, and quickly the family grew, stretching his meagre finances to the limit. His application to the university in December 1949 to rewrite the final year exams he had already failed three times was rejected.

Even after passing the attorneys' admission exam on 8 August 1951, he pushed to continue his LLB. Despite his leading role in the Defiance Campaign of 1952[i] he tried again to persuade the University of the Witwatersrand to take him back, until, on his thirty-fourth birthday, I. Glyn Thomas of the University wrote to him saying he had been excluded from classes until he paid the £27 he owed.

While imprisoned at Pretoria Local Prison in 1962 he signed up to London University to continue his studies, and faced challenges at every turn. Studying at night after almost eight hours toiling in the quarry, digging out lime from 1965 to 1978, was not his biggest obstacle. His correspondence reveals that he often did not receive the correct study materials or not on time. The scenario he would sketch for university officials from the University of London, and during his subsequent studies through the University of South Africa, went on for many years. He finally achieved the degree in 1989, months before his release from prison.

---

i   Initiated by the ANC in December 1951, and launched with the South African Indian Congress on 26 June 1952 against six apartheid laws, the Defiance Campaign Against Unjust Laws (known as the Defiance Campaign for short) involved individuals breaking racist laws such as entering premises reserved for 'whites only', breaking curfews, and courting arrest. Mandela was appointed national volunteer-in-chief and Maulvi Cachalia as his deputy. Over 8,500 volunteers were imprisoned for their participation in the Defiance Campaign.

To the commanding officer, Robben Island

30th November 1964

The Commanding Officer
Robben Island

URGENT

I must pay today Rd 16.0 to the Cultural Attache, British Embassy, Hill Street, Pretoria, in respect of examination entry fees for Part I of the Final LL.B of the University of London.

Last month I wrote to the university for the entry forms and to my wife for the necessary funds. On the 9th of this month, I wrote a further letter to the Cultural Attache for the forms. In neither case have I received an acknowledgement or reply.

I am writing to ask you to wire today Rd 16.0 to the Cultural Attache and to ask him to send me the forms for completion. I may not have sufficient funds for this purpose, and Ahmed Kathrada, Prisoner No. 468, would be prepared, subject to your approval, to cover the entry fees and costs of the telegram.

As the entries for these examinations close today, I shall appreciate it if you would kindly treat the matter as extremely urgent.

Nelson Mandela
[Signed NRMandela]
Prisoner no. 466/64

[A note in English in red pen and in another hand] I have no objection to the wiring of the R16.00 but I am not prepared that prisoners can borrow money from each other. [Initialled and dated 30.11.]

◇◇◇◇◇◇◇◇◇◇

Mandela studied the Afrikaans language in prison in search of a better knowledge of the history and culture of the ruling National Party and its followers. He believed this would help him to communicate more effectively with his enemy.

It worked. It assisted in breaking down barriers with prison guards and later with government officials and even the country's president, P.W. Botha.[i]

---

i   P.W. Botha, president of South Africa 1978–84 and state president 1984–89 – see the glossary.

Here, while making the point that legitimate requests are often ignored, he is reiterating his plea to be able to prepare for his exams by studying past papers of an organisation which promoted Afrikaans, an official South African language from 1925, as well as asking for back copies of an Afrikaans-language women's magazine, Huisgenoot.

To Major Visser, prison official

[Stamp dated 25.8.1965]

Major Visser,

During the inspection on the 14th August 1965, I tried to speak to you but you did not give me the opportunity of doing so. While the inspection was in progress Chief Warder Van Tonder, who accompanied you, promised to tell you that I had some requests to make, but you left without seeing me. I am now writing to you because the matter has become urgent.

1. I am preparing to write an examination on the 29th October 1965. In March this year and early in May, I had made written applications to the Commanding Officer for leave to order old examination papers from the Saamwerk-Unie of Natal as part of my preparation for this examination. You have repeatedly assured me that you have written to the SWU and ordered the required papers and that you awaited their reply. Although the examination is now 2 months away I still have not received the papers.

2. I owe the University of South Africa the sum of R40.0 being the balance of fees for an Honours Degree course which I had planned to write in February 1966. In terms of the contract this amount must be paid before the 1st September 1965. On the last occasion I discussed the matter with you, you informed me that you had written to the university. A few days ago, I received the account for this amount and I am anxious to have the matter finalised before it is too late. In this connection I might add that I ordered my study books from Messrs Juta & Co. I asked them to order them if they did not have them in stock and to advise me when they would have them available to enable me to plan my work. I have not heard from them and I would be glad if you would kindly advise me whether the matter has been attended to.

3. You also told me that you had ordered the old *Huisgenoot*[i] numbers I required for purposes of study and I wish to remind you that I have not yet received them.
4. Several times last year and early this year I applied for a loan of books from the State Library and for enrolment forms. I have not heard from them.

I am seriously considering whether in view of the difficulties I have mentioned above, I should write the forthcoming examinations, and I should be pleased if you would give me the opportunity to discuss the whole matter with you.

[Signed NRMandela]

To the commissioner of prisons[ii]

The Commissioner of Prisons
PRETORIA

I am grateful for the concession you made on the 13th October 1965, when you informed me that you had no objection to us exchanging study books among ourselves. This relief will considerably reduce the expenses for pre-scribed textbooks, which most of us cannot afford, and will make available to all those who are studying more adequate sources of information and reference.

If the privilege to study is to be of any value, certain conditions are absolutely essential. Their importance applies to all students, especially to those who have to pursue their courses by correspondence and, therefore, lack the all-important direct communication between teacher and student. Academic assistance in the form of recommendation of literature, exchange of ideas, constant and personal review and criticism is implied amongst the students who have the opportunity of direct and free communication with their teachers and fellow students. Indeed correspondence colleges, as well as the University of South Africa, try in some measure to eliminate the obvious disadvantage suffered by their students by arranging annual vacation schools and emphasizing their importance to students.

i   *Huisgenoot* is an Afrikaans-language magazine.
ii   There are two versions of this letter. A typed version, which was presumably the one sent to the commissioner, is dated 10 October 1965. The date of the handwritten letter is cut off, apparently in the photocopying for this collection.

For prisoners preparing themselves for the same examination as people who are able to take advantage of such vacation schools and other forms of direct and unrestricted communication with their tutors, other experienced academicians and other students, the permitting and encouraging of mutual assistance among prisoners themselves would be a reasonable measure of compensation and entirely compatible with the Prisons Act. Such mutual assistance would involve free discussions on [the] part of [the] prisoner with others who are able to assist him. This would apply especially where he is studying language, law and the Humanities. Discussion sharpens one's interest in any subject and accordingly inspires reading and corrects errors. The cumulative effect of all this would be to facilitate the retention in the mind of what has been read.

Moreover, the preparation of exercises and essays for others to correct and advise on would be a constant stimulus to the student who otherwise could not have a proper check on his progress. In both respects, prisoners, particularly in this prison, are at a tremendous disadvantage and one in which they will never attain parity with other students outside to whom are available adequate facilities. In this connection I would point out that in 1963, while at the Pretoria Jail, I started a language course and I took advantage of the prison school there. I found it very helpful in correcting my mistakes and in enabling me to pick up the language fairly quickly.

To allow us free discussion and the other forms of assistance discussed above would, taken together with the concession you have already made, go a long way to remove our present difficulties. In this regard I would like to repeat the undertaking I made to you on the 13th instant that we will endeavour not to use the concessions you have already granted, as well as those you may still grant, for any improper purpose.

Finally, I would like to refer to your decision rejecting the request I made on the 14th March 1965 relating to the account for the eye test. No reasons were furnished for the refusal and I am consequently unable to give you fresh reasons to support my request. I would, however, ask you to reconsider the matter afresh and grant me the relief asked for.

[Signed NRMandela]

∞∞∞∞∞∞

Apart from the letters they were allowed to write to officials and their lawyers, prisoners could only initially write to direct family members. In the beginning it was one letter of 500 words every six months. They were also only allowed one family visit every six months. Children over two years old could only visit

their fathers when they turned sixteen. By the time of Mandela's first imprison-
ment in 1962, his five children – two boys and three girls – were aged between
twenty-three months and seventeen years old. He mentions all five in this letter:
Thembi, Makgatho (Kgatho), Maki (Makaziwe), Zeni (Zenani) and Zindzi
(Zindziswa). The first three were born during his first marriage to Evelyn Mase
and the youngest two during his marriage with Winnie Madikizela.

To Winnie Mandela,[i] his wife

[In another hand it says 'Special letter'][ii]

When replying put at the top of your letter "Reply to special letter"[iii]

NELSON MANDELA No 466/64   17 February 1966

Darling,

I should be pleased if you would kindly instruct Messrs Hayman & Aron-
sohn not to proceed with the action against the Prison Authorities.

On the 8th February 1966 I had an interview with the Chief Magistrate of Cape Town who came on the instruction of the Secretary for
Justice. He asked me to give him an affidavit relating to any complaints or
representations that I wished to make on my treatment. I was unable to give
him an affidavit, but I gave him a written statement in which I indicated
that I was anxious to take advantage of the opportunity of repeating my
representations to higher authorities. I pointed out, however, that I would
like to consult my attorney on the matter.

On the 14th February I had another interview, this time with the Commissioner of Prisons, in the course of which he promised to put my requests
to the Minister of Justice. It has been my attitude right from the beginning
to endeavour to explore all the channels available within the Department. I
accordingly decided to take advantage of the opportunity of my representations being placed before the Minister. I should, therefore, be pleased if you
would kindly advise Miss Hayman of this arrangement and instruct her not
to proceed, to her know that I am very grateful for her prompt action and

---

i   Nomzamo Winifred Madikizela-Mandela (1936–) – see the glossary.
ii   Special letters were not deducted from a prisoner's quota.
iii Replies to special letters were not deducted from a prisoner's quota.

I shake her hand very warmly. You also acted with equal speed for which I compliment you.

I have now received Niki's[i] 2 telegrams and was shocked by the news of C.K's[ii] illness and greatly relieved to learn of his recovery. Do write and tell him that I wish him complete recovery and many years of good health and prosperity. The Commanding Officer has given me permission to receive a letter from Niki, and I should be pleased if you would kindly tell her to write.

I have passed the Hoër Afrikaanse Taaleksamens[iii] and have now enrolled for Afrikaans-Nederlands Course 1[iv] with the University of South Africa. The fees and cost of text books have been prohibitive and my funds have run out. Tell G. Please do not pay from your account.

Your Xmas card could not be traced Mhlope.[v] I hope you received my January letter. I had written to Nkosikazi Luthuli[vi] on New Year and I got an inspiring reply. I will keep it for you.

The law exams begin on the 13 June, the day before our 8th wedding anniversary. This is a very difficult period of hard and heavy swotting. It will be such a relief when it is all over at last. I hope you have not abandoned your studies and that in your next letter you will be able to report progress.[vii]

My love to Niki and Uncle Marsh,[viii] Nali,[ix] Bantu[x] and hubby, Nyanya[xi] and all our relatives and friends. Do tell Nali to pass my regards to Sefton.[xii]

Tons and tons of love to you darling and a million kisses. Tell Thembi, Kgatho, Maki, Zeni and Zindzi[xiii] that I miss them very much and that I send my love.

Devotedly,
Dalibunga

Nkosikazi Nobandla Mandela,
House no 8115, Orlando West,
Johannesburg

---

i   Niki Xaba (1932–1985), Winnie Mandela's eldest sister – see the glossary.
ii   Columbus Kokani Madikizela, Winnie Mandela's father – see the glossary.
iii   Higher Afrikaans Language Exams.
iv   A course in a more traditional form of the Dutch language.
v   One of Winnie Mandela's names.
vi   *Nkosikazi* means 'Mrs.' in isiXhosa. He is referring to Albert Luthuli's wife.
vii Winnie Mandela had a diploma in social work and she was studying sociology.
viii Marshall Xaba, husband of Niki Xaba, Winnie Mandela's eldest sister (for Niki Xaba, see the glossary).
ix   Nali Nancy Vutela, Winnie Mandela's sister.
x   Nobantu Mniki, Winnie Mandela's sister.
xi   Nonyaniso (Nyanya) Madikizela, Winnie Mandela's youngest sister.
xii Sefton Vutela, Nali's husband.
xiii Mandela's children.

◇◇◇◇◇◇◇◇

Still struggling to receive study materials, Mandela writes directly to the registrar of the University of South Africa, using the man's native tongue of Afrikaans. This letter implies that he is aware he has the right to make such an enquiry and also displays that he has managed to maintain the dignity the prison system conspired to place from his reach. He would also have been aware that this letter would make clear to officials, particularly those in the censors' office, that he was not prepared to give up this battle.

To the registrar, University of South Africa

[Translated from Afrikaans]

22 August 1966

The Registrar,
University of South Africa,
PO Box 392
Pretoria

Reference no MB072

Dear Sir,

Please be so good as to allow me to postpone the AFRIKAANS-NED-ERLANDS exam till next year. I am struggling to obtain some of the pre-scribed books and I believe it to be dangerous to attempt the exam without these books.

    Sincerely,
[Signed NRMandela]
NELSON R.[i] MANDELA

---

i   The letter R stands for his given name, Rolihlahla.

To the secretary, American Society of International Law

31.8.66

The Secretary,
American Society of International Law,
2223 Massachusetts Avenue, N.W.
WASHINGTON D.C. 2008
20008

Dear Sir,

I have not received the July 1966 issue of the *American Journal of International Law*. Presumably because my subscription has lapsed.

I would have enclosed with this letter the annual subscription fee but I unfortunately do not know what amount is due because a friend had originally paid for me.

I am preparing to write an examination in Public International Law shortly and I should, therefore, be pleased if you would kindly advise me by return of post whether the subscription has expired and the amount now due.

Yours faithfully,
[Signed NRMandela]

To the commanding officer, Robben Island

NELSON MANDELA 466/64.   8th September 1966.

The Commanding Officer,
Robben Island

I have broken the lens of my reading glasses and I should be pleased if you would kindly arrange for the glasses to be sent for repairs to Dr Sachs of Cape Town who prescribed them.

Kindly deduct the costs of repairs from my account.[i]

---

i   Upon entering prison, a list was made of the belongings a prisoner had with them. Details of the amount of cash a prisoner may have brought with them were recorded in an individual account under the name of the prisoner (this was not a bank account but simply a separate bookkeeping record). Thereafter, any funds reaching the prison in the name of that prisoner were recorded in that account and so too were any disbursements made in the name of the prisoner. When they were discharged from prison, the prisoner was given what remained in the account.

[Signed NRMandela]
NELSON MANDELA

◇◇◇◇◇◇◇◇

It is unclear whether this was a smuggled letter as the addressee, Cecil Eprile, was not a member of Mandela's family, or whether by that stage he was permitted to write to friends. Eprile was a friend of Mandela and had been editor of the Golden City Post, *a Johannesburg newspaper aimed at black South Africans. Eprile's son, Tony, is convinced his father never received this letter. It was written at the time the Eprile family had left South Africa for London where Cecil worked as editor-in-chief of Forum World Features. They settled in the United States in early 1972.*

To Cecil Eprile,[i] **a friend and former** *Golden City Post* **editor**

[in another hand] 46664 Nelson Mandela

466/64   11/2/67

Dear Cecil,

I need R150.00 for studies; may I exploit you. During the last 4 years I parasited on Winnie. She has been out of employment since April '65 and I haven't the heart to squeeze her further. Last year she sent me R100.00 and it has all vanished.

I must also burden you with yet another of my personal problems. My son, Makgatho, was expelled from St Christopher's, Manzini, apparently after a student strike there. Luckily he managed to secure a first-class pass in the Junior Certificate, and I believe he now attends a local school. I fear that the sudden change may affect his progress and standard of performance. He may also be feeling lonely and unhappy here because all his sisters and friends are over there. Could you try and help him be readmitted or fixed up in another boarding school there. He is a clever fellow and should be able to catch up with others even though he may return late. I believe his health has recently become indifferent and it may be that, in

---

i   Cecil Eprile (1914–93) – see the glossary.

the circumstances, it is considered advisable that he should not be far from Baragwanath Hospital. Perhaps it may be better to call him to your office and discuss the matter with him first and ascertain his views on the matter. You may also have a chat with Winnie; anyway I leave the matter in your able hands.

I was sorry to learn of the death of Nat,[i] it was a cruel blow for we regarded him with a great deal of affection. He was a man of undoubted competence and an asset to us all. Often, after reading his articles, I came away with the feeling that indeed, the pen was mightier than the sword. I hope you found somebody just as capable to replace him.

I was happy to know of the rapid growth and expansion of the enterprise you have piloted so skilfully, as well as of your own progress and achievement. I know that all of this will be embarrassing to you. But [there is a water stain over the word] the consolation that I will not be there to see you blush. As for myself I feel on top of the world in more senses than one. I am keeping well and fit in flesh and spirit and am looking forward to the day when I will again see you enjoy once more the happy moments we have spent together in the past.

My fondest regards to you and Leon and tons of love to your wife[ii] and Zelda.[iii]

Sincerely,
Nelson

PS: Please tell Winnie that in arranging the next visit, she must give preference to Madiba or Makgatho[iv] if she will not be coming down in person.

N

Cecil Eprile Esq,
c/o Mrs Winnie Mandela
House no, 8115 Orlando West
Johannesburg

---

i   Nat Nakasa who wrote for the *Golden City Post* and who was a friend of Eprile. Nakasa left South Africa for the United States and died in New York City on 14 July 1965. Mandela probably learnt of Nat's death some time after it happened as the prisoners were forbidden from having access to news until 1980.
ii   Liesl Eprile, a refugee from Nazi Germany who married Eprile in South Africa.
iii Leon and Zelda Street, friends and neighbours of the Epriles who lived in the same apartment block, Riviera Mansions. When he was on the run, Mandela took over the bedroom of their daughter, Laura, when he stayed with them for a few weeks.
iv   His sons, Madiba Thembekile (1945–69) and Makgatho Mandela (1950–2005) – see the glossary.

27th February 1967.

The Commanding Officer,
Robben Island.

      I am preparing to write an examination on the 10th June 1967. Entries for this examination ought to have been received by the British Embassy by 1st December 1966. I handed in the entry forms early in November 1966 with a request that the forms together with the sum of R800 be sent to Pretoria. In spite of several enquiries I made, I am still uncertain whether my entry has now been approved.

In February 1966 I ordered a prescribed text-books from a London book firm to prepare for this same examination, and although I had been assured that the money to cover the cost of the books as well as postage had been sent, I never received them. In October last year I placed another order for the same books and I still have not received them, a fact which has seriously handicapped me in preparation for the forthcoming examination.

In September 1966 I had ordered from the same book-firm a number of text books but my letter was posted without the necessary amount for the payment and postage of these books. I subsequently received an account from them after they had sent the books on credit.

I had also written to the Registrar of the University of London and requested that R1·00 be enclosed in my letter. I have received no reply to this letter either.

Finally, in December last year I made written

from 2nd Jan. 1965

application for a detailed statement of accounts & and I have not been supplied with this information. I should accordingly be pleased if you would kindly advise me at the earliest opportunity what progress, if any, has been made in regard to five (5) items mentioned above.

NRMandela.
Prisoner no. 466/64.

'The Commanding officer.

To the commanding officer, Robben Island

27th February 1967

The Commanding Officer
Robben Island.[i]

I am preparing to write an examination on the 10th June 1967. Entries for this examination ought to have been received by the British Embassy by 1st December 1966. I handed in the <u>entry forms early in November 1966</u> with a request that the forms together with the <u>sum of R8.00</u> be sent to Pretoria.[ii] In spite of several enquiries I made, I am still uncertain whether my entry has now been approved.

In <u>February 1966</u> I ordered prescribed <u>text-books</u> from a <u>London book firm</u> to prepare for this same examination, and although I had been assured that the money to cover the cost of the books as well as postage had been sent, I never received them. <u>In October last year</u> I placed another order for the same books and I still have not received them, a fact which has seriously handicapped me in preparation for the forthcoming examination. In <u>September 1966</u> I had ordered from the same book firm a number of text books but my letter was posted without the necessary amount for the payment and postage of these books. I subsequently received an accountry from them after they had sent the books on credit.

I had also written to the <u>Registrar of the University</u> of London and requested that R1.00 be enclosed in my letter. I have received no reply to this letter either.

Finally, <u>in December</u> last year, I made written application for a <u>detailed statement of account</u> as from 2nd January 1965 and I have not been supplied with this information. I should according[ly] be pleased if you would kindly advise me at the earliest opportunity what progress, if any, has been made in regard to five (5) items mentioned above.

[Signed NRMandela]
Prisoner no. 466/64

---

i   It looks as if the words have been underlined by Mandela himself as they are in the same ink.
ii   All the underlining in this letter is in the same pen and is, therefore, probably Mandela's own underlining.

To, Frank, Bernadt & Joffe, his attorneys

Copy[i]

21st March 1967

Messrs Frank, Bernadt & Joffe
PO Box 252
Cape Town

Attention: Mr Brown

Dear Sirs,

I am charged with being lazy, careless or negligent in my work[ii] and the case has been set down for hearing on the 4th April 1967. In this connection I should be pleased if your Mr Brown would kindly appear for me.

My defence will be that I suffer from high blood pressure for which I have been receiving treatment in this prison since the 14th June 1964 and that, in the circumstances, pick-and-shovel work, which I do at the lime quarry, is strenuous and dangerous to my health.

I propose calling as a witness a Cape Town physician, Dr. Kaplan, who gave me a thorough examination on the 15th April 1966 with the aid of technical instruments. I mentioned this matter to the official who gave me the charge sheet, and pointed out, at the same time, that I did not have the funds to cover the fees of the physician. I asked that the Prison Department should undertake responsibility for payment of these fees. This request was refused and I ask you to consider the possibility of making an urgent application to the Supreme Court for an order directing the Prison Department to pay these charges, if you consider that such an application would have a fair chance of success. The prison doctor, who has throughout treated me with kind consideration, checks my blood pressure regularly and gives me treatment for it as well as for swelling feet, but he will naturally not be in a position to give evidence on the examination by the physician on the 15th April as such evidence would be hearsay.

Finally, having regard to the atmosphere that prevails in this place, details of which will be supplied to you during consultation if necessary, I consider it not compatible with the interests of justice that my trial should

---

i   The word 'copy' is in Mandela's hand.
ii   Mandela was charged with Eddie Daniels, Laloo Chiba, and Neville Alexander (see the glossary for notes on these individuals) with what he called 'trumped up charges' (Nelson Mandela in conversation with Richard Stengel, December 1992, CD 5, Nelson Mandela Foundation, Johannesburg) because they were seen as spokespeople for other prisoners. They were convicted and sentenced to a period of isolation and a diet of rice water (water in which rice had been boiled, three times a day for three days).

be heard by a prison official and I ask that you demand trial by a magistrate. I will be able to raise the funds to cover your fees.[i]

Yours faithfully,
[Signed NRMandela] (NELSON MANDELA)

◇◇◇◇◇◇◇◇◇

This letter marks the first salvo in what turned out to be a long, drawn-out war with state officials over attempts to have Mandela disbarred as an attorney. In the first attempt the authorities relied on his 1952 conviction under the Suppression of Communism Act,[ii] a law to outlaw the Communist Party of South Africa from 1950. Its secondary role was to taint all opponents of apartheid as Communists and thereby punish and at least neutralise them. On 2 December 1952 Mandela and nineteen others were convicted for their participation in the 1952 Defiance Campaign Against Unjust Laws, commonly known as the Defiance Campaign. It was a creation of the ANC and the South African Indian Congress as a popular initiative to highlight six of the laws the National Party created after it won power in 1948 and brought in the policy of apartheid.

Looking back some twenty-five-years later, while in conversation with American writer Richard Stengel, Mandela remembered being defended at no charge by Walter Pollak, then the Chair of the Bar Council. 'The court dismissed the application of the Law Society on the ground that to be convicted for your political convictions does not make a person who is unfit to be a lawyer.'[46]

The second attempt turned on his conviction for sabotage, essentially in terms of a certain section of the Internal Security Act. On that occasion, Mandela decided to conduct his own defence and demanded to be let off hard labour to prepare his case. 'I wanted tables, chairs, proper chairs, proper lighting for me to prepare the case. I also wanted to be taken to Pretoria where the case was going to be heard, so that I could have access to the library.'[47]

After much correspondence, the case was withdrawn. The prison authorities had refused Mandela's demand to be let off the back-breaking work in the lime quarry from 7:30 a.m. to 4:00 p.m. on weekdays, they didn't want to provide better food to aid his concentration, and they would not transfer him to Pretoria for the duration of the case.

'Throughout my imprisonment, when I threatened to go to court, they pulled back. They didn't mind me briefing a lawyer, they didn't mind me getting

---

i   During his incarceration, Mandela received financial support from people such as the British newspaper publisher David Astor (1912–2001) and Lady Elinor Birley and her husband Sir Robert Birley (1903–82), the former headmaster of Eton College and at the time the visiting professor of education at the University of the Witwatersrand.

ii   For the Suppression of Communism Act, see the glossary.

a lawyer to argue my case, but when I said I don't want a lawyer, I want to
appear in court myself, they did not want that, and they pulled back,' he said.
　　'Because they were afraid of the publicity?' Stengel enquired.
　　'Yes. They wanted the people to forget about me as much as possible.'[48]

––––––––––

To Joel Carlson,[i] his attorney

[Note in another hand] 466/64 Nelson Mandela　　　letter to attorney[ii]

Mr J Carlson　　　　　　　　　　　　　　　　　[Stamp dated 1967]
PO Box 8533
Johannesburg

Dear Sir,

On 19th June 1967, about an hour after my interview with you, a member
of the security staff handed me a letter, signed by the Liquidator appointed
in terms of the Suppression of Communism Act (Act No 44 of 1950),[iii]
drawing my attention to a judgment delivered on 2.12.52 by Justice Rumpff
in the Witwatersrand Local Division. In the opinion of the Liquidator the
findings and verdict in this case were conclusive of my having contravened
Section 11(b) of the above act. Copy of the aforementioned judgment was
attached. On the basis of this judgment he proposed to include my name on
the list of office-bearers, members or active supporters of the Communist
Party of South Africa, and he invites me to make representation within 30
days from the date of the letter (i.e. from 23.5.67).

　　I am instructing you to handle this matter on my behalf. I would have
preferred a personal interview with you. In fact the same day I received the
Liquidator's letter, I wrote to the Commanding Officer and asked him to
telephone urgently, and at my expense, to ask you to return to the Island for
a consultation on this matter, but permission to communicate with you was
granted only yesterday. I cannot give you proper instructions by correspondence and I should be pleased if you would kindly arrange a consultation.
I assume that it will not be possible for you to come down and I should,
therefore, be pleased if you would kindly instruct your Cape Town corre-

––––––––––

i　　Joel Carlson (1926–2001) – see the glossary.
ii　　This note indicates that this is a special letter which will not come off his quota.
iii　　For the Suppression of Communism Act, see the glossary.

spondent, Mr Brown of Frank, Bernadt & Joffe to see me. I should further be pleased if you would communicate with the Liquidator and advise him that you are now handling the matter.

Yours faithfully,
[Signed NRMandela]
NELSON MANDELA

P.T.O.
The judgment relied upon by the Liquidator is the one where I was convicted with 19 others for the part we played in organising the Campaign for the Defiance of Unjust Laws.
[Initialled NRM]

―――――――――――――

To the liquidator, Department of Justice

[Stamped 23 October 1967 by the Robben Island prison reception office]
The Liquidator
Department of Justice,
Pretoria.

Sir,

Re: Communist Party of South Africa

I have received your letter of the 23rd May 1967 to which you attach copy of a judgement delivered on the 2nd December 1952 by the Honourable Justice Rumpff in the Witwatersrand Local Division of the Supreme Court in which case I was one of twenty accused.

You state that the findings and verdict in that case were in your mind conclusive of my having contravened Section 11 (b) of Act No. 44 of 1950 as charged.[i]

Finally you advise that I may submit to you further representations in this regard.

At the outset, I wish to reiterate the statement I made in previous

―――――――――

i   The Suppression of Communism Act. Section 11(b) states that there will be penalties for any person who 'advocates, advises, defends or encourages the achievement of any such object or any act or omission which is calculated to further the achievement of any such object', the object being communism.

correspondence with you that I have never been an officer-bearer, officer, member or active supporter of the Communist Party of South Africa. I further deny that my conviction in the above case entitles you to include my name in the list of persons who were members or active supporters of the Communist Party and I will strenuously contest any efforts on your part to do so. It is my firm belief that the allegation that I was a member or active supporter of the Communist Party is an act of persecution and a propaganda manoeuvre intended to distort my political beliefs and to justify the removal of my name from the roll of attorneys. It is not in any way inspired by any honest belief that I am a Communist. A study of the correspondence in this matter confirms my view.

In your letter of the 1st July 1966, you advised me that the Minister of Justice had in terms of subsection (10) of section 4 of Act No 44 of 1950 directed you to complete a list of persons who were or had at any time before or after the commencement of the said Act been office-bearers, officers, members or active supporters of the Communist party which was by subsection (1) of section 2 of the said Act declared to be an unlawful organisation. In that letter you further advised me that evidence had been placed before you that I had been a member and active supporter of the said Communist Party. You then afforded me opportunity, in terms of section 4, to show why my name should not be included in the abovementioned list.

In my letter of the 15th July 1966, I emphatically denied that I was a member of the Communist Party. I pointed out that since you had given me no particulars in regard to this allegation, I could do no more at that stage than merely to make a bare denial. I accordingly asked you to furnish me with full particulars of such evidence as had been placed before you. Your reply of the 27th July 1966 stated expressly that sworn evidence had been placed before you to show that I had been a member [of] the Communist Party since 1960 and that I had taken part in its activities, inter alia, by attending conferences of the said Party. On the . . . [sic] August I wrote and asked you to furnish me with detailed particulars. After a silence of almost four months, I received your letter of the 15th December 1966 in which you informed me that it had been decided not to include my name in the list of office-bearers, officers, members or active supporters of the Communist Party at that stage. No reference whatsoever was made to my letter of the . . . [sic] August 1966 and the particulars I had asked for.

Five months thereafter you wrote me your letter of the 23rd May 1967 and confronted me with a completely new allegation. Now it was proposed listing me because of my conviction in December 1952 for contravening section 11(b) of the above Act. The original allegation that I was a member of the Communist Party since 1960 was abandoned and I was deprived of the opportunity of clearing my name by publicly demonstrating its falsity. Now it was maintained by inference, that I had been such a member since 1952. If it is seriously contended that the 1952 judgement made me a member or active supporter of the Communist Party, why then was it necessary first to proceed against me on the ground that I had been a member since 1960?

It is my contention that the first allegation was abandoned simply because it was from the beginning untrue and because the particulars I asked for could not be supplied. I contend further that the fact that it has taken fifteen years before proceedings were started to list me suggests that throughout this period, the above conviction was not considered to have put me in the category of persons who were members or active supporters of the Communist Party. I feel obliged to point out that the proposal to include my name in the said list is an act of victimisation and has nothing whatsoever to do with the fulfilment of duties imposed by section 4 of the above Act.

As more fully appears from the copy of the judgement attached to your letter of the 23rd May 1967, I and nineteen others were sentenced for the part we played in organising the Campaign for the Defiance of Unjust Laws. The Campaign was organised and directed by a National Action Council which was composed of representatives of the African National Congress and the South African Indian Congress, and was based on the principles of non-violence which were adopted by Mahatma Gandhi and Pandit Nehru in India. It was a protest against certain selected apartheid legislation which we considered harsh and unjust. The actual demonstrations were peaceful and disciplined and it was because of this consideration that the Learned Judge decided to suspend sentence [sic]. The Campaign had nothing whatsoever to do with Communism. Its object was to secure a redress of the just and legitimate grievances of the African, Indian and Coloured people of this country.

To the best of my knowledge and belief, of the twenty accused in the above case, ten had already been listed under the above Act when they were convicted on the 2nd December 1952, all of them having been members of the Communist Party before it was dissolved in 1950. Of the remaining ten, with the exception of myself, I am not aware of any proceedings that have been taken to list any one of them because of the above conviction. I have been singled out and treated differently from my co-accused in that case, some of whom held, at the time, more senior positions in the political organisations than I did. The only inference I can draw from this differential treatment is that in my case the above conviction is considered to have made me a member or active supporter of the Communist Party, whereas the same conviction carries no such implications as far as the rest of the accused were concerned.

Even in my case for fifteen years after the conviction, it was apparently not deemed necessary to put my name on the list. Only now that I am a prisoner serving a life sentence was it considered expedient to do so. I am forced to the conclusion that in making the original allegation advantage was being taken of my disabilities as an incarcerated person and it was apparently thought that I would consequently be unable to contest the allegation. It is my considered opinion that resort is now being made to the 1952 conviction for the purpose of saving face.

In any event the Communist party was dissolved in 1950 shortly before Act no 44 of 1950 was promulgated and was re-formed only in 1953. This information was given to me by Messrs Govan Mbeki,[i] Raymond Mhlaba[ii] and Elias Motsoaledi[iii] all of whom are prisoners serving life sentences in Robben Island. Mr Mhlaba informs me that up to June 1950 when the Communist Party was dissolved at a Conference held in Cape Town, he was secretary of the Port Elizabeth District of that body, and that he attended the dissolution conference. Mr Motsoaledi, who was at that time Group's Secretary in Johannesburg, confirmed Mr Mhlaba's statement. Mr Mbeki who, prior to his arrest in July 1963, was a member of the Port Elizabeth District Committee, informs me that a new Communist Party was formed in 1953 and bore the name South African Communist Party. There was thus no Communist Party between June 1950 and 1953. I could, therefore, not be a member or active supporter of an organisation that did not exist. I accordingly submit that the above conviction does not entitle you to include my name in the list of persons who were members or active supporters of the Communist Party.

The case of R V Adams 1959 (1) S.A. 646 (Special Court), which is popularly referred to as the Treason Trial,[iv] and in which I was one of the accused, is relevant. The Crown, as it then was, alleged a conspiracy to overthrow the existing state by violence and to replace it with a Communist state. The indictment, as far as I can remember, covered the period of 1st December 1952 to December 1956, and included a count under Act no 44 of 1950. Amongst the bodies that were involved in this case were the African National

---

i   Govan Mbeki (1910–2001), MK activist and Rivonia trialist who was imprisoned with Mandela – see the glossary.
ii   Raymond Mhlaba (1920–2005), MK activist and Rivonia trialist who was imprisoned with Mandela – see the glossary.
iii Elias Motsoaledi (1924–94), trade unionist, ANC member, and Rivonia trialist who was imprisoned with Mandela – see the glossary.
iv   The Treason Trial (1956–61) was a result of the apartheid government's attempt to quell the power of the Congress Alliance, a coalition of anti-apartheid organisations. In early-morning raids on 5 December 1956, 156 individuals were arrested and charged with high treason. By the end of the trial in March 1961 all the accused either had the charges withdrawn or, in the case of the last twenty-eight accused (including Mandela), were acquitted.

Congress and the South African Indian Congress, the same organisations that organised the Defiance Campaign[i] in 1952. I was one of the witnesses that were called for the defence, and who were cross-examined by counsel for the Crown. The verdict was given on the 29th March 1961 when all the accused were acquitted. The reasons for judgement were handed in about a month thereafter. I never saw any report, official or otherwise, of the reasons for the judgement. But I read press reports according to which it appeared that the same Justice Rumpff who convicted me on the 2nd December 1952, and on whose judgement you now rely, made observations which seemed to indicate that he did not consider me to be a Communist. If this be correct, then I contend that such a finding would be conclusive of the fact that I was not, during the period covered by the indictment, a member or active supporter of the Communist Party.

As far as the question of my political beliefs is concerned, I have always regarded myself, first and foremost, as a nationalist, and I have throughout my political career been influenced by the ideology of African nationalism. My one ambition in life is, and has always been, to play my role in the struggle of my people against oppression and exploitation by whites. I fight for the right of the African people to rule themselves in their own country.

Although I am a nationalist, I am by no means a racialist. I fully accept that principle stated in the report of the Joint Planning Council of the African National Congress and the South African Indian Congress which is quoted on page 5 of the judgement attached to your letter of the 23rd May 1967 that all people irrespective of the national group they may belong to, are entitled to live a full and free life on the basis of the fullest equality.

I have read Marxist literature and I am impressed by the idea of a classless society. I am firmly convinced that only socialism can do away with the poverty, disease and illiteracy that are prevalent amongst my people, and that maximum industrial development is the result of central planning and the nationalisation of the key industries of the country. But I am not a Marxist. As far as South Africa is concerned, I believe that the most immediate task facing the oppressed people today is not the introduction of a workers' government and the building of Communist society. The principal task before us is the overthrow of white supremacy in all its ramifications, and the establishment of a democratic government in which all South Africans, irrespective of their station in life, of their colour or political beliefs will live side by side in perfect harmony.

---

i   Initiated by the ANC in December 1951, and launched with the South African Indian Congress on 26 June 1952 against six apartheid laws, the Defiance Campaign Against Unjust Laws (known as the Defiance Campaign for short) involved individuals breaking racist laws such as entering premises reserved for 'whites only', breaking curfews, and courting arrest. Mandela was appointed national volunteer-in-chief and Maulvi Cachalia as his deputy. Over 8,500 volunteers were imprisoned for their participation in the Defiance Campaign.

The one organisation which appeared to me best suited to undertake the task of uniting the African people, and that would eventually win back our freedom, was the African National Congress. I joined it in 1944 and in 1952 I became its Transvaal president and Deputy National President. In 1953 I was served with a notice in terms of the above Act calling upon me to resign from the African National Congress and never again to take part in its activities. It was formed in 1912 to strive for the liberation of the African people. Throughout its history it was inspired by the idea of African nationalism. In 1956 it adopted the Freedom Charter[i] a policy document which embodies the principles upon which the African National Congress will build a new South Africa. At the Treason Trial the Crown alleged that the Charter was a blue-print for a Communist state and called expert evidence to substantiate the allegation. On the other hand, the defence contended that the Charter was not a Communist document, but that its terms embodied the demands of a movement of national liberation. Amongst the evidence led by the defence to refute the allegation made by the prosecution was an article which I had written in the monthly magazine *Liberation* of June 1956 in which I posed precisely this same question, namely, whether the Charter was a blue-print for a Communist state.[ii] In that article, I had endeavoured to show that, apart from the clauses dealing with the nationalisation of mines, banks and other monopolies, the Charter was based on the principle of free enterprise, and that when its terms were implemented, capitalism amongst Africans would flourish as never before. In the press reports referred to above, Mr Justice Rumpff was reported to have expressly referred to this article and relied partly on it in holding that the Crown had not proved the allegation that the Charter was a Communist document. The African National Congress is a nationalist, and not a Marxist organisation, and, unlike the Communist Party whose membership is open to all national groups, it is an organisation exclusively for Africans.[iii]

Although it is not a Marxist organisation, the African National Congress had often co-operated with the Communist Party on matters of common concern. Such cooperation became possible because the Communist Party supported the liberation struggle of the African people. Instances of such cooperation between national movements and Marxist parties are to

i   A statement of the principles of the Congress Alliance (see the glossary), adopted at the Congress of the People in Kliptown, Soweto, on 26 June 1955. The Congress Alliance rallied thousands of volunteers across South Africa to record the demands of the people. The Freedom Charter espoused equal rights for all South Africans regardless of race, land reform, improved working and living conditions, the fair distribution of wealth, compulsory education, and fairer laws. It was a powerful tool used in the fight against apartheid.

ii   The article Mandela wrote for the publication is headlined 'In Our Lifetime'. In it, he writes: 'Whilst the [Freedom] Charter proclaims democratic changes of a far-reaching nature it is by no means a blue-print for a socialist state but a programme for the unification of various classes and groupings amongst the people on a democratic basis.' *Liberation: A Journal of Democratic Discussion* was sold for one shilling.

iii   The ANC opened its membership to non-Africans in 1969.

be found all over the world. For example, in the struggle for national independence in India, the All-India National Congress Cooperated with the Communist Party of India.

Communists have always been free to join the African National Congress and many of them are members, and some of them even serve on its national, provincial and local committees. Inside the African National Congress, and in my political work generally, I have worked closely with Communists, especially Messrs Moses Kotane,[i] J.B. Marks[ii] and Dan Tloome.[iii] It is easy to understand why Communists are admitted as members of the African National Congress when one takes into account the fact that this organisation is not a political party but a political organisation in which various shades of opinion are permitted. It is a parliament of the African people. Just as there are Communist Parliamentarians in France, Italy and other western countries, so do we find Communists in the membership of the African National Congress. But the cooperation referred to between the Communists mentioned above and me has been limited to such matters as I considered to be within the framework of the policy of the African National Congress or as furthered the general struggle against racial oppression. But in no way have Communists, either as an organisation or as individuals, exercised any control over my political beliefs or activities nor did I, at any time, support their objects or programme.

Before I was banned in 1953, I had also taken part in the activities of the South African Peace Council,[iv] of which I was one of the vice-Presidents. The Reverend D.C Thompson was at the time, its national chairman and its object was the preservation of world peace. It ran specific campaigns centering around the question; as for example the campaign to induce the Five Big Powers to conclude a Pact of Peace. It was not a Communist movement but Communists like Messrs A. Fischer,[v] A.M. Kathrada, and Miss Hilda Watts,[vi] served on its committees! In 1953 the Minister of Justice ordered me to resign from the Council.

In March 1961 I was the main speaker at an All-in African Conference which was held at Pietermaritzburg. The Conference had been called

---

i   Moses Kotane (1905–78), ANC member and secretary-general of the South African Communist Party.
ii   J. B. Marks (1903–72), ANC member and a leader in the 1952 Defiance Campaign (for the Defiance Campaign, see the glossary).
iii   Dan Tloome (1919–92), ANC and South African Communist Party member who spent decades in exile in Zambia where he rose to leadership positions in the ANC and served as the official chairman of the South African Communist Party.
iv   Established in the 1950s, the South African Peace Council promoted peace both in South Africa and internationally and ran campaigns against the development of the atomic bomb, the militirisation of South Africa, the rearming of Germany, and the wars in Korea and Kenya.
v   His lawyer Abram (Bram Fischer) – see the glossary.
vi   Hilda Bernstein (née Watts) (1915–2006), author, artist, and anti-apartheid and women's rights activist. She was a founding member of the South African Peace Council and of the Federation of South African Women. After her husband, Lionel (Rusty), was acquitted in the Rivonia Trial, they crossed into neighbouring Botswana on foot.

to protest against the decision of the Government to establish a Republic without consulting Africans. The Conference was attended by Africans from various walks of life – sportsmen, churchmen and politicians. A resolution was adopted demanding that the Government call a national Convention of all South Africans, black and white, to draw up a new democratic constitution for the country. The resolution called for mass demonstrations on the 29th, 30th and 31st May 1961 if the Government failed to summon the Convention. I was the Honorary Secretary of the Conference and took the lead in organising the general strike on the eve of the declaration of the Republic. A year later I was convicted and sentenced to three years imprisonment for organising this strike, and I have been in jail ever since. There was nothing in the Conference that was Communistic nor could it be argued that the above resolution advocated an object of Communism.

I played a leading role in the formation of Umkhonto weSizwe in November 1961 which planned and directed the acts of sabotage in this country. The formation of Umkhonto was the direct result of the policy of the Government to rule the country by force, a policy which made all forms of constitutional struggle impossible. The Communist Party was represented on the National High Command, the governing body of Umkhonto. But its representatives formed a minority and did not in any way direct its policy.

Early in January 1962 I left the country to attend the conference of the Pan-African Freedom Movement for Central, East and Southern Africa which was to be held in Addis Ababa in February that year. This was a conference of African nationalists called for the purpose of examining problems and of formulating plans for the liberation of the oppressed people in the Pafmecsa[i] area. After the conference I toured Africa and visited England. I did not visit any of the Communist countries. In 1962 I was convicted and sentenced to two years imprisonment for leaving the country without a passport.

A study of my political background demonstrates that I have never been a member or active supporter of the Communist Party of South Africa or of its successor, the South African Communist Party. On the contrary, that background shows that I am a nationalist. One ambition has dominated my thinking, my political beliefs and my political actions. This is the idea of exploding the myth of white supremacy and of winning back our country. The only body which has enabled our people to forge ahead in our freedom struggle in the past, and which will lead us to our final goal in the future is, and has always been, the African National Congress with its dynamic

---

i   An initialism for the Pan-African Freedom Movement of East, Central and South Africa.

creed of African nationalism. All my efforts to help advance the struggle of my people have been made through the African National Congress. If on occasions I served on other bodies it was because I considered that those bodies and their work helped to speed the liberation of the African people.

Finally, I deny that my conviction of the 2nd December 1952 entitles you to include my name in the list of persons who were members or active supporters of the Communist Party.

Yours faithfully
[Signed NRMandela]
N.R. Mandela

―――――――――――

To the registrar of the Supreme Court

[Typed]

Private Bag,
ROBBEN ISLAND.
CAPE PROVINCE.
6th December 1967.

The Registrar of the Supreme Court,
PRETORIA

Dear Sir,

Re: SECRETARY FOR JUSTICE vs NELSON ROLIHLAHLA MAN-
DELA: APPLICATION FOR REMOVAL FROM THE ROLL OF
ATTORNEYS. M 1529/1967

I have to advise that I am opposing the above application and it is my intention to attend the hearing in order to submit my argument in person. Formal notice of opposition will be filed in due course.

As indicated in paragraph 2 of [the] applicant's affidavit, I am at present serving a sentence of life imprisonment at Robben Island. The material that I require for [the] purpose of preparing the answering Affidavit and argument is located in the Transvaal Province, and it will be impossible for me to prepare the case from Robben Island.

It will be equally impossible for me to attend the hearing unless the prison authorities make the necessary arrangements for me to do so. I have accordingly written to the Commissioner of Prisons today requesting him to transfer me immediately to Pretoria for purposes of preparing the said Affidavit. I have further requested the Commissioner to make arrangements to enable me to attend the hearing.

In this connection I enclose copies of letters written to [the] applicant's Attorney and to the Commissioner respectively[i] so that the court may be aware of my difficulties in this matter, I particularly wish to draw attention to the letter addressed to [the] applicant's Attorney in which I ask for an extension of the time within which I should file the Affidavit.

Should [the] Applicant's Attorney refuse my request I shall have no alternative but to apply to court for such an extension.[ii]

Yours faithfully,
[Signed Nelson R. Mandela]

◇◇◇◇◇◇◇◇

It is clear from correspondence in Mandela's prison files held by the National Archives and Records Service of South Africa, that he wrote on several occasions to Adelaide Tambo, the wife of his former law partner and the president of the ANC, Oliver Tambo, who was living in exile with his family in London, and running the organisation from abroad. It is unlikely that Adelaide Tambo received the letters before the latter part of his prison sentence. In 1968 Mandela wrote to her care of his wife and used her African name, Matlala, and the surname Mandela. A note in Afrikaans at the end of one of the letters shows that the prison authorities had worked out the identity of the real recipient because someone has written 'A Tambo' on the letter. Just this information would have been enough for them to hold it back. It is highly probable that all the underlined text in this letter is the work of the prison censors, drawing attention to individuals that are known to them or whom they want to identify.

---

i   This text has been crossed out and signed by someone else.

ii   In his response on 13 December 1967, J. H. du Toit agreed to extend until the end of March 1968, the period within which Mandela had to serve and lodge his answering affidavit. He added that this extension was 'subject to the court's approval'. Mandela signed this reply, acknowledging that he received it on 14 December 1967.

To Adelaide Tambo,[i] friend, anti-apartheid activist, and the wife of Oliver Tambo, ANC president and Mandela's former law partner[ii]

5.3.68

[Note in another hand says 'My sister'.]

Kgaitsedi yaka,[iii]

I send you my warmest love. You, Reginald,[iv] Thembi, and Dalindlela[v] the baby have been in my thoughts during the past five years, and it gives me great pleasure to be able to tell you this.

I hope you have all been keeping well. Zami[vi] gives me scraps of information about you in her letters and whenever she comes down, but the last occasion I heard from you directly was when I received Reggie's[vii] inciting telegram during my first case. I was tremendously inspired. It arrived almost simultaneously with that from the late Chief, and both messages gave a new dimension to the issues.

News of the widespread efforts made by our household[viii] during the first half of '64 played a similar role. Such efforts fortified our spirits and relieved the grimness of that period.

But I must return to you Matlala.[ix] Just exactly where do I start? Certainly not from the day in the early fifties when Reggie and I drove to the Helping Hand[x] where you presented him with a smart jersey that you had especially knitted for the occasion. That would take us far back. Suffice to say that I thought you played your cards very well. Nor do I wish to remind you [of] the pertinent observations you used to make during the numerous consultations we attended together with the late Rita, Effie[xi] and others on matters that vitally affected the interests of your profession,[xii] the savoury meals I enjoyed when I visited you in the East shortly after your wedding as well as in June '62 over there.[xiii] The correspondence we had in '61 was stimulating and was widely discussed among us at the time. These and

---

i   Adelaide Tambo (1929–2007) – see the glossary.
ii   The underlining of words appears to have been done by the censor to question the names of the people he mentions.
iii   'My sister' in both Sesotho and Setswana.
iv   Oliver Reginald Tambo (1917–93) – Mandela's friend, former law partner, and the president of the ANC – see the glossary. His middle name was Reginald.
v   The Tambo's son, Dali.
vi   Zami is one of Winnie Mandela's names.
vii   Oliver Reginald Tambo (his middle name Reginald was shortened to Reggie).
viii 'Our household' is code for the ANC.
ix   'Matlala', a nickname for Adelaide Tambo.
x   Adelaide Tambo and Winnie Mandela both stayed at the Helping Hand Hostel in Hans Street, Jeppestown, when they moved to Johannesburg.
xi   Possibly Effie Schultz, a medical doctor and activist.
xii   He might be referring to Adelaide Tambo's vocation as a nurse. Also see footnote i on page 53.
xiii He is referring to his visit to London where he saw the Tambos in June 1962 while on his clandestine trip out of South Africa.

numerous other incidents have flashed across my mind on many occasions and I love to recall them.

I was sorry to learn that you had abandoned your studies.[i] In July '62 I had mentioned the matter to Xamela[ii] and others, and the news of which they approved fully, had much excited them. In fact we were calculating only the other day that you had either completed or [were] at least doing the final year. Anyway I am sure you and Reggie must have weighed the matter very carefully and, there must have been a good reason for terminating the studies.

Thembi, Dali and the baby[iii] must have grown and I would love to hear about them. Please give them my love. I hope Thembi still remembers the Saturday morning when you and herself visited Chancellor House.[iv] In the general office and with all the clients around I complimented her on her new dress, whereupon she promptly [displayed] the dress, boasting that "i ne stiffening" to the amusement of everybody there.

I also think of Malume and the heavyweight from the western areas[v] and hope that they still find time to dye their hair. Incidentally, during our sojourn with Reggie, I remarked that he was beginning to turn grey and drew from him the grave comment: "Please don't tell me that, don't tell me that". I am sure my good friend Gcwanini,[vi] always polite and peaceful for the [first] five days of the week and who always allowed himself relaxation from these virtues and a bit of rioting on weekends still will remember the night we spent at home together with Peter. Then there is the nocturnal Ngwali, who never got tired of waking us up at midnight to burden us with numerous problems, and the ubiquitous Bakwe.[vii] I believe problems of weight have slowed down the activities of both. Madiba of Orlando East, the two Gambus, Alfred, Mzwayi, Tom, Dinou, Maindy,[viii] and Gabula, I remember them all. I hope you still see Tough Guy and Hazel. Has he produced anything new after "The Road to . . . ?" Any new literature from Todd

---

i   Adelaide Tambo was a nurse and matron at the hospital where she worked. She had a master's degree in gerontology from the University of Oxford and after being encouraged by the doctors at the hospital, enrolled to study medicine. She discontinued her studies when it became apparent that she would need to give up her job, the income from which her family relied on. (Dali Tambo in an email to Sahm Venter, 28 November 2017.)

ii   Walter Sisulu (1912–2003), ANC and MK activisit and fellow Rivonia trialist who was imprisoned with Mandela – see the glossary. Mandela is referring to him by his clan name Xamela (sometimes spelt by Mandela as Xhamela) as he is not permitted to write about other prisoners.

iii   The Tambos' children.

iv   Chancellor House was the building in which Mandela and Oliver Tambo started their law practice, Mandela and Tambo, in 1952.

v   Mandela is possibly speaking about people in code here.

vi   Advocate Duma Nokwe (1927–78), political activist and advocate – see the glossary. Gcwanini is possibly his clan name.

vii   Bakwe (Joe) Matthews (1929–2010), political activist and son of Frieda and Z. K. Matthews – see the glossary for these three individuals.

viii   Maindy Msimang, also known as Mendi Msimang, was an administrative officer of the ANC in London.

and Esme,[i] or musical composition? Do you hear of Cousin, Mlahleni, and Mpumi?[ii] I would like to be remembered to all of them.

Our family has always attached a great deal of importance to education and progress, and the widespread illiteracy facing us has always been a matter of grave concern. Efforts to overcome this problem have always been frustrated by lack of funds and of adequate facilities for academic and vocational training. Now these problems are being gradually tackled and solved and increasing numbers of school-going youths are finding their way into boarding schools and technical colleges. It flatters one's pride to know that those who have completed their courses and who have been given posts and assignments are doing so exceptionally well. Heartiest congratulations and fondest regards to all.

The pronoun "I" has been prominent in this correspondence. I would have preferred "we". But I am constrained to use terminology acceptable to the practice of this establishment, however much it may be incompatible with my own individual [taste]. I am sure you will pardon me for the egotism.

Once again, I wish you to know that you, Reggie, the kids and all my friends are constantly in my thoughts. I know you must be worried about my incarceration. But let me assure you that I am well, fit and on top of the world, and nothing would please me more than to hear from you.

In the meantime my warmest to you and fondest regards to all.

Sincerely,
Nel

[Written in another hand in Afrikaans] (Contents from inside the envelope).

[Envelope]
Miss Matlala Mandela,[iii]
8155, Orlando West,
Johannesburg.

---

i   Todd Matshikiza (1920–68), writer and musician who composed the musical score for the internationally successful South African musical *King Kong* (1959) and his wife Esme Matshikiza, a social worker.
ii   Mlahleni is Professor Nyisani and his wife Mpumi.
iii   Using Adelaide Tambo's nickname and the surname Mandela indicates further that he wishes to disguise her identity.

To the commanding officer, Robben Island

29th April 1968

The Commanding Officer,
Robben Island

Attention: Capt. Naude

As more fully appears from the accompanying letter to the Cultural Attaché, British Embassy, Pretoria, I have decided to withdraw my name from the list of candidates this year. I might add that in terms of the Regulations of the University of London I am expected to write Part II within two years after completing Part I which I did only in 1967. I had, however, planned to attempt it within one year of completing Part I. In view of the late arrival of the study books, however, I have elected to postpone the examination until June 1969.

[Signed NRMandela]
NELSON MANDELA 466/64

To the cultural attaché, British Embassy

[In Mandela's hand] Copy

29th April 1968

The Cultural Attaché,
The British Embassy,
Pretoria.

Attention: Mrs S Goodspeed

Dear Sir,

I will not be able to sit for the University of London LL.B Examination Part II of the Final year. On the 25th January 1968 I placed an order with the London book firm of Messrs Sweet & Maxwell, Spon, Limited for certain law books which I needed for purposes of preparations for the above Examinations. These books were only delivered to me on the 23rd April 1968 and

I now consider it unwise to tackle the examination.

I propose presenting myself in June 1969 and I should be pleased if you would kindly withdraw my name from this year's examination list.

Yours faithfully,
[Signed NRMandela]
NELSON MANDELA

To the commanding officer, Robben Island

16th September 1968

The Commanding Officer
Robben Island

Attention: Major Kellerman

I should be pleased if you would grant me leave to write to Brigadier Aucamp[i] in connection with the under-mentioned matter.

I intend applying to the Registrar of the University of South Africa for permission to postpone the examinations in Afrikaans Course I from the 15th October next to February 1969 on the grounds of ill-health. In terms of the University Regulations such application must be accompanied by a medical certificate specifying the nature of the illness. The Prison Doctor is willing to issue the certificate[ii] but the hospital orderly, H/W Embiek[iii], drew his attention to the fact that such a certificate can only be issued with the approval of Capt Naude. A few days thereafter, H/W Embiek informed me that Capt Naude had told him that it was not necessary for me to produce a medical certificate to postpone the forthcoming examination. On the 30th August 1968, and in pursuance of the information given me by the aforesaid head warder, I wrote and requested Capt Naude to authorise the issue of the certificate. On the 9th September Capt Naude informed me that the issue of a medical certificate was a matter entirely in the hands of the doctor and had nothing to do with him – a statement which flatly contradicted that of head warder Embiek. On the same day I consulted the doctor and acquainted him with Capt Naude's attitude and he promised to go into the

---

i   Brigadier Aucamp, commanding officer of Robben Island – see the glossary.
ii   This appears to have been underlined by officials.
iii   It is not clear from Mandela's handwriting of the exact spelling of the head warder's name.

matter. Subsequently, the head warder told me he would discuss the matter with Capt Naude. I have heard nothing since.

On the 4th September I had discussed the matter with Brigadier Aucamp who adopted a reasonable and helpful attitude, pointing out in the course of the conversation that he had dealt with such applications in Pretoria, and promised to take up the matter with the Captain. I must assume that, due to pressure of business, he forgot to discuss it, and I should accordingly be pleased if you would grant me leave to place the whole matter before him again.

[Signed NRMandela]
NELSON MANDELA: 466/64

Attention: Major Kellerman
              The Commanding Officer,
              Robben Island

[Notes in Afrikaans from prison officials]

Major,

For your information [Signed] 16/9/68
Lt. Good. He can write to Brig. Aucamp. It must be sent unofficially.

[Signed] 17/9/68

◇◇◇◇◇◇◇◇

For Nelson Mandela, 1968 marked the beginning of the most harrowing of his years in prison. On 26 September his mother, Nosekeni, died and he was forbidden from attending her funeral. Despite a measured and rational written request to the authorities promising to return to prison after the funeral, he was denied the possibility. He was restricted to writing to those who had attended the funerals offering his deep relief and gratitude.

To K. D. Matanzima,[i] his nephew, a Thembu chief, and chief minister for the Transkei

[in another hand]: 466/64 Nelson Mandela

[Stamp dated Reception Office Robben Island 14.10.1968]

WHEN ACKNOWLEDGING RECEIPT HEREOF, PLEASE WRITE THE FOLLOWING WORDS AT THE TOP OF YOUR LETTER: "REPLY TO SPECIAL LETTER".

Nyana Othandekayo,[ii]

My brother-in-law, Timonthy Mbuzo, visited me two days ago and reported that you attended my mother's funeral. Your presence at the graveside, in spite of your many preoccupations, means a lot to me, and I should like you to know that I deeply appreciate it.

I last saw my mother on September 9 last year. After the interview I was able to look at her as she walked away towards the boat that would take her to the mainland, and somehow the idea crossed my mind that I would never again set my eyes on her. Her visits had always excited me and the news of her death hit me hard. I at once felt lonely and empty. But my friends here, whose sympathy and affection have always been a source of strength to me, helped to relieve my grief and to raise my spirits. The report on the funeral reinforced my courage. It was a pleasure for me to be informed that my relatives and friends had turned up in large numbers to honour the occasion with their presence and was happy to be able to count you amongst those who paid their last respects to her. Nangomso![iii]

In this connection I consider it proper to let you know that I have been kept fully informed of your continued interest in my affairs and those of the family over the last six years. During one of her visits my mother told me that twice you travelled all the way to Qunu to advise her of my conviction. Your visits to [my] Johannesburg home and other acts of hospitality towards the family have all been repeatedly reported by Nobandla.[iv] This interest stems not only from our close relationship, but also from the long and deep friendship that we have cultivated since our student days kuwe la kwa Rarabe.[v]

---

i   K. D. Matanzima (1915– 2003) – see the glossary.
ii   'Beloved son' in isiXhosa.
iii   'Nangomso' is an isiXhosa word that expresses deep gratitude to a person who has gone beyond the call of duty. Mandela sometimes spelled it nangomso.
iv   Nobandla is one of Winnie Mandela's names.
v   *Kuwe* – 'to you'; *la kwa* – 'from Rarabe'. Rarabe is a subgroup of the Xhosa nation, House of Phalo.

I have written to your brother and Head of the Xumbu Royal House, Jonguhlanga,[i] to thank him for undertaking the strenuous task of organising and planning the funeral and for the heavy disbursments that he personally made on this occasion in spite of his declining health and [?] commitments. His painstaking concern and care for my mother's welfare during the past six years and his touching devotion generally have created a profound impression on me and I owe him an immense debt. I only hope his health will improve.

I am also writing to Mr Guzana.[ii]

This is a special letter allowed me only for the purpose of thanking you for attending the funeral and it is not possible to discuss other matters. I need only request you to give my love to Amakhosikazi Nozuko, Nobandla, No-Gate,[iii] and to Mthetho,[iv] Camagwini[v] and Wanda; and my fondest regards to Chief Mzimvubu,[vi] Thembekile, Dalubuhle's heir, Manzezulu, Gwebindlala and Siyabalala; and to Bros Wonga, Thembekile, Headman Mfebe and Mr Sihle.

I would have much liked to write to my father-in-law and to Ma[vii] and thank them directly for their own share on this occasion, but it will not be possible to do this, and I must accordingly ask you to do so on my behalf.

Yours very sincerely,
Dalibunga.

Chief K.D. Matanzima
Chief Minister for the Transkei
Umtata[viii]

---

i   King Sabata Jonguhlanga Dalindyebo (1928–86), paramount chief of the Transkei homeland and leader of the Democratic Progressive Party, the opposition party in Transkei which opposed apartheid rule – see the glossary.

ii   Knowledge Guzana (1916–), attorney and leader of the Democratic Party in the Transkei – see the glossary.

iii   Matanzima's wives. *Amakhosikazi* means 'married women' in plural form in isiXhosa and isiZulu.

iv   Chief Mthetho Matanzima (d. 1972), Mandela's nephew K. D. Matanzima's son and chief of the Noqayti region – see the glossary.

v   K. D. Matanzima's daughter.

vi   George Matanzima, K. D. Matanzima's brother.

vii   He is mostly likely referring to his mother-in-law.

viii   Umtata (now called Mthatha) was the capital of the Transkei homeland.

To Knowledge Guzana,[i] attorney and leader of the Transkei homeland's Democratic Party[ii]

[Stamp dated 14.10.1968]

WHEN ACKNOWLEDGING RECEIPT HEREOF PLEASE WRITE THE FOLLOWING WORDS AT THE TOP OF YOUR LETTER: "REPLY TO SPECIAL LETTER."

Dear Dambisa,[iii]

Two days ago my brother-in-law, Timothy Mbuzo,[iv] informed me that you attended my mother's funeral and I should like to thank you for this considerate gesture.

Only a keen sense of public duty would enable a man in your position, and on whom there must be heavy and pressing demands for his services, to find time to devote himself to the public good, and I should like you to know that I am greatly indebted to you.

It was never easy for one anywhere to lose a beloved mother. Behind bars such misfortune can be a shattering disaster. This could easily have been the case with me when I was confronted with these tragic news on September 26, which ironically enough was my wife's birthday. Fortunately for me, however, my friends here, who are endowed with virtues far in excess of anything I can hope to command, are remarkable for their ability to think and feel for others. I have always leaned heavily on their comradeship and solidarity. Their offers of goodwill and encouragement enabled me to face this tragic loss with resignation.

Sibali[v] Mkhuze told me that my relatives and friends responded admirably and rallied to the graveside. This was a magnificent demonstration of solidarity which gave me a shot in the arm, and it is a source of tremendous inspiration for me to count you amongst those who gave me this encouragement.

I have also written to your friend and head of the Tembu[vi] Royal House,[vii] Jonguhlanga, to thank him for undertaking the strenuous task of planning

---

i   Knowledge Guzana (1916–) – see the glossary.
ii   The Democatic Party, which was formed in 1963, rejected 'independence' of black homelands or Bantustans and was the official opposition party in the Transkei. Guzana led the party from 1966 until 1976.
iii Knowledge Guzana's clan name.
iv   Sibali Timothy Mbuzo, a close relative of Mandela's brother-in-law Daniel Timakwe and a long-standing leading member of the ANC in the Transkei homeland.
v   *Sibali* means 'brother-in-law' in isiXhosa.
vi   More commonly this is spelt 'Thembu'.
vii Mandela was a member of the Thembu royal house – see the glossary. In a letter to Fatima Meer, dated 14 June 1989, Mandela said the correct spelling was Thembu.

the funeral, and this in spite of his declining health and heavy commitments. His touching devotion to his relatives, friends and people generally has created a profound impression far and wide. I only hope that his health might improve.

This is a special letter allowed me only for the purpose of thanking you for attending the funeral and it is not possible to refer to wider issues. It is sufficient for me to say that I am happy to note that the interest you showed in public affairs as a student at S.A.N.C[i] 30 years ago has not flagged. I hope that in this note I have succeeded in placing on record not only my deep gratitude to you for honouring the occasion with your presence but also in indicating to you the regard I have for you and family.

Bulisa elusasheni na ku[ii] [name is difficult to read]. Na ngomso![iii]

Yours very sincerely,
Nelson

K Guzana, Esq.,
Ncambedlana,
P.O. Umtata.[iv] Transkei

To Mangosuthu Buthelezi,[v] family friend and Zulu prince

[In another hand] 466/64 Nelson Mandela

                    [Stamp dated and signed] Censor Office4–11–1968
My dear Chief,

I should be pleased if you would kindly convey to the Royal Family my deepest sympathy on the death of King Cyprian Bhekuzulu.[vi] His passing away took me completely by surprise for I did not have even the slightest hint of the King's fatal illness. Although a few years back I had heard that his health was somewhat indifferent, a friend had later informed me that he

---

i   South African Native College, another name for University College of Fort Hare.
ii   'Give my regards to the family' in isiXhosa.
iii   'Nangamso' is an isiXhosa word that expresses deep gratitude to a person who has gone beyond the call of duty. It is usually spelled nangamso, sometimes Mandela spelled it nangomso and in this case, na ngomso.
iv   Umtata (now called Mthatha) was the capital of the Transkei homeland.
v   Mangosuthu Buthelezi (1928–) – see the glossary.
vi   King Cyprian Bhekuzulu kaSolomon, king of the Zulu nation – see the glossary.

had much improved, a fact which seemed to be confirmed by photographs that I subsequently saw in various publications and which on the face of it appeared to indicate that he was in good health. The unexpected news consequently shocked me immensely, and I have since been thinking of the Royal Family in their bereavement.

You and the late King were closely related and bound to each other by a long and fruitful friendship, and his death must have been a severe blow to you. I met him twice only; in my Johannesburg home and in my office, and on both occasions he was accompanied by you. It afforded me great pleasure to note how deeply he valued your friendship and how highly he appreciated your advice. In him we caught glimpses of the astuteness and courage that was the source of so much of the glittering achievements of his famous ancestors. In serving him as you did, you were carrying on the tradition established by my chiefs, Ngqengelele and Mnyamana, your ancestors, whose magnificent role in the task of national service is widely acknowledged.

The vast crowds that must have attended the funeral, the words of comfort delivered at the graveside and the messages of sympathy from organisations and individuals all over the country would by now have fully demonstrated that the Royal Family is not alone in mourning his unfortunate loss to the country.

The death of a human being, whatever may be his station in life, is always a sad and painful affair; that of a noted public figure brings not only grief and mourning to his family and friends, but very often entails implications of a wider nature. It may mean tampering with established attitudes and the introduction of new ones, with all the uncertainty that normally accompanies the change of personalities at the head of affairs. In due course Amazulu will no doubt be summoned to the Royal capital to deliberate over the whole situation and to make the necessary decisions. I am confident that the statesmen and elders whose vast wealth of wisdom, ability and experience have guided the fortunes of this celebrated House in the past, will, on this occasion, offer solutions which will be inspired by the conviction that the interests and welfare of all our countrymen is the first and paramount consideration. In this regard, your immense knowledge and able advice will be as crucial now as it has been in the past.

Incidentally, in December 1965 I wrote a special letter to Nkosikazi Nokhukhanya[i] and requested her, amongst other things, to mention me to your late cousin and to you. I indicated then that on my release I would visit Zululand to pay my respects to my traditional leader. I hope the message

---

i   Nokhukhanya Luthuli, widow of Chief Albert Luthuli – see the glossary.

was received. This resolution remains unchanged, and although it will no longer be my privilege to pay homage to the late King personally, it will be an honour for me to visit Nongoma[i] and thereafter Mahlabatini.[ii]

Finally, I should like you to know that I think of you and Umndlunkulu[iii] with warm and pleasant memories, and sincerely wish you great happiness and good health. My fond regards to Umntwana,[iv] your mother, and to your mother-in-law.

Yours very sincerely,
[Signed NR Mandela]
NELSON R[v] MANDELA

Chief Mangosuthu Buthelezi
P.O. Box 1, Mahlabatini
Zululand

=========

To Zenani and Zindzi Mandela,[vi] his middle and youngest daughters

4.2.69

My Darlings,

The nice letter by Zindzi reached me safely, and I was indeed very glad to know that she is now in Standard 2. When Mummy came to see me last December, she told me that both of you had passed your examinations and that Zeni was now in Standard 3. I now know that Kgatho[vii] and Maki[viii] have also passed. It pleases me very much to see that all my children are doing well.

I hope that you will do even better at the end of the year.

I was happy to learn that Zeni can cook chips, rice, meat, and many other things. I am looking forward to the day when I will be able to enjoy all that she cooks.

Zindzi says her heart is sore because I am not at home and wants to know when I will come back. I do not know, my darlings, when I will return.

---

i   Residence of the Zulu King and the seat of the royal family.
ii   Buthelezi's birthplace and residence.
iii   A royal reference to Mangosuthu Buthelezi's wife, Irene Buthelezi.
iv   'The child' in isiZulu.
v   The initial R stands for his given name, Rolihlahla.
vi   Zenani Mandela (1959–) and Zindziswa Mandela (1960–) – see the glossary.
vii   Makgatho (Kgatho) Mandela (1950–2005), Mandela's second-born son – see the glossary.
viii   Makaziwe (Maki) Mandela (1954–), Mandela's eldest daughter – see the glossary.

You will remember that in the letter I wrote in 1966, I told you that the white judge said I should stay in jail for the rest of my life.

It may be long before I come back; it may be soon. Nobody knows when it will be, not even the judge who said I should be kept here. But I am certain that one day I will be back at home to live in happiness with you until the end of my days.

Do not worry about me now. I am happy, well and full of strength and hope. The only thing I long for is you, but whenever I feel lonely I look at your photo which is always in front of me. It has a white frame with a black margin. It is a lovely photo. For the last 2 years I have been asking Mummy to send me a group photo with Zindzi, Zeni, Maki, Kgatho, Nomfundo[i] and Kazeka. But up to now I have not received it. The photo will make me even more happy than I am at the present moment.

Many thanks for the wonderful Christmas cards you sent me. Apart from yours, I received one from Kgatho and another from Mummy. I hope you received more.

Mummy visits me two or three times a year. She also arranges for Kgatho and others to see me. Father Long of the Roman Catholic Church, St Patrick, Mowbray, Cape Town, still visits me once a month. In addition, I am allowed to receive and write one letter every month. All these things keep me happy and hopeful.

Please pass my fondest regards to Father Borelli and tell the Mother Superior[ii] that I am greatly indebted to her and all the sisters there for the help and guidance they are giving you. Perhaps someday I may be able in some small way to return this kindness.

In December 1965 I received a letter from Zeni in which she also asked me to come back home, just as Zindzi says in hers. The English was good and the handwriting clear. But I was completely surprised to get one from Zindzi. Her English was also good and the writing was just as clear. You are doing well, my darlings. Keep it up.

With lots and lots of love and a million kisses.

Affectionately,
Tata[iii]

MISSES ZENI & ZINDZI MANDELA
HOUSE NO. 8115 ORLANDO WEST
JOHANNESBURG

---

i   Olive Nomfundo Mandela, daughter of Mandela's sister Notancu.
ii   Zindzi and Zenani were at a Catholic school in neighbouring Swaziland.
iii   'Father' in isiXhosa.

To Makaziwe Mandela,[i] his eldest daughter

16.2.69

My Darling,

I was indeed very happy to learn that you, Kgatho, Zeni & Zindzi[ii] had passed your respective examinations. Please accept my warmest congratulations. Your success in all the examinations that you have written up to now show that all of you have the ability to study and I do hope this will inspire you to work even harder this year. You are now doing the final year of the Junior Certificate and I feel that when the time comes to sit for the examinations at the end of the year, you will again pass, provided you work hard and continuously right from the beginning. I expect you to tell me in your reply your subjects this year, and the titles of the English and Xhosa/Zulu set works. I should like to read them. But for the time being I say: "Well done!"

I believe you, Tembi[iii] & Kgatho were expected to go down to Umtata[iv] to visit Makhulu's[v] grave and to pay your last respects to her. Did you succeed? I was very sorry to receive the news of her death for I had hoped to be able to look after her in her last days on earth and to bury her when she died. But Mummy and others tell me that relatives and friends, led by Paramount Chief Sabata,[vi] attended in large numbers and gave a burial that aroused deep feelings. I know that Zeni & Zindzi attended and would be equally happy to be told that you were also able to do so.

I hope you received the Xmas card I sent you and Kgatho and that you enjoyed your Xmas and New Year. It was a real pleasure for me to get your undated letter in November 1967. The language and style were good and the writing clear. It pleased me very much to hear that you were enjoying yourself in school and that you liked English the best. I was also happy to know that your ambition is to become a doctor or scientist. Both are strenuous professions and you must work hard and steadily during school terms and have a good rest during school holidays. I see that you are afraid of

---

i   Makaziwe Mandela (1954–) – see the glossary.
ii   Mandela's son Makgatho (1950–2005) and his daughters Zenani (1959–) and Zindziswa (1960–).
iii   Mandela's eldest son, Madiba Thembekile (1945–69). Mandela variously shortened it to 'Thembi' or 'Tembi'.
iv   Umtata (now called Mthatha) was the capital of the Transkei homeland.
v   'Grandmother' in isiXhosa. Here Mandela is referring to his mother, Nosekeni Mandela, who died in 1968.
vi   King Sabata Jonguhlanga Dalindyebo (1928–86), paramount chief of the Transkei homeland and leader of the Democratic Progressive Party, the opposition party in Transkei which opposed apartheid rule – see the glossary. The term 'paramount chief' was developed by the British colonisers as the highest title in a region with a chief-based system. Paramount Chief Sabata was actually a king. The British maintained that only the British monarch could hold that title.

being kidnapped one day when you have discovered a dangerous drug. Do not worry much, darling, about kidnappers. Their world is getting smaller and smaller and their friends fewer. One day there will be a new world when all of us will live in happiness and peace. That world will be created by you and me; by Kgatho, Zeni & Zindzi; by our friends and countrymen. When you become a doctor or scientist and use your knowledge, training and skill to help your people who are poor and miserable and who have no opportunity to develop, you will be fighting for that new world.

In your letter you told me that Kgatho was doing first year matric and that he was doing well at school. The reports I have received both before and after your letter confirm your statement. I am pleased to learn that Kgatho is keen on his studies and that he is making good progress. You also told me that Thembi was working, and that he had a 2 year baby who was plumpy and lovely. You ended your letter on this point, by pointing out that Thembi was helping in every way, that he was buying clothes and all that you needed. It pleased me much to be informed that he is of assistance to you. Anything that eases your difficulties and that adds to your happiness fills my heart with joy, and I am really grateful to Thembi for all that he does for you.

I am however sorry to learn that he elected to leave school before he had obtained even the Junior Certificate. I wrote to him in 1967 and advised him to return to school together with his wife, or to continue the studies by correspondence. I received no reply from him nor have I any information on just what work he is doing.

I thank you for letting me know that But' Sitsheketshe[i] is married and that he stays in Pimville.[ii]

I have been trying for the last 2 years to get a group photo of you, Kgatho, Zeni, Zindzi, Nomfundo[iii] and Chief Mdingi's daughter.[iv] I should be grateful if you would help in arranging for the photo to be taken and sent down as soon as possible.

Please ask Mme Ngakane[v] to give me, through you, the respective qualifications, profession or trade of Mookamedi[vi] Makgatho, Letanka, Msane and Mabaso. You will give me this information in your reply.

The sentiments you expressed in the last paragraph of your letter were

i   Mandela's cousin.
ii   A suburb of Soweto.
iii Olive Nomfundo Mandela, daughter of Mandela's sister Notancu.
iv   Chief Mdingi is a relative of Mandela's and the Thembu chief who named Mandela's two younger daughters. The eldest he named 'Zenani' meaning 'What have you brought?', and the Madikizelas (Winnie Mandela's family) named her Nomadabi Nosizwe – 'battlefield of the nation'. Mdingi named the youngest daughter Mantu Nobutho Zindziswa.
v   Neighbours of the Mandelas.
vi   'President' in Sesotho. Although we haven't been able to identify to whom Mandela is referring, it is probably not an actual president.

very sweet and they gave me a lot of inspiration and strength, darling. You are now 14 and the day is not far off when you will be able to visit me. I am told that you have grown tall and charming and I am anxious to see you. In the meantime I should like you to know that I think of you, Kgatho, Zeni, and Zindzi every day and your school progress makes me happy and proud of you. With lots and lots of love.

Affectionately,
Tata

29.7.69

I had written the above letter & handed it in for posting to you on February 16 this year but for some reason or other it was not sent away. I have already written to your mother and Kgatho and Zeni and Zindzi giving you all my deepest sympathy, darling. My application for permission to attend the funeral was not granted, and I hope it was possible for you and Kgatho to do so.

In March I received the group photo I asked for, and you need no longer worry about it. I had previously been promised a photo of Thembi and his family, and will write to Molokozana[i] about it as soon as Kgatho gives me the particulars I had asked for.

With much love,
Tata

◇◇◇◇◇◇◇◇

While battling his grief at the passing of his mother and ensuring that he'd written to all who needed to be comforted or thanked, Mandela continued with life behind bars and its daily struggles.

The perennial tussle with the authorities for the study materials he was entitled to took up a lot of his time. The problem persisted throughout his time on Robben Island, and he refused to stop calling to account the authorities who were obliged to follow the regulations.

---

i   'Daughter-in-law' in isiXhosa. He is referring to Thoko Mandela, his son Thembi's widow.

To Captain Huisamen, commanding officer, Robben Island

[In another hand] File

28.2.69

The Commanding Officer
Robben Island

Attention: Capt. Huisamen

On 25th February 1969, Warder De Jager informed us that instructions had been received from Pretoria to the effect that in future we could only order study books if such books were prescribed and that recommended works would not be allowed.

In this connection we wish to advise you that precisely the same instructions were issued to us towards the end of 1965. In February 1966, in the presence of the Commanding Officer of that time, Major Kellerman, I discussed the whole matter with the Commissioner of Prisons, General Steyn, and asked him to reconsider his decision. In support of my request I drew his attention to the fact that I was studying for the LL.B Degree of the University of London, and that according to the Regulations of that university there were no prescribed books for that course, all the books I was required to read for examination purposes being recommended and not prescribed. I pointed out that in regard to the Honours Courses, the tutorial letters expressly warned students to read widely and not to confine themselves to the list of books provided in the study guides. I further pointed out that education was not intended merely to prepare people to write and pass the examinations; its main function was to enable them to be specialists in their respective fields, a fact which made it absolutely imperative to read extensively. I invited the Commissioner to bear in mind that on release from prison we would compete for appointments with people who had a free and unrestrained access to all sources of information on a particular subject, and that the enforcement of the new instructions would seriously handicap us. The Commissioner accepted these arguments and instructed Major Kellerman to restore the privilege to order recommended works. For some time thereafter we experienced no difficulties whatsoever in this matter.

Early in 1967, however, the officer in charge of studies at the time reissued the instructions and informed us that we would not be allowed to order recommended books. On the 15th February the same year I discussed the matter again with [the] Commissioner and the privilege was again restored and we have enjoyed it ever since.

We assume that you are not aware of this background and we request you to reconsider the matter.

[Signed NRMandela]
NELSON MANDELA: 466/64

[In another hand in Afrikaans] Discuss. Do not accept responsibility for prescribed books and they must be very well considered when they are ordered. [Signed] 2/3/69

◇◇◇◇◇◇◇◇

It appears that by the end of the 1960s, Mandela was allowed to write to those outside his family circle. But such correspondence was not exempt from the obstacles that had become a hallmark of the prisoner and his lifeline to the world. In this series of letters, Mandela has rewritten his original letter with its original date, and then explained this to the recipient in a postscript.

To Lilian Ngoyi,[i] his friend & comrade

3.3.69

Kgaitsedi yaka, yaratehang[ii]

I wrote to you before I was sentenced in Nov 1962. You also heard from me sometime thereafter when I asked you, as the eldest daughter in the family, always to play the role of peacekeeper. Since then I have been anxious to write to you but the main difficulty has always been the fact that you would not have been able to reply.[iii] Now, however, you are free to communicate with me & I should like you to know that I always think of you, the Old Lady,[iv] Hlatse,[v] Memo[vi] & Oupa[vii] with warm & affectionate memories. I hope you are all keeping well & am looking forward to hear something on each one of you.

---

i   Lilian Ngoyi (1911–80), politician, and anti-apartheid and women's rights activist – see the glossary.
ii   'My dear sister' in Sesotho or Setswana.
iii She wouldn't have been able to reply due to the fact that she was not family and also that she was a known political activist.
iv   Annie, Lilian Ngoyi's grandmother.
v   Lilian Ngoyi's daughter.
vi   Peletsi 'Memory' Mphahlele, Lilian Ngoyi's adopted daughter.
vii Edith's son Tebogo and Lilian Ngoyi's nephew.

I was very sorry to hear of the death of Percy[i] & was even more so that I was unable to attend the funeral. He was not only your brother but a friend whose kindness and charm made him dear to me & I regretted very much when I heard that he was no more. Even though years have passed since the happening of this event, I should be pleased if you would kindly give the Old Lady my deepest sympathy.

It was very sweet of you to send Hlatse to the Rivonia Trial. We deeply appreciated the trouble she took in travelling the 32 miles to Pretoria & accepted her presence in court as an act of solidarity from you and family that gave us much courage & inspiration. In all the important issues that we took up you were always in the forefront, sharing common hardships with your friends & giving them encouragement & hope. Your humble contribution was made in the Defiance Campaign,[ii] COP,[iii] Women's Protest March to Pretoria[iv] & the Treason Trial,[v] to mention but a few.

We knew that although you could not be present in person you were, nevertheless fully, with us in spirit as we went through that memorable case, & were indeed very glad to see Hlatse there. Is Sonny[vi] keeping well?

You may not be in a position to give my fondest regards to Helen.[vii] I should like her to know that I think of her as well. I have always respected her for her noble ideas & immense courage. We travelled together almost daily to & from Pretoria during the Treason Trial & we became very close to each other. Together we worked in Pretoria Prison preparing her evidence during the State of Emergency[viii] & I watched her as she was mercilessly being hammered by the prosecution for several days.[ix] She did very well

---

i   Lilian Ngoyi's brother.
ii   Initiated by the ANC in December 1951, and launched with the South African Indian Congress on 26 June 1952 against six apartheid laws, the Defiance Campaign Against Unjust Laws (known as the Defiance Campaign for short) involved individuals breaking racist laws such as entering premises reserved for 'whites only', breaking curfews, and courting arrest. Mandela was appointed national volunteer-in-chief and Maulvi Cachalia as his deputy. Over 8,500 volunteers were imprisoned for their participation in the Defiance Campaign.
iii   The Congress of the People, held on 25–26 June 1955 in Kliptown, Johannesburg, was attended by 3,000 delegates and was the culmination of a year-long campaign where members of the Congress Alliance visited homes across the length and breadth of South Africa recording people's demands for a free South Africa. These were included in the Freedom Charter, which was adopted on the second day of the Congress of the People, and which espoused equal rights for all South Africans regardless of race, along with land reform, improved working and living conditions, the fair distribution of wealth, compulsory education, and fairer laws.
iv   On 9 August 1956, 20,000 women marched to the government's Union Buildings in Pretoria to protest against the extension of passes to African women.
v   The Treason Trial (1956–61) was a result of the apartheid government's attempt to quell the power of the Congress Alliance, a coalition of anti-apartheid organisations. In early-morning raids on 5 December 1956, 156 individuals were arrested and charged with high treason. By the end of the trial in March 1961 all the accused either had the charges withdrawn or, in the case of the last twenty-eight accused (including Mandela), were acquitted.
vi   Edith Ngoyi's husband.
vii   Helen Joseph (1905–92), teacher, social worker, and anti-apartheid and women's rights activist – see the glossary.
viii Declared on 30 March 1960 as a response to the Sharpeville Massacre, the 1960 State of Emergency was characterised by mass arrests and the imprisonment of most African leaders. On 8 April 1960 the ANC and Pan Africanist Congress were banned under the Unlawful Organisations Act.
ix   When the South African government declared a State of Emergency in 1960, the accused in the Treason Trial who had been on bail were taken into custody. The defence team withdrew in protest and those accused who were lawyers assisted their colleagues in preparing for the trial. Mandela provided legal assistance to his fellow trialist Helen Joseph.

indeed & my confidence in her grew deeper. Her training as a social worker, & probably her experience as an army officer, made her very sensitive to the welfare of her needy colleagues & she was always ready to offer some kind of material help. Now & again I get some snatches of information about her & I am happy to know that my confidence in her was not misplaced. My only regret was that I was unable to see her book on the Treason Trial after it was published.[i]

I was privileged to read the manuscript & found it very stimulating. I would have liked to see the finished article. Perhaps now that she is living in semi-retirement she may be devoting her good talents to more writing.

My fondest regards also go to Ntsiki,[ii] Greta,[iii] Doreen, Muriel, Joana, Caroline, Catherine, Mrs Taunyane, Lily Seroke, Virginia,[iv] Onica & Dorcas, my cousin Nobelungu & Hilda.[v] All of them are courageous girls & I regard it as a privilege to have been associated with them in the past.[vi]

I am presently reading on the great African Chiefs, Sekukuni & Mampuru, sons of Sekwati,[vii] & on the struggle between them for the Bapedi Throne. Even by modern standards these were intelligent & capable men who loved their country & people. The role of Sekukuni in the history of the country is known far & wide, but I have often wondered what the course of that history would have been if these & other chiefs in the country had sunk their differences & tried to solve their mutual problems through common efforts. Ngoana waKgosi Godfrey[viii] has every reason to be proud of the achievements of his famous grandfather. I hope he and his family are keeping well. It is quite some time since I last heard of Motsoala John. May he also be in good health & as lively as we knew him to be.

In January 1966 I received a sweet & inspiring letter from Ma Nokukanya,[ix] in which she informed us that we were always in her thoughts. Her words of encouragement did us a world of good. When the chief died I was allowed to write a special letter of condolence, but it never reached. I hear that her son-in-law is in hospital & I should be glad to hear about his condition. Once again I should like you to know that I think of you & family

---

i   Helen Joseph, *If This Be Treason* (Cape Town: Kwagga Publishers, 1963).
ii   Albertina Sisulu (1918–2011), anti-apartheid and women's rights activist, and wife of Mandela's comrade Walter Sisulu – see the glossary. Ntsiki is short for Nontsikelelo, her African name.
iii   Greta Ncapayi, an ANC Women's League activist and friend of Albertina Sisulu.
iv   Virginia Mngoma, political activist.
v   Hilda Bernstein (1915–2006), author, artist, and anti-apartheid and women's rights activist. She was a founding member of the South African Peace Council and of the Federation of South African Women. After her husband, Lionel (Rusty), was acquitted in the Rivonia Trial, they crossed into neighbouring Botswana on foot.
vi   All these women are likely to have been friends and associates of Mandela's who were anti-apartheid activists.
vii   Sekukuni or Matsebe Sekhukhune (1814–82) and Mampuru were sons of Bapedi king Sekwati and became rivals for the throne following his death in 1861. Sekhukhune was killed by Mampuru in 1882, and Mampuru was executed the following year. His remains have never been found.
viii   Godfrey Mogaramedi Sekhukhune became a freedom fighter with the ANC's military wing Umkhonto weSizwe, and at some point was imprisoned on Robben Island.
ix   Nokhukhanya Luthuli, widow of Chief Albert Luthuli.

with warm & affectionate memories & nothing would please me more than to hear from you.

> With love,
> Yours very sincerely,

Nel

Mrs Lilian Ngoyi
c/o Miss Nonyaniso Madikizela,[i]
House No. 8115, Orlando West,
Johannesburg.

29.7.69

This letter had been written & handed in for posting to you on March 3 this year. I now know that you never received it. Here it is again & though much has occurred since I wrote it, I have nevertheless preferred to reproduce it exactly as it was when I first wrote it. I can only hope that this time it will reach you.

Thank you very much for your moving message of condolence which has given me much strength & inspiration. I received the tragic news on July 16 & my reaction was the same as yours. I could hardly believe that Thembi was really gone. My application to attend the funeral was not approved, just as happened on the occasion of my mother's death 10 months ago. In both cases I was denied the opportunity to pay my last respects to those who are dearest to me. But my colleagues did all they could to soften the blow & make me happy. Your message has meant much to me & the sentiments it expresses have given me mighty courage. Once more I feel on top of the world and ready to face whatever the fates may have in store for me. Nel

---

To Gibson Kente,[ii] his nephew and a renowned playwright and composer[iii]

For the month of February 1969 B.I.P. V.B[iv]

---

i   Winnie Mandela's sister.
ii   Gibson Kente (1932–2004) – see the glossary.
iii   Because Gibson Kente came from the Madiba clan, as Mandela did, he called him a nephew.
iv   These initials are in Mandela's handwriting. It is not clear what the initials stand for.

3.3.69

My dear Nephew,

Zami[i] has told me of my niece, Evelyn,[ii] your wife. Unfortunately, the time allowed for visits is never long enough to enable us to cover fully such family matters as we should like to discuss & she was consequently unable to give me all the information I need know about her. I have not had the privilege of meeting her before but I am sure she must be a talented & charming girl to win your affection & I should be glad to receive her family background. I am looking forward to seeing both of you one day. In the meantime I wish you a fruitful marriage & happy future.

I should like to know whether the Union of S. A. Artists[iii] is still growing strong. Who are the present officials & what is the name of their publication (if any) & subscription fee? I am collecting albums of African songs[iv] – Sotho, Zulu & Xhosa – but I am experiencing difficulties. I am aware of Mohapeloa's[v] collection but I was unable to obtain them from the Cape Town firm which specialises in this field. I managed to get a look at choral folk songs for mixed voices by Williams & Maselwa,[vi] but I am more interested in albums of modern African music. Perhaps you may advise me how to go about it.

I learn from various sources that you have been doing rather well these days in drama & that *Sikalo*[vii] and *Lifa*[viii] have drawn fairly big audiences. This is quite an achievement for which I give you my warmest congratulations & good luck in future efforts. I should have much liked to see both plays; perhaps one day it may be possible for me to at least read the scripts. It was not clear from the reports whether you wrote both the scripts & produced the plays, & whether the audiences were drawn mainly from Africans or whites. I am interested to know the impact of drama on Africans generally.

---

i   Zami is one of Winnie Mandela's names.

ii Nomathemba Evelyn Kasi, a top model, was married to Gibson Kente, her second husband, from 1969 to 1974. She later moved to the USA and married attorney Alan Jackman, becoming known as Thembi Jackman. She went missing in South Africa in 2008 and was presumed dead by court order in 2012.

iii The Union of South African Artists was formed in 1952 and by 1958 was one of the most successful entertainment promotional bodies in South Africa.

iv When asked if the Robben Island prisoners had access to music, fellow Robben Island prisoner and former comrade of Mandela's, Mac Maharaj (see the glossary), recalls that 'There was a brief (very short) period in the late sixties (I think) when the authorities installed a speaker system in our section which they used to play music from the control room in the main office. If I recall correctly we then asked to be allowed to select and buy records that could be played by the officers for us over the broadcast system. The records were kept by the prison authorities, we made requests as to which piece of music and song should be played. The authorities discontinued within a few months. But up to the time of my departure (1976), we were not allowed to buy and keep and music albums in our cells, (Mac Maharaj in an email to Sahm Venter).

v   Joshua Pulomo Mohapeloa (1908–82), a lyricist and Sesotho composer who worked with Gibson Kente on his musical productions (Sahm Venter, telephonic conversations with Gibson Kente's niece, Vicky Kente, 23 July 2017).

vi H. C. N. Williams and J. N. Maselwa (New York: G. Schirmer, 1960), *Choral Folksongs of the Bantu, for Mixed Voices*.

vii Commercially successful musical *Sikalo* (Lament) was produced by Gibson Kente in 1965. The story centres upon a young man who tries to avoid becoming part of a gang but ends up going to jail.

viii Lifa was also a successful show produced by Gibson Kente in 1967.

I believe *Nongqawuse*[i] was quite a draw; who wrote the script? Are these available as publications?

I believe Miriam[ii] continues to do well overseas & that she is either engaged or married to Carmichael.[iii] She has shown great talent & her views on social questions seem to be more advanced than I ever knew. I am told that Dolly[iv] is also in the States. I hope that she will be as lucky & make as great an impact as Miriam has done. In London I met Dambuza, Joe & Rufus.[v] At the time, they were planning to tour Africa & I hope they succeeded. I was sorry to miss Gwigwi,[vi] who made quite an impression to our fellows abroad & I should like to be remembered to him if he is back. We hardly hear anything about Peggy Phango[vii] & Hugh Masekela[viii] & hope they are doing well. All these are talented artists for whom we have the greatest regard, & nothing would please us more than to know that they are making full use of the opportunities now available to them.

Who are the new stars at home & how good are they? Who are the respective secretaries of the B.M.S.C.,[ix] the D.O.C.C.,[x] & Moroka Centres? I served for several years on the Board of Trustees & Board of Management of the D.O.C.C. & was able to gain some insight into the value of such institutions provided the secretary is a man with a go.

Now & again Zami gives me details of how helpful you are to her &

---

i   Legendary figure Nongqawuse has been written about frequently. She was a young Xhosa prophetess who delivered an instruction in 1856 to kill all the cattle and burn all the grain in order for the dead to come back to life so that they could assist the Xhosa in living free of European rule. However, as a result of carrying out her instructions the Xhosa people suffered a severe famine and the British enforced colonial rule. The first play about the Xhosa, *UNongqause*, written by Mary Waters, was produced in 1925. It is likely that Mandela was referring to a contemporary version of the Nongqawuse story here.

ii   Zenzile Miriam Makeba (1932–2008), South African singer, actor, United Nations goodwill ambassador, and activist.

iii   Stokely Carmichael (1941–98), Trinidadian-American involved in the US Civil Rights and Pan-African movement, who became the 'Honorary Prime Minister' of the Black Panther Party and later of the All-African Peoples Revolutionary Party.

iv   Dolly Rathebe (1928–2004), South African jazz singer and actress.

v   Nathan 'Dambuza' Mdledle (1923–95), Joe (Kolie) Mogotsi (1924–2011), and Rufus Khoza – three of four members of the Manhattan Brothers, a popular South African jazz band of the 1940s and 1950s that incorporated Zulu harmonies and African choral music into its music. They were the first band to have a Billboard Top 100 hit in the United States with their song 'Lovely Lies' in 1956.

vi   Gwigwi Mrwebi (1936–73) , founder of the Union of South African Artists. A saxophonist, he was a member of The Jazz Maniacs, Harlem Swingsters, and Jazz Dazzlers.

vii   Peggy Phango (1928–98), South African jazz singer and actor who played the female lead in the musical *King Kong* on London's West End in 1961.

viii   Hugh Ramopolo Masekela (1939–), South African trumpeter, singer, and composer who has written anti-apartheid songs including 'Bring Him Back Home', recorded in 1986, which demands the release of Nelson Mandela. He went into exile following the Sharpeville Massacre of 1960, in which 69 protesters were shot dead, and studied music in London, then New York.

ix   The Bantu Men's Social Centre (BMSC), founded in Sophiatown, Johannesburg, in 1924, was an important cultural, social, and political meeting place for black South Africans. Its facilities included a gym and a library, and it hosted boxing matches, political meetings, and dances. Mandela and four others founded the ANC Youth League there in 1944.

x   The Donaldson Orlando Community Centre was a community space in Soweto that hosted dances, concerts, and boxing matches. It was built by the Donaldson Trust, established in 1936 by Lieutenant Colonel James Donaldson D.S.O. to 'advance the status, improve the conditions and remove the disabilities suffered by the black African population of South Africa; and generally to seek their benefit and betterment'. Nelson Mandela used to box there in the 1940s and 1950s and spent many of his evenings training at the gym with his eldest son, Thembi.

children, & I should like you to know that I deeply appreciate the interest that you continue to show. Nangomso![i] I think of you with warm & pleasant memories. Lots of love to Evelyn, Zami & kids.

Yours very sincerely,
Uncle Nel

29.7.69 P.S. Temba (Union Wide) remembers you.

Mr Gibson Kente
c/o Mrs Nobandla Mandela, House no. 8115, Orlando West,
Johannesburg

29.7.69 P.S. This letter had been written & handed in for posting to you on March 3 this year. I know that you never received it. Here it is again & though much has occurred since I wrote it, I have, nevertheless, preferred to reproduce it exactly as it was when I first wrote it. I can only hope that this time it will reach you.

Uncle Nel

=========

To Chief Mthetho Matanzima,[ii] a relative[iii]

[In another hand in Afrikaans, in red] Special letter to his nephew
[in red in his hand] WHEN REPLYING PLEASE PUT AT THE TOP OF YOUR LETTER THE WORDS "REPLY TO SPECIAL LETTER."[iv]

17.3.69

Mntan'omhle,[v]

---

i   'Nangomso' is an isiXhosa word that expresses deep gratitude to a person who has gone beyond the call of duty. Mandela sometimes spelled it nangomso.
ii Mthetho Matanzima (d.1972) – see the glossary.
iii Taken from an A4 hardcover notebook in which Mandela copied some of his letters.
iv Special letters and their replies were not taken off the prisoner's quota.
v   'Beautiful child' in isiXhosa.

My wife informs me that you have been installed & I write to congratulate & wish you a happy & fruitful reign. The elders that spoke at the ceremony will have given you much advice on how you should wield power and dispense justice to your people. Perhaps they even reminded you that you assume chieftaincy in a far better position than most chiefs as you have to your credit a legal training & a sound education which should normally enable you to aspire to independent thinking & to see far into the future. Further advice on these matters would certainly be redundant. It is sufficient for me to say that I was indeed very happy to know that Jonguhlanga[i] honoured the occasion with his presence & that he personally installed you. The late Chief Jongintaba[ii] never tired of stressing the importance of good & harmonious relations between Jonguhlanga and Daliwonga,[iii] & I am glad to see the possibility of full cooperation between the two leading houses of Mtirara[iv] on matters falling within the ambit of the tribe. I hope this cooperation will develop into a closer & more intimate association & I regard it as part & parcel of the wider unifying ideal for which we all strive.

I very often think of the impact made by your famous ancestor, Matanzima, who in the course of his colourful reign, tasted both honour & humiliation, comfort & hardship. He knew the pleasure & responsibility of being the respected symbol of tribal unity, the centre of his people's loyalty & affections.

He also experienced the longing & loneliness of one who had to be away from his home, family & people & from all that was dear to his heart. Although he lived in the 19th century and had nothing of the learning opportunities of the present generation, he was a wise and talented patriot who was inspired by noble aspirations. He, Siqungathi,[v] Gungubele & Dalisile[vi] are among the numerous traditional leaders in our country who have made a worthy contribution to the monumental task of arousing our national pride & who have made us proud of our history, our culture & everything that is our own. It is the efforts & achievements of men like these that make the history & aspirations of the Tembus part of the ideas & hopes of the human family.

When King Cyprian died I sent a letter of sympathy to the Royal House. I received an interesting letter from a well known Chief in Zululand

---

i   King Sabata Jonguhlanga Dalindyebo (1928–86), paramount chief of the Transkei homeland and leader of the Democratic Progressive Party, the opposition party in Transkei which opposed apartheid rule – see the glossary.

ii   Chief Jongintaba Dalindyebo (d. 1942), the chief and regent of the Thembu people. He became Mandela's guardian following his father's death – see the glossary.

iii   K. D. Matanzima (1915– 2003), Mandela's nephew, a Thembu chief, and chief minister for the Transkei – see the glossary.

iv   Mtirara is a royal family of the Thembu people. The different houses relate to the households of different wives.

v   A brother of King Ngangelizwe (c.1846–84) who in the nineteenth century sought to unite the various Thembu clans. He never fought against the British but his brothers, Siqungathi and Mtirara, did. K. D. Matanzima was Ngangelizwe's grandson.

vi   A Thembu chief.

& a close friend of the late King. Amongst the documents enclosed was a card that bore the Royal coat-of-arms, & once again I caught something of the spirit of national consciousness for which that celebrated House will always be remembered.

Incidentally, one of the very first remarks made by Leopold Senghor[i] when I met him in his capital in 1962 was that he was busy studying the fascinating story of the founder of the Zulu nation. Our history is rich with national heroes & those who are destined for public careers have many models upon which to shape their own outlook & thoughts.

All that remains for me to do is to wish you once more a happy & fruitful reign.

The letter from the Royal House reported that Jonguhlanga's health was causing much concern. The last letter I received from him was written from a Durban hospital & he indicated then that his condition had much improved. I hope it continues to be better. I expressed my concern over this matter to both Jonguhlanga and Daliwonga when I wrote to them on 14.10.68 in connection with my mother's death & funeral. I do not know if they received my letters.

I should like to be remembered to Chiefs Daliwonga, Mzimvubu, Dalubuhle's son, Thembekile, Vulindlela, Manzezulu, Gwebindlala, Headman Mfebe & Thembekile & Kulo lonke ikomkhulu.[ii] My fondest regards to Amakhosikazi Nobandla, Nozuko, Nogate[iii] & to Nkosazana Camagwini[iv] who I believe is now teaching.

Tell Nobandla[v] I have not forgotten how useful she was the last time I came down; she went as far as Ezibeleni.[vi] That concern was an expression of the kindness & warm love she has always shown for those who are close to her. I will always think of her.

Bayete,[vii]
Dalibunga

CHIEF MTHETO MATHANZIMA,[viii] THE GT. PLACE, QAMATA, COFIMVABA

---

i   President of Senegal, 1960–80.

ii   'The entire royal house' in isiXhosa.

iii   *Amakhosikazi* means 'married women' in plural form in isiXhosa and isiZulu.

iv   *Nkosazana* means 'Miss' or 'princess' in isiXhosa.

v   Mandela is not referring to Winnie Mandela, his wife, who is also called Nobandla but one of K. D. Matanzima's five wives. Nobandla is a common isiXhosa name.

vi   A town in Transkei.

vii   A traditional Zulu royal salute.

viii   The correct spelling is Matanzima but sometimes Mandela spelled it Mathanzima.

2. 4. 69.

Darling,

I was taken completely by surprise to learn that you had been very unwell as I did not have even the slightest hint that you suffered from blackouts. I have known of your past occasional pleurisy attacks. I am however happy to hear that the specialists have diagnosed the particular condition you suffer from, that the blackouts have now disappeared. I should like to be given details of the doctors' diagnosis. I am pleased to know that our family doctor has been wonderful as usual. I wish you speedy & complete recovery Ngutyana & all that is best in life. "The Power of Positive Thinking" & "The Results of Positive Thinking" both written by the American psychologist, Norman Vincent Peale, may be rewarding to read. The municipal library should stock them. I attach no importance to the metaphysical aspects of his arguments, but I consider his views on physical & psychological issues valuable. He makes the basic point that it is not so much the disability one suffers from that matters but one's attitude to it. The man who says: I will conquer this illness, live a happy life, is already half-way through to victory. Of the talents you possess, the one that attracts me most is your courage & determination. This makes you stand head & shoulders above the average & will in the end bring you the triumph of high achievement. Do consciously keep this constantly in mind.

Last nov. I wrote to Chief Buthelezi, cousin of the late King Cyprian & asked him to convey our sympathies to the Royal family. I received an interesting reply plus a letter of condolence for mas's death. The Dec. letters went to Mali & Kgatho, Jan. to Wonga, & in feb. I wrote to Maki, & zeni & zindzi. Lily & Gibson should by now have received the March letters. Advise me whether they were all received. On 17/3 I wrote a special letter to Mthetho & am glad to note that the family rift has been settled. Sabata has not replied 2 letters I wrote him. The relative to whom funds could be sent was mentioned in Kgatho's letter. On 8/3 I was due for a visit that did not come off. Who was it? Why did he not come? Funds have run out. Have received the American journal. Have you had from Marrykled about Sweetie & maxwell. I hear that my brother Regie is experiencing difficulties with the knees & that malome is ill. Can you elaborate? Fondest regards to our friends Messrs Maud.

Page from a letter to Winnie Mandela, 2 April 1969, see opposite.

To Winnie Mandela,[i] his wife

2.4.69

Darling,

I was taken completely by surprise to learn that you had been very unwell as I did not have even the slightest hint that you suffered from blackouts. I have known of your heart condition & pleurisy attacks.

I am however happy to hear that the specialists have diagnosed the particular condition you suffer from & that the blackouts have now disappeared. I should like to be given details of the doctors' diagnosis.

I am pleased to know that our family doctor has been wonderful as usual & I wish you speedy & complete recovery Ngutyana[ii] & all that is best in life.

"The Power of Positive Thinking"[iii] & "The Results of Positive Thinking",[iv] both written by the American psychologist Dr Norman Vincent Peale, may be rewarding to read. The municipal library should stock them. I attach no importance to the metaphysical aspects of his arguments, but I consider his views on physical & psychological issues valuable.

He makes the basic point that it is not so much the disability one suffers from that matters but one's attitude to it. The man who says: I will conquer this illness & live a happy life, is already halfway through to victory.

Of the talents you possess, the one that attracts me most is your courage & determination. This makes you stand head & shoulders above the average & will in the end bring you the triumph of high achievement. Do consciously keep this constantly in mind.

Last Nov. I wrote to Chief Butelezi [sic], cousin of the late King Cyprian, & asked him to convey our sympathies to the Royal Family. I received an interesting reply plus a letter of condolence for ma's death.

The Dec. letters went to Nali & Kgatho; Jan. to Wonga,[v] & in Feb. I wrote to Maki, & Zeni & Zindzi. Lily[vi] & Gibson[vii] should by now have received the March letters. Advise me whether they were all received. . . .

Sabata[viii] has not replied [to] 2 letters I wrote him.

---

i   Nomzamo Winifred Madikizela-Mandels (1936–) – see the glossary.
ii   One of Winnie Mandela's names. She comes from the amaNgutyana clan.
iii   Norman Vincent Peale, *The Power of Positive Thinking* (New York: Prentice-Hall, Inc., 1952).
iv   Norman Vincent Peale, *The Amazing Results of Positive Thinking* (New York: Fawcett Crest, 1959).
v   K. D. Matanzima (1915– 2003), Mandela's nephew, a Thembu chief, and chief minister for the Transkei – see the glossary. His middle name was Daliwonga, which was abbreviated to Wonga.
vi   Lilian Ngoyi (1911–80), politician, and anti-apartheid and women's rights activist – see the glossary.
vii   Gibson Kente (1932–2004), playwright, composer, and director. Like Mandela, he was from the Madiba clan, so Mandela referred to him as a nephew – see the glossary.
viii King Sabata Jonguhlanga Dalindyebo (1928–86), paramount chief of the Transkei homeland and leader of the

The relatives to whom funds could be sent were mentioned in Kgatho's letter.

On 8/3 I was due for a visit that did not come off. Who was it? Why did he not come? My funds have run out. Have received the *American Journal*.

Have you heard from Mary[i] & Paul[ii] about Sweet & Maxwell?[iii] I hear that my brother Regie[iv] [*sic*] is experiencing difficulties with the kids & that Malome[v] is ill. Can you elaborate?

Fondest regards to our friends Moosa & Maud.[vi] . . .

A family photo at last 'what a masterpiece'. Kgatho & sisters are terrific & it gave me such joy to see ma's photo. Your small picture almost created an upheaval. "Ayingo Nobandla lo!"[vii] "Is this not her younger sister!" "Madiba has been too long in jail, he does not know his sister-in-law," all these & other remarks were flung at me from all directions.

To me the portrait aroused mixed feelings. You look somewhat sad, absent-minded & unwell but lovely all the same. The big one is a magnificent study that depicts all I know in you, the devastating beauty & charm which 10 stormy years of married life have not chilled. I suspect that you intended the picture to convey a special message that no words could ever express. Rest assured I have caught it. All that I wish to say now is that the picture has aroused all the tender feelings in me & softened the grimness that is all around. It has sharpened my longing for you & our sweet & peaceful home.

These days my thoughts have wondered far & wide; to Hans St[viii] where a friend would jump into a blue van & unburden herself of all the solemn vows that are due from fiancée to her betrothed & immediately thereafter dash across to an Olds on the opposite end of the block with vows equally sweet & reassuring; the skill with which she manipulated her evening 'studies' in Chancellor House[ix] & made it possible to receive & entertain old friends as soon as new ones proceeded to a boxing gym. All these have come back over & over again as I examine the portrait.[x]

Democratic Progressive Party, the opposition party in Transkei which opposed apartheid rule – see the glossary.

i   Mary Benson (1919–2000), friend, author, journalist, and anti-apartheid activist – see the glossary.

ii   Paul Joseph.

iii Bookshop in London from which Mandela ordered legal books for his studies.

iv Oliver Reginald Tambo (1917–1993) – Mandela's friend, former law partner, and the president of the ANC – see the glossary. His middle name was Reginald and Mandela referred to him as Reggie.

v   'Uncle' in isiXhosa.

vi Moosa Dinath and his wife Maud Katzenellenbogen. Mandela first met Moosa Dinath when he was a member of the Transvaal Indian Congress and businessman in Johannesburg. They renewed their acquaintance in prison in 1962 while Mandela was awaiting trial and Dinath was serving a sentence for fraud. He and Maud Katzenellenbogen, who befriended Winnie, hatched a plan to free Mandela from prison, but it was shelved after Winnie became suspicious of it.

vii 'This is not Nobandla' in isiXhosa.

viii Winnie Mandela stayed at the Helping Hand Hostel in Hans Street, Jeppestown, when she moved to Johannesburg. Mandela is reminding her of when he would pick her up from there.

ix Winnie would do her studies at Mandela's law firm in Chancellor House when he worked after hours.

x   Nelson and Winnie Mandela met in 1956 and went on their first date on 10 March that year. They married on 14 June 1958 in Winnie's home town of Bizana. In a letter to Fatima Meer dated 14 June 1989, he wrote: 'The

Finally Mhlope,[i] I should like you to know that if in the past my letters have not been passionate, it is because I need not seek to improve the debt I owe to a woman who, in spite of formidable difficulties & lack of experience, has nonetheless succeeded in keeping the home fires burning & in attending to the smallest wants & wishes of her incarcerated life companion. These things make me humble to be the object of your love & affection. Remember that hope is a powerful weapon even when all else is lost. You & I, however, have gained much over the years & are making advances in important respects. You are in my thoughts every moment of my life. Nothing will happen to you darling. You will certainly recover and rise.

A million kisses & tons & tons of love.
Dalibunga

NKOSIKAZI NOBANDLA MANDELA.
HOUSE NO. 8115, ORLANDO WEST.
JOHANNESBURG.

[PS] Good luck to Kgatho in his exams & tell Mtshana Nomfundo,[ii] that I am glad to note that she is not discouraged. Let her remember that perseverance is key to success. I hope you managed to forward the letter to Cecil.

◇◇◇◇◇◇◇◇

Mandela ran his relationship with the prison authorities on the basis of respect seasoned with the wry observation that an ordinary guard made the difference between an extra blanket in winter or not. The basis of all these interactions, however, was the recognition of the humanity of the other, all the while being sure to maintain his own dignity and to protect his rights.

His many letters to the prison authorities for requests to see an eye specialist or a dentist, or pushing for more study rights, were not obligatory. Prisoners were presented every week with the opportunity of making complaints or requests to an officer. But, according to his comrade and fellow prisoner Mac Maharaj, while prisoners had an opportunity to make verbal requests, they were not given the opportunity to elaborate on them or provide any background information. Mandela probably wanted to keep a written record and at the same time was

wedding party left Johannesburg at midnight on 12 June and reached Bizana the next day in the afternoon. As we were expected to reach the bride's place, Mbongweni, at dusk we spent some time at Dr Gordon Mabuya's place where he and his wife, Nontobeko, entertained us.'
i   One of Winnie Mandela's names.
ii   *Mtshana* means 'niece' or 'nephew' in isiXhosa. He is referring to Olive Nomfundo Mandela, his niece.

shrewdly managing each request for possible improvements from which the other prisoners may benefit.[49]

 He also boldly wrote to senior officials and, in some cases, the minister of justice himself. Just less than five years into his prison sentence he wrote to the minister of justice demanding that he and his colleagues be released or treated as political prisoners according to rules of the Geneva Convention. His knowledge of the battles between the Afrikaners and the British colonial powers was brought to bear to support his arguments.

 Comparing his plight and that of his fellow prisoners with the way in which the Afrikaner freedom fighters had been treated in jail, Mandela made a solid case for their freedom. But his captors were not the British; and the apartheid regime, which ran the country on force and oppression, was fearful that letting Mandela go would weaken it in the eyes of its supporters.

To the minister of justice, c/o the commissioner of prisons

[Typed]

The Commissioner of Prisons,
PRETORIA.

I should be pleased if you would kindly approve of the following letter to the Minister of Justice.

22.4.69

The Minister of Justice,
Parliament Buildings,
CAPE TOWN.

Dear Sir,

My colleagues have requested me to write and ask you to release us from prison and, pending your decision on the matter, to accord us the treatment due to political prisoners. At the outset we wish to point out that in making this application we are not pleading for mercy but are exercising the inherent right of all people incarcerated for their political beliefs.

The persons whose names appear in schedule A attached to this letter live in the Single Cell Section of Robben Island Prison and are completely isolated from the rest of the prisoners on the Island. For this reason we are unable to furnish you with a full list of all the persons on this Island and in other prisons on behalf of whom this application is made.

Prior to our conviction and imprisonment we are[i] members of well-known political organisations which fought against political and racial persecution, and which demanded full political rights for the African, Coloured and Indian people of this Country. We completely rejected as we still do, all forms of white domination, and more particularly the policy of separate development, and demanded a democratic South Africa free from the evils of Colour oppression, and where all South Africans, regardless of race or belief, would live together in peace and harmony on a basis of equality.

All of us, without exception, were convicted and sentenced for political activities which we embarked upon as part and parcel of our struggle to win for our people the right of self-determination, acknowledged throughout the civilized world as the inalienable birthright of all human beings. These activities were inspired by the desire to resist racial policies and unjust laws which violate the principle of human rights and fundamental freedoms that form the foundation of democratic government.

In the past the governments of South Africa have treated persons found guilty of offences of this nature as political offenders who were released from prison, in some cases, long before their sentences expired. In this connection we refer you to the cases of Generals Christiaan De Wet, JCG Kemp and others who were charged with high treason arising out of the 1914 Rebellion.[ii] Their case was in every respect more serious than ours. 12,000 rebels took to arms and there were no less than 322 casualties. Towns were occupied and considerable damage caused to government installations, while claims for damage to private property amounted to R500,000. These acts of violence were committed by white men who enjoyed full political rights, who belonged to political parties that were legal, who had newspapers that could publicise their views. They were freely to move up and down the country espousing their cause and rallying support for their ideas. They had no justification whatsoever for resorting to violence. The

---

i   The letter was typed by a prison official and the word 'are' rather than 'were' must have been typed by mistake.
ii   During World War I the British government called on its dominions to assist it. South Africa was specifically asked to fight against Germany in the neighbouring South West Africa. While Prime Minister Louis Botha supported Britain, a number of his generals did not and rebelled against the South African government.

leader of the Orange Free State rebels, De Wet, was sentenced to 6 years' imprisonment plus a fine of R4,000. Kemp received a sentence of 7 years and a fine of R2,000. The rest were given comparatively lighter sentences.

In spite of the gravity of their offences, De Wet was released within 6 months of his conviction and sentence, and the rest within a year. This event occurred a little more than half a century ago, yet the Government of the day showed much less intransigence in its treatment of this category of prisoner than the present Government seems prepared to do 54 years later with black politicians who have even more justification to resort to violence than the 1914 rebels. This Government has persistently spurned our aspirations, suppressed our political organisations and imposed severe restrictions on known activists and field workers.

It has caused hardship and disruption of family life by throwing into prison hundreds of otherwise innocent people. Finally it has instituted a reign of terror unprecedented in the history of the Country and closed all channels of constitutional struggle. In such a situation, resort to violence was the inevitable alternative of freedom fighters who had the courage of their convictions. No men of principle and integrity could have done otherwise.[i] To have folded arms would have been an act of surrender to a Government of minority rule and a betrayal of our cause. World history in general, and that of South Africa in particular, teaches that resort to violence may in certain cases be perfectly legitimate.

In releasing the rebels soon after their convictions the Botha Smuts Government acknowledged this vital fact. We firmly believe that our case is no less different, and we accordingly ask you to make this privilege available to us. As indicated above, there were 322 casualties in the Rebellion.

By way of contrast, we draw attention to the fact that in committing acts of sabotage we took special precautions to avoid loss of life, a fact which was expressly acknowledged by both the trial Judge[ii] [and] the prosecution in the Rivonia case.[iii]

---

i   At the time of Mandela's arrest, Umkhonto weSizwe (MK), which was launched on 16 December 1961, had set off explosive devices after hours, to avoid loss of life, at locations including municipal and post offices, pass offices, a resettlement office, and an electricity substation. At that stage there was no loss of life.

ii   'Counsel for the defence successfully convinced the judge that MK – and therefore the defendants – was not responsible for all the acts of sabotag', wrote Kenneth S. Braun in *Saving Nelson Mandela: The Rivonia Trial and the Fate of South Africa* (Oxford University Press: Oxford, 2012), p. 147. 'This fact was also acknowledged by the court during closing argument and lent support to another – perhaps even more important – point in the judge's failure to sentence them to death. No act of sabotage actually attributed to them or their organizations had resulted in death or injury to any person.' (Ibid.)

iii   Attorney Joel Joffe wrote that his colleague Arthur Chaskalson showed that 'of the 193 acts of sabotage which the

An examination of the attached schedule shows that if we use De Wet's case as the standard, then every one of us ought to have been released by now. Of the 23 persons whose names are listed therein, 8 are doing life imprisonment, 10 are serving sentences ranging from 10 to 20 years, and 5 between 2 and 10 years.

Of those doing imprisonment for life, 7 have completed 4 years 10 months and 1 has done 4 years and 4 months. The man with the longest sentence amongst those serving terms between 10 and 20 years is Billy Nair[i] who has already completed ¼ of his sentence. Joe Gqabi,[ii] Samson Fadana and Andrew Masondo,[iii] the first to be convicted in this group have each completed 6 years of their respective sentences of 12, 8 and 13 years. The last men to be sentenced in the same group were Jackson Fuzile[iv] and Johannes Dangala who received 12 and 7 years respectively. Fuzile has completed a ¼ of the sentence whereas Dangala will have done exactly half of his on 19th May 1969. Every one of those serving terms between 2 and 10 years has at least completed ¼ of his sentence.

Our claim for release becomes even stronger when examined in relations to the cases of Robey Leibrandt,[v] Holm,[vi] Pienaar, Strauss[vii] and others. Leibrandt, a national of the Union of South Africa,[viii] arrived in the Union from Germany at a time when that country was at war with the Union. He then proceeded to set up a para-military underground organisation with the purpose of overthrowing the Government and establishing in its place one modelled on that of Nazi Germany. He was found guilty of high treason and sentenced to death, later commuted to imprisonment for life. Holm, Pienaar and Strauss were also imprisoned for high treason, it

---

State had proved to have happened, only about a dozen had been proved legally' and 'not one involved any danger whatsoever to human life'. Joel Joffe, *The State vs. Nelson Mandela: The Trial that Changed South Africa* (London: One World Publications, 2007), pp. 238 and 239.

i   Billy Nair (1929–2008), comrade and MK member who was charged with sabotage in 1963. He was held in B Section with Mandela on Robben Island and was released in 1984 – see the glossary.

ii   Joe Gqabi (1929–81) was convicted of sabotage for MK activities and was imprisoned on Robben Island for ten years.

iii   Andrew Masondo (1936–2008) was convicted of sabotage for MK activities and was imprisoned on Robben Island for thirteen years.

iv   Mxolisi Jackson Fuzile (1940–2011) was convicted of sabotage for his activities on behalf of the ANC and sentenced to imprisonment for twelve years.

v   Sidney Robey Leibbrandt (1913–66), a South African Olympic boxer of German and Irish descent, was a Nazi supporter who, after training with the Germany army, became a central part of Operation Weissdorn, a plan approved by Hitler, to assassinate General Jan Smuts, the head of South Africa's government, and bring about a coup d'etat in South Africa. He was initially sentenced to death for treason, but Smuts later commuted this to life imprisonment. When the National Party came to power in 1948, he was pardoned and released.

vi   Eric Holm was engaged by Zeesen Radio which broadcast Nazi propaganda to South Africa.

vii Possibly Mandela is referring to Strauss von Moltke, a former leader of the Greyshirts, a South African fascist organisation which sympathised with German Nazis, who handed over documents stolen from the Jewish Board of Deputies to anti-Semitic elements in South Africa's National Party.

viii The Union of South Africa was formed in 1910 from the four self-governing British colonies of the Cape, Natal, the Transvaal, and the Orange River Colony.

being alleged that they collaborated with the enemy in prosecuting the war against the Union and its allies. On coming to power, however, the present Government released these and other prisoners sentenced for treason and sabotage, notwithstanding the fact that they had been arrested in circumstances which made them appear to many South Africans as traitors to their own country. Again, by way of contrast, we draw attention to the fact that our activities were at all times actuated by the noblest ideals that men can cherish, namely, the desire to serve our people in their just struggle to free themselves from a Government founded on injustice and inequality.

We further wish to remind you that in 1966 your predecessor released Spike de Keller,[i] Stephanie Kemp,[ii] Allan Brooks[iii] and Tony Trew,[iv] all of whom originally appeared jointly with Edward Joseph Daniels[v] (whose names appear in the schedule) on a charge of Sabotage. Kemp, Brooks and Trew pleaded guilty to an alternative charge and a separation of trial was ordered. The case against Daniels and De Keller proceeded on the main charge and on 17th November 1964 they were found guilty and sentenced to 15 and 10 years respectively. Kemp, Brooks and Trew were found guilty on the alternative and sentenced to 5, 4 and 4 years respectively, each of which was partly suspended. We are informed that De Keller was released after he had served approximately 2 years, or less, of his sentence of 10 years, whilst Kemp, Brooks and Trew were also released before they had completed their sentences.

We do not in any way begrudge those who were fortunate enough to be released and who escaped the hardship of prison life and are happy to know that they now lead a normal life. But we refer to their case for the limited purpose of showing that our request is reasonable, and also to stress that a Government is expected to be consistent in its policy and to accord the same treatment to its citizens.

There is one important difference between our case and that of De Wet and Leibrandt. They were released only after the rebellion had been crushed and after Germany had been conquered and they were thus no

---

i   David 'Spike' de Keller, member of the African Resistance Movement and the Liberal Party, who spent a year in prison.
ii   Stephanie Kemp (1941–), member of the African Resistance Movement and the Communist Party, who spent a year in prison.
iii   Allan Brooks (1940–2008), member of the African Resistance Movement and the Communist Party, who spent a year in prison..
iv   Tony Trew (1941–), member of the African Resistance Movement who spent a year in prison..
v   Eddie Daniels (1928–2017), member of the African Resistance Movement who spent fifteen years on Robben Island – see the glossary.

threat to the safety of the State when they were freed. In our case, however, it may be argued that our revolution is planned for the future and that security considerations require that we be treated differently. Add to this fact that our convictions have not changed and our dreams are still the same as they were before we were jailed. All of which would seem to confirm the opinion that our case is distinguishable from all previous ones. We feel sure, however, that you will not be tempted to think along these lines, as such an argument would carry sinister implications. It would mean that if security considerations today require that we should be kept in prison, we would not be released when we complete our respective sentences, if the present situation remains unaltered, or if the position worsens. The plain truth is that the racial strife and conflict that seriously threatens the country today is due solely to the short-sighted policies and crimes committed by this Government.

The only way to avert disaster is not to keep innocent men in jail but to abandon your provocative actions and to pursue sane and enlightened policies. Whether or not evil strife and bloodshed are to occur in this country rests entirely on the Government. The continued suppression of our aspirations and reliance on rule through coercion drives our people more and more to violence. Neither you nor I can predict [what] the country will have to pay at the end of that strife. The obvious solution is to release us and to hold a round table conference to consider an amicable solution.

Our main request is that you release us and, pending your decision, to treat us as political prisoners. This means that we should be provided with good diet, proper clothing outfits, bed and mattresses, newspapers, radios, bioscope,[i] [and] better and closer contact with our families and friends here and abroad. Treatment as political prisoners implies the freedom to obtain all reading material that is not banned and to write books for publication, we would expect to be given the option to work as one desires and to decide the trades one would like to learn. In this connection we wish to point out that some of these privileges were enjoyed both by the 1914 rebels as well as by Leibrandt and colleagues, all of whom were treated as political prisoners.

The prison authorities attempt to answer our demand for treatment as political prisoners by pointing out that we were convicted by the courts for contravening the laws of the county, that we are like any other criminals and, therefore, cannot be treated as political offenders.

---

i   A cinema or film.

This is a spurious argument which flies in the face of the facts. On this view De Wet, Kemp, Maritz, Leibrandt and others were ordinary criminals. Treason, sabotage, membership of an illegal organisation were criminal offences then as now. Why then were they treated differently? It seems to us that the only difference between the two cases is one of colour.

Serious differences of opinion on a specific issue had emerged amongst the whites, and those who lost in the contest that flowed from those differences eventually found themselves behind bars. On all other issues, especially on the major question of colour, both victor and vanquished were in agreement. The conflict having been solved it was possible for the Government to adopt a conciliatory attitude and to extend to the prisoners all sorts of indulgences. But today the position is altogether different. This time the challenge comes, not from white men, but mainly from black politicians who disagree with the Government on almost everything under the sun. The victory of our cause means the end of white rule.

In this situation the Government regards the prison not as an institution of rehabilitation but as an instrument of retribution, not to prepare us to lead a respectable and industrious life when released, and to play our role as worthy members of society, but to punish and cripple us, so that we should never again have the strength and courage to pursue our ideals. This [is] our punishment for raising our voices against the tyranny of colour. This is the true explanation for the bad treatment we receive in prison – pick and shovel work continuously for the last 5 years, a wretched diet, denial of essential cultural material and isolation from the world outside jail. This is the reason why privileges normally available to other prisoners, including those convicted of murder, rape and crimes involving dishonesty are withheld from political offenders.

We get no remission of sentence. Whilst the ordinary prisoner is classified in C group on admission, political offenders are put in D which carries the least privileges. Those of us who managed to reach A group are denied privileges normally enjoyed by criminals in the same group. They are compelled to do pick and shovel work, are not allowed newspapers, radios, bioscope, contact visits and even groceries are given grudgingly.

As already indicated in the second paragraph above, I make this application on behalf of all my colleagues on the Island and in other jails and I trust that any concessions that may be granted will be made available to all without exception.

The Prisons Act 1959 gives to you the necessary powers to grant the relief we seek. Under its provisions you are entitled to release us on parole or probation. De Wet and others were released under the former method.

In conclusion we place on record that the years we have spent on this Island have been difficult years.[i] Almost every one of us has had [our] full share in one way or another of the hardships that face non-white prisoners. These hardships have at times been the result of official indifference to our problems, other times they were due to plain persecution. But things have somewhat eased and we hope even better days will come. All that we wish to add is that we trust that when you consider this application you will bear in mind that the ideas that inspire us, and the convictions that give form and direction to our activities constitute the only solution to the problems of our country and are in accordance with the enlightened conceptions of the human family.

Yours faithfully,
[Signed N. Mandela]

––––––––––––

To Mrs. P. K. Madikizela, Winnie Mandela's stepmother[ii]

466/64: Nelson Mandela: Letter in lieu of visit for April 1969.

4-5-69

Our dear Ma,

I am able to write to you at last! I had planned to do so sometime towards the end of last year, but the shocking news of ma's death completely upset that arrangement. Zami[iii] wrote to me immediately she returned from home and gave me full details of the help you and Bawo[iv] gave her and all that you did in connection with the funeral. On October 12, Sibali Timothy Mbuzo[v]

---

i   By 1969, Mandela and the other accused Rivonia trialists incarcerated on Robben Island had been there for almost five years.

ii   Winnie Mandela's mother died when she was ten years old. Her father remarried nine years later to a school principal, Nophikela Hilda Madikizela.

iii   Zami is one of Winnie Mandela's names.

iv   Columbus Kokani Madikizela, Winnie Mandela's father – see the glossary.

v   Sibali Timothy Mbuzo, a close relative of Mandela's brother-in-law Daniel Timakwe and a long-standing leading member of the ANC in the Transkei homeland. *Sibali* means 'brother-in-law' in isiXhosa.

had travelled all the way from Umtata[i] to see me. In his report he had particularly drawn attention to your presence on this occasion.

These reports brought me some measure of relief and peace. I had never dreamt that I would never be able to bury ma. On the contrary, I had entertained the hope that I would have the privilege of looking after her in her old age, and be on her side when the fatal hour struck. Zami and I had tried hard to persuade her to come and live with us in Johannesburg, pointing out that she would be nearer Baragwanath Hospital which would ensure for her regular and proper medical attention, and that moving to the Reef[ii] would enable Zami to give her effective and all-round attention. I further discussed the matter with ma when she visited me on 6/3/66 and again on 9/9/67. But she spent all her life in the countryside and became attached to its plains and hills, to its fine people and simple ways. Although she had spent some years in Johannesburg, she found it very difficult to leave the home & family graves. Though I fully appreciated her views & feelings I still hoped I might eventually succeed in persuading her to go up.[iii]

Her last visit aroused mixed feelings in me. I had always looked forward to these visits and was indeed very happy to see her once more. But her physical condition worried me. She had lost a lot of weight and looked unwell.

I watched her as she walked away slowly to the boat that would take her back to the mainland, and I feared I had seen her for the last time. Thereafter I wrote and pleaded with her to consider my advice that she move to the Rand.[iv] In a cheerful and charming reply she assured me that she was well and succeeded in allaying my fears. I was beginning to feel that my anxiety was unfounded when I received the tragic news. I was however relieved by Zami's and Sibali Timothy's reports and particularly by the knowledge that the family and friends had turned up in large numbers. Your own presence on this occasion and the personal interest you took has a significance for me which no pen can accurately describe. All that I wish you to know is that I think of you and Bawo with the greatest affection.

I was happy to hear that Bawo had retired. His strenuous official duties were a cause of concern to Zami and me and we were really relieved when he lay down to begin a well-earned rest which I hope will ultimately lead to complete recovery. This will also give you the opportunity to nurse and render all the help and attention necessary to contain the illness. I

---

i   Umtata (now called Mthatha) was the capital of the Transkei homeland.
ii   The Reef in Johannesburg refers to the gold reef where gold was first discovered by Australian George Harrison in 1896. That gold rush gave birth to Johannesburg, which is now part of Gauteng province.
iii   Mandela is referring to his mother going up to Johannesburg.
iv   An abbreviated name for the Witwatersrand, a 56-kilometre-long ridge in the Gauteng province of South Africa where Johannesburg is based.

have confidence that Sibali Mpumelelo & Nyawuza,[i] Niki and Marsh,[ii] Nali and Sef,[iii] Bantu and hubby,[iv] Lunga, Nyanya, Msutu and Tanduxolo[v] probably share these sentiments. In one of her letters Zami reported that you were also unwell. I look forward to your letter which will tell me that you have recovered.

In March last year Bawo wrote and advised that he intended paying me a visit when he retired. In my present circumstances, a visit, especially from the family, is something you first have to be behind bars to be able to fully appreciate its value and importance. Nothing would please me more than to see Bawo. But I'm wondering whether in view of his health and age it would not be too risky for him to make this strenuous journey. I should be glad if you would consider the matter in this light.

Zami informs me that Bawo received a special letter from this Department advising him not to send the Reports I had asked for. On receipt of this information I immediately contacted Major Kellerman who was then Commanding Officer of this place, and who had given me permission to obtain this material, and he told me he knew nothing about the matter but would make enquiries from Pretoria. Unfortunately, he left a few days thereafter on transfer. As I did not wish to burden the new C.O. with this affair, I decided not to pursue it any further and I propose that we regard it as closed. I am sorry for any expenses Bawo may have incurred and for any inconvenience I might have caused. I believe that both Msutu and Tanduxolo were endorsed out of Johannesburg. Where are they now and what are they doing? I was very disappointed by this information as both of them were extremely helpful to Zami. I spend a lot of time thinking of her, the painful experiences she is having and the numerous problems that face her as a result of my absence. My confidence and regard for her has risen considerably. My only hope is that one day I may be able to give her the peace, comfort and happiness that will compensate for her dreadful hardship.

By the way, and in spite of the tragic nature of the occasion, it was a wonderful experience for her to come down home and to meet you, Bawo and members of my family. She and the children were the centre of genuine love and affection which benefited them immensely.

I learnt that the letter I wrote to Mpumelelo shortly before Nyawuza visited me on 30/12/67,[vi] and in which I was discussing family matters

---

i   See note vi below.
ii   Niki Xaba (1932–1985), Winnie Mandela's eldest sister (see the glossary), and her husband Marshall Xaba.
iii   Nancy Vutela, Winnie Mandela's sister, and her husband Sefton Vutela.
iv   Nobantu Mniki, Winnie Mandela's sister, and her husband Earl Mniki.
v   Msutu and Tanduxolo are Winnie Mandela's brothers.
vi   In his record of family visits he notes Sibali Manyawuza as having visited on that day. Mandela confused his clan name and referred to him as Manyawuza. *Sibali* means 'brother-in-law' in isiXhosa.

N. Mandela.   S.B.
                    90.

ONTVANGST-INTOU?
RECEPTION OFFICE
20. -5.
PRIVAATSAK/PRIVATE B. 0
ROBBENEILAND/ROBBEN ISLAND
P R I S O N

Messrs Frank, Bernadt & Joffe,
P. O. Box 252.
Cape Town.
Dear Sirs,   Attention: Mr Brown

   I understand that my wife has been arrested with several
other persons in Johannesburg and that she is presently under detention.
   In this connection I should be pleased if you would kindly
instruct your Johannesburg correspondent to furnish me with the
following information:

1. The date of the arrest and the nature of the charge.
2. Whether or not she has been released on bail and the amount thereof?
3. The full names and addresses of her co detainees.
4. Whether she received my letter of 4th April?
5. The name of the person, if any, who is now in charge of our Johannesburg
home.

   Your prompt attention will be highly appreciated.

               Yours faithfully.
               NRMandela.
               NELSON MANDELA.

Letter to attorneys Messrs Frank, Bernadt & Joffe, 20 May 1969, see page 94.

and friends, never reached. There has been no reply to another I wrote to Dr Mbekeni[i] of Tsolo last December. I am taking the precaution of registering this one to make sure that you get it.

And now ma; I should like you to know that I think of you and the children with warm affection. Fondest regards to Mpumelelo & Nyawuza, Uncle Silas,[ii] Mleni, Headman Madikizela and to Amasogutya Onke[iii] and, of course, not forgetting Bawo.

Your affectionate son,
Nelson

MRS P.K. MADIKIZELA
MBONGWENI BUS SERVICE
BIZANA,
TRANSKEI.

◇◇◇◇◇◇◇◇

In May 1969, Mandela's wife Winnie was hauled from her Soweto home in darkness in front of their two terrified small daughters and spent the following fourteen months in solitary detention which she called 'tortuous mental agony'.[50] *In prison she suffered anaemia, bronchitis, and heart problems.*

During this time the couple did not know who was taking care of the children and in what condition they were forced to live. Mandela could not be sure that his letters ever reached her. And we can only be sure that any letters were received once there was a reply referring to previous correspondence. While his wife was no stranger to police harassment, one can only imagine the anxiety of two imprisoned parents trying to take care of their children.

He wrote to his wife, their children and various family members in desperate attempts to find out what was happening in their parentless lives outside prison.

---

i   Mandela's cousin.
ii   Winnie Mandela's uncle.
iii Referring to her whole family.

To Frank, Bernadt & Joffe, his attorneys

[In another hand] N. Mandela   S.B[i]

[Stamped] Reception Office Robben Island, 20 May 1969

Messrs Frank, Bernadt & Joffe
PO Box 252.
Cape Town.

Dear Sirs,

Attention: Mr Brown

I understand that my wife has been arrested with several other persons in Johannesburg and that she is presently under detention.

In this connection, I should be pleased if you would kindly instruct your Johannesburg correspondent to furnish me with the following information:

1. The date of the arrest and the nature of the charge.
2. Whether or not she has been released on bail and the amount thereof?
3. The full names and addresses of her co-detainees.
4. Whether she received my letter of 4th April?
5. The name of the person, if any, who is now in charge of our Johannesburg home.

Your prompt attention will be highly appreciated.

    Yours faithfully,
[Signed NRMandela]
NELSON MANDELA

---

i   S.B. indicates that this is a special letter. B stands for 'Brief' in Afrikaans. Special letters were not taken off a prisoner's quota.

Zenani and Zindzi Mandela,[i] his middle and youngest daughters

23.6.69

My Darlings,

Once again our beloved Mummy has been arrested and now she and Daddy are away in jail. My heart bleeds as I think of her sitting in some police cell far away from home, perhaps alone and without anybody to talk to, and with nothing to read. Twenty-four hours of the day longing for her little ones. It may be many months or even years before you see her again. For long you may live like orphans without your own home and parents, without the natural love, affection and protection Mummy used to give you. Now you will get no birthday or Christmas parties, no presents or new dresses, no shoes or toys. Gone are the days when, after having a warm bath in the evening, you would sit at table with Mummy and enjoy her good and simple food. Gone are the comfortable beds, the warm blankets and clean linen she used to provide. She will not be there to arrange for friends to take you to bioscopes, concerts and plays, or to tell you nice stories in the evening, help you read difficult books and to answer the many questions you would like to ask. She will be unable to give you the help and guidance you need as you grow older and as new problems arise. Perhaps never again will Mummy and Daddy join you in House no. 8115 Orlando West,[ii] the one place in the whole world that is so dear to our hearts.

This is not the first time Mummy goes to jail. In October 1958, only four months after our wedding, she was arrested with 2000 other women when they protested against passes in Johannesburg[iii] and spent two weeks in jail. Last year she served four days, but now she has gone back again and I cannot tell you how long she will be away this time. All that I wish you always to bear in mind is that we have a brave and determined Mummy who loves her people with all her heart. She gave up pleasure and comfort for a life full of hardship and misery because of the deep love she has for her people and country. When you become adults and think carefully of the unpleasant experiences Mummy has gone through, and the stubbornness with which she has held to her beliefs, you will begin to realise the importance of her contribution in the battle for truth and justice and to the extent

---

i   Zenani Mandela (1959–) and Zindziswa Mandela (1960–) – see the glossary.
ii   The family home in Soweto.
iii   In the mid-1950s the National government began issuing black women with pass books which they were required to carry at all times. This led to a series of organised protests and campaigns which led to thousands of arrests. In a speech given in 1976 after the Soweto Uprising, Winnie Mandela was reported as saying: 'We have to carry passes which we abhor because we cannot have houses without them, we cannot work without them, we are endorsed out of towns without them, we cannot register births without them, we are not even expected to die without them.'

to which she has sacrificed her own personal interests and happiness.

Mummy comes from a rich and respected family. She is a qualified Social Worker and at the time of our marriage in June 1958[i] she had a good and comfortable job at the Baragwanath Hospital. She was working there when she was arrested for the first time and at the end of 1958 she lost that job. Later she worked for the Child Welfare Society in town, a post she liked very much. It was whilst working there that the Government ordered her not to leave Johannesburg, to remain at home from 6pm to 6am, and not to attend meetings, nor enter any hospital, school, university, courtroom, compound or hostel, or any African township save Orlando where she lived. This order made it difficult for her to continue with her work at the Child Welfare Society and she lost this particular job as well.

Since then Mummy has lived a painful life and had to try to run a home without a fixed income. Yet she somehow managed to buy you food and clothing, pay your school fees, rent for the house and to send me money regularly.

I left home in April 1961 when Zeni was two years and Zindzi three months. Early in January 1962 I toured Africa and visited London for ten days, and returned to South Africa towards the end of July the same year. I was terribly shaken when I met Mummy. I had left her in good health with a lot of flesh and colour. But she had suddenly lost weight and was now a shadow of her former self. I realised at once the strain my absence had caused her. I looked forward to some time when I would be able to tell her about my journey, the countries I visited and the people I met. But my arrest on August 5 put an end to that dream.

When Mummy was arrested in 1958 I visited her daily and brought her food and fruits. I felt proud of her, especially because the decision to join the other women in demonstrating against the passes was taken by her freely without any suggestion from me. But her attitude to my own arrest made me know Mummy better and more fully. Immediately I was arrested our friends here and abroad offered her scholarships and suggested that she leave the country to study overseas. I welcomed these suggestions as I felt that studies would keep her mind away from her troubles. I discussed the matter with her when she visited me in Pretoria Jail in October 1962. She told me that although she would most probably be arrested and sent to jail, as every politician fighting for freedom must expect, she would nevertheless remain in the country and suffer with her people. Do you see now what a brave Mummy we have?

Do not worry, my darlings, we have a lot of friends; they will look after

---

i   They married on 14 June 1958 in Winnie Mandela's home village of Bizana in the Transkei.

you, and one day Mummy and Daddy will return and you will no longer be orphans without a home. Then we will also live peacefully and happily as all normal families do. In the meantime you must study hard and pass your examinations, and behave like good girls. Mummy and I will write to you many letters. I hope you got the Christmas card I sent you in December and the letter I wrote both of you on February 4 this year.

    With lots & lots of love and a million kisses.

    Yours affectionately,
Daddy

MISSES ZENI & ZINDZI MANDELA
C/O MRS IRIS NIKI XABA.[i]
P.O. BOX 23,
DUBE VILLAGE
SOWETO, JOHANNESBURG.

To Winnie Mandela,[ii] his wife

23.6.69

My Darling,

One of my precious possessions here is the first letter you wrote me on Dec. 20, 1962, shortly after my first conviction. During the last 6½ years I have read it over and over again & the sentiments it expresses are as golden & fresh now as they were the day I received it. With the aspirations & views that you hold & the role you are playing in the current battle of ideas, I have always known that you would be arrested sooner or later. But considering all that I have gone through, I had somehow vaguely hoped that such a calamity would be deferred & that you would be spared the misfortune & misery of prison life. Accordingly when the news of your arrest reached me on May 17, in the midst of feverish preparations for my finals, then only 25 days away, I was quite unprepared & felt cold & lonely. That you were free & able within limits to move about meant much to me. I looked forward to all your visits & to those of members of the family & friends

---

i   Winnie Mandela's eldest sister – see the glossary.
ii   Nomzamo Winifred Madikizela-Mandela (1936–) – see the glossary.

which you organised with your characteristic ability & enthusiasm, to the lovely birthday, wedding anniversary & Xmas cards which you never failed to send, & to the funds which in spite of difficulties you managed to raise. What made the disaster even more shattering was the fact that you had last visited me on Dec. 21 & I was actually expecting you to come down last month or in June. I was also awaiting your reply to my letter of Apr. 2 in which I discussed your illness & made suggestions.

For some time after receiving the news my faculties seemed to have ceased functioning & I turned almost instinctively to your letter as I have always done in the past whenever my resolution flagged or whenever I wanted to take away my mind from nagging problems:

> "Most people do not realise that your physical presence would have meant nothing to me if the ideals for which you have dedicated your life have not been realised. I find living in hope the most wonderful thing. Our short lives together, my love, have always been full of expectation . . . In these hectic & violent years I have grown to love you more than I ever did before . . . Nothing can be as valuable as being part & parcel of the formation of the history of a country."

These are some of the gems this marvellous letter contains & after going through it on May 17 I felt once more on top of the world. Disasters will always come & go, leaving their victims either completely broken or steeled & seasoned & better able to face the next crop of challenges that may occur. It is precisely at the present moment that you should remember that hope is a powerful weapon & one no power on earth can deprive you of; & that nothing can be as valuable as being part & parcel of the history of a country. Permanent values in social life & thought cannot be created by people who are indifferent or hostile to the true aspirations of a nation. For one thing those who have no soul, no sense of national pride & no ideals to win can suffer neither humiliation nor defeat; they can evolve no national heritage, are inspired by no sacred mission & can produce no martyrs or national heroes. A new world will be won not by those who stand at a distance with their arms folded, but by those who are in the arena, whose garments are torn by storms & whose bodies are maimed in the course of contest. Honour belongs to those who never forsake the truth even when things seem dark & grim, who try over & over again, who are never discouraged by insults, humiliation & even defeat. Since the dawn of history, mankind has honoured & respected brave & honest people, men & women like you darling – an ordinary girl who hails from a country village hardly shown in most maps,[i] wife of a kraal,[ii] which is the humblest even by peasant standards.

My sense of devotion to you precludes me from saying more in public than I have already done in this note which must pass through many hands. One day we will have the privacy which will enable us to share the tender thoughts which we have kept buried in our hearts during the past eight years.

In due course you will be charged & probably convicted. I suggest that you discuss matters with Niki[iii] immediately you are charged & make the necessary arrangements for funds for purposes of study, toilet, Xmas groceries & other personal expenses. You must also arrange for her to send you as soon as you are convicted photos with suitable leather picture frames. From experience I have found that a family photo is everything in prison & you must have it right from the beginning. From this side you will have all my monthly letters, darling. I have written a long letter to Zeni & Zindzi, care of Niki, explaining the position in an attempt to keep them informed & cheerful. I only hope they received my earlier letter of Feb. 4. Last month I wrote to Mummy[iv] at Bizana[v] & to Sidumo.[vi] This month I will write to Telli[vii] & to Uncle Marsh.[viii] I have heard neither from Kgatho,[ix] Maki,[x] Wonga,[xi] Sef,[xii] Gibson,[xiii] Lily,[xiv] Mthetho[xv] & Amina[xvi] to whom I wrote between Dec. & April.

It has been possible to write this letter by kind permission of Brig. Aucamp[xvii] & I am sure he will be anxious to help you should you desire to reply to this letter whilst you are still under detention. If you succeed, please confirm whether you received my April letter. Meanwhile, I should like you to know that I am thinking of you every moment of the day. Good luck, my darling. A million kisses & tons & tons of love.

Devotedly,
Dalibunga

---

i   Winnie Mandela's home village is Mbongweni, Bizana, Transkei.
ii   A *kraal* is an Afrikaans word for a traditional collection of huts surrounded by a fence for enclosing cattle.
iii   Niki Xaba (1932–1985), Winnie Mandela's eldest sister – see the glossary.
iv   Winnie Mandela's mother.
v   The district in which she was born.
vi   Sidumo Mandela, his cousin.
vii   Telia (Telli or Tellie) Mtirara, a relative of Mandela's.
viii   Husband of Niki Xaba, Winnie Mandela's eldest sister (for Niki Xaba, see the glossary).
ix   Makgatho Mandela (1950– 2005), Mandela's second-born son – see the glossary.
x   Makaziwe Mandela (1954–), Mandela's eldest daughter – see the glossary.
xi   K. D. Matanzima (1915– 2003), Mandela's nephew, a Thembu chief, and chief minister for the Transkei – see the glossary. His middle name was Daliwonga, which was abbreviated to Wonga.
xii   Sefton Vutela, his brother-in-law.
xiii   Gibson Kente (1932–2004), playwright, composer, and director. Like Mandela, he was from the Madiba clan, so Mandela referred to him as a nephew – see the glossary.
xiv   Lilian Ngoyi (1911–80), politician, and anti-apartheid and women's rights activist – see the glossary.
xv   Chief Mthetho Matanzima (d. 1972), Mandela's nephew K. D. Matanzima's son and chief of the Noqayti region – see the glossary.
xvi   Amina Cachalia (1930–2013), friend and anti-apartheid and women's rights activist – see the glossary.
xvii   Brigadier Aucamp, commanding officer of Robben Island – see the glossary.

To Niki Xaba,[i] his wife's sister

15.7.69

My dear Niki,

I had originally planned to write this letter to Uncle Marsh.[ii] But I consider you mother to Zami[iii] & not just her eldest sister, & when I received the news of the detention of Nyanya,[iv] in addition to that of Zami, I realised just how much the whole affair must have disturbed you. In the circumstances I decided to send the letter to you instead.

In the letter I wrote to Ma[v] at Bizana on May 4, I told her I spent a lot of time thinking of Zami, the painful experiences she was having & the numerous problems that face her as a result of my absence. I pointed out that my confidence & regard for her had risen considerably, & that my only hope was that one day I might be able to give her the peace, comfort & happiness that would compensate for her dreadful hardships. Little did I know at the time that only 8 days thereafter Zami would be back in jail. Her arrest is a real disaster to the family & I must confess that I am very concerned. She is unwell[vi] & prison might worsen her condition. When I was arrested I had the fortune that she was outside & free. Before I was convicted she saw me on every visiting day without exception, brought me delicious provisions & clean clothes, & wrote me sweet & charming letters, & never missed a single day of my 2 trials to which she brought many friends & relatives, including my mother. I will never forget the day of sentence in the Rivonia Case for, besides the immense crowds of supporters & well-wishers that turned up, there sat behind us Zami, Ma, Nali[vii] & Nyanya. It was a rare moment which comes seldom in a man's career & it deepened my love & respect for Zami & drew me closer to my relatives – to Ma, Nali, Nyanya & to all of you. During my 5 years on this island Zami has visited me no less than 9 times & organised 10 other visits which brought me into contact with relations & friends I much value & respect. Even when difficulties on her side were growing, when she was without a job and her health was giving trouble, she thought first & foremost of me & my happiness & never failed to send me funds,

---

i   Niki Xaba (1932–1985), Winnie Mandela's eldest sister – see the glossary.
ii   Niki Xaba's husband, Marshall Xaba.
iii   Zami is one of Winnie Mandela's names.
iv   Winnie Mandela's youngest sister, Nonyaniso Madikizela, who was also known as Nyanya.
v   Nophikela Hilda Madikizela, Winnie Mandela and Niki Xaba's stepmother – see the glossary.
vi   Winnie Mandela had a heart condition.
vii   Nali Nancy Vutela, Winnie Mandela's sister.

wonderful letters, birthday & wedding anniversary cards. All these things have meant much to me. One has to be a prisoner to appreciate fully the true value of many things we take much for granted in life outside prison. During the nearly 7 years of my imprisonment Zami has been truly at my side. Now it is her turn & she needs all my love & affection, all my sympathy & help, & yet I can do absolutely nothing for her. She can look forward to no visit from me that would bring some welcome change from the depressing routine to which she is now subjected, no tasty provisions that would suit her indifferent health, no warm & affectionate letters that would bring back happy memories. If she should ultimately be charged, it will not be possible for me to show solidarity through physical presence, & none of the countless things she did for me as prisoner shall I be able to do for her.

The tender faces of small children, distorted by fear & drowsiness, seeing their dear mother escorted away in the dead of night, & unable to understand the issues involved is a memory that could haunt the most fearless mother. Add to this picture the fact that for years her children may live like orphans & that she may be completely deprived of the opportunity of giving her children the help & guidance which they would need in the most critical years of their lives. I know how Zami is devoted to the children & if there is one thing that would do further harm to her health it is the uncertainty & insecurity that now threatens them. These are the reasons why I regard her arrest as a family disaster, Niki. I am not in a position to make any predictions as to how she will face up to the situation & I shall certainly not risk any prophecy. But her record up to now has shown her as a woman of great courage who has stuck to her principles in spite of severe trials. My only hope is that she will find it possible to survive even this one in spite of her indifferent health. I am equally proud of Nyanya & have grown to love her much more than I ever did in the past. I sometimes think that if I were at home these last 8 years she would have made good progress both in her studies & ideas in life. In my last letter to Bawo I expressed my concern over the fact that she was idling at home & suggested that she should at least be given some vocational training. I hope she will also benefit from this experience.

At the time of writing to Ma I was actually expecting a visit from Zami as I had last seen her in December & I had had no visit since then. Our friend Radebe (Mgulwa)[i] was due to visit me in February but for reasons unknown to me he did not come. I had looked forward to that visit because it offered me the only opportunity of hearing something about Zami & the kids as apparently none of the letters I have written monthly since

---

i   Alfred Mgulwa (Radebe is his clan name), Winnie Mandela's uncle.

December last has reached its destination. On June 28 another good friend, Moosa Dinath,[i] who was coming down from Johannesburg for the express purpose of discussing family problems caused by Zami's detention, also failed to turn up & again the prison authorities were unable to give me an explanation for this mysterious behaviour on the part of my visitors. I now know that before May 12 Zami had applied for a visiting permit for Kgatho for May 24. The authorities never even told me of this particular visit. The result is that I have been completely cut off from my family & friends at a time when such contact has been absolutely essential. On June 23 I wrote Zeni & Zindzi a long letter which I sent to Brig. Aucamp[ii] of the Headquarters, Pretoria, & asked him to forward it to you. I hope at least this one has reached you. In December I wrote to Nali, February to Zeni & Zindzi, March, to my nephew Gibson Kente[iii] and to Lilian.[iv] All these letters were addressed to 8115, Orlando West. The fact that I received no acknowledgement compels me to infer that the letters were not received & perhaps Uncle Marsh[v] will make the investigations & let you know. I have also written to Tellie[vi] requesting her to find out about the letters to Kgatho[vii] & Maki[viii] in January & February. I was sorry to hear that you were involved in a car accident in which you fractured a leg. I hope you are recovering & am anxious to get some details in your next letter. How are the children getting on & what are their names? How old are they? How many children has Bantu?[ix] Love and fondest regards to Marsh, Bantu & hubby, Tellie, Mfundo, etc.

Sincerely,
Nel

MRS NIKI IRIS XABA, 8115, ORLANDO WEST, JOHANNESBURG

---

i   Mandela first met Moosa Dinath when he was a member of the Transvaal Indian Congress and businessman in Johannesburg. They renewed their acquaintance in prison in 1962 while Mandela was awaiting trial and Dinath was serving a sentence for fraud.
ii   Brigadier Aucamp, commanding officer of Robben Island – see the glossary.
iii Gibson Kente (1932–2004), playwright, composer, and director. Like Mandela, he was from the Madiba clan, so Mandela referred to him as a nephew – see the glossary.
iv   Lilian Ngoyi (1911–80), politician, and anti-apartheid and women's rights activist – see the glossary.
v   Marshall Xaba, husband of Niki Xaba, Winnie Mandela's eldest sister (for Niki Xaba, see the glossary).
vi   Telia (Telli or Tellie) Mtirara, a relative of Mandela's.
vii Makgatho (Kgatho) Mandela (1950–2005), Mandela's second-born son – see the glossary.
viii Makaziwe (Maki) Mandela (1954–), Mandela's eldest daughter – see the glossary.
ix   Nobantu Mniki, one of Winnie Mandela's sisters.

To Tellie Mtirara, a relative

Letter in lieu of visit for June 1969.

15.7.69

My dear Nkosazana,[i]

There is hardly a single person I know of who welcomes problems. This is understandable since problems often interfere with one's plans, pleasure & happiness. Worse still, they may bring a lot of hardship & suffering. The detention of Nobandla[ii] has really disturbed me precisely because it carries just these dangers. She may be kept in jail for years without trial. If she is at last charged she may be given a heavy sentence. In either case this would mean many years of forced separation from the children, relations & friends, many years of toiling & sweating & the denial to her of the privileges of a free person. This is a heavy price to pay. But though always painful & unpleasant, problems may have the advantage of reminding one of those trustworthy and devoted members of the family to whom one instinctively turns when hard times come. Ever since I saw you in court during the Rivonia Case, & especially after you accompanied Nobandla to Cape Town in Aug, '64. It has been my intention to write & thank you for the ready & unfailing assistance that you have given at home. But the very fact that you are a member of the family induced me to take it for granted that you will always know that I have the highest regard for you & that I am fully conscious of the important role you are playing at home in my absence. This in turn gave me the excuse of postponing writing to you until I had attended to what appeared to be the more urgent cases. But Nobandla's arrest has now cut me off from home, my friends & relatives and now I must rely on you & Niki.[iii] The two of you will have to arrange my visits as well as those of Nobandla when she becomes entitled to them.

I have already written & requested Niki to investigate whether the letters I wrote to Zeni & Zindzi,[iv] Nali,[v] Gibson[vi] & to Lilian[vii] were received. I should like you to give me a report on whether Kgatho,[viii] Maki[ix] & Mrs

---

i   *Nkosazana* means 'Miss' or 'princess' in isiXhosa.
ii   One of Winnie Mandela's names.
iii   Niki Xaba (1932–1985), Winnie Mandela's eldest sister – see the glossary.
iv   Zenani (1959–) and Zindzi (1960–) Mandela, his youngest daughters – see the glossary.
v   Nali Nancy Vutela, Winnie Mandela's sister.
vi   Gibson Kente (1932–2004), playwright, composer, and director. Like Mandela, he was from the Madiba clan, so Mandela referred to him as a nephew – see the glossary.
vii Lilian Ngoyi (1911–80), politician, and anti-apartheid and women's rights activist – see the glossary.
viii Makgatho Mandela (1950–2005), Mandela's second-born son – see the glossary.
ix   Makaziwe Mandela (1954–), Mandela's eldest daughter – see the glossary.

Amina Cachalia[i] got their letters which were written in January, February and April respectively. I require the following additional information on Kgatho: How is his health? Did he go for circumcision?[ii] Did he pass the supplementary examinations which he wrote in March? What work is he doing at present & what are his future plans? Perhaps it may be advisable for him to come down so that we could discuss the whole matter. I should also like to know whether Nobandla still possessed the car & the house telephone, as well as what arrangements, if any, have been made for the payment of the accounts? As you know, we have a family attorney who has handled all Nobandla's matters in the past & I should be pleased if you would kindly let me have the name of the lawyer or lawyers who are watching her interests at present & who will appear for her when she is charged. In my letter to Niki I mentioned that this year I expected visits from Kgatho, Moosa Dinath[iii] & Alfred Mgulwa[iv] & none of them turned up & I should be glad to be informed why they failed to come. Last December I wrote to Dr Wonga Mbekeni,[v] P.O. Tsolo,[vi] thanking him for attending my late mother's funeral & for his contribution towards the expenses of the ceremony. I also gave him my condolences on the death of Nkosazana Nozipho[vii] & asked him to send me some information which I indicated. As he did not reply I assume he never received this important letter. You must, however, answer this particular one immediately without waiting for Wonga's answer. This can be sent later when you hear from him.

Do you happen to know where Nyanya[viii] is being kept? If you are able to communicate with her, do give her my love & let her know I am very proud of her indeed. You should also give my love & fondest regards to Amakhosazana Nombulelo & Nobatembu[ix] & let me know whether Nombulelo is still working at the eiderdown factory in Selby. Then there is Nkosazana Nqonqi[x] for whom I have the greatest admiration and respect. She has always been a tower of strength to me. Way back in 1942 she stayed next to the power station in Orlando East. Then she moved next to the Communal Hall, later to

i   Amina Cachalia (1930–2013), friend and anti-apartheid and women's rights activist – see the glossary.
ii   Circumcision was a traditional rite of passage into manhood. Mandela undertook it at the age of sixteen.
iii   Mandela first met Moosa Dinath when he was a member of the Transvaal Indian Congress and businessman in Johannesburg. They renewed their acquaintance in prison in 1962 while Mandela was awaiting trial and Dinath was serving a sentence for fraud. He and his wife, Maud Katzenellenbogen, who befriended Winnie, hatched a plan to free Mandela from prison, but it was shelved because Winnie became suspicious of it.
iv   Winnie Mandela's uncle.
v   A cousin of Mandela's who negotiated his marriage to Winnie Madikizela with Winnie's uncles or other male elders in her family, and who was at the time the president of the Medical Association of Transkei.
vi   Post office in Tsolo, Transkei.
vii   *Nkosazana* means 'Miss' or 'princess' in isiXhosa. Nozipho Mbekeni was a nurse and the sister of Wonga Mbekeni, a cousin of Mandela's.
viii   Nonyaniso (Nyanya) Madikizela, Winnie Mandela's youngest sister.
ix   *Amakhosazana* means 'the Misses'. Nombulelo Judith Mtirara is a sister of Sabata Jonguhlanga Dalindyebo (see the glossary) and Nobatembu is Nelson Mandela's cousin's daughter.
x   Nqonqi Mtirara, a cousin of Mandela's.

Jabavu & finally to Killarney. I frequented these places & she always treated me very warmly as she has frequently done to members of the family. When I married Nobandla she lived with her at her Killarney home. One of my wishes is that she may live long until I am released so that I can have the opportunity of thanking her for what she has done for me & Nobandla. You will of course tell me everything about the child who must be very big now.

Last year I received very inspiring letters from Jonguhlanga,[i] Nkosikazi NoEngland,[ii] & from Chief Vulindlela.[iii] In the course of the nearly 7 years that I have spent in prison I have received several letters from friends in various parts of the country, all of which I value. But letters from the family have special significance for me, particularly when they come from people such as the Abahlekazi[iv] & Nkosikazi[v] above, who have made tremendous sacrifices on my behalf & whom I trust completely. As for you, Nkosana,[vi] I need only mention that I have lived with you since the early fifties & one of the striking quality [sic] you possess in full measure is honesty, love & devotion to the family. The free & open manner in which you discussed problems with me & the valuable & constructive criticisms you made of myself, all created a deep impression which I have not forgotten up to the present day. With people like you and Niki round the home I have little cause to worry. I am fully confident that both of you will do your best to keep things steady & even. Love & fondest regards to Nkosazana Samela[vii] & husband, & to Mtsobise.[viii]

Very sincerely,
Tat'omncinci[ix]

MISS TELLIE MTIRARA,
8115 ORLANDO WEST, JOHANNESBURG.

◇◇◇◇◇◇◇◇

As if 1969 could not have got any worse, a telegram came, carrying devastating news. Mandela's firstborn child, Madiba Thembekile 'Thembi', had been killed

---

i   King Sabata Jonguhlanga Dalindyebo (1928–86), paramount chief of the Transkei homeland and leader of the Democratic Progressive Party, the opposition party in Transkei which opposed apartheid rule – see the glossary.

ii   Wife of the regent Chief Jongintaba Dalindyebo who was Mandela's guardian after his father died when he was twelve (see the glossary).

iii   Chief Vulindlela Mtirara/Matanzima, a Tembu chief and relative of Mandela's.

iv   'The gentlemen above' in isiXhosa, referring to Jonguhlanga and Chief Vulindlela Mtirara.

v   'Mrs' in isiXhosa, referring to the regent's wife.

vi   'Miss' in isiXhosa.

vii   Samela Mtirara, one of Mandela's relatives. *Nkosazana* means 'Miss' or 'princess' in isiXhosa.

viii   Olive Nomfundo Mandela, daughter of Mandela's sister Notancu.

ix   'Youngest uncle' or 'sibling from the same clan' in isiXhosa.

in a car accident in Cape Town. His wife, Thoko, had survived the collision but his passing left his two little daughters fatherless. Mandela had not yet met his daughter-in-law or his two granddaughters, Nandi and Ndileka. He would have to wait until they had reached sixteen, the required visiting age, for that privilege.

Winnie Mandela was still in prison, and he poured out his sorrow to her and Thembi's mother – his first wife, Evelyn – and many other members of the family. Letters remained the only tool for his remote control parenting and they were not enough, notwithstanding their unpredicatable journey into the outside world. Unable to physically console anyone or to stand at the grave as his son was buried, Mandela had to rely on his comrades for comfort and his own inner strength.

Once they were free, Mandela's colleagues were able to relate their own anguish at seeing him wrapped tightly in a brown prison-issue blanket, sitting in his cell alongside his friend Walter Sisulu.[i]

To Winnie Mandela,[ii] **his wife**

Special letter to Zami[iii]

16.7.69

My Darling,

This afternoon the Commanding Officer received the following telegram from attorney Mendel Levin:[iv]

"Please advise Nelson Mandela his Thembekile[v] passed away 13th instant result motor accident in Cape Town."

I find it difficult to believe that I will never see Thembi again. On February 23 this year he turned 24. I had seen him towards the end of July 1962, a few days after I had returned from the trip abroad. Then he was a lusty lad of 17 that I could never associate with death. He wore one of my trousers which was a shade too big & long for him. The incident was significant & set me thinking. As you know he had a lot of clothing, was particular about his dress & had no reason whatsoever for using my clothes. I was deeply touched for

---

i   Walter Sisulu (1912– 2003), ANC and MK activisit and fellow Rivonia trialist who was imprisoned with Mandela – see the glossary.

ii   Nomzamo Winifred Madikizela-Mandela (1936–) – see the glossary.

iii   Special letters were not taken off a prisoner's quota. Zami is one of Winnie Mandela's names.

iv   Mendel Levin was a lawyer Winnie Mandela's friend Maud Katzenellenbogen proposed to defend Winnie Mandela. After consultation with Mandela she did not use him and eventually chose Joel Carlson instead.

v   Madiba Thembekile (Thembi) Mandela (1945–69), Mandela's eldest son – see the glossary.

the emotional factors underlying his action were too obvious. For days there-after my mind & feelings were agitated to realise the psychological strains & stresses my absence from home had imposed on the children. I recalled an incident in December 1956 when I was an awaiting trial prisoner at the Johannesburg Fort. At that time Kgatho[i] was 6 and lived in Orlando East. Although he well knew that I was in jail he went over to Orlando West & told Ma[ii] that he longed for me. That night he slept in my bed.

But let me return to my meeting with Thembi. He had come to bid me farewell on his way to a boarding school. On his arrival he greeted me very warmly, holding my hand firmly & for some time. Thereafter we sat down & conversed. Somehow the conversation drifted to his studies, & he gave me what I considered, in the light of his age at the time, to be an interesting appreciation of Shakespeare's *Julius Caesar* which I very much enjoyed. We had been corresponding regularly ever since he went to school at Matatiele & when he later changed to Wodehouse.[iii] In December 1960 I travelled some distance by car to meet him. Throughout this period I regarded him as a child & I approached him mainly from this angle. But our conversation in July 1962 reminded me I was no longer speaking to a child but to one who was beginning to have a settled attitude in life. He had suddenly raised himself from a son to a friend. I was indeed a bit sad when we ultimately parted. I could neither accompany him to a bus stop nor see him off at the station, for an outlaw, such as I was at the time, must be ready to give up even important parental duties. So it was that my son, no! my friend, stepped out alone to fend for himself in a world where I could only meet him secretly & once in a while. I knew you had bought him clothing & given him some cash, but nevertheless I emptied my pockets and transferred to him all the copper and silver that a wretched fugitive could afford. During the Rivonia Case he sat behind me one day. I kept looking back, nodding to him & giving him a broad smile. At the time it was generally believed that we would certainly be given the extreme penalty & this was clearly written across his face. Though he nodded back as many times as I did to him, not once did he return the smile. I never dreamt that I would never see him again. That was 5 years ago.

During the intervening period, you gave me many interesting reports on him in your letters & during your visits. I was particularly pleased to note his attachment to the family & the personal interest he took in matters affecting his relations. This attachment & interest is demonstrated by the warm letter he wrote you in June 1967, meeting you at the airport when

i   Makgatho Mandela (1950–2005), Mandela's second-born son – see the glossary.
ii   He is most likely referring to his mother, Nosekeni Fanny Mandela, who stayed with them for a while.
iii   Wodehouse Junior Secondary School in Cofimvaba, Transkei.

Special letter

16. 7. 69

Dear Evelyn,

This afternoon the Commanding Officer informed me of a telegram received from attorney Mendel Levin of Johannesburg in which he reported the death of Thembi in a motor accident in Cape Town on July 13.

I write to give you, Kgatho & Maki my deepest sympathy. I know more than anybody else living, today just how devastating this cruel blow must have been to you for Thembi was your first born & the second child that you have lost. I also am fully conscious of the passionate love that you had for him & the efforts you made to train & prepare him to play his part in a complex modern industrial society. I am also fully aware of how Kgatho & Maki adored & respected him, the holidays & good time they spent with him in Cape Town. In his letter written in October 1967 Maki told me that Thembi helped you in buying them all they needed. My late ma gave me details of the warm hospitality she received the received from him when she visited me on the Island. Throughout the last five years up to March this year, Nobandla gave me interesting accounts of his attachment & devotion to the family & the personal interest he took in all his relatives. I last saw him five years ago during the Rivonia trial & I always looked forward to these accounts for they were the main channel through which I was able to hear something of him.

The blow has been equally grievous to me. In addition to the fact that I had not seen him for at least sixty months, I was neither privileged to give him a wedding ceremony nor to lay him to rest when the fatal hour had struck. In 1967 I wrote him a long letter drawing his attention to some matters which I thought it was in his interest to attend to without delay. I looked forward to further correspondence to & to meeting him and his family when I returned. All these expectations have now been completely shattered for he has been taken away at the early age of 24 and we will never again see him. We should all be consoled & comforted by the fact that he had

Pages from a special letter to Evelyn Mandela, 16 July 1969, see pages 111–12.

many good friends who join with us in mourning his passing away. He fulfilled all his duties to us as parents and has left us with an inheritance for which every parent is proud – a charming Molokazana & two lovely babies Once more I extend to you, Kgatho & Maki my sincere condolences and trust that you will muster enough strength and courage to survive this painful tragedy fondest regards to Sam & Khezi, to Nomanage, hutu, Phindi, Ntsesi, Nicolisi, Mongezi & waza. Nobandla joins me in this message of sympathy.

Yours very sincerely,
Nelson.

you visited me the same month, looking after Ma[i] in Cape Town & bringing her to the Docks to board the Island boat, visiting you when he recently came up to Johannesburg with his family & taking Zeni & Zindzi[ii] out. I do not know whether he managed to go down to see Ma's grave. He has sent messages through Kgatho & gave me the parental honour of asking me to name his baby. Maki[iii] also told me that he bought Kgatho & herself clothing & all the other things they need. I know what a shattering blow his death is to you darling & I write to give you my deepest sympathy. I have sent Ntoko[iv] our condolences. Though taken away so early in his life, he will rest in peace for he has done his duty to his parents, brother & sisters & to his relations. We will all miss him. It is a pity that neither you nor I could pay him the last respects that are due from parents to a beloved son who has departed. To lose a mother & a first-born, & to have your life partner incarcerated for an indefinite period, and all within a period of ten months, is a burden too heavy for one man to carry even in the best of time. But I do not at all complain my darling. All I wish you to know is that you are my pride & that of our wide family.

Never before have I longed for you than at the present moment. It is good to remember this in this day of bitter misfortunes & bitter reverses. The writer, P. J. Schoeman, told the story of an African Commander-in-Chief who took his army of magnificent black warriors for a hunt. During the chase the son of the Commander was killed by a lioness & the Commander himself was badly mauled by the beast. The wound was then sterilised with a red-hot spear & the wounded dignitary writhed with pain as the wound was being treated. Later Schoeman asked how he felt & he replied that the invisible wound was more painful than the visible one. I now know what the commander meant. I think of you every moment of the day. Tons & tons of love & a million kisses, Mhlope.[v]

Devotedly,
Dalibunga

NKOSIKAZI NOBANDLA MANDELA. 8115 ORLANDO WEST JOHANNESBURG

---

i   Nelson Mandela's mother and Thembi's grandmother who passed away in September 1968.
ii   Zenani (1959–) and Zindzi (1960–) Mandela, his youngest daughters – see the glossary.
iii   Makaziwe mandela (1954–), Mandela's eldest daughter – see the glossary.
iv   Evelyn Ntoko Mandela (1922–2004), Mandela's first wife (1944–1958) and the mother of Thembi – see the glossary.
v   One of Winnie Mandela's names.

To Evelyn Mandela,[i] his former wife and mother of Thembi[ii]

16.7.69

Special letter[iii]

Dear Evelyn,

This afternoon the Commanding Officer informed me of a telegram received from attorney Mendel Levin of Johannesburg in which he reported the death of Thembi in a motor accident in Cape Town on July 13.

I write to give you, Kgatho & Maki[iv] my deepest sympathy. I know more than anybody else living today just how devastating this cruel blow must have been for you for Thembi was your first-born & the second child that you have lost.[v] I am also fully conscious of the passionate love that you had for him & the efforts you made to train & prepare him to play his part in a complex modern industrial society. I am also aware of how Kgatho & Maki adored & respected him, the holidays & good time they spent with him in Cape Town. In her letter written in October 1967 Maki told me that Thembi helped you in buying them all they needed. My late Ma gave me details of the warm hospitality she received from him when she visited me on the Island. Throughout the last five years up to March this year, Nobandla[vi] gave me interesting accounts of his attachment & devotion to the family & the personal interest he took in all his relatives. I last saw him five years ago during the Rivonia Trial & I always looked forward to these accounts for they were the main channel through which I was able to hear something of him.

The blow has been equally grievous to me. In addition to the fact that I had not seen him for at least sixty months, I was neither privileged to give him a wedding ceremony nor to lay him to rest when the fatal hour had struck. In 1967 I wrote him a long letter drawing his attention to some matters which I thought was in his interest to attend to without delay. I looked forward to further correspondence & to meeting him and his family when I returned. All these expectations have now been completely shattered for he has been taken away at the early age of 24 and we will never again see

---

i Evelyn Ntoko Mandela (1922–2004), Mandela's first wife (1944–1958) and the mother of Thembi – see the glossary.

ii Madiba Thembekile (Thembi) Mandela (1945–69), Mandela's eldest son – see the glossary.

iii Special letters were not taken from a prisoner's quota.

iv His remaining living children with Evelyn Mandela – Makgatho (Kgatho) Mandela (1950–2005), Mandela's second-born son (see the glossary) and Makaziwe (Maki) Mandela (1954–), Mandela's eldest daughter (see the glossary).

v His first daughter with Evelyn died of an illness at the age of nine months. She was named Makaziwe. They susequently gave the same name to their second daughter.

vi One of Winnie Mandela's names.

him. We should all be consoled & comforted by the fact that he had many good friends who join with us in mourning his passing away. He fulfilled his duties to us as parents and has left us with an inheritance for which every parent is proud – a charming Molokazana[i] & two lovely babies. Once more I extend to you, Kgatho & Maki my sincere condolences & trust that you will muster enough strength & courage to survive this painful tragedy.

Fondest regards to Sam & Tshezi,[ii] to Nomanage, Lulu, Phindi, Nosisi, Mxolisi, Mongezi & Waza.[iii] Nobandla joins me in this message of sympathy.

Yours very sincerely,
Nelson.

To Colonel Van Aarde, commanding officer, Robben Island

July 22, 1969

The Commanding Officer
Robben Island

Attention Col. Van Aarde

My eldest son, Madiba Thembekile,[iv] aged twenty-four, passed away in Cape Town on July 13, 1969, as a result of injuries he sustained in a motor-car accident.

I wish to attend, at my own cost, the funeral proceedings and to pay my last respects to his memory. I have no information as to where he will be buried, but I assume that this will take place either in Cape Town, Johannesburg or Umtata.[v] In this connection I should be pleased if you would give me permission to proceed immediately, with or without escort, to the place where he will be laid to rest. If he will already have been buried by the time you receive this application, then I would ask that I be allowed to visit his grave for the purpose of "laying the stone", the traditional ceremony reserved for those persons who miss the actual burial.

It is my earnest hope that you will on this occasion find it possible to approach this request more humanely than you treated a similar application

i   isiXhosa for 'daughter-in-law'. He is referring to his late son Thembi's wife, Thoko Mandela – see the glossary.
ii   Evelyn Mandela's brother and sister-in-law.
iii   Members of Evelyn Mandela's family.
iv   Madiba Thembekile (Thembi) (1945–69), Mandela's eldest son – see the glossary.
v   Umtata (now called Mthatha) was the capital of the Transkei homeland.

I made barely ten months ago, in September 1968, for leave to attend my mother's funeral. Approval of that application would have been a generous act on your part, and one which would have made a deep impression on me. Such a humanitarian gesture would have gone a long way in softening the hard blow and painful misfortune of an imprisoned man losing a mother, and would have afforded me the opportunity to be present at the graveside. I might add that I saw my late son a little more than five years ago and you will readily appreciate just how anxious I am to attend the funeral.

Finally, I should like to point out that precedent exists when Governments have favourably considered applications of this nature.[i]

NELSON MANDELA[ii]

To Makgatho Mandela,[iii] his second-born son

28.7.69

My dear Kgatho,

I have been shown your telegram of July 17 in which you advised me of Thembi's[iv] death in a car accident. The previous day the Commanding Officer had received a similar telegram from Attorney Mendel Levin of Johannesburg. I hope your mother[v] has by now received the letter I wrote on July 16 expressing my condolences to her and to you and Maki.[vi]

It is a wise rule never to brood over past calamities, however disastrous they may appear to be, and we should try to reconcile ourselves to the grim fact that Thembi, your beloved brother, is no more and that never again shall we see him. None the less, his passing away is a serious loss to the family and it has left a deep and painful wound that may take many years to heal.

I think of your mother who must have been severely shocked to lose a son so early in his life and who had already begun to take over some of the

---

i   He is likely referring to the first prime minister of India Jawaharlal Nehru (1889–1964) and elaborates on this more fully in his letter to Nolusapho Irene Mkwayi on 29 September 1969 (see page 127) and the accompanying note number.
ii   In his letter to Nolusapho Irene Mkwayi on 29 September 1969 (see page 127), he writes that his application to attend the burial of Thembi was 'simply ignored'.
iii Makgatho Mandela (1950–2005) – see the glossary.
iv   Madiba Thembekile (Thembi) (1945–69), Mandela's eldest son – see the glossary.
v   Evelyn Ntoko Mandela (1922–2004), Mandela's first wife (1944–1958) – see the glossary.
vi   Makaziwe (Maki) Mandela (1954–), Mandela's eldest daughter – see the glossary.

heavy duties of a parent that will now press on her from all sides. I think more particularly of you and Maki because I realise fully just how hard a blow Thembi's death must have been to both of you. He sincerely loved you, and you, in turn, were very fond of him. He was not just a brother but the person to whom you naturally turned for advice and assistance. He was the shield that protected you against danger, and that helped you to build up the self-confidence and courage you need to deal with the numerous problems that you meet as you grow. You could take him into confidence in regard to many matters a child would hesitate to disclose to his parents, and now that he is gone you must be feeling lost, lonely and sad. In Cape Town he provided a home for you where you could happily spend exciting holidays, meet new friends and learn more about your country and people. His death means that no more will you be able to enjoy these advantages and that from now on you will have to fight and win your own battles and to depend on your own resources.

I think it fit and proper to highlight but one striking virtue of his which created a deep impression on me. His love and devotion to you, Maki, Zeni,[i] Zindzi[ii] and to relatives generally, created the image of a man who respected family ties and who was destined to play an important role in the upbringing, education and development of the children. He had already developed himself to a position where he had become the object of his sisters' love, admiration and respect and a source of pride to the family.

From 8115[iii] I was kept constantly informed of his unflagging interest in all of us and details of his hospitality during his recent visit with his family to Johannesburg were outlined. The late Granny[iv] never missed the chance of saying something complimentary about him whenever she visited me here and I sincerely regret that death has denied him the opportunity to bring this magnificent gift of his in full play in the service of the family.

I hate giving lectures, Kgatho, even to my own children and I prefer discussing matters with everyone on a basis of perfect equality, where my views are offered as advice which the person affected is free to accept or reject as it pleases him. But I would be failing in my duty if I did not point out that the death of Thembi brings a heavy responsibility on your shoulders. Now you are the eldest child and it will be your duty to keep the family together and to set a good example for your sisters, to be a pride to your parents and to all your relatives. This means that you will have to work harder on your studies, never allow yourself to be discouraged by difficulties or setbacks,

---

i   Zenani (Zeni) Mandela (1959–), Mandela's middle daughter.
ii   Zindziswa (Zindzi) Mandela (1960–), Mandela's youngest daughter.
iii   Mandela's house in Vilakazi street, Orlando West, Soweto.
iv   Nelson Mandela's mother, Nosekeni Fanny Mandela, who died in 1968 – see the glossary.

and never give up the battle even in the darkest hour. Remember that we live in a new age of scientific achievement, the most staggering of which is the recent landing of man on the moon. That is a sensational event that will enrich man's knowledge of the universe and that may even result in a change or modification of many fundamental assumptions in many fields of knowledge. The younger generation must train and prepare themselves so that they can easily grasp the far-reaching repercussions of developments in the realm of space. This is an era of intense and vicious competition in which the richest rewards are reserved for those who have undergone the most thorough training and who have attained the highest academic qualifications in their respective fields. The issues that agitate humanity today call for trained minds and the man who is deficient in this respect is crippled because he is not in possession of the tools and equipment necessary to ensure success and victory in service of country and people. To lead an orderly and disciplined life, and to give up the glittering pleasures that attract the average boy, to work hard and systematically in your studies throughout the year, will in the end bring you coveted prizes and much personal happiness. It will inspire your sisters to follow the example of their beloved brother, and they will benefit greatly through your scientific knowledge, vast experience, diligence and achievements. Besides, human beings like to be associated with a hardworking, disciplined and successful person, and by carefully cultivating these qualities you will win yourself many friends. This is what I should like to stress. Perhaps you would like to discuss the matter with Sisi Tellie[i] in 8115 who will arrange a permit[ii] for you to come down so that we can discuss future plans relating to your education.

Last January I wrote you a lengthy letter discussing precisely this matter and other personal questions. I wrote Maki a similar one on February 16. Your failure to reply made me suspect that both of you had not received the letters. I made enquiries and found that there was no evidence that the letters had been posted to you. I was indeed shocked to hear that my letters do not reach you and other members of the family & friends as they are the only means I have to communicate with you. I hope at least this one will reach you. Please let me know about your supplementary results.

Finally I must thank you most earnestly for advising me of the death of Thembi and I will think of you in this family tragedy. Do let me have the full name of Molokazana,[iii] her present address as well as the names of Abazukulu.[iv] Fond regards to all.

---

i   Telia (Telli or Tellie) Mtirara, a relative of Mandela's. *Sisi* means 'sister' in isiXhosa and is often used to refer to a woman in the samge age group.

ii   Permits were required by all visitors.

iii   'Daughter-in-law' in isiXhosa. He is referring to Thembi's wife, Thoko Mandela – see the glossary.

iv   'Grandchildren' in isiXhosa and isiXulu. Mandela is referring to Thembi and Thoko Mandela's children Ndileka

Affectionately
Tata.[i]

MR MAKGATHO LEWANIKA MANDELA, HOUSE NO. 8115 ORLANDO WEST, JOHANNESBURG.

─────────

To Sefton Vutela, the husband of Nancy (Nali) Vutela, Winnie Mandela's sister

28.7.69

My dear Sef,

I have been shocked to discover that almost every letter I have written since December last to members of my family, relations & friends has not reached its destination, including one I wrote you 7 months ago. I hope this one will reach safely & that the invisible forces that have been responsible for the mysterious but systematic disappearance of my correspondence, & that have completely cut me off from my family and relations will be prompted by considerations of fairplay & sportsmanship to give me a break & let this one through.

I owe you a debt which I may find difficult to repay. The day my colleagues and I were sentenced in the Rivonia Trial,[ii] Nali, Zami,[iii] my late mother and Nyanya[iv] sat amongst the audience. The offence for which we had been convicted the previous day carried a capital sentence, & there were many who feared that we would in due course be condemned to the countless legions of the dead. As a matter of fact, on the very first day of consultations, counsel felt obliged to inform us that the prosecution had indicated that they would demand the extreme penalty, at least against some of the accused. The gravity of the situation was sufficiently stressed & we were duly warned to prepare ourselves for this grim and grievous end to all our dreams. I am neither brave nor bold, & since the days of my youth, I have been stalked by the chronic weakness of being anxious to

---

(1965–) and Nandi (1968–) Mandela – see the glossary.
i   'Father' in isiXhosa.
ii   See the glossary.
iii   Another name for Winnie Mandela.
iv   Nonyaniso (Nyanya) Madikizela, Winnie Mandela's youngest sister.

live & be an eye-witness to the introduction of the radical developments for which my countrymen have fought so bravely in the course of the last three centuries. As disciplined and dedicated comrades fighting for a worthy cause, we should be ready to undertake any tasks which history might assign to us however high the price to be paid may be. This was the guiding principle throughout our political careers, & even as we went through the various stages of the trial. I must, however, confess that for my own part the threat of death evoked no desire in me to play the role of martyr. I was ready to do so if I had to. But the anxiety to live always lingered. But familiarity does breed contempt even for the hideous hand of death. The critical phase lasted a few hours only, & I was a worried & exhausted man as I went to bed the day I heard of the Rivonia swoop.[i] But when I got up in the morning the worst was over & I had somehow mustered enough strength & courage even to rationalise that if there was nothing else I could do to further the cause we all so passionately cherished, even the dreadful outcome that threatened us might serve a useful purpose on wider issues. This belief served to feed & replenish my slender resources of fortitude until the last day of the proceedings. It was reinforced by the conviction that our cause was just & by the wide support we received from influential bodies & individuals on both sides of the Colour line. But all the flourish of trumpets & the hosannas sung by us & our well-wishers in the course of the trial would have been valueless if courage had deserted us when the decisive moment struck.[ii] The immense crowds that turned up when sentence was pronounced on June 12 gave us real inspiration. As we entered the courtroom that morning my eyes immediately fell on Nyanya, Nali, Ma & Zami. Ma & Zami have always been a tower of strength to me & have very often succeeded in spurring me to accomplish much more than my limited talents warranted. I was delighted to see them on this occasion. But for me Nali's attendance was a shot in the arm; it had a significance that went somewhat beyond the mere physical presence of a sister-in-law. I regarded it as an act of solidarity on your part because of the major principle that was at stake. I shall always remember that day.

In 1967 Nali travelled the 1,000 miles between Johannesburg & Cape Town reaching the Island on February 4. She brought me a visit which really excited me. She looked well & terrific & I was indeed very happy to see her once more.

Some time before that you had personally packed & sent me the liter-

---

i   The police raid on Liliesleaf Farm on 11 July 1963 in which most of Mandela's fellow Rivonia Trialists were arrested.

ii   Mandela and his comrades received much support from within and outside South Africa during the Rivonia Trial. The courage he is referring to here is related to the expectation that they would be sentenced to death.

ature I needed for my studies & your pencil signature in the books meant much to me. Above all is the invaluable help you have given Zami, the details of which she repeatedly placed before me through correspondence & during her visits. It may not be out of place to make the point here that often in normal life, when happy & free, we build for ourselves ivory towers into which we retreat & within which we swell with pride & conceit & treat with indifference & even contempt the generosity & affection of friends. Behind iron bars such artificial towers easily crumble & acts of hospitality become priceless jewels. I do want to assure you in all sincerity that I deeply appreciated all that you and Nali did for me & Zami. The northern areas are miles away from your native village in the Transkei, from the plains & hills where your childhood was spent, & from your kith & kin. Often I have sat down & thought long & deeply over you & Nali, & the ideas that have crossed my mind have been legion, all that I need say at the present moment is that I wish both of you & the children (about whom I should like to hear when you reply) good health, strength & much luck & fortune in the days that lie ahead.

Zami also told me of the help given by Cameron,[i] my suave brother-in-law, & I should be pleased if you would kindly tell him that his assistance made a profound impression on me. I have not had the privilege of meeting his wife & I do look forward to seeing her one day. I think of Kha & Tami as well. I do not know if I would find it easy to recognise her as I saw her once or twice, but I still remember that she is a beautiful girl, as all the Madikizela females are, otherwise how do you think they succeeded in dragging you, Tami & me to the altar?

Fondest regards to Tshutsha, NKOMO & VUYIZANA Dabane, Mthuthu & his Joyce.[ii] Warmest love to Nali.

Yours very sincerely,
Nel

MISS NANCY MADIKIZELA,
C/O MRS NIKI IRIS XABA.[iii]
HOUSE NO. 8115 ORLANDO WEST, JOHANNESBURG

---

i　One of Winnie Mandela's brothers.
ii　Nothuthuzelo and Joyce Mgudlwa, Winnie's relatives.
iii　Niki Xaba (1932–1985), Winnie Mandela's eldest sister – see the glossary.

To Zenani and Zindzi Mandela,[i] his middle and youngest daughters

August 3, 1969

My Darlings,

On July 17 I received a telegram from Kgatho[ii] in which he told me that Buti[iii] Thembi, your beloved brother, had died in a car accident. The accident occurred in Touws River, near Cape Town, on July 13. I am told that apart from him two Europeans, who recently came to this country from Italy, also died. Your brother will be buried in Johannesburg today. In his telegram Kgatho informed me that he was sending the full details of how Thembi died. But my letters take a very long time to reach me and, at the time of writing Kgatho's letter, had not arrived, and I am thus not in a position to give you more particulars on the matter.

I write on behalf of Mummy and myself to give you our deepest sympathy. All of us were very fond and proud of Thembi, and he, in turn, was devoted to us, and it is indeed very sad to think that we will never see him again. I know just how he loved you. Mummy wrote to me on March 1 and advised me that he spent his holidays with his family in Johannesburg, and that during that period he took you out several times and gave you much pleasure and joy.

Mummy has also informed me that he had invited you to spend the forthcoming December holidays with him in Cape Town and that you were looking forward to a lot of fun. There you would have seen the sea; places like Muizenberg and the Strand where you could swim. You would also have seen the Castle, a large stone fort which was completed about the year 1679. Here the Governors of the early Cape lived. It was also here that the famous African king, Cetywayo, was kept for a while after the Battle of Isandhlwana in January 1879 where the Zulu army defeated the English. In Cape Town you would also have seen Table Mountain which is about 3,549 feet high. From the top of the mountain you would see Robben Island across the waves. Thembi's death means that you will not be able to spend your December holidays down there, and you will also miss the pleasures and beautiful places I have mentioned above, and we are all very sorry that our Thembi is really gone. He meant much to us and we will miss him.

It was not possible for Mummy and myself to attend his funeral. Both of us are in jail and our request for permission to go to the funeral was not granted. You also did not attend, but when you return from school Kgatho

---

i   Zenani Mandela (1959–) and Zindzi Mandela (1960–) – see the glossary.
ii   Makgatho (Kgatho) Mandela (1950–2005), Mandela's second-born son – see the glossary.
iii   'Brother' in isiXhosa and isiZulu.

will arrange for you to be taken to see the grave and bid your departed brother farewell. Perhaps one day Mummy and I will be able also to visit the grave. But now that he is gone, we must forget about the painful fact of his death. Now he sleeps in peace, my darlings, free from troubles, worries, sickness or need; he can feel neither pain nor hunger. You must continue with your schoolwork, play games and sing songs.

This time I have written you a sad letter. On June 23 I had written you another letter which was just as sad, because it dealt with the arrest of Mummy. This year has been a bad one indeed for us, but happy days will come when we will be full of joy and laughter. What is even more important is that one day Mummy and I will come back and live happily together with you in one house, sit at table together, help you with the many problems you will experience as you grow. But until then Mummy and I will write to you regularly. Tons and tons of love, my darlings.

Affectionately,
Tata.[i]

MISSES ZENI AND ZINDZI MANDELA
C/O MRS NIKI IRIS XABA,[ii]
HOUSE NO. 8115 ORLANDO WEST, JOHANNESBURG.

———————

To Irene Buthelezi,[iii] a friend and the wife of Chief Mangosuthu Buthelezi[iv]

3-8-69

Our dear Mndhlunkulu,[v]

I was moved by the message of condolence contained in the telegram sent by my chief, Mangosuthu, on behalf of the family & which I received on July 18 (my birthday), & I should like him to know that I deeply appreciate it. 1968 & 1969 had been difficult & trying years for me. I lost my mother only 10 months ago. On May 12 my wife was detained indefinitely under the Terrorist Act, leaving behind small chdn as virtual orphans, & now my

---

i   'Father' in isiXhosa.
ii   Niki Xaba (1932–1985), Winnie Mandela's eldest sister – see the glossary.
iii   See the glossary.
iv   Chief Mangosuthu Buthelezi (1928–), Zulu prince and politician – see the glossary.
v   An isiXhosa reference to royalty.

eldest son is gone never to return. Death is a frightful disaster no matter what the cause & the age of the person affected. Where it approaches gradually as in the case of normal illness, the next-of-kin are at least forewarned & the blow may not be so shattering when it ultimately lands. But when you learn that death has claimed a strapping & healthy person in the prime of his life, then one must actually live through the experience to realise how completely paralysing it can be. This was my experience on July 16 when I was first advised of my son's death. I was shaken from top to bottom & for some seconds I did not know exactly how to react. I ought to have been better prepared for Thembi was not the first child I lost. Way back in the forties I lost a nine months baby girl.[i] She had been hospitalised & had been making good progress when suddenly her condition took a grave turn & she died the same night. I managed to see her during the critical moments when she was struggling desperately to hold within her tender body the last sparks of life which were flickering away. I have never known whether or not I was fortunate to witness that grievous scene. It haunted me for many days thereafter & still provokes painful memories right up to the present day; but it should have hardened me for similar catastrophes. Then came Sept. 26 (my wife's birthday) when I was advised of my mother's death. I had last seen her the previous Sept. when she visited me on the Island at the ripe age of 76,[ii] having travelled all alone from Umtata.[iii] Her appearance had much distressed me. She had lost weight & although cheerful & charming, she looked ill & tired. At the end of the visit I was able to watch her as she walked slowly towards the boat which would take her back to the mainland, & somehow the thought flashed across my mind that I had seen her for the last time. But as the months rolled by, the picture I had formed on her last visit began to fade away & was altogether dispelled by the exciting letter she wrote thereafter testifying to her good health. The result was that when the fatal hour struck on Sept. 26 I was again quite unprepared & for a few days I spent moments in my cell which I never want to remember. But nothing I experienced in the late forties & in Sept. last year can be likened to what I went through on July 16. The news was broken to me about 2:30 p.m. Suddenly my heart seemed to have stopped beating & the warm blood that had freely flown in my veins for the last 51 years froze into ice. For some time I could neither think nor talk & my strength appeared to be draining out. Eventually, I found my way back to my cell with a heavy load on my shoulders & the last place where a man stricken with sorrow should be. As

i   Mandela's first daughter with his wife Evelyn died of an illness at the age of nine months. She was named Makaziwe. They susequently had another daughter together to whom they gave the same name.

ii   His mother visited him twice on Robben Island, on 6 March 1966 and on 9 September 1967.

iii   Umtata (now called Mthatha) was the capital of the Transkei homeland and is around 625 miles from Robben Island.

usual my friends here were kind & helpful & they did what they could to keep me in good spirits. My second son, Kgatho,[i] sent me a telegram on July 17 & I felt even much better. The telegram from the Chief created a deep impression on me & greatly contributed to my complete recovery from the shock. I should like to assure him that I will always remember his inspiring message of sympathy, as well as the one he sent on the occasion of my mother's death. I feel mighty & strong & confident because of the good wishes & messages of solidarity that have come from my trusted friends, amongst whom I am privileged to include you & the Chief.

My thoughts very often go back to the forties when I lived at Mzilikazi[ii] where I first met your parents. Your father, the son of Mzila, was really a grand old man I admired & respected in all sincerity. He was dignified, courteous & confident & throughout the 4 years of my stay at Mzilikazi we were on friendly terms. The conversations I had with him indicated a man who was proud of the traditions & achievements of his people, & this aspect, more than anything else, fascinated me. But though he loved & respected his own history & culture he was sensitive to modern & progressive ideas & valued education. In this respect you & your brother should be witnesses. He was often seen at the Bantu Men's Social Centre[iii] in his black & gold regalia, decorated with medals & ribbons, playing drafts [sic] & other games with remarkable skill against distinguished sportsmen of that city. I will always remember him as a man who gave me much encouragement & help in my struggling days. I have not forgotten the Old Lady & the warm smile with which she always greeted me. I valued it even then, but you have to be behind bars for at least 7 years to appreciate fully just how precious human kindness can be. It gave me much pleasure to be able to act on her behalf when the Old Man's estate was wound up. Always remember that I highly value my association with your family & that I hold the Chief in esteem. My fondest regards to you all & to Dr. Dotwane[iv] & your sister-in-law.

Once again, many thanks to the Chief for his inspiring message.

Yours very sincerely.
Nelson.

---

i   Makgatho Mandela (1950–2005) – see the glossary.
ii   Mandela is referring to a mine compound where he lived while working as a gold mine security guard in the early 1940s. The name Mzilikazi is likely to be a nickname emanating from the surname of the mine compound's manager in charge, Mzila, who was Irene Buthelezi's father. Mandela had known her since she was child.
iii   The Bantu Men's Social Centre (BMSC), founded in Sophiatown, Johannesburg, in 1924, was an important cultural, social, and political meeting place for black South Africans. Its facilities included a gym and a library, and it hosted boxing matches, political meetings, and dances. Mandela and four others founded the ANC Youth League there in 1944.
iv   Dr. Mafu Dotwana was the husband of Mandela's relative Dili Mtirara.

MRS IRENE BUTHELEZI
"KWAPHINDANGENE", P.O. BOX 1,
MAHLATHINI, ZULULAND

To Brigadier Aucamp,[i] c/o the commanding officer, Robben Island

August 5, 1969

The Commanding Officer
Robben Island

Attention: Col Van Aarde.

Kindly approve of the enclosed urgent letter to Brig. Aucamp.

[Signed NRMandela]
NELSON MANDELA. 466/64

[Handwritten note in another hand] Send in the ordinary way to Brig Aucamp. [Signed and dated] 5/8/69

August 5, 1969

[Handwritten note in another hand] Nelson Mandela 466/64 Letter to Brig Aucamp

August 5, 1969

The Commissioner of Prisons   EXTREMELY URGENT
Private Bag, Pretoria.

Attention: Brig Aucamp

I should be pleased if you would approve of the attached letter to my wife, which [discusses] the important and urgent question of legal representation. Kindly arrange with the [Security police] staff for delivering to her at the earliest possible convenience.
    I should further be pleased if you would now grant me the permission

---

i   Brigadier Aucamp, commanding officer of Robben Island – see the glossary.

I have been seeking since May 20 to communicate with the firm of Messrs. Frank, Bernadt and Joffe. I should like to remind you that since the arrest of my wife, none of the 12 letters I have written up to last June had reached its destination. Four successive visits which had been arranged for me for [the] past six months failed to materialise. Even letters addressed [to me] were delayed unreasonably, a discriminatory practice which contrasts sharply with the treatment afforded my fellow prisoners. A letter that arrived on the island on Apr 24 was only delivered to me 44 days thereafter on June 7. Another one which was received by the Post Office on June 17 was handed to me 39 days later on July 26. I should add that at the time of writing I have received no authentic information on the death of my son. My younger son telegraphed to me on July 17 – four days after the fateful accident – and advised that he was sending me the full particulars. But in accordance with previous practice, I probably will not be allowed to receive it timeously not withstanding its nature. By way of contrast I refer to a letter that was written to a fellow prisoner on June 16 and which reached him 6 days thereafter. Another one [written to the] same man on July 13 reached him again 6 days after it had been written. In the circumstances it is reasonable for me to urge you to grant my application without further delay. It is undesirable that I should be kept ignorant about questions which are so important to me and the family, and I appeal to you to expedite the matter. In this connection, I should like you to know that I deeply appreciate the opportunity you are giving me to communicate with my wife. The approval of the permission sought above will enable me to deal with all domestic problems caused by my wife's detention, and will be an appropriate and logical complement to the help you have already granted me and my wife.

[Signed NRMandela]
Nelson Mandela. 466/64

To Olive Nomfundo Mandela, his niece

8.9.69

My dear Mtshana,[i]

I was indeed very shocked to hear that you, a little girl in her teens, in a

---

i   'Niece' or 'nephew' in isiXhosa.

rough and cruel city like Johannesburg, have for the past four months lived all alone, exposed to all kinds of danger, and that those who took away your Auntie[i] from home did not even take the simple and reasonable steps of making sure that you will at least be safe by arranging for some elderly person to look after you and the home.[ii] How you get your food, buy your clothing and soap, travel to and from school, pay for your school fees and books, and all the many things a child of your age needs, is regarded by them as something which is no concern of theirs. I can well imagine just how hard and difficult things must be for you these days. All domestic work such as cooking, cleaning the house and polishing the stoop must now be done by you alone, leaving you hardly any time to attend to your school work. Add to this the strain caused by many hours of loneliness, uncertainty as to how long Auntie will be away from home, and fear of the unknown. Perhaps some days you wake up in the morning and go to school without having eaten, or drank tea, because there is no money to buy meat, milk, eggs, sugar, bread, butter, mealie meal,[iii] coal or paraffin.

It is possible that you have sat for long moments wondering why you are so unfortunate, comparing yourself with the happy and well-fed children you meet at school, and in Soweto, children who live with their parents, who are always full of laughter, who have never suffered in their lives and who have none of the problems that now worry you. May be that at times you doubt whether you will ever see Auntie and myself again, and that it is even difficult to understand why all this human suffering should occur in the Christian world of the 20th century. There have been moments in my life when in spite of my old age I have had these doubts and difficulties too. The little education that I have, enables me to follow with real interest the progress which man has made over the one million years of his history on earth, developing from a backward and superstitious savage to the cultured individual he now is supposed to be. Yet the cruel experiences you and other members of the family have had, and their suffering and misery, make me wonder whether it is correct to talk of any human being as being Christian or civilised. Today, you are an orphan living for the greater part of the day in loneliness, sadness and fear, because your Auntie and myself, who are alive and well, and who would have given you the chances in life that you deserve, have been jailed by other human beings, by our own countrymen who, like true Christians and cultured beings, should treat us with love and kindness. We were seized and thrown into prison not because we have killed, stolen or

i   Winnie Mandela.
ii   Daughter of Mandela's sister Notancu, Olive Nomfundo Mandela lived in the family home at 8115 Orlando West for a time and was left all alone when Winnie Mandela was arrested.
iii   An ingredient made from ground maize, also known as maize meal, which is combined with boiling water to make a porridge.

committed some other crime, but because we stand for truth, justice, honour and principle and because we will never agree that any human being is superior to us. If my whole life and that of Aunt Nobandla[i] should be spent here and we should never see you again; if we should never have the chance of sending you to university as we had hoped, of giving you a decent wedding when the time comes for you to get married, and of helping you to start your own home, then dear Mtshana, you will at least know the true story about us. It will not be because we did not love you, Kgatho, Maki, Zeni and Zindzi,[ii] or that we were not conscious of our duties as parents. That will be due to the fact that we loved you so much that we could never allow that you should be denied in your own country the rights and opportunities which human beings elsewhere have enjoyed for many centuries. This is the real truth that explains why we are prisoners, why we are away from home, and why you now sit alone in 8115 Orlando West.

Whatever difficulties you may be having now, Mtshana, do not be discouraged and leave your studies. Though in jail, we will do everything in our power to keep you in school and send you to varsity. Make sure that you pass at the end of the year. Though you may be living under great difficulties at the present moment, you will not die of starvation or loneliness. Sisi Tellie,[iii] Uncle Marsh and Aunt Niki[iv] will always be ready to help you. Besides, we have many good and trusted friends, like Aunt Gladys,[v] on whom you may rely for advice and assistance. One day we will be back home and you, just as the other children at school and [in] Soweto do, will live happily with us. Gone will be your loneliness, miserable life and fear of the unknown, and the dangers to which you are now exposed will be no more. You will struggle less than you do now, eat better food and be able to laugh with joy. In the meantime, we should like you to know that we are very proud to have you as our Mtshana, a brave and clever girl like you, and nothing would please us more than to know that you have passed your examinations.

My love and fondest regards to Kgatho, Maki, Zeni, Zindzi, Matsobiyane,[vi] and to Sisi Tellie, Uncle Marsh, Aunt Niki and Aunt Gladys.

Good luck! Tons and tons of love, Mtshana.
Your Malume[vii]

---

i   Nobandla is one of Winnie Mandela's names.
ii   Mandela's children Makgatho, Makaziwe, Zenani, and Zindziswa.
iii   Telia (Telli or Tellie) Mtirara, a relative of Mandela's. *Sisi* means 'sister' in isiXhosa and is often used to refer to a woman in the samge age group.
iv   Marshall Xaba and his wife Niki Xaba, Winnie Mandela's eldest sister (for Niki Xaba, see the glossary).
v   Winnie Mandela's aunt.
vi   The granddaughter of Mandela's cousin.
vii   'Uncle' in isiXhosa.

MISS NOMFUNDO MANDELA
HOUSE NO. 8115 ORLANDO WEST
JOHANNESBURG

To Nolusapho Irene Mkwayi, wife of fellow prisoner Wilton Mkwayi[i]

29.9.69

Our dear Nolusapho,

I was indeed encouraged by the touching message of sympathy you sent me on the occasion of the death of my eldest son, Thembi.[ii] Both the printed text of the condolence card, as well as the soothing sentiments you scribbled down next to the text, were singularly appropriate & they did much to inspire me.

I received the tragic news on July 16, & six days thereafter I applied to the Commanding Officer for leave to attend the funeral, at my own cost, & with or without escort.[iii] I added that, if Thembi would have been buried by the time my application was received, I should in that event be allowed to visit his grave for the purpose of 'laying the stone' (ukubek'ilitye[iv]) – the traditional ceremony that is reserved for those who miss the actual burial.

Ten months before this I had made a similar application when my mother passed away, & though the authorities had then adopted a hard line in refusing what I considered in all the circumstances to be a reasonable request, I nonetheless vaguely hoped that this time the death of two members of the family occurring so soon after the other would probably induce the authorities to give me the one opportunity I had in life of paying my last respects to Thembi. In the letter of application I expressly referred to the fact that I had been refused leave to be present at the graveside when my mother was laid to rest, pointing out at the same time, that approval of that application would have been a generous act on their part and one that would have made a deep impression on me. I drew attention to the fact that I had seen Thembi five years ago, & expressed the hope that they would appreciate how anxious I was to attend the funeral.

I was of course aware that 30 years ago the British had imprisoned

---

i   Wilton Mkwayi (1923–2004), trade unionist, political activist, and political prisoner – see the glossary.
ii   Madiba Thembekile Mandela (1945–69) – see the glossary.
iii See his letter to Colonel Van Aarde of 22 July 1969, page 112.
iv   Ukubek'ilitye literally means 'to place a stone', and is a ceremony for those who missed the actual burial.

a famous freedom fighter in one of the colonies, a man who later became Prime Minister when his country gained full independence in 1947.[i] He was in jail when his wife's health worsened, & when it became necessary for him to accompany her to Europe for medical treatment.

British imperialism has brought untold misery and suffering to millions of people throughout the world, & when the English withdrew they left behind them countries which had been plundered, and whose people were condemned to many years of poverty, famine, disease and illiteracy. This period forms the black chapter of British history & many historians have justly censured Britain. On the other hand, the English are widely known by friend & foe for their broad outlook & sensible approach to human problems, & for their deep respect for men who are ready to give up their lives for a worthy cause. Often in the course of political conflicts with leaders of national movements in their former colonies, they were able to treat political offenders humanely, & to render them genuine & substantial help whenever necessary. So it was that when the politician referred to above was faced with the problem of the illness of his wife, the English released him to travel abroad. Unfortunately, the wife died after reaching Europe & thereafter the bereaved man returned to his country to serve the balance of his sentence. This is how an enlightened government is expected to treat its citizens, & this is how the British Government responded to an application made on compassionate grounds by political opponents a little more than 30 years ago.

In the case of both my late mother & Thembi, I was faced not with the problem of illness but that of death. I asked for permission not to travel abroad, but to another part of my own country which was under the constant surveillance of a strong & experienced Security Force. In Thembi's case my application was simply ignored & I was not even favoured with the courtesy of an acknowledgement. A further request for permission to obtain copies of press reports on the fatal accident was turned down, & up to now I have no authentic information whatsoever as to how Thembi died. All my efforts to obtain the services of an attorney to investigate the question of legal responsibility for the accident, any claims arising there out & the estate generally, have been unsuccessful. Not only was I deprived of the

---

i   Mandela is referring to Jawaharlal Nehru. Later, in a conversation with Richard Stengel in 1993, he recalled: 'Firstly, I had to pay my respects to my mother's grave, who died in '68 when I was in prison. I had asked the prison authorities to allow me to attend the funeral and I quoted the case of Pandit Nehru, that is before he actually was a prime minister, before independence – before the independence of India. His wife was ill, she had contracted TB, and Nehru was in jail, and he then asked the British for permission to take his wife to Germany which apparently was reputed to . . . have the most advanced methods of curing tuberculosis at the time. The British agreed and he left prison and took his wife to Germany. Unfortunately the wife died but he then returned to jail and the British decided to release him because of the tragedy.' (Conversation with Richard Stengel, 13 January 1993, CD 15, Nelson Mandela Foundation, Johannesburg.)

opportunity of seeing for the last time my eldest son & friend, & the pride of my heart; I am kept in the dark on everything relating to him & his affairs.

On Sept. 6 I received a report on my household affairs which greatly disturbed me. My niece, Nomfundo,[i] who is still in her teens, lives in the house virtually alone, & I believe that the lady who stayed there after Zami's[ii] arrest was frightened away. This indifference completely astonished me & kept wide open the painful wounds which the dreadful hands of death had made in my heart.

Your message must be seen in the light of these facts; of the obstacles & frustrations that surround me. Fortunately, my numerous friends here & outside prison have showered me with messages of sympathy & encouragement & the worst is now over. Among these is your own message; you, Nolusapho, the wife of the Amagqunukhwebe,[iii] the children of Khwane,[iv] Cungwa, Pato and Kama.[v] I should like you to know that I deeply appreciate your wonderful message. Though I have not yet had the privilege of meeting you, I have the picture of one who genuinely loves her people & who always places the welfare & happiness of others above hers. That you were able to send me this message in spite of your own illness & personal problems says a lot more in your favour than language can express. I sincerely wish you a speedy & complete recovery.

Many thanks for the lovely Xmas cards you & Nomazotsho sent me. Love & fondest regards to Georgina,[vi] Nondyebo,[vii] Beauty,[viii] Squire,[ix] & Vuyo.

Yours very sincerely,
Nelson

TO: NOLUSAPHO IRENE MKWAYI.
HOUSE NO. 11842 ORLANDO WEST EXTENSION.
JOHANNESBURG.

---

i   Olive Nomfundo Mandela, daughter of Mandela's sister Notancu.

ii   One of Winnie Mandela's names.

iii   The Amagqunukhwebe are a sub-group of the Xhosa nation.

iv   Khwane kaLungane, a counsellor and a warrior of King Tshiwo (1670–1702) of amaXhosa, headed the chiefdom of amaGqunukhwebe, and established the Khwane dynasty.

v   Descendants of Khwane who succeeded him as king.

vi   Winnie Mandela's friend who served as one of her bridesmaids.

vii   Nondyebo Jane Bam, a nurse and anti-apartheid activist. She was a sister of Brigalia Bam (1933–), who Mandela later appointed head of South Africa's Independent Electoral Commission when he was president, and Fikile Bam (1937–2011), who was also imprisoned on Robben Island from 1964–75.

viii   Nobantu Mniki, one of Winnie Mandela's sisters.

ix   Henry Makgothi (1928–2011), a school teacher who was fired for his political activities. He was elected Transvaal ANC President in 1954 and was an accused in the Treason Trial. He was arrested while trying to leave the country and sentenced to ten years in prison. After his release he lived in exile and worked for the ANC. He returned to South Africa in 1990 and served as ANC chief whip in the National Council of Provinces until 1999.

To the external registrar, University of London

1 October 1969

The External Registrar,
University of London
Senate House,
London, W.C.1.

Dear Sir,

I should be pleased if you would kindly credit me with having passed Juris-prudence and Legal Theory, and allow me to write the remaining three sub-jects for Part II of the LL.B course on two separate occasions, i.e., I should like to write Public International Law in June 1970, and the remaining two subjects in June 1971.

As a prisoner who is doing hard labour, I am experiencing consider-able difficulty in preparing to write four subjects in one examination, and any concession you might make in this regard will give me a fair chance of showing competent knowledge in each subject I offer.

I might add that one of my main problems has been to obtain the latest editions of the recommended text-books, and to consult the reference works, as well as the journals that would enable me to keep abreast of the development of the law in each subject. The total cost of the study material I require for purposes of preparing for the examinations is, in my circum-stances, prohibitive. I could afford such costs only if the remaining course is phased out as indicated above.

Yours faithfully,
[Signed NRMandela]
NELSON MANDELA

To the commanding officer, Robben Island

October 9, 1969

The Commanding Officer
Robben Island

Attention: Major Huisamen

I have to advise you that on May 21, 1969, I had an interview with Brigadier Aucamp[i] in the course of which I endeavoured to persuade him to reconsider the decision to terminate post-degree studies at the end of 1969.

He outlined the reasons why the Government had taken this step, and regretted that he was not in a position to assist us in the matter. But he made the important reservation that the above decision would apply only to those who were doing post-degree courses with the University of South Africa, and not to those who were studying with overseas universities. He pointed out that the Department of Prisons had made arrangements with Unisa[ii] to enable those whose post-degree courses had been interrupted as a result of the above decision to proceed with their studies after they had completed their respective terms of imprisonment.

In so far as I am registered with Unisa as a BA (Honours) student in Political Science, the decision applies to me. But Brigadier Aucamp had further pointed out that I would be allowed to complete my law studies with the University of London, and gave reasons why this concession had been made to me. I have planned to complete the remaining courses on the basis of the information given to me by the Brigadier, and I trust that it will be possible for you to forward all my correspondence to London University.

I might add that from experience I have found it very strenuous, and well-nigh impossible, to sit for four final year subjects at one time, and my only hope of success is to spread the remaining examinations over two years.

I should also like to draw attention to the fact that the prescribed literature is voluminous and expensive and not available in South Africa. To buy it in bulk is far beyond my financial resources and the only alternative is the relief I seek from the Registrar as set out in the enclosed letter.

[Signed N. R. Mandela]
NELSON MANDELA. 466/64

---

i   Brigadier Aucamp, commanding officer of Robben Island – see the glossary.
ii   University of South Africa.

To Adelaide Sam Mase, the sister-in-law of his first wife, Evelyn Mandela[i]

3.11.69

My dear Tshezi,[ii]

I am grateful to Sibali Sam[iii] for the message of sympathy contained in his letter of August 20. Thembi's death was a painful experience to all of us. This was particularly so for me, especially when one takes into account the fact that I had not seen him for 5 years, and that my application for permission to attend the funeral was not granted. I will never forget Thembi.[iv]

On September 6, the same day I received Mqwati's[v] affectionate letter, my niece, Tellie,[vi] visited the Island and gave me an account of the funeral, and it was some sort of consolation for me to know that the public response was good. Tellie's report was confirmed by my sister-in-law, Mrs. Xaba,[vii] who was at the airport when the corpse arrived from Cape Town, and who was present at the graveside. I was happy to know that you travelled all the way to the Rand[viii] for the occasion, and to hear of the excellent contribution made by the people of Engcobo[ix] to whom I am greatly indebted.

I read the fresh and meaningful passages from the scriptures to which Mqwati[x] kindly referred me. He is an expert on religious matters, a fact which makes me respect his views on all questions relating to the gospel. All that I wish to say here is that the importance of the passages quoted by him lies in the fact that they tell us of a way of life which would have brought us peace and harmony many centuries ago, if mankind had fully accepted and faithfully practised the teachings they contain. They visualise a new world where there will be no wars, where famine, disease and racial intolerance will be no more, precisely the world for which I am fighting, the world painted by the prophet Isaiah where the wolf and the lamb shall dwell together, the leopard and the kid, the calf and the young lion and the fatling shall all live peacefully.[xi] Of course Mqwati and I have not always seen eye to eye as to how this world will come about.[xii] In the numerous discussions

---

i   Evelyn Ntoko Mandela (1922–2004) – see the glossary.
ii   Adelaide Mandela's clan name.
iii   *Sibali* means 'brother-in-law' in isiXhosa. Mandela is referring to Adelaide's husband, Sam.
iv   Madiba Thembekile Mandela (1945–64) – see the glossary.
v   Evelyn Mandela's clan name. She was married to Mandela from 1944 until 1957.
vi   Telia (Telli or Tellie) Mtirara, a relative of Mandela's.
vii   Niki Xaba (1932–1985), Winnie Mandela's eldest sister – see the glossary.
viii   An abbreviated name for the Witwatersrand, a 56-kilometre-long ridge in the Gauteng province of South Africa where Johannesburg is based.
ix   Evelyn Mandela was born in Engcobo in the Transkei.
x   Mqwati is name of Evelyn Mandela's clan. Here it is assumed this reference is to Sam Mase, Evelyn's brother.
xi   He is loosely paraphrasing from Isaiah 11:6.
xii   Evelyn Mandela was a Jehovah's Witness.

that I had with him I persistently tried to hammer one central point: that the new world will be born as a result of our own toil and tears, our sacrifices and struggles. The progress made by man during the 500,000 years from the primitive and simple forms of social organisation to the advanced and complex systems of the modern age, and more especially the rapid and tremendous advances made over the last 50 years or so, show very clearly that in the foreseeable future mankind will inherit the kingdom described by the prophet Isaiah.

The lives and actions of prominent religious men show that those who fight for a new order need not divorce theory from practice. Moses shared common hardships with his countrymen in Egypt and eventually led them physically from slavery to the Promised Land. In his efforts to establish the Christian Church, St. Paul came into conflict with established authority and vested interests. The advocate who prosecuted him is reported to have said: "The plain truth is that we find this man a perfect pest; he stirs up trouble amongst the Jews the world over, and is ringleader of the Nazarene Sect."[i] Thereafter this "Nazarene Sect" was to spread to almost every corner of the globe and be embraced by many nations as their state religion. The man who was described as a perfect pest later became a saint loved and respected by millions of Christians throughout the world. You will, however, appreciate that it is not possible to discuss in full important problems such as these through correspondence and I will say no more here than merely to indicate that the spread of the Christian faith and the new world it created was accomplished by the physical labours of the vast and fearless army of the gospel. All I should like to add is that I was deeply moved by Mqwati's[ii] affectionate letter, and I know that Thembi's death was as painful to you as it was for me.

Some months ago I learnt that your brother, Justice, who worked for the Information Department in the Transkei, had passed away. He and I were close friends at Healdtown[iii] and the news of his death greatly shocked me. Though we had not met or corresponded for 20 years, I never forgot him and it gave me some pleasure to get a bit of news about him. Please give my belated condolences to his family. Similar condolences are due to Temba Mdaka on the death of his first wife Nomayeza. They were also at Healdtown at the same time as the late Justice and me. She was a very warm and refined lady and [I] was indeed sorry to learn that she was no more. Chief Dumalisile Mbekeni[iv] is a man for whom I have the highest regard. I

---

i   Acts 24:5.
ii   Evelyn Ntoko Mandela (1922–2004), Mandela's first wife (1944–1957) – see the glossary.
iii The Wesleyan college in Fort Beaufort, just outside the Ciskei homeland, that Mandela attended as a young man – see the glossary.
iv   A cousin of Mandela's and brother of Dr. Mbekeni.

spent a lot of time with him at the Royal Kraal at Mqekezweni[i] and I was greatly impressed by his vast knowledge and oratory. Give him the assurance that I have not forgotten him. One day I will be back and I really look forward to seeing him. In the meantime I should like to be remembered to him and his entire family, and more especially to Mgcawezulu.[ii] I have never congratulated my Chief, Sakhela's son,[iii] on his appointment as chief of Amaqwati, and I should be pleased if you would kindly give me his full name and address, including isikhahlelo.[iv]

Fondest regards to Mqwati, Gordon, Jani,[v] Sodinga Gcanga[vi] and Danile Xundu.[vii]

Sincerely,
Nelson.

MRS ADELAIDE SAM MASE,
PO BOX 43,
ENGCOBO.

To Winnie Mandela,[viii] his wife

16.11.69

Dade Wethu,[ix]

I believe that on Dec. 21 you and 21 others will appear in the Pretoria Supreme Court under the Sabotage Act,[x] alternatively, for contravening the provisions of the Suppression of Communism Act.[xi] I am informed that you have all instructed Mr. Joel Carlson to act in the matter.

---

i   Also spelt Mqhekezweni, it is the Thembu royal palace where Mandela was raised from age twelve when he was entrusted to the care of Chief Jongintaba Dalindyebo following the death of his father.
ii   A relative of Chief Dumalisile Mbekeni.
iii A relative of Evelyn Mandela's.
iv   'Praise name' in isiXhosa.
v   Relatives of Evelyn Mandela.
vi   An activist from the Defiance Campaign (for the Defiance Campaign, see the glossary).
vii A priest in Port Elizabeth.
viii Nomzamo Winifred Madikizela-Mandela (1936–) – see the glossary.
ix   Normally written as one word, this means 'sister' in isiXhosa.
x   The General Law Amendment Act, No. 76, is also known as the 'Sabotage Act' of 1962. It provided for ninety days' detention without trial. Mandela's co-accused in the Rivonia Trial, who were arrested in 1963, were held under 'Ninety Days'. It also widened the definition of sabotage to include stikes, making them a capital offence.
xi   An Act passed on 26 June 1950, in which the state banned the South African Communist Party and any activities it deemed communist, defining 'communism' in such broad terms that anyone protesting against apartheid would be in breach of the Act.

16.11.69

Dade Wethu,

I believe that on Dec 1 you & 21 others will appear in the Pretoria Supreme Court on a charge under the Sabotage Act, alternatively for contravening the provisions of the Suppression of Communism Act. I am informed that you have all instructed Mr Joel Carlson to act in the matter.

From the particulars of the charge it would seem that you would require me to give evidence on your behalf & I look forward to an early consultation with you and Counsel. I would certainly consider it irregular & unjust & contrary to the elementary principles of natural justice to force you to start a long and protracted trial on a serious charge without arrangements having first been made for us to meet. We have not seen each other since Dec. last year & a meeting between us would go a long way towards easing the strains & stresses of the last 5 months & putting you in a better physical condition & frame of mind. Only after such a meeting could you have something approximating a fair trial, & I sincerely hope it will be possible to arrange it. I am also keen to discuss the question of how you should conduct your defence & to anticipate the tactics the State will most certainly use.

Since our wedding day in June 1958, you have, under some pretext or other, been dragged 5 times before the Criminal courts & once before a Civil one. The issues involved, at least in part of this litigation, are better forgotten than recalled. They caused us much grief & concern. This will be the 5th occasion, & I suspect that here there is much that lies beneath the surface, & the proceedings are likely to be the bitterest experience of your entire life to date. There will be those whose chief interest will be to seek to destroy the image we have built over the last decade. Attempts may be made to do now what they have repeatedly failed to achieve in former cases. I write to warn you in time of what lies ahead to enable you to prepare yourself both physically & spiritually to take the full force of the merciless blows that I feel certain will be directed systematically at you from the beginning to the end of the trial. In fact the trial & the circumstances surrounding it, may so far influence your thoughts & actions that it might well constitute an important landmark in your entire career, compelling you to re-examine very carefully values you once firmly cherished & to give up pleasures that once delighted your heart.

Already the months you spent in detention have been a severe test for you & when you come to the end of the case, you will have got a deeper underst—

A letter to Winnie Mandela, 16 November 1969, see opposite and pages 139–42.

...nding of human nature & its frailties & what human beings can do to others once their privileged position is endangered. When this threat emerges all the lofty virtues of western democracy about which we read so much in books are brushed aside. Neither the moral standards of modern civilisation, the teachings of the Christian faith, the universal idea of the common brotherhood of men, nor pure sense of honour will deter the privileged circles from applying the multitudinous pressures at their disposal on those who fight for human dignity. Those who are in the front-line should be willing and ready to draw the fire on to themselves in order to inspire their colleagues & make things easier for them. In the battle of ideas the true fighter who strives to free public thinking from the social evils of his age, need never be discouraged if, at one & the same time, he is praised & condemned, honoured & degraded, acclaimed as saint & cursed as an irredeemable sinner. In the course of your short but lively political career you have been the object of all these contradictory labels, but you have never wavered, instead you held firmly to your conviction. Today even a bigger test faces you for a conviction will certainly entail many years of sorrow & suffering behind iron doors. But I have not the slightest doubt whatsoever that you will fight to the bitter end with all the tenacity & earnestness that you have shown on previous occasions, for you know only too well that substantial victories will be won by those who stand on their feet & not by those who crawl on their bellies.

In planning your own case & working out your strategy it will be important to bear in mind that you are engaged in a contest with an adversary who possesses vast resources in wealth & means of propaganda & who will be able to give facts any twist which he considers expedient. In such a situation your best defence, & one no power on earth can ever penetrate, is truth, honesty & courage of conviction. Nothing must be done or said which might imply directly or indirectly a repudiation of your principles & beliefs. The rest I propose discussing with you if & when I see you. That moment may or may not come. I do hope it will. If it doesn't, then I know that you will nevertheless be in good hands & that you will be able to manage even without my help & advice. For the present, I send you all my good wishes & fondest regards. I will keep my fist clenched, & will do anything to assist you, Ngutyana. How is our dear Nyanya? Do tell me something about her.

I have just received the tragic news that Cameron in Botswana had a stroke

A letter to Winnie Mandela, 16 November 1969, see pages 139–42.

which resulted in paralysis & the amputation of a leg. To be struck down by
such a fatal illness far away from your country & people is a disaster that might
well make recovery difficult. I think of just how helpful he has been to you in
my absence & regret it very much that we are not in a position to assist him. As
far as I know, as an awaiting-trial prisoner, you can write as many letters as
you please & I suggest that you immediately write to tell him that we wish
him speedy recovery. Kepthe visited me on Oct. 25, following upon Nkosazana
Jethe who was here on Sept 6. On Nov. 8 I received a disturbing letter from
her in which she bitterly complains for having been left behind when
relatives visited you on Oct. 28. She is very good to us, & is receiving rough
treatment from certain quarters. I hope it will be possible for you to let
her know that she means much to us.

I received a stimulating letter from Amina & she paid you flattering
compliments. I am sure you will be happy to know that your friends have
not forgotten you. I believe Lily has at last got my letter. In July she sent
me a warm & moving message of sympathy. I also received an equally
inspiring condolence card from Irene. She seems to be a wonderful girl &
has built up an impressive image. This month I wrote to Mrs Adelaide
Mase, the wife of Mamgwali's brother at Engcobo, thanking them for the
letter they wrote me in August. Mamgwali also wrote in Oct. in reply to
the message I sent to her on behalf of you & I.

The salutation to this letter will not surprise you. In the past I have
addressed you in affectionate terms for then I was speaking to Nobandla,
wife of Ama-Dlomo. But on this occasion, I can claim no such prerogatives
because in the freedom struggle we are all equal & your responsibility is
as great as mine. We stand in the relationship, not of husband & wife, but of
sister & brother. Until you return to 8115, or some other appointed place, This is
how I will address you; O.K? Perhaps this arrangement will provide
~~room~~ for the legions of students, medical or otherwise, that have crossed the
life of one or other of us

Finally, Mhlope, I do wish you to know that you are the pride of my heart
& with you on my side, I always feel I am part of an invincible force
that is clearly to win new worlds. I am confident that, however dark &
difficult times might seem to be now, one day you will be free & able
to see the beautiful birds & lovely fields of our country, bath in its

marvellous sunshine & breathe its sweet air. You will again see the picturesque scenery of the land of Faku where your childhood was spent, & the kingdom of Ngubengcuka where the ruins of your own kraal are to be found.

I miss you dearly! Tons & tons of love & a million kisses

Devotedly,
Dalibunga.

NKOSIKAZI NOBANDLA MANDELA
c/o BRIGADIER AUCAMP.
PRETORIA.

A letter to Winnie Mandela, 16 November 1969, see pages 139–42.

From the particulars of the charge it would seem that you would require me to give evidence on your behalf & I look forward to an early consultation with you and Counsel. I would certainly consider it irregular & unjust & contrary to the elementary principles of natural justice to force you to start a long and protracted trial on a serious charge without arrangements having first been made for us to meet. We have not seen each other since Dec. last year & a meeting between us would go a long way towards easing the strains & stresses of the last 5 months & putting you in a better physical condition & frame of mind. Only after such a meeting could you have something approximating a fair trial, & I sincerely hope it will be possible to arrange it. I am also keen to discuss the question of how you should conduct your defence & to anticipate the tactics the state will most certainly use. Since our wedding day in June 1958, you have, under some pretext or other, been dragged 3 times before the criminal courts & once before a civil one.[i] The issues involved, at least in part of this litigation, are better forgotten than recalled. They caused much grief & concern. This will be the 5th occasion, & I suspect that here there is much that lies beneath the surface, & the proceedings are likely to be the bitterest experience of your entire life to date. There will be those whose chief interest will be to seek to destroy the image we have built over the last decade. Attempts may be made to do now what they have repeatedly failed to achieve in former cases. I write to warn you in time of what lies ahead to enable you to prepare yourself both physically & spiritually to take the full force of the merciless blows that I feel certain will be directed systematically at you from the beginning to the end of the trial. In fact, the trial, & the circumstances surrounding it, may so far influence your thoughts & actions that it might well constitute an important landmark in your entire career, compelling you to re-examine very carefully values you once fondly cherished & to give up pleasures that once delighted your heart.

Already the months you spent in detention have been a severe test for you & when you come to the end of the case, you will have got a deeper understanding of human nature & its frailties & what human beings can do to others once their privileged position is endangered. When this threat emerges all the lofty virtues of western democracy about which we read so much in books are brushed aside. Neither the moral standards of modern civilisation, the teachings of the Christian faith, the universal idea of the common brotherhood of men, nor pure sense of honour will deter the priv-

---

i   Winnie Mandela was arrested in October 1958 and held in prison for two weeks for participating in a protest against the extension of pass laws to women. She was arrested in 1963 for attending a gathering and was acquitted. In 1967 she was accused of resisting arrest and was acquitted. She was then sentenced to twelve months' imprisonment for violating her banning order.

ileged circles from applying the multitudinous pressures at their disposal on those who fight for human dignity. Those who are on the front-line should be willing and ready to draw the fire on to themselves in order to inspire their colleagues & make things easier for them. In the battle of ideas the true fighter who strives to free public thinking from the social evils of his age need never be discouraged if, at one & the same time, he is praised & condemned, honoured & degraded, acclaimed as saint & cursed as an irredeemable sinner. In the course of your short but lively political career you have been the object of all these contradictory labels, but you have never wavered; instead you held firmly to your convictions. Today even a bigger test faces you for a conviction will certainly entail many years of sorrow & suffering behind iron doors. But I have not the slightest doubt whatsoever that you will fight to the bitter end with all the tenacity & earnestness that you have shown on previous occasions, for you know only too well that substantial victories will be won by those who stand on their feet & not by those who crawl on their bellies.

In planning your own case & working out your strategy it will be important to bear in mind that you are engaged in a contest with an adversary who possesses vast resources in wealth & means of propaganda & who will be able to give facts any twist which he considers expedient. In such a situation your best defence, & one no power on earth can penetrate, is truth, honesty & courage of conviction. Nothing must be done or said which might imply directly or indirectly a repudiation of your principles & beliefs. The rest I propose discussing with you if & when I see you. That moment may or may never come. I do hope it will. If it doesn't, then I know you will, nevertheless, be in good hands & that you will be able to manage even without my help & advice. For the present, I send you all my good wishes & fondest regards. I will keep my fist clenched, & will do anything to assist you, Ngutyana.[i] How is our dear Nyanya?[ii] Do tell me something about her.

I have just received the tragic news that Cameron[iii] in Botswana had a stroke which resulted in paralysis & the amputation of a leg. To be struck down by such a fatal illness far away from your country & people is a disaster that may well make recovery difficult. I think of just how helpful he has been to you in my absence & regret it very much that we are not in a position to assist him. As far as I know, as an awaiting trial prisoner, you can write as many letters as you please & I suggest that you immediately write

---

i   One of Winnie Mandela's names. She comes from the amaNgutyana clan.
ii   Nonyaniso (Nyanya) Madikizela, Winnie Mandela's youngest sister.
iii   One of Winnie Mandela's brothers.

to tell him that we wish him speedy recovery. Kgatho[i] visited me on Oct. 25, following upon Nkosazana Tellie[ii] who was here on Sept. 6. On Nov. 8 I received a disturbing letter from her in which she bitterly complains of having been left behind when relatives visited you on Oct. 28. She is very good to us, & is receiving wrong treatment from certain quarters. I hope it will be possible for you to let her know that she means much to us.

I received a stimulating letter from Amina[iii] & she paid you flattering compliments. I am sure you will be happy to know that our friends have not forgotten you. I believe Lily[iv] had at last got my letter. In July she sent me a warm & moving message of sympathy. I also received an equally inspiring condolence card from Irene.[v] She seems to be a wonderful girl & has built up an impressive image. This month I wrote to Mrs. Adelaide Mase,[vi] the wife of Mamqwati's[vii] brother at Engcobo, thanking them for the letter they wrote me in August. Mamqwati also wrote in Oct. in reply to the message I sent to her on behalf of you & I.

The salutation to this letter will not surprise you. In the past I have addressed you in affectionate terms for then I was speaking to Nobandla,[viii] wife of Ama-Dlomo.[ix] But on this occasion, I can claim no such prerogatives because in the freedom struggle we are all equals & your responsibility is as great as mine. We stand in the relationship, not of husband & wife, but of sister & brother. Until you return to 8115, or some other appointed place, this is how I will address you, OK? Perhaps this arrangement will provide room for the legions of students, medical or otherwise, that have crossed the life of one or other of us.

Finally, Mhlope,[x] I do wish you to know that you are the pride of my heart, & with you on my side, I always feel I am part of an invincible force that is ready to win new worlds. I am confident that, however dark & difficult times might seem to be now, one day you will be free & able to see the beautiful birds & lovely fields of our country, bath in its marvellous sunshine & breathe its sweet air. You will again see the picturesque scenery of the land of Faku[xi] where your childhood was spent, & the kingdom of

---

i   Makgatho Mandela (1950–2005), Mandela's second-born son – see the glossary.
ii   Telia (Telli or Tellie) Mtirara, a relative of Mandela's. *Nkosazana* means 'Miss' or 'princess' in isiXhosa.
iii   Amina Cachalia (1930–2013), friend and anti-apartheid and women's rights activist – see the glossary.
iv   Lilian Ngoyi (1911–80), politician, and anti-apartheid and women's rights activist – see the glossary.
v   Possibly Irene Buthelezi, an old friend and the wife of Chief Mangosuthu Buthelezi, or Irene Mkwayi, wife of fellow prisoner Wilton Mkwayi (see the glossary).
vi   See letter from 3 November 1969, page 132.
vii   Evelyn Ntoko Mandela (1922–2004), Mandela's first wife (1944–1958) – see the glossary. Maqwati was her clan name, spelled by Mandela here as Mamqati.
viii   Nobandla is one of Winnie Mandela's names.
ix   Mandela belonged to the AmaDlomo clan.
x   One of Winnie Mandela's names.
xi   King Faku controlled all of Pondoland. In 1854 he signed a treaty with the British which allowed him to reign supreme. Winnie Mandela's great-grandfather Madikizela was the last chief to sign a treaty with the British.

Ngubengcuka[i] where the ruins of your own kraal are to be found.

I miss you badly! Tons & tons of love & a million kisses.

Devotedly,
Dalibunga.

NKOSIKAZI NOBANDLA MANDELA.c/o BRIGADIER AUCAMP.[ii]
PRETORIA.
24.3.70: Rewritten & handed in for posting per registered mail.
4.4.70: Registered slip given to me by H/W Joubert.

===

To the external registrar, University of London

18th November 1969

The External Registrar,
University of London,
Senate House, London, W.C.1.

Dear Sir,

On the 1st October 1969, I wrote you the letter quoted below to which you did not respond:

"I should be pleased if you would kindly credit me with having passed Jurisprudence and Legal Theory, and allow me to write the remaining three subjects for Part II of the LL.B course on two separate occasions, i.e., I should like to write Public International Law in June 1970, and the remaining two subjects in June 1971.

"As a prisoner who is doing hard labour, I am experiencing considerable difficulty in preparing to write four subjects in one examination, and any concession you might make in this regard will give me a fair chance of showing competent knowledge in each subject I offer.

"I might add that one of my main problems has been to obtain the latest editions of the recommended text-books, and to consult the reference works, as well as the journals that would enable me to keep abreast of the development of the law in each subject. The total cost of the study material

---

i   King Ngubengcuka was the great-grandfather of Mandela's father, Nkosi (chief) Mphakanyiswa Gadla Hendry (d. 1930).

ii   Brigadier Aucamp, commanding officer of Robben Island – see the glossary.

I require for purposes of preparing for the examinations is, in my circumstances, prohibitive. I could afford such costs only if the remaining course is phased out as indicated above."

I should now be pleased if you would kindly let me have your reply at your earliest possible convenience, together with a certificate of approval of candidature for the Public International Law Examination next June, should you approve of my application.

Yours faithfully,
[Signed N. R. Mandela]

NELSON MANDELA

[Notes in Afrikaans in other hands]
1. Colonel (for your information)
    Study section. Deel Mandela so mee[i]
2. Brig Aucamp[ii] told me personally by telephone on 26/11/69 that Mandela must finalise his exams in 1970. This request cannot be agreed to.

[Signed]
Maj. 27.11.69
[another signature and date 9.1.70]

<hr />

To Paul Mzaidume,[iii] Winnie Mandela's uncle

19.11.69

My dear Radebe,[iv]

I have received disturbing reports that my son, Makgatho,[v] 8115 Orlando West, is not keen to go to Fort Hare[vi] next year. He should have registered at the beginning of this year, but he had to write a supplementary examination in March & apparently thought he could not be admitted for a degree

---

i   'Share with Mandela' in Afrikaans.
ii   Brigadier Aucamp, commanding officer of Robben Island – see the glossary.
iii   In 1958 Mandela and Winnie Madikizela celebrated their engagement at the home of her Aunt Phyllis and Uncle Paul Mzaidume whom Winnie was living with at the time.
iv   Paul Mzaidume's clan name.
v   Makgatho (Kgatho) Mandela (1950–2005), Mandela's second-born son – see the glossary.
vi   University College of Fort Hare, Alice in the Ciskei homeland – see the glossary.

course. It would be tragic if he were to miss yet another year & I should be glad if you would do everything in your power to get him to College in February at all costs.

He visited me on Oct. 25 & assured me that he had already filled in & forwarded to the Registrar the relevant application forms. We also discussed the question of fees & allowance whilst at College, & gave him the names of two friends in Johannesburg who, I believe, will be keen to help in this connection. Kgatho will be able to give you their names & addresses, & I would advise that you see them in person & thrash out the whole matter with them.

You may indicate to Kgatho that in appealing to you to assist on this question, I do not in any way wish to suggest that I doubt the assurance he gave me. I have complete confidence in his personal integrity & sense of honour & do not believe that he would ever deliberately wish to mislead me on matters relating to his future career. I am, however, a thousand miles away from Johannesburg, & it is natural & reasonable that I should feel concerned about any information which tends to indicate that he is not acting with the prudence and diligence that I expect from him. I also make allowance for the fact that he may have special problems which, because of my present circumstances, he is not keen to confide to me. I have even wondered whether he does not find it humiliating or embarrassing to discuss financial assistance with persons who are strangers to him, & I am asking you to take a personal interest in the matter, as I believe that the intervention of a relative, who will negotiate on his behalf on these delicate questions; will at least save him this embarrassment.

At present he has a good job & earns a steady income which enables him to assist in the maintenance of the family & in paying for the education of his sisters. He may consequently doubt the wisdom of throwing away a lucrative post which makes it possible for him to shoulder important family responsibilities, only to start again from scratch some years later. Add to this his age. At 19 any young man in his position may not find it at all easy to resist the glittering attractions of a golden city. I mention all these things because I believe that you should be fully informed on the sort of problems that may be influencing the trend of his thinking & actions, & to enable you to know how to handle the situation. Anyway I leave the whole matter to you & to Mzala,[i] Khathi.[ii]

Incidentally, last Saturday I received a sweet letter from my eldest daughter, Maki,[iii] who is doing J.C.[iv] at the Orlando High School. She had

---

i   'Cousin' in isiXhosa.
ii   Khathi is Kathazwa, Mandela's cousin's daughter.
iii   Makaziwe Mandela (1954–), Mandela's eldest daughter – see the glossary.
iv   Junior Certificate.

been keen on science but the death of her eldest brother, Thembi,[i] to whom she looked for financial support, has clearly affected her plans. She now informs me that she is no longer keen to be a scientist because funds will not be available for this purpose. When I left home in April '61 we had made arrangements for the education of all the children & things went very well until the end of 1967. Even after that date, Zami,[ii] with all her formidable difficulties, just managed to keep things fairly even. But now that she is away things seem to be going into pieces. You may mention this aspect to my friends as well.

I never like to allow my thoughts to dwell much on Zeni & Zindzi.[iii] It was hard enough for them that I should be away from home. It should even be more so now that Zami has followed. I cannot be sure that this disruption of our family life may not have seriously affected them. I wrote to them in June & July but I learn that neither letter reached. I hear very little about them & this increases my anxiety & concern. But I am always consoled by the fact that you, Khathi, Marsh,[iv] Niki[v] and many of our friends are there to give them all the warm love & affection & protection that they need. If there is one thing that contributed to Zami's deteriorating health, it is precisely the plight of the children at the present moment, to whom she is deeply attached. But you will be happy to know that she counts you amongst those who will spare no efforts in making the children forget that they are orphans.

I hear from her now and again & it is a pleasure for me to be able to tell you that in spite of her indifferent health, she is in a grand mood. What a girl! She was brave enough to drag me to the altar, but I never once suspected that her courage would take her so far. I feel very humble indeed when I compare my own insignificant efforts with the heavy sacrifices she is making. My only worry is to know how C.K.[vi] and Niki have taken the whole thing. Radebe, it was a real pleasure for me to receive your moving letter exactly 12 months ago, & to hear something about abazala[vii] & Granny. It's amazing how fast children go [sic]. I found it difficult to believe that Khathi was going to varsity. As a matter of fact I had planned to write to her & hear something about Fort Hare, but Kgatho's case compelled me to write to you instead. Love & fondest regards to all.

---

i   Madiba Thembekile Mandela (1945–69), Mandela's eldest son – see the glossary.
ii   One of Winnie Mandela's names.
iii   Zenani Mandela (1959–) and Zindziswa Mandela (1960–), Mandela's middle and youngest daughters – see the glossary.
iv   Winnie Mandela's brother-in-law Marshall Xaba, husband of Niki Xaba.
v   Niki Xaba (1932–1985), Winnie Mandela's eldest sister – see the glossary.
vi   Columbus Kokani Madikizela, Winnie Mandela's father – see the glossary.
vii   'Cousins' in isiXhosa.

Sincerely,
Madiba

MASHUMI PAUL MZAIDUME
7012 ORLANDO WEST
JOHANNESBURG

24.3.70: Rewritten & handed in for posting per registered post.
4.4.70: Registered slip given to me by H/W Joubert.
[i]

To Thoko Mandela,[ii] his daughter-in-law & the widow of his son Thembi[iii]

29.11.69

My dear Thoko,

I have written no less than 7 letters on the death of Thembi either to express my condolences to members of the family or to thank those who kindly sent me messages of sympathy. On such an occasion I would have liked to communicate with you immediately upon receiving the tragic news, but I could not do so because I did not have your address.

Last July I wrote Kgatho for the address & other essential particulars but he gave me this information only when he visited me on Oct. 25. The previous month I had asked my niece, Tellie,[iv] to apply on your behalf for a visiting permit, my intention at that time being to write to you after you had been here. Beryl's[v] letter made me hope that I would see you today. Instead Lulu[vi] came & although I look forward to seeing you in December, I feel I can no longer delay this note.

Since the occurrence of the fatal accident, members of the family & speakers at the graveside as well as friends in various parts of the country will have said much that helped to raise your spirits & to bring some sort of peace & hope in your bereavement.

---

i   This was written by Mandela in the margin of the first page of the letter.
ii   See the glossary.
iii   Madiba Thembekile (Thembi) Mandela (1945–69), Mandela's eldest son – see the glossary.
iv   Telia (Telli or Tellie) Mtirara, a relative of Mandela's.
v   Beryl Lockman, Walter Sisulu's niece, who was living with Thoko. She later married Thoko's brother, Leonard Simelane.
vi   Lulama (Lulu) Mgudlwa was the niece of Mandela's former wife Evelyn Mandela.

Those who knew Thembi well may have spent the greater part of their remarks of reminding you of his talents & achievements, his devotion to you & the children & his parents. Some may have emphasised that he was only 24 years when death claimed him, leaving behind a widow & two very young children to face all alone the grim & tricky world in which we live, & without the help, support & guidance a diligent husband & father would always be ready to give his family.

Others may have stressed the important fact that death comes to each & every family, striking down today either a beloved father or mother or child, brother or sister, [and] that what is essential is not so much the particular calamity that befalls you, but the attitude you adopt towards it. These and many other remarks of a similar nature will have been addressed to you by able & experienced speakers & I do not think it possible to enlarge on them; except to say that I was particularly happy to learn of the contribution made by your parents, the people of Cape Town & Johannesburg, & the large numbers that accompanied our Thembi to eternal rest.

Perhaps some day I will be privileged to meet your parents & thank them personally & directly for the love & help they gave him whilst he lived & for honouring him when he passed away. For the time being I would ask you to acquaint them with these sentiments.

The theme that I wish to discuss with you is one that you may have already thought of & perhaps even started to carry out. Thembi was only 19 when I last saw him, then attending school in Swaziland where I believe you met him. It was a difficult period in the life of any young person when all kinds of ideas were crossing the mind. I had been in jail for almost 2 years & had been unable to help him sort out the numerous problems that he was encountering.

Consequently, I never knew what your ambitions in life were nor am I familiar with your plans at the time of his death nor the resolutions & vows that you may have taken together. But according to Maki's[i] recent letter, both of you aimed high, a statement which confirms similar opinions given me by Mom Winnie. I will always remember him and will reserve July 13 every year as his day. Convey my sympathies to your brother on the death of his wife.

Perhaps the best way to remember Thembi is to do those things which he valued most in life, the things that made life enjoyable & meaningful to him & to carry out any of your joint resolutions as circumstances allow. In my letter to Thembi in '66 or '67, I suggested that both of you should be careful not to neglect your education & that if you found it difficult to go

---

i   Makaziwe Mandela (1954–), Mandela's eldest daughter – see the glossary.

back to boarding school, you should enrol for tuition with a Correspondence College. I want to repeat this suggestion for your consideration. Today there are millions of people throughout the world who are studying privately & who are making excellent progress. By raising their level of education, they increase their knowledge and become more valuable in serving their country & people. For you, Molokazana,[i] advanced studies would serve a double purpose. It would keep your mind engaged in some fruitful occupation which, in turn, will guarantee you some measure of security & independence. Secondly, it would make it easier for you to carry out your life dreams.

But you must bear in mind that this letter comes from one who has been in jail for a little more than 7 years & who is out of touch with developments in the country. You are the best judge & I leave the whole matter in your able hands. Remember that whether or not you accept my advice will not in any way affect my attitude towards you. You are my daughter-in-law of whom I am very proud. You are dear to me & I do look forward to seeing you next month. I hope your arm continues to improve & wish you complete recovery & good luck.

It was very nice for Lulu to motor down all the way from the Reef[ii] to visit me. I had not seen her ever since I was arrested & I spent 60 minutes of real pleasure & joy. In my present circumstances, it is very heartening to know that your relations think of you. I was also happy to have a glimpse of Beryl as she walked out. I was very impressed when I was given the report that she was living with you at this sad moment in your life. From various sources we continue to hear pleasant accounts of her. She seems to have inherited all the good qualities of her late mother who was very close to me[iii] & whose friendship I really valued. Love & fondest regards to Ndindi, Nandi[iv] and your parents. Yours very affectionately, Daddy

MRS LYDIA THOKO MANDELA
"HILLBROW"
SEVENTH AVENUE, RETREAT.

◇◇◇◇◇◇◇◇

In the following letter to Winnie Mandela, who was then on trial, Mandela reports on a review of a book by a South African author portraying the trial of

---

i   'Daughter-in-law' in isiXhosa.
ii   The Reef in Johannesburg refers to the gold reef where gold was first discovered by Australian George Harrison in 1896. That gold rush gave birth to Johannesburg, which is now part of Gauteng province.
iii   Rosabella (Barbie) Sisulu, Walter's sister, who married Thomas Lockman.
iv   Ndileka (1965–) and Nandi (1968–) Mandela, the daughters of his late son Thembi (for Thembi Mandela, see the glossary).

Christ. According to Winnie Mandela's attorney, Joel Carlson, the first time he got to see her and her twenty-one co-accused, they had not been allowed to take a bath or a shower for 'nearly two hundred days'.[51] *By the time Mandela wrote this letter to her their trial had started. They were accused with furthering the aims of the ANC and conspiring to commit sabotage, although no acts of violence were alleged.*

Mandela was aware that this was quite literally the trial and test of his young wife's life, and his attempt at cheering her saw him dig deep into the story of the injustice of the trial of Christ, and by extension of her and other freedom fighters. If this letter reached her it would indeed have provided strength from an island at the end of the country.

To Winnie Mandela,[i] **his wife**

466/64 Nelson Mandela [in another hand]

January 1, 1970

Dade Wethu,[ii]

A novel by Langenhoven, *Skaduwees van Nasaret* (Shadows of Nazareth),[iii] depicts the trial of Christ by Pontius Pilate when Israel was a Roman dependency & when Pilate was its military governor. I read the novel in 1964 & now speak purely from memory. Yet though the incident described in the book occurred about 2000 years ago, the story contains a moral whose truth is universal & which is as fresh & meaningful today as it was at the height of the Roman Empire. After the trial, Pilate writes to a friend in Rome to whom he makes remarkable confessions. Briefly this is the story as told by him &, for convenience, I have put it in the first person:

As governor of a Roman province I have tried many cases involving all types of rebels. But this trial of Christ I shall never forget! One day a huge crowd of Jewish priests & followers, literally shivering with rage and excitement, assembled just outside my palace & demanded that I crucify Christ for claiming to be king of the Jews, at the same time pointing to a man whose arms & feet were heavily chained. I looked at the prisoner & our eyes met. In the midst of all the excitement & noise, he remained perfectly calm, quiet & confident as if he had millions of people on his side. I told the priests

---

i   Nomzamo Winifred Madikizela-Mandela (1936–) – see the glossary.
ii   The usual spelling is Dadewethu, meaning sister.
iii   C. J. Langenhoven, *Skaduwees van Nasaret* (Nasionale Pers, 1927).

that the prisoner had broken Jewish, & not Roman law & that they were the rightful people to try him. But in spite of my explanation they stubbornly persisted in demanding his crucifixion, immediately realised their dilemma. Christ had become a mighty force in the land & the masses of the people were fully behind him. In this situation the priests felt powerless & did not want to take the responsibility of sentencing & condemning him. Their only solution was to induce imperial Rome to do what they were unable to do.

At festival time it has always been the practice to release some prisoners & as the festival was now due, I suggested that this prisoner be set free. But instead, the priests asked that Barabas, a notorious prisoner, be released & that Christ be executed. At this stage I went into Court & ordered the prisoner to be brought in. My wife & those of other Roman officials occupied seats in the bay reserved for distinguished guests. As the prisoner walked in my wife & her companions instinctively got up as a mark of respect for Christ, but soon realised that this man was a Jew & a prisoner, & whereupon they resumed their seats. For the first time in my experience I faced a man whose eyes appeared to see right through me, whereas I was unable to fathom him. Written across his face was a gleam of love & hope; but at the same time he bore the expression of one who was deeply pained by the folly & suffering of mankind as a whole. He gazed upwards & his eyes seemed to pierce through the roof & to see right beyond the stars. It became clear that in that courtroom authority was not in me as a judge, but was down below in the dock where the prisoner was.

My wife passed me a note in which she informed me that the previous night she had dreamt that I had sentenced an innocent man whose only crime was that of messiah to his people. "There before you, Pilate is the man of my dream; let justice be done!" I knew that what my wife said was quite true, but my duty demanded that I sentence this man irrespective of his innocence. I put the note in my pocket & proceeded with the case. I informed the prisoner what the charge was against him, & asked him to indicate whether or not he was guilty. Several times he completely ignored me & it was clear that he considered the proceedings to be an utter fuss, as I had already made up my mind on the question of sentence. I repeated the question & assured him that I had authority to save his life. The prisoner's gleam dissolved into a smile & for the first time he spoke. He admitted that he was king & with that single & simple answer he totally destroyed me. I had expected that he would deny the charge as all prisoners do, & his admission brought things to a head.

You know, dear friend, that when a Roman judge tries a case in Rome, he is guided simply by the charge, the law & the evidence before the court, & his decision will be determined solely by these factors. But here in the provinces, far away from Rome, we are at war. A man who is in the field of battle is interested only in results, in victory & not in justice, & the judge is himself on trial. So it was, that even though I well knew that this man was innocent, my duty demanded that I give him the death sentence & so I did. The last time I saw him he was struggling towards Calvary amidst jeers, insults & blows, under the crushing weight of the heavy cross on which he was to die. I have decided to write you this personal letter because I believe that this confession to a friend will at least salve my uneasy conscience.

This in brief is the trial of Jesus & comment is unnecessary; save to say that Langenhoven wrote the story in the twenties (?)[i] to arouse the political consciousness of his people in a South Africa where & at a time when, in spite of the formal independence his people enjoyed, the organs of government, including the judiciary, were monopolised by Englishmen. To the Afrikaner, this story may recall unpleasant experiences & open up old wounds, but it belongs to a phase that has passed. To you and I it raises issues of a contemporary nature. I hope you will find it significant & useful, & trust it will bring you some measure of happiness. Molokazana[ii] paid me a visit this Saturday. She is a charming girl & I was really pleased to see her. On 14.1.70 she will be in Johannesburg for the "Kulula" ceremony.[iii] I am writing to Ntambozenqanawa[iv] to ask him & Jongintaba Mdingi[v] to help her in this task. Last month I wrote to her, & to Vuyo Masondo[vi] & gave the latter our condolences on the death of her brother at Umtata. Tons & tons of love, Mhlope,[vii] and a million kisses. May good luck be on your side!

Devotedly, Dalibunga.

NKOSIKAZI NOBANDLA MANDELA, C/O BRIGADIER AUCAMP,[viii]
PRETORIA

---

i   Mandela's own question mark.
ii   He is most likely referring to Thoko Mandela, his son Thembi's widow – see the glossary.
iii A ceremony to mark the removal of mourning clothes. It was eighteen months since Thembi Mandela's death.
iv   Mandela's cousin, Chief Ntambozenqanawa Nkosiyane.
v   The brother of Chief Mdingi who named Mandela's children Zenani and Zindziswa.
vi   The wife of fellow prisoner Andrew Masondo.
vii One of Winnie Mandela's names.
viii Brigadier Aucamp, commanding officer of Robben Island – see the glossary.

To Chief Ntabozenqanawa Nkoyisane, his cousin[i]

[Translated from isiXhosa]

January 1, 1970

sent 8.1.70

A! Ntambozenqanawa,

I received the report that the burial ceremony of my eldest son on the 3rd of August was undertaken by you and my chiefs Jongintaba and Vulindlela.[ii] I was deeply saddened when I received the news of his passing, even more so that I couldn't be at his bedside to bid him farewell. It came as a relief to hear that most of our relatives were able to attend the funeral. I would like to express my gratitude to you, Zondwa and Tshawe[iii] for the exceptional role that you two play in affairs relating to my family. The same gratitude also extends to Chief Jongintaba and all our family and friends.

I understand how busy you are and that you might not always have time to write back. It would please me when you find the time to write to me to tell me about Balisile, where he is, his health and how often you see him. The last time I checked, his son was completing his Matric, what is he doing now? What was the last you heard of Ntabayitshe? He is someone I trust and has shown to be a man of courage and of high intelligence. He makes me proud. I was deeply disappointed that he could not come to visit me. Please pass my regards to him and Zwelidumile.

Chief Msungulwa Mgudlwa's daughter was here last month, informing me that Jonguhlanga[iv] is there. I would also like to hear about his health. My daughter-in-law[v] came to visit me last Saturday. On the 14th of January, she will be in Johannesburg to have a ceremony symbolising the end of her mourning period. I assured her that I would speak to you and Chief Jongintaba so you could assist her with the ceremony. My ex-wife is now a member of a church that does not believe in animal sacrifice.[vi] I therefore leave this ceremony in your capable hands. *

Best regards.

---

i   Taken from the A4-sized hard-cover book in which he copied some of his letters
ii   Chief Vulindlela Mtirara/Matanzima, a Tembu chief and relative of Mandela's.
iii   Mandela's cousins.
iv   King Sabata Jonguhlanga Dalindyebo (1928–86), paramount chief of the Transkei homeland and leader of the
       Democratic Progressive Party, the opposition party in Transkei which opposed apartheid rule – see the glossary.
v   Thoko Mandela, his son Thembi's widow – see the glossary.
vi   Evelyn Mandela was a Jehovah's Witness.

Yours faithfully,
Dalibhunga

*My younger brother, Marshall Xaba,[i] 1086 Mofolo, promised to visit me. I really look forward to seeing him when he gets the time. I would also appreciate it if he would let me know if my mother-in-law, Nobandla's[ii] mother in Bizana, received the letter I wrote to her on the 4th of May. I would also like a report on the children's health and their performance at school.

Chief Ntabomzenqanawa Nkoyisane
c/o Makgatho Mandela[iii]
House No 8115 Orlando West
Johannesburg

◇◇◇◇◇◇◇◇

It is not known whether this letter in 1970 would have reached Adelaide Tambo[iv] as Mandela uses her real name and address as opposed to a code name such as the one he used for her in 1968 when he wrote to her as Matlala Mandela and sent the letter to his home address in Soweto (see his letter on page 52). In 1970, ANC president Oliver Tambo[v] remained a top enemy of the South African government and was still running an illegal organisation,[vi] working for the apartheid regime's downfall.

═══════════

To Adelaide Tambo,[vii] friend, anti-apartheid activist, and the wife of Oliver Tambo, ANC president and Mandela's former law partner

[In another hand in Afrikaans] 466/64 Nelson Mandela S/Letter[viii] to Adelaide Tambo[ix]

---

i   Husband of Niki Xaba, Winnie Mandela's eldest sister (for Niki Xaba, see the glossary).
ii   Nobandla is one of Winnie Mandela's names.
iii Makgatho (Kgatho) Mandela (1950–2005), Mandela's second-born son – see the glossary.
iv   Adelaide Tambo (1929–2007), friend, anti-apartheid activist, and wife of Oliver Tambo, Mandela's former law partner and president of the ANC – see the glossary. The Tambos were living in exile in London.
v   Oliver Reginald Tambo (1917–93), friend, former law partner, and the president of the ANC – see the glossary.
vi   The ANC was a banned organisation from 1960 until 1990.
vii Adelaide Tambo (1929–2007) – see the glossary.
viii S/Letter denoted special letter which would not have been taken from his quota.
ix   It is interesting that in this instance the prison authorities were aware that the letter was to Adelaide Tambo and that it seems as if they would have sent it.

January 31, 1970

Kgaitsedi yaka yoratehang,[i]

I last saw Zami[ii] in Dec, '68, and it is probable that years may roll before we meet again. She was collared last May, a week or so before she was due to come down & as I was preparing to write this letter to you. Her absence completely upset my plans, compelling me to communicate, at the rate of 1 letter a month, with friends & relations on a wide variety of urgent family matters. Kgatho[iii] visited me yesterday & brought along with him a host of fresh problems, but I have nevertheless decided not to postpone writing to you.

Maki,[iv] who will visit me next June, is doing Form IV at the Orlando High School. Zeni & Zindzi[v] are at Our Lady of Sorrows, a Roman Catholic boarding school in Swaziland, & spend the holidays with our mutual friend, Allan.[vi] Unfortunately, it has not been possible for me to get any information on their examinations.

I was very sorry indeed to learn that you could not proceed with your medical studies. OR[vii] & I had fully discussed the matter during the tour[viii] & on my return I had raised the subject with Xhamela[ix] & others, indicating to them that I had suggested to OR that you should be encouraged to undertake the course, a view with which they fully agreed. As a matter of fact, only a few days before we heard that you had abandoned the studies, there were speculations here to the effect that you might have already completed, & though the reasons advanced for your decision were perfectly understandable, we were sorry that Dali & sisters[x] had deprived you of this opportunity. Actually, I should be glad to hear something of their school progress & special interests. I have been hoping that you would send me a homely family photo not more than 6" x 8" in size. But I know that OR lives perpetually beyond the seas & that this may not be possible. I feel sure, however, that Thembi, Dali & Dudu[xi] would love to pose for me.

We were really delighted to get a bit of information about you all. For days thereafter we discussed and rediscussed the various items amidst

---

i   'My dear sister' in Sesotho and Setswana.
ii   One of Winnie Mandela's names.
iii Makgatho Mandela (1950–2005), Mandela's second-born son – see the glossary.
iv   Makaziwe Mandela (1954–), Mandela's eldest daughter – see the glossary.
v   Zenani Mandela (1959–) and Zindziswa Mandela (1960–), Mandela's middle and youngest daughters – see the glossary.
vi   Dr. Allen Nxumalo, a medical doctor and an old friend of the Mandela's. Leader of the Swaziland Democratic Party which was dissolved after independence in 1968, and Swaziland's first minister of health.
vii Her husband (1917–93), Oliver Reginald Tambo, Mandela's friend, former law partner, and the president of the ANC – see the glossary.
viii Mandela is most probably referring to his clandestine tour of Africa and London, in 1962.
ix   Fellow Rivonia trialist Walter Sisulu's clan name.
x   The Tambos' children.
xi   The Tambos' children.

great excitement & many reminiscences, some of course a bit coloured here & there, & others distorted by advancing age, were recalled. I even remembered how one day in the late fifties I returned from Chancellor House[i] to be entertained by Zami's uncle with a tale that offered me much amusement. He had just come from a country dorp[ii] in the Free State where OR had defended a case. In the course of an altercation with the presiding magistrate, so goes the story, the official made a ruling against which my erstwhile partner vigorously protested, switching in the process from English to Latin. This, Zami & I were told with a flourish, stopped the judicial officer in his tracks. Juicy anecdotes of this sort are also told about Gcwanini's[iii] short but brilliant legal career. I recall listening one morning to a detailed review of his escapades in the courtroom told by an enthusiastic & imaginative admirer. A prominent Transvaal judge was reported to have said that in the course of a long career as practitioner & judge he had not met or heard of a barrister who could match Gcwanini's devastating power of cross-examination. There is a whole catalogue of lovely stories about you there, Nkunzebomvu, Malome, Mqwati & others[iv] which, however magnified & romantic they may appear to be, are based on some factual incident & which indicate the powerful impact that you were making in our individual and collective capacities on the masses of the people even as far back as the late fifties. We were equally happy to hear about Bakwe,[v] Gambu Bros, Mpandla, Temba, Mzwai[vi] (whose Arabic I hope has improved), Mainrad, Raymond,[vii] Tough Alfie & Moloi, as well as our Amazons: Maggie,[viii] Radi, Long Ruta Jozi & Fiki. We think of Mhlekazi Madiba of OE, Pulatsheka, Hector, Dinone, Joe Joseph Sejake,[ix] piccanin Ruta, Florence, Kay, Edith & all our colleagues there without exception. We hear that Malome's health & that of Nkunzebomvu is not too bright but have the confidence that their cheerful disposition & tremendous courage will enable them in due course to pull through & recover completely.

I am anxious to write to Dave[x] to express my appreciation for all that he has done for me, but I am not sure whether in view of the circumstances this

---

i   Chancellor House was the building in which Mandela and Oliver Tambo started their law practice, Mandela and Tambo, in 1952.
ii   'Town' in Afrikaans.
iii   Advocate Duma Nokwe – see the glossary.
iv   Friends and comrades.
v   Bakwe (Joe) Matthews (1929–2010), political activist and son of Frieda and Z. K. Matthews – see the glossary for these three individuals.
vi   Possibly Esme Matshikiza, a social worker and the wife of Todd Matshikiza (1920–68), a writer and musician who composed the musical score for the internationally successful South African musical King Kong (1959). They were living in London.
vii   Raymond Mhlaba (1920–2005), MK activist and Rivonia trialist who was imprisoned with Mandela – see the glossary.
viii   Wife of an ANC activist in London.
ix   Friends based in Lesotho.
x   David Astor (1912–2001), British newspaper publisher and ANC supporter.

would be the right thing to do. Perhaps you might advise me in your reply. At any rate, I like him to know that I always think of him, Mary,[i] Michael, Colin,[ii] Thony[iii] & Freda.[iv] I should also be pleased if you would kindly let me have the address of Bakwe's ma.[v] I sent a message to her through Zami on the death of Prof[vi] & I should like to write to her as soon as that can be arranged. I hope Mary Letele,[vii] Tristie & Ezme[viii] are keeping well & that time has helped to heal their wounds.

The particulars submitted by Wamba to Europa Publications, 18 Bedford Square, W.C.1, require to be checked, amended or otherwise supplement.ed by OR. The better course would have been to send them directly to him but, as you know, this was not possible. The matter is now in his hands.

In Dec. '68 and again in '69 I sent you & family Xmas cards & hope you received them. For the first time since my conviction 8 years ago, I received no cards from Zami & children nor a letter from her. I felt there was something missing as I "celebrated" the great day ngombona namarewu.[ix]

Time was when I would have found it very difficult to manage without seeing Zami indefinitely & without receiving letters or hearing from her & the children. But the human soul & human body has an infinite capacity of adaptation & it is amazing just how hardened one can come to be; & how concepts which we once treated as relatively unimportant suddenly become meaningful & crucial.

I never dreamt that time & hope can mean so much to one as they do now. An important personage commented on the death of Ma & Thembi[x] & on the incarceration of Zami & said: for you it never rains but pours. That is how I also felt at the time. But the numerous messages of condolence & solidarity that we received gave us a lot of encouragement & spirits are as high as you have always known them to be. Hope is a powerful weapon even

---

i   Mary Benson (1919–2000), friend, author, journalist, and anti-apartheid activist – see the glossary.
ii   Canon Collins (1905–1982), Anglican priest appointed as a canon of St Paul's Cathedral, London in 1948. In 1956 he committed his organisation Christian Action to raise funds for the defence of the 156 accused in the Treason Trial (for the Treason Trial, see the glossary) in South Africa. This gave rise to the Defence and Aid Fund for Southern Africa.
iii   Anthony Sampson (1926–2004), author, anti-apartheid activist, and friend who was living in London.
iv   Freda Levson (1911–2004), South African anti-apartheid activist who went into exile in England. She administered the Defence and Aid Fund with Mary Benson (see the glossary) and Ruth Mompati.
v   Frieda Matthews (1905–98), one of the first black women to earn a university degree in South Africa – see the glossary.
vi   Frieda Matthews's husband, Professor Z. K. Matthews (1901–68), academic, politician, and anti-apartheid activist – see the glossary.
vii   Wife of Dr. Letele who participated in the Defiance Campaign (for the Defiance Campaign, see the glossary).
viii   Possibly Esme Matshikiza, a social worker and the wife of Todd Matshikiza (1920–68), a writer and musician who composed the musical score for the internationally successful South African musical *King Kong* (1959). They were living in London.
ix   He is referring in isiXhosa to the meal of corn (*ngombona*) and a non-alchoholic drink (*rewu*) made of slightly fermented maize-meal porridge. In this context, *nama* means 'with'.
x   Madiba Thembekile (Thembi) Mandela (1945–69), Mandela's eldest son – see the glossary.

when nothing else may remain. What has sustained me even in the most grim moments is the knowledge that I am a member of a tried & tested family which has triumphed over many difficulties. In such a large & broad family opinions can be diverse on almost everything but we have always succeeded in sorting out things together & going forward all the same. This fact endows my spirits with powerful wings. Fondest regards to all & with much love to you, OR, Thembi, Dali & Dudu.

    Yours very sincerely,
Nel

Mrs Adelaide Tambo, c/o Mr Aziz Pahad, 83, North End House, Fitzjames Avenue, London W14

◇◇◇◇◇◇◇◇◇

Mandela called his Soweto home at 8115, on the corner of Vilakazi and Ngakane streets, Orlando West, Johannesburg, 'the centrepoint' of his world.[52] He and his first wife, Evelyn, and their baby, Thembekile, moved there in 1946. They raised their children there and Mandela's mother stayed there from time to time. The three-room house cost 17s. 6d. per month in rent (black people weren't allowed to own property). It was at 8115 that Mandela and his second wife, Winnie, were welcomed back after their wedding in June 1958 and where their children were also raised. It was to 8115 that he returned when he was released from prison. He described it in his autobiography as 'identical to hundreds of others built on postage-stamp size plots on dirt roads. It had the same standard tin roof, the same cement floor, a narrow kitchen, and a bucket toilet at the back. Although there were streetlamps outside, we used paraffin lamps inside as the homes were not yet electrified. The bedroom was so small that a double bed took up almost the entire floor space.'[53]

*   It was from 8115 that Winnie Mandela was arrested on several occasions while her husband was in prison. During those times, family members were brought in to take care of the house.*

To Marshall Xaba, husband of Niki Xaba,[i] Winnie Mandela's eldest sister

February 3, 1970

Sent 18.2.70

<u>Registered Airmail</u>

My dear Uncle Marsh,

Please avoid any arrangement about House No. 8115 Orlando West, which would have the effect of depriving Kgatho and sisters of a home during our absence.

Kgatho[ii] saw me last Saturday and appeared terribly upset over the fact that someone, who is not a relative and who is not acceptable to him and Tellie,[iii] should be given charge of the house. He prefers my niece, Lulu,[iv] who paid me a visit on November 29. I am in favour of Kgatho's suggestion provided that it is acceptable to Zami,[v] and I should be pleased if you would kindly acquaint her with my views. I must confess that Kgatho's anxiety over the whole affair has worried me ever since he raised the matter on January 31, and I consider it most undesirable that he should at any time feel wronged and insecure. He told me that the matter might be finalised with the municipal authorities this week, and I hope that this letter will reach you in time and before you commit yourself to a decision which may cause ill-feeling. I should like you to show this letter to Kgatho and put his mind at rest before he leaves for Fort Hare.[vi]

It is not necessary for me, Uncle Marsh, to assure you that I am fully aware that you and Niki have no ulterior motive in this matter and that your sole purpose is to safeguard our interests, and I am sure that now that you are aware of my views on the matter you will do everything in your power to settle it amicably and satisfactorily.

The time was so short when I saw Kgatho that I forgot to ask about Zeni and Zindzi's[vii] school reports and health. Please give me some information when you reply. In her September letter Niki indicated that you had applied to come down and I have been hoping that I would see you. I am

---

i   Niki Xaba (1932–1985), Winnie Mandela's eldest sister – see the glossary.
ii   Makgatho (Kgatho) Mandela (1950–2005), Mandela's second-born son – see the glossary.
iii Telia (Telli or Tellie) Mtirara, a relative of Mandela's.
iv   Lulama (Lulu), the niece of his former wife Evelyn Mandela.
v   Winnie Mandela, his wife.
vi   University College of Fort Hare, Alice in the Ciskei homeland – see the glossary.
vii Zenani Mandela (1959–) and Zindziswa Mandela (1960–), Mandela's middle and youngest daughters – see the glossary.

also anxious to know whether Ma of Bizana[i] received my letter of May last. Let Bantu[ii] know that she is free to visit me, and I would indeed be happy to see her. I hope Nali's[iii] letter, which I wrote in July last year, was received.

I will write to my dear friends, the Ngakanes,[iv] at the earliest possible opportunity, and add to your explanation.

Fondest regards and much love to you, Niki and family.

Yours very sincerely,
Nel

MR MARSHALL XABA,
P.O. Box 23, Jabavu,
Johannesburg

To Tellie Mandela, a relative

March 6, 1970

Sent 17.3.70

My dear Nkosazana,[v]

I received your letter which was posted in Johannesburg on October 22 and in which you reported that Joel[vi] had agreed to appear for Nobandla.[vii]

I also received your second letter written on October 28 in which you informed me that Joel had actually appeared when the case was remanded the same day. I am very grateful for all the efforts that you are making to straighten out our domestic problems, and more particularly for the important role that you have played in obtaining the services of Joel. Whatever may be the final outcome of the painful episodes in which Nobandla is now engaged, nothing pleases me more than the fact that the case and our affairs are handled by a man in whom I have the fullest confidence; and for this I am greatly indebted to you, Nkosazana.

---

i   Nophikela Hilda Madikizela, Winnie Mandela's stepmother.
ii   Nobantu Mniki, Winnie Mandela's sister.
iii   Nali Nancy Vutela, Winnie Mandela's sister.
iv   Neighbours from Soweto.
v   '*Nkosazana* means 'Miss' or 'princess' in isiXhosa.
vi   Joel Carlson, the Mandelas' lawyer – see the glossary.
vii   Winnie Mandela, his wife.

I was very disturbed to hear that you were unable to see her in the court cells when she and her friends appeared for remand.[i] In my present circumstances, Madiba,[ii] problems which I could have otherwise easily solved become extremely difficult to handle. You, Uncle Marsh and Niki,[iii] are all very close to Nobandla and me, and all of you are trying your very best to help us in every possible way. . . .

As you know, Kgatho[iv] saw me on January 31 and mentioned the problem of who should look after the home when he goes to Fort Hare,[v] stressing at the same time that the matter was extremely urgent. I had hoped that the visit would, as usual, last for an hour but, unfortunately, we were given only 30 minutes and the interview was terminated before I had given my views. I would have preferred to send a telegram to Kgatho and Marsh,[vi] setting out my views but these things are not always possible here, and notwithstanding the urgency of the matter, I had to be content with an airmail letter to Marsh only and which I am not even so sure whether it ever reached its destination.

In this letter I asked Marsh to avoid any arrangement about the house which would have the effect of depriving Kgatho and sisters of a home during our absence. I informed him that I considered Lulu[vii] to be the most suitable person for this purpose, provided Nobandla approved of the arrangement. I hope this matter has now been satisfactorily settled.

In your letter of October 28 you report that the house was owing R34 and that you made means to have the money paid. Kgatho also told me that you had also bought dresses for Zeni and Zindzi.[viii] No words that I may write here can adequately give expression to our gratitude to you. Perhaps one day we may be privileged with the opportunity of returning your kindness, however humble our own act of reciprocity may be.

Incidentally, I should like you to know that it gave me much joy to hear that you felt quite different after you had seen me in October last year, that the cloud of depression had cleared, and that you were now looking at the brighter side of things. That is the correct spirit. It has been rightly said that when you laugh the whole world laughs with you, but when you weep you do so alone. Remember that!

---

i   On 16 February 1970, the charges against Winnie Mandela and her twenty-one co-accused were suddenly withdrawn, but in the short period where they were technically 'free to go' they were rearrested in the courtroom. They went back into custody, and on 4 August 1970, Winnie Mandela and nineteen others were formally charged in court. Three of her previous co-accused were not there. One had suffered a breakdown and two had disappeared after being released.

ii   Madiba is a clan name and anyone from the clan can be called it.

iii   Marshall Xaba, husband of Niki Xaba, Winnie Mandela's eldest sister.

iv   Makgatho (Kgatho) Mandela (1950–2005), Mandela's second-born son – see the glossary.

v   University College of Fort Hare, Alice in the Ciskei homeland – see the glossary.

vi   Marshall Xaba, husband of Niki Xaba, Winnie Mandela's eldest sister.

vii   Lulama (Lulu) was the niece of his former wife Evelyn Mandela.

viii   Zenani (1959–) and Zindzi (1960–) Mandela, his middle and youngest daughters – see the glossary.

On January 1, I wrote to Vulindlela[i] straight to Umtata[ii] and to Ntamboz-enqanawa,[iii] care of Kgatho. On November 19 I had written to Nobandla's uncle, Mr Paul Mzaidume,[iv] 7012 Orlando West. I am anxious to establish whether any of my letters do reach their destination and I should be pleased if you would kindly check whether[v] Ntambozenqanawa and Nobandla's uncle received theirs.

Finally I should like Joel to know that I urgently need R100 for purposes of studies and I should be pleased if he will kindly raise the amount on my behalf. There is nothing else that I can do with Nobandla away.

Once again I thank you for all that you are doing and more especially for having made it possible for Joel to act for Nobandla. Fondest regards to all and with much love to you.

Yours very sincerely,
Buti[vi] Nel

MISS TELLIE MANDELA.
HOUSE NO. 8115 ORLANDO WEST.
JOHANNESBURG

To Makgatho Mandela,[vii] his second-born son

31.3.70

Sent 2.4.70

My dear Kgatho,

I have spent a lot of time these past few months thinking of you. Although you last visited me on January 31, it seems as if I have not seen you for a decade, so badly do I miss you. I hope it will be possible for us to meet before the year is out to discuss confidential family matters which cannot be suitably handled through correspondence.

---

i   Chief Vulindlela Mtirara/Matanzima, a Tembu chief and relative of Mandela's.
ii   Umtata (now called Mthatha) was the capital of the Transkei homeland.
iii   Mandela's cousin, Chief Ntambozenqanawa Nkosiyane.
iv   See his letter on page 143.
v   A note in pencil here that appears to be in another hand reads 'This is where I must start'.
vi   'Brother' in isiXhosa.
vii   Makgatho (Kgatho) Mandela (1950 2005) – see the glossary

Forced separation from the family has always been a tragic & painful experience, & during the past 7 years of my imprisonment I have come to realise how frustrating it can be to be completely unable to give guidance & help to your children in the maze of problems they meet as they grow. In 1966 I received reports that the late Thembi[i] had lost interest in his studies, preferring a driver's job to an academic career. Early in 1967 I wrote and urged him to resume his studies either by returning to a boarding institution or by enrolling with a correspondence college. I assured him that proper arrangements for payment of fees & for personal allowance would be made. I also warned him to refrain from a course of conduct which would have the effect of depriving him of the opportunity of obtaining a worthy & successful career, & whereby he would remain always inferior to others on matters of general scientific knowledge, condemned forever to the degrading status of being subservient to, & the object of exploitation by other human beings. Though you brought me a message from him in October 1967, he never in fact responded to my advice. Yet Thembi was a good boy, full of promise & talent. The late Granny,[ii] Ma Nobandla[iii] & other relatives & friends always gave me good accounts on Thembi when they visited or wrote to me. I sincerely believe that if I were home in 1966, he would not have succumbed to the temptation that induced him to leave school at a critical age in his life.

On July 28 last year I wrote you a long note[iv] on the important family responsibilities that fall on your shoulders now that Thembi is gone. I pointed out that you are now the eldest child, & that it would be your duty to keep the family together & to set a good example to your sisters. I particularly drew your attention to the fact that the issues that interest mankind today call for trained minds, & the man who is without this training cannot effectively serve his people & country. I emphasised further that to lead an orderly & disciplined life & to give up the glittering pleasures that attract the average boy, to work hard & systematically in your studies throughout the year would in the end bring you coveted prizes & much personal happiness. On October 25 you informed me you had passed your supplementary examinations & indicated at the same time that you had renewed your application to Fort Hare.[v] I made suggestions on the question of fees & during your last visit you reported that everything had been arranged & that you would leave for varsity on February 14. I am now informed that

---

i   Madiba Thembekile (Thembi) Mandela (1945–69), Mandela's eldest son who died in a car accident – see the glossary.
ii   Mandela's mother, Nosekeni Fanny Mandela, who died in 1968.
iii   Nobandla is one of Winnie Mandela's names.
iv   See his letter from 28 July 1969, page 113.
v   University College of Fort Hare, Alice in the Ciskei homeland – see the glossary.

you have neither gone to Fort Hare nor have you registered with Unisa.[i] Even more unpleasant rumours & comments made by young & old have come to my notice. Of course I have the fullest confidence in you Kgatho & I will make no conclusion one way or the other until you have given me a full explanation.

I am, however, convinced that the basic cause of your present troubles is my absence from home, as well as the fact that in my present circumstances I do not have the proper facilities of remaining in close contact with you & your current problems. Perhaps if we were together my advice & guidance would probably have saved the 2 valuable years of your life that you have already wasted. I should be glad to hear from you immediately you receive this note, but in the meantime I must warn you not to follow any course of conduct which will finally damage your health & ruin your career whatever temporary pleasure & joy it may give you now. A lot of talent & promise lie buried in you, dear Kgatho, & there is certainly a bright future for you if only you would give yourself a chance. You passed your J.C.[ii] with honours; you are tactful & gentle in handling problems. This is not the time to allow talent to accumulate rust. The youth of your own age, some much younger, are distinguishing themselves in the field of education, in sport, music & in other important spheres. In making these achievements they are inspired by their personal pride, by their desire to enhance the good name & reputation of their respective families & by their love & devotion to the cause of the people. What are you doing? Have you neither pride nor conscience, strong will & independence? Anybody, young or old, who is keeping you away from Varsity & from your studies is not a genuine friend but a fraud & a danger to you. Look out: take stock of the position before it is too late! Go to Fort Hare this year if they will accept you & do reply by return of post.

When you visited me in January you raised the disturbing question of the house. I had hoped at the time that our visit would last for an hour as usual, but as you know, the interview was stopped abruptly & without prior notice after 30 minutes had expired & I was consequently unable to give you my views on the urgent matter you wished to discuss with me. The following Monday I tried desperately to communicate with you before you left Cape Town.[iii] I also tried to contact Mr. Xaba[iv] the same day to tell him to

---

i   University of South Africa.
ii   Junior Certificate.
iii In *Long Walk to Freedom*, Mandela described the visiting room on Robben Island as 'cramped and windowless'. He wrote, 'On the prisoner's side was a row of five cubicles with small square pieces of glass that looked out on identical cubicles on the other side. One sat in a chair and looked through the thick, smudged glass that had a few small holes drilled into it to permit conversation. One had to talk very loudly to be heard. Later the authorities installed microphones and speakers in front of the glass, a marginal improvement.' (NM, *Long Walk to Freedom*, p. 476.)
iv   Marshall Xaba, the children's uncle and the husband of Winnie Mandela's sister Niki Xaba (for Niki Xaba, see the glossary).

do nothing that would have the effect of depriving you and your sisters of a home in our absence.[i] But my efforts were unsuccessful & the registered airmail letter that I wrote him on February 3 appears not to have reached. Tell Lulu[ii] in the meantime that I am trying to arrange for her to remain in the house. I expect Maki[iii] this June. Fondest regards & love to you all. Yours very affectionately, Tata[iv]

Makgatho Lewanika Mandela, 8115, Orlando West, Johannesburg.

To the commanding officer, Robben Island

2nd April 1970

The Commanding Officer
Robben Island

Attention: Medical Officer

My skin becomes very dry and develops cracks on every occasion after taking a bath, a condition which worsens during winter.

In 1967 the physician, Dr Kaplan, recommended that I apply Pond's Cold Cream which I had constantly used prior to my conviction. Thereafter I discussed the matter with the local medical officer who gave me some type of Vaseline. But quite apart from its unsuitability and the inconvenience it occasioned, it did not help me and I was reluctantly compelled to abandon its use. I should accordingly be pleased if you would allow me to order, at my own expense, and for as long as is reasonably necessary, the aforementioned Cold Cream.

[Signed NRMandela]
NELSON MANDELA: 466/64

[Note presumably by a prison official] In my considered opinion Ponds Cold Cream is made up with a base cream called Lanolin. Adeps Lanal, which contains Lanolin, is as good for this patient's skin problem. 2.4.70

---

i   See his letter from 3 February 1970, page 158.
ii   Lulama (Lulu), the niece of his former wife Evelyn Mandela.
iii Makaziwe Mandela (1954–), Mandela's eldest daughter – see the glossary.
iv   'Father' in isiXhosa.

[In another hand] Approved as requested 22.4.70

[In Afrikaans] Colonel.
He also spoke to me about this. The recommendation from the doctor below. [Signed and dated 22.4.70]

Hospital,

For your information and handling

<hr>

To the commanding officer, Robben Island

20 April 1970

Commanding Officer
Robben Island

Attention: Col Van Aarde

I am greatly disturbed and shocked by the way the Censors' office is handling my visits, and I would ask you to investigate the matter personally, at your earliest possible conveniene, and put a stop to these unwarranted irregularities.

Molly de Jager,[i] my daughter-in-law, "Hillbrow", 7th Avenue, Retreat, Cape Town, has for almost three months been battling to obtain a permit to visit me. She made the first application at the very beginning of February and advised me of this fact in a letter which was received by the Censors' Office on the 12th of the same month. Last month I was informed by the Censors' Office that her letter of application had not been "received". She applied again at the beginning of this month and I was warned to expect a visit from her on Saturday 18th April. She did not turn up.

But Beryl Lockman who visited her uncle, Walter Sisulu,[ii] last Saturday and who lives at the same address as my daughter-in-law, informed her Uncle that she and my daughter-in-law had applied for visiting permits

<hr>

i   Thoko Mandela, his late son Thembi's wife (for both Thoko and Thembi Mandela, see the glossary). She adopted the surname De Jager from a relative so that she could live in Retreat, an area for coloured people ('Honouring Thembekile Madiba', Nelson Mandela Foundation, 22 February 2012, https://www.nelsonmandela.org/news/entry/honouring-thembekile-mandela).

ii   Walter Sisulu (1912– 2003), ANC and MK activisit and fellow Rivonia trialist who was imprisoned with Mandela – see the glossary.

the same day. She received her own permit which did not contain the only essential information a permit should have, namely, the date for which the visit had been arranged. Beryl informed the uncle that my daughter-in-law had not come because her permit had not arrived. I am expecting her to come on the 25th instant and I ask you to ensure that the visit is not obstructed again.[i]

I need hardly give you the assurance that this letter is not intended to be a reflection against Lt. Nel, the officer who is directly in charge of the Censors' Office and who treats every one of my requests sympathetically. [Signed NR Mandela]

To Makaziwe Mandela,[ii] his eldest daughter

1 May, 1970

My Darling,

I was pleased to hear from Kgatho[iii] that you had passed your J.C.[iv] Examinations, and that you are now proceeding with matric.

The good progress that you are making in your studies shows that you are a talented and keen student, capable of obtaining the highest qualifications and of winning the best prizes provided of course you work hard and systematically from the beginning of the school term until the examination. I hope that in your next letter it will be possible to give me the symbols that you obtained in each subject you wrote, as well as your aggregate. I know only too well that it is not always easy for an African child to study as a day scholar.

The average African family lives in poverty, in a small and crowded house, without the privacy that a scholar needs to concentrate on her studies, and cannot afford to employ domestic assistants to clean the house, to cook the family food and wash the dishes. All the duties must fall upon the shoulders of the child, with the result that she is never fresh enough in the evenings when she comes to do her homework. By comparison, a child who studies at a boarding-school enjoys many advantages as against a day

---

i   It is not known whether this underlining was done by Mandela or the authorities.
ii   Makaziwe (Maki) Mandela (1954–) – see the glossary.
iii Makgatho (Kgatho) Mandela (1950–2005), Mandela's second-born son and Makaziwe's brother – see the glossary.
iv   Junior Certificate.

scholar. There the environment and atmosphere are altogether different. She has ample time for study, can and very often discusses problems with her classmates, get help from senior students, converse for most of the time in the medium in which subjects are taught, find plenty of recreation in games, gymnastics and music, and have a high standard of performance in her examinations at the end of the year.

These difficulties are much lessened in the case of those scholars whose parents are fortunate enough to have a fairly high level of education and who keep abreast of modern developments in the field of education by reading widely. They can ease the problems of the child by giving her assistance and guidance. Kgatho would undoubtedly have been of great help if you lived together. I would also have added my own bit if I were free. I am accordingly aware of the handicaps that you must be having in pursuing your studies. It is in the light of these difficulties that I see your examination results. I am inclined to the view that you would probably have done much better if you were at a boarding-school. You have done well and I give you my heartiest congrats!

In your undated letter which reached me on the 15th November last year you say that you no longer want to be a scientist because funds will not be available for you to study for this profession. We will discuss this matter more fully when you visit me next June and when I will make definite suggestions. In the meantime I should like to give you the assurance that in spite of my present circumstances, I will do everything in my power to organise the funds required for your degree studies. I do not believe that any of my children who is really keen on her studies, can be prevented from proceeding to varsity because of lack of funds. You should remember that with a father who is serving a life sentence you and Kgatho are like orphans. To both of you education is more than a question of status. It is a matter of life and death. As long as there is money for your studies, you ought to seize the opportunity with both hands. Only in this way will you have security and a bright future. Only when you have the best qualifications will you be able to get good occupations and relieve your mother of her present responsibility and heavy burden. Anyway we will settle the details next month.

I did hear that Mom Winnie is in jail and I agree with you that it will be a long time before she comes out. She will be completing a full year on the 12th of this month. She is in fine spirit. Nyanya[i] has also done very well and I feel proud of them. I cannot give you a clear and straightforward answer as to who is taking care of the children. But you, Kgatho, Sisi Tellie,[ii]

---

i   Nonyaniso (Nyanya) Madikizela, Winnie Mandela's youngest sister.
ii   Telia (Telli or Tellie) Mtirara, a relative of Mandela's. *Sisi* means 'sister' in isiXhosa and is often used to refer to a woman in the samge age group.

Makazi Niki,[i] and our numerous friends are there to look after them. As for me, I have tried during the past 14 months to take advantage of the only opportunity that I have of keeping in touch with them – writing them letters. I did so on the 4th February, 23rd June and 3rd August, but to my greatest disappointment not one of these letters appears to have reached them.

I was happy to hear that you visited Granny's grave and of the hospitality of Paramount Chief Sabata.[ii] He is a wonderful person and I do not know how I will repay him for all that he has done for me. I read somewhere that you attended Mthetho's[iii] wedding last January. The trip down to the ceremony itself must have been an exciting experience. I am glad to note that you are keeping in close touch with members of the family. Such firm ties can give you much strength and inspiration. Are Chief Mdingi and wife keeping well? How old is their daughter and what is she doing. On the 3rd November last year I wrote to Ma-Tshezi[iv] thanking them for the letter of condolence that she and Uncle Sam[v] sent me on the death of Thembi.[vi] I also gave Ma-Tshezi my sympathy on the death of her brother Justice. I received no reply and do not know whether they got the letter.

Lulu[vii] wrote in March asking for permission to stay at our home in Orlando West. I had already written the previous month to Uncle Xaba[viii] asking him to avoid any arrangement about the house which would have the effect of depriving Kgatho and sisters of a home. I informed him that I preferred Lulu to stay in the house, provided Mom-Winnie agreed with this arrangement. Do tell Lulu this.

Today is 1st May, your birthday. Lots of luck and fortune and may you see many more, Darling. Hope you received the birthday card I sent last month.[ix] Affectionately,
Tata[x]

Miss Maki Mandela,
House No. 5818, Orlando East
Johannesburg

---

i   Niki Xaba (1932–1985), Winnie Mandela's eldest sister – see the glossary. *Makazi* means 'sister of your mother' in isiXhosa.
ii   King Sabata Jonguhlanga Dalindyebo (1928–86), paramount chief of the Transkei homeland and leader of the Democratic Progressive Party, the opposition party in Transkei which opposed apartheid rule – see the glossary.
iii   Chief Mthetho Matanzima (d. 1972), K. D. Matanzima's son and chief of the Noqayti region – see the glossary.
iv   Adelaide Mase, the sister-in-law of Mandela's first wife, Evelyn, and Makaziwe's aunt; see his letter, page 132.
v   His first wife Evelyn Mandela's brother Sam.
vi   Madiba Thembekile Mandela (1945–69), Mandela's eldest son – see the glossary.
vii   Lulama (Lulu), the niece of his former wife Evelyn Mandela.
viii Marshall Xaba, husband of Niki Xaba, Winnie Mandela's eldest sister – see his letter from 3 February 1970, page 158.
ix   At some stage during his imprisonment Mandela was allowed to order greeting cards to send on special occasions.
x   'Father' in isiXhosa.

To the commanding officer, Robben Island

[Note in another hand] Censors kindly discuss [Signed and dated 3.6.70]

29th May 1970

The Commanding Officer,
Robben Island.

Attention: Col Van Aarde

Yesterday, I advised you that on the 4th May I wrote you two letters, one relating to matters which are being handled by Brigadier Aucamp,[i] and the second dealt with issues of a local nature, most of which have already received your attention.

There are, however, two matters which were mentioned in the second letter on the 4th May and which are still outstanding.

1. [ii]In June I expect my daughter, Makaziwe,[iii] to pay me a visit for the first time in her life since I was arrested, and I am anxious that the visit should be arranged for next month when she will be on vacation.

2. The second matter that is still outstanding is the special letter to Marshall Xaba[iv] which[v] I handed in for posting on 3rd February with a request that it should be sent by express airmail. Apparently the letter was sent by ordinary post of February 18 notwithstanding the importance of its contents and urgency. You will recall that during the interview on 24th May, I informed you that by the 10th March the letter had not reached its destination, from which fact I inferred that it had probably gone astray.[vi]

[Signed NRMandela]
NELSON MANDELA: 466/64

---

i   Brigadier Aucamp, commanding officer of Robben Island – see the glossary.
ii   There are two horizontal lines on the left side of this paragraph. Possibly the work of a prison official.
iii Makaziwe Mandela (1954–), Mandela's eldest daughter – see the glossary.
iv   Husband of Niki Xaba, Winnie Mandela's eldest sister (for Niki Xaba, see the glossary). See his letter to Adelaide Mase on page 132.
v   It is likely that this underlining is by a prison official.
vi   Ibid.

To Leabie Makhutshwana Piliso,[i] his youngest sister

1st June, 1970

My dear Nkosazana,[ii]

Your letter of March 9, 1969 duly reached me and I was pleased to hear of the role that Jonguhlanga[iii] continues to play in helping to solve the difficulties which my absence from home have brought on you and the rest of the family.

I received the news of your marriage with mixed feelings. A happy marriage is the ambition of all human beings, and that you had found your life-partner gave me real joy. As I have already expressed my feelings and views in a previous letter which contained my congratulations to you and Sibali,[iv] I do not consider it necessary to add here anything on this aspect of the matter. It is sufficient to say that it is a source of real pride to me to have yet another brother-in-law. My only regret is that many years may pass before I see him. Although the news of your marriage pleased me very much, mine was pleasure mingled with worry and concern because I know well how uneasy a girl with national pride could be when the conclusion of the marriage was not accompanied by the usual traditional rites. Accordingly, it was a great relief for me when I heard that Jonguhlanga had bought you the required articles and that he had arranged for you to be formally escorted to your new kraal. Jonguhlanga has a large family and heavy responsibilities, and it is a measure of the deep love and devotion to us all that he was able, in spite of his numerous obligations, to give you the assistance you describe in your letter.

In October 1968 I sent a long letter thanking him for organising Ma's[v] funeral and for the heavy expenses he personally incurred on that occasion. Nobandla[vi] wrote and gave me a lengthy report on the proceedings. About a week before I received Nobandla's letter Sibali Timothy Mbuzo[vii] had visited me for the express purpose of giving me a first-hand account of the passing away and of the funeral of Ma. It afforded me much consolation to hear from him that large crowds had turned up to honour her at the graveside. I was particularly happy to be told that you were able to attend. Ma was

---

i   Leabie Makhutshwana Piliso (1930–97).

ii   *Nkosazana* means 'Miss' or 'princess' in isiXhosa.

iii   King Sabata Jonguhlanga Dalindyebo (1928–86), paramount chief of the Transkei homeland and leader of the Democratic Progressive Party, the opposition party in Transkei which opposed apartheid rule – see the glossary.

iv   Leabie Makhutshwana Piliso (1930–97).

v   Nosekeni Fanny Mandela, his mother, who died in 1968.

vi   Winnie Mandela, his wife.

vii Sibali Timothy Mbuzo, a close relative of Mandela's brother-in-law Daniel Timakwe and a long-standing leading member of the ANC leader in the Transkei homeland. *Sibali* means 'brother-in-law' in isiXhosa.

very attached to you and her death must have been exceedingly painful for you. I hope that you have now completely recovered. Tellie[i] came down last October and told me that you and Baliwe[ii] had managed to attend Thembi's funeral in Johannesburg, another family disaster which shook me violently. I should have liked to attend both ceremonies, but in my current circumstances it is not easy to carry out such wishes. Incidentally, in connection with Ma's funeral I also wrote to Daliwonga,[iii] Nkosikazi NoEngland,[iv] Vulindlela,[v] Wonga,[vi] Thembekile ka Tshunungwa[vii] and Guzana[viii] and thanked them for their own role.

I thought I would discuss the question of the child with Nobandla when she visited me in May last year. I fully grasped the importance of the whole question of removing her from Mount Frere[ix] and had hoped to arrange with Nobandla that she be sent to the same boarding school as Zeni and Zindzi.[x] But as you are now aware she was arrested on May 12 almost a fortnight before she was due to visit me, and she is still in prison. Since her arrest I have experienced considerable difficulties in arranging our household affairs. Almost every one of the letters I write appears not to reach its destination. I have not been able to establish contact even with Zeni and Zindzi in spite of repeated efforts I am making and of several letters that I have written to them. I shall keep on trying to contact a friend who, in Nobandla's absence, will be the most suitable person to help straighten out our affairs, and shall keep the question uppermost in my mind. By the way, Zeni and Zindzi must feel at times very lonely and homesick, and I feel sure that a cheerful letter from you once or twice a year would keep them bright and hopeful. You could always write to them care of Mrs Iris Niki Xaba,[xi] PO Box 23, Jabavu, Johannesburg.

In March I wrote to Sibali, Mrs Timothy Mbuzo.[xii] Today I am sending a special letter to Mhlekazi Sidumo.[xiii] He never replied to the one I sent him in May 1969. I suspect that his was one of the numerous letters from

---

i   Telia (Telli or Tellie) Mtirara, a relative of Mandela's.

ii   One of Mandela's sisters.

iii   K. D. Matanzima (1915– 2003), Mandela's nephew, a Thembu chief, and chief minister for the Transkei – see the glossary. His middle name was Daliwonga.

iv   Wife of the regent Jongintaba Dalindyebo, she raised Mandela as one of her own children when he went to live with them after the death of his father.

v   Chief Vulindlela Mtirara/Matanzima, a Tembu chief and relative of Mandela's.

vi   Wonga Mbekeni was a student at nearby Lovedale College when Mandela was at University College of Fort Hare.

vii An ANC activist and member of the Thembu royal family, he was on trial with Mandela in the 1956 Treason Trial (for the Treason Trial, see the glossary).

viii Knowledge Guzana (1916–), attorney and leader of the Democratic Party in the Transkei – see the glossary.

ix   A town in the Transkei.

x   Zenani Mandela (1959–) and Zindziswa Mandela (1960–), Mandela's middle and youngest daughters – see the glossary.

xi   Winnie Mandela's eldest sister – see the glossary.

xii Sibali Timothy Mbuzo's wife.

xiii Sidumo Mandela, a cousin of Mandela's. *Mhlekazi* means 'sir' or 'honourable sir'.

me that inevitably "go astray", especially since Nobandla's arrest. You may phone or write to Sisi Connie Njongwe,[i] Station Road, Matatiele, and tell her that it was a real pleasure to receive her inspiring letter and to get news about the family. Let her know that in August last year I received a letter of condolence from Robbie and Zuki, and was disturbed to learn that Jimmy[ii] had removed a disk and subsequently fractured a leg. Connie never even as much as hinted at this in her letter. Tell them that I know just how tough and courageous Jimmy is, and that I have not the slightest doubt but that he is still the same cheerful man who is always full of self-confidence and hope. I will be writing as soon as that can be arranged. Connie will inform Robbie that I was just about to reply to their sweet and encouraging letter when weather conditions in their territory worsened. I shall drop them a line as soon as conditions improve. Tons and tons of love.

Yours very affectionately, Buti[iii] Nel

Mrs Nowam Leabie Piliso
P.O. Mkemane Store, Mount Frere

To Nkosikazi Nokukhanya Luthuli, widow of former president-general of the ANC Chief Albert Luthuli[iv]

8th June 1970

Our dear Ma,

In July 1967 Major Kellerman, then Commanding Officer of this prison, gave permission for me to write you a special letter of condolence on behalf of all of us here on the occasion of the passing of the late Chief.

Under normal circumstances we would have certainly attended the funeral to pay homage directly to the memory of a great warrior as he passed from the stage into history. A veteran of many campaigns who was deeply loved by his people and respected far and wide as an outstanding champion of those who carried on their shoulders the curse of poverty

---

i   Connie Njongwe, wife of Dr. James 'Jimmy' Njongwe (1919–76), medical doctor, ANC leader, and organiser of the
      Defiance Campaign (for the Defiance Campaign, see the glossary) in the Eastern Cape – for Jimmy Njongwe, see
      the glossary. *Sisi* means 'sister' in isiXhosa and is often used to refer to a woman in the samge age group.
ii   James 'Jimmy' Njongwe.
iii   'Brother' in Afrikaans.
iv   See the glossary.

and want, who were afflicted by disease and ignorance, who never knew real happiness and peace, and to whom opportunities for advancement and fulfilment were beyond reach. For a decade and a half he dominated the country's public life, and led us with great skill during one of the most difficult phases in our struggle for higher ideals and a better life. The Chief was in many ways a remarkable man. He was a true nationalist whose feet were firmly planted in his native soil and who drew much strength and inspiration from the traditional background but who, nevertheless, had a progressive outlook and without the slightest trace of racial arrogance or parochialism. His forceful personality and keen brain were tempered by humility, modesty and unequivocal acceptance of the principle of collective leadership. Although he was always calm and restrained, those who came into contact with him were inspired by his warmth and friendship and by his readiness to appreciate other people's good work and talents. He was a national leader in the full sense of the term and especially qualified to lead a broad national movement. He was free of all sectarian tendencies, a dreadful disease which has crippled and even destroyed powerful movements, and which has at various times in our history raised its ugly head. It was a pleasure to watch him in action either as he addressed a public gathering, participated in a committee meeting (or as he gave his memorable evidence in the Treason Trial). His public speeches were simple and frank, and were delivered or expressed without any violent appeal to the emotions of the audience. In committee discussions he had the capacity to listen patiently and carefully to others and when he ultimately spoke he would highlight those issues which would bring about the widest possible measure of agreement. He never fell foul of the temptation of trying to display his knowledge, nor did he ever attempt to prove himself superior to any of his colleagues. Notwithstanding his training as teacher and his former position as tribal Chief, I have never had cause to feel that he approached his public duties with over-caution and conservatism. On the contrary, he consistently gave the impression of a patriot who was moved by radical and advanced ideas and who kept abreast with the most revolutionary of the younger generation.

(His death was a severe setback to our efforts to live decent and honourable lives.) To you it was a disastrous loss for it meant many years of loneliness, of toil and sweat without the expert and experienced help of a life-partner who was deeply attached to you. His death also deprived the children of the guidance of a father who was well-equipped to discharge the duties of parenthood because he was in the centre of public activity and highly sensitive to progressive ideas. We regretted his loss to you and the family and to the community as a whole and gave you our sincere sympathy. We were certain, however, that the immense courage that you had shown throughout the most dangerous period of the Chief's public career, would carry you through that unfortunate experience. We also expressed the hope that the huge crowds that would turn up at the funeral and the numerous messages of condolence that would come from various parts of the world, might serve as a tonic to your wounded feelings.

That letter was in our current circumstances the only means we had of conveying to you and the family the sentiments expressed above, and we did not have the slightest suspicion that you would not receive it. How great was our disappointment when we learnt that it did not reach you! About three months after I had handed in the letter for posting away, I wrote to Alan[i] and gave him our sympathy on the death of his wife. We felt that fate had treated him very savagely in taking away his wife so soon after the death of his friend, the Chief. (We praised the firm stand he had taken on many public questions and thanked him for the evidence in mitigation that he gave on our behalf at the Rivonia Trial[ii]), and concluded the letter by telling him that we were confident that neither family tragedy nor advancing age would induce him to lay down the harness. We now know that Alan's letter never reached also. We cannot imagine that anybody would deliberately interfere with condolence letters and prevent them from reaching the bereaved. I am, however, taking the precaution of having this one registered to ensure its safe arrival. In our present environment kind words achieve an impact that is not easy or wise to analyse. It is sufficient to say that they achieve far more than the mere act of boosting morale. Your short but sweet note of January 1966 exceedingly excited us. It pleased us much to hear that the world, our people and particularly your Ma think of us every day. Your letter is amongst my most treasured possessions. Fondest regards and love to Norman, Fana, Ntombazana, and Kwena, Thandeka and Tulani; Sibongile and Dr Ngobese[iii] and to all the young children.

Yours very sincerely,
Nelson

Nkosikazi Nokukhanya Luthuli
P.O. Groutville, Stanger, Natal

---

i   Alan Paton (1903–88), author and founder and leader of South Africa's anti-apartheid Liberal Party. He gave evidence in mitigation of sentence for Mandela and his co-accused at the Rivonia Trial – see the glossary.

ii   Alan Paton said that like everyone else, African people aspired 'to live a decent life' and that Mandela was heir apparent to ANC president-general Chief Albert Luthuli. Speaking of the accused, he said, 'I have never had any doubt about their sincerity, their deep devotion to the cause of their people, and their desire to see that South Africa became a country in which all people could participate.' (Joel Joffe, *The State vs. Nelson Mandela: The Trial That Changed South Africa* (London: One World Publications, 2007) p. 249.)

iii   All fellow activists, including Dr Helen Ngobese, a friend of Winnie Mandela's who was one of her bridesmaids.

To Winnie Mandela,[i] his wife

20th June 1970

Dade Wethu,[ii]

Indeed, "the chains of the body are often wings to the spirit." It has been so long, and so it will always be. Shakespeare in <u>As You Like It</u>[iii] puts the same idea somewhat differently:
> "Sweet are the uses of adversity,
> Which like a toad, ugly and venomous,
> Wears yet a precious jewel in the head."[iv]

Still others have proclaimed that 'only great aims can arouse great energies.'

Yet my understanding of the real idea behind these simple words throughout the 26 years of my career of storms has been superficial, imperfect & perhaps a bit scholastic. There is a stage in the life of every social reformer when he will thunder on platforms primarily to relieve himself of the scraps of indigested information that has accumulated in his head; an attempt to impress the crowds rather than to start a calm & simple exposition of principles & ideas whose universal truth is made evident by personal experience & deeper study. In this regard I am no exception & I have been victim of the weakness of my own generation not once but a hundred times. I must be frank & tell you that when I look back at some of my early writings & speeches I am appalled by their pedantry, artificiality and lack of originality. The urge to impress & advertise is clearly noticeable. What a striking contrast your letters make, Mhlope![v] I hesitate to heap praises on you but you will pardon my vanity and conceit, Ngutyana.[vi] To pay you a compliment may amount to self-praise on my part as you & I are one. Perhaps under the present conditions this type of vanity may serve as a powerful lever to our spirits.

During the 8 lonely years I have spent behind bars I sometimes wished we were born the same hour, grown up together and spent every minute of our lives in each other's company. I sincerely believe that had this been

---

i   Nomzamo Winifred Madikizela-Mandela (1936–) – see the glossary.
ii   Normally written as one word, this means 'sister' in isiXhosa.
iii   This is likely to be Mandela's underlining.
iv   William Shakespeare, *As You Like It*, Act 2, scene 2.
v   One of Winnie Mandela's names.
vi   One of Winnie Mandela's names. She comes from the amaNgutyana clan.

the case I would have been a wise man. Every one of your letters is a precious possession & often succeeds in arousing forces I never suspected to be concealed in my being. In your hands the pen is really mightier than a sabre. Words flow out freely & naturally & common expressions acquire a meaning that is at once challenging & stimulating.

The first paragraph of your moving note, & more especially the opening line, shook me violently. I literally felt every one of the millions of atoms that make up my body pulling forcefully in all directions. The beautiful sentiments you have repeatedly urged on me since my arrest & conviction, & particularly during the last 15 months, are clearly the result more of actual experience than of scholasticism. They come from a woman who has not seen her husband for almost 2 years, who has been excluded from her tender children for more than 12 months & who has been hard hit by loneliness, pining & illness under conditions least conducive for recovery, & who on top of all that must face the most strenuous test of her life.

I understand perfectly well, darling, when you say you miss me & that one of the few blows you found hard to take was not hearing from me. The feeling is mutual, but it is plain that you have gone through a far more ravaging experience than I have ever had. I tried hard & patiently to communicate with you. I sent you a long note on Nov. 16;[i] thereafter a Xmas card, and again a letter on Jan. 1[ii] – all were written at a time when you were an awaiting-trial prisoner. After Feb. 13 I was informed that I could not communicate with you & my earnest plea for a relaxation of this particular restriction was unsuccessful.

Your illness has been stubborn & persistent, and I would have expected to be given a proper medical report by the Prisons' Department to help ease my mind. Brig. Aucamp[iii] gave me a very generalised account which disturbed me intensely. I was shocked to learn that you had to be hospitalised & to actually see evidence of your present state of health in your sloppy handwriting. I believe you completely when you say that you have shrunk to Zeni's[iv] size. It was some sort of relief to hear that you have been seen by numerous specialists & that blood tests have been taken. But I know, Mntakwethu,[v] that every piece of your bone, ounce of flesh & drop of blood; your whole being is hewed in one piece out of granite, & that nothing whatsoever, including ailment, can blow out the fires that are burning in your heart. Up on your feet! Onward to duty! My love and devotion is your armour & the ideal of a free South Africa your banner.

---

i　See his letter on page 134.
ii　See his letter on page 149.
iii　Brigadier Aucamp, commanding officer of Robben Island – see the glossary.
iv　Zenani Mandela (1959–), their eldest daughter – see the glossary.
v　A term of endearment in isiXhosa.

A few days after your arrest in May last year I asked for a special letter to my attorney[i] in connection with the following urgent matters:

1. The appointment of a caretaker for the house & for the payment of rent;
2. The appointment of a legal guardian for the children;
3. The making of arrangements for the maintenance, upbringing & education of the children;
4. The making of arrangements for the raising of funds for your education, toilet & other requirements in the event of your being found guilty and imprisoned;
5. The making of arrangements for the raising of funds for my own education, toilet & other requirements during your absence in jail.

Although I have made repeated representations on several occasions, the application was not granted. I have, however, now instructed Mr Brown of the firm of Frank, Bernadt and Joffe[ii] in Cape Town to give immediate attention to these matters. I agree with your suggestion that Father Leon Rakale & Uncle Mashumi[iii] be appointed joint guardians of the children. I should like to add Uncle Marsh's[iv] name. I wrote him an urgent letter on February 3 in connection with the house.[v] I doubt if he ever received it. He never responded. When Kgatho[vi] visited me on Jan. 31 he indicated that he & Tellie[vii] were in favour of Lulu[viii] (Mxolisi's sister) moving into the house. I informed Uncle Marsh of this fact & indicated that I would be happy if she did, provided you approved. Mxolisi visited me last Saturday & she says they have not heard from Marsh. Perhaps you would like to discuss the matter with him & Niki[ix] when they next pay you a visit. I also doubt if Mashumi received my note written on Nov. 19[x] & rewritten on Apr. 4. I asked him to give me a report on Zeni & Zindzi[xi] and to help get Kgatho to varsity. I received no reply from Mashumi as well. Kgatho is at home and I have no proper information as to why he failed to go to Fort Hare.[xii] I made the necessary arrangements for payment of fees & allowance & when he

---

i   See his letter to Messrs Frank, Bernadt & Joffe, 20 May 1969, page 94, although not all the points he mentions here were actually included in that letter.
ii   His attorneys.
iii   Winnie Mandela's uncle, Paul Mzaidume.
iv   Marshall Xaba, husband of Niki Xaba, Winnie Mandela's eldest sister (for Niki Xaba, see the glossary).
v   See page 158.
vi   Makgatho (Kgatho) Mandela (1950–2005), Mandela's second-born son – see the glossary.
vii   Telia (Telli or Tellie) Mtirara, a relative of Mandela's.
viii   Lulama (Lulu) was the niece of his former wife Evelyn Mandela.
ix   Niki Xaba (1932–1985), Winnie Mandela's eldest sister – see the glossary.
x   See his letter on page 143.
xi   Zindziswa Mandela (1960–), his youngest daughter – see the glossary.
xii   University College of Fort Hare, Alice in the Ciskei homeland – see the glossary.

came down in Jan. he confirmed that everything had been fixed & that he would leave for varsity on Feb. 14. I believe he is not working. My letter to him on March 31st produced no response.

I have written 3 letters to Zeni & Zindzi. I now know that the first 2 never reached them. The 3rd one was written on June 1st. I have received no information whatsoever on them since your arrest save & except the reports you gave me. Of course Niki's letter of Sep. 9 informed me that they were well.

I, however, hope to straighten out the whole affair with Mr. Brown soon & will arrange for you to be regularly informed.

I have raised the question of my paying you a visit once more & I can tell you nothing at present apart from saying that Brig. Aucamp has promised to discuss the matter with the Commissioner. Speaking frankly, I think the Commissioner has been unusually hard & has not shown the consideration & assistance that I normally expect from him in circumstances of this nature.

Dade Wethu, I wish I could have been in a position to tell you something that could gladden your heart & make you smile. But as I see it we may have to wait a long time for that bright & happy moment. In the meantime we must 'drink the cup of bitterness to the dregs.' Perhaps, no I am sure, the good old days will come when life will sweeten our tongues & nurse our wounds. Above all remember March 10. That is the source of our strength. I never forget it.

Tons and tons of love, Mhlope, [i] and a million kisses.
Devotedly.
Dalibunga

Nkosikazi Nobandla Mandela
Pretoria Prison

To Winnie Mandela,[ii] his wife

1 July 1970

Dade Wethu,[iii]

---

i   One of Winnie Mandela's names.
ii   Nomzamo Winifred Madikizela-Mandela (1936–) – see the glossary.
iii Normally written as one word, this means 'sister' in isiXhosa.

Thoko[i] saw me again last April. In Feb. she sent me R10 for 'pocket money' as she put it. The second visit was much easier than the first. Then she still bore signs of one whose energy had been drained by the shock of death & whose nerves have been wrecked by prolonged brooding over the ghastly experience that had befallen her so early in her married life. Although I was meeting her for the first time, it was easy to notice that I was seeing a shadow of her real self. The visit almost upset my own balance, especially when she showed me Thembi's picture. The feeling of anguish & depression that had hit me so viciously when I received the horrible news of his death returned and began to gnaw away mercilessly at my insides. Once again I had come face to face with the ugly reality of life. Here was a green girl who had just turned 25 & who looked up to me to say something that could console her; something that might take away her mind from grief & give her some hope. This was one of those occasions which tend to emphasise just how little we know about real life & its problems in spite of all the literature that we read & the stories we listen to.

Things were altogether different in April. She looked grand & cheerful and could even use her injured arm. I thoroughly enjoyed the visit. When I think of the disasters that had invaded us over the past 21 months, I very often wonder what gives us the strength & courage to carry on. If calamities had the weight of physical objects we should long have been crushed down, or else, we should by now have been hunch-backed, unsteady on our feet, & with faces full of gloom & utter despair. Yet my entire body throbs with life & is full of expectations. Each day brings a fresh stock of experiences & new dreams. I am still able to walk perfectly straight & firmly. What is even more important to me is the knowledge that nothing can ever ruffle you & that your step remains as fleet & graceful as it has always been – a girl who can laugh heartily & infect others with her enthusiasm. Always remember that this is how I think of you.

I believe that you have been charged and that you will appear again on Aug. 3. On June 19 I met Brig. Aucamp[ii] & he gave me the assurance that I am free to discuss the case with you & to give you the necessary advice & encouragement. In the first charge I was a co-conspirator & a count[iii] referred to certain conversations which were to have taken place when you visited me. I am ready to testify on behalf of all of you whether or not I am still cited as a co-conspirator, as long as counsel deems my evidence relevant & necessary. It will be a real pleasure for me to be of some help to you & your fearless comrades in striking the blows you have waited so

---

i   Thoko Mandela, his son Thembi's widow – see the glossary.
ii   Brigadier Aucamp, commanding officer of Robben Island – see the glossary.
iii Meaning 'charge'.

long to deliver & in turning the tables against those responsible for the multitude of wrongs that are being wantonly committed against you. The various pleas tendered during the last trial were quite appropriate & pleased me very much – my fist is clenched. They portrayed you as determined & conscious freedom fighters who are fully alive to their social responsibilities & who have no delusions whatsoever about the sort of justice dispensed by the country's courts nowadays, both inferior & superior. The first trial collapsed because you pulled no punches & asked for no mercy. The onslaught against you this time may be more vicious & vindictive than in the last trial, & more calculated to smear rather than to establish guilt in the usual way. You people have shown extraordinary alertness & amazing stamina during the last 13 months, & my remarks may be altogether redundant. But in these hectic days when the adversary is plotting cunningly & laying traps in all directions, we are called upon to be extremely cautious & vigilant; & there is nothing wrong in drawing attention to the dangers that lie ahead, even though such dangers may be plain for all of us to see. We fight against one of the last strongholds of reaction on the African Continent. In cases of this kind our duty is a simple one – at the appropriate time to state clearly, firmly & accurately the aspirations that we cherish & the greater South Africa for which we fight. Our cause is just. It is a fight for human dignity & for an honourable life. Nothing should be done or said which may be construed directly or indirectly as compromising principle, not even the threat of a more serious charge & severe penalty. In dealing with people, be they friends or foe, you are always polite & pleasant. This is equally important in public debates. We can be frank and outspoken without being reckless or abusive, polite without cringing, we can attack racialism & its evils without ourselves fostering feelings of hostility between different racial groups.

These are matters we ought to discuss in absolute confidence & no third person ought ever to know about them. Any impression that I lecture or give pious advice will fill me with a sense of shame. You know, darling, that I never even attempted to do so before. That I have to run this risk today is a measure of the unusual times in which we live & the great issues that are at stake. It is men & women like yourselves, Mhlope,[i] that are enriching our country's history & creating a heritage for which future generations will feel really proud. I know that, even though on the morning of Aug. 3 you may have shrunk to a size much smaller than that of Zeni,[ii] & even though life itself may be oozing out of you, you will try to muster just enough strength to be able to drag your thinning body to the courtroom to defend the ideals

---

i   One of Winnie Mandela's names.
ii   Zenani Mandela (1959–), their eldest daughter – see the glossary.

for which many of our patriots over the last 500 years have given their lives. I have already written to Brown[i] re the children & am expecting him soon. Is Nyanya[ii] in or out?[iii] Can she visit me?[iv] Tons and tons of love & a million kisses, darling.

Devotedly, Dalibunga

To Winnie Mandela,[v] his wife

August 1, 1970

Dade Wethu,[vi]

Can it be that you did not receive my letter of July 1? How can I explain your strange silence at a time when contact between us has become so vital?

In June I learnt for the first time that you had been confined to bed for 2 months & that your condition[vii] was so bad that you did not appear with your friends when the case came up for formal remand. Is your silence due to a worsening of your health or did the July letter suffer the fate of the 39 monthly letters, letters in lieu of visits & specials that I have written since your arrest on May 12 '69, all of which, save 2, seemed not to have reached their destination? Not even Kgatho, Maki, Zeni, Zindzi,[viii] Tellie,[ix] Ma of Bizana,[x] Marsh[xi] & Mashumi[xii] responded. I am becoming increasingly uneasy every day. I know you would respond quickly if you heard from me & I fear that you have not done so because you either did not receive the letter or you are not fit to write.

The crop of miseries we have harvested from the heartbreaking frustrations of the last 15 months are not likely to fade away easily from the mind. I feel as if I have been soaked in gall, every part of me, my flesh,

---

i   Brown was Mandela's Cape Town attorney.
ii   Nonyaniso (Nyanya) Madikizela, Winnie Mandela's youngest sister.
iii   Nonyaniso Mandela had been imprisoned for being in Johannesburg without a pass. He is asking if she is still in prison.
iv   Mandela's record of family visits contains a note that on 26 December 1971 'Nyanya refused visit' meaning she had been denied permission to visit him.
v   Nomzamo Winifred Madikizela-Mandela (1936–) – see the glossary
vi   'Sister' in isiXhosa.
vii   Winnie Mandela had a heart condition.
viii   His four children.
ix   Telia (Telli or Tellie) Mtirara, a relative of Mandela's.
x   Nophikela Hilda Madikizela, Winnie Mandela's stepmother.
xi   Marshall Xaba, husband of Niki Xaba, Winnie Mandela's eldest sister (for Niki Xaba, see the glossary).
xii   Winnie Mandela's uncle, Paul Mzaidume.

bloodstream, bone & soul, so bitter am I to be completely powerless to help you in the rough & fierce ordeals you are going through. What a world of difference to your failing health & to your spirit, darling, to my own anxiety & the strain that I cannot shake off, if only we could meet; if I could be on your side & squeeze you, or if I could but catch a glimpse of your outline through the thick wire netting that would inevitably separate us. Physical suffering is nothing compared to the trampling down of those tender bonds of affection that form the basis of the institution of marriage & the family that unite man & wife. This is a frightful moment in our life. It is a moment of challenge to cherished beliefs, putting resolutions to a severe test.

But as long as I still enjoy the privilege of communicating with you, even though it may only exist in form for me, & until it is expressly taken away, the records will bear witness to the fact that I tried hard & earnestly to reach you by writing every month. I owe you this duty & nothing will distract me from it. Maybe this line will one day pay handsome dividends. There will always be good men on earth, in all countries, & even here at home. One day we may have on our side the genuine & firm support of an upright & straightforward man, holding high office, who will consider it improper to shirk his duty of protecting the rights & privileges of even his bitter opponents in the battle of ideas that is being fought in our country today; an official who will have a sufficient sense of justice & fairness to make available to us not only the rights & privileges that the law allows us today, but who will also compensate us for those that were surreptitiously taken away. In spite of all that has happened I have, throughout the ebb & flow of the tides of fortune in the last 15 months, lived in hope & expectation. Sometimes I even have the belief that this feeling is part & parcel of my self. It seems to be woven into my being. I feel my heart pumping hope steadily to every part of my body, warming my blood & pepping up my spirits. I am convinced that floods of personal disaster can never drown a determined revolutionary nor can the cumulus of misery that accompanies tragedy suffocate him. To a freedom fighter hope is what a life-belt is to a swimmer – guarantee that one will keep afloat & free from danger. I know, darling, that if riches were to be counted in terms of the tons of hope & sheer courage that nestle in your breast (this idea I got from you) you would certainly be a millionaire. Remember this always.

By the way, the other day I dreamt of you convulsing your entire body with a graceful Hawaiian dance at the B.M.S.C.[i] I stood at one end of the

---

i   The Bantu Men's Social Centre (BMSC), founded in Sophiatown, Johannesburg, in 1924, was an important cultural, social, and political meeting place for black South Africans. Its facilities included a gym and a library, and it hosted boxing matches, political meetings, and dances. Mandela and four others founded the ANC Youth League there in 1944.

famous hall with arms outstretched ready to embrace you as you whirled towards me with the enchanting smile that I miss so desperately. I cannot explain why the scene should have located at the B.M.S.C. To my recollection we have been there for a dance only once – on the night of Lindi's[i] wedding reception. The other occasion was the concert we organised in 1957 when I was courting you, or you me. I am never certain whether I am free to remind you that you took the initiative in this regard.[ii] Anyway the dream was for me a glorious moment. If I must dream in my sleep, please hawaii for me. I like to see you merry & full of life.

I enjoyed reading Fatima's "Portrait of Indian S. Africans"[iii] – a vivid description of Indian life written in a beautiful & simple style. With characteristic modesty she describes the title in the preface as still pretentious for a book that only skims the surface. But the aspects that form its theme are skilfully probed. She raises an issue of wider interest when she points out that "differences that divide are not differences of custom, of rituals & tradition, but differences of status, of standard of living, of access to power and power-gaining techniques. These are the differences that have at all known times determined the destinies of persons & people, and the same people and the same cultures have at one point enjoyed high privilege and at another none." The book contains chapters which touch on other fundamental matters & I fear that some of her observations on current public questions may spark off animated debates. I welcome the brutal frankness of her pen, but it may be that once she elects to raise such matters her duty is not only to comment but to inspire, to leave her fellow countrymen with hope & something to live for. I hope you will be able to read the book before the case ends. It is a brilliant work written by a brilliant scholar. I thoroughly enjoyed it.

Mr Brown, our Cape Town attorney, should have been here on July 29 in connection with the question of guardianship of the children. The sea was very rough & this may probably be the reason for his failure to turn up. I am hoping that he will come soon. In the meantime I am writing to our friend, Duggie Lukhele,[iv] requesting him to check on them & to give us a detailed report. I shall certainly keep you informed of developments. Do not allow yourself to be agitated by the chaos in our household affairs & by the difficulties we are having in communicating officially & openly with each other. This is a phase in our life that will pass & leave us still

---

i   One of Lionel Ngakane's sisters.
ii   Mandela met Winnie Madikizela when she was consulting with his colleague Oliver Tambo in 1957. They went on their first date on 10 March 1957 and married on 14 June 1958.
iii Fatima Meer, *Portrait of Indian South Africans* (Durban: Avon House, 1969).
iv   Douglas Lukhele, Harvard-educated Swazi lawyer who did his articles at Mandela and Oliver Tambo's law firm in the 1950s. He was the first Swazi attorney-general and high court judge in Swaziland.

there, & perhaps even growing stronger. I almost forgot to tell you that my second application to see you was summarily rejected, notwithstanding the fact that I had cited your present illness as one reason for renewing the application. The Commissioner did not even consider it his duty to allay my fears by giving me a report on your condition.[i] There was a time when such experiences would make me wild; now I can take them calmly. I have become used to them. Keep well, my darling; do not allow yourself to be run down by illness or longing for the children. Fight with all your strength. My fist is firm. Tons & tons of love & a million kisses. Devotedly, Dalibunga

Nkosikazi Nobandla Mandela, Central Prison, Pretoria

To Senator Douglas Lukhele,[ii] friend and former colleague

August 1, 1970

My dear Duggie,

Our children, Zeni & Zindzi,[iii] aged 11 & 10 respectively, are at "Our Lady of Sorrows," a Roman Catholic boarding school at Hluti.[iv] We are extremely disturbed because, since Zami's[v] detention on May 12 last year, we have heard nothing about them. Information reached me that they spend their holidays with Allan. I should have liked to write directly to him & wife, to thank them for the hospitality, but I am not sure whether, having regard to his present position, I am free to do so. I [would] like them to know that Zami & I are sincerely grateful. I believe Mrs Birley,[vi] now lecturing in a British university, had arranged scholarships for the children at Waterford[vii] for next year. I have written them 3 letters & sent a birthday card, but none seems to have reached. Please investigate & give me a detailed report, preferably by registered letter, at your earliest possible convenience. Letters from

---

i   Brigadier Aucamp was also in touch with Winnie Mandela as he was in charge of security at all prisons where there were inmates held for politically related offences.
ii   Harvard-educated Swazi lawyer Douglas Lukhele did his articles at Mandela and Oliver Tambo's law firm in the 1950s. He was the first Swazi attorney-general and high court judge in Swaziland.
iii   Zenani Mandela (1959–) and Zindziswa Mandela (1960–), Mandela's middle and youngest daughters – see the glossary.
iv   Hluti is in Swaziland.
v   One of Winnie Mandela's names.
vi   Lady Elinor Birley (Mandela misspelled her name as 'Eleanor') whose husband Sir Robert Birley (1903–82), was the former headmaster of Eton College and at the time the visiting professor of education at the University of the Witwatersrand. Whilst there, the Birley's worked to acquire books to establish a library in Soweto, which then became known as the Birley Library.
vii   Waterford Kamhlaba school in neighbouring Swaziland.

me hardly ever reach destination & those addressed to me fare no better. I am hoping that the remorseless fates, that consistently interfere with my correspondence & that have cut me off from my family at such a critical moment, will be induced by considerations of honour & honesty to allow this one through. I know that once it reaches your hands my troubles will be virtually over.

You know that I am essentially a rustic like many of my contemporaries, born & brought up in a country village[i] with its open spaces, lovely scenery & plenty of fresh air. Although prior to my arrest & conviction 8 years ago I lived for two decades as a townsman, I never succeeded in shaking off my peasant background, & now & again I spent a few weeks in my home district as a means of recalling the happy moments of my childhood. Throughout my imprisonment my heart & soul have always been somewhere far beyond this place, in the veld[ii] & the bushes. I live across these waves with all the memories & experiences I have accumulated over the last half century – memories of the grounds in which I tended stock, hunted, played, & where I had the privilege of attending the traditional initiation school.[iii] I see myself moving into the Reef[iv] in the early forties, to be caught up in the ferment of the radical ideas which were stirring the more conscious of the African youth. (Incidentally it was at this stage that I first met Allan, then a clerk at Union College.) I remember the days when I served articles, licking stamps daily, running all sorts of errands, including buying hair shampoo & other cosmetics for white ladies. Chancellor House![v] It was there that OR[vi] & I became even more intimate than we were as college mates & as Leaguers.[vii] Around us there developed new & fruitful friendships – Maindy,[viii] Zubeida Patel & Winnie Mandleni, our first typists;[ix] the late Mary Anne, whose sudden and untimely death greatly distressed us, Ruth,[x] Mavis, Godfrey,[xi]

---

i   Qunu in the Transkei.

ii   'Field' in Afrikaans.

iii   Mandela describes the importance of initition into manhood in *Long Walk to Freedom*: 'For the Xhosa people, circumcision represents the formal incorporation of males into society. It is not just a surgical procedure, but a lengthy and elaborate ritual in preparation for manhood. As a Xhosa, I count my years as a man from the date of my circumcision.' (NM., p. 30.)

iv   The Reef in Johannesburg refers to the gold reef where gold was first discovered by Australian George Harrison in 1896. That gold rush gave birth to Johannesburg, which is now part of Gauteng province.

v   Chancellor House was the building in which Mandela and Oliver Tambo started their law practice, Mandela and Tambo, in 1952.

vi   Oliver Reginald Tambo (1917–93), friend, former law partner, and the president of the ANC – see the glossary.

vii   Members of the ANC Youth League established in 1944. More militant African youth like A. P. Mda (1916–93), Anton Lembede (1914–47), Walter Sisulu (1912–2003), Jordan Ngubane (1917–85), Victor Mbobo, William Nkomo (1915–72), David Bopape (1915–2004), Oliver Tambo (1917–93) and Mandela helped to found the organisation proposed by Dr. Lionel Majombozi (d. 1949).

viii   Maindy Msimang, also know an Mendi Msimang, was an administrative officer of the ANC in London.

ix   For the law firm Mandela and Tambo.

x   Ruth Mompati (1925–2015) was also one of Mandela and Tambo's typists. She became a member of the ANC and was one of the leaders of the 1956 Women's March to protest pass laws for black women.

xi   Godfrey Pitje (1917–97), former ANC Youth League president and lawyer who served his articles at Mandela and Tambo.

boxing Freddy & Charlie the upright & popular caretaker & cleaner who never missed a day at Mai-Mai.[i] For some time you battled almost alone & against formidable difficulties to keep the firm afloat when OR and I were immobilised by the Treason Trial. I even recall the strange incident that occurred when you visited Zami & I at our home in Orlando West in Dec. '60. As you approached the gate a bolt of lightning split out with such tremendous force that Zeni, then only 10 months, was flung to the ground where she remained motionless for some seconds. What a relief it was when she came round & started yelling; it was a close shave. Your presence at the D.O.C.C.[ii] on that occasion put a new & deeper meaning to your magnificent stand at Winburg[iii] & added more weight & lustre to the eulogies that have since been heaped on you in memory of your outstanding service to the womenfolk.

Lenvick! There you established yourself with Manci as articled clerk & ably assisted by the smooth & energetic Joe Magame. I have not forgotten the good things you did for me personally those days. I was still involved in the T.T.[iv] & during adjournments you kept me busy by giving me work, & it thus became possible for me to assist Zami in some way to keep the home fires burning. I hope one day I shall be able to reciprocate. Anyway I was very happy when I was informed that your fatherland,[v] the beautiful country which is full of so much promise & potential, could now avail itself of your talents to the fullest extent. I was even more pleased to be told that you were now [a] member of your country's Senate. But I knew at the same time that it must have been a grievous blow for you to sever connections with a country you had chosen to be your permanent home & to be cut off from a community you had served so faithfully & courageously. These & other reminiscences, occupy the long & difficult moments of my present life. Spiritual weapons can be dynamic & often have an impact difficult to appreciate except in the light of actual experience in given situations. In a way they make prisoners free men, turn commoners into monarchs, & dirt into pure gold. To put it quite bluntly, Duggie, it is only my flesh & bones that are shut up behind these tight walls. Otherwise I remain cosmopolitan

---

i   One of the oldest traditional medicine markets in Johannesburg.

ii   The Donaldson Orlando Community Centre was a community space in Soweto that hosted dances, concerts, and boxing matches. It was built by the Donaldson Trust, established in 1936 by Lieutenant Colonel James Donaldson D.S.O. to 'advance the status, improve the conditions and remove the disabilities suffered by the black African population of South Africa; and generally to seek their benefit and betterment'. Nelson Mandela used to box there in the 1940s and 1950s and spent many of his evenings training at the gym with his eldest son, Thembi.

iii   He is possibly referring to a protest at Winburg in the Orange Free State (now called Free State).

iv   The Treason Trial (1956–61) was a result of the apartheid government's attempt to quell the power of the Congress Alliance, a coalition of anti-apartheid organisations. In early-morning raids on 5 December 1956, 156 individuals were arrested and charged with high treason. By the end of the trial in March 1961 all the accused either had the charges withdrawn or, in the case of the last twenty-eight accused (including Mandela), were acquitted.

v   Douglas Lukhele was from Swaziland.

in my outlook, in my thoughts I am as free as a falcon. The anchor of all my dreams is the collective wisdom of mankind as a whole. I am influenced more than ever before by the conviction that social equality is the only basis of human happiness. We & the children of Mswati[i] & Mbandzeni[ii] are linked by a million threads. We have a common history & common aspirations. What is precious to you touches our own hearts. It is in this light that we think of Sept. 6[iii] – an historic event that marks the close of an epoch & the rise of a people whose national pride & consciousness helped them to survive the changes of fortune brought by the imperialist era to our Continent. It is around these issues that my thoughts revolve. They are centred on humans, the ideas for which they strive; on the new world that is emerging, the new generation that declares total war against all forms of cruelty, against any social order that upholds economic privilege for a minority & that condemns us the mass of the population to poverty & disease, illiteracy & the host of evils that accompany a stratified society. Remember me to Ntlabati, Leslie's wife, Andrew & wife, Stanley Lollan,[iv] Maggie Chuene, Regina Twala, Wilson & Gladys[v] if they are still around. I am particularly grateful to Wilson for looking after my son, Kgatho,[vi] after he had been expelled from school for organising a strike, & for all the help he & Gladys gave him. Let everyone keep well & be of good cheer; my fist is firm! Yours very sincerely, Nel

Senator D. Lukhele, Parliament, Lobamba, Swaziland

To Winnie Mandela,[vii] his wife

August 31, 1970

Censors asked me to shorten the letter on the ground that it exceeded 500 words.[viii]

Dade Wethu,[ix]

---

i	Mswati II (c.1820–68), king of Swaziland 1840–68.
ii	Ingwenyama Mbandzeni (1855–1899), the son of Mswati II and Nandzi Nkambule. King of Swaziland, 1875–89.
iii	Swaziland became independent from British rule on 6 September 1968.
iv	A former Treason trialist (for the Treason Trial, see the glossary) who then lived in Swaziland.
v	Friends of Mandela's.
vi	Makgatho Mandela (1950–2005), Mandela's second-born son – see the glossary.
vii	Nomzamo Winifred Madikizela-Mandela (1936–) – see the glossary.
viii	This appears at the bottom of the first page.
ix	Normally written as one word, this means 'sister' in isiXhosa.

Your note of July 2 was shown to me on Aug. 14 – 1 month and 12 days after you wrote it. It was the sweetest of all your letters, surpassing even the very first one of Dec. 20, '62. If there was ever a letter which I desperately wished to keep, read quietly over and over again in the privacy of my cell, it was that one. It was compensation for the precious things your arrest deprived me of – the Xmas, wedding anniversary and birthday cards – the little things about which you never fail to think.[i] But I was told to read it on the spot & was grabbed away as soon as I had reached the last line.

Brig. Aucamp[ii] attempted to justify this arbitrary procedure with the flimsy excuse that in the letter you gave his name for your address instead of your prison. He went on to explain that my letters to you were handled in exactly the same way, & that you were not allowed to keep them. When I pressed him for an explanation he was evasive. I realised there were important issues at stake which necessitate to the making of serious inroads on your right as an awaiting-trial prisoner to write and receive letters & a curtailment of my corresponding privilege. Our letters are subject to a special censorship. The real truth is that the authorities do not want you to share the contents of the letters I write you with your colleagues there, & vice versa. To prevent this they resort to all means, fair or foul. It is possible that communications between us may be whittled down still further, at least for the duration of the trial. As you know, the privilege as far as my normal monthly letters to & from friends & relations practically disappeared with your arrest. I have been trying to communicate with Matlala[iii] since January last[iv] & with Nolusapho[v] since November. On June 19 Brig. Aucamp explained that another department had instructed him not to forward these letters, adding at the same time that he was not in a position to give me reasons for these instructions, but that such instructions were not influenced by the content of the letters. This revelation solved the riddle of the disappearance of most of the letters I wrote over the past 15 months. The matter entails even more serious implications. I should like to be in the position where I could always rely on what officials tell me, but I'm finding it increasingly difficult to square up wishes with experience. Twice during July & early this month, I was informed that your letter had not arrived. I have now established that the letter was actually here when I was being given assurances to the contrary. I was also disgusted to hear from you

---

i   This sentence appears in the margin in Mandela's original letter.
ii   Brigadier Aucamp, commanding officer of Robben Island – see the glossary.
iii Adelaide Tambo (1929–2007), friend, anti-apartheid activist, and wife of Oliver Tambo, Mandela's former law partner and president of the ANC – see the glossary. The Tambos were living in exile in London, United Kingdom.
iv   See his letter of 31 January 1970, page 153.
v   Nolusapho Irene Mkwayi, wife of fellow prisoner Witton Mkwayi (see the glossary).

that Marsh[i] had been applying for a permit to see me and that he had been informed by the prisons department that there were long queues of visitors for me. Nothing could be further from the truth. I had only three visits during the past 8 months – in January, April & June.[ii] It is easy to understand why they are reluctant to allow Marsh to come down. He is in touch with you & a visit from him would not suit Liebenberg[iii] and the S.B.[iv] who wish to cut me off from you. I have had numerous experiences of this nature and each one leaves me sad and disappointed.

Incidentally, I was told that you and your colleagues now enjoy better privileges. I asked for more details & was shocked to learn that even after you had been formally charged you were not allowed a change of clothing & food from outside.[v] How can any honest & intelligent person justify this barbarism? To the best of my knowledge & belief, as an awaiting-trial prisoner you are entitled to clean garments & to food from relations & friends. These are not privileges but legal rights. The tragedy of the whole situation is the blissful ignorance on the part of the officials concerned of the implications of the offensive utterances they often make. I deeply resent to be told of so-called concessions which are invariably made so late in the day & which are so trivial as to cause more harm & bitterness than gratitude and appreciation.

But your marvellous letter! There are moments in the life of every couple that are not easily forgotten & the occasions which you describe so feelingly, I recall with equal affection & I always think of them. The information on Zeni & Zindzi's[vi] manners & tastes interested me much. I should like to know more about them, & it will be a real joy for me when I break through & succeed in establishing contact with them. By the way, the other day I was reading the terrific telegram you sent 2 years ago on the occasion of my 50th birthday. It dawned on me that it will not be long before I become elder, the highest title which even ordinary men automatically acquire by virtue of advanced age. Then it will be quite appropriate for me to purchase some measure of corpulence to bloat my dignity & give due weight to what I say. If obesity were my dream, I would have all the means of fulfilment at my disposal. To be able to swing my own pot belly all I need to do is take things easy & pack my wretched stomach with carbohydrates – mealie-pap

---

i   Marshall Xaba, husband of Niki Xaba, Winnie Mandela's eldest sister (for Niki Xaba, see the glossary).
ii   On 31 January 1970 he had an hour-long visit from his son Makgatho; on 28 April 1970 he was visited by his son Thembi's widow Thoko for thirty minutes, and on 13 June 1970 he received a visit of an hour from Mxolisi, a nephew of Evelyn Mandela's and the brother of Mandela's niece Lulu.
iii   Possibly a policeman from the security branch of the South African Police.
iv   'Security branch' (of the South African Police).
v   Winnie Mandela was held in solitary confinement for ten months, given barely edible food, and interrogated for five days and five nights in a row.
vi   Zenani (1959–) and Zindzi (1960–) Mandela, their daughters – see the glossary.

at sunrise, mealies for lunch & mealie-pap[i] at supper. But the trouble is your letters. They form a solid wall between me and senility. After reading one of them the natural processes seem reversed, & I am never certain whether I'm ageing or rejuvenating. The latter feeling appears dominant.

How I long for Amasi,[ii] thick and sour! You know, darling, there is one respect in which I dwarf all my contemporaries or at least about which I can confidently claim to be second to none – a healthy appetite.[iii] There was a time when I could polish off enormous quantities of food in any order. I could start from pudding backwards & feel just as happy & contented at the end of it all. I well remember the painful remarks of a housewife who was also medical student at the time. She & hubby had invited me for dinner one day. I had built quite some formidable reputation as a meat-eater. After watching my performance for some time & as the heavily laden dishes on the table rapidly vanished one after the other, & I concentrating more especially on the meat, she decided to share with me the benefit of her immense learning. Bluntly she told me I would die of coronary thrombosis probably in my early forties. I was foolish enough to challenge her statement, & tried to support my argument with the sweeping declaration that thrombosis was unknown amongst our forefathers in spite of the fact that they were great meat-eaters; whereupon she promptly produced a huge textbook out of which she read out emphatically & deliberately the relevant passage. It was a galling experience. Almost immediately I felt a million pains in the region of the heart. That tip, raw and tactless as it was, made me cautious, & although I still relished meat I reduced its consumption. But my appetite was still as sharp as ever & I did not lose my colours as hero in this field. I long for the wonderful meals you could prepare so carefully at home, putting your whole heart into it – fresh homemade bread, macaroni with mince meat, egg & cheese, ox tongue & tail, chops, liver & steak, porridge & honey with the high flavour that was always mixed with your dishes. Above all I long for Amasi – the food for which I loved to sharpen my teeth & to stretch out my tummy, the one act that I really enjoyed, that went straight into my blood & into my heart & that produced perfect contentment.[iv] A human being, whatever his colour

---

i   Porridge made from ground corn.
ii   A traditional African fermented milk drink that has a consistency somewhere between yoghurt and cottage cheese and a tart flavour. In *Long Walk to Freedom*, Mandela describes how his fondness for this drink nearly blew his cover when he went underground in 1961. While hiding in the flat of Congress of Democrats member Wolfie Kodesh in the white suburb of Berea, Johannesburg, Mandela would sometimes leave a bottle of milk on the windowsill to ferment. One evening he overheard some young men outside querying in Zulu, 'What is "our milk" doing on that window ledge.' Knowing it seemed odd for a black man to be making *amasi* in a white suburb, Mandela realised he'd aroused suspicion, and moved on the next night (p. 329).
iii   Due to the fermenting process, amasi has a high lactic acid content, giving it many of the benefits of probiotic foods including improved digestion.
iv   Due to the fermenting process, *amasi* has a high lactic acid content, giving it many of the benefits of probiotic foods including improved digestion.

may be, whether he lives under a regime of Christians, Pharisees, hypocrites, heathens, or those who chose to flirt openly with the devil, ought never to be compelled to regard the taking of meals as a mere duty. This is likely to be the case if the diet is poor, monotonous, badly prepared and tasteless. If I can only have Amasi. You remember how we carried a calabash on our way back from Mbongweni.[i] What a lovely trip, Mhlope![ii] I'm sure we will do it again. In the meantime I know that your courage will rise with danger & that you'll fight with all your might. Fight, just as your gallant forefathers did from the Zuurveld to Ngwavuma,[iii] from Nxuba Ntaba Busuku, the Lulu to the land of Nyabela.[iv] Fight as worthy heirs of Mafukuzela,[v] Seme,[vi] Makgatho,[vii] Rubusana[viii] and the constellation of heroes that have defended the birthright of our people. This Sept. 26 will be your second birthday in jail. May the next one find you free. I think of you always, Ngutyana.[ix] I will join battle and do my best when counsel calls. A million kisses and tons and tons of love to you. Devotedly, Dalibunga.

To Makgatho Mandela,[x] his son

August 31, 1970

Heit my Bla,[xi]

I don't know whether I should address you as son, mninawa[xii] or, as we would say in the lingo, *my sweet brigade. The bond of parent & child that has kept us together for 2 decades gradually weakens as you grow full size, whilst that of friendship becomes stronger & deeper. I'm beginning to see in you

---

i   The village of Mbongweni is Winnie Madikizela-Mandela's birthplace in the district of Bizana, Transkei.
ii   One of Winnie Mandela's names.
iii Armed clashes between the Boers and the Xhosa over land and cattle began in the Zuurveld in the 1780s. Ngwavuma is a town in KwaZulu-Natal province close to where assassinated Zulu king Dingane was buried.
iv   King Nyabela fought against the Boers in the Mapoch War from 1982–83. He was defeated and sentenced to life in prison.
v   A praise name for John Langalibalele Dube (1871–1946), the first president of the South African Native National Congress (which later became the ANC).
vi   He is most likely referring to Pixley ka Isaka Seme (c. 1881–1951), South Africa's first black lawyer and a founder and president of the South African Native National Congress (which later became the ANC).
vii Sefako Mapogo Makgatho (1861–1951), second president of the South African Native National Congress (which later became the ANC). Makgatho Mandela (1950–2005), Mandela's second-born son, was named after him.
viii Walter Rubusana (1858–1936), a minister, intellectual, and co-founder of the South African Native National Congress (which later became the ANC) who led a delegation to London, in 1914 to protest the Natives Land Act of 1913, which limited land ownership by Africans.
ix   One of Winnie Mandela's names. She comes from the amaNgutyana clan.
x   Makgatho (Kgatho) Mandela (1950–2005), Mandela's second-born son – see the glossary.
xi   It's a greeting that says something like 'Hello, my brother'. More Tsotsitaal than Afrikaans.
xii 'Young brother' in isiXhosa.

an intimate colleague with whom I can discuss hopes & despairs, setbacks & achievements, one with whom I can chat as an equal; to whom I can open my heart. It is to such a friend that I now write; to you Lewanika, **my bla, as the guys up on the Rand[i] would put it. To you I can write freely & forget about formal or elevated language. You must be frightfully busy; I have not heard from you these past 7 months. I know you'll write as soon as you can. I should have liked to leave you alone, but I long for you and am anxious to hear how you are getting on. What is even more important is that this September 8th you will turn 20 & that alone is sufficient excuse for me to intrude. Naturally, it will not be possible for me or Mummy to be at home to organise a birthday party, give you our warmest love & special wishes, to sit round the family table & feast, sing merrily, tell stories & rejoice with you with a full heart. But we will be thinking of you. The family is very proud of you & watches your progress with real interest. May good things come to you, fortune & the best of health & achievement. I hope you now received the card that contains our greetings & good wishes.

I have been reminiscing a great deal these days & events from the past in which you prominently featured come to mind – active moments in the gymnasium with Jerry Moloi,[ii] Simon Tshabalala***, Joe Motsepe, Joe Mokotedi, Eric Ntsele, Freddie Ngidi, Selby Msimang & other wonderful boys;[iii] the pennies we spent to provide you with the pleasure of swimming at the Huddlestone Pool,[iv] accompanying Nyanya[v] to see the presentation of *King Kong*[vi] at Milner Park, the amount of fish you consumed as we travelled together from Qamata to Johannesburg[vii] & legions of other episodes. I remember all these as if they occurred only the other day. Those were the days when you lived a happy life free of problems & fenced from all hardships & insecurity by parental love. You did not work, grub was galore, clothing was plentiful & you slept good. But some of your playmates those days roamed around completely naked & dirty because their parents were too poor to dress them & to keep them clean. Often you brought them home

---

i   An abbreviated name for the Witwatersrand, a 56-kilometre-long ridge in the Gauteng province of South Africa where Johannesburg is based.

ii   A boxer Mandela trained with.

iii In the 1940s and 1950s, Mandelaa trained at the Donaldson Orlando Community Centre, a community space in Soweto that hosted dances, concerts, and boxing matches.

iv   The only swimming pools for blacks in Johnnesburg was in Orlando West, Soweto. It was established by Father Trevor Huddlestone (1913–98) in the 1950s.

v   Nonyaniso (Nyanya) Madikizela, Winnie Mandela's youngest sister.

vi   An African jazz opera with an all-black cast created by Todd Matshikiza and Pat Williams, *King Kong* is the story of real-life boxing champion Ezekile Dlamini, whose ring name was King Kong, and is set in Sophiatown, a multiracial Johannesburg suburb where blacks could own property freehold. It played from 1959 to record-breaking and multiracial audiences. It moved to London's West End in 1961 for a 200-show run, and launched the international careers of Miriam Makeba and Hugh Masekela among others. Mandela attended the opening night on 2 February 1959 at the Great Hall of the University of the Witwatersrand.

vii Qamata is a small town that was formerly part of the Transkei and before that part of western Thembuland. It is approximately 830 km from Johannesburg by car.

& gave them food. Sometimes you went away with double the amount of swimming fees to help a needy friend. Perhaps then you acted purely out of a child's affection for a friend, & not because you had become consciously aware of the extremes of wealth & poverty that characterised our social life. I hope you're still as keen today to help those who are hard-hit by want as you were then. It's a good thing to help a friend whenever you can; but individual acts of hospitality are not the answer. Those who want to wipe out poverty from the face of the earth must use other weapons, weapons other than kindness. There are millions of poverty-stricken & illiterate people, masses of unemployed people, men & women who are grossly underpaid, who live in dirty & overcrowded dwellings, who feed mainly on dikgobe, papa, mngqusho , motoho & marhewu,[i] whose children never drink milk & who are exposed to all sorts of disease.

This is not a problem that can be handled by individual acts of hospitality. The man who attempted to use his own possessions to help all the needy would be permanently ruined & in due course himself live on alms. Experience shows that this problem can be effectively tackled only by a disciplined body of persons, who are inspired by the same ideas & united in a common cause. Most of us never had the opportunities which are enjoyed by the present youth – a wide variety of progressive literature dealing with man's struggle to master nature's physical resources; the immortal classics that stress, on the one hand, the dependence of human beings upon one another, & on the other hand, the social conflicts that flow from the distinctive interests that split society into various strata. I was almost 35 when I began reading works of this nature systematically, & what a difference it brought to my own outlook! You appear more militant & a better democrat than I was at your age & hope you'll be selective in your readings. We shall discuss the letter more fully on your next visit. In the meantime, I hope you'll enjoy "And Quiet Flows the Don" by Sholokhov.[ii] Did Tellie[iii] get her letter of March 6, 1970?[iv] I also wrote you 31.3.70[v] & to Maki[vi] on 1.5.70.[vii] Once again, hearty congrats on your 20th birthday. Keep den 8115 safe & clean.

---

i	Traditional South African food. *Dikgobe* is cooked corn. *Papa* is a porridge made from maize meal. *Umngusho* is samp and sugar beans. *Motoho* is a fermented sorghum meal porridge. *Marhewu* is a fermented drink made of maize meal and sugar.
ii	An award-winning novel by Russian author Mikhail Aleksandrovich Sholokhov's which came out in four volumes between 1928 and 1940 and which deals with the lives of Don Cossacks during the Russian Revolution and civil war. Sholokhov won the Nobel Prize in Literature for the work in 1965. At some stage during his imprisonment, Mandela was allowed to order book (see, for instance, his letter to Vanguard Booksellers, 26 September 1971, page 242).
iii	Telia (Telli or Tellie) Mtirara, a relative of Mandela's.
iv	See his letter on page 159.
v	See his letter on page 161.
vi	Makaziwe Mandela (1954–), Mandela's eldest daughter – see the glossary.
vii	See his letter on page 166.

14th September 1970.

The Minister of Justice,
Union Buildings
Pretoria.

My wife was detained on May 12, 1970 and has been in custody ever since

I last saw her in December 1968. Twice after her arrest, I asked the Commissioner of Prisons to make arrangements for me to meet her. The second application was made after I had received information that she had been hospitalised as a result of deteriorating health. Both applications were refused. I now make a special appeal to you to approve the request

These are important and urgent domestic problems which we cannot properly solve without coming together. In examining the matter you will bear in mind that there is nothing in the law or administration of justice to preclude me as husband from having consultations with her while she is facing trial, political or otherwise. On the contrary it is my duty to give her all the help that she requires. The fact that I am a prisoner ought not of itself to deprive me of the opportunity of honouring the obligations that I owe her. You will also bear in mind that she has been in custody for more than 15 months, 10 of which were spent in solitary confinement — a frightful experience which must have been primarily responsible for the worsening of her condition. I sincerely believe that the pleasure she would derive from a meeting between us would induce a speedy and complete recovery, and put her in a better position to stand trial

In considering both applications, General Steyn failed to show that high sense of values and human feeling that I have come to associate with him as an individual during the last 8 years. I am willing to hope that you, as executive head of the Department of Justice, are well instructed in the principles of rightness and equity not to turn a deaf ear to this appeal, and that the whole bent of your mind will be used to uphold those virtues that your office symbolises.

NRMandela.
NELSON MANDELA: 466/64

A letter to the minister of justice, 14 September 1970, see opposite and overleaf.

Affectionately,
Tata[i]

Makgatho Lewanika Mandela, 8115, Orlando West, Johannesburg.

*Pronounced meyi[ii]
**Pronounced meyi
***He was brutally tortured by the Security Police in 1964, resulting in the breaking down of his health.

To the minister of justice[iii]

14th September 1970

The Minister of Justice,
Union Buildings
Pretoria.

My wife was detained on May 12, 1969 and has been in custody ever since.

I last saw her in December 1968. Twice after her arrest, I asked the Commissioner of Prisons[iv] to make arrangements for me to meet her. The second application was made after I had received information that she had been hospitalised as a result of deteriorating health. Both applications were refused. I now make a special appeal to you to approve the request.

There are important and urgent domestic problems which we cannot properly solve without coming together. In examining the matter you will bear in mind that there is nothing in the law or administration of justice to preclude me as husband from having consultations with her while she is facing trial, political or otherwise. On the contrary, it is my duty to give her all the help that she requires. The fact that I am a prisoner ought not of itself to deprive me of the opportunity of honouring the obligations that I owe her. You will also bear in mind that she has been in custody for more than 15 months, 10 of which were spent in solitary confinement – a frightful experience which must have been primarily responsible for the worsening of her condition.[v] I sincerely believe that the pleasure she would derive from

---

i   'Father' in isiXhosa.
ii   He is providing the Afrikaans pronounciation of the word 'my', which has the same meaning as it does in English.
iii   South Africa's minister of justice from 1966 to 1974 was Petrus Cornelius Pelser.
iv   General Steyn.
v   Winnie Mandela had a heart condition

a meeting between us would induce a speedy and complete recovery, and put her in a better position to stand trial.

In considering both applications, General Steyn failed to show that high sense of values and human feeling that I have come to associate with him as an individual during the last 8 years. I am willing to hope that you, as executive head of the Department of Justice, are well instructed in the principle of rightness and equity not to turn a deaf ear to this appeal, and that the whole bent of your mind will be used to uphold those virtues that your office symbolises.

[Signed NR Mandela]
Nelson Mandela: 466/64

◇◇◇◇◇◇◇◇◇

Winnie Mandela was released on 15 September 1970 after 491 days in custody. Two weeks later her banning orders – effective house arrest – were renewed for another five years. She was forced to remain at home from 6 p.m. to 6 a.m. on weekdays and from 2 p.m. to 6 a.m. on weekends. She was not allowed to have visitors other than her own children. She applied for permission to visit her husband in prison whom she had last visited on 28 September 1968 for one hour. The local magistrate rejected her application. She eventually got permission and was allowed to see him on 7 November 1970 for thirty minutes.

To Winnie Mandela,[i] his wife

October 1, 1970

My Darling,

A respite at last! I received your unexpected telegram in which you informed me of your release. I'm sure you were as surprised to be acquitted as I was when I received the wonderful news. I should have liked to reply also by telegram immediately upon receiving yours, but these conveniences are not available for me even on so important an occasion as an acquittal on a capital charge. I had to wait for 2 weeks before I could send you my warmest congratulations for serving 491,[ii] & still emerge the lively girl you are, & in high spirits.

---

i   Nomzamo Winifred Madikizela-Mandela (1936–) – see the glossary.
ii   Winnie Mandela had served 491 days in prison.

To you & your determined friends I say welcome back! Were I at home when you returned I should have stolen a white goat from a rich man, slaughtered it & given you ivanya ne ntloya[i] to down it. Only in this way can a beggar like myself fete and honour his heroes.

You are back & in accordance with my promise I bid good-bye to "dadewethu"[ii] & return to "My darling", to you dear Mhlope.[iii] This is the salutation I have used since Aug. '62,[iv] & I regretted it much when I had to abandon it.

Now that you are back I long for you even much more than I did when you were in. I fought hard to see you in the knowledge that such a meeting would do you a lot of good. But I did so also to save myself from catastrophe. There were times when I felt & responded like one in whom something had suddenly snapped. I could hardly concentrate & the picture of you rotting away in some dingy & isolated apartment with nothing to read & nobody to whom you might talk was unbearable. Your release has relieved me, but it has worsened my pining. I can no longer wait. I want to see you badly; it is now my turn to shrink to a size less than that of Zeni.[v] When will you come? How I wish I could have a contact visit, where I could hug you, feel the warmth of your blood, smile straight into your eyes, chat to you normally, without having to shout before I could be heard, as happens at present. I long to see you in a peaceful & decent atmosphere, as a man & wife should when discussing tender domestic affairs after a separation of almost 2 years. But those who bear the cross ought never to squeal if the going is uphill, & I shan't. How is your health? Have you seen Zeni & Zindzi?[vi] What news will you bring me?

Incidentally, several hours before I received your exciting message I had handed in a letter addressed to the Minister of Justice asking him to allow us to meet. I imagine me still fighting long after the battle had been won. If your plea had been dismissed by the Court & my application to the Minister refused, I would probably have appealed to a bone-thrower, or beseeched the Divinitus or turned to Marx. Luckily I did not have to choose amongst these alternatives. I was sorry to learn that Ramotse[vii] remained

---

i   A traditional southern African welcome drink that is served hot to guests. It is made from the sediment of a
     traditional maize and sorghum beer, called *umqombothi*, mixed with *intloya*, the watery part of *amasi* (sour milk
     drink).
ii   'Sister' in isiXhosa. He was making a point of referring to her in this way because he was treating her as a comrade
     in the struggle against apartheid.
iii One of Winnie Mandela's names.
iv   Mandela was arrested on 5 August 1962.
v   Zenani Mandela (1959–), Mandela's middle daughter.
vi   Zenani Mandela (1959–) and Zindziswa Mandela (1960–), Mandela's middle and youngest daughters – see the
     glossary. The girls were at boarding school in Swaziland.
vii MK activist Benjamin Ramotse was seriously injured in December 1961 in one of the first MK explosions that
     killed fellow combatant Petrus Molefi. Ramotse was arrested and put on trial but escaped the country while on
     bail. In his book *No Neutral Ground*, Joel Carson describes how Ramotse 'conducted guerrilla activities on the

behind. May he also have luck when the case goes to trial.

You have heard by now that our friend Mr Denis Healey,[i] accompanied by the British ambassador, saw me on Sept. 19. I was pleased to see him again. He told me that you had paid a visit to Helen[ii] & Shanti.[iii] He also told me that that evening you would attend a ball given in his honour. I was very happy to hear this because after the ugly experience you had recently, you need relaxation & a lot of fun. Do enjoy yourself but beware of sprees if you can. It is a strange coincidence that you should have chosen to visit the Josephs and the Naidoos at the moment when they were very much in my thoughts. I wish you had met Shanti's father, Naran,[iv] a courageous person who was widely known for his dedication & simplicity. We were arrested together in June 1950 & detained for some hours before we were released. When we reached their Doornfontein[v] residence we were hungry & tired. Amma,[vi] wearing that free and easy smile of hers, presented us with a meal of crab & rice. It was my first time to see these creatures cooked, & the mere sight of them made me sick & everything inside me – my gizzard included – began protesting violently. You know, darling, that I never give up easily on such matters. I tried to be as graceful as was possible in the circumstances & even dared to chew 1 leg or 2. It was a delicate adventure. Thereafter I became much attached to the Naidoos and enjoyed crabs very much. Shanti was then a mere nipper. I was to see her grow into a fearless girl who followed closely on the father's footsteps. But I never suspected that she had such strength of character, pluck & endurance.

As for our friend, Helen,[vii] I believe she is one woman who would continue to swing the sword even beyond the grave; that is if death allows her victims freedom to engage in these posthumous activities. With her background, qualifications, social status & opportunities she hardly had any reason to ruin her brilliant career by following the course she chose.[viii] She had the franchise, could belong to any of the respectable parties and express herself fully & freely on any public questions. Only a highly principled per-

---

borders of South Africa for the next eight years when he was kidnapped from Botswana and brought through Rhodesia to South Africa to be tried finally in 1970'. (London: Davis-Poynter Ltd, 1973, p. 117).

i   Denis Healey (1917–2015), British Labour Party politician who Mandela first met during his short visit to London in 1962. Later Healey visited him in prison.

ii   Helen Joseph (1905–92), teacher, social worker, and anti-apartheid and women's rights activist – see the glossary.

iii Shanti Naidoo (1935–), anti-apartheid activisit – see the glossary. With another activist, Nondwe Mankahla, she refused to testify against Winnie Mandela and was sentenced to two months in prison. Shandi Naidoo's brother Indres Naidoo (1936–2016) served a long prison sentence on Robben Island – see the glossary.

iv   Thambi Naransamy 'Naran' Naidoo (1901–53), also known as Roy, was the son of an early collaborator of Mahatma Gandhi.

v   A suburb in downtown Johannesburg.

vi   Shanti Naidoo's mother.

vii Helen Joseph.

viii British-born teacher Helen Joseph worked in the Women's Auxillary Air Force during World War II and then went to South Africa to work as a social worker. She became aware of the reality of life under apartheid and became politically involved.

son, completely dedicated to the ideals of freedom would make this fatal decision. I have the highest regard for her. She certainly will be one of the very first persons I shall visit when I return, just as you & Nomvula[i] did the day after your release. She can dish out & take punches, & I'm sure she will still be slogging it out when the people of S.A of all races lay her remains to eternal rest. Give her, Amma & Shanti my warmest love. . . .

To come back to you, darling, your friends have impressed me tremendously. I was not the least surprised by David, Elliot, Mqwati, Rita, Douglas, Thoko, Martha, & Livingstone. One day I shall have the opportunity of hearing something on Samson, Jackson, Nomvula, Paulos, Joseph, David Dalton, Victor, George, Joseph Chamberlain, Simon, Owen & Samuel & Peter.[ii] Fondest regards to them all.

I'm proud of you darling & you are more to me than the world. I expect wonderful stories from you when I return home. One day we will pack up. Then we will be free from the troubles of this world. Even then there will be hope for us. I do hope we will be allowed to sleep side by side as we have done in the privacy of our bedroom during the 4 years of our married life that we managed to live together. A million kisses & tons & tons of love.

Devotedly, Dalibunga

Nkosikazi Nobandla Mandela, 8115, Orlando West, J.H.B.

―――――――――   ―――――――――

To the minister of justice[iii]

[Translated from Afrikaans][iv]

19 November, 1970

The Honourable Minister of Justice
Pretoria

---

i   Joyce Nomafa Sikhakane (1943–), journalist and anti-apartheid activist – see the glossary.
ii   Winnie Mandela's comrades who had been charged with her.
iii South Africa's minister of justice from 1966 to 1974 was Petrus Cornelius Pelser.
iv   It is likely that Mandela was writing to the minister of jusice in Afrikaans in a bid to appeal to the oppressor. In conversation with Richard Stengel in 1992, he explained that he studied Afrikaans in prison because 'as a public figure you do want to know the two main languages, official languages of the country and Afrikaans is an important language, spoken by the majority of the white population in the country and by the majority of the coloured people, and it's a disadvantage not to know it. Because when you speak [a] language, English . . . many people understand you, including Afrikaners, but when you speak Afrikaans, you know you get, go straight to their hearts. So it's important to know the language. Especially in prison, it was very important.' (NM in conversation with Richard Stengel, 9 December 1992, CD 5, Nelson Mandela Foundation Johannesburg.)

I should greatly appreciate it if you would grant me an interview at a time convenient to you to discuss the following matters:

1. My wife's health condition [i]
   I have been informed that my wife suffered a heart attack on November 8, 1970. Up to the time of writing I have not received particulars about the gravity of her illness, and I do not know in which hospital she is being treated. I should like to visit her, hoping that the visit will cheer her up and hasten her recovery.

2. Our domestic affairs
   You have afforded me a thirty-minute visit on November 7. Before that I saw her on December 21, 1968, and the duration of the first-mentioned visit was insufficient for us to properly discuss our domestic affairs. In this regard I should want to assure you that this request is not an effort to misuse a privilege I enjoyed twelve days ago. Under the circumstances a visit of two hours would not be unreasonable. Please take into account that her heart condition will preclude her from visiting me in the near future.

3. The implications of new charges against my wife
   I have been informed that my wife, along with her sister Nonyaniso Madikizela, have been charged in the Johannesburg magistrate's court with contravening the terms of the Suppression of Communism Act, No 44 of 1950,[ii] as amended. The charge compels her to spend twelve hours every night all by herself. I fear the exertion exacted by this kind of situation, as well as the additional court case against her by the state, may exacerbate her condition. Of course, the case is sub judice[iii] and I shall not make any requests in this regard.

In this communication I am mentioning only the main points that would form the basis of the interview, and I have not attempted a comprehensive exposition of the arguments that could support me in addressing the above issues.
NELSON MANDELA 466/64

---

i   The underlining in this letter was likely done by Mandela.
ii   An Act passed on 26 June 1950, in which the state banned the South African Communist Party and any activities it deemed communist, defining 'communism' in such broad terms that anyone protesting against apartheid would be in breach of the Act.
iii Meaning that a case is still under judicial consideration and unable to be discussed publicly elsewhere.

To Sanna Teyise,[i] proprietor of the Blue Lagoon restaurant

[Translated from Afrikaans]

December 1, 1970

My dearest sister,

I have wondered many times if the Blue Lagoon[ii] is still standing strong at 10 Von Wieilligh or whether it is lying somewhere abandoned and alone. In any other location it will never be the same place we once knew. Elsewhere it will be but a shadow of the bustling meeting place that kept us together the past 25 years.

Your Lagoon was not simply a name where one could order a delicious meal. It was an institution with a rich history; with historical links to Motortown, the Bantu and Wemmer sports facilities, the BMSC,[iii] Dorkay House,[iv] the Rio[v] and Uno[vi] bioscopes, Mai-Mai,[vii] Mayibuye Restaurant, and all the activities that took place in and around these facilities. Even Charlie's dilapidated shop across from Melrose Street and Kruger's butchery constituted important parts of your popular café.

Your café was the institution around which people's lives turned. Well known people, including Seretse Khama,[viii] Oliver Tambo,[ix] Eduardo Mondlane,[x] Joshua Nkomo,[xi] repeatedly dined and relaxed there. The Motieloas, Twalas, Moikangoas, Nongawuzas, Xakanas, Malis, Hermanus, Leleti, Dlambulo, Mzondeki, Njongwe Magoa, Magagane [and] Zibi were at one time or another intimate members of the Lagoon[xii] family, and they derived much benefit from their interaction with you, as you did from your friendship with them. As far as my association with the café is concerned I should at this stage rather not say anything. I shall never be in a position to compensate you for what you had done for and meant to me.

In 1952 I hosted an important American professor in your café. And,

---

i   Elsewhere he refers to her surname as 'Thys' rather than Teyise.
ii   A restaurant in Johannesburg frequented by Mandela when he lived there.
iii The Bantu Men's Social Centre (BMSC), founded in Sophiatown, Johannesburg, in 1924, was an important cultural, social, and political meeting place for black South Africans. Its facilities included a gym and a library, and it hosted boxing matches, political meetings, and dances. Mandela and four others founded the ANC Youth League there in 1944.
iv   Home to the African Music and Drama Association in the 1950s and a rehearsal space used by prominent musicians such as Hugh Masekela and Miriam Makeba.
v   Rio Cinema in Johannesburg hosted a number of boxing matches in the 1950s.
vi   Uno Cinema, Johannesburg.
vii One of the oldest traditional medicine markets in Johannesburg.
viii Seretse Khama (1921–80) became the first president of an independent Botswana in 1966.
ix   Oliver Reginald Tambo (1917–93), friend, former law partner, and the president of the ANC – see the glossary.
x   Eduardo Mondlane (1920–69) was the founding president of the Mozambique Liberation Front (FRELIMO), which was established in 1962.
xi   Joshua Nkomo (1917–99) was the founder and leader of the Zimbabwe African People's Union (ZAPU), which was established in 1961.
xii These are all friends and associates who frequented the Blue Lagoon restaurant.

from the same country, there was the social worker who was your regular customer for about three months. My memory is not as good as it used to be but was it not in the same year that a prominent British parliamentarian ate at your place? Perhaps the years 1952–53 also constituted the period in which you made your single most important contribution to the progress and happiness of our nation. Twice a day, and over a period of six months, you fed almost 100 of our colleagues at the general hospital – out of your own pocket![i] With this the Lagoon fully answered its calling and so it created a powerful comradeship among us all. I have now mentioned your contribution to our welfare. See, we did not forget. If you think that, you are wrong, my girl. We were of the opinion that the meals you served were priced too low, and some of us advised you to increase your prices. But you bluntly refused to do it. The reasons you proffered proved to us you have insight and empathy and a chord of love that bound you to your fellow human beings. However, the magnitude of your sacrifice must be measured against the fact that your landlord exploited your legal dilemma to unreasonably hike the rent. Your restaurant holds and exudes both cosmopolitan and parochial characteristics. Sometimes it felt as if I were in Griquatown, in the heart of the Postmasburg district[ii] where I saw the gathered Thys family[iii] and relatives: Tukkie, JoJo, Nomyo,[iv] Nomanto, Platman, Phinatjie, Tooi, Lilly, Andries, Bella, Bella's sister and her brother the pastor,[v] Nontombi,[vi] Klaasie, Maye, Ouboetie and Ma, Aletta, Esther[vii] and Ma, Willem and the lost daughter, Qadi.[viii] Perhaps by now Qadi had become a nursing sister or a matron. Where is she stationed? And what about my cute brother, JoJo, who never had any difficulty licking the last drops from the bottom of a bottle! Do you still remember how Phinatjie's good looks once saved her when we had to appear before the Classification Board?[ix] It was a sheer pleasure for me to help your family avert what could have been a catastrophe. Does Phinatjie and her boss* still live in Pretoria? I hope her back problems have eased.

I will never forget how Bella's brother once put an end to my arguments when I had the audacity to challenge his authority in religious matters.

Sanna, I wish I could discuss the present or future with you. What man

---

i	The Blue Lagoon was known to have provided meals free of charge at times, and it's possible this was during the the Defiance Campaign of 1952.
ii	In the Cape Province.
iii	Sanna Teyise's family – they also used the surname Thys.
iv	Nomvuyo Vuyiswa 'Tiny' Nokwe (1928–2008), the wife of Advocate Duma Nokwe (see the glossary for Duma Nokwe). In an email communication with Sahm Venter on 11 December 2017, Nomvuyo Nokwe writes, 'I believe this is a coded reference to our mother Vuyiswa Nokwe, nee Malangabi (1929-2008)'.
v	Friends.
vi	Friend.
vii	Esther Maleka, a ANC activist who worked for the organisation underground.
viii	Friends and relatives of the Thys family.
ix	He is most likely referring to the Population Registration Act of 1950 where every South African citizen was expected to go before a classification board to be classified according to their racial characteristics.

with deep yearnings and ambition wants to live in the past? But I have no choice in this particular matter. In order to discuss viable issues one must have authentic sources of information and enjoy greater freedom to express himself. I have neither one nor the other. Do you now understand why I must unearth the skeletons of beloved ones now late, and why I'm talking about things that occurred a long time ago? I wish I could freely discuss the future with you! I miss you and your family, and now that I've written this letter, I am sure the yearning will recede.

I do not have the requisite training to understand the ways of man, and prefer to leave matters of the human soul to the pious Tukkie. But I can talk with authority about my own feelings, and I say: I'm as fresh as the morning dew and quick as the wind. My very being spills over with hope and I have no doubt that the good old days we spent together will return, maybe during this decade, within five years or even next year. Be of firm belief, my friend, and have courage. An industrious and optimistic girl such as yourself has no reason whatsoever to despair. When life tries you on all sides, remember you have many friends who admire and congratulate you.

Affectionately
Boet Nel[i]

*Naturally her husband

To: Sanna Teyise, c/o Mrs Nobandla Mandela, 8115, Orlando West, Johannesburg.

––––––––––

To the commanding officer, Robben Island

24th December 1970

The Commanding Officer,
Robben Island.

Attention: Medical Officer

My medical report will show that my blood-pressure has for several months remained dangerously high, and I frequently complained of headaches and dizziness.

---

i   'Brother Nel' in Afrikaans.

I have been put on a daily treatment of 6 improved Rantrax (50) and 6 Aldimets, the effect of which is to make me tired and sleepy during working hours. On several occasions when I go out with the span,[i] I have to ask the warder-in-charge, much against my will, to allow me to lie down both in the fore- and afternoon. To the best of my knowledge and belief, the pressure has not risen beyond the level it reached on 14 September 1970. On the contrary, there has been a slight improvement and even the headaches are abating.

I contribute the improvement to the treatment and the complete rest that I am having. I have explained my position fully and frankly to the Medical Officer, Chief Warder Fourie and the warder-in-charge of the Section. Some time back I was ordered to remain inside for a specified period, and when that period lapsed, I returned to work but fared no better. The headaches and dizziness reappeared as well as the feelings of fatigue and drowsiness. I stayed inside and immediately reported to Dr Going who promised to go into the matter.

I am restating the position because I consider it proper that you should be fully aware of my health condition, and I trust that in examining the position you will be influenced solely by health and humanitarian considerations.

[Signed NRMandela]
NELSON MANDELA: 466/64

<hr>

To the commanding officer, Robben Island

24 December 1970

The Commanding Officer
Robben Island

Attention: Medical Officer

I should be pleased if you would kindly reconsider your decision rejecting my application for leave to order 4lbs of honey per month on health grounds.

I have been shown your comment on my previous application in which you stated that I did not need the honey requested. You will recall that I had

---

i   Afrikaans word for 'team' that was used in prison.

earlier shown you a pamphlet of the S.A.B.C.[i] which contained an address by Dr McGill. I drew your attention to some paragraph but missed the crucial statement contained in page 5 thereof which I am anxious that you should read.

A perusal of my medical report will reveal that although I have been put on treatment with a higher potency, and although the rising of the pressure has been halted, it is far from being normalised. In reexamining the whole question, I ask you to bear in mind that applications of this nature raise not only medical issues, but also those of psychology, etc. I trust that you will give me an opportunity to discuss the matter with you again if you consider this second application inadequate for the purpose of inducing you to reconsider your decision.

[Signed NRMandela]
NELSON MANDELA

[Handwritten note]
O.C.[ii]

The treatment he is on is the best that modern medicine can provide. Honey is not a therapeutic substance for hypertension. I therefore refer you to my previous comment on this matter. I am prepared to see Mandela at any time to recheck his blood pressure.

To Winnie Mandela,[iii] his wife

Dec. 28, 1970

My Darling,

You always speak affectionately of Ma of Bizana,[iv] the way a devoted daughter should feel about her mum. You are perfectly justified in your attitude for she has mothered you & helped in your upbringing. What she did for us during the wedding & when I returned to fetch Nyanya justifies the love &

---

i   South African Broadcasting Corporation.
ii   Officer Commanding.
iii   Nomzamo Winifred Madikizela-Mandela (1936–) – see the glossary.
iv   Nophikela Hilda Madikizela, Winnie Mandela's stepmother.

respect you have for her. You speak in similar vein of Sibali Manyawuza[i] & my own experiences with her confirm your impression.

You'll probably recall many moments in your childhood when you doubted whether they were sufficiently warm to you, when you felt you needed more love, a bit of appreciation for what you had done or a little present. That makes no difference whatsoever. We have much evidence now that you are always in their thoughts. There was much more in their recent trip to Pretoria than mere interest in a trial in which their daughter was involved, & the effect of their presence there was evident in the punchy letter you wrote me soon thereafter. I'm sorry they do not seem to be getting my letters. I'm more indebted to them than umkhwenyana[ii] normally is.

Many times I have speculated on what would have happened if the daughter of Mzaidume[iii] still lived. I'm inclined to think that our personal problems would have been much less & your struggle to stay alive not so desperate. She would virtually be living with you just as the daughter of Nkedama[iv] did on & off, & would probably have organised many visits & presents for Zeni & Zindzi,[v] to make them forget our absence. Many a time I've pondered over the host of difficulties a girl experiences who grows [up] without a mother. I'm able to appreciate this problem because I was about 10[vi] when my own Dad died. Chief Jongintaba, the Regent of the tribe,[vii] supported a large family in addition to his heavy tribal responsibilities. He looked after me with the diligence of a natural father & gave me opportunities in life which my own Dad would have found difficult to provide. Yet with all the love & attention the chief gave me, there were moments when I longed for my own father & even felt as an orphan would. You probably experienced a similar feeling. Ma-Radebe[viii] should have been alive today. I would have someone to take a bit, just a wee bit, of the damaging load from my high pressured heart. We would have grieved together & could have burdened her with much that I hesitate to confide even with our dear Niki.[ix] At times I see in Zami[x] the reactions of one who missed that intensive & precious training, care & love which a mother can give a beloved daughter & make childhood really delightful, something which one may recall with fond memories.

---

i   Sibali Nyawuza. Mandela confused his clan name and referred to him as Manyawuza. *Sibali* means 'brother-in-law' in isiXhosa.

ii   'Son-in-law' in isiXhosa.

iii   Winnie Mandela's mother, Nomthansanqa Gertrude Mzaidume, who died when she was ten years old.

iv   It is likely that Mandela is referring to his mother Nosekeni Fanny whose father was called Nkedama.

v   Zenani (1959–) and Zindzi (1960–) Mandela, their daughters – see the glossary.

vi   His father died in 1930, the year in which he turned twelve.

vii Chief Jongintaba Dalindyebo (d. 1942), the chief and regent of the Thembu people. He became Mandela's guardian following his father's death – see the glossary.

viii Winnie Mandela's mother, Nomthansanqa Gertrude Mzaidume.

ix   Niki Xaba (1932–1985), Winnie Mandela's eldest sister – see the glossary.

x   One of Winnie Mandela's names.

You concentrate all your attention on me & spend little time on yourself. Even now, Mhlope,[i] you're not showing the caution & vigilance that is required. You owe us a duty to be extraordinarily alert – a duty to those who love & think of you all the time; those to whom you are a source of inspiration & pride: Ama-Dlomo[ii] & Amagutyana,[iii] Kgatho,[iv] sisters, & nieces, Nyanya,[v] Tellie,[vi] Nomvula[vii] & many others, & above all to yourself & me.

Consultation, full & frank as is possible under the circumstances, has become vital, even on matters that at other times we should consider relatively unimportant. You have not grasped this fact at all. You never once stop to think that even your own shadow may tell tales, leave clear footmarks & give you away. Be careful darling, & give us, you & me, the chance to attend to those urgent matters which we both have had to neglect altogether these last 6 years. I have noted & fully accepted what you intended to tell me in your Nov. 30th tattered letter. I have been happier & ever since my hopes have risen.

I shall be pleased to hear in your next letter that you continue to advise our cousin honestly & fearlessly all along the line. Let her be realistic, speak from the heart & not merely with her tongue, trim her sails to the wind, live simply & resist her love of entourage. Will you? She is a terrific girl & needs your help; you, who can act as her mirror. You cross-examined me very closely on my health on Dec. 12. I tried everything to put you off but you would not let go. It was clear you were acting on definite information. Who has been spying for you? Spies are no good even when they be honest men. Don't be disturbed, darling, I hope to outlive Methuselah & be with you long after you have reached the menopause, when not even Zeni & Zindzi will fuss over you, when all the gloss you now have will be gone & your body, your lovely face included, will be all wrinkles, skin as tough as that of a rhinoceros. I shall nurse and look after you in every way. Now & again we shall visit the farm, walk around with the fingers of my left hand dovetailing with those of your right, watching you dart off to pluck some beautiful wild flowers, just as you did on Sunday March 10.[viii] You were dazzling in that black white-spotted nylon dress. Every day will always be March 10 for me. What does age or [a] little blood pressure matter to us. Nothing! Are you happy now? Say yes; that's what I like of you! I've always known you to be a good girl. Keep just there.

---

i   One of Winnie Mandela's names.
ii   Dlomo is one of the 'houses' that Mandela is descended from.
iii   Winnie Mandela was born into the AmaNgutyana clan.
iv   Makgatho Mandela (1950–2005), Mandela's second-born son – see the glossary.
v   Nonyaniso (Nyanya) Madikizela, Winnie Mandela's youngest sister.
vi   Telia (Telli or Tellie) Mtirara, a relative of Mandela's.
vii   Joyce Nomafa Sikhakhane (1943–), journalist and anti-apartheid activist – see the glossary.
viii   Nelson and Winnie Mandela's first date was on 10 March 1957.

But you are a witch! Always casting spells on your man; ubethelela izik-honkwana[i] & taking no chances. Are you so unsure of yourself? Have you forgotten what we have gone through together, & the remark with which I greeted you on Nov. 7? You could have worn your Ncora[ii] Mazawatee goggles[iii] that you once used for reading purposes & I would have adored you just as passionately. Why did you give me that enchanting photo? It has made me homesick.

Fancy dragging poor Nyanya into this affair. How is it possible for the 2 of you to be so confident, free, jovial and pretty in spite of everything that is happening all around you. Nyanya has become a fine lady. Tell me something about her fiancé, first name, occupation & domicile. I wrote to Nali[iv] in Dec. 68, rewrote through Niki on 28/7/69. Did they not receive it? What do you hear about them?

I've suspended Afrikaans studies till I complete law. What are you doing?

Thanks for the funds.

I'm holding thumbs for January 15. Be in the best of health & spirit!

Miss you very much. Looking forward to seeing you again. Meanwhile write to me every month long & sweet letters. What rapture your visits & letters bring.

Tons & tons of love & a million kisses. Devotedly, Dalibunga.

Nkosikazi Nobandla Mandela, 8115 Orlando West, Johannesburg

∞∞∞∞∞∞

Joyce Sikhakhane (1943–) was a journalist and anti-apartheid activist who was put on trial with Winnie Mandela and twenty others in 1969. She never received this letter and only heard of it when she was contacted in 2008 by Ruth Muller, then a staff member at the Nelson Mandela Foundation. Sikhakhane hadn't actually met Mandela before he went to prison but had played with the children from his first marriage, as she lived close to them.

Sikhakhane was engaged to marry Samson 'John' Fadana a relative of Mandela's. When they went to the Magistrates Court to be married the security police threatened to charge her as she was breaking her banning orders to do

---

i   He is expressing in isiXhosa how in love and happy he is with her.
ii   For her second practical social work assignment, Winnie Mandela went to the Ncora Rural Centre in the District of Tsolo.
iii   He is referring to round spectacles Winnie Mandela wore at the time, which resembled the spectacles worn by an old lady and a child in an advertisement for Mazawattee tea.
iv   Nali Nancy Vutela, Winnie Mandela's sister.

this. They then 'endorsed' Fadana out of Johannesburg and sent him back to the Transkei. Under apartheid 'influx control' laws, an African person had to have permission to live in a city and authorities had the power to remove anyone from the city by 'endorsing' them out. Fadana later married someone else in the Transkei.

Mandela must have heard that Sikhakhane was a journalist, which is why he refers to a string of well-known journalists in this letter, mostly from the influential Drum *magazine which launched the careers of many black journalists and represented a new black urban identity in contrast to the apartheid regime's tribal and pastoral stereotyping of black people. Sikhakhane had started working as a journalist in December 1963, soon after matriculating.*

<hr>

To Joyce Sikhakhane,[i] comrade of Winnie Mandela

PLEASE SEE POSTSCRIPT BEFORE YOU READ THIS LETTER

January 1, 1971

My dear Nomvula,[ii]

Re roba matsoho[iii] for you & John![iv] Is it true? Can you two really do this to me, take such momentous decisions without even as much as giving me a hint? I must have missed heaps of meat & pudding at the engagement party. To your wedding I would have been accepted just as I am, without having to sport a frock coat, starched shirt & top hat. What is even more important to me, your wedding would have been one occasion in which I could have shined at last. I rehearse daily on a penny whistle; everyone around here calls it that though it cost R2.00. I'm still on the d.t.l.-stage but with more practice I could have tried Handel's *Messiah* on it on the great day.

You have guts in the proper sense of the term. Was it love, love of adventure or both that made you take such a gamble? There is no insurance house anywhere in the country that could secure you against such an obvious risk. One as hopeful & as ambitious as John is will most probably not allow the sweet pleasures of an ordered family life to interfere with his

<hr>

i   Joyce Nomafa Sikhakhane (1943–), journalist and anti-apartheid activist – see the glossary.
ii   Mandela calls her Nomvula as she was engaged to his relative John Fadana.
iii   Meaning 'applause' in Sesotho.
iv   Samson John Fadana whom Mandela had been in prison with.

pattern of thoughts and doings. Besides, even at a distance, association with a Nomvula would tend to keep him on the ball most of the time. What do you expect the poor fellow to do when you are actually entrenched right inside his mansion, your ears on the ground and feeling the pulse as usual, now questioning this, condemning that & demanding action all along the line? He will run wild.

They tell the story of a woman (I believe she lives in your street)[i] who has terrific reserves of will-power & initiative, & who made a deal as fatal & remarkably similar to the one you are now contemplating. The going was uphill right from the beginning. Hardly 4 months after the wedding bells had tolled, some hue & cry on the Reef[ii] forced her to live for a fortnight with the matron at Ameshoff St. Yena nowakwakhe[iii] tight-roped for 48 months when their dreams of a well-organised domestic life abruptly ended. Hubby went & real chaos reigned in her soul & everything around her. She now lives like a swimmer in a rough sea, battered & tossed about by giant waves & treacherous currents. Is this the miserable life you now wish to lead?

I suspect you'll immediately retort by pointing out that on questions of this nature I ought to address myself not to your brains but to your breast, persuade not your head but your heart, for it is the latter that John has won; or are you the conqueror? If this be your retort then say I: Hallelujah! benissimo!! Sermons on such matters, even from well-meaning friends, are out of place. What the heart feels may very often be the sole justification for what we do. I have known John since the forties & I regard him very highly. He is human & generous & possesses a lively & sober mind. I sincerely believe that in him you've found an ideal partner who will make life for you happy & enjoyable, & who will encourage you to sharpen the abilities that you undoubtedly possess. You've caught a big fish, little sister! Or are you going to prove me wrong once again by saying: Buti, I'm a modest person but I can't help thinking that John is a lucky fellow. It's him, not me, who has caught a big fish. I am the creation's rarest fish, the Coelacanth!

This is a duel to be fought between you two & I'll stay out of it. But I do wish you to know that: Siqhwabizandla![iv] May the wedding day be bright & lovely & the night lit by a golden moon.

I should have liked to have written to both of you, but I deliberately avoided such a course. John & I are very close & I can speak frankly to him on personal matters without hurting him. If I spoke directly to him I might be tempted to ignore everything I have said here about delivering sermons.

---

i   He is referring to Winnie Mandela.
ii   A name for the Johannesburg area that refers to the Witwatersrand gold reef where gold was first discovered by Australian George Harrison in 1896.
iii   This is isiXhosa for a person and his or her romantic partner.
iv   'We congratulate you. Literally we are clapping hands' in isiXhosa.

My letter might both be congratulations & reprimand, a demand for explanations which might make consciences itch. But to you I can truly speak as
I have done here, & this is how I should like things to be. Remember that
both of you are very dear to me.

Thanks for the Xmas card you sent in Dec. 69. That I never received it
makes no difference whatsoever to my sense of gratitude. My only regret is
that I was denied the opportunity of possessing a precious souvenir which
would have made John & others shrink with jealousy. It was most kind of
you, Thoko,[i] Rita,[ii] Miriam & our sister to think of me. Give them my fondest regards. Have you seen our sister lately?[iii] I'm worried over hr. I have
watched all kinds of storm break loose upon her. The harm occasioned by
the ceaseless bombardment to which she has been subjected over a lengthy
period is shown by the decline in her health. But it gives me some pleasure
to notice that she is taking things well. Give her all my love.

You are probably in touch with an old friend I never forget, Benjy.[iv]
I have wanted to write to him but on every occasion I have hesitated for
reasons you would readily appreciate. He is brilliant & fearless, the type of
man who must rise to the top of his profession. His dare-devilry reminds
me of another friend for whom I had great admiration, Henry Nxumalo,[v]
another go-getter. Give him my greetings.

Do you ever hear of Cecil?[vi] I once wrote to him[vii] but he was already
settled in New York when my letter reached the Rand.[viii] I'm sorry he had to
leave because he played a special role which made him very valuable indeed.
In the important media he controlled, he stressed those issues that keep us
together as a community. In his office & home he kept a dialogue with those
who repeatedly found themselves in disagreement on vital questions & he
used his resources to narrow the gaps & to caution against separatism.

Recently I read a stimulating contribution by Lewis Nkosi[ix] on cultural

---

i   Thoko Mngoma, an ANC activist in Alexandra township. She was also detained and stood trial in what is known
as the Trial of the Twenty-two, when Winnie Mandela and twenty-one others were detained and then charged with
working for the banned ANC. The trial started on 1 December 1969, and on 16 February 1970 the charges were
withdrawn. Before they could leave court they were rearrested. On 3 August 1970 Winnie Mandela and nineteen
others were recharged. They were acquitted on 14 September 1970.

ii   Rita Ndzanga (1933–), an ANC activist and trade unionist. She was also one of the accused in the Trial of the
Twenty-two. Her husband, Lawrence, was murdered in detention by the security police. Her two sons were in MK
but died after 1994.

iii   This is most probably a reference to Winnie Mandela.

iv   Most probably this is Benjamin Pogrund (1933–), former editor of the *Rand Daily Mail* and Mandela's friend
– see the glossary.

v   Henry Nxumalo (1917–57) was an investigative journalist for *Drum* magazine and wrote stories exposing racial
inequality. He was murdered while investigating a story. His killers were never found.

vi   Cecil Eprile (1914–93), friend, journalist, and newspaper editor – see the glossary.

vii See his letter from 11 February 1967, page 34.

viii An abbreviated name for the Witwatersrand, a 56-kilometre-long ridge in the Gauteng province of South Africa
where Johannesburg is based.

ix   Lewis Nkosi (1936–2010), South African author who started out as a journalist writing for *Ilanga Lase Natal*
(Natal Sun), *Drum* magazine and *Golden City Post*. He criticised the apartheid government and his works were
subsequently banned.

problems & I was happy to note that he is still magnificent. My thoughts immediately went back to the mid-fifties, to other friends in the same profession – the late Can Themba, Todd Matshikiza[i] & Nat Nakasa, to Bloke Modisane, Benson Dyantyi, Robert Resha, . . . Leslie Sehume, Arthur Maimane, Simon Mogapi, Bob Gosani, Harry Mashabela, Casey Motsisi, Ronnie Manyosi, Layton Plata, Doc Bikitsha, Mayekiso & Ikaneng, all of whom we miss.[ii]

Many of them are top chaps & compare very well with their counterparts across the colour line – Ruth First, Stanley Uys, Brian Bunting, Margaret Smith, Charles Bloomberg & others.[iii] Needless to say, I did not agree with everything they said, but I patiently listened to them because they often spoke a language I well understood & drew attention to concrete problems. I hope they still try to uphold these high standards. What new faces are there? How is Owen?[iv] I have seen a couple of your manuscripts.[v] You'll not feel offended if I tell you that I was highly impressed. One or two lines caused me concern, but my confidence in you helps me to hope that you would certainly be able to give me an explanation which I could accept.

Re roba matsoho! With love, very sincerely,
Buti[vi] Nel

Miss Joyce Sikakane, c/o Nkosikazi Nobandla Mandela, 8115 Orlando West, Johannesburg

Postscript: This letter will amuse you. I received information that you were engaged to one of my great friends, hence this note. Though Zami[vii] corrected the error, I let it go as originally drafted.[viii]

---

i   Todd Matshikiza (1920–68), writer and musician who composed the musical score for the internationally successful South African musical *King Kong* (1960).
ii   Apart from Bob Gosani, who was a photographer, these are mostly South African journalists and editors who worked for *Drum* magazine.
iii   White journalists who were active in or supported the anti-apartheid struggle.
iv   Owen Vanqa, a journalist from the Eastern Cape who was tried with Joyce Sikhakhane, Winnie Mandela, and twenty others in 1969 and 1970.
v   When Sikhakhane was interviewed by the Nelson Mandela Foundation about this letter in 2008 she said that she thought Mandela was referring to magazine articles published under her byline. ('The Lost Letter', Nelson Mandela Foundation, 22 July 2008, https://www.nelsonmandela.org/news/entry/the-lost-letter).
vi   'Brother' in isiXhosa.
vii   One of Winnie Mandela's names..
viii   Sikhakane did marry Samson Fadana but a day later the security police told her that she 'would be charged for entering the Magistrates Court illegally and having been in the presence of more than one person. They told me that my so-called marriage was null and void because it was done illegally. That was the end of the marriage.' ('The Lost Letter', Nelson Mandela Foundation, 22 July 2008, https://www.nelsonmandela.org/news/entry/the-lost-letter).

To Nomabutho Bhala,[i] a friend

January 1, 1971

*Ntombi yakowethu,[ii]

Many thanks indeed for your unexpected but very kind letter of June last year. I had hoped to reply earlier than now, but you know only too well what were my difficulties all along.

Although the bulk of the load has been lifted away, temporarily at least, there are still knotty problems to be solved. However, I shall not postpone this reply any further.

Your letter was one of the shortest I ever received, the entire contents consisting only of one compound sentence. Yet it is one of the best letters I had read for a long time. I had thought that our generation of rabble rousers had vanished with the close of the fifties. I had also believed that, with all the experience of almost 30 years behind me, in the course of which I attentively listened to many persuasive speakers, and read first class biographies of some of the world's most prominent public figures, it would not be easy for me to be carried away by mere beauty of prose or smooth flow of one's oratory. Yet the few lines that you scrawled carefreely across that modest sheet of writing material moved me much more than all the classics I have read. Many of the personalities that featured in your remarkable dream lived, simply and without written records, some 3 centuries ago. Neither you nor I ever saw them plan the operations that were to make them famous in history, nor did we watch as they went into action. For most of them there is not even one authentic photograph which would at least give us a faint idea of their physical features or personality. Yet even a polished urbanite like yourself, who lives in the second half of the 20th century, with all the fantastic progress and achievement that mark it, and who is cut off from the influence of tribal life, cannot wipe away from your thoughts, plans and dreams the rugged and fierce heroes of the Neolithic age. They were unusual men – the exceptions that are found elsewhere in the world; in so far as their economy and implements were concerned they lived in the Stone Age, and yet they founded large and stable kingdoms by means of metal weapons. In the conflicts that were later to rock the country, they gave a good account of themselves, holding at bay for a continuous

---

i   Taken from the A4 hardcover book in which he copied some of his letters.
ii   'Our sister' in isiXhosa.

period of more than one hundred years a community millennia in advance of themselves in economic organisation and technology, and which made full use of the scientific resources at their disposal.

I find the explanation for your dream in the simple fact that you read deeper lessons into our ancestry. You regard their heroic deeds during the deathless century of conflicts as a model for the life we should lead today. When their country was threatened they showed the highest standard of patriotism. Just as they refused to use the primitiveness of their economic system and ineffectiveness of their weapons as an excuse for shirking their sacred duty, so the present generation shall not allow itself to be intimidated by the disparities current internal alignments seem to entail.

*

The 14 great names that you mention in your letter have become legendary in our history, and we trust that future generations will continue to pay homage to their immortality. But the full story of our past heritage remains incomplete if we forget that line of indigenous heroes who acted as curtain raisers to the major conflicts that subsequently flamed out, and who acquitted themselves just as magnificently.

The Khoi-khoi,[i] from whom the bulk of our Coloured folk is descended, were skilfully led by Autshumayo[ii] (S.A.'s first black political prisoner to be exiled to Robben Island), Odasoa[iii] and Gogosoa.[iv] During the 3rd Liberation War in 1799 Klaas Stuurman[v] took the unprecedented step of joining forces with Cungwa, Chief of [the] Amagqunukhwebe.[vi]

Many people, including freedom fighters with a long record of struggle and sacrifice, speak contemptuously of [the] Abatwa.[vii] Yet several S.A. historians have written objective and warm accounts on their unconquerable spirit and noble qualities. Those who have read reports of the Sneeuberg battles between Abatwa and the Boers, and more especially that between Abatwa, led by their chief, Karel, and a commando of more than 100 Boers

---

i   The Khoikhoi make up one of the four groups who were the original inhabitants of South Africa. They were a pastoral people who depended on their cattle and sheep for subsistence.

ii   Autshumao (spelt by Mandela as Autshumayo) was a Khoikhoi leader in the seventeenth century. He learnt English and Dutch and then worked as an interpreter during the Dutch settlement of the Cape of Good Hope in 1652. He and two of his followers were banished by Cape Town's first colonial administrator, Jan van Riebeeck, to Robben Island in 1658 after waging war with Dutch settlers. He was one of the first people to be imprisoned on Robben Island and the only person to ever successfully escape.

iii   Odasoa was chief of the Cochoqua (Saldanhars) in the 1600s.

iv   Gogosoa was paramount chief of the Goringhaiqua during the seventeenth century.

v   A leader of the Khoi people, who is estimated to have been born between 1743 and 1803.

vi   The Amagqunukhwebe are a sub-group of the Xhosa nation. Cungwa was a descendant of Khwane kaLungane, a counsellor and a warrior of King Tshiwo (1670–1702) of amaXhosa, who headed the chiefdom of amaGqunukhwebe, and established the Khwane dynasty.

vii   Also known as the Batwa and Abathwa, they live in the Democratic Republic of Congo, Eastern Uganda, and Rwanda. Historically they have been referred to as 'pygmy people' due to their small stature and have been widely discriminated against.

around the great cave at Poshuli's Hoek,[i] will have an idea of the important contribution made to S.A. history by a community that once were the sole occupants of our beautiful country. In numerous engagements they showed unusual courage and daring and would continue to fight desperately even after the last arrow had been fired.

These are the men who strove for a free S.A. long before we reached the field of battle. They blazed the trail, and it is their joint efforts that supply the source of the vast stream of S.A. history. We are the heirs to a three-stream heritage; an inheritance that inspires us to fight and die for the loftiest ideals in life. The title "African hero" embraces all these veterans. Years later more articulate and sophisticated personalities were to follow and, in the process, the tableau of history was enriched a thousand times – the Selope Themas,[ii] Jabavus,[iii] Dubes,[iv] Abdurahmans,[v] Gools,[vi] Asvats,[vii] Cachalias,[viii] and now you and your generation have joined this legion of honour.

I am very fond of great dreams and I particularly liked yours; it was very close to my heart. Perhaps in your next dream, there will be something that will excite not only the sons of Zika Ntu, but the descendants of all the famous heroes of the past. At a time when some people are feverishly encouraging the growth of fractional forces, raising the tribe into the final and highest form of social organisation, setting one national group against the other, cosmopolitan dreams are not only desirable but a bounden duty; dreams that stress the special unity that hold the freedom forces together – a bond that has been forged by common struggles, sacrifices and traditions. I have tried hard to resist the wonderful prose in your letter and to grasp

---

i   A description of the battle at Poshuli's Hoek appears in *The Native Races of South Africa: A History of the Intrusion of the Hottentots and Bantu into the Hunting Grounds of the Bushmen, the Aborigines of the Country,* George W. Stow (published 1905), which Mandela read and transcribed while in prison.

ii   Selope Thema (1886–1955), leading member of the South Africa Native National Congress and secretary of the deputation on behalf of black South Africans to the Versailles Peace Conference and the British government in 1919.

iii   John Tengo Jabavu (1859–21), academic, writer, newspaper editor, and political activist. Father of Davidson Don Tengo Jabavu. Established the first black-owned newspaper, *Imvo Zabantsundu* (Black opinion), in 1884. Assisted in the establishment of the South African Native College (University College of Fort Hare) in 1916. Davidson Don Tengo Jabavu (1885–1959), son of John Tengo Jabavu. Academic, poet and political and anti-apartheid activist. First black professor at the University College of Fort Hare, Alice. President of the All-African Convention(AAC), established in 1935 in opposition to segregationist legislation. Educator and co-founder of the South African Native National Congress (renamed as the ANC in 1923).

iv   John Langalibale Dube (1871–1946). Educator, publisher, editor, writer, and political activist. First president general of the South African Native National Congress (renamed as the ANC in 1923) established in 1912. Established the Zulu Christian Industrial School at Ohlange. Established the first Zulu/English newspaper *Ilanga lase Natal (Sun of Natal)* in 1904. Opponent of the 1913 Land Act. Member of the executive of the AAC, 1935. Mandela voted at the Ohlange school in 1994 for the first time in his life, and then visited Dube's grave to report that South Africa was now free.

v   Abdullah Abdurahman (1872–1940), the first coloured person to be elected to the Cape Town City Council in 1904 and the Cape Provincial Council in 1914. President of the African Political Organisation, which fought racial oppression against coloureds.

vi   Cissie Gool (1897–1963), daughter of Abdurahman. Founder and first president of the National Liberation League, president of the Non-European United Front in the 1940s, and the first coloured woman to graduate from law school in South Africa and be called to the Cape Bar.

vii   Zainab Asvat (*c*.1920), political activist, member of the Transvaal Indian Congress and medical doctor.

viii   The Cachalia family has been prominent in the anti-apartheid struggle in South Africa.

mainly its important message. Some say that chauvinism is one of my weak-nesses. They may be right. True enough, my blood and brain do not often synchronise. Very often reason induces me to approach cautiously what excites my feeling. I can only hope that I shall succeed in maintaining this proper balance. Finally, we all know that the price you have already paid is high, and I fear to speculate on what you still have to pay. Your courage has moved me immensely and makes my own sacrifices a mere trifle in comparison to yours. Fondest regards to you, your family and all.

Ozithobileyo,[i] Nelson

*Original in Zulu

Mrs Nomabutho Bhala, 588L KwaMashu, Durban

To the commanding officer, Robben Island

[Translated from Afrikaans]

2 January, 1971

The Commanding Officer,
Robben Island.

Attention C/O Fourie

New Year's Day is never an appropriate occasion to announce disappointing news. Unfortunately both of your letters denying my request for a visit and the censoring of the letter from my wife reached me on this significant day.

I don't suppose I'd complain about it, except to say that the guitar player must have a special talent to persuade his listeners to listen carefully to him. He must always try to hold the attention of his audience, to draw them unto him. Only a person armed with love for his fellow human beings, and who cares about others, will succeed where force and power will be applied in vain. This simple principle is applicable to ordinary matters also, and is valid even in institutions where strict discipline has to be maintained.

---

i   'Yours obediently' in isiXhosa.

[Signed NR Mandela]
Nelson Mandela 466/64

———————————

To Tim Maharaj, wife of fellow prisoner Mac Maharaj

February 1, 1971

My dear Ompragash,[i]

Twice I tried to catch a glimpse of your face at the visitors' booths & twice I failed; first last year when you seemed equally determined to deny me the pleasure, & then on Dec. 5, 1970 when you eluded me altogether.

Hardly have I ever had a better chance of witnessing once again just how mighty is the force of tradition. Who could have suspected that the shadow of the purdah[ii] could induce a world-wise girl like yourself to bend down to its power. Yet this is what happened on every occasion I came near you. For me yours is a face behind the curtain, true intangible, but a curtain all the same. I was anxious to verify the claim repeatedly made by one lad here that the country's brightest & most charming wifey is to be found in Durban's Wakuff Buildings.[iii] I was also keen to compare the live face with the attractive photo that is proudly displayed in exquisite leather for me somewhere here; to contrast the original with the carbon copy. I have now despaired, hence this note. Perhaps through this medium I might accomplish more than would a fleeting glance at a young lady draped in the latest fashion & skilfully touched up by beauticians. I might penetrate past the well-mannered Tim to the plain Ompragash.

By the way, I almost forgot to confide that one day an innocent jester removed the photo from the rack, & believe me the world almost went up in flames.[iv] A young man, for whom I otherwise have the highest regard, went livid with rage (or was it jealousy?) & ransacked almost every cell, mine included. I say mine included as your Oompie[v] I ought to be immune to all kinds of molestation from those we both hold dear. But in case you get a

———

i   She was Hindu and this is a Hindu name. Tim was her nickname.
ii   A practice in some Hindu and Muslim societies where women are screened from men or strangers by a curtain.
iii At the time she was sharing a flat with her brother George in Wakuff's Building off Queen's Street in Durban.
     These different ways of identifying or referring to the same person were intended to confuse the prison censors.
iv   At this stage, prisoners were only allowed one photograph. Mandela is poking fun at the rection of Tim's husband,
     fellow prisoner Mac Maharaj, when someone removed Tim's photo from his cell.
v   Mandela is referring to himself as Oompie, an endearing, dimunitive form of the Afrikaans word oom, which
     means 'uncle'. Mandela called Mac neef, meaning 'nephew'. In an email communication with Sahm Venter on
     22 August 2017, Maharaj writes, 'Here he is claiming that Mac should not have searched his cell. In fact it was
     Madiba who pilfered the photo from Mac's cell!!!'

distorted picture, I hasten to point out that spiritually he is still as grand as he was during the hectic four months preceding the never-to-be-forgotten Dec. 18.[i] He is as tough as steel & tries to be flexible as a quince stick. Of course, nothing would be as easy as to criticise another, & maybe that your man has faults galore. But if he has, you would know them better than I do. Or better still, you might snap my nose off & tell me that even gods, messiahs & saints have been criticised by some & cursed by others; why should he be any different? I am completely on your side. Our respect for him increases the longer we stay together & I would be perfectly content to let age & experience soften his impatience &, if during the 1976 Xmas sprees echoes of his sharpness are heard, I'm sure you would be able to handle the situation.[ii]

Writing to a friend in Durban reminds me of some amusing incidents. In '61 I visited the city incognito and stayed with another friend.[iii] They had a lovely daughter of about 6 with whom I immediately struck up friendship. In the morning I took a bath & thereafter straightened out my hair & beard with a comb. Satisfied that I was quite clean & presentable I walked into the sitting room & took her on my lap. She gave me one look & exclaimed: You have a dirty face, go & wash! More was to follow. As my host & his wife had to go out to work, I spent the day at their mother's place. A jovial old lady whose knowledge of English was minimal. All that my host could say in introducing me to her was: This is our friend; we collect him this evening. As subsequently turned out, the old lady was suspicious & determined to sort out this puzzle in her own way. I spent the whole day inside & had not ventured out. Little did I know I had met one a hundred times wiser than I was. The dialogue between us went something like this: Q. Where you from? A. Pietersburg. Q. When you come? A. Yesterday. Q. You see Durban first time? A. Yes. Q. When you go back? A. Tomorrow. I was becoming uneasy when fortunately the interrogation ceased & I thought my troubles were over. Lunch was delightful & the rich flavour of the afternoon tea strongly appealed to me. I was enjoying the day & beginning to relax when the old lady entered my room & resumed her investigations. She invited me to accompany her to the shopping centre. I could not & politely declined. She

---

i   'The four months preceding December 18 refer to the four months that Mac was in detention without trial and was heavily tortured. The references to "spiritually" and "tough" and "flexible" are brought into play to reassure Tim that Mac is in good shape despite the torture he endured.(Note: It was reported that Mac was at that time one of the detainees who had undergone the most severe forms of torture.) Hence Mandela was at pains to assure Tim that Mac was psychologically and physically fit.' (Mac Maharaj in an email to Sahm Venter, 22 August 2017.)

ii   He is referring to the fact that Mac Maharaj was due to be released on 18 December 1976, hence his use of 'Christmas spree'. 'He is informing Tim that Maharaj is raring to get back into the struggle and she should brace herself for that . . . and he knows she will stand by him, when he says, "I am sure you would be able to handle the situation."' (Mac Maharaj in an email to Sahm Venter, 22 August 2017.)

iii   Mandela is referring to the period when he was on the run from the police during which time the media coined him 'The Black Pimpernel'.

then asked how far Pietersburg was. I wasn't sure but took a guess: About 600 miles, I said. Then came the question I least suspected: You come very far & spend whole holiday reading book in one room? I was convinced that she had seen through everything & I found it difficult to answer. I changed the subject. I visited Durban several times thereafter but preferred to stay away from her & starve rather than risk another interrogation. I hope she is keeping well.[i]

Niggie,[ii] you have been in our thoughts ever since you advised Mac of your intention to have the op. Under normal conditions many of us would have paid you a visit in hospital & brought you flowers, or sent a message of good wishes which might reach you during the period of recuperation. But in our present circumstances none of these things were possible & we could do no more than to express our sympathies directly to Neef here.

Zami's[iii] brief respite enables me to give expression to the sentiments that I have harboured since the painful news reached us. I sent you this letter in the hope that it may help brighten everything around you, keep your spirits high, bring hope to your heart & enable you to enjoy as full a life as possible under the circumstances. It has been said a thousand and one times that what matters is not so much what happens to a person than the way such person takes it.[iv] It may sound silly for me to burden you with what is a matter of more than common knowledge. Yet whenever it is my turn to be the victim of some misfortune, I forget precisely these simple things, & thereby let hell break loose upon me. We think of you and hope you thoroughly enjoyed the trip to & your stay in Cape Town.

Fondest regards to Phyl[v] & kids. I really admire her ability to handle situations by remote control. She sent two family photos. The first, homely & lovely, brought MD[vi] to his feet again. But it is more the second that did the trick. It is the prettiest portrait of her that I've seen. Its message is clear & unambiguous: Darling I'm the centre of the universe; sheet anchor of all your dreams! Never again did I hear MD complain of any ailment. On the contrary, he now walks on springs, & shows something of the brilliant young man who went with Monty[vii] & others to Pretoria in the mid-forties and who gave us a stimulating report on the mission at the Gandhi Hall.[viii]

---

i   We haven't been able to find out who this person was. Mandela clearly wanted his regards to be sent to her family.

ii   Niggie is the Afrikaans word for 'niece', which is how he is addressing Tim since he calls her husband 'nephew'.

iii One of Winnie Mandela's names.

iv   He refers to his wife's release from detention and the collapse of her trial to inspire Tim to have strength for her surgery.

v   Phyllis Naidoo, wife of fellow prisoner M. D. Naidoo and Tim's sister-in-law.

vi   M. D. Naidoo, a member of the South African Communist Party and the South African Indian Congress who was imprisoned on Robben Island for five years and was in B Section with Mandela. He was Tim Maharaj's brother.

vii Monty Naicker (1910–78), doctor, politician, and anti-apartheid activist – see the glossary.

viii Gandhi Hall was in Fox Street, Ferreirastown, Johannesburg. It was used for political meetings in the 1940s and 1950s. The report Mandela refers to was given by M. D. Naidoo at a meeting at the Gandhi Hall to comrades in

What is it a woman can't do to a man! Finally, I'd like you to know that you'll always be in our thoughts. I only hope the next time we meet the purdah will be off. Zami joins me in this message of good wishes. With love, Oom Nel

Mrs Tim Maharaj, P.O. Box 346, Dalbridge, Natal

--- ---

To Ishmael & Martha Matlhaku,[i] friends

February 1, 1971

My dear Ishy & Mohla,[ii]

Kgele banna![iii] Do you forget your friends so easily? Why are you not writing? The way you behave towards me these days gives me the impression that you gave up your beautiful home at Phomolong[iv] and trekked only to be rid of me. You know nothing would please me more than to hear from you, and that Zami[v] would never grouse if you dropped me a line once in a while. But you've never let me down in the past, and I can find no reason why you should do so now. May it be that the fault lies with me; that you are not writing because you expect me to do so first? Very well then, here's my letter, when may I expect yours?

I love to think of the happy times we spent together in the past; the days in the early forties when I came to the Reef[vi] fresh from the country and met Mohla. She was then secretary to an estate agent, Nkomo, and was one of the very first persons to befriend me in the Golden City.[vii] At that time she moved in the circles of Marjorie Pretorius, Dorothy Qupe,

---

the then Transvaal on the progress of the Passive Resistance Campaign. This was waged by the Transvaal and Natal Indian Congresses from 1946 to 1948 against the Asiatic Land Tenure Act of 1946 which sought to confine Asian ownership of land to particular areas. Dr Monty Naicker, president of the Natal Indian Congress, was among the first batch of protesters against the Act who resisted racial laws and courted arrest. (Paraphrased from an email from Mac Maharaj to Sahm Venter, 22 August 2017.)

i   Also spelled Matlaku.
ii   Martha Matlhaku once worked as Mandela's personal secretary. Her husband, Ishmael, often transported comrades or activists to the Botswana border; and he had also been trusted with the transportation of the leadership, including Mandela. When he realised his activities were being monitored, he moved to Botswana and stayed in Mochudi as a refugee. He was later joined by Martha. He continued to assist activists from South Africa who crossed into Botswana.
iii   'I am shocked' in Setswana.
iv   A suburb of Soweto.
v   One of Winnie Mandela's names.
vi   A name for the Johannesburg area that refers to the Witwatersrand gold reef where gold was first discovered by Australian George Harrison in 1896.
vii   Johannesburg is called the Golden City due its origins as a gold-mining town in the nineteenth century.

Nomvula Sitimela, Meisie Dingane, Florence Mosenyi, Edith Ntisa and Emily Gabushane.[i] Later she became Xamela's[ii] secretary and moved into new court chambers and new circles. Now and again she travelled on official business to various parts of the country, and came into contact with many of our public figures. Her charming manner and kindness endeared her to many of us and made her the ideal person to serve in an office which sought to cater for people from all walks of life. She worked hard and overtime, and scarcely ever complained. Do you still remember the occasion a few weeks before June 26, 1950 when Nomvula and her Lami nearly strangled me for being slave-driver? We had a lot of work to clear and our call for volunteers from the youth brought a good number to the chambers, Nomvula and Lami being amongst them. When we pushed them right past 10pm even this fine couple could not take it. To save myself I immediately ordered tshayile.[iii]

Mohla was a member of the Johannesburg International Club[iv] and when in 1951 I became its secretary she spent a lot of her spare time assisting in the planning of activities, raising funds and typing for us. It was during this period that you hit headlines in the press when a well-known Johannesburg legal firm sent you to type a record in the Vereeniging[v] Magistrate's Court. Remember? Perhaps your broad outlook and love of progress and reform were much influenced by your experiences during this same period of contacts with members of various population groups. You are always moving forward, and in the process, finding means of being useful to the community at large. One of your gifts is a sharp eye for those finer things in life which take our minds away from our troubles and fill our hearts with feelings of joy. Of course, all of us are in varying degrees guilty of selfish tendencies and Mohla has her own shortcomings of this kind. She spends quite some time and money on herself, packing her wardrobe with quality garments, driving around in the latest car models, and fitting her house with choice furniture.

When all this has been considered, the dominant impression I have about Mohla is that of a girl who tries to live for others, a fact which should make her useful wherever she is.

Mohla and I have known each other before Zami and Ishy came into our lives. The friendship between our respective families was built on the foundations laid by you and I. First came Ishy who pulled you out of your

---

i   Friends and associates of Mandela.
ii   Walter Sisulu's clan name (for Walter Sisulu, see the glossary).
iii   In Fanekalo, a pidgin language used in the mines and based primarily on isiZulu, English, and some Afrikaans, Mandela is saying that he decided to announce that it was home time.
iv   Established in 1949 as a meeting place of people of all nationalities and races to meet and communicate. It held debates and hosted international guests. Mandela was at one time its secretary.
v   A city in the Transvaal province (now the Gauteng province).

Kraaipan[i] retreat and brought you back into circulation. By the way, you have not yet given us the full story of how Ishy discovered you. Perhaps one day we shall have the pleasure of listening to you deliver the memorable address. Shall I invite the Mof for the occasion?

Ishy has played a role no less significant. He brought us into contact with men like David Motsamayi,[ii] Sydney Kgaje, Cecil Ntoeli and other socialites who form an important part of the public opinion of the Rand,[iii] and readily offered his services whenever we required them. By the way, I hope Bra[iv] Dave did not mind me using him as my cover name. If I had had the opportunity, I would have consulted him about it.

But to return to our theme, Zami came into the picture only in '57 and our friendship at once deepened into a solid comradeship. She has always shown respect for my feelings and treats all my friends affectionately. I can think of no single case in which she has even indirectly tried to influence me against any of my numerous friends. From our own side the closeness of our relationship is due in large measure to her sweet temper and love for you.

Do you still remember the last time I saw you? There at the Fort in Sept. '62[v] you brought heaps of good food and presented me with an expensive hanky which I hope Zami has kept for me. She told me you looked after her and kids right up to the day of your departure. She was indeed very sorry to know that she would not see you for a long while, be unable to visit you, or have the pleasure of welcoming you at Westcliffe.[vi]

Though I was 1000 miles away when you left, your departure upset me considerably, and I felt quite lonely. It had been consolation for me to know that in the case of emergency Zami could always count on you. Moreover, the removal costs and those of settling down must have eaten too deeply into your reserves. It must have been a painful moment for you to turn your backs to your home, your friends and the places where you were born.

As for me, I shall miss Ishy's infectious smile, Mohla's juicy jokes, the hot cup of tea, delicious food and soft drinks that were always available when I called at Phomolong. Do you realise now what you are to us, to Zami and me, and what your letter will mean? When can I expect it?

Mohla, I prefer to say nothing now on our dear Nyinyi who now lies in a field far from Phomolong. One day you'll tell me all about this tragedy.

---

i   A town in the Transvaal province, which is now part of the North West province.
ii   David Motsamayi was a client of Mandela's, and when Mandela went underground he borrowed his name. This name appears also in his Ethiopian passport.
iii An abbreviated name for the Witwatersrand, a 56-kilometre-long ridge in the Gauteng province of South Africa where Johannesburg is based.
iv Colloquial form of 'brother'.
v   He is referring to when he was held at the Old Fort Prison in Johannesburg after he was arrested while on the run in 1962.
vi Mandela is referring to the suburb of Westcliff in Johannesburg but has misspelt it as 'Westcliffe'.

Perhaps I'll be able to hold your hand and take you for a short walk in silence. In the meantime let's try and forget

Remember, I await your letter which I hope will be as sweet and enjoyable as those you wrote me from Kraaipan. Let my sister-in-law and hubby, the Vutelas, know that I think of them and hope they received my letter of 28th July 69. I also think of Ngwana wa Kgosi, David Moiloa, of Edna who has not seen Mike for 4 years, Nana and hubby, and the veteran Dan. Are Peter and Jerry still around? To all of them I send my fondest regards.

Finally, I should like Fish[i] and wife to know I shall ever remain indebted to them for all they did for me. I felt completely at home with them.

With all my love.
Ke nna Madiba, Moforutse ya'binang tshwene morena li Mofu Magadi.[ii]

Ishmael & Martha Matlhaku

To Zenani Mandela,[iii] his middle daughter

March 1, 1971

My Darling,

Friday the 5th February this year was your 12th birthday and in January I sent you a card containing my congratulations and good wishes. Did you get it? Again I say: many happy returns.

It is not easy for me to believe that our Zeni, who was only a baby when I last saw her, is now a big girl in Standard V at a Boarding School, and doing subjects I never learnt in school, like French, Physical Science and Maths. I still remember clearly the night when you were born in 1959. On February 4th that year I returned home very late and found Mummy highly restless. I rushed for the late Aunt Phyllis Mzaidume, and the two of us drove Mummy to Baragwanath Hospital. There was a remarkable coincidence. Aunt Phyllis herself was born on 5th February and on our way to Bara she hoped you would be born on the same date, and that is exactly what happened. When she heard of the news of your

---

i   Fish Keitsing (1919–2005) was a Botswana-based activist who accommodated and helped Mandela on his 1962 tour.
ii   In the Sesotho language this meaning of this phrase is 'My name is Madiba, whose totem is a baboon, gentleman and lady'. *Mofumagadi* means the chief's wife/queen mother, and is loosely used to show respect to a married woman.
iii Zenani Mandela (1959–) – see the glossary.

arrival, she was as happy as if she had created you.

Your birth was a great relief to us. Only three months before this, Mummy had spent fifteen days in jail under circumstances that were dangerous for a person in her condition.[i] We did not know what harm might have been done to you and to her health, and were happy indeed to be blessed with a healthy and lovely daughter. Do you understand that you were nearly born in prison? Not many people have had your experience of having been in jail before they were born. You were only 25 months old when I left home and, though I met you frequently thereafter until January 1962 when I left the country for a short period, we never lived together again.

You will probably not remember an incident that moved me very much at the time and about which I never like to think. Towards the end of 1961 you were brought to the house of a friend and I was already waiting when you came.[ii] I was wearing no jacket or hat. I took you into my arms and for about ten minutes we hugged, and kissed and talked. Then suddenly you seemed to have remembered something. You pushed me aside and started searching the room. In a corner you found the rest of my clothing. After collecting it, you gave it to me and asked me to go home. You held my hand for quite some time, pulling desperately and begging me to return. It was a difficult moment for both of us. You felt I had deserted you and Mummy, and your request was a reasonable one. It was similar to the note that you added to Mummy's letter of the 3rd December 1965 where you said: "Will you come home next year. My mother will fetch you with her car." Your age in 1961 made it difficult for me to explain my conduct to you, and the worried expression that I saw in your face haunted me for many months thereafter. Luckily, however, you soon cooled down and we parted peacefully. But for days I was lost in thought, wondering how I could show you that I had not failed you and the family. When I returned to South Africa in July 1962 I saw you and Zindzi[iii] twice and this was the last time we met. In 1964 you were brought to the Supreme Court in Pretoria and I was quite disappointed when you were not allowed to see me.[iv] I have been longing to see you ever since. You will be able to pay me a visit me in 1975 when you will have turned sixteen. But I am growing impatient and the coming five years seem longer than eternity. What a lovely letter you wrote me last month! Merci beaucoup! I have started 1971 with a real bang. Yours was the first and only letter I got from the family this year and I read it over

---

i   Winnie Mandela was arrested in October 1958 and held in prison for two weeks for participating in a protest against the extension of pass laws to women.
ii   Mandela is referring to the period in 1961 when he was on the run from the authorities and living apart from his family.
iii Zenani's sister, Zindziswa Mandela (1960–) – see the glossary.
iv   He is referring to the Rivonia Trial – see the glossary.

and over again. I shall keep it as a souvenir. It pleased me very much to know your subjects for this year and hope you will work hard right from the beginning of the year and pass. French is an important language. On the African continent more people speak French than English. Latin, Zulu, Physical Science, Maths and Geography are also useful and you should pay a great deal of attention to them. I was also pleased to hear that you take walks to the mountains and about the beautiful scenery that you describe.

I saw the note that you wrote at the back of the letter asking the postman to send the letter away at once and to "be like Elvis, go man, go." The music of Elvis is very lively and popular and I am glad to note that you are fond of it too. I hope that you also love the music of Miriam Makheba [*sic*],[i] Mohapeloa,[ii] Caluza,[iii] Tyamzashe,[iv] Paul Robeson,[v] Beethoven,[vi] Tchaikovsky.[vii] What is even more important, I trust that one day you will be able to compose, sing and play your own music, or do you prefer to be a ballet star in addition to being a scientist, doctor or lawyer?

What games do you play? Basketball, swimming or athletics, especially track events (i.e. running), would keep you healthy and strong, and give you the pleasure of helping your college win victories. Try your luck, darling.

May this letter bring you the same joy and happiness that yours gave me.

Give my love to Zindzi, Maki,[viii] Kgatho,[ix] and abazala[x] Andile, Vuyani, Kwayiyo and Maphelo, and of course to you and Mummy.

Lots of love and plenty of kisses.

Yours affectionately,

Tata[xi]

Miss Zeni Mandela, 8115 Orlando West, Johannesburg

---

i   Zenzile Miriam Makeba (1932–2008), South African singer, actor, United Nations goodwill amabassador, and activist.

ii   Joshua Pulomo Mohapeloa (1908–82), a lyricist who worked with Gibson Kente on his musical productions (Sahm Venter, telephonic conversations with Gibson Kente's niece, Vicky Kente, 23 July 2017).

iii   R. T. Caluza (1895–1969), Zulu composer and musician who transcended many musical genres, including hyms, ragtime and vaudeville. He wrote the South African Native National Congress's first anthem, 'iLand Act', protesting against the 1913 Native Land Act.

iv   Benjamin Tyamzashe (1890–1978), South African composer, choir conductor, organist, and teacher.

v   Paul Robeson (1898–1976), American bass singer who was involved with the civil rights movement.

vi   Ludwig van Beethoven (1770–1827), German composer and pianist.

vii   Pyotr Ilyich Tchaikovsky (1840–93), Russian composer of the romantic period.

viii   Makaziwe Mandela (1954–), Mandela's eldest daughter – see the glossary.

ix   Makgatho Mandela (1950–2005), Mandela's second-born son – see the glossary.

x   'Cousins' in isiXhosa.

xi   'Father' in isiXhosa.

To Christine Scholtz,[i] friend

[Translated from Afrikaans]

March 1, 1971

My dear Kiesie,[ii]

I always knew of the town of Worcester.[iii] To me it was the place where they manufactured vinegar, or is it sauce,[iv] that popular liquid that makes our food so delectable and which a handsome mate sprinkled on my fish the other day. Of the people of Worcester, their yearnings, struggles, and contribution to our progress and happiness,[v] however, I knew nothing. In December 1947 I took my vacation in Cape Town. Naturally the train stopped at your station, but even on that occasion Worcester was a mere name just as the many others through which we had travelled. In the forties John Alwyn's name was bandied about, and when I returned to the Boland[vi] in '55 I visited him.

Do you still remember our friend from bygone days, Greenwood, the Capetonian from the Transkei, who was forever sporting a red necktie. Yes, he! He accompanied me. By that time events and circumstances had taken their toll on Alwyn, but it was nevertheless my pleasure to be able to shake hands with him. I had contact with a person who had made a laudable effort in the interest of social progress. Later on he went astray, but we cannot for this reason delete his name from history.

December 5, 1956, brought me, Ayesha Dawood, Joseph Mphoza, Joseph Buza[vii] and others together. For two years we sat in the Drill Hall in Johannesburg, organised outings, discussed problems, and spoke the contents of our hearts. At one time a good friend and I received bunches of sweet grapes from Ayesha and we really enjoyed it. In April 1961 Archie Sibeko[viii] and I spent the entire day there and were glad for the opportunity to be able to chat with their parents and family. From that time Worcester was no longer a little dot on the map of South Africa. It was the hometown of dear comrades with opinions and feelings I respected. I know of course that they are now dispersed. Ayesha is in London, and Busa in King William's

---

i   Taken from the A4 hardcover book in which he copied some of his letters..
ii   Diminutive of Christine in Afrikaans
iii   A town in the Western Cape province.
iv   The Union Vinegar Company was established in the town in 1913. As well as making vinegar, it also produced Worcester sauce (which originates from the city of Worcester in the UK rather than the town in South Africa).
v   Many anti-apartheid activists came from the town of Worcester.
vi   A region of the Western Cape province.
vii   Three of the accused in the Treason Trial (for the Treason Trial, see the glossary) who came from the town of Worcester. Most of the 156 accused were arrested on 5 December 1956.
viii A fellow accused in the Treason Trial of 1956–61.

Town.[i] I am sure that wherever they are they will remember Worcester with fondness.

I was informed of the tragic circumstances in which Ayesha's father had died. It must have been a terrible blow to her. I hope she and her old husband and children are in the best of health and flourishing. Do you now realise how closely my heart is bound to Worcester and its people? The bond between you and me, Kiesie, is one of the reasons why I am writing you this letter! By the way, do you know that our paths almost crossed last December? I looked forward to your visit because I was hoping to convey my warm regards personally to you. Maybe it was I who disappointed you.

A long time ago I was a shepherd[ii] and I really enjoyed my duties. To this day I dream of my days as a shepherd. However, I should note I was not a shepherd under modern conditions, where a person has his own fenced farm and pasturage as vast as the world – a situation which would make one selfish and sectarian, and thinking of one's own welfare only. No, I was a shepherd in the Reserves, among poor folk who lived on government land and who had to share communal grazing lands. People think that to care for one's herds is the only task of a herder. Yes, it is true that to care for one's flock and its increase is the main task of a herder, but an equally important task for those dependent on communal pasturage is the maintenance of harmony among the various herders. They have to cooperate in building dams and dipping tanks and in joint action against common enemies. In such circumstances there is little opportunity for selfishness and sectarian tendencies. People in other occupations could perhaps draw lessons from this experience.

Ah, how I went off on a tangent, away from Worcester and my comrades? Let me return to my theme then. I know a korrelkop[iii] whose birthday is February 8. He might be an unknown chap to many people, but he made profound impression on those who know him well. As far as I'm concerned I should rather say nothing. Unfortunately his point of view and mine coincide on a number of pertinent issues; we conduct our affairs under the same umbrella and any praise or criticism I might offer will reflect directly on me. Also, neither you nor I claim to be a prophet and as such we won't succumb to engage in idle speculation. What I can say is that the three years I have spent with him increased my expectations of him and I consider him a worthy addition to the coterie of friends I have in your town. He is the chord that binds me, on the one hand, to you, Jose, Soes and all the friends you love, and even the avocado tree in front of your house, on the other – the link between me and the pasturage of my childhood.

---

i   A town in the Eastern Cape province.
ii   When he was a child growing up in the Transkei.
iii   An Afrikaans word to describe someone with curly hair.

The past four years must have been a terrible time for you, a period of all manner of hardship – of struggling with troubles and burdens that made heavy demands on the family finances, and moments of concern, loneliness, and yearning for loved ones not there, as well as the regular difficult trips which brought cheer and relief, yet not sufficiently so because when you reached your destination you could not speak your heart's content, could not completely relieve yourself of your burdens. Maybe the stormy times also greatly excited you and pearls started appearing in your hair. You poor women! During her last visit my Zami[i] also complained that she was fast greying. Of course, it can be no consolation to you that this is happening to other families also. Pain hurts, even if it assails lot of victims at the same time. But at least you now have relief which I hope you'll thoroughly enjoy. Give our korrelkop a katkop,[ii] puza,[iii] and now and then hake with sauce. I'm sure he'll make his own arrangements for Oom Tas wine.[iv] Wedding day! When? It's a pity I won't be able to enjoy the pleasure of being your master of ceremonies.

Love and warm wishes.
Affectionately,
Nel.

Miss Christine Scholtz,
14 Hammer Street,
Worcester

To Fatima Meer,[v] friend and comrade

March 1, 1971

My dear Fatima,

This letter should have gone either to Shamim, Shehnaz or Rashid.[vi] To hear directly from them would give me a deeper insight into the shifts in the patterns of thought & outlook amongst the young folk.

---

i   One of Winnie Mandela's names.
ii   'Bread' in Afrikaans.
iii   'A drink' in Afrikaans.
iv   He is referring to Tassenberg, a popular dry red wine in South Africa.
v   Fatima Meer (1928–2010), writer, academic, and anti-apartheid and women's rights activist – see the glossary.
vi   Fatima and Ismail Meer's children.

My son, Kgatho,[i] one of my best pals, visits me twice yearly. We seem to be in agreement on major issues, but now & again he clears the cobwebs from my mind by taking a different view on matters which I have come to regard as axiomatic. At times I have suspected that he sees in me something of a useful relic from the past, a sort of souvenir to remind him of the days when he regarded me as knowing everything under the sun, & when he gulped down anything I told him. His independence of mind & fresh ideas have made my conversations with him enjoyable, & this is what I believe that I would get if I spoke directly to the children. You realise now why I prefer Rashid & sisters to you?

I have lived with my generation all these years, a generation that is inclined to be conservative & to lean backwards most of the time. I'm keen to know a bit more about the new ideas stirring among the modern youth. But news about the children tends to remind me of problems about which I prefer never to think. When I'm told that our Shamim is at varsity, constructing beautiful house models, the full weight of my 52 years bears down upon me. She appears on page 70 of the "Portrait[ii] . . ." I suspect Shehnaz to be the second on her left. If I'm wide of the mark let her remember that she was only a little more than a toddler when I last saw her, & her features must have changed a lot after she has grown big enough to be in Standard IX. I have searched in vain for Rashid & have even made wild guesses amongst the boys on page 40. I was very sorry to learn that he could not go to Waterford[iii] as he could have acted [as] elder brother to my Zeni & Zindzi.[iv] I have not forgotten about the beautiful face cloth with which they presented me on the last occasion I was there & I should love to hear from them whenever they can spare some time for writing letters.

I could have addressed the letter to Ismail,[v] my very first friend across the race curtain, comrade of my youth. You know we practically lived together at Kholvad[vi] & it was him who brought me into contact with

---

i   Makgatho (Kgatho) Mandela (1950–2005), Mandela's second-born son – see the glossary.
ii   *Portrait of Indian South Africans* by Fatima Meer (Durban: Avon House, 1969).
iii   Waterford Kamhlaba school in neighbouring Swaziland.
iv   Zenani (1959–) and Zindzi (1960–) Mandela, Mandela's middle and youngest daughters – see the glossary.
v   Ismail Meer (1918–2000), Fatima's husband and a lawyer and anti-apartheid activist – see the glossary.
vi   Kholvad House, an apartment block in downtown Johannesburg where Ismail Meer had an apartment. Mandela writes in *Long Walk to Freedom*, 'At Wits I met and became friends with Ismail Meer, J.N. Singh, Ahmed Bhoola, and Ramlal Bhoolia. The centre of this tight-knit community was Ismail's apartment, Flat 13, Kholvad House, four rooms in a residential building in the centre of the city. There we studied, talked and even danced until the early hours of the morning, and it became a kind of headquarters for young freedom fighters. I sometimes slept there when it was too late to catch the last train back to Orlando.' (p. 105.)

Dadoo,[i] Naicker brothers,[ii] the Cachalias,[iii] Nana Sita,[iv] Naidoos,[v] Pahad,[vi] Nathie,[vii] the Singhs,[viii] Hurbans,[ix] Poonen,[x] Nair,[xi] Seedat,[xii] AI Meer[xiii] & other eminent leaders of the Indian community. To him I should like to chat freely & openly about the past. But the trouble, my difficulty is you, behn.[xiv] I hesitate to put bhai[xv] in a position where he would have to withhold from you my letters to him, or when you would feel obliged to rifle his pockets. I've not the slightest doubt what would happen if you saw any of such letters you would roast him alive. I often wonder whether you and Radi[xvi] ever stop to think just how much you owe to me for the peace of mind & happiness that surround you. Remember Ismail, J.N. [Singh] & I have been a solid trio for almost 30 years. I shall stick to our vow: never, never under any circumstances, to say anything unbecoming of the other. They will readily agree that I have not once given away the show. Anyway, what it is that I could ever think of divulging? Talk of angels! Your men & I are & have always been. The trouble, of course, is that most successful men are prone to some form of vanity. There comes a stage in their lives when they consider it permissible to be egotistic & to brag to the public at large about their unique achievements. What a sweet euphemism for self-praise the English language has evolved! Autobiography, they choose to call it,

---

i   Dr Yusuf Dadoo (1909–83), medical doctor, anti-apartheid activist, and orator. President of South African Indian Congress, deputy to Oliver Tambo on the Revolutionary Council of MK, and chairman of the South African Communist Party – see the glossary.

ii   Monty Naicker (1910–78), doctor, politician, and anti-apartheid activist – see the glossary. M. P. Naicker (1920–77), anti-apartheid activist, journalist, leader, and organiser for the Natal Indian Congress, South African Communist Party, and the Congress Alliance. The Naickers were not brothers, but comrades.

iii   Maulvi Cachalia (1908–2003), anti-apartheid activist and leading member of the South African Indian Congress, Transvaaal Indian Congress, and ANC – see the glossary. Yusuf Cachalia (1915–95), brother of Maulvi Cachalia. Political activist and secretary of the South African Indian Congress – see the glossary. Their families were also involved in fighting apartheid.

iv   Nana Sita (1898–1969), president of the Transvaal Indian Congress, a follower of Gandhi's philosophy of *satyagraha* (non-violence).

v   The Naidoo family of Rocky Street, Yeoville, in Johannesburg. Naransamy Roy (1901–53) and Ama Naidoo (1908–93) and the family.

vi   Goolam Pahad, executive committee member of the Transvaal Indian Congress and the father of activists Essop (1939–) and Aziz (1940–) Pahad.

vii   Solly Nathie (1918–79), executive committee member of the Transvaal Indian Congress.

viii J. N. Singh (d. 1996), member of the Transvaal Indian Congress and the Natal Indian Congress. He studied towards his LLB degree with Nelson Mandela at the University of Witwatersrand. His wife was Radhi Singh (d. 2013), anti-apartheid activist, teacher, and attorney.

ix   Gopal Herbans – treasurer of the Natal Indian Congress and an accused in the Treason Trial (for the Treason Trial, see the glossary).

x   George and Vera Poonan.

xi   Billy Nair (1929–2008), comrade and MK member who was charged with sabotage in 1963. He was held in B Section with Mandela on Robben Island and was released in 1984 – see the glossary.

xii   Dawood Seedat (1916–76) was an accused in the Treason Trial of 1956, and detained in the 1960 State of Emergency (for both the Treason Trial and the 1960 State of Emergency, see the glossary). He was vice-president of the Natal Indian Congress. He and his wife, Fatima, were banned for five years in 1964, then the order was exended to 1974.

xiii The uncle of I. C. Meer (1918–2000) (for I. C. Meer, see the glossary).

xiv 'Sister' in Gujarati.

xv   'Brother' in Gujarati.

xvi Wife of J. N. Singh, an activist who was on the executive committees of both the Natal Indian Congress and the South African Indian Congress.

where the shortcomings of others are frequently exploited to highlight the praiseworthy accomplishments of the author. I am doubtful if I will ever sit down to sketch my background. I have neither the achievements of which I could boast nor the skill to do it. If I lived on cane spirit every day of my life, I still would not have had the courage to attempt it. I sometimes believe that through me Creation intended to give the world the example of a mediocre man in the proper sense of the term. Nothing could tempt me to advertise myself. Had I been in a position to write an autobiography, its publication would have been delayed until our bones had been laid, & perhaps I might have dropped hints not compatible with my vow. The dead have no worries, & if the truth & nothing but the whole truth about them emerged, the image I have helped to maintain through my perpetual silence was ruined, that would be the affair of posterity, not ours. You now see what a risk would be entailed in writing to Ismail? Anyway you know he is a heavyweight, moves slowly & I would probably whistle for a reply.

I can almost hear you ask the pertinent question: Where to does this verbosity lead us? Quite a sensible question! The truth is that I am trying to find an excuse for writing to you. How can I resist talking to you, behn, you who has always treated me so kindly? You, Ismail & I have wrenched ourselves free from the inhibitions of our Caucasoid & Negroid ancestries & established firm & warm relations which not even the tempestuous decade of the sixties could shake or chill. We have forged our own kutum: silusapho lendw'enye.[i] Remember the numerous occasions I have lived with you since the early fifties there at Umngeni Road;[ii] were Pamela's parents your next door neighbours then? I moved with you to Sydenham.[iii]

Now & then Zami[iv] tells me some good news about you. Although your application to visit me was refused I was happy to know that I'm in your thoughts. I have read & re-read the "Portrait".[v] Splendid! A moving story & skilfully handled; it is a mine of information for me. The fact that you wrote it obliged me to read it as if you were conversing informally with me. I almost read the 235 pages at one sitting, & it helped me begin the attempt to overcome a weakness which I have never been able to shake off. I'm one of those who possess scraps of superficial information on a variety of subjects, but who lacks depth & expert knowledge in the one thing in which I ought to have specialised, namely the history of my own country &

---

i   An isiXhosa phrase meaning 'We come from one family'. *Silusapho* means 'We are family' and *lendw'enye* means 'one house'.

ii   Where Ismail and Fatima Meer lived from 1951 to 1958 before they moved into their home in Burnwood Road in Sydenham, Durban.

iii   The suburb in Durban to which the Meers later moved.

iv   One of Winnie Mandela's names.

v   *Portrait of Indian South Africans.*

people. I have tried to read anything relating to African history carefully & with real interest, but have tended to neglect that of other national groups. It was when I read the "Portrait . . ." I had the opportunity to appreciate the fascinating human story which begins in 1860.[i] I asked Zami to try & get the book & indicated to her my own views on the issues raised in Chap. III. Our interpretations may not altogether coincide & I hope to refer to the whole question in my next letter.

In the meantime I say Mubarak![ii]

With all my love to you, Ismail & kids,[iii] Radhi & J.N,[iv] Molly & Monty,[v] Alan & wife,[vi] G.R.[vii] & family, Dawood & Fatima.[viii]

Very sincerely,
Nelson

Mrs Fatima Meer, 148 Burnwood Road, Sydenham, Durban

To the commanding officer, Robben Island

31st March 1971

The Commanding Officer,
Robben Island

Attention: Col Badenhorst

I have to advise that two long hard cover notebooks in which I have kept

---

i   Although there were Indian people in South Africa earlier, between November 1860 and 1911 (when the system of indentured labour was stopped) around 152,000 indentured labourers from across India arrived in Natal. After serving their indentures, the first category of Indians were free to remain in South Africa or to return to India.

ii   'Congratulations' in Gujarati.

iii Ismail Meer and their children.

iv   J. N. Singh (d. 1996), member of the Transvaal Indian Congress and the Natal Indian Congress. He studied towards his LLB degree with Nelson Mandela at the University of Witwatersrand. His wife was Radhi Singh (d. 2013), anti-apartheid activist, teacher, and attorney.

v   Monty Naicker.

vi   Alan (1926–2013) and Beata Lipman (1928–2016), their friends. Alan, an architect, designed their house in Sydenham.

vii G. R. Naidoo, a South African photographer. He attended a party at the Meers' home in Durban which Mandela attended the day before he was arrested on 5 August 1962.

viii Fatima Seedat (1922–2003) was the twin of Rahima Moosa, one of the leaders of the 1956 Women's March. A member of the Natal Indian Congress and ANC, Fatima was jailed for her role in the Passive Resistance Campaign waged by the Transvaal and Natal Indian Congresses from 1946 to 1948 against the Asiatic Land Tenure Act of 1946 which sought to confine Asian ownership of land to particular areas. She was jailed again in 1952 for participating in the Defiance Campaign (for the Defiance Campaign, see the glossary). Natal Indian Congress and ANC member.

copies of my correspondence since February 1969 have been removed from my cell. The second notebook contains loose pieces of paper in which I was drafting the three letters for April 1971.[i]

I have to advise further that I received permission from the Commanding Officer of the time to use this particular material to keep copies of this correspondence. I must further point out that the Commissioner of Prisons, General Steyn, Brigadier Aucamp[ii] and Chief Warder Fourie are aware that I keep copies of all letters that I write.

[Signed NRMandela]

NELSON MANDELA: 466/64

[Note in Afrikaans in another hand]

Colonel,

I am not 'aware'[iii] of Sunday evening when I caught him. He can go and blow bubbles. The other people were too afraid. I am not afraid of anything. Good reading material for the shredder.

[Signed and dated 31.3.71]

To Thoko Mandela,[iv] his daughter-in-law and the widow of his son, Thembi[v]

April 1, 1971

My dear Thoko,

I wish I had some means to influence the invisible force that governs our lives and determines our fortunes and misfortunes.

A broken family, a young widow wrecked by grief and battling all alone against heavy odds, 2 orphaned children deprived of the security of a stable home and father's love, and hungry most of the time are cruel penalties that make life tough and bitter. I have many a time wondered whether the marvellous inventions and progress brought by science make us more secure

---

i   The group or grade in which a prisoner was put by the authorities came with varying degrees of privilege. There is no official list noting when Mandela was in which group or grade, but we can establish from what he wrote at the top of some of his letters that he was in B grade in 1972 and in A grade from 1973.

ii   Brigadier Aucamp, commanding officer of Robben Island – see the glossary.

iii   While the note is in Afrikaans, 'aware' is in English in single quotation marks.

iv   See the glossary.

v   Madiba Thembekile (Thembi) Mandela (1945–69), Mandela's eldest son – see the glossary.

and happier than were our ancestors a hundred thousand years ago. Sure, there have been significant milestones in man's battle against ignorance, poverty and disease. Means are being found to make us less dependent on nature and its moods, to have greater control over our environment and, in the process, we have come to have relatively higher living standards.

But fate continues to be treacherous and to bring us suffering and misery that we do not deserve. The family has had an alarming quantity of catastrophes. Why should Mkozi[i] die so soon after Thembi? During his last visit Kgatho told me that you had attended Kapadika's funeral, one of Thembi's close friends and who spoke on behalf of Cape Town on Aug. 3, 1969.[ii] Why should all these things happen to you at one and the same time? I can imagine the awkward questions Ndindi and Nandi must be asking: Shall we never see our Daddy again? Is he now together with Grandpa of Diepkloof.[iii] Will Tatomkulu[iv] never return from Robben Island? Who will now bring us dresses and chocolates? And many more similarly unanswerable enquiries. The news of your father's death disturbed me. I would have been more troubled if I had not had the privilege of having witnessed how courageous and dignified you can be in the face of personal tragedy. I know that you are not the type of person who will allow sorrow to overwhelm you. In spite of all that has happened you have not lost everything. There are many people who have no mothers, step-fathers, father- and mother-in-laws, no host of relations and friends such as you have, friends and relations who think of you and wish you well. Besides, you have the opportunity to make your future and that of Ndindi and Nandi bright and meaningful. You are young and in good health and full of talent. Do remember this, Thoko.

As you know, I have not met Lennard[v] but all the reports that have reached me indicate that he is equally brave and calm. My deepest sympathy to both of you. Are you sending me a report on the funeral? When did you return from Johannesburg? Are you working?

In March last year I wrote to Lennard and gave him a number of messages. I never heard from him. Perhaps your reply will include this information.

I hope you have not forgotten the matter I raised in my letter of 29th November 1969[vi] relating to your own personal position. I hope at your next visit you will give me some progress report. I am anxious that you put your-

---

i   This is likely to be Thoko Mandela's father.
ii   Mandela must be referring to Thembi Mandela's funeral. His body arrived in Johannesburg from Cape Town on 29 July 1969. (Sophie Tema, 'Mandela's Son's Body Arrives', *The World*, 30 July 1969.)
iii   A suburb in Soweto, Johannesburg.
iv   'Granddad' in isiXhosa.
v   Thoko's brother, Leonard Simelane. Mandela misspelt his name.
vi   See his letter on page 146.

self in a position whereby you will be able to guide the children in the choice of careers and in preparing them for such careers. The home atmosphere must exist which will encourage them to strive for the highest ideals in life, and this depends largely on you. Today your mother and mother-in-law are there to help you bring up Ndindi and Nandi, but sooner or later they will also pass to eternal rest, leaving you to fight all alone, and to face the difficult task of supervising the progress of the children. I shall say more on this matter when you come. In the meantime please read the letter again.

Nandi really looks fine in her maroon and white outfit. The green vegetation that forms the background to the photo is beautiful and reminds me of the happy and romantic days of my childhood. I can almost smell the sweet perfumes that must have filled the area where she posed. I have taken particular note of her mischievous smile. It is a charming picture and I am happy you sent it. I put it alongside that of Zeni and Zindzi[i].

Many thanks for the beautiful Xmas card you sent me. You must have combed the whole of Cape Town to get it. I like its bright red background and its artistic arrangement. I also received Ntombi's with the chocolate belle on the cover. The two of you must be little witches. You seem to know my tastes better than I do. They are really wonderful and I was happy to receive them.

What is happening? Why have you not come? You wrote as far back as November and told me that you had applied for a visiting permit. Four full months have passed and you have not turned up. Did you apply by registered letter? Do know I am looking forward to seeing you soon? Perhaps it may be advisable before you renew your application to phone Mum Winnie, Orlando 113, and find out if she has not already applied to come down.

My fondest regards to your mother and step-father and love to you, Ndindi, Ntombi and Lennard.

Yours affectionately,
Tata[ii]

Mrs Lydia Thoko Mandela, "Hillbrow", 7th Avenue, Retreat

---

i   Zenani Mandela (1959–) and Zindziswa Mandela (1960–), Mandela's middle and youngest daughters – see the glossary..

ii   'Father' in isiXhosa.

To 'Sisi'[i]

April 1, 1971

My dear Sisi,[ii]

Thinking about you and home does me a lot of good. For most of the time such thoughts give me plenty of fun. I am able to recall many amusing incidents of my teenage days.

One evening the Chief stormed out of his bedroom dragging a formidable stick to punish Justice[iii] for having forgotten his portmanteau at Umtata.[iv] Cenge, besides whose car we stood, jumped to the wheel and raced away at top speed, while Justice took to his feet and vanished into the dark night. I was not involved, so I thought, and remained standing where I was. But as the Chief approached I suddenly realised that I had been left to handle the baby. "I am not Justice!" I loudly protested. Came back the terrifying retort: "You are!" You know the rest of the story.

Then there was the unforgettable occasion when you scolded me for stealing green mealies[v] from Rev. Matyolo's garden. That evening the chief was indisposed and you conducted the family prayers. We had hardly said "Amen" when you turned to me and boomed: "Why do you disgrace us by stealing from a priest?" I had a perfectly straightforward [answer], namely, that stolen food was to me sweeter than all the lovely dishes I got effortlessly from you. But the way you timed your unexpected rebuke made me speechless. I felt that all the angels of heaven were listening, horrified by my infernal crime. Never again did I tamper with the property of clergymen, but mealies from other gardens still continued to tempt me. There are dozens of such incidents which I recall in the solitude of my cell.

But why should I yearn so much for you? There are times when my heart almost stops beating, slowed down by heavy loads of longing. I miss you, Umqekezo[vi] and its people. I miss Mvezo where I was born and Qunu where I spent the first 10 years of my childhood. I long to see Tyalara

---

i   Taken from the A4 hardcover book in which he copied some of his letters.
ii   Sisi may be the wife of the regent Chief Jongintaba Dalindyebo (see the glossary). In his original autobiography written in prison, Mandela says that a woman called Sisi rebuked him for talking during prayers when he lived at the Great Place at Mqhekezweni after his father died when he was twelve.
iii Justice Dalindyebo, Jongintaba Dalindyebo' s son and Mandela's nephew who was about four years older than him. They grew up together as brothers at the Great Place at Mqhekezweni. They ran away together to Johannesburg in 1941 when the regent began arranging marriages for them.
iv   Umtata (now called Mthatha) was the capital of the Transkei homeland.
v   Fresh corn.
vi   It is another name for Mqhekezweni, or the Great Place, where Mandela was raised by the regent Jongintaba Dalindyebo after his father died.

where Justice, Mantusi,[i] Kaiser[ii] and I underwent the traditional rites of manhood. I would love to bathe once more in the waters of Umbashe,[iii] as I did at the beginning of 1935 when we washed off ingceke.[iv] When will I again see Qokolweni, and Clarkebury,[v] the school and institution which enabled me to see the distant and dim outlines of the world in which we live? I often wonder whether Miss Mdingane,[vi] who taught me the alphabet, is still alive. I miss Bawo[vii] Mdazuka, Menye,[viii] Pahla,[ix] Njimbana, Mbanjwa,[x] the Mvulanes[xi] and all the other wise and eloquent councillors of the Mqekezweni Court.[xii] I think of Chief Jongintaba who made it possible for me to be where I am. He inspired me to set goals for myself, which I hope will be judged to be in accord with the interests of the community as a whole. Our hopes and aims centre around this ideal. Above all I miss Ma with her kindness and modesty. I thought I loved her when she lived. But it is only now that she is gone that I think I could have spent more time to make her comfortable and happy. You know what I owe to her and the Chief. But how and with what could a prisoner repay a debt owed to the deceased?

You and all the members of the family are my special pride. Nothing moves me more than the knowledge that all of you are my flesh and blood. But there are moments when I become extremely worried over you. In fact, there have been occasions when I wish I was born of an ant-hill or came from the legendary stork, when I wished I had no relations, never had a life companion, children or family responsibilities. Repeatedly I have asked the question: Is one justified in neglecting his family on the ground of involvement in larger issues? Is it right for one to condemn one's young children and aging parents to poverty and starvation in the hope of saving the wretched multitudes of this world? Is the public welfare not something remote and secondary to that of one's family?[xiii] Does the principle charity begins at home not apply to social questions? Ma was hardpressed until the very last day of her life. The letter you wrote me in November 1968 showed

---

i   Mandela writes of the initiation in *Long Walk to Freedom*: 'The traditional ceremony of the circumcision school was arranged principally for Justice. The rest of us, twenty-six in all, were there mainly to keep him company.' (p. 30.)
ii   K. D. Matanzima (1915– 2003), Mandela's nephew, a Thembu chief, and chief minister for the Transkei – see the glossary.
iii   A river in the Transkei.
iv   A white clay substance that is smeared over the body during the traditional initiation into manhood.
v   Mandela attended Clarkebury Boarding Insitute in the town of Engcobo, Transkei, from the age of sixteen.
vi   His first school teacher who gave him the name Nelson.
vii   'Bawo' is a term of respect for an elder.
viii   Mandela's friend.
ix   A traditional clan name.
x   A friend of Mandela's.
xi   In-laws of Justice Dalindyebo.
xii   The Great Place or royal palace in Mqhekezweni, Transkei, where Mandela was raised from the age of twelve.
xiii   Mandela wrote this sentence in the margins and he linked to it by including an asterisk after the word 'questions' at the end of the following sentence.

that you faced similar problems. Are the ideas that move us fair compensation for your current hardships? These are questions that torment me daily. Add to this the fact that many of my dreams as an individual have collapsed as I became more committed on wider issues; many of my illusions have been shattered, not to mention the host of opportunities that I have lost. By contrast I have watched many of my childhood friends and college mates develop protruding tummies and "ample bottoms", living well and complacently and enjoying many of the pleasures that I should like to have for myself. But the attempt to answer these pertinent questions has dissolved the doubts that I have had, and led to greater certainty as to the correctness of my stand. I hope I have in the process gained a priceless reward – an objective and activated conscience, the ability to dream of golden ages, to live for what could be.

I live in the hope of receiving warm and affectionate letters and visits from family and friends, from you, Hlamba ngobubende.[i] I hope your next letter will be as full and informative as your last one. Above all I live in the immediate hope of returning home one day; to Mqekezweni[ii] and Qunu[iii] and to be welcomed by you and to enjoy incum, isandlwana, iqeba ne thumbu.[iv]

Fondest regards to Justice and his wife, Lala and husband, to Lulu, Sandile, Mlungiseleli, Nokwezi, Lindehru Nomqopiso, Zabonke and family.[v] Last but not least, to you Nyawuza.[vi] I hope Jonguhlanga[vii] received my condolence letter.

Yours affectionately, Dalibunga

To the commanding officer, Robben Island

4 April 1971

The Commanding Officer,
Robben Island

---

i   Mandela is referring to a clan name.
ii   In *Long Walk to Freedom* he spelt this name Mqhekezweni.
iii   The village where Mandela spent his childhood.
iv   Different parts of meat in isiXhosa. *Incum* is a soft part from the chest, *isadlwana* is a specific type of intestine, *iqeba* is the soft part under the chin and *ithumbu* is the general intestine. It can be seen as a special dish prepared to welcome someone.
v   Friends.
vi   Nyawuza or Mnayawuza refers to members of the Nyawuza clan Mandela knew from his childhood.
vii   King Sabata Jonguhlanga Dalindyebo (1928–86), paramount chief of the Transkei homeland and leader of the Democratic Progressive Party, the opposition party in Transkei which opposed apartheid rule – see the glossary.

Attention: Lt Badenhorst

Further to my letter addressed to you on the 31st March 1971, I have to advise that yesterday morning I became aware for the first time that two of my foolscap hard cover notebooks, in which I keep copies of my correspondence, had been surreptitiously removed from my cell.

I immediately reported the matter to the Head Warder Carstens in the presence of Warder Meyer. They both emphatically denied that they had searched my cell the previous day and removed the missing notebooks. They further added that they had no information whatsoever as to the identity of the person who removed the books. I asked H/W Carstens to investigate the matter and thereafter acquaint me with his report.

On the night of the 31st March I decided to make a thorough search of my cell to find out what other articles, if any, were missing and I was greatly shocked to observe that my silver Parker T Ball point pen has also disappeared. I had last used it in December 1970 but I continued to see it in the box where I kept it until just the other day. In the morning of the 1st April I reported the fact to Warder Meyer, H/W Carstens being off duty.

I strongly suspect that the person who removed the books from the cell also took the pen and I ask you to investigate the matter and have this article replaced. The disappearance of my pen has greatly disturbed me. Mine is the fifth one to disappear within the first three months of this year. I have lived in the Single Cell section for seven years and this is the first time for us to suffer such losses.

I should also be pleased if you would kindly give me the following information:

1.   The name of the official, if known to you, who removed the notebooks from my cell.
2.   The reason or reasons for removing them
3.   The date when they will be returned to me

I might add that one of the notebooks contains the completed drafts of two of the three letters which I intended to write for this month. The removal of this particular book means that I will have to delay the dispatch of the aforementioned letter until I have access to it.

I should also be pleased if you would allow me to write to Brigadier Aucamp in connection with a letter which I wrote to the Minister of Justice last year[i] relating to my household affairs. Some aspect of the request I made was attended to, and he asked me to raise the matter with him again.

---

i   See his letter from 14 September 1970, page 195.

In this connection I should like to draw attention to the fact that a copy of this letter, which I should like to consult before I write to Brig Aucamp,[i] is in one of the missing books, and I should be much indebted to you if you would allow me to have access to it.

[Signed NR Mandela]
NELSON MANDELA: 466/64

—————————

To the commanding officer, Robben Island

14th June 1971

The Commanding Officer,
Robben Island

Attention: Major Huisamen

I refer to the letter I addressed to you in March this year, and in which I advised that my preparations for the University of London's Final LL.B Examinations in June 1971 had been hampered by illness which forced me much against my will, to suspend studying completely for several months.[ii]

By February this year my health had improved to such an extent that I resumed preparations for the above examinations, but I discovered that I had lost my power of concentration and stamina, and the headaches that had worried me during the second half of 1970 reappeared. I discussed the matter with Dr Poleksi, the Medical Officer, and it was after consultation with him that in March I wrote to you and to the Cultural Attaché. In response to my letter you informed me then that you had referred the matter to your Headquarters and, at the same time advised me to continue preparing for the examinations.

I tried hard to comply with your advice and exerted myself to the utmost, but found that although my health continued to improve the rate of recovery was not fast and complete enough to enable me to make satisfactory progress in my work, the main difficulty being, as always, recurring headaches. Postural hypertension, from which I suffer, is an illness which is aggravated by tension and mental exertion, both of which naturally fol-

—————————

i   Brigadier Aucamp, commanding officer of Robben Island – see the glossary.
ii   While on trial in 1962 Mandela had a blackout in prison and was diagnosed with high blood pressure.

low from concentrated study and preparation. In such circumstances I was compelled to consider the best way of continuing with the studies without impeding the rate of recovery, and the obvious answer was to spread the course over two years with the aim of completing the course in June 1972. Your insistence that I complete in 1971 was to call upon me to attempt what was entirely beyond my physical condition.

I might perhaps add that I should have completed in June 1970 and I did not do so because the Prison Department failed to forward to the university documents which would entitle me to enter for the above examinations.

The Department sought to justify its action on the ground that my permission to study with this particular university had lapsed. As you are aware I was only informed in September that I could resume my studies. Even if I were in the best of health it would have been quite difficult for me to obtain a pass with only 8 months of preparation for a final year course where I had to take 4 wide and complicated subjects at one sitting.

I must accordingly ask you to allow me a further 12 months to complete the degree. I should like you to know that, according to the regulations governing this course, if I fail to satisfy the examiners this June in any one of the 4 outstanding subjects, I will be forced to repeat not only these, but also the other 4 that I have completed for Part I of the Final. A perusal of the General Notes and Reading Lists for the guidance of students and the syllabus will show that these examinations require prolonged and intensive preparations. I am accordingly most reluctant to tackle the forthcoming examination as my preparations were hampered and I hope you will reconsider your decision and grant the request made above. I need hardly stress that your refusal of my request will involve me in heavy financial loss.

[Signed NRMandela]
NELSON MANDELA: 466/64

[note in Afrikaans in another hand]
21/6/71

Colonel,
His request for extension has already been rejected by Brig. Aucamp. His studies have now ended and his books put with his property.

To Vanguard Booksellers[i]

26th September 1971

The Manager,
Vanguard Booksellers,
123 Commissioner Street,
Johannesburg.

[Handwritten note in Afrikaans] Head warder De Jager, this sort of thing is not allowed.

Dear Sir,

I enclose herewith the sum of R5.00 and should be pleased if you would kindly send, at your earliest possible convenience, the following birthday presents to the persons mentioned below, together with a plain card containing the words indicated under each title:

1. NKOSIKAZI NOBANDLA MANDELA, House no. 8115 Orlando West, JHB. "THE JUNGLE"[ii] by Upton Sinclair.
   My darling,
   For your Birthday. A million kisses & tons & tons of love.
   Dalibunga

2. MR KGATHO MANDELA, HOUSE no 8115 OW; JHB "FOR WHOM THE BELL TOLLS"[iii] BY Ernest Hemmingway [*sic*]
   For you my bro'
   If you want to remain a clever and cute "cat", read this book.
   Brother (alias) Dad

3. MISS MAKI MANDELA, 8115, OW; JHB "THE PEARL"[iv] by Steinbeck
   My darling,
   With all my love!
   Tata

---

i   His friend and comrade Helen Joseph (1905–92) worked there (for Helen Joseph, see the glossary).
ii   Sinclair's *The Jungle* (Doubleday, 1906) portrays the harsh working conditions and exploitation of immigrants living in Chicago, USA.
iii   Hemingway's *For Whom the Bell Tolls* (Charles Scribener's Sons, 1940) tells the story of a young American working with a guerrilla unit in 1937 during the Spanish civil war.
iv   John Steinbeck's *The Pearl* (Viking Press, 1947) tells the story of a pearl diver, Kino, and explores themes of the destructive force of greed, racisim, and destiny.

If these titles are not available, please supply suitable ones from stock and thereafter advise me. Kindly credit the balance, if any, to my account.

Yours faithfully,
[Signed NRMandela]
NELSON MANDELA

To the commanding officer, Robben Island

27th March 1972

The Commanding Officer,
Robben Island

Attention: C/W Van der Berg[i]

The right-hand screw of the spectacles enclosed here is loose and needs to be tightened or replaced. Kindly send them to the optician for attention at my own cost.

[Signed NRMandela]
NELSON MANDELA: 466/64

[Notes in Afrikaans]
R5.00 gevrees[ii] [and signature]

Colonel,

For your decision please [and signature]

Hospital,
Show H/K
GPO B 11 (8) (b)
[Signature] 27/3/72
Approved for his own cost

---

i   This name is crossed out and signed by someone else and dated 27.3.72.
ii   'Frozen' in Afrikaans (normally spelt 'gevries'), which could mean that the authorities have frozen this amount from Mandela's funds for this purpose.

[Signature]
10/4/72

[Note at the top in another hand]

466/64 Nelson Mandela (B Group)

◇◇◇◇◇◇◇◇

In 1971 Winnie Mandea had been sentenced to twelve months in prison for communicating with a banned person in her house. She successfully appealed both the conviction and sentence. The following year she won her appeal against sentences of six and twelve months for receiving visitors.

═══════════════

To Winnie Mandela,[i] his wife

[Note in another hand at the top of the letter] 466/64 Nelson Mandela (B Group)

JUNE FIRST 1972

My darling,

Once again your letters are not coming through, and when they do, they are surprisingly late. That of JANUARY 30 was given me on MARCH 4 whilst that of FEBRUARY 26 I received on APRIL 15.

On FEBRUARY 25 I had discussed the whole question of our correspondence with the Commissioner of Prisons, General Steyn, pointing out to him that I had received only 3 of the 12 you wrote me in 1971, & that you had also got only 3 of the letters I wrote you during the same period.

I told him then that I had had this difficulty since 1969 & that the Commanding Officer had repeatedly explained to me that all my outgoing letters had been sent off & that I had been given all the correspondence that had arrived. The C.O.P.[ii] emphatically repudiated my suggestion that our correspondence was being interfered with in the course of transit through the G.P.O.[iii] and promised that he would have the matter investigated.

---

i   Nomzamo Winifred Madikizela-Mandela (1936–) – see the glossary.
ii   Commissioner of Prisons.
iii General Post Office.

About a week thereafter I discussed the same matter with Brig Aucamp[i] to whom it had been referred by the C.O.P. At the end of the discussion he promised that he would instruct the relevant official to tell him (Brig Aucamp) as soon as a letter from you had been received by the prison. This arrangement, he assured me, would solve my difficulties in this particular regard, an assurance which I completely accepted. But now we are exactly where we were before I made these representations to the head of the C.O.P. & to Brig Aucamp. Though on APRIL 8 Lt. Fourie had told me in your presence that he had received your FEBRUARY & MARCH letters only that for FEBRUARY has been delivered & I still await that of MARCH. Those for APRIL & MAY are also overdue. I am disturbed to note that my representations to the head of the Prison Dept & an assurance from Brig. Aucamp, in regard to an issue which they can easily straighten out, should turn out to be fruitless.

One ought not to experience difficulties of this sort in communicating with his family.

As you know none of the birthday cards that you have sent me since 1969 have reached. I have not had the courage to tell you that not even the Xmas cards sent by the children on 1st December arrived. I cannot even be sure that Maki[ii] got the birthday card I sent her last month. I suggest that you urgently communicate with the C.O.P. in Pretoria, or if he is not there, then through his Cape Town address, and bring the whole matter to his attention again. [?] you register all your letters & you should have little difficulty in finding out from the G.P.O. where they were dispatched, whether they reached their destination, who received them on what date?

It is right that you should know that your letters to me are heavily censored. You do not number the pages and it is often difficult to know whether I have been given the whole letter but lines 43, 44, 45, 46 & 47 on the second page of the letter of January 30 were obliterated. With the exception of the words "lives in prison" the whole of line 12 on the first page of that of FEBRUARY 26 was also obliterated. Lines 30, 31 and 32 on page 2 of this letter were deleted & the last SEVEN lines cut out.

You now keep copies of all the letters you write to me and from now on you will be better able to know what things you must avoid in future letters. My second letter has gone to Thoko[iii] & the third to Shadrack & Nyanya.[iv] Please check up whether Uncle Allen got my April letter. Have you now information about the one I wrote to Douglas Lukhele?[v] It would seem that

---

i   Brigadier Aucamp, commanding officer of Robben Island – see the glossary.
ii   Makaziwe Mandela (1954–), Mandela's eldest daughter – see the glossary.
iii   Thoko Mandela, the daughter of his late son Thembi (for Thembi Mandela, see the glossary).
iv   Nonyaniso (Nyanya) Madikizela, Winnie Mandela's youngest sister.
v   Douglas Lukhele, Harvard-educated Swazi lawyer who did his articles at Mandela and Oliver Tambo's law firm in

Lily[i] plans to visit me this November. She would naturally be free to come down if you approve. I intend writing to her, perhaps next month, care of you again, to indicate that it would be desirable for her to arrange the visit through you. November is, however, not a suitable occasion for her because it is the time when you or the children would like to come along. By the way, last year I asked you to arrange for Kgatho[ii] to be here in Dec for I thought you had chosen November because you would not be able to come down on Xmas. Anyway please let me know soon how you feel about the intended visit in November. In November 1970 Joe's mum[iii] P/B 36, Gaborone promised to send me ALBERTI'S ACCOUNT OF THE XHOSA IN 1807.[iv] I wrote back immediately to tell her that the officer in charge of studies then had agreed that I could receive the book. I never heard from her again. Are you keeping in touch with Sef & Nali?[v] Remember what they have done for you? Tell Zeni & Zindzi[vi] that I shall write to them soon. In the meantime tons & tons of love and a million kisses, darling.

Devotedly, Dalibunga

Nkosikazi Nobandla Mandela, 8115 Orlando West, Johannesburg

To the commanding officer, Robben Island

NELSON MANDELA: 466/64

7th March 1973

The Commanding Officer,
Robben Island.

My tooth-feeling is giving me trouble, it is painful and now and again bleeds when I eat. Further it is sensitive to heat and cold.

---

the 1950s. He was the first Swazi attorney-general and high court judge in Swaziland. See Mandela's letter to him on page 184.
i   Lilian Ngoyi (1911–80), politician, and anti-apartheid and women's rights activist – see the glossary.
ii   Makgatho (Kgatho) Mandela (1950–2005), Mandela's second-born son – see the glossary.
iii   This is probably Frieda Matthews (1905–98), friend and wife of his university professor Z. K. Matthews, as she was from Botswana and her son Bakwe Matthews (1929–2010) was also known as Joe – see the glossary for these three individuals.
iv   Ludwig Alberti, *Ludwig Alberti's Account of the Xhosa in 1807*, translated by W. Fehr (Cape Town: A.A. Balkema, 1968).
v   Nancy and Sefton Vutela, Winnie's sister and her husband.
vi   Zenani (1959–) and Zindzi (1960–) Mandela, their daughters – see the glossary – who were at boarding school in Swaziland.

In this connection I should be pleased if you would kindly arrange for a dentist to attend to me at the earliest possible convenience. I have sufficient funds to cover his expenses.

NELSON MANDELA: 466/64
[Signed NRMandela]

To the commanding officer, Robben Island

7th March 1973

The Commanding Officer,
Robben Island.

My eyes were last tested for reading glasses in November 1970, and I should be pleased if you would kindly arrange for my eyes to be tested at the earliest possible convenience. I have enough funds to cover the costs of such a test.

NELSON MANDELA: 466/64
[Signed NRMandela]

To Helen Suzman,[i] opposition member of Parliament in South Africa

Nelson Mandela 466/64   A Group   March 1, 1974

Dear Doctor Suzman,

I have just learnt with sincere pleasure that the University of Oxford has honoured you with the Degree of Civil Laws, and I write to give you my warmest congratulations.

   I do not exactly know when the degree was conferred, whether you were able to travel there to receive it, nor have I even the faintest idea of the

---

i   Helen Suzman (1917–2009), academic, politician, anti-apartheid activist, and MP for the opposition party – see the glossary.

address, if any, which you delivered on that occasion. Of course, views on important questions of principle and method do not always coincide even amongst those who are inspired by the same ideals and whose goal in life is substantially the same. Your reservations in regard to much that I consider natural and inevitable are well-known and even understandable. Nonetheless, yours would be an address which, for obvious reasons, I would have read very carefully. It would attempt to present the point of view of a large segment of liberal opinion that has remained stubbornly vocal. Perhaps one day there will be opportunity to see it.

In the meantime, I hope you will not consider it out of place for me to say that this is an honour which you thoroughly deserve. A public career such as the one you have chosen, and taking into account all the circumstances, offers many challenges that would deter the average man. It requires a thick skin and strong nerves which you possess in abundance. It means constant hard work, rough passage all along the line, many days, weeks and even months away from your loved ones, and results which, though we hope will come in our lifetime, may in fact be enjoyed only by posterity long after those who laboured for them will have passed from the scene. It is always a source of great comfort to know that your efforts are widely appreciated. Oxford has given you a shot in the arm, an event which must have come as a source of great pleasure to your family and the wider cause that you serve. Perhaps you will permit me a bit of selfishness in hoping that this will even tempt you to cross over to this side more often than you have done in the past.[i]

S.A. has produced a rich crop of eminent women who have played an independent role in our history. At the beginning of the last century 'Manthatisi[ii] rose to command what was by the standards of the time, a powerful army which influenced the course of events in this country, particularly in the Free State and the N.W. Cape. Olive Schreiner[iii] was a militant liberal with a dynamic pen. Even today some of her writings and speeches could turn jelly into solid rock. On the other hand, Cissie Gool[iv] operated within a comparatively narrow compass, but her stand on matters essentially local had repercussions far beyond the W. Cape. A contemporary of yours, Elisabeth Eybers,[v] has written some of the most beautiful poetry

i   Suzman continuously raised the issue of political prisoners in Parliament and first met Mandela and his comrades on Robben Island in 1967.
ii   Queen Manthatisi led the Tlôkwa people during the period of the Difiqane/Mefacane wars, 1815–40, until her son, Sekonyela was old enough to rule.
iii   Olive Schreiner (1855–1920), South African author, feminist, socialist, and pacifist.
iv   Cissie Gool was the founder and first president of the National Liberation League, president of the Non-European United Front in the 1940s, and the first coloured woman to graduate from law school in South Africa and be called to the Cape Bar.
v   Elisabeth Eybers (1915–2007), South African poet who mainly wrote in Afrikaans.

in the country and, as "Dertiger", blazed the trail in the sphere of literature. Foremost amongst the women who today are making a significant contribution in the educational, literary, political and sociological field is Fatima Meer[i] who is attracting attention from far and wide, whilst Ray Alexander,[ii] an active trade unionist since the thirties, has been a commanding figure in the struggle of the workers for a better life.

These are but a few of the many women in S.A. who have made, and are making, a definite mark in public affairs. The link that unites them all is the fine tradition they have built. May be that is that fine tradition which has consciously or unconsciously inspired you to venture out of the sanctuary of your comfortable and happy home into the storms and frustrations of your present life. If today that fine tradition still finds echo inside the most important organ of governance here, it is mainly because you had the courage to step out into the arena when many would prefer to remain on the sidelines.

Perhaps at times you have been driven to near-despair by what seems to be a hopeless endeavour – a task undertaken by a single hand where a whole legion is required. I trust that any doubts you might have entertained have now been completely dispelled, that you will consider both the honour, as well as the numerous messages of congratulations I assume you received, as a tangible expression of the crucial value of your efforts. You have many friends and well-wishers.

Once more, my warmest congratulations! May the coming month be a day of joyful occurrence for you and colleagues. Fondest regards to you and family.

Yours very sincerely,
[Signed NR Mandela]

Dr Helen Suzman, M.P., c/o Nkosikazi Nobandla Mandela, House no 8115, Orlando West, P.O. Phirima, Johannesburg

---

i   Fatima Meer (1928–2010), writer, academic, and anti-apartheid and women's rights activist – see the glossary.
ii   Ray Alexander was born in Latvia and arrived in South Africa on 6 November 1929 where she joined the Communist Party of South Africa at age sixteen.

1/3/74

SECRET[i]

LETTER FROM PRISONER MANDELA TO MRS H SUZMAN, MP.

THE HONOURABLE THE DEPUTY MINISTER OF PRISONS.

1. Attached hereto is a typewritten copy of a letter from prisoner Nelson Mandela, addressed to Mrs. H Suzman, MP. Via Nkisikazi[ii] [*sic*] Nobandla Mandela[iii] or Orlando West, for your information.
2. As the letter does not convey any domestic affairs, but is dressed with political suggestions and ideas, it has not been released

JC STEYN

COMMISSIONER OF PRISONS
CHIEF DEPUTY COMMISSIONER (FUNCTIONAL)

Copy for your information

[Signed]

COMMISSIONER OF PRISONS

[Stamp dated] 3-4-1974

<><><><><><>

In 1973 Winnie Mandela was sentenced to twelve months for having lunch with her children in the presence of a banned person, photographer Peter Magubane. Six months were shaved off the sentence when she appealed, and she was forced to serve the remaining six months in Kroonstad Prison in Kroonstad in the Orange Free State (now the Free State).

　　　When she was not in prison she lived in a state of insecurity at home where more than once she was physically attacked in the dead of night. Mandela did everything in his power that he could, including petititioning the minister of justice to provide her with protection.

---

i　　It is not immediately clear why the official marked this cover note as 'Secret' other than that he intended for it to remain secret that it was not sent.
ii　　Correct spelling should be *Nkosikazi*, meaning 'Mrs.' in isiXhosa.
iii　　Nobandla is one of Winnie Mandela's names.

To the minister of justice

[Message in another hand in Afrikaans at the top of the letter] 466/64 N. Mandela. Special letter to Commissioner about how his wife is being handled

13 May 1974

The Honourable Advocate J Kruger,[i]
Minister of Justice
Pretoria.

Dear Sir,

I should be pleased if you would treat this matter as one of the utmost urgency. I should have liked to have made these representations more than three months ago, but due to my current circumstances and the measured pace at which government departments are accustomed to move, it has not been possible for me to write earlier than today.

1

In this connection, I should be grateful if you would:

a) grant my wife, Mrs Winnie Mandela, House no 8115 Orlando West, Johannesburg, a permit to acquire a firearm for purposes of self-defence;

b) request the Minister of Police to order members of the South African Police in dealing with my wife to confine themselves strictly to the execution of their duties according to law.

c) use your influence with the City Council of Johannesburg to relax their influx control regulations and to allow my brother-in-law Mr Msuthu Thanduxolo Madikizela,[ii] and his wife to live permanently with my wife at 8115 Orlando West, Johannesburg.

d) arrange with the Minister of Police for members of the South African Police to guard the house daily from 7 pm to 6 am until my brother-in-law and his family join my wife.

---

i   James (Jimmy) Kruger (1917–87), minister of justice and police, 1974–79 – see the glossary.
ii   One of Winnie Mandela's brothers.

466/64. N. Mandela.   A/B. aan Komm. oor sy vrou se behandel g.

81/142289

Robben Island Prison.
Robben Island.
13 May 1974.

The Honourable Advocate J. Kruger,
Minister of Justice
Pretoria.
Dear Sir,

I should be pleased if you would treat this matter as one of the utmost urgency. I should have liked to have made these representations more than two months ago, but due to my current circumstances and the measured pace at which government departments are accustomed to move, it has not been possible for me to write earlier than today.

In this connection, I should be grateful if you would:
(a) grant my wife, Mrs Winnie Mandela, House no. 8115 Orlando West, Johannesburg, a permit to acquire a firearm for purposes of self-defence;
(b) request the Minister of Police to order members of the South African Police in dealing with my wife to confine themselves strictly to the execution of their duties according to law.
(c) use your influence with the City Council of Johannesburg to relax their influx control regulations and to allow my brother-in-law, Mr Msuthu Thanduxolo Madikizela, and his wife to live permanently with my wife at 8115 Orlando West, Johannesburg.
(d) arrange with the Minister of Police for members of the South African Police to guard the house daily from 7 p.m. to 6 a.m. until my brother-in-law and his family join my wife.
(e) to request the Minister of Interior to furnish my wife with a passport to enable her to holiday abroad.
(f) grant my wife and me a two-hour contact visit for the purpose of discussing the special problems outlined here.

2

My wife is a person upon whom notice has been served under the provisions of the Suppression of Communism Act, 44 of 1950. I have not had the opportunity of seeing the actual text of the abovementioned notice, but to the best of my knowledge and belief, she is prohibited from

GPS-(7)-B

A letter to the minister of justice, 13 May 1974, see pages 251–264.

2

attending gatherings, entering a factory, an educational centre or similar places. Though she is free to take up employment within the urban area of Johannesburg, she is otherwise ~~compelled~~ confined to Orlando Township and is not permitted to enter the rest of the area in Johannesburg known as Soweto.

3

In terms of the abovementioned notice, and with the exception of our two daughters now aged 15 and 13 respectively, no person is allowed to visit the house during certain specified hours. As the children were then, and still are, away at a boarding school for the greater part of the year, this meant that she had to live all alone in the house.

4

Towards the end of 1970 and again on 27 May 1971 I wrote to your predecessor, Mr P C Pelser, requesting him to grant me an interview to enable me to discuss with him my wife's house-arrest and its implications. In this connection I wish to refer you to the following passage in my letter of 27 May 1971:

"I consider it dangerous for a woman and detrimental to her health to live alone in a rough city like Johannesburg. She suffers from an illness which is caused by worry and tension and which has on occasions rendered her unconscious. Believe me when I say that I have since September last year lived in a real nightmare. She has visited me thrice since her release from prison, and the harmful effects of many nights of loneliness, fear and anxiety are written across her face. She looks frail and spent. I am further told that her hardships have been carefully and fully explained to you, without success, by herself as well as her legal representative. I cannot get myself to accept that you could remain indifferent where the very life of another human being is actually involved, and I ask you to relax the notice to enable her to live with friends and relatives."

In addition, I raised other family problems which I considered serious and repeated the request for an interview.

5

I was informed by the Commanding Officer at the time, and by Brigadier Aucamp, that both letters had been forwarded to your predecessor.

e) to request the Minister of Interior to furnish my wife with a passport to enable her to holiday abroad.

f) grant my wife and me a two-hour contact visit for the purpose of discussing the special problems outlined here.

2

My wife is a person upon whom notice has been served under the provisions of the Suppression of Communism Act, 44 of 1950. I have not had the opportunity of seeing the actual text of the abovementioned notice, but to the best of my knowledge and belief, she is prohibited from attending gatherings, entering a factory, an educational centre or similar places. Though she is free to take up employment within the urban area of Johannesburg, she is otherwise confined to Orlando township and is not permitted to enter the rest of the area in Johannesburg known as Soweto.

3

In terms of the abovementioned notice, and with the exception of our two daughters now aged 15 and 13 respectively, no person is allowed to visit the house during certain specified hours. As the children were then and still are, away at a boarding school for the greater part of the year, this meant that she had to live all alone in the house.

4

Towards the end of 1970 and again on 27 May 1971 I wrote to your predecessor, Mr P.C. Pelser,[i] requesting him to grant me an interview to enable me to discuss with him my wife's house-arrest and its implications. In this connection I wish to refer you to the following passage in my letter of 27 May 1971:

> "I consider it dangerous for a woman and detrimental to her health to live alone in a rough city like Johannesburg. She suffers from an illness which is caused by worry and tension and which has on occasions rendered her unconscious. Believe me when I say that I have since September last year lived in a real nightmare. She has visited me thrice since her release from prison, and the harmful effects of many nights of loneliness, fear and anxiety are written across her face. She looks pale and spent. I am further told that her hardships have been carefully and fully explained to you, without success, by herself as well

---

i   See his letters from 14 September 1970 and 19 November 1970, pages 195 and 199.

as her legal representative. I cannot get myself to accept that you could remain indifferent where the very life of another human being is actually involved, and I ask you to relax the notice to enable her to live with friends and relatives."

In addition, I raised other family problems which I considered serious and repeated the request for an interview.

5

I was informed by the Commanding Officer at the time, and by Brigadier Aucamp,[i] that both letters had been forwarded to your predecessor.
I regret to advise you, however, that Mr Pelser did not even favour me with the courtesy of an acknowledgement to say nothing of a reasoned reply.
However, some time after the May 1971 letter had been forwarded my wife informed me that the notice had been relaxed and that she could now live with such relatives or friends as were qualified to remain within the urban area of Johannesburg in terms of its influx control regulations. She further informed me that although the terms of the notice were still restrictive, some of the problems about which I had complained in my second letter had somewhat eased.

6

In pursuance of the abovementioned relaxation our friends, Mr and Mrs Madhlala, came to live with my wife. To the best of my knowledge and belief, the Madhlalas were not associated with any of the political organisations that fight against racial oppression generally and the policy of separate development in particular. In spite of this, the Security Police repeatedly dragged them to their headquarters and subjected them to gruelling interrogation. As a result of this harassment they were reluctantly compelled to leave our place. The news of the experiences of the Madhlalas at our house spread far and wide and people, including close friends who would readily agree to reside with my wife, took fright and are now unwilling to do anything that may attract the attention of the Security Police, so much so that today there is hardly any person who is willing to share the type of life my wife is forced to lead.

7

The one and only person who is still prepared to live with my wife is Mr Madikizela, and I must request you to use your influence with the City

---

i   Brigadier Aucamp, commanding officer of Robben Island – see the glossary.

3

I regret to advise you, however, that mr Pelser did not even favour me
with the courtesy of an acknowledgment to say nothing of a reasoned
reply. However,

* Some time after the May 1971 letter had been forwarded my wife
informed me that the notice had been relaxed and that she could now live
with such relatives or friends as were qualified to remain within the urban
area of Johannesburg in terms of its influx control regulations. She further
informed me that although the terms of the notice were still restrictive,
some of the problems about which I had complained in my second
letter had somewhat eased.

6

In pursuance of the aforementioned relaxation our friends, mr and mrs
Madhlala, came to live with my wife. To the best of my knowledge and
belief, the Madhlalas were not associated with any of the political
organisations that fight against racial oppression generally and the policy
of Separate Development in particular. In spite of this, the Security Police
repeatedly dragged them to their headquarters and subjected them to
gruelling interrogation. As a result of this harassment they were
reluctantly compelled to leave our place. The news of the experiences of
the Madhlalas at our house spread far and wide and people, including
those close friends who would readily agree to reside with my wife, took
fright and are now unwilling to do anything that may attract the
attention of the security Police, so much so that today there is hardly
any person who is willing to share the type of life my wife is forced
to lead.

7

The one and only person who is still prepared to live with my wife
is mr Madikizela, and I must request you to use your influence with
the City Council of Johannesburg to give him permission to live at
8115 Orlando West. I must add that prior to her endorsement out of
the urban area of Johannesburg, mr Madikizela, stayed with my
wife.

8

The fears I expressed in my letters to your predecessor were not
unfounded. On several occasions my wife has been the subject of brutal

A letter to the minister of justice, 13 May 1974, see pages 251–64.

4

night attacks from criminals whose identity is unknown to us. In this connection I wish to quote from a letter she wrote to me on 6 December 1972:

"You must have perhaps heard from our mutual informer of the serious events which have left me quite shaken. Briefly, the house was broken into whilst I went home with the children to see my sick father. All our little valuable possessions were taken, the strange thief did extensive damage to the house, smashed to pieces what he could not take, tore down paintings from the walls, broke our glass partition, smashed the glass doors, removed books and personal documents...

"Then at 3.30 am Sunday morning two weeks ago, three black men gained entry into the house through the same window which I had not fixed because the police had not taken the statement of the burglary. They tried to strangle me with a cloth. Had he not taken a deep breath as he bent over my neck to tie the cloth I would not have heard anything I did not know I could scream so much, they switched off the lights & fighting them off in the dark saved me. I sustained slight injuries. I was given police protection for a few days whilst an urgent application was made for someone to stay with me. My attorneys applied for Msuthu & Nonyaniso & her husband temporarily whilst the Minister is deciding on Msuthu. However, I was subsequently granted permission for a Mr & Mrs Nsikonisko whom I met at work, they have been given 7 days at a time & their permit is expiring tomorrow. Our problem is that no one is prepared to share my kind of life, the situation is far worse now."

I also quote from her letter of 20 March 1974:

"The last attempt on my life on the 9th [i.e. 9 February] has left me quite speechless.... The damage to the house was quite speechless extensive. I have been battling to repair what can be repaired, the garage doors need complete replacement. The hatred with which iron doors were torn apart like pieces of wood is indescribable. It is a mystery to me how the house doors took so long to give in with such heavy impact on them."

These events show that the effect of the restrictions placed upon my

Council of Johannesburg to give him permission to live at 8115 Orlando
West. I must add that prior to his endorsement out of the urban area of
Johannesburg, Mr Madikizela stayed with my wife.

8

The fears I expressed in my letters to your predecessors were not unfounded.
On several occasions my wife has been the subject of brutal night attacks
from criminals whose identity is unknown to us. In this connection I wish
to quote from a letter she wrote me on 6 December 1972:

> "You must have perhaps heard from our mutual informer of
> the serious events which have left me quite shaken. Briefly, the
> house was broken into whilst I went home with the children
> to see my sick father. All our little valuable possessions were
> taken, the strange thief did extensive damage to the house,
> smashed to pieces what he could not take, tore down paintings
> from the walls, broke our glass partition, smashed the glass
> doors, removed books and personal documents . . .[i]

> "Then at 3.30 am Sunday morning two weeks ago, three black
> man gained entry into the house through the same window
> which I had not fixed because the police had not taken the state-
> ment of the burglary. They tried to strangle me with a cloth. Had
> he not taken a deep breath as he bent over my neck to tie the
> cloth I would not have heard anything. I did not know I could
> scream so much, they switched off the light & fighting them
> off in the dark saved me. I sustained slight injuries. I was given
> police protection for a few days whilst an urgent application was
> made for someone to stay with me. My attorneys applied for
> Msuthu & Nonyaniso[ii] and her husband temporarily whilst the
> Minister is deciding on Msuthu. However I was subsequently
> granted permission for a Mr & Mrs Ntsokonsoko whom I met
> at work, they have been given 7 days at a time and their permit
> is expiring tomorrow. Our problem is that no one is prepared to
> share my kind of life, the situation is far worse now."

I also quote from her letter of 20 March 1974:

> "The last attempt on my life on the 9th (i.e. 9 February) has
> left me quite speechless . . . The damage to the house was quite
> extensive. I have been battling to repair what can be repaired,

---

i   Mandela's own ellipsis.
ii   Nonyaniso (Nyana) Madikizela, Winnie Mandela's youngest sister.

the garage doors need complete replacement. The hatred with which iron doors were torn apart, like pieces of wood is indescribable. It is a mystery to me how the house doors took so long to give in with such heavy impact on them."

These events show that the effects of the restrictions placed upon my wife, and the persistent refusal of the Johannesburg City Council to allow Mr Madikizela to stay with her, have made her an easy target to a mysterious type of thugs. An Alsatian dog, which she acquired at the end of 1970, was poisoned and killed quite obviously by a person who has considerable experience in dealing with dogs that are trained to do police duties and to accept food from one person only.

All the fears I expressed to your predecessor have been confirmed and today my wife lives in perpetual danger and acute anxiety. I am reluctantly compelled to request you to give her a permit to acquire a firearm for purposes of self-defence, a request which I hope you will consider fair and reasonable, having regard to all the circumstances. I might add, that last year a man attempted to stab her in the streets of Johannesburg in broad daylight and she was saved only by the intervention of friends. The man was subsequently arrested, but I have been told that the charge was later withdrawn.

9

In the light of my wife's experiences I must ask you to arrange for the house to be guarded by members of the South African Police daily from 7 pm to 6 am. Until Mr Madikizela moves in.

I must point out that from all the reports I have received the Security Police have acted towards my wife in a manner which I cannot accept as a proper execution of their duties. She is shadowed wherever she goes, taxi men whom she hires to convey her to and from work are frequently interrogated, and those who come to stay with her persistently harassed. Generally their attitude is hostile and on occasions positively provocative. Your intervention could give her some respite and ease the strain.

10

In spite of all her bitter experiences my wife has no intention whatsoever of leaving the house. But I think it advisable for her to be furnished with a passport to enable her to travel abroad on holiday. Getting away from Orlando for a month or two might ease the strain and benefit her health immensely.

B

wife, and the persistent refusal of the Johannesburg City Council to allow
Mr Madikizela to stay with her, have made her an easy target to a mysterious
type of thugs. An alsation dog, which she acquired at the end of 1970, was
poisoned and killed quite obviously by a person who has considerable
experience in dealing with dogs that are trained to do police duties and to
accept food from one person only.

All the fears I expressed to your predecessor have been confirmed and
today my wife lives ~~under~~ perpetual danger and acute anxiety. I am
reluctantly compelled to request you to give her a permit to acquire a
firearm for purposes of self-defence, a request which I hope you will
consider fair and reasonable, having regard to all the circumstances. I
might add that last year a man attempted to stab her in the streetz of
Johannesburg in broad daylight and she was saved only by the
intervention of friends. The man was subsequently arrested, but I have
been told that the charge was later withdrawn.

9

In the light of my wife's experiences I must ask you to arrange for
the house to be guarded by members of the South African Police daily from
7 p.m to 6 am. until Mr Madikizela moves in.

I must point out that from the reports I have received the security
police have acted towards my wife in a manner which I cannot accept
as a proper execution of their duties. She is shadowed wherever she goes,
taximen whom she hires to convey her to and from work are frequently
interrogated, and those who come to stay with her persistently harassed.
Generally their attitude is hostile and on occasions positively provocative.
your intervention could give her some respite and ease the strain.

10

In spite of all her bitter experiences my wife has no intention whatsoever
of leaving the house. But I think it advisable for her to be furnished
with a passport to enable her to travel abroad on holiday. Getting
away from Orlando for a month or two might ease the strain and
benefit her health immensely.

11

I must add that although I have now completed eleven years of
my sentence, and although I have reached 'A' Group, the highest

A letter to the minister of justice, 13 May 1974, see pages 251–64.

6.   problems

classification a prisoner may attain, I have never been given the privilege
of a contact visit with my wife. I have been forced to discuss serious domestic *
across a glass partition, and under difficult conditions where I have to
shout to be heard even in regard to highly confidential matters. Moreover,
the one hour allocated for the visit is too short a period, if account is
taken of our special problems. I must accordingly ask you to allow me
a two-hour contact visit, with all the normal liberties and courtesies
associated with such visits, for the purpose of discussing these special
problems.

12.

I am quite certain that if you think that my representations are
reasonable and substantial, and you consider it your duty to help, all
red tape will be brushed aside and our problems could be solved with a
stroke of the pen.

13.

It would be quite easy for you to reject each and every one of the
requests I have made. You could, for example, point out that the
question of the relaxation of influx control regulations is a matter
outside your competence and within the jurisdiction of the Johannesburg
City Council. You could adopt the same attitude towards my request
in regard to the South African Police and passports, and tell me that
my wife and I should apply directly to the appropriate authorities. You
could even go further to rub it in by adding that my wife, in
fighting racial oppression, has deliberately invited all the troubles
she is now experiencing, and that the Security Police, in giving
more than ordinary attention to her movements and activities, are
carrying out their normal duties under the law.

14.

I am well aware that, in view of all the circumstances, my
representations will have to be approached cautiously and carefully,
and that a decision either way will carry a heavy responsibility. Your
official capacity may demand that you should pay attention to policy
and security considerations which will result in grave injustices to
specific individuals. I am also aware that the decision you arrive at
in your ministerial capacity may frequently clash with your own

GPS-(F)-8

11

I must add that although I have now completed eleven years of my sentence, and although I have reached 'A' Group, the highest classification a prisoner may attain, I have never been given the privilege of a contact visit with my wife. I have been forced to discuss serious domestic * problems across a glass partition, and under difficult conditions where I have to shout to be heard even in regard to highly confidential matters. Moreover, the one hour allocated for the visit is too short a period, if account is taken of our special problems. I must accordingly ask you to allow me a two-hour contact visit, with all the normal liberties and courtesies associated with such visits, for the purpose of discussing these special problems.

12

I am quite certain that if you think that my representations are reasonable and substantial, and you consider it your duty to help, all red tape will be brushed aside and our problems could be solved with the stroke of a pen.

13

It would be quite easy for you to reject each and every one of the requests I have made. You could, for example, point out that the question of the relaxation of influx control regulations is a matter outside your competence and within the jurisdiction of the Johannesburg City Council. You could adopt the same attitude towards my request in regard to the South African Police and passports, and tell me that my wife and I should apply directly to the appropriate authorities. You could even go further to rub it in by adding that my wife, in fighting racial oppression, had deliberately invited all the troubles she is now experiencing, and that the Security Police, in giving more than ordinary attention to her movements and activities, are carrying out their normal duties under the law.

14

I am well aware that, in view of all the circumstances, my representations will have to be approached cautiously and carefully, and that a decision either way will carry a heavy responsibility. Your official capacity may demand that you should pay attention to policy and security considerations which will result in grave injustices to specific individuals. I am also aware that the decisions you arrive at in your Ministerial capacity may frequently clash with your own personal feelings in matters of this nature.

7

personal feelings in matters of this nature.

15

The representations contained in this letter are made in the knowledge and certainty that they can be approved in such manner and under such conditions as will not endanger the security of the State or the public interest.

Above all, is the fact that the central issue in this matter is that the life of another human being, of a citizen, is at stake. I feel confident that in examining my requests you will allow humanitarian considerations to override all others, and do everything in your power to enable my wife to lead at last a normal and happy life

Yours faithfully,
NRmandela.
NELSON MANDELA. 466/64.

A letter to the minister of justice, 13 May 1974, see pages 251–64.

15

The representations contained in this letter are made in the knowledge and certainty that they can be approved in such manner and under such conditions as will not endanger the security of the State or the public interest. Above all, is the fact that the central issue in this matter is that the life of another human being, of a citizen, is at stake. I feel confident that in examining my requests you will allow humanitarian considerations to override all others, and do everything in your power to enable my wife to lead at last a normal and happy life.

  Yours faithfully,
[Signed NRMandela]
NELSON MANDELA 466/64

To the minister of justice

[Partly illegible note in another hand in Afrikaans] 466/64. Special Letter

25 May 1974

The Honourable Advocate J Kruger,[i]
Minister of Justice, Prisons and Police,
Pretoria.

Dear Sir,

Further to my letter of 13 February 1974[ii] in connection with the attempts made on my wife's life, I have to advise that on 22 May 1974 I received the following disturbing telegram from her:

> "Another vicious attack 12 am today police investigation no arrest one face assailant seen house helper nearly died we are all right children returning school 26/5 cheer up you are our force [Source][iii] of strength all our love"

In my letter of 13 February I should have added the following passage from my wife's letter of 29 April 1974:

---

i   James (Jimmy) Kruger (1917–87), minister of justice and police, 1974–79 – see the glossary.
ii   He is most likely referring to his letter of 13 May 1974 rather than 13 February. See his letter on page 251.
iii   Mandela wrote 'sorce' in square brackets.

"I hope you have taken some steps towards the question of my younger brother Msuthu. The state of anxiety in which I always am when the children are around is unbearable. Although I have learnt to expect anything to happen to me, I cannot bear the thought of the dangers my children are exposed to. My would be killers struck four days after the children left for school last time. As a result they did not settle down at all this term, especially Zindzi who seems to be more scared than Zeni."[i]

You will readily appreciate when I say that I am very concerned about the whole matter and should be pleased if you would treat it as one of the utmost urgency.

Yours faithfully,
[Signed NRMandela]
NELSON MANDELA 466/64

To the West Rand Board

18 June 1974

The Manager
West Rand Board

Dear Sir,

I am the registered tenant of House No 8115 Orlando West, Johannesburg, and now serving a sentence of life imprisonment. This is an application for permission for my brother-in-law, Mr Msuthu Thanduxolo Madikizela, and his wife to live with Mrs Nobandla Winnie Mandela, my wife, at the above house.

My wife is a person upon whom notice has been served under the Suppression of Communism Act, 44 of 1950. I have not had the opportunity of seeing the actual text of the abovementioned notice, but to the best of my knowledge and belief, she is prohibited from attending gatherings, entering a factory, an educational centre or similar places. Though she is free to take

---

i   Zindziswa Mandela (1960–) and Zenani Mandela (1959–), Mandela's youngest and middle daughters – see the glossary.

up employment within the urban area of Johannesburg, she is otherwise confined to Orlando Township and is not permitted to enter the rest of the area in Johannesburg known as Soweto.

In terms of the notice mentioned above, and with the exception of our two daughters now aged 15 and 13 respectively, no person is allowed to visit the house during certain specified hours. As the children then were, and still are, away at a boarding school for the greater part of the year, this meant that she had to live all alone in the house.

On several occasions my wife has been the victim of night attacks from criminals whose identity is unknown to us. But from all the reports I have received it seems clear that these attacks were inspired, and that although the actual persons employed to undertake the sordid work of attempting to assassinate an innocent and defenceless woman may be criminals, they are in fact no more than mere agents of powerful interests. In this connection I wish to quote from a letter my wife wrote to me on 6 December 1972:

> "You must have perhaps heard from our mutual informer of the serious events which have left me quite shaken. Briefly the house was broken in whilst I went home (i.e. Transkei) with the children to see my sick father. All our valuable possessions were taken; the strange thief did extensive damage to the house, smashed to pieces what he could not take, tore down paintings from the walls, broke our glass partition, smashed the glass doors, removed books and personal documents . . .[i]

> "Then at 3.30 am Sunday morning [sic][ii] two weeks ago, three black men gained entry into the house through the same window which I had not fixed because the police had not taken the statement of the burglary. They tried to strangle me with a cloth. Had he not taken a deep breath as he bent over my neck to tie the cloth, I would not have heard anything. I did not know I could scream so much, they switched off the light and fighting them off in the dark saved me. My attorneys applied for Msuthu,[iii] Nonyaniso[iv] and her husband temporarily whilst the Minister is deciding on Msuthu. However, I was subsequently granted permission for a Mr and Mrs Ntsokontsiko whom I met at work, they have been given 7 days at a time & their permit is

---

i   Mandela's own ellipsis.
ii   Mandela's own 'sic' in square brackets.
iii   Msuthu Tanduxolo Madikizela, Winnie Mandela's brother.
iv   Nonyaniso (Nyana) Madikizela, Winnie Mandela's youngest sister.

expiring tomorrow. Our problem is that no one is prepared to share my kind of life, the situation is far worse now."

I also quote from her letter on 20 March 1974.

"The last attempt on my life on 9th (i.e. 9 February) has left me quite speechless . . . The damage to the house was quite extensive. I have been battling to repair what can be repaired, the garage doors need complete replacement. The hatred with which iron doors were torn apart like pieces of wood is indescribable. It is a mystery to me how the house doors took so long to give in with such a heavy impact on them."

Then on 29 April 1974 she wrote:

"I hope you have taken some steps towards the question of my younger brother Msuthu. The state of anxiety in which I always am when the children are around is unbearable. Although I have learnt to expect anything to happen to me, I cannot bear the thought of the dangers my children are exposed to. My would-be killers struck four days after the children left for school last time. As a result they did not settle down at all this term, especially Zindzi who seems to be more scared than Zeni."[i]

Finally, I wish to quote the following disturbing telegram from my wife sent on May 22:

"Another vicious attack 12am today police investigation no arrest one face assailant seen house helper nearly died we are all right children returning school 26/5 cheer up you are our force [sic][ii] of strength all our love."

Shortly after my conviction and my imprisonment, Mr Madikizela came to live with my wife at Orlando West but was later endorsed out of the urban area, thus compelling my wife to live all alone. The persistent refusal of the local authority to allow him to return has made her an easy target to a mysterious type of thug. An Alsatian dog she acquired at the end of 1970 was poisoned and killed, quite obviously by a person or persons with considerable experience in dealing with dogs trained to do police duties and to accept food from one person only.

---

i   Zindziswa Mandela (1960–) and Zenani Mandela (1959–), Mandela's youngest and middle daughters – see the glossary.
ii   Mandela's own 'sic' in square brackets.

I might add that last year a man attempted to stab her in the streets of Johannesburg in broad daylight and she was saved only by the intervention of friends. Although this particular aspect has no direct bearing on the request I am making to you, I have deemed it proper to mention it so that you could see our special problem in a wider context. During 1971 and after I had made written representations to Mr P.C. Pelser, then Minister for Justice,[i] the restrictions imposed on my wife were relaxed, and she could now live with such relatives or friends as were qualified to remain within the urban area of Johannesburg.

In pursuance of the abovementioned relaxation, our friends, Mr and Mrs Madhlala, came to live with my wife in Orlando West. To the best of my knowledge and belief, the Madhlalas were not, and are not, associated with any of the political organisations that fight against racial oppression generally, and the policy of Separate Development in particular. In spite of this, the Security Police repeatedly dragged them to their headquarters and subjected them to gruelling interrogation. As a result of this persistent harassment, the Madhlalas were reluctantly compelled to leave our place. The news of the experiences of the Madhlalas at our house spread like wild fire and people, including close friends who would have readily agreed to reside with my wife, took fright and are now unwilling to do anything that might attract the attention of the Security Police, so much so that today there is hardly any person who is willing to share the type of life my wife is forced to lead.

The one and only person who is still prepared to risk his life and stay with my wife is Mr Madikizela. As he is not entitled to remain in your urban area for more than 72 hours, I must request you to relax your influx control regulations and allow him and his wife to live together with my wife.

I am well aware that if you wished to refuse this application, you would have a multitude of excuses, technical and otherwise. For one thing, you could deal with the matter formally as the Chief Magistrate of Johannesburg and the South African Police have repeatedly done, and point out that she is free to live with anybody who is entitled to be within the urban area. You could also take up the position that it is against the policy of your Board to make exceptions and advise her to leave Johannesburg instead. But I make this application in the hope that you will consider the matter on its merits and from a humanitarian angle.

Lastly, I must request you to allow us to erect a jackal fence around the house, that is, a fence of approximately eight feet high and so constructed as to prevent scaling by trespassers.

---

i   See his letters from 14 September 1970 and 19 November 1970, pages 195 and 199.

Please treat the matter as urgent.

Yours faithfully,
[Signed NRMandela]
NELSON R MANDELA

To the commanding officer, Robben Island

26 June 1974

The Commanding Officer
Robben Island

In accordance with your instructions I have attempted either to delete or to rephrase these paragraphs to which you object.[i]

I must point out, however, that in making the allegations contained in my first letter to the West Rand Board I had no desire to make propaganda or statements calculated to reflect against any particular individual or government organ. The three paragraphs you require me to delete are either statements based on facts whose accuracy cannot be challenged and which have been given wide publicity in the local and foreign press or they are necessary and obvious inferences from plain facts, e.g. the poisoning of the Alsatian. The effect of your refusal that I cite them as I had done in the first letter can only be to prevent me from relying on facts which [are] material and even decisive on the granting of my application.

I must, however, assure you that I appreciate your special problems and obligations in this regard.

[Signed NR Mandela]

[In another hand]
Censors
Dispatch please
[Signed]
27/6/74

---

i   He was instructed by the censors to rewrite his letter to the West Rand Board of 18 June 1974 (see page 265), omitting three paragraph deemed unacceptable. We do not know which paragraphs they were.

To Fatima Meer,[i] friend and comrade

Nelson Mandela, 466/64   A Group   Nov 1, '74[ii]

Wahali[iii] Fatimaben

Even if you had not sent that marvellous telegram of 14/10 I would have
been quite sure that you & Ismail would take care of the girls, that they
would not be orphans as long as you were alive, that in Zami's[iv] absence
there would be someone to whom they could turn when problems arise,
someone conversant with our background, outlook, aspirations & dreams
&, perhaps one should add, even our shortcomings. In this regard there
is hardly anybody more qualified than you. Naturally I would have liked
to discuss certain problems raised by Zami's imprisonment face to face
with you. For one thing, Zami & I were discussing the possibility of the
girls[v] holidaying in America this Dec. Cousin Njisana,[vi] who is well-known
to you, was working on the project together with Prof. Gwen Carter[vii] &
Lady Birley,[viii] London. The girls have written to me several times about the
matter. I quite appreciate their keenness to holiday abroad. They attend
school with chdn of well-to-do families who can easily afford holidaying
overseas &, judging from the girls' letters, travelling to Europe & America
has become quite a craze at their school. Now & again in discussing matters
of this nature, I am tempted to remind them not to forget that they are my
chdn, a fact that may place insurmountable difficulties in their path. But
hard reality does not often coincide with people's wishes, especially when
those people are chdn. I do not know how far our cousin had gone with the
arrangements but Zami's imprisonment may now have upset those plans.
Besides, there are those intimate problems which young girls meet as they
grapple with natural urges. Often Zami & I have tried to discuss these, but
attitudes on such questions move fairly fast & tend to shift from day to day.
She will have to swot up a lot of information on her return to be useful to
the girls. They are good girls but, I must confess, still too young to handle
such problems alone. Durban is more than 1,000 miles away & the cost of

---

i   Fatima Meer (1928–2010), writer, academic, and anti-apartheid and women's rights activist – see the glossary.
ii   The letter was stamped 'Censors Office Robben Island 19-11-74'.
iii   *Vehalie* means 'dear' in Gujarati. He probably would have asked one of his fellow prisoners who was fluent in
       Gujarati like Laloo Chiba. Mandela spelled it various ways including as *wahalie*. *Ben* means 'sister' in Gujarati.
iv   One of Winnie Mandela's names.
v   Zenani (1959–) and Zindzi (1960–) Mandela, his and Winnie Mandela's daughters – see the glossary.
vi   Winnie Mandela's cousin.
vii   Professor Gwendolen M. Carter (1906–91), Canadian–American political scientist and scholar of African affairs.
       She was a benefactor.
viii   Lady Elinor Birley whose husband Sir Robert Birley (1903–82), was the former headmaster of Eton College and
       at the time the visiting professor of education at the University of the Witwatersrand.

coming down is frightening. I do not have the courage to ask even you to come. Yet there are problems that would better be discussed face to face than by correspondence. As you know, only relatives in the first degree are permitted to come, but your special position in regard to the family generally & to the girls in particular, would entitle your application to be considered on merit.

I should like to add that my son, Kgatho,[i] 24, owes 2 subjects for his matric. He did very well up to J.C.,[ii] passing with honours, though he wrote the exams several mths after he had been expelled from the boarding school for organising (so it was alleged) a student strike. He has since lost all his sharpness & has through private tuition twice attempted matric without success. The real trouble is that at his age & in my absence he finds it a bit hard to resist the attractions of city life. I have been trying to get him back to a boarding school – Clarkebury or St John's, both in the Transkei – where he would be able to study fulltime far from the influences that make it difficult for him to concentrate on his work. He has a powerful argument to fall back upon: A comfortable job which he may lose if he accepts my suggestion & is also engaged. There is an important detail which I do not feel free to mention here. However, I suggested that he could take study leave for a yr to complete at least matric. Thereafter, I told him, we would discuss further plans. I gained the impression that we had at last convinced him & Zami was busy organising funds for him & fiancée to return to college. Unfortunately these plans will now have to be put off as well. I had discussed the matter with Danapathy[iii] & suggested that he invite Kgatho over to Durban, to take him round to places like Ngoye, Westville, your university[iv] & M.L. Sultan College[v] to see at first-hand what young people are doing elsewhere. I had hoped such an opportunity would arouse his ambitions & induce him to resume his studies more seriously. I appreciate the unfortunate crcs[vi] which might have made it very difficult for Danapathy even to think of such matters. Perhaps you & Ismail could invite Kgatho to spend a weekend with you so that you could take him round & discuss the whole matter with him. He is interested in a legal career & Ismail would be the ideal person to put the sparks into him. He lives at House No, 5818 Orlando East, J.H.B. & is employed by the Federated Insurance Co. You may also reach him through a personal call via our home. Otherwise Yusuf's Amina[vii] could contact him

---

i   Makgatho (Kgatho) Mandela (1950–2005), Mandela's second-born son – see the glossary.
ii   Junior Certificate.
iii   Fellow prisoner M. D. Naidoo.
iv   Fatima Meer worked at the University of Natal in the homeland of Natal (now KwaZulu-Natal).
v   Universities in Durban.
vi   'Circumstances'.
vii   Yusuf and Amina Cachalia – see the glossary.

on your behalf. I can entrust these problems neither to the divinities or the fates. They are all beyond my reach.

According to my records there are 630,000 S. Africans of Indian origin, 70,000 being in the Tvl & 20,000 in the Cape. How is it that in your province there are only 8 manag committees as against 25 in Tvl & 3 in Cape? Who is more or less enthusiastic than who? I expect a reply to my letter of 1/7 which I am told was forwarded to you; or must I assume that my plea for forgiveness fell on deaf ears, that you have now forgotten that we never hit one who has surrendered? Grannie Nic's health is a matter of great interest to all members of the family, & it is a source of real inspiration to hear that in spite of her great age she is still active & busy. Very few people can at 80 walk straight up, so firmly & confidently as we believe she still does. As social worker & wayfarer who, for the greater part of her life, has concerned herself almost exclusively with solving social problems of a crucial nature, bringing some relief & security to people in different walks of life, she has become something of a living symbol. She has built ties far more stronger than those of historical origin, language & even blood. For decades she has travelled up & down with nose always on the ground like a keen-scented bloodhound. She keeps to the beaten track but has hardly ever failed to muster resources & initiative to cut open a new path whenever a blind-alley loomed ahead. By now she should know every stream in that province, every valley, hill, hole & blade of grass. We are fairly confident that Mrs Monty, M.J. & Co will pull their skill & experience to keep the old girl on her feet till we meet again. Warmest love & fondest regards to her, Shamim, Shehnaz, Rashid,[i] your boyfriend[ii] &, of course, to you, ben.

Register your letters.

Very sincerely, Nelson

Mrs Fatima Meer, 148 Burnwood Rd, Sydenham, Durban

To the commanding officer, Robben Island

[In another hand and partly illegible] N. Mandela 466/64

---

i   Fatima Meer's children.
ii   Ismail Meer (1918–2000), Fatima's husband and a lawyer and anti-apartheid activist – see the glossary.

1 December 1974

The Commanding Officer,
Robben Island.

Attention: Col. Roelofse

I should be pleased if you would allow me to appeal to the Commissioner of Prisons against your decision in which you refused me permission:

1. to write to the Minister of Justice and advise him on the attack made on my home in Johannesburg on 18 September 1974 in the course of which the garage was burgled and the car damaged.
2. to write to the C.O.P.[i] and ask for reasons, if any, why my letter to Dr Helen Suzman[ii] M.P. dated 1 March 1974,[iii] in which I congratulated her for having been awarded the Degree of Doctor of Laws, was placed in my file.

You are now aware that on 13 May 1974 I wrote[iv] and requested the Minister of Justice to

(a) grant my wife a permit to acquire a firearm for purposes of self-defence;
(b) request the Minister of Police to order members of the South African Police in dealing with my wife to confine themselves strictly to the execution of their duties according to law;
c) to use his influence with the City Council of Johannesburg and ask them to relax their Influx Control regulations so as to enable my brother-in-law to live permanently with my wife in our Johannesburg home.
(d) arrange with the Minister of [the] Interior to furnish my wife with a passport to enable her to holiday abroad.
(e) to arrange with the Minister of Police for members of the South African Police to guard the house daily from 7 pm to 6 am until my brother-in-law joins my wife.
(f) grant my wife and me a two-hour contact visit for the purpose of discussing the special problems outlined above.

---

i   'Commissioner of Prisons'.
ii   Helen Suzman (1917–2009), academic, politician, anti-apartheid activist, and MP for the opposition party – see the glossary. Suzman continuously raised the issue of political prisoners in Parliament and first met Mandela and his comrades on Robben Island in 1967.
iii See his letter on page 247.
iv   See his letter on page 251.

On 25 May I was forced to write a second letter to the Minister[i] because of yet another vicious attack on my family and other inmates of my home.

Shortly thereafter the Head of the Prison, Lt. Terblanche, advised me that the Minister had referred the issues raised in my letters to the appropriate state departments for attention and that I would be advised of the outcome in due course.

In September I was informed by Lt. Terblanche that the application by my wife for a passport would be considered on merit, and that she was at liberty to submit a formal application to the Commissioner of the area in which she resides. I was further informed that the Minister was unable to accede to the request for a two-hour contact visit. Although more than six months have elapsed since the matter was brought to the Minister's attention I have had no reply in regard to the requests made in (a), (b), c) and (e) of the letter to the Minister.

In the meantime, a further attack was made on the home on September 18. In this connection I quote from a letter I received from my wife and dated September 29.

> "Our friends the "Bantu Youths" came to bid us goodbye by attacking the garage and just concerning themselves with the car on the 18th. The only consolation is that they bring it back whatever damage it has suffered."

I also quote from my wife's letter of October 8 to indicate to you the systematic persecution that she has experienced and her anxiety and concern for the safety of the children and our property whilst away in jail.

> "As said it is 1 am on the above date. I am waiting for the "Bantu males" to attack, an enemy I can do nothing about. I am sitting up because the memory of those cruel blows, shattering of glass, vicious knocking off of the doors, etc., would shatter me. I would like to imagine that there would be no theft of documents and clothes or above incidents in my absence. The horror of the same happening to our matchbox home, because the children are back from school is my source of great concern."

I must also refer you to a passage from a letter written by my sister-in-law, Mrs Mniki,[ii] and dated November 7. She and her husband now live in the house.

---

i   See his letter on page 264.
ii   Nobantu Mniki, Winnie Mandela's sister.

".... she (my wife) asked us to take care and possession of the house, so we just had to take it buti, there was no alternative because there were already complications about the house otherwise we are having it very tough."

In the course of my professional work prior to my conviction & sentence, I have had interviews with public officials, and as a prisoner I have had discussions with the C.O.P., General Steyn, the former Security Chief, Brigadier Aucamp,[i] other senior officials from the Headquarters and with all the Commanding Officers of this prison since 1964. It is my considered opinion that the interview I had with you on November 23 was one of the most frustrating and embarrassing experiences I have had with any government official. Not only were the reasons you advanced in refusing what I consider to be a perfectly reasonable and logical request based on humanitarian grounds astonishing, but your whole attitude in the matter was in sharp contrast to the humane, cautious and enlightened approach General Steyn frequently shows in dealing with such issues. I may be wrong, but I feel confident that, having regard to all the circumstances, he would never deny me the opportunity of advising the Minister of the attack made on our home on September 18 and of the type of life led by my wife even after I have asked the Minister to give the matter urgent attention. In the circumstances, I must ask you to allow me to put the full position before the C.O.P. The fact that my wife is presently serving a term of imprisonment is irrelevant for, judging from the letter from my sister-in-law, attacks of one kind or another are still taking place on the home.

On March 1 1974 I wrote a letter to Dr Helen Suzman, M.P., in which I congratulated her for having been awarded the Honorary Degree of Doctor of Laws. The letter was placed in my file on the instructions of the C.O.P. No reasons were given to me for disallowing the letter. In May Col. Willemse advised me to discuss the matter directly with the C.O.P. and promised to arrange for him to visit the single cell section during the Parliamentary Session. Six months have elapsed since then and I should be pleased if you would allow me to discuss the matter with him by letter. In particular, I should like the Commissioner to advise me

(a) Whether or not I am at liberty to write to Dr Suzman. If, as Col. Willemse suggested, such letter can only be written with the approval of the C.O.P., I now formally apply for such permission.

(b) Whether the letter was disallowed because of its contents.

---

i   Brigadier Aucamp, commanding officer of Robben Island – see the glossary.

(c) To avoid further misunderstanding in the future, would the Commissioner advise me of the principles the Prison Department uses in censoring prisoners' letters and the considerations I should bear in mind in writing letters.

Finally on June 18 I wrote to the Manager, West Rand Central Board,[i] which has now taken over from the Johannesburg City Council the jurisdiction over African townships in that area. I have never had any acknowledgement of this particular letter and should be pleased if you would advise me when it was posted and to what address it was sent.

[Signed NRMandela]
NELSON MANDELA: 466/64

To Winnie Mandela,[ii] his wife

[Note in Afrikaans in another hand] Keep 913 [the number of Mandela's file]

Nelson Mandela 466/64   A Group   1.2.75

Dadewethu,[iii]

This is the 5th & last letter I'll write to you before you leave jail.[iv] I fear that the March letter may reach Kroonstad after you'll have been drafted & I'll accordingly send it straight home. I'll do the same with that of Apr. My other letters for Feb have gone to Zeni,[v] Ndindi[vi] (Thembi's[vii] eldest daughter who will be 9 on 20/2), Sisi Phathiwe & Florence Matanzima.[viii] Sisi Phathiwe is Mrs Nkala & now matron of the Mditshwa High School in Ncambele[ix] & probably the first in the Dalindyebo[x] family to qualify as a teacher. She was

---

i   West Rand Administration Board, see his letter on page 265.
ii   Nomzamo Winifred Madikizela-Mandela (1936–) – see the glossary.
iii   'Sister' in isiXhosa.
iv   Winnie Mandela was still serving her six-month sentence in Kroonstad Prison for being in the presence of another banned person.
v   Zenani Mandela (1950–), their eldest daughter – see the glossary.
vi   Ndileka Mandela (1965–), Mandela's eldest grandchild.
vii   Madiba Thembekile (Thembi) Mandela (1945–69), Mandela's eldest son – see the glossary.
viii   A wife of K. D. Matanzima (for K. D. Matanzima, see the glossary).
ix   A village about 20 km outside Mthatha in the Transkei (now Eastern Cape province).
x   Chief Jongintaba Dalindyebo (d. 1942), the chief and regent of the Thembu people. He became Mandela's guardian following his father's death – see the glossary.

at Shawbury.[i] As you know, Florence is our Molokazana.[ii]

I told Judy[iii] in my Nov letter to her that I should like to see Zeni alone as soon as she turns 16. I would suggest that for her 16th birthday you attempt something a little more than usual, say, slaughter a sheep & call together AmaDlomo[iv] & friends. You should consult Kgatho,[v] Jongintaba, Ntatho,[vi] Lily,[vii] Dorcas,[viii] Marwede & others. Such an affair may give her a lot of pride, self-confidence & joy. But you should keep it within bounds. There's still the more important 21st birthday when you'll have to go all out to launch the girl into a new life as an independent person.

Visits from across the Kei[ix] affect me in a special sort of way. Seeing the old lady,[x] Mabel,[xi] Luvuyo, Bambilanga,[xii] Chief of the Qulunqu,[xiii] Mbuzo, George[xiv] & others revived many fond memories. But there is a gap which has not been filled. One of the fervent hopes I have nursed these last 10 yrs is that of seeing Amangutyana[xv] from Mbongweni, a hope which was kindled by Manyawuza's[xvi] visit & by C.K.[xvii] himself in the one & only letter I ever received from Bizana (dated 12/3/68). Of course Niki, Nali & Bantu[xviii] have been here, but they are all townsmen to whom the approach & idiom of people from the village has now become foreign. I was tempted to believe that Nyawuza's visit would be the first in a series that would come from Amangutyana. I also thought that 14/10 would shake up Ma[xix] & bring her over there & here at once. Maybe she is well aware of our almost expectations but I suspect that the poor soul is experiencing pretty formidable problems. I've never received a single line from her & Mpumelelo in spite of several letters I've written home. But it would be unwise, & even unfair, to suggest that she should come. The beauty about these things is the knowledge that your people think of you on their own.

---

i   A high school run by Methodists.
ii   'Daughter-in-law' in isiXhosa.
iii   Nombulelo Judith Mtirara is a sister of Sabata Jonguhlanga Dalindyebo (for Sabata Jonguhlanga Dalindyebo, see the glossary).
iv   Mandela was part of the AmaDlomo clan.
v   Makgatho Mandela (1950–2005), Mandela's second-born son – see the glossary.
vi   Nthato Motlana (1925–2008), friend, medical doctor, businessman, and anti-apartheid activist – see the glossary.
vii   Lilian Ngoyi (1911–80), politician, and anti-apartheid and women's rights activist – see the glossary.
viii   Possibly Dorcas Nongxa, an ANC Women's League activist.
ix   Kei River in the Transkei.
x   Possibly he means his mother.
xi   Mabel Notancu Timakwe (1924–2002), Mandela's sister.
xii   Bambilanga (also known as Nxeko) is the brother of King Sabata Jonguhlanga Dalindyebo, paramount chief of the Transkei homeland.
xiii   The Qulunqu people were from the district of Engcobo in the Transkei.
xiv   George Matanzima (1918–2000), K. D. Matanzima's brother, Transkei leader and chief. While Mandela was at University College of Fort Hare with KD, George studied at nearby Lovedale College.
xv   Members of Winnie Mandela's family who come from the amaNgutyana clan.
xvi   Sibali Nyawuza. Mandela confused his clan name and referred to him as Manyawuza. Sibali means 'brother-in-law' in isiXhosa.
xvii   Columbus Kokani Madikizela, Winnie Mandela's father – see the glossary.
xviii Three of Winnie Mandela's sisters.
xix   He is most likely referring to Nophikela Hilda Madikizela, Winnie Mandela's stepmother.

A million thanks for the beautiful Xmas card, almost identical with that of Alan Paton[i] which arrived the same day. The rest came from Judy, Rochelle & sisters,[ii] Tellie[iii] & Mafu,[iv] Leabie & hubby,[v] Nolusapho, Gwen Curry, Anne & Benjie,[vi] Phyllis & kids, Mkentane family, Monica Kobus, Euphemia Mhlatuzana.[vii] Nothing from the chdn & Thoko.[viii] Apart from yours, which I hope you've got, I sent cards to the ff.[ix] Kgatho & Reyne,[x] the girls, Maki, Ma & Camagu,[xi] Ndindi & Nandi,[xii] Thoko,[xiii] Buyelekhaya,[xiv] Judy & kids, Bantu & Earl,[xv] Lily, Fatima & Ismail,[xvi] & Tim. By the way, in my last letter I spoke of Esther,[xvii] instead of Jane, to whom I intend writing in March.

The discreetness of Hans St[xviii] in regard to family matters impresses me very much. There have been a few notable occasions in which caution has been thrown to the winds. But I have the hope & confidence that this will be avoided in future. There are affairs in life where third parties, no matter who they are, should not be let in at all. Incidentally, you may find that the cell is an ideal place to learn to know yourself, to search realistically & regularly the process of your own mind & feelings. In judging our progress as individuals we tend to concentrate on external factors such as one's social position, influence & popularity, wealth & standard of education. These are, of course, important in measuring one's success in material matters & it is perfectly understandable if many people exert themselves mainly to achieve all these. But internal factors may be even more crucial in assessing one's development as a human being. Honesty, sincerity, simplicity, humility, pure generosity, absence of vanity, readiness to serve others – qualities which are within easy reach of every soul – are the foundation of one's spiritual life.

Development in matters of this nature is inconceivable without serious

i   Alan Paton (1903–88), author and founder and leader of South Africa's anti-apartheid Liberal Party. He gave evidence in mitigation of sentence for Mandela and his co-accused at the Rivonia Trial – see the glossary.
ii   Nombulelo Judith Mtirara's daughters.
iii   Telia (Telli or Tellie) Mtirara, a relative of Mandela's.
iv   One of Winnie's brothers.
v   Leabie Makhutswana Piliso (1930–97), Mandela's sister, and her husband.
vi   Anne and Benjamin Pogrund (1933–), friends. Anne is an artist and Benjamin was former editor of *the Rand Daily Mail* – see the glossary.
vii   A friend of Mandela's.
viii   Thoko Mandela, his son Thembi's widow, and their two daughters.
ix   'And the following'.
x   Makgatho (Kgatho) Mandela (1950–2005), Mandela's second-born son – see the glossary – and his then wife, Rose Rayne Mandela, known as Rennie.
xi   Makaziwe Mandela (1954–), Mandela's eldest daughter – see the glossary. and her husband.
xii   Ndileka (1965–) and Nandi (1968–) Mandela, the daughters of his late son, Thembi (for Thembi Mandela, see the glossary.
xiii   Thoko Mandela, the daughter of his late son, Thembi.
xiv   Buyelekhaya Dalindyebo (1964), son of Sabata Jonguhlanga Dalindyebo – see the glossary.
xv   Winnie Mandela's sister Nobantu and her husband Earl Mniki.
xvi   Fatima (1928–2010) and Ismail Meer (1918–2000), friends. Fatima was a professor, author, and anti-apartheid activist and Ismail was a lawyer and anti-apartheid activist – see the glossary for both these individuals.
xvii   Esther Maleka, an ANC activist who worked in the underground.
xviii   Hans Street is where the Helping Hand boarding house was located. Winnie Mandela stayed there when she arrived in Johannesburg in 1953.

introspection, without knowing yourself, your weaknesses & mistakes. At least, if for nothing else, the cell gives you the opportunity to look daily into your entire conduct, to overcome the bad & develop whatever is good in you. Regular meditation, say about 15 minutes a day before you turn in, can be very fruitful in this regard. You may find it difficult at first to pinpoint the negative features in your life, but the 10th attempt may yield rich rewards. Never forget that a saint is a sinner who keeps on trying.

You should also think seriously about the new life you'll have to lead after Apr. 13. The bit of warm sunshine in which you once bathed may be gone & the atmosphere more chilly & glum than you may imagine. There certainly will be no trumpets to announce your return & perhaps there'll hardly be a soul to meet you at the Fort, & sharp arrows may come from unexpected quarters, even from those who adore you. Maybe that even resuming old jobs may be a milestone in your life in which the most elaborate explanations to those who have been on your side would be pointless.

But even on such occasions the opportunities for challenge, initiative & success are tremendous. Difficulties break some men but make others. No axe is sharp enough to cut the soul of a sinner who keeps on trying, one armed with the hope that he will rise & win in the end. I have every reason to love you. There are treasures buried deep inside you & I live in the hope that you'll be able to unlock them some day. My most tender thoughts centre always on you. A million kisses & tons & tons of love.

Devotedly,
Dalibunga

Your Dec letter never arrived. Have written to you monthly since Oct. Nkosikazi Nobandla Mandela, C/o Major Van Zyl, Women's Prison, Kroonstad (9500)

To the minister of justice, J. Kruger[i]

12 February 1975

The Honourable Adv. J. Kruger,
Minister for Justice, Police and Prisons,
Pretoria.

---

i   James (Jimmy) Kruger (1917–87), minister of justice and police, 1974–79 · see the glossary.

Dear Sir,

Extracts from your letter of 13 January 1975 addressed to the Commanding Officer were read out to me.

I note a) that my request for my wife to be granted a firearm licence was
carefully considered but that you were unable to approve it; b) that no complaint against any member of the South African Police (the Security Branch
included) had been made by my wife and that no member of the South
African Police (the Security Branch included) was specifically employed to
watch her activities; c) that due to shortage of manpower, the request that
you arrange for members of the S.A.P.[i] to guard the house daily could not be
acceded to, and that if protection was really deemed necessary by my wife,
she could be advised to approach one of the numerous private organisations
which undertake services of this kind; d) that the request that my brother-in-
law be permitted to live with her was still under consideration.

In this connection I should be pleased if you would be good enough to
reconsider your decision on the question of the firearm licence. It should
be a matter of real concern to the police authorities that, despite persistent
attacks on the house and family, the S.A.P. with all their training, skill and
experience, and with all the vast resources and modern facilities at their
disposal for tracking down criminals, the culprits involved in this particular
case should still be at large. I have no clear information to indicate who is
really responsible for persecuting my family. When I discussed the matter
with you on 27 December 1975[ii] you repudiated any suggestion that the
S.A.P. might in any way be involved and, in the absence of concrete evidence one way or the other, I could not take the matter any further. I must
also accept your statement that, owing to shortage of manpower, the S.A.P.
cannot guard the house as requested. But I cannot appreciate why you
should be reluctant to assist my wife in acquiring a firearm when the police
have been totally unable to give her protection in the face of a serious threat
to her life.

There are literally thousands of South African women, including
blacks, who have lawful access to firearms in spite of the fact that they lead
normal family lives, enjoying the protection of able-bodied men whose residential areas are, comparatively speaking, well-patrolled by members of the
S.A.P. and who are not exposed to any kind of danger whatsoever. You even

---

i   South African Police.
ii   Mandela was visited on Robben Island by Minister of Justice Jimmy Kruger who offered to release him into the
      Transkei on condition that he recognised the Transkei homeland and settled there. In a conversation with Richard
      Stengel on 22 December 1992 Mandela said, 'I just discussed the matter seriously and rejected it. That I don't
      believe in the Bantustans, I belong to Johannesburg and I'm not going to go to the Bantustans.' (CD 11, Nelson
      Mandela Foundation, Johannesburg.)

seem to doubt whether protection is really deemed necessary by my wife notwithstanding the detailed particulars on the matter already furnished.

Bearing in mind the viciousness of the last two attacks in particular, growing concern on my part for the safety of the family is, to say the least, not unreasonable. Her health has already broken down and there are disturbing reports that the children are finding the strain difficult to bear. It seems to me that the only solution in these circumstances is to grant her a permit to acquire a firearm. I should add that even if you should be good enough to arrange for my brother-in-law to join her, which I trust you will do at your earliest possible convenience, she will still require possession of the weapon. He cannot be expected to defend the family against armed thugs with bare hands. I believe my wife would be willing to submit to any reasonable conditions subject to which you might grant the permit. The firearm could for instance, be inspected at the house by the S.A.P. at their convenience. Alternatively, she would probably be prepared to hand it to the S.A.P. at 7 am and collect it at 5 pm daily. The second alternative would be quite onerous and would also deprive her of protection during the daytime, and I hope you will not impose it. But it may be that she would be prepared to accept even such a stringent condition if she would thereby be able to defend herself at night. These conditions should meet any security problems the S.A.P. might have in this regard. I might also add that I am unable to advise her to approach any kind of the private organisations which undertake services of this kind, solely because she cannot afford the fees charged by such organisations. She is due to be released from prison on April 13 and I must tell you that I am deeply troubled by the fact that she may have to go back to the house to face all over again the ordeals she has experienced in the past before anything is done to ensure her safety.

I was sorry to learn that you were unable to grant me permission to write to Mr Bram Fischer concerning his illness.[i] I must remind you once more that he is a friend of long standing and has been good to me and [my] family in numerous ways. I am told that his illness is a serious one and fear that I may never see him again. Writing to him now may be the only chance I have to tell him just how much his friendship has meant to me, and to let him know that at this critical time in his life my sympathy and thoughts are with him. Few things would be sweeter in his adversity than little words of comfort and encouragement from a well-wisher. Such sentiments may give him the courage and strength to fight back, and perhaps even help to save him altogether. The fact that my letter would be subjected to a double censorship should allay the anxiety that anything objectionable on security grounds may pass

---

i   He was diagnosed with cancer in prison.

between us. I leave the matter entirely in your good hands again.

It was indeed very kind of you to allow me to acquire Piet Meiring's "Ons Eerste Ses Premiers".[i] I am really eager to go through it. The only difficulty I might experience in this regard is that reading such material often tends to whet one's appetite. Perhaps one day I may be able to thank you personally for your kind gesture.

Finally, I should like you to know that it was a pleasure for me to be able to exchange views with you on matters of mutual concern. Your statement that the problems of our country will be solved by blacks and whites together coincides with my own views. Carried to its logical conclusion, and objectively applied, such an approach could provide a solid basis for harmonising the common efforts of all South Africans in working out lasting solutions. I sincerely hope your efforts in this regard may bring rich rewards. Mag dit u goed gaan![ii]

Yours sincerely,
[Signed NRMandela]
NELSON MANDELA 466/64

To Yusuf Dadoo,[iii] comrade in exile in London

NELSON MANDELA 466/64   A. GROUP.

1.11.75

My dear Motabhai,[iv]

Since Jan. '73 I've written the family, relatives & friends 190 letters &, during the past 13 yrs have amassed a precious fortune of 199 letters that contain inspiring sentiments of love & devotion, solidarity & hope. Some of these are disturbingly realistic & sober whilst others are highly idealistic.

Do you still remember the '52 D.C.[v] with its apostolic themes of

i   Piet Meiring, *Ons Eerste Ses Premiers, 'n Persoonlike Terugblik ('Our six prime ministers, a personal retrospective')* (Cape Town: Tafelberg, 1972).
ii   'Go well' in Afrikaans.
iii Dr Yusuf Dadoo (1909–83), medical doctor, anti-apartheid activist, and orator. President of South African Indian Congress, deputy to Oliver Tambo on the Revolutionary Council of MK, and chairman of the South African Communist Party – see the glossary.
iv   'Big brother' in Gujarati. *Mota* means someone older than you – a sign of respect – and Dadoo was known as Mota.
v   Initiated by the ANC in December 1951, and launched with the South African Indian Congress on 26 June 1952 against six apartheid laws, the Defiance Campaign Against Unjust Laws (known as the Defiance Campaign for short) involved individuals breaking racist laws such as entering premises reserved for 'whites only', breaking

"Crossroads" and "in our lifetime"? Of course you do. I can still see [word very difficult to read] as black as nicotine in khaki outfit & with baton in hand, singing with his congregation those thrilling hosannas & ready to foot it all the way to heaven. My letters are rich with such sentiments.

My aunt, who is fond of me & whom I last saw 20 yrs ago, writes lively letters. "A hothead is tamed by his own people," says she in one of them & then goes on to urge perfect submission on my part in the hope that such an attitude will lead to a change of heart in relevant quarters. Others turn to the last weapon of those who have no concrete suggestion to offer & advise that we pray hard & sincerely because, so they argue, the divinities can never let down those who seek their protection. The third category stresses while you've repeatedly urged on formal & informal occasions in the past & what has influenced me in the last 30 yrs. This is the rich harvest I've gathered in the last decade. But none of these letters contains a note of despair or pessimism & all of them assume that one day we'll be back to share all the pleasures of a free life. Each one of them is a powerful tonic that keeps my blood clean & my head clear. Each one that comes makes me feel stronger & more confident than the day before.

It is mainly for this reason that Saturdays are so important here. Our post is always delivered on this day. Almost all eyes are usually fixed on the main gate to the Section, & officials that bring the letters are for the moment as popular as film stars. When they appear, otherwise ponderous fellows & who normally move around like confident pontiffs, suddenly become alert ready to dart forward to find out whether there's something for them. Smiles immediately light the faces of those who are lucky, whilst a few amongst them even hum a ditty out of pure joy. The rest stroll away bravely hoping for better luck next time. If Matlala,[i] Reggie,[ii] Muggie, Adie & Barbra knew all this, they would long have acknowledged my letters. Did Ruth[iii] receive hers?

A substantial percentage of my outgoing correspondence consists of condolence letters. It may well be that death has always been as common as it is at this distance & that in the old days pressure of work gave me little time to think about such matters. It is also possible that my present circumstances have made death appear far more tragic than I saw it before I was jailed. Certainly the death of members of the family & other relatives has

curfews, and courting arrest. Mandela was appointed national volunteer-in-chief and Maulvi Cachalia as his deputy. Over 8,500 volunteers were imprisoned for their participation in the Defiance Campaign.

i   A nickname for Adelaide Tambo (1929–2007), friend, anti-apartheid activisit, and wife of Oliver Tambo, Mandela's former law partner and president of the ANC – see the glossary. The Tambos were living in exile in London.

ii   Oliver Tambo's middle name was Reginald and Mandela referred to him as Reggie.

iii   He could be referring to anti-apartheid and women's rights activist Ruth First (1925–82) who was also in exile in London.

hit me very hard. I was equally shaken by that of friends like A.J.,[i] Amina, Debi, Hymie, Jimmy, Mike, Miriam, Molly & your successor, Nana, Z.K.[ii] & others I remember with fond memories. Such losses inevitably make one feel alone when one has become thoroughly accustomed to group life. I've found it hard to live away from old friends & even harder to be away from those I'll never see again.

I told Amina in a letter to her today that I remember all the memorable days from 52 onwards. Of course I've nothing to prod the memory – photos. I can pull out of the drawer, records I can consult & landmarks that show the future direction of affairs. Nevertheless I often think of '46 the year when Ismail introduced me to you. By the way, he & I still keep together as we did during our varsity days.[iii] Fatima[iv] writes regularly & even visited me in '73. I think of 47, the yr of the medical congress in which you, Xuma[v] and Monty[vi] prominently featured.[vii] Does James still remember that occasion? I also remember the day in the Broadway Cinema in '52 when we gave you & Dave[viii] a boisterous send-off & everything that followed thereafter. You know the score quite well.

I think much of the days to come, the problems of adjustment, & of picking up the old threads. It is mainly in this regard that I never really live on this island. My thoughts are ever travelling up & down the country, remembering the places I've visited. The *Oxford Atlas* in spite of its old age – having acquired it in '63 – is one of my greatest companions, & in the process I've come to know the world & my country far better than when I was free.

But the purpose of this note is not to talk about correspondence, past memories or the *Oxford Atlas*, but to tell you that I never forget Sept 5[ix] to wish you many happy returns. We think of you with far more pride than words can express. The birthday parties we used to hold for you are amongst the memorable occasions Ahmed[x] and I often talk about. We realise only too well that perhaps now it may not be possible for you to celebrate

---

i   Chief Albert Luthuli (1898–1967), president-general of the ANC, 1952–67 – see the glossary.
ii   Professor Z. K. Matthews (1901–1968), academic, politician, anti-apartheid activist, and ANC member – see the glossary.
iii   He is indicating to Dadoo who was in exile that he is still close to Ismail Meer.
iv   Ismail Meer's wife.
v   Albert Xuma (1893–1962), first black South African to become a medical doctor, president-general of the ANC 1940–49.
vi   Monty Naicker (1910–78), doctor, politician, and anti-apartheid activist – see the glossary.
vii   He is mostly likely referring to 'The Doctors' Pact' of 1947 signed by Dr. Yusuf Dadoo, Dr. Alfred Xuma, and Dr Monty Naicker about cooperation between the ANC, the Transvaal Indian Congress, and the Natal Indian Congress and calling for the right of freedom of movement, education, the right to vote, and equal opportunities for all 'non-European' South Africans.
viii David Bopape (1915–2004), ANC and South African Communist Party member.
ix   Yusuf Dadoo's birthday.
x   Ahmed Kathrada (1929–2017), leading member of the ANC and South African Communist Party, and fellow Rivonia trialist who was imprisoned with Mandela – see the glossary.

in the usual way. But even so I hope you'll at least find time to gather a few friends and have a bit of relaxation. In particular I hope that you, the 2 Reggies[i] and Toni's Pa[ii] are keeping together like quadruplets. I always think of you in this way.

For god's sake don't tell me that you gave up indlamu[iii] which you used to dance so well in Soweto in the fifties. It's a typical S. African dance – as typical as "daar kom die Alabama",[iv] the tickiedraai[v] & the Bharat natium.[vi] But I'd like to try the very oldest of our traditional dances: the Basaxwa[vii] ceremonial hunting dance & the Khoikhoi askoek.[viii] Not only will they keep you as fit & fearless as one strives to be, but will give you a more realistic insight into why the aborigines loved life so intensely & why they defended themselves so stubbornly & long against the vicissitudes of nature & of human folly.

Finally, I wish to remind you of the many ties that hold us together, not the least of which is the Winnies on our side[ix] – the most wonderful creatures on earth. Once more many happy returns. I look forward to seeing you some day. In the meantime I send you fondest regards & my very best wishes to your Winnie, Shireen[x] & everybody.

Sincerely, Nelson

Mr Mota D, Mothabhai,[xi] c/o Mrs Amina Cachalia, PO Box 3265, Johannesburg

---

To the commanding officer, Robben Island

Nelson Mandela 466/64

Re Flask

---

i   One of the Reggies Mandela is referring to is probably Oliver Reginald Tambo.
ii   Mandela is possibly referring to comrade Rusty Bernstein (1920–2002) – see the glossary – who was acquitted in the Rivonia Trial. His daughter's name was Toni.
iii A traditional Zulu dance.
iv   An Afrikaans folk song.
v   A traditional Afrikaans dance.
vi   A genre of classical Indian dance.
vii A ceremonial hunting dance perfomed by the Basarwa people.
viii A dance step of the San people.
ix   Both their wives were named Winnie.
x   Yusuf and Winnie Dadoo's daughter.
xi   By using Dadoo's nickname, Mandela is trying to disguise his identity.

What Maj. Sandburg requires is an endorsement to the effect I still require one flask on medical grounds.
He will then take up the question of two flasks himself.

[Signed NRMandela]
15.12.75

[Signed in another hand and dated 5.12.76]

To Fatima Meer,[i] friend and comrade

NELSON MANDELA 466/64   1.1.76

Wahali Fatimaben[ii]

A good head & a good heart are always a formidable combination. But when you add to that a literate tongue or pen then you've something very special & a simple story one has heard repeatedly suddenly evokes significant moral lessons. Interest me in mythology? I'd try even magic if only you recommend it. As for mythology my interest in that particular field has a long history, my mother having fed me on it from the earliest dys of my childhood. I'd plenty of it at a college but outside the lecture room mythology can be even more challenging & absorbing & that is why I've found your theme so particularly exhilarating.

An element of hindsight cannot be completely eliminated in statements made after the happening of a relevant event. But I'd like you to know that since Oct. '74 I've mused a great deal on the idea of the goddess Zamona descending into the 3rd heaven repeatedly preoccupied me. This was then nothing more than a mere whim which came & passed like the winds & I attached no significance whatsoever to it. Only when I got your marvellous letter & that of Zami[iii] did the thought occur whether the whim was a premonition or not. Perhaps we ought not to pursue this point much further less we end up in the supernatural world.

---

i   Fatima Meer (1928–2010), writer, academic, and anti-apartheid and women's rights activist – see the glossary.
ii   *Vehalie* means 'dear' in Gujarati. He probably would have asked one of his fellow prisoners who was fluent in
       Gujarati like Laloo Chiba. Mandela spelled it various ways including as *wahalie*. *Ben* means 'sister' in
       Gujarati.
iii   One of Winnie Mandela's names.

Suffice to say that this particular narrative, rendered with characteristic skill, has dispelled all the pessimism that might flow out of the belief that all sparks have been drained off the Voras, Kolas, Hadas, Kalas & Biharas, & that the evil spirits are invincible. The simple lesson of religions, of all philosophies & of life itself is that, although evil may be on the rampage temporarily, the good must win the laurels in the end. Your story expresses this truth very well. I've always regarded the multiplicity of gods in Greek mythology as yet another manifestation of the widespread belief that the destiny of all natural & human affairs is in the hands of the divinities whose superhuman excellence is a source of inspiration & hope to all creation – an excellence which will ultimately rule the world.

We, who were brought up in religious homes, & who studied in missionary schools, experienced the acute spiritual conflict that occurred in us when we saw the way of life we considered sacred being challenged by new philosophies & when we realised that amongst those who dismissed our beliefs as opium were clear thinkers whose integrity & love of their fellowmen was beyond doubt. But at least there was one thing in which both the adherents of the scriptures as well as atheists accept: that belief in the existence of beings with superhuman powers indicates what man would like to be & how throughout the centuries he has fought against all kinds of evil & strived for a virtuous life.

You say that myths are not to be taken at their face value & that underlying are the great moral lessons. I accept that completely & whatever shifts may have occurred in my own outlook, I realise more than ever before the dynamic role of mythology in the exposition of human problems & in the moulding of human character. A few yrs ago I was browsing hurriedly through a review of the works of Euripides, Sophocles & other Greek scholars when I came across the statement that one of the basic tenets we've inherited from classical Greek philosophy was that a real man was one who could stand firmly on his feet & never bend his knees even when dealing with the divine. Passage of time tends to blur even immortal teachings such as these & your story has revived all my interest in symbolic abstraction. If I had access to the Vedas[i] & Upanishads[ii] I'd plough through them with all zest. I believe Chota & Choti[iii] are off to Mecca. Perhaps it's now time for Ismail[iv] to leave his pampered roses & also go on pilgrimage. I hope I'll hear from you again.

---

i The oldest Hindu texts which were written toward the end of the second millennium BCE.

ii Written between 600–900 BC, the Upanashids constitute a section of Vedic literature and are considered to be the oldest philosophical works.

iii Dr. Mahomed 'Chota' Motala (1921– 2005), Natal Indian Congress member. His wife was Rabia 'Choti' Motala. They were from Pietermaritzburg. Chota is the Gujarati term for the youngest male and Choti for the youngest female. As he was known as Chota Motala, his wife became known as Choti. Chota Motala was a relative of Ismail and Fatima Meer's.

iv Ismail Meer (1918–2000), Fatima's husband and a lawyer and anti-apartheid activist – see the glossary.

I had a lovely time on Dec. 27 with Zeni & Zindzi.[i] I was seeing Zeni for the 3rd time & the youngest for the first since '62. She has a lot of fire in her & I hope she'll exploit it fully. They told me that they & mum spent a lovely weekend with you & Ismail & looked forward to seeing you again, this time for a little longer. They added that you've now gained a few pounds but that you remain as agile & charming as ever. It pleases me much to know that Zami can now move around freely & see old friends. The suggestion that you & her should travel to India & Britain enjoys my full support, though I doubt very much if she'll get the travelling documents. Taking the girls[ii] along will be too expensive & I'd suggest that you leave them behind. They're young & their chance will come in due course. I never know how to end a letter to a couple that's been so wonderful to me & family. Merely to say "many thanks" seems formal & flat. Perhaps nothing expresses more clearly just what you mean to us than this perpetual difficulty. Love & fondest regards to Ismail, the children & you.

Sincerely, Nelson

Mrs Fatima Meer, c/o Nobandla Mandela, House no 8115 Orlando West, P.O. Phirima [1898]

To the commissioner of prisons

[In another hand] 466/64 Nelson Mandela – S/letter[iii] to B/O about his studies

23 January 1976

The Commissioner of Prisons,
Private Bag.
Pretoria.

Attention: Brigadier Du Plessis

I have now been informed of your refusal to grant my application to com-

---

i   Zenani Mandela (1959–) and Zindziswa Mandela (1960–), Mandela's middle and youngest daughters – see the glossary.
ii   Zeni and Zindzi.
iii Special letter. These were not deducted from a prisoner's quota.

plete the final year of the LL.B Degree of the University of London or of the University of the Witwatersrand or to study for this course with the University of South Africa.[i] In this connection I should be pleased if you would be good enough to reopen the matter and to allow me to proceed with the same course with Unisa.

I hope in considering this application you will take into account the fact that although I have been studying the LL.B Degree with the University of London for the last 12 years, I have had considerable difficulties in obtaining the prescribed literature and this has been the real cause of my negative results. Unfortunately, even where I could have obtained the required literature there have been considerable administrative difficulties in sending cash to London, especially during the last 3 years. This statement is not in any way made in the spirit of criticism but solely to enable you to see my application in proper context.

In addition I should like to point out that the Dean of the Faculty of Law is prepared to grant me exemption from at least 7 courses and I may be able to complete the course in 4 years. I should accordingly be pleased if you would grant me the permission to register for this course.

[Signed NRMandela]
NELSON MANDELA 466/64

<hr/>

To D. B. Alexander,[ii] mother of a former prisoner, Neville Alexander

[The first and last sentences of this letter are translated from Afrikaans]
Nelson Mandela 466/64   A Group   1.3.76

Kgaitsedi,[iii]

You are often in my thoughts and it does me good to write to send you my best wishes.

It disturbed me a great deal when a few years back I heard that your health was not so good. But I was confident that the woman who produced such lovely children as Myrtle, Dorothy, Janette, Boy & Edward[iv] would rise

<hr/>

i   He was petitioning the authorities to allow him to continue studying for his LLB.
ii   This is most likely to be Dimbiti Bisho Alexander, the mother of his fellow prisoner Neville Alexander (1936–2012).
iii 'My sister' in both Sesotho and Setswana.
iv   Neville's second name was Edward and he was one of five children. Mandela is probably referring to him as

& move around again inspiring all those who come into contact with her. I do hope that with Edward and Dorothy now back from holiday,[i] you feel even better.

Today I wrote and told a friend who has been sending me Xmas cards that last year I had hoped also to send her a card, but that I couldn't do so because the family is scattered all over and monopolises all my cards. This is what I should like to tell you as well. I trust you will accept this brief note in the spirit in which it is written. It contains all my love & thanks.

One of my favourite hobbies is to examine all the cards I've received during the previous year & only the other day, I was looking at the one you sent me last Dec. It contains only 4 printed words to which you added 3 in a clear & bold script. That economy in words is characteristic of all the seasonal messages I've received from you & yet they're full of warmth & inspiration & each time I feel far younger than kleinseun[ii] Leo. Dankie, Schwester![iii]

Have you been to Cradock[iv] recently?

Visiting that world will remind you of your younger days & rest your lungs from the foul air of the city. I also hope you're still in regular contact with the children. They must all be missing you, especially Janette and Leo. I hope Edward's research project is going on well & that his findings will be as worthy and fruitful as his past academic record.[v] Please give all the children my fondest regards & thank Gwen for the Dec 74 card.

I wish you well and good health and luck for '76 and for years thereafter. With love.

Sincerely,
Nelson

Mrs D.B. Alexander
No 2, First Avenue,
Lotus River.
Grassy Park (7800) Cape Town.

    Edward rather than Neville to avoid alerting the authorities to the fact that he is writing about another prisoner, which wasn't allowed.

i   Neville Alexander was released from prison in April 1974. He was then placed under house arrest until 1979. Mandela is probably referring to his release from prison as a 'holiday' to avoid alerting the authorities to the fact that he is writing about another prisoner.

ii   'Grandson' in Afrikaans.

iii   German for 'sister'.

iv   The town in the Eastern Cape where Neville Alexander was born.

v   Before he was imprisoned, Neville Alexander completed his doctorate at Tübingen University in Germany. In 1979 he published the book *One Azania, One Nation: The National Question in South Africa* (London: Zed Press), which was written under the pseudonym No Sizwe because he was banned.

To Felicity Kentridge, lawyer and wife of Advocate Sydney Kentridge[i]

Nelson Mandela 466/64   A Group   Robben Island

9.5.76

Dear Felicity,[ii]

[There is a line through the first two paragraphs below.]

My grand niece, Xoliswa Matanzima, Deckerts Hill, P.O. Qamata (5327) daughter of the Transkei Chief Minister[iii] is presently studying for the final yr of the B Juris at Fort Hare.[iv] She intends spending 2 yrs in America & will thereafter return to do her LLB.

Her father is not happy that she should study law & argues that women have not been particularly successful in this field. Nevertheless, she's keen on a legal career & the family has asked for my advice. I've been out of action for 16 yrs now & my views may be outdated. But I've never regarded women as in any way less competent than men in this & many other professions &, subject to what her father will finally say, I've encouraged Xoliswa to qualify as a lawyer. But I've told them that I'd ask for your opinion on the matter & I'm sure your views will be of great help to her & highly appreciated by the family.

After my letter had been sent off to Qamata,[v] I was almost taken aback to learn that you've now retired from the Bar to become a housewife. Have you forgotten that last yr it was '75 when women decided to stand on their feet & free themselves from the tyranny of males? Fortunately, I also learnt at the same time that Sidney [sic] has become an internationalist after all. How else can I describe a Johannesburger who has lectured in Harvard & who I'm told has recently appeared at an international arbitration in Paris?

You & your family, relatives & scores of friends both of you have won in the course of your practice at the Bar & elsewhere have every reason to be proud of him. He made a formidable impression on us during the Syna-

---

i   Felicity (d. 2015) and Sydney Kentridge (1922–) were lawyers. Sydney was part of the defence team in the Treason Trial (for the Treason Trial, see the glossary). They moved to London in the 1970s.

ii   Mandela wrote in a list of his outgoing correspondence that he handed in this letter for posting on 9 May; it was returned to him on 4 June; he rewrote it and handed it in for posting on 21 July. It was finally returned to him on 9 August 'on the ground that they now object to the person'.

iii K. D. Matanzima (1915– 2003), Mandela's nephew, a Thembu chief, and chief minister for the Transkei – see the glossary.

iv   University College of Fort Hare, Alice in the Ciskei homeland – see the glossary.

v   Qamtata is a small town that was formerly part of the Transkei and before that part of western Thembuland. It is approximately 830 km from Johannesburg by car.

gogue dys [i] & I'm glad to note that he has fulfilled the high expectations he aroused from those who admired his ability at the time.

When I visited you in the late Fifties you had one child, a handsome son.[ii] I hope you and Sidney [*sic*] were not so cruel as to condemn him to life-long loneliness by depriving him of the pleasure of company & trust that he now has at least a sister or brother.[iii] He should now be at varsity & a source of pride and joy to both of you.

I still remember clearly the last occasion I saw you in June '64 when you seemed glued to your seat in the jury box & listening attentively to the proceedings like a layman who was attending such proceedings for the very first time in life. I look forward to seeing you, Sidney[iv] and your son when I hope to shake hands very warmly & say: thank you. In the meantime I send you & family my very best wishes & fondest regards,

Sincerely,
Nelson

Mrs Felicity Kentridge, c/o Nkosk Nobandla Mandela, 8115 Orlando West, P.O. Phirima [1848] Johannesburg

◇◇◇◇◇◇◇◇◇

The year 1976 in South Africa was marked by a growing unease among young people frustrated by their parents' lack of resistance to apartheid.

The clampdown of the 1960s, which followed the arrest and imprisonment of a range of freedom fighters, was intended to have permanently suppressed opposition to the regime. The rise of Black Consciousness from the late sixties culminated in the student uprising in Soweto on 16 June 1976 against a plan to have black students taught in Afrikaans, the language of the oppressor. The police responded to the peaceful protests with live ammunition, killing hundreds. Hundreds more were arrested, many of them ending up as sentenced prisoners; even more fled the country to swell the ranks of the exiled armies of the liberation movements. Cut off from news media until 1980, the prisoners on Robben Island only became aware of what had happened in August 1976 when the first of the young people began arriving with sentences to serve.

The following long letter to the prison authorities detailing the continuing abuses of authority can also be read as Mandela's way of trying to improve

---

i   He is referring to the Old Synagogue in Pretoria which served as a court for the 1956 Treason Trial in which Sydney Kentridge was one of the defence lawyers.

ii   William Kentridge (1955), one of South Africa's most famous artists and filmmakers.

iii   The Kentridges had four children.

iv   Sydney Kentridge was a friend of some of the Rivonia Trial defence lawyers.

conditions for all prisoners, including the new group of angry young men. He and
his comrade Walter Sisulu[i] stood out for their efforts to talk down the firebrands
and advise them on a better path to survival in prison.[54]

To the commanding officer, Robben Island

12 July 1976

The Commanding Officer
Robben Island

Attention: Col. Roelofse

The attached letter is for the personal attention of the Commissioner of
Prisons, General Du Preez, and I should be pleased if you would approve
and forward it to him.

I am putting it in a sealed envelope addressed to you and marked
"Confidential and for the personal attention of Col. Roelofse." But once I
hand it over to the official-in-charge of the section, I have no further control
over it and cannot guarantee that it will reach you in the condition in which
it left me.

[Signed NRMandela]

To the commissioner of prisons

12 July 1976

The Commissioner of Prisons
Pretoria

Attention: General Du Preez

---

i   Walter Sisulu (1912– 2003), ANC and MK activisit and fellow Rivonia trialist who was imprisoned with Mandela
    – see the glossary.

I must draw your attention to the abuse of authority, political persecution and other irregularities that are being committed by the Commanding Officer of this prison and members of his staff. Although this letter raises complaints of a personal nature, some of them affect other prisoners as well and it may, therefore, be necessary to mention certain names by way of illustration of these irregularities.

During the past 14 years of my incarceration I have tried to the best of my ability to cooperate with all officials, from the Commissioner of Prisons to the Section warder, as long as that cooperation did not compromise my principles. I have never regarded any man as my superior, either in my life outside or inside prison, and have freely offered this cooperation in the belief that to do so would promote harmonious relations between prisoners and warders and contribute to the general welfare of us all. My respect for human beings is based, not on the colour of a man's skin nor authority he may wield, but purely on merit.

Although I did not agree with the approach of General Steyn on the country's major problems and the policy of the Department of Prisons I, nevertheless, respected him as head of this Department and as an individual and have never had occasion to question his integrity. Even though I think he could have done more that he did to promote the welfare of prisoners here and elsewhere in the country, his genial and unassuming manner made it easy for me to discuss with him otherwise delicate matters and, in spite of many disagreements I had with him from time to time on the actual decisions he made on specific issues, he was often prepared to give a reasoned motivation for his actions.

I met your immediate predecessor Gen Nel, when he came to the Island in 1970 with Mr Dennis [sic] Healey[i] and, bearing in mind the few remarks we exchanged on that occasion, I have no reason to think that as head of this Department he fell short of the standard set by his predecessor in regard to the manner in which he handled problems I brought to his attention. Unfortunately I have not had the pleasure of an interview with you but I have assumed throughout this letter that you would do everything in your power to improve prisoner-warder relations and to promote our welfare.

I have now had no less than 3 interviews with Brigadier Du Plessis, head of the security section and, in spite of the fact that every one of my complaints was not rectified, he nevertheless tried to give reasonable explanations for his actions and outlined the policy of the Department on the matters we discussed as patiently as time allowed.

---

i   Denis Healey (1917–2015), British Labour Party politician who Mandela first met on a short visit to London in 1962. Later Healey visited him in prison.

As I understand it, one of the principal functions of this Department is to maintain good order, discipline and the proper administration of the prison. In terms of the Prison Rules, special attention shall be accorded to the preservation of good relationships between a prisoner and his relatives in the best interests of both parties. This object is normally attained through visits, letters, telegrams, birthday, Easter and Christmas cards.

A public department is a creation of a law and should be run in accordance with the governing legal rules. The actions of both the officials and prisoners in every field of activity should be based on rules that can easily be ascertained and, even where officials are given a wide discretion on a particular point, respect for the principles of natural justice would demand a clear indication of the considerations that will be taken into account in the exercise of that discretion. This rule is observed in many countries throughout the world by public bodies which deal with human problems so as to remove or minimize the dangers of injustice though malice, caprice, arbitrariness, corruption, pettiness and other improper motives.

The actions of the Commanding Officer and his staff that are mentioned below have nothing to do with the maintenance of good order, discipline and the proper administration of the prison, nor with the promotion of harmonious relations between prisoners and officials, such actions are incompatible with the preservation of good relations between a prisoner and his relatives and constitute abuse of authority, political persecution and vindictiveness.

The absence of clearly defined rules that lay down how the discretion enjoyed by local officials is to be exercised in the particular cases indicated below has given them wide scope for malice, arbitrariness and other improper motives.

On several occasions I have tried in vain to draw the attention of Col. Roelofse to these problems and it is because he and the head of the prison Lt. Prins, and the official in charge of censoring, W/O Steenkamp have fallen short of the high standard of morality required from those who are entrusted with the running of a public department that I now feel compelled to place the whole matter before you.

1. Abuse of authority
   (a) On December 27, 1974 the Minister of Prisons, Advocate J. T. Kruger, in the presence of the C.O.;[i] granted me permission to purchase Piet Meiring's "Ons Ses Eerste Premiers"[ii] and, at the same time, informed the C.O. that there was nothing in the book he

---

i   Commissioner of Prisons.
ii   See his letter to the minister of justice from 12 February 1975, page 279.

considered objectionable. In pursuance of this permission I ordered the book, but, as it was out of print at the time, it only arrived on the Island on February 16 this year. In spite of the fact that permission to acquire the book was given by the Minister himself, and in spite of repeated efforts on my part to get it, the C.O. failed to release the book until April 27, exactly 2 months 11 days after it had arrived. I probably would not have got it if Brigadier Du Plessis had not intervened on my behalf.

(b) Both Col. Roelofse and Lt Prins have been systematically practicing racialism to prisoners in the Single Cell Section and trying to foment feelings of hostility among us.

(i) At the meeting of the Prison Board this year, the C.O. asked a coloured prisoner from this section what he thought of the level of civilisation of the 'Bantu' in the section and how the coloured prisoners were getting on with the 'Bantu'.[i] When this particular prisoners replied that his African colleagues in this section were educated and cultured men for whom he had good respect and that we all got on with one another, the C.O. made disparaging remarks describing Africans as being from a low level of civilisation and as people who walked about the country half naked.

(ii) On two previous occasions W/O Prince, as he then was, made remarks to 2 Indian prisoners, speaking to each one on a different occasion, to the effect that Africans were uncivilized and that when they were in power they would attack whites, coloured and Indians alike, and stressed that the best course for Indians would be to join whites. To one of them he added that he always thought politically on these matters.

It is dangerous to entrust the task of promoting the welfare of prisoners to officials who hold racialistic views, and it is an abuse of authority to take advantage of their official positions to try and create feelings of hostility amongst prisoners of different population groups. We totally reject apartheid in all its forms and the C.O. had no right whatsoever to attempt to sell us an idea we regard as diabolical and dangerous.

In this connection, I should like to add that the conduct of these officials is not only improper but also contrary at least to the avowed official policy. Government spokesmen, including

---

i   While the word 'Bantu' comes from 'Abantu' meaning people, it can be seen as offensive in a context such as this one where the speaker is using it as a racial description. It was used under apartheid to refer to Africans.

the present Premier, have repeatedly repudiated the idea that any particular population group in the country is superior to others.

2. Improper interference with Social Relationships

(a) My youngest daughter, Zindziswa,[i] sent me photographs on 3 different occasions, one of which I actually saw in my file in 1974 when W/O Du Plessis and I were looking for the copy of a letter I had written to a former Minister of Justice. When I asked for the photo, he told me we should deal with one thing at a time and, for that day, I left the matter there. When I subsequently asked for it, the photo had disappeared.

I mentioned the matter to Lt. Terblanche then head of the prison, who told me he would investigate it. Later, I received 2 other letters in which my wife reported that my daughter had sent other photos. As I had not received them, I immediately placed the matter before Lt Prins. Although I mentioned it to him twice thereafter, I have never heard from him again.

I might add that I had no trouble with letters from my daughters until Zindziswa complained to the United Nations about the systematic persecution of her mother by the Government and I believe that the difficulties that have since arisen with her correspondence with me and that of her elder sister, Zenani,[ii] is a pure act of vindictiveness from the C.O. acting in collaboration with the Security Police.

(b) In January this year my 2 daughters wrote me letters which they sent by registered post. Although both Lt Prins and Sgt Fourie of the Censors Office have assured me that they have not been received, I have been given the same information before and later discovered that in actual fact, the letters had already been received when such assurances were given.

(c) Two children who live with my wife also sent me 2 registered letters about the same time. A month or so after that, my wife advised me of this fact and Sgt Fourie assured me as usual that they had not been received. I warned him of the seriousness of telling me an untruth in regard to letters sent by registered post and asked him to make further investigation. He later informed me that he had checked as requested but reiterated his earlier assurance.

---

i   Zindziswa Mandela (1960–), Mandela's youngest daughter – see the glossary.
ii   Zenani Mandela (1959–), Mandela's middle daughter – see the glossary.

I then reported the matter to Lt Prins who subsequently acknowledged that the letters had been received some weeks before I spoke to Sgt Fourie. Lt Prins than formally advised me that the letters would not be given to me because they were militant and written by children who did not know me. One is related to my wife and I was already in prison when she was born. The other was only 5 when I was sentenced. Lt Prins refused to tell me why I was given untruthful explanations about the letters by Sgt Fourie. *Precisely the same thing happened with the letters from Mrs Adelaide Joseph[i] and again the abovementioned 2 officials were involved.

(d) Letters written by my wife to her relative, Mr Sandi Sejake, also in this section and those written by him to her do not reach their destination.

(e) There are many cases of this nature, but I should like to cite that of my fellow prisoner Theophilus Cholo, who was convicted in 1973 and who has not received a visit from his wife since then, their only means of contact being through letters. He last received one from her in February this year and in May Lt. Prins refused to give him a 3 page letter from her on the ground that its contents were objectionable, and at the same time prohibited him from telling her that her letter was withheld from him. I now consider the untruthful explanations that are repeatedly made by the local officials about our correspondence and the so-called objection either to the contents of the letter or person who wrote it as a mere technique to deprive us of the legal right of preserving good relationships between ourselves and our relatives and friends.

3. Censorship of outgoing mail
    The following examples will demonstrate to you the type of difficulties we are having due to over-suspicion on the part of your officials and maybe even to their difficulty of understanding the language and its idiom.

    (a) On July 1, 1975 I sent a birthday card to a friend who is in his early thirties and ended the message of felicitations with the greeting in phonetic script: "Me-e-e-e-i Bra-a-a!" which is a corruption of the Afrikaans "My Broer" and which form of greeting is commonly used by today's urban youth. I was told to rewrite the whole birthday message and to leave out the words quoted above. I was asked for no explanation and put to the unnecessary expense of using another card.

---

i   The wife of Paul Joseph (1930–), a South African political activist exiled in London. When Mandela was arrested in 1962 she brought him food in prison.

(b) As has often happened in the past, the birthday card I sent to my daughter Zindziswa, on December 1 last year did not reach her. On February 1 I wrote to my wife:

> "These are the only occasions when I sometimes wish science could invent miracles and make my daughter get her missing birthday cards and have the pleasure of knowing that her Pa loves her, thinks of her and makes efforts to reach her whenever necessary. It is significant that repeated attempts on her part to reach me and the photos she has sent have disappeared without trace whatsoever."

Again I was ordered to omit this passage and when I asked Sgt Steenkamp, as he then was, for an explanation he discourteously told me that the letter would not go if I did not rewrite it.

c) My daughter Zindziswa plays rugby at school and has openly discussed her sport interests both during her visits and in her letters. In her letter of February 8 this year which came through the normal official channels, she complained about loss of weight. On April 15 I wrote back to her:

> "But if you really want to be in top condition for such strenuous games as rugby, which require tremendous reserves of energy and speed, you'll have to pay due attention to your diet – eat well, I repeat, eat well! Although I do not know where Mum will raise all the cash for that."

The passage was disallowed and Lt Prins refused to give me any explanation about the matter.

(d) My grandniece, Xoliswa Jozana,[i] wishes to study LL.B with a view of practising as a lawyer and the parents asked for my advice as to whether it would be wise for her to do law. On April 15 I wrote back to them encouraging my grand-niece to proceed as she wished, but at the same time advised the parents that I have been out of practice for 16 years and would accordingly consult Mrs F Kentridge, who formerly practised at the Johannesburg Bar. On May 9 I wrote to Mrs Kentridge[ii] along the lines indicated above and, on June 4, Lt Prins arrogantly told me that I should rewrite the letter and leave out the facts mentioned above, adding that the Matanzimas could get the advice from somebody else.

---

i   Xoliswa Jozana, daughter of K. D. Matanzima (1915– 2003), Mandela's nephew, a Thembu chief, and chief minister for the Transkei – see the glossary. His middle name was Daliwonga.

ii   See his letter on page 291.

It was the hostility with which he spoke more than his unreasonable explanation that struck me. In addition, I wondered what had happened to my letter of April 15. Whatever they did with it they acted improperly. If they sent it to the Matanzimas then they allowed me to make a promise to my relatives which they knew in advance they would not permit me to fulfill. If the letter was held back, I should have been told about the matter, which was not done.

To prevent me from telling my wife that I sent my daughter a birthday card which did not reach her, that I always think of her and that the photos she had posted to me had disappeared is an unreasonable act based neither on security considerations nor on the desire to maintain good order and discipline nor to promote my welfare. The same applies to my letter to Mrs Kentridge in which I requested her to advise my grandniece on her desire to become a lawyer.

4.   Censorship of incoming correspondence

But the worst abuses in regard to the censoring of letters are committed in regard to incoming correspondence and, in this connection, the C.O. and his staff have gone rampant. The censoring is malicious and vindictive and again is motivated by considerations of security and discipline not the desire to promote our welfare.

I regard it as part of a campaign of systematic political persecution and an attempt to keep us in the dark about what goes on outside prison & about our own family affairs. What the C.O. is trying to do is not only to cut us off from the powerful current of goodwill and support that has ceaselessly flown in during the 14 years of my incarceration in the form of visits, letters, cards and telegrams, but also to discredit us to our family and friends by presenting us to them as irresponsible people who neither acknowledge letters written to them nor deal with important matters referred to us by our correspondents.

In addition the double standards used in censoring letters is cowardly and calculated to deceive the public into the false impression that our outgoing mail is not censored. In the case of outgoing letters we are required to rewrite them whenever there is any matter to which the prison authorities object, so as to remove any evidence that they have been heavily censored whilst incoming ones are badly cut or scratched out as the censors please. Nothing will best convey to you the extent of the damage caused to our incoming mail more than an actual inspection by you in person. Many of the letters from my wife consist of strips of incoherent information that are difficult to keep together even in a file.

My wife has been in prison several times and not only knows the relevant Prison Rules well, but also the sensitivity of your local officials to anything they might consider objectionable. She makes a conscious effort to confine herself to family affairs, yet hardly a single one of her letters escapes mutilation.

On November 24 1975 she wrote me a 5-page letter and only the remains of 2 pages finally reached me. The censorship policy adopted here is not followed even by your own officials in other jails. As you are aware, my wife has recently served a 6 months sentence in Kroonstad. Some of her letters were passed by the C.O. of that prison but heavily censored this end.

But what I intensely detest is to force us to be parties to a practice based on our plain falsehood. It is immoral for the C.O. to destroy or withhold letters from our families and friends and at the same time prevent us from telling them about what he does with them. I consider it callous to allow our people to continue wasting money, time, energy, goodwill and love by sending us letters and cards which the C.O. knows will never be given to us.

Between December 1974 and April 1976 no less than 15 letters for Mr A Kathrada were withheld. Among them were those from members of his family, from Prof Rampol, Messrs Ismail Bhoola, Essop Pahad[i] and Navraj Joseph.[ii] Lt Prins refused Mr Kathrada permission to tell his people to stop writing to him, adding that he found their letters interesting. When Mr Kathrada said he supposed the security police were also interested, Lt. Prins, although he did not say so categorically, indicated that they would be so interested. This is a clear case of abuse of authority and you ought to issue a public statement in which you clearly define the policy of your Department, and set out, more particularly, what you consider objectionable and the categories of persons who may not write or send us money or messages of goodwill.

5.   Disappearance of letters in transit
The number of letters that disappear in transit is far too large to be explained on the basis of the inefficiency of the Post Office Department and, from the unreasonable and persistent refusal of the C.O. to allow us to register our letters, I must draw the inference that their disappearance is not accidental. In this regard the C.O. recently made

---

i   Essop Pahad (1939–), political activist in exile in London.
ii   Paul Joseph, a political activist in exile in London.

a bad mistake which confirmed my suspicion that in these matters he and subordinates are not acting openly.

On March 1 I wrote to Mr Q Mvambo, care of my wife, and at the same time advised her about it. She replied that she had not received the letter to Mr Mvambo and the C.O. had that information cut out from my wife's letter so as to keep me in the dark about the fact. If the C.O. were not implicated about the disappearance of this particular letter why did he deliberately try to conceal the fact?

The registration of outgoing mail will partly solve this particular problem and the introduction of this practice will not increase the work of the local officials at all. A post office book for the bulk registration of mail can be used as in all big firms and we are prepared to do the secretarial work under the supervision of the Sgt in charge of the section and all that the censors would be required to do would be exactly what they are doing now, namely, to enter the letters in the official records and post them away.

6. Visits

Even here the measures taken by the C.O. in supervising conversations between prisoners and their visitors go beyond the security requirements. To put four and sometimes even six warders on duty to one visitor, breathing into her face or staring threateningly at her is a blatant form of intimidation.

It is my duty to tell you that there is a widespread belief amongst my fellow prisoners that at these visits there is a listening device that records all conversations, including confidential matters between husband and wife. If this be the case there is hardly any justification for the show of force now generally displayed during such visits. I might add that I encountered repeated opposition from the warder-in-charge when, during one of her visits, I kept on reminding my daughter not to allow herself to be distracted by these strong-arm tactics. For several years in the past only one or two warders were on duty during these visits and I request you to reintroduce this system.

In addition, we were also allowed to use memory aids to make certain that nothing of importance would escape attention and to deny us that privilege after we have enjoyed it for more than a decade is to deprive us of all the advantages of a planned and systematic conversation. We have repeatedly assured the C.O. that we would be prepared to submit these aids for inspection before and after the visit. Moreover, as there are always warders on duty, the danger of passing on objectionable information does not exist at all.

Mandela on the roof of Kholvad House, Johannesburg in 1953, where both Ismail Meer and Ahmed Kathrada lived during the late 1940s and early 1950s, and which became an informal meeting place for anti-apartheid activists.

A contact sheet of Nelson and Winnie on their wedding day in June 1958.

Mandela's Robben Island cell as it has been recreated by the Robben Island Museum. When Mandela lay down, his head touched one wall, and his feet almost the other.

This photograph of Mandela's Robben Island cell was taken in 1977 when the apartheid government organised a visit to the Island by media to showcase how 'well' the political prisoners were being treated. Over the years the prisoners struggled for better prison conditions and by 1977 Mandela was allowed to have books related to his study.

30th November 1964

The Commanding Officer.
Robben Island

<u>URGENT</u>

I must pay today Rd 16·0 to The Cultural Attaché, British Embassy, Hill Street, Pretoria, in respect of examination entry fees for Part I of the Final LL·B of the University of London.

Last month I wrote to the university for the entry forms and to my wife for the necessary funds. On the 9th of this month, I wrote a further letter to the Cultural Attaché for the forms. In neither case have I received an acknowledgment or reply.

I am writing to ask you to wire today Rd 16·0 to the Cultural Attaché and to ask him to send me the forms for completion. I may not have sufficient funds for this purpose, and Ahmed Kathrada, prisoner no. 468, would be prepared, subject to your approval, to lend me the necessary amount, to cover the entry fees and costs of the telegram.

As the entries for these examinations close today, I shall appreciate it if you would kindly treat the matter as extremely urgent.

Nelson Mandela
N Mandela
Prisoner no. 466/64

Accts —
I have no objection to the wiring of the R16.00 but I am not prepared that prisoners can borrow money from each other

30/11

Letter from Mandela to the commanding officer of Robben Island requesting permission to borrow money from fellow inmate Ahmed Kathrada to cover examination entry fees. A note in another hand, reads: "I have no objection to the wiring of the R16.00 but I am not prepared that prisoners can borrow money from each other" (see page 26).

23. 6. 69

My darlings,

Once again our beloved Mummy has been arrested and now she and Daddy are away in jail. My heart bleeds as I think of her sitting in some police station far away from home, perhaps alone and without anybody to talk to, and with nothing to read. Twenty-four hours of the day longing for her little ones. It may be many months or even years before you see her again. For long you may live like orphans, without your own home and parents, without the natural love, affection and protection Mummy used to give you. Now you will get no birthday or Christmas parties, no presents or new dresses, no shoes or toys. Gone are the days when, after having a warm bath in the evening, you would sit at table with Mummy and enjoy her good and simple food. Gone are the comfortable beds, the warm blankets and clean linen she used to provide. She will not be there to arrange for friends to take you to bioscopes, concerts and plays, or to tell you nice stories in the evening, help you read difficult books and to answer the many questions you would like to ask. She will be unable to give you the help and guidance you need as you grow older and as new problems arise. Perhaps never again will Mummy and Daddy join you in House no. 8115 Orlando West, the one place in the whole world that is so dear to our hearts.

This is not the first time Mummy goes to jail. In October 1958, only four months after our wedding, she was arrested with 2000 other women when they protested against passes in Johannesburg and spent two weeks in jail. Last year she served four days, but now she has gone back again and I cannot tell you how long she will be away this time. All that I wish you to always bear in mind is, that we have a brave and determined Mummy who loves her people with all her heart. She gave up pleasure and comfort in return for a life full of hardship and misery, because of the deep love she has for her people and country. When you become adults and think carefully of the unpleasant experiences Mummy has gone through, and the stubbornness with which she has held to her beliefs, you will begin to realise the importance of her contribution in the battle for truth and justice and the extent to which she has sacrificed her own personal interests and happiness.

Mummy comes from a rich and respected family. She is a qualified Social

Pages from a letter from Mandela to daughters Zindzi and Zenani dated 23 June 1969, after learning that Winnie had been arrested (see pages 95–7).

Misses Zeni + Zindzi Mandela
c/o Mrs Iris Niki Xaba
P.O. Box 23,
Orlando VILLAGE
SOWETO JOHANNESBURG

worker and at the time of our marriage in June 1958 she had a good and comfortable job at the Baragwanath Hospital. She was working there when she was arrested for the first time and at the end of 1958 she lost that job. Late she worked for the Child Welfare Society in town, a post she liked very much. It was whilst working there that the Government ordered her not to leave Johannesburg, to remain at home from 6 p.m to 6 a.m, and not to attend meetings, nor enter any hospital, school, university, courtroom, compound or hostel, or any African townships save Orlando where she lived. This order made it difficult for her to continue with her work at the Child Welfare Society and she lost this particular job as well.

Since then mummy has lived a painful life and had to try and run a home without a fixed income. Yet she somehow managed to buy you food and clothing, pay your school fees, rent for the house and to send me money regularly. I left home in April 1961 when Zeni was two years and Zindzi three months. Early in January 1962 I toured Africa and visited London for ten days, and returned to South Africa towards the end of July the same year. I was terribly shaken when I met mummy. I had left her in good health with a lot of flesh and colour. But she had suddenly lost weight and was now a shadow of her former self. I realised at once the strain my absence had caused her. I looked forward to some time when I would be able to tell her about my journey, the countries visited and the people I met. But my arrest on August 5 put an end to that dream. When mummy was arrested in 1958 I visited her daily and brought her food and fruits. I felt proud of her especially because the decision to join the other women in demonstrating against passes was taken by her freely without any suggestion from me. But her attitude to my own arrest made me know mummy better and fully. Immediately I was arrested our friends here and abroad offered her scholarships and suggested that she leave the country to study overseas. I welcomed these suggestions as I felt that studies would keep her mind away from her troubles. I discussed the matter with her when she visited me in Pretoria Jail in October 1962. She told me that although she would most probably be arrested and sent to jail, as every politician fighting for freedom, must expect, she would nevertheless remain in the country and suffer with her people. Do you see now what a brave mummy we have?

Do not worry, my darlings, we have a lot of friends, they will look after you, and one day mummy and daddy will return and you will no longer

be orphans without a home. Then we will also live peacefully and happily as all normal families do. In the meanwhile you must study hard and pass your examinations and behave like good girls. mummy and I will write to you many letters. I hope you get the Christmas card I sent you in December and the letter I wrote to both of you in February of this year. Your affectionately Mum with lots and lots of love and a million kisses. Daddy

In April 1977 the government invited South African journalists to Robben Island to dispel rumours about harsh treatment of political prisoners. Photographs were taken of Mandela and his comrades as part of a manufactured spectacle for the media.

take and send our photographs to our own families.

We stress the fact that the way in which the Minister planned this visit in no way differs from previous ones. IN August 1964 re= porters from "The Daily Telegraph" found those of us who were here at the time "mending clothes" instead of our normal work at the time of knapping stones with 5 lb. hammers. As soon as the re= porters left we were ordered to crush stones as usual. At the end of August 1965 Mrs. I.*da Parker from "The Sunday Tribune" found us wearing raincoats on our way back from the lime quarry - raincoats which were hurriedly issued to us at work on the very day of her visit, and which were immediately taken away when she left. The rain coats were not issued to us again until a year or so later.

We emphatically state that under no circumstances are we willing to cooperate with the Department in any manoeuvre on its part to distort the true state of affairs obtaining on this island. With few exceptions our span has been kept inside for several months now, but our normal work is still that of pulling sea-weed, and the Department has given no assurance that we will never be sent out to the quarry again.

We also cite the example of the cupboards we have in our cells. Any television-viewer is likely to be impressed with this furniture and would naturally give all the credit to the Department. It is unlikely that such telefision-viewers and newspaper readers would be aware that the cupboards have been painstakingly built with crude tools in a crude "workshop" from cardboard cartons and from driftwood picked up on the beaches by prisoners, that the costs for beautifying them have been borne by the prisoners themselves, and that they have been built by a talented fellow prisoner, Jafta Masemola, working approximately 8 hours a day on weekdays at the rate of R1,50 (One Rand fifty Cents) a month.

Rubbish!

The same for other prisoners

At all times wer are willing to have press and television inter= views, provided that the aim is to present to the public a balanced picture of our living conditions. This means that we would be allowed to express our grievances and demands freely, and to make comments whether such comments are favourable or otherwise to the Department.

We are fully aware that the Department desires to protect a favourable

3/......

Page from a letter written by prisoners to the head of the prison complaining about the journalists' visit of 1977 and the inherent abuse of their rights. Note the comments in the margin: "Rubbish!" and "The same for other prisoners" (see pages 340–4).

Above: Robben Island prisoners were made to sit in rows in the prison courtyard and smash stones into gravel.

Above: Members of the team appointed by Minister of Justice Kobie Coetsee to hold meetings with Mandela while he was in prison: l–r General Willemse, commissioner of prisons; Mandela; Dr Niël Barnard, head of the National Intelligence Service; Kobie Coetsee, and Fanie van der Merwe, director-general of justice.

7. Language qualifications of the censors

The man who is directly in charge of censoring of our mail and magazines is W/O Steenkamp who was previously in charge of this section. Although he may have passed matric English, he is certainly no more proficient in that language than I am in Afrikaans and I doubt if Sgt Fourie is any the better in this regard. I would certainly consider it an injustice to entrust me with the task of censoring Afrikaans letters. Neither of the officials in the Censors Office is properly qualified for the job.

Even the C.O. finds it difficult to express himself in English. In fact, during the 14 years of my imprisonment I have met no C.O. whose English is as poor as that of Roelofse; who commands a prison where the overwhelming majority of prisoners are English-speaking and who have no knowledge of Afrikaans at all.

The poor language qualifications of the local officials, especially in the Censors Office, may be one of the contributing factors to the unreasonably heavy censoring of our letters and it is proper for you to review the whole position and appoint censors who are thoroughly conversant with English, Herero, Ovambo,[i] Sotho, Tswana, Xhosa and Zulu.[ii]

8. Ban on correspondence with political supporters

Lt Prins has now told me that we are no longer allowed to communicate with any people known to the Department to be our political associates nor to relatives of other prisoners, irrespective of the contents of the letter. He accordingly refused me permission to write a condolence letter to Mrs N Mgabela, wife of a fellow prisoner on this island, who lost a grandchild. He also did not allow a letter to Mrs Lilian Ngoyi,[iii] a lifelong friend, who helped look after the house and the children when my wife was jailed. A letter I wrote to her on January 1, 1975 and in which I thanked her for her gesture never reached. The failure of all my attempts to acknowledge the help she freely gave and her hospitality to the children is a constant worry to me and I must request you to allow me to send her a copy of the letter of January 1. I am equally anxious to send Mrs Mgabela my condolences and undertake not to say anything in the letter to which any reasonable objection might be made by the C.O.

---

i   Herero and Ovambo are languages from Namibia.
ii   Sesotho is the language of the Sotho people, Setswana is the language of the Tswana people, isiXhosa is the language of the Xhosa people and isiZulu is the language of the Zulu people.
iii Lilian Ngoyi (1911–80), politician, and anti-apartheid and women's rights activist – see the glossary.

9. Telegrams and Easter Cards

(a) the C.O. has introduced a new practice of not allowing us to see the actual telegrams sent to us. He has given us no reasons for departing from a practice that has been followed for many years. But I have had two experiences in which the local officials have been quite negligent and failed to deliver telegrams punctually.

(i) In 1972 when Col Willemse was C.O., I expected a visit on a Saturday from my eldest daughter, Makaziwe.[i] That Saturday I was actually taken to the visiting rooms but she did not arrive. Later she wrote and referred me to a telegram she had sent postponing the visit. In response to my enquiry, the telegram was delivered two weeks after it had been received here. Col Willemse, however, gave me an explanation which exonerated him from any blame in his personal capacity and we settled the matter amicably.

(ii) Last year I was given a telegram announcing the death of the brother of the Paramount Chief Sabata Dalindyebo[ii] and advising me of the day when he would be buried. Although the telegram was received before the funeral, it was given to me about 6 days after the burial and I now strongly protested at what I considered to be plain irresponsibility.

What happens now is that we are given a message scrawled on a piece of paper, sometimes in writing that is difficult to read, and without the date when the telegram was sent and received as well as other essential information. Again the current belief is that some of these telegrams are first referred for scrutiny to the Security Police before delivery to the addressee and in order to cover up the delay in handing over, the C.O. has introduced this practice.

The people who send these telegrams pay more money in order to ensure a speedy transmission of the message and it is a matter of public concern when a government department deliberately frustrates the smooth and efficient operation of a public service for which citizens pay an appropriate fee.

(iii) For several years now I have received Easter cards from a number of friends but this year none arrived. Last month and again in response to my enquiries Lt. Prins told me that one had arrived but that he objected to the person who sent it and refused to

---

i   Makaziwe Mandela (1954–), Mandela's eldest daughter – see the glossary.
ii   King Sabata Jonguhlanga Dalindyebo (1928–86), paramount chief of the Transkei homeland and leader of the Democratic Progressive Party, the opposition party in Transkei which opposed apartheid rule – see the glossary.

disclose the identity of the sender. Against the background set out above I did not find it easy to accept the truthfulness of that statement.

10. Money received for prisoners

There is a general impression amongst prisoners here that the CO and the Security Police are running a racket with our moneys. Although I have no evidence to substantiate this allegation, I should like to draw your attention to the following aspects:

(a) Last December my wife told me that our friends, Mr and Mrs Matlhaku, from Botswana,[i] had sent me R20.00. I immediately enquired from Lt Prins and on several occasions this year he assured me as usual that the money had not been received. Early in May the accounts section, in response to an earlier request, furnished me with my balance and statement of moneys credited to my account[ii] as from February 1975 to this year.

On May 31 Lt Prins sent a message to the effect that an amount of R30.00 was received from the Matlhakus on November 5 1975. No explanation as to why this year he repeatedly told me that the money had not been received nor why the money was not shown as having been credited to my account in the statement supplied to me by the accounts sections, nor about the covering letter from the Matlhakus. I assume that in due course I will be given the usual flippant excuse that the C.O. objects either to the Matlhakus or the contents of the letter.

(b) I have repeatedly complained about the amount of R40.00 which, according to my wife, was sent to me by my nephew from Cape Town and even mentioned the matter to Brigadier Du Plessis on April 28, as I had done with that of the Matlhakus. Lt Prins asked me to produce proof that this amount had been sent by my nephew and I showed him one letter from my wife and promised to produce a second one, also from my wife, which was not immediately available when I gave him the first. Early in May I offered to show him the second letter and he indicated that he would tell me when he wanted. To the best of my knowledge and belief the matter has received no further attention.

---

i   Ishmael and Martha Matlhaku, political activists and friends. They went into exile in Botswana.

ii   Upon entering prison, a list was made of the belongings a prisoner had with them. Details of the amount of cash a prisoner may have brought with them were recorded in an individual account under the name of the prisoner (this was not a bank account but simply a separate bookkeeping record). Thereafter, any funds reaching the prison in the name of that prisoner were recorded in that account and so too were any disbursements made in the name of the prisoner. When they were discharged from prison, the prisoner was given what remained in the account.

(c) For several years now, Mr G Mlyekisana and friends in Cape Town have been sending me and some of my fellow prisoners Christmas presents in the form of small amounts. None of us received any of these sums last year. This cannot be a pure coincidence. I believe the C.O., acting in consultation with the Security Police, has done something to prevent us from getting the moneys which he does not wish us to know.

(d) My friend, Mr Robert Matji, from Lesotho wrote some time last year and promised to send me and another fellow prisoner money for study purposes and, despite repeated enquiries, I have not been told whether or not that money came.

I must tell you that in the negligent manner in which my complaints have been investigated and the lengthy delays involved in extracting simple information on what are essentially trust moneys, is a matter of serious concern which you ought to investigate as soon as you can to clear the reputation of your Department at least in this particular respect. In the light of my experiences with the amount from the Matlhakus, you will readily appreciate my present state of mind on this question.

11. Problems relating to health matters

(a) About July last year and as a result of a knee injury I sustained last year whilst working at the seaside,[i] Dr Edelstein recommended that I should be provided with a sanitary pail lighter than the standard one I am presently using. Sgt Schoeman of the local hospital duly communicated the doctor's recommendation to the head of the prison. When difficulties arose, I personally interviewed Lt Prins on the matter. Although the injury has now healed, I was never provided with the pail as recommended by the doctor.

(b) On July 17 this year and again on health grounds, Dr Edelstein recommended that I could acquire at my own cost a pair of pyjamas and this recommendation by a competent medical practitioner was turned down by the C.O. on the ground, I learn, that prisoners are only allowed to buy sports equipment. With due respect to the C.O., it seems to me ridiculous to allow us to buy outfits for mere recreation, a concession we naturally appreciate, and refuse us permission to buy nightwear recommended by an experienced doctor.

As a matter of fact the C.O. knows only too well that his decision is arbitrary and inconsistent with a practice he himself has

---

i   The prisoners collected seaweed.

followed. My skin is sensitive to brackwater[i] used on the Island, and on the recommendation of [the] doctor, I have been using a special cream since the Sixties to keep the skin soft.

On July 5 I discussed the matter with Dr Edelstein and he was surprised that I encountered difficulties in this matter and promised to take up the issue with the C.O. directly. I have since been informed that he could not move Col Roelofse. With his surprisingly backward views on race relations, I believe the C.O. fears that if I acquire the pair of pyjamas as recommended by Dr Edelstein, the Senior Medical Officer on the Island, I will virtually become a white man.

In this country only white prisoners have the right to sleep in pyjamas with the exception of those fellow prisoners who are hospitalised locally and who are provided with a nightshirt which in many cases barely reaches ones knees. Black prisoners here sleep naked with only blankets as a cover. This is the real reason for the unusual step of a mere layman vetoing the considered decision of a competent professional man in his own field. When I saw Dr Edelstein on June 17 Sgt Schoeman had suggested that the prison hospital could provide me with a nightshirt which the doctor found unsuitable. It was after this offer that had been made that Dr Edelstein made his recommendation.

For 13 years I have slept naked on a cement floor that becomes damp and cold during the rainy season. Although I am physically fit and active, such unhealthy conditions have caused some damage. I will certainly not embarrass Dr Edelstein who has treated me well by discussing the matter with him again. But I need the outfit urgently and I must request you to allow me to purchase the recommended pyjamas at the earliest possible convenience.

I hope, General, you will not consider it as a threat directly or indirectly when I say that I have the legal right to take measures to protect my health and, once the medical officer is of the opinion that these measures will best improve a man's health, the C.O. has no jurisdiction whatsoever in the matter.

13. Political discussions at the sittings of the Prison Board[ii]

It has been the practice for several years now at the sittings of the Prison Board for its members to engage prisoners in political discus-

---

i   Brackish water – fresh water mixed with saltwater.
ii   Point 12 of Mandela's original letter was missing, he must have mis-numbered when writing it.

sions. Political discussions are welcome and may even be fruitful if they are properly arranged by the right people. The correct premise for any such discussions is the clear recognition that we are loyal and disciplined members of political organisations that have definite policies, and that on fundamental political problems we cannot act as individuals but as representatives of our organisations.

Secondly, if the discussions are to be profitable, we must be told about them beforehand, be furnished with the actual topic for discussion, the names of the persons who will conduct such discussions with us and their principal aim. It is certainly not the function of the Board to conduct discussions of a political nature and I consider the whole practice improper and request you to stop it. Its function is to submit reports to the COP on the conduct, training, aptitude and maturity of a prisoner and to make recommendations for his classification, release without conditions, or on probation or parole.

It is also the firm opinion of my fellow prisoners that these discussions are used by the Board for the purpose of victimising those who are opposed to the policy of separate development by not upgrading them.

14. Other acts of victimisation

Throughout our stay here we have been constantly subjected to various forms of victimisation for a variety of reasons connected with political events outside the prison or with the usual tensions that characterise relations between prisoners and warders. Many examples can be quoted to illustrate the point, but for purposes of this letter, it is sufficient to mention 3 of the current or recent cases.

(a) As you are aware the churches have provided us with an inter-communication system to supply us with music from records bought by ourselves. Since the installation of the service we have invested in more than R1,000 worth of records. The service has been out of action for about 5 months now and we do not accept the explanation that the main difficulty in restoring it is the C.O. cannot obtain the necessary spare parts.

(b) On July 3 we expected to see a film in accordance with a programme which has been in operation for some time now. It was not shown and the only explanation given by W/O Du Plessis was that it was not worth seeing.

(c) A hot water system was installed last year and, on several occasions since its installation, the electric geyser failed but the electrician was able to fix it in a matter of minutes. For more than a week now, it has been out of order and the 'breakdown' coincides with a spell of cold weather on the Island. The remarkable thing about the matter is that, although we repeatedly reported the matter to the authorities, the electrician has not even come to examine the apparatus to see what is wrong with it, with the result that we have been deprived[i] of hot water at the one time of the year when it is most needed.

The coincidence between the disorder in the geyser and the spell of cold weather becomes even more significant when considered against the surrounding circumstances. The general practice in the past has been to keep the span[ii] inside on rainy days but on July 7 the span was sent out to pull out bamboo[iii] from the sea although it was raining. They returned about lunchtime all wet and cold. By the morning of July 8 a few had contracted a cold. With the possible exception of the severe winter of 1964, this was certainly the coldest day on the Island in the last 12 years. Nevertheless the span was again sent out to the same spot which was the most exposed in the whole of this area from about 8am to 3.30 pm. The span shivered from cold and many were almost numb on their return. On July 9 a delegation consisting of Messrs Billy Nair,[iv] John Pokela and JB Vusani discussed the whole matter with Lt. Prins who promised that throughout the winter the span would not again be sent to work on that spot. He also arranged for hot water to be brought in drums from the kitchen.

15. Complaints against juniors

Lt. Prins, W/O Du Plessis and Steenkamp and Sgt. Fourie are all too junior to be expressly mentioned in a letter from me to you. But they are the officials in charge of our affairs and it is through them that the C.O. abuses his authority and persecutes us.

I have repeatedly brought to his attention most of the complaints discussed above without success. It is clear that he considers it his duty to support almost everything done by his officials against prisoners, however wrong that official may be, and I see no useful purpose whatsoever in pursuing these issues with him any longer.

---

i   Mandela includes a note in the margin to see footnote 22 and writes at the end of the letter: 'In regard to this matter I speak purely as a layman and from experience of what actually happened in the past when the geyser was out of order. It may well be that the electrician has some more reliable means of identifying the fault without actually inspecting the apparatus itself.'

ii   Afrikaans wrod for 'team' that was used in prison.

iii   This is actually a type of seaweed which had the Afrikaans name of *bambous*. (Christo Brand, *Doing Life with Mandela* (Johannesburg: Jonathan Ball, 2014, p. 38.)

iv   Billy Nair (1929–2008), comrade and MK member who was charged with sabotage in 1963. He was held in B Section with Mandela on Robben Island and was released in 1984 – see the glossary.

As already indicated, I have had no less than 3 interviews with Brigadier Du Plessis and, in spite of his friendliness and courtesy it is clear that the situation is in many respects beyond his control, and what has happened since his last visit and my interview with him seems to have fanned the abuse of authority and political persecution.

Had I not been a Black prisoner born and brought up in South Africa, and who has been subjected in his daily life to all the excesses of racial prejudice, I would not have believed that normal human beings could be associated with such a mania for persecuting their fellow men. It is a mean type of cowardice to wreak vengeance on defenceless men who cannot hit back. An honourable warrior is no peacetime hero who concentrates his attacks on those who carry no weapons and he prefers to use his sword against those who are similarly armed.

16.   The C.O.P.'s failure to visit political prisoners on Robben Island

The abuses described above are aggravated by your failure personally to visit the Island and to give us the opportunity to discuss these problems directly with you. The C.O. told us in the course of an interview with him early this year, that Gen Nel's term as C.O.P. would be expiring soon and that he was not likely to visit the Island before his retirement. This was unfortunate because regular visits by the C.O.P. are in themselves a means of checking abuses by subordinates and the knowledge that he would not be coming down made the C.O. unrestrained in his actions.

When Gen. Steyn was C.O.P. he visited us at least once a year and listened to complaints and requests. Then he brought Col. Badenhorst who tried to terrorise us and, in order to give him a free hand to transgress the law, Gen. Steyn stayed away from the Island whilst we were being persecuted, tortured, beaten up and humiliated in various ways. In 1972 I gave judges Steyn, Theron and Corbett,[i] in the presence of Gen. Steyn and Col. Badenhorst, details of the persecution we had received whilst the latter was C.O., stressing that in spite of my repeated requests to Gen Steyn to continue visiting the prison regularly he had kept away. I told the judges that he had stayed away because he realised that he could not defend the illegalities that were being committed by his subordinates. I got the distinct impression that the judges were as much concerned about the General's failure to carry out his duties in this particular regard as I was.

i   Justice Michael Corbett (1923–2007) was the judge who administered Mandela's oath of office when he became president of South Africa in 1994.

A visit by other officials from Headquarters, whatever their ranks may be, can be no substitute for a visit by the Department Head in person. As already indicated, our treatment here is much influenced by political events outside prison and, in a way, the C.O. treats us like hostages. Whenever South Africa is under heavy attack for its racial policies, prison officials try to vent their anger and frustration on us.

In addition, any substantial complaint from a political prisoner, however genuine, tends to be regarded as a threat to the survival of the white man and even high ranking officials consider it their duty to resist it at all costs. In the prevailing political atmosphere in which it is being denounced by the whole world, no officials from Headquarters who still look forward to promotions and other lucrative benefits after retirement, are to burn their fingers by checking the abuses of a C.O. and upholding the complaints of the men who have played a part in mobilising opposition to apartheid. Only you and you alone, is in a position to take a bold line and confine the actions of the C.O. within the four corners of the law.

It is my earnest opinion that his actions fall outside the scope of the Prison Rules. A C.O. and Head of the Prison who still try today to perpetuate the myth of the superiority of the white man, who equate civilisation with a white skin and the clothing one wears, are not the fit and proper persons to be in charge of an institution, one of whose principal aims is the promotion of the welfare of Black prisoners.

One of the main causes of the friction here is the link between this Department and the Security Police and one of the first steps in your attempt to redress our grievances is to cut out that link completely. Honest officials from the Department frankly admit that in many respects we, as political prisoners, fall outside the scope of the Department and are the responsibility of the Security Police. The latter have no legal right to interfere in the internal administration of this institution and I hope that, in this regard, you will be able to assert yourself far more than your predecessors were able to do, and stop this unwarranted practice. Our treatment should be the responsibility of your Department not just in theory but in actual practice as well. The duty of the Security Police is to ensure that we are kept in a maximum security prison and their authority should go no further.

Many prisoners regard the C.O.P. in relation to all matters concerning us as a mere figurehead, and that the real boss is the Chief of the Security Police who order the C.O.P. not only what to do but how to do it. It is the Security Police that have induced your Department to want to isolate us from the people outside prison, to deny us the love of our wives and children and the good wishes from our friends by cutting down visits to the so-called first degree relations, trying to terrorise our visitors, not allowing us to use notes at visits, through malicious censoring of letters, cards and other material, false information in regard to letters, cards and money received on our behalf and the unprecedented 'disappearance' of letters in the post.

I have been wondering for some time now whether I should continue to be party to a practice I consider unethical and which gives the impression that I still enjoy rights and privileges which have been whittled away so much so that they have become practically useless. In particular, I have considered the question whether I should allow my wife and children to come down the 1000 miles from Johannesburg at great expense only to see me under such humiliating conditions, whether I should allow them to waste time, energy and money to write letters that 'disappear' in transit and whose remains that reach me are quite disconnected and meaningless. I resent the fact that before every visit they should receive lectures from swaggering and vindictive officials as to what they may or may not say when they talk to me.

Since January 1973 to June this year I have received 42 letters from my wife. Of the 6 I got in 1973 only 3 were mutilated. Off the 11 which came in 1974 7 were heavily censored and in 1975 6 out of the 16. But the picture for 1976 is totally different. Of the 9 I have received since the beginning of the year only 1 reached me unscathed. It is this situation that makes me wonder whether I should continue enduring these indignities.

But I still believe that you, as Head of this Department, who holds the rank of General, will not allow or condone these underhand methods and, until your actual decision on the matter proves me wrong, I shall continue to act in the belief that you are not aware of what is going on in this prison.

It is futile to think that any form of persecution will ever change our views. Your Government and Department have a notorious reputation for their hatred, contempt and persecution of the Black man, especially the African, a hatred and contempt which forms the basic principle of a multiplicity of the country's statutes and cases. The cruelty of this Department in subjecting our people to the indecent practice of thawuza according to which a prisoner was required to strip naked and display his anus for inspection by an official in the presence of other prisoners, the equally obscene practice of a warder poking a finger into a prisoner's rectum, of brutally assaulting them daily and without provocation, was curbed by the Government after it had erupted in a national scandal.

21.

P 71 81/143198

wife. Of the 6 I got in 1973 only 3 were mutilated. Of the 11 which came in 1974 7 were heavily censored and in 1975 6 out of 16. But the picture for 1976 is totally different. Of the 9 I have received since the beginning of the year only 1 reached me unscathed. It is this situation that makes me wonder whether I should continue enduring these indignities.

But I still believe that you, as Head of this department who holds the rank of General, will not allow ~~this dubious practice to~~ or condone these underhand methods and, until your actual decision on the matter proves me wrong, I shall continue to act in the belief that you are not aware of what is going on in this prison.

It is futile to think that any form of persecution will ever change our views. Your Government and department have a notorious reputation for their hatred, contempt and persecution of the Black man, especially the African, a hatred and contempt which forms the basic principle of a multiplicity of the country's statutes and cases. The cruelty of this ~~practice~~ department in subjecting our people to the indecent practice of tauwza according to which a prisoner was required to totally ~~naked and~~ display his anus for inspection by an official in the presence of other prisoners, the equally obscene practice of a warder poking a finger into a prisoner's rectum, of brutally assaulting them daily and without provocation, was curbed by the Government after it had erupted into a national scandal.

But the inhumanity of the average South African warder still remains; only now it has been diverted into other channels and has taken the subtle form of psychological persecution, a field in which some of your local officials are striving to become specialists. You are no doubt aware that many psychologists regard psychological persecution in circumstances such as ours as even more dangerous than plain assault. I have the hope that a man of your rank and experience will immediately grasp the gravity of this ~~practice~~ dangerous practice and take adequate measures to stop it.

It is pointless and contrary to this country's historical experience to think that our people will ever forget us. Although 160 years have passed since the Slachters Nek executions, 74 since the internment camps of the Anglo-Boer War and 61 since Jopie Fourie made his last speech, I will certainly never

I believe ...

Page from a letter to the commissioner of prisons, 12 July 1976, see pages 293–315.

But the inhumanity of the average South African warder still remains, only now it has been diverted into other channels and has taken the subtle form of psychological persecution, a field in which some of your local officials are striving to and becoming specialists. You are no doubt aware that many psychologists regards psychological persecution in circumstances such as ours as more dangerous than plain assault. I have the hope that a man of your rank and experience will immediately grasp the gravity of this dangerous practice and take adequate measures to stop it.

It is pointless and contrary to this country's historical experience to think that our people will ever forget us. Although 160 years have passed since the Schlachters Nek executions,[i] 74 since the internment camps of the Anglo Boer War[ii] and 61 since Jopie Fourie[iii] made his last speech, I will certainly never believe you when you tell me that you have now forgotten those Afrikaner patriots, the men whose sacrifices helped to free you from British Imperialism and to rule the country, and for you in particular to be Head of this Department.

It is certainly quite unreasonable for any man to expect our people, to whom we are national heroes, persecuted for striving to win back our country, to forget us in our lifetime at the height of the struggle for a free South Africa. Your people are slaughtering mine today and not a century and a half ago. It is present South Africa that is a country of racial oppression, imprisonment without trial, of torture and harsh sentences and the threat of internment camps lies not in the distant past but in the immediate future. How can our people ever forget us when we fight to free them from all these evils?

In South Africa, as in many other countries, various issues divide prisoners and officials. I do not agree with the policy of the Department of which you are the Head. I detest white supremacy and will fight it with every weapon in my hands. But even when the clash between you and me has taken the most extreme form, I should like us to fight over principles and ideas and without personal hatred, so that at the end of the battle, whatever the results might be, I can proudly shake hands with you because I feel I have fought an upright and worthy opponent who has observed the whole code of honour and decency. But when

---

i   In 1815 a Boer farmer named Bezuidenhout refused to answer to charges of having mistreated his workers. He was shot by a British soldier when they came to arrest him. His supporters attempted to have revenge and were arrested. Six were executed by hanging at Schlachters Nek.

ii   The British ran concentration camps for Boer women and children during the South African War (1899–1902) and separate ones for black prisoners.

iii   'Jopie' Fourie (1879–1914), an Afrikaner rebel, was the last person to be put to death by firing squad in South Africa after he rebelled against the government which had chosen to support the British in the First World War rather than the Germans.

your subordinates continue to use foul methods then a sense of real bitterness and contempt becomes irresistible.

[Signed NRMandela]
NELSON MANDELA

∞∞∞∞∞∞

Winnie Mandela was also detained in August 1976 when she came out strongly in support of the students and their uprising. She visited police stations to search for missing students, helped to arrange funerals for those killed, and consoled families.

To the commanding officer, Robben Island

[In another hand]
466/64
Special letter[i] to apply to speak personally to the Colonel in connection with his wife

18 August 1976

The Commanding Officer,
Robben Island
Attention: Col. Roelofse

This morning Chief Warder Barnard advised me that my wife would not be able to receive the telegram I handed in for dispatch to her on August 12 on the ground that she has been arrested.

In this connection, I should be pleased if you would grant me, at your earliest possible convenience, an interview to enable me to discuss the matter. I should like to draw your attention to the fact that my wife has been arrested on several occasions before and served [a] sentence twice already. On the first occasion when she was arrested, General Steyn, then Commissioner of Prisons, ruled that it was humanitarian and reasonable that I should be given full particulars about her arrest, detention, charge, sentence and place where she was kept in custody.

---

i   Special letters were not deducted from a prisoner's quota.

I might add that from May 1969 to September 1970 she was detained under the Terrorism Act but throughout that period I was allowed to correspond with her. In this regard, I should be pleased if you would grant me an interview this morning to discuss the whole matter with you.

[Signed NRMandela] 466/6

To Winnie Mandela,[i] his wife

Nelson Mandela 466/64   A Group   Aug. 76

Dadewethu,[ii]

The contents of your telegram requiring details of the subjects still owing for the final yr of the LLB of the University of London were conveyed to me on Aug. 4 & mine was handed in for dispatch to you on Aug 12 – which I hope you've now received.

My main difficulty in completing the English degree is that of obtaining the prescribed literature, especially the text books, law reports & journals. Jurisprudence is essentially a philosophic subject & requires reference to comparatively few cases, but Administrative Law, in the International Law & Company Law are fast-moving subjects & almost every yr there's some important case that changes one or other established principle. Without access to this literature I consider it a sheer waste of time, energy & money to continue with the English degree.

The best thing for me to do would be to complete the six subjects outstanding for the final LLB of Wits. All of them are fairly familiar & I'd be able to take them in one sitting & thereafter tackle Latin which has since been added. In '74 the Registrar advised that they'd have no objection to me completing the remaining courses & indicated that they'd ask the Minister (of Education, I suppose) for me to sit for the exams. It'd not be necessary for me to obtain the D.P. Certificates as I've already attended classes & attempted all these particular subjects. Latin I could be done through Unisa[iii] & then apply to Wits for exemption.

Failing that I'd prefer to do the Unisa LL.B even though it is a course

---

i   Nomzamo Winifred Madikizela-Mandela (1936–) – see the glossary.
ii   'Sister' in isiXhosa.
iii   University of South Africa.

of 26 subjects & for which the Dean of the Law Faculty is prepared to grant me seven exemptions. But permission for me to study law with London, Wits or Unisa was refused by the Commissioner of Prisons on Dec 18 '75. I subsequently discussed the matter with Brig. du Plessis on Jan. 23, '76, & as a result of that discussion I made a second application, this time to do the Unisa LL.B only. For one thing, the course would be far more interesting than London & I'd have comparatively less difficulties about literature. But again permission was refused by the Commissioner last February.

As far as your own personal position is concerned I'd like you to know that since '70 I've made repeated representations for the relaxation of your banning orders & until last mth for Msuthu[i] to be allowed to live with you. Towards the end of '70 & on May 27, '71 I sought an interview with Mr P.C. Pelser, then Minister of Justice, to discuss our domestic affairs, particularly your restrictions & the breakdown of your health due to the weird experiences that you sustained.[ii] He never replied.

On May 13, '74 I wrote a seven-page letter to the present Minister, Mr J. T. Kruger,[iii] in which I asked him to (a) grant you a firearm for self-defence purposes, (b) order the police in dealing with you to confine themselves strictly to the execution of their duties according to law, (c) assist to obtain a permit for Msuthu to live with you, (d) put a police guard at home daily from 7 pm to 6 am until Msuthu joins you, (e) request the Minister of Interior to grant you a passport to enable you to travel abroad, (f) give you & me a 2 hr contact visit to enable us to discuss our household affairs.

On May 25 '74 I had to write another letter to the Minister[iv] because of the vicious attack on the old lady & house reported in your telegram the same mth. In Sept. the Head of the Prison informed me that your application for a passport would be considered on merit & that you were at liberty to submit a formal application to the Commissioner of the place where you resided. The Minister refused the request for a 2hr contact visit.

In a letter to the Commanding Officer on Dec. 1 '74 I explained the attack on the car on Sept. 18 as described in your letter of Sept. 29. I also quoted from that of Oct. 8 which you wrote at 1am whilst waiting for the "'Bantu Males' to attack", an enemy you could do nothing about.[v] I added a paragraph from Bantu's[vi] letter of Nov. 7 where she spoke of the very

---

i   Msuthu Tanduxolo Madikizela, Winnie Mandela's brother.
ii   It is likely that he is referring to the home invasions made on Winnie Mandela's residence.
iii See his letter, page 251.
iv   See his letter, page 264.
v   He quotes from Winnie Mandela's letters in his letter to the commanding officer dated 1 December 1974 (see page 272).
vi   Nobantu Mniki, Winnie Mandela's sister.

tough time they were having in the house in your absence.[i] Although your restrictions have now been removed, all the other representations have been rejected.

On Feb 12 I asked the Minister to reconsider his decision in regard to the question of the firearm & urged that it should be a matter of real concern that despite persistent attacks on the house & family by the S.A.P.[ii] with all their training, skill & experience in tracking down criminals, the culprits involved in this particular case should still be at large.[iii] I told Mr Kruger that I could not appreciate why he should be reluctant to assist you in acquiring a firearm when the police had been totally unable to give you protection in the face of a serious threat to your life. I could not move him.

I hope you got my letters of July 18, Aug 1, copies of the letter & birthday card to you & Zindzi[iv] both dated Dec 1 '75. Your problems'll remain & you & the children [will] never have a real home until a close relative lives with you. Although I strongly feel that my original representations in this regard merited serious consideration, I now wish to approach the same matter from another angle & await the information requested in my letter of July 18.

On Aug. 4 I got another telegram from Justice's wife, Nozolile, announcing the death of Nkosk. NoEngland[v] & that she'd be buried on July 31. On Aug. 12 I sent her a condolence telegram. Last Saturday Mabel came down from Mthatha[vi] & gave me details of the funeral which Sabata[vii] handled very well. I've also written to Nomafu giving her our sympathies. Zindzi sent me a lovely birthday card which made up for the fact that the very last letter I got from you was that of June 27. It looks quite strange not to get a birthday card from you & Zeni.[viii]

Hope you're studying hard & have cut down all other engagements until after the exams. I LOVE YOU! I MISS YOU & HOPE TO BE WITH YOU ON YOUR NEXT BIRTHDAY. Devotedly, Dalibhunga

Nkosk, Nobandla Mandela, 8115 Orlando West, P.O. Phirima [1848], JHB

---

i   He quotes from Nobantu Mniki's letter in his letter to the commanding officer dated 1 December 1974 (see page 272).
ii   South African Police.
iii   See note ii above.
iv   Zindziswa Mandela (1960–), Mandela's youngest daughter – see the glossary.
v   Wife of the regent Chief Jongintaba Dalindyebo who was Mandela's guardian after his father died when he was twelve.
vi   Alternative spelling of Umtata (now officially called Mthatha), which was the capital of the Transkei homeland.
vii   King Sabata Jonguhlanga Dalindyebo (1928–86), paramount chief of the Transkei homeland and leader of the Democratic Progressive Party, the opposition pary in Transkei which opposed apartheid rule – see the glossary.
viii   Zenani Mandela, Mandela's middle daughter – see the glossary.

To Winnie Mandela,[i] his wife

Nelson Mandela, 466/64   Aug 19. '76

Dadewethu,[ii]

Yesterday I'd just finished writing & explaining to you the position relating to my studies & giving you a brief account of the representations I'd made in regard to the restrictions previously imposed on you as well as about Msuthu[iii] when I learnt from the Commanding Officer that you'd been arrested, but gave me no further information.

Up to now I don't know where & when you were apprehended, the law under which you're held in custody, where you're kept & the charge, if any, against you. What I do know now is that the brief spell of [freedom] you've enjoyed for just 10 mnths in 13 yrs has come & gone barely 2 mths before your birthday; gone in '76 less than a ¼ century to 2000 which you'll see certainly in your lifetime. I've, however, requested the Commissioner of Prisons to give me information on your arrest.

In my letter of Aug. 1, which I doubt if you received, I warmly thanked you for joining me on my birthday & tried to entice you to come down by reminding you that Sept 25 & 26, just like July 17 & 18,[iv] would fall on a Saturday & Sunday & I'd vaguely hoped that you might bite, funds being available. I now know that that is not possible. Still & especially because of that, it's always a dy to which I look forward very keenly as if you're still coming. For me it's always a dy I value & honour more than all the dys in the history of this world. I'll remember you more than you shook me that March 10.[v]

It's always given me plenty of satisfaction & joy to write to you. I sincerely don't know whether you'll ever get this particular one nor those of July 18, Aug 1 & 18 &, if you do, when that'll be. Nonetheless, the act of writing to you at this moment removes all the tensions & impurities in my feelings & thoughts. It's the only time I ever feel that some dy in the future it'll be possible for humanity to produce saints who will really be upright & venerable, inspired in everything they do by genuine love for humanity & who'll serve all humans selflessly. Since yesterday I feel closer & more proud of you than ever before & I'm sure the girls also feel the same.

I've no false illusions whatsoever, my darling Mum, & know only too well

---

i   Nomzamo Winifred Madikizela-Mandela (1936–) – see the glossary.
ii   'Sister' in isiXhosa.
iii   Msuthu Tanduxolo Madikizela, Winnie Mandela's brother.
iv   He is referring to their birthdays – 26 September for Winnie Mandela's and 18 July for Mandela.
v   The date of their first date.

Nelson Mandela, 466/64.   Aug. 19, '76

Dadewethu,

Yesterday I'd just finished writing & explaining to you the position relating to my studies & giving you a brief account of the representations I'd made in regard to the restrictions previously imposed on you as well as about Monday when I learnt from the Commanding Officer that you'd been arrested, but gave me no further information.

Up to now I don't know where & when you were apprehended, the law under which you're held in custody, where you're kept & the charge, if any, against you. What I do know now is that the brief spell of you've enjoyed for just 10 mths in 13 yrs has come & gone barely 2 miles before your bicketry, gone in '76 less than a ½ century to 2000 which you'll see certainly in your lifetime I've however, requested the Commissioner of Prisons to give me information on your arrest.

In my letter of Aug. 1, which I doubt if you received, I warmly thanked you for joining me on my birthday & tried to entice you to come down by reminding you that Sept 25 & 26 just like July 17 & 18, would fall on a Saturday & Sunday & I'd vaguely hoped that you might bite, funds being available. I now know that that is not possible. Still & especially because of that V, 18 a day to which I look forward very keenly as if you're still coming. For me it's always a day I value & treasure more than all the days in the history of this world. I'll remember you more than you should me that treasured 10.

It's always given me plenty of satisfaction & joy to write to you. I sincerely don't know whether you'll ever get this particular one nor those of July 18, Aug 1 & 18 &, if you do, when that'll be. Nonetheless, the act of writing to you at this moment removes all the tensions & impurities in my feelings & thoughts. It's the only time I ever feel that some day in the future it'll be possible for humanity to produce saints who will really be upright & venerable, inspired in everything they do & genuine love for humanity & who'll serve all humans selflessly. Since yesterday I feel closer & more proud of you than ever before & I'm sure the girls also feel the same.

I've no false illusions whatsoever, my darling mum, & know only too well the ghastly schemes you've had in the past 14 yrs & the horrid accounts that've been repeatedly blazed about you & that'd completely shattered another woman. Do you think I've forgotten '63/64, may 13 & the 18 mths that followed, Oct. '70 in particular, Apr. '75 to Aug last mth, the venomous telegrams, reports, some sent anonymous by others & by well-meaning people known to both of us, all full of alarming & vile information?

It has been valuable experience for me to watch powerful organisations & highly-placed individuals clubbing together for the specific purpose of destroying a virtually widowed woman; how all these can stoop so low as to bring to my notice all sorts of details

Pages from a letter to Winnie Mandela, 19 August 1976, see previous page and overleaf.

calculated to dim the clear image I have about the most wonderful friend I have on earth. *Completely baffles me:* My consolation has always been that you've kept your head, held the family tight together & made us as happy & optimistic as circumstances would allow a girl who's lived under heavy & sustained pressure from all directions. Of course, dear Mum, we're but human – Zami, Zindzi & I & we'd like you to be highly praised by all & all the time, just like the lady who rose from the valley of the Caledon in the 1820's. But the more you're slandered the more attached to you do I become. These are not the things we should even mention in our correspondence to each other. But we live 1000 miles apart, see each other rarely & for short periods & with all the jazz around your ears you may even wonder what Madiba thinks. Only because of this do I think I should nevertheless, hint to you that I love you & Always.

Strength of affection & rising admiration for you, Mhlophe, create stalemate situations. Concern & adoration frequently intermingle & at times I'm not at all certain which is dominant. Your health, the intense longing for & anxiety about the girls, the many hrs, mths & even yrs living alone far away from the open air & the warm sunshine in which she was brought up, who likes the company of others & can laugh very well, who has lost a comfortable job, the chance to write a university exam for which so much money had been sunk, hard work, energy & precious time had been spent, the uncertainty when I'll see you again all make the heart heavy. As to why I adore you particularly at this hr you know exactly why. Do you still remember when I first addressed you as Nkosazana & why I've stubbornly stuck to it all these yrs? Yes, yes, you do, Ngutyana. Your optimism & wonderful smile have put more steel in me than all the famous classics of this world. You're my darling & in moments such as these, it's reasonable to speak frankly & sincerely. Although I can't be certain my own hope is that these 2 letters will reach you duly & in the form in which I've written them.

I'm writing to the girls to put them at ease & to assure them that you're now a veteran who can take care of herself & to wish them good luck in the exams. I believe Zeni & Bantu still hold on each other but that Zeni has broken with poor Thelza & has had a new gold strike in Mafeta Oupa about whom she says you'll tell me a lot. I don't who to suggest about whom they'd spend their Dec. holidays in your absence. There's of course Kgatho & Rennie, the ever-willing Kgatho, Fatu, Niki & Bantu. But I'll wait until I've a clearer picture of the situation before I make positive suggestions. Who did you live behind with the children? You told me the name of Zizwe's Mum but have now forgotten it. I'll also ask Ntatho & Sally to visit you if they can get permits & to look after the house & kids. On Aug. 1 I wrote to your sister Connie a condolence letter & asked you to redirect it to her. I'll now ask Rennie to do so. Devotedly, Dalibhunga & I love you Always!

the ghastly shocks you've had in the past 14 yrs & the lurid accounts that've been repeatedly blazed about you & that'd completely shattered another woman. Do you think I've forgotten '63/'64, May 13 & the 18 months that followed, Oct '70 in particular, April '75 to last mth, the venemous telegrams, reports, some sent anonymously, & others from well-meaning people known to both of us, all full of alarming & vile information?[i]

It has been a valuable experience for me to watch powerful organisations & highly-placed individuals clubbing together for the specific purpose of destroying a virtually widowed woman; how all these can stoop so low as to bring to my notice all sorts of details calculated to dim the clear image I have about the most wonderful friend I have in life completely baffles me. My consolation has always been that you've kept your head, held the family tight together & made us as happy & optimistic as circs.[ii] would allow a girl who's lived under heavy & sustained pressure from all directions. Of course, dear Mum, we're but human – Zeni, Zindzi[iii] & I & we'd like you to be highly praised by all & all the time, just like the lady who rose from the valley of the Caledon in the 1820's. But the more you're slandered, the more attached to you do I become. These are not the things we should even mention in our correspondence to each other. But we live 1000 miles apart, see each other rarely & for short periods & with all the jazz around your ears you may even wonder what Madiba thinks. Only because of this do I think I should, nevertheless, hint to you that I LOVE YOU ALWAYS.

Strength of affection & rising admiration for you, Mhlope,[iv] create stalemate situations. Concern & adoration frequently intermingle & at times I'm not at all certain which is dominant. Your health, the intense longing for & anxiety about the girls, the many hrs, mths & even yrs living alone for the one who loves the open air & the warm sunshine in which she was brought up, who likes the company of others & can laugh very well, who has lost a comfortable job, the chance to write a university exam for which so much money had been sunk, hard work, energy & precious time had been spent, the uncertainty when I'll see you again, all make the heart heavy. As to why I adore you particularly at this hr you know exactly why. Do you still remember when I first addressed you as Dadewethu[v] & why I've stubbornly stuck

---

i   Mandela may be referring to such events in *Long Walk to Freedom* when he writes: 'Some of the nastiest items were known to me because when I would return from the quarry, I would often find neatly cut clippings about Winnie that had been anonymously placed on my bed by the warders.' (p. 504) and 'I had also learned from a newspaper clipping that a Special Branch officer broke into our Orlando house while Winnie was dressing and she reacted angrily, pushing the officer out of the bedroom.' (p. 505.)

ii   Circumstances.

iii   Zenani Mandela (1959–) and Zindziswa Mandela (1960–), Mandela's middle and youngest daughters – see the glossary.

iv   One of Winnie Mandela's names.

v   'Sister' in isiXhosa.

to it all these yrs? Yes, yes, you do, Ngutyana.[i] Your optimism & wonderful smile have put more steel in me than all the famous classics of this world. You're my darling & in moments such as these, it's reasonable to speak frankly & sincerely. Although I can't be certain, my own hope is that these 2 letters will reach you duly & in the form in which I've written them.

I'm writing to the girls to put them at rest & to assure them that you're now a veteran who can take care of herself & to wish them good luck in the exams. I believe Zeni & Bahle still hold on each other but that Zeni has broken with poor Fidza & has had a new gold strike in Mafuta oupa about whom she says you'll tell me a lot. I don't know who to suggest about where they'd spend their Dec. holidays in your absence. There's of course Kgatho & Rennie,[ii] the ever-willing Fatu,[iii] Niki[iv] and Bantu.[v] But I'll wait until I've had a clearer picture of the situation before I make positive suggestions. Who did you leave behind with the chdn? You told me the name of Zizwe's Mum but [I] have now forgotten it. I'll also ask Ntatho & Sally[vi] to visit you if they can get permits & to look after the house & kids. On Aug. 1. I wrote to your sister Connie a condolence letter[vii] & asked you to redirect it to her. I'll now ask Rennie to do so. Devotedly, Dalibhunga.
I LOVE YOU ALWAYS!

Nkosk Nobandla Mandela, c/o Commissioner of Prisons. Pretoria

---

To Winnie Mandela,[viii] his wife

[Translated from isiXhosa]

Sept. 1, 1976

My Dearest Sister,
As a family, we honour and respect you deeply – you are our pride and joy.

i   One of Winnie Mandela's names. She comes from the amaNgutyana clan.
ii   His son Makgatho (Kgatho) Mandela (1950–2005), Mandela's second-born son – see the glossary – and his then wife, Rose Rayne Mandela, known as Rennie.
iii   Fatima Meer (1928–2010), writer, academic, and anti-apartheid and women's rights activist – see the glossary.
iv   Niki Xaba (1932–1985), Winnie Mandela's eldest sister – see the glossary.
v   Nobantu Mniki, Winnie Mandela's sister.
vi   Nthato Motlana (1925–2008), friend, medical doctor, businessman, and anti-apartheid activist – see the glossary, and his wife Sally.
vii   This was probably a condolence letter on the death, in 1976, of Connie Njongwe's husband Dr. James 'Jimmy' Njongwe (1919–76), medical doctor, ANC leader, and organiser of the Defiance Campaign (for the Defiance Campaign, see the glossary) in the Eastern Cape – for Jimmy Njongwe, see the glossary.
viii   Nomzamo Winifred Madikizela-Mandela (1936–) – see the glossary.

It almost feels as though I haven't seen you in a long time even though I saw you recently on the 17th and 18th July. Your picture has been a source of comfort when I think of you, looking at it over and over again is the only thing that gives me comfort when love and remembrance engulf me.

The state of your health and that of the children, their examinations and all that is troubling your soul concerns me. With all of these concerns, I am reminded of how mature you are for your age, but you have shown brilliance, strong character, stability, determination and resilience. Hence I trust you this much.

Accept your present circumstances, do not concern yourself about things you cannot change. Do not worry about the girls, they are mature now, can fend for themselves and can plan for their future. My wish is to one day embrace them to show them they are not alone.

I will write to the Dlomos, the Ngutyanas[i] and other relatives as well to request their assistance with the livelihood and daily expenses of the girls.

I will ask that they invite them over for the school holidays, and also to bear the costs; to cover their transport to and from school, and transport costs for them to come and visit you.

Forget about these responsibilities; the house, rent, car, furniture and the telephone bills. I have written to Rennie,[ii] asking her to provide a detailed report on all of these. I have asked Kgatho[iii] to get Marsh,[iv] Earl,[v] Zwelidumile and Mr Mdingi to look for a reliable person to look after the house as well as to care for the children.

Forget altogether about employment, the costs incurred and the dreams and hopes that you had of providing for yourself and the girls. Now is the time for you to forget about cultural expectations from you as a Dlomo wife, chin up! Love, best wishes and success wherever you are.

Since July I have written five letters to you; July 18, Aug 01 and a copy that I sent on Dec 09 using the home address. The letter dated August 19[vi] were sent via the Commissioner of Prisons asking him to send them to you if that is allowed.

I was reading the letters you wrote to me dated September/October 1974, after the Appeal Court gave its ruling. You wrote these on your 40th birthday which you nearly spent in Kroonstad.[vii] They brought bitter sweet feelings, however I did not let my emotions overcome me.

---

i   Winnie Mandela's family. They come from the amaNgutyana clan.
ii   His son Makgatho's wife.
iii   Makgatho (Kgatho) Mandela (1950–2005), Mandela's second-born son – see the glossary.
iv   Marshall Xaba, husband of Niki Xaba, Winnie Mandela's eldest sister (for Niki Xaba, see the glossary).
v   Earl Mniki, husband of Nobantu Mniki, Winnie Mandela's sister.
vi   See his letter, page 319.
vii   Kroonstad Prison.

Your letter of the 29 September highlights the fact that over the past ten years each birthday wish you received has a unique message. In the letter dated the 09 October, you mention your plans to come and visit, however you are concerned that the Special Branch[i] would foil these plans.

On September 26 you will be turning 42. Although you will not be home and have the usual celebrations, remember that this is your big day, and my wish is that it finds you well, and that you stay strong.

I sincerely hope you have not forgotten the promise I made to you during the eighteen (18) months you were away from home, where you found the house in a mess upon your return, I still stand by it.

I do miss and love you my dearest.

The other letters are for Kgatho, Zeni and Zindzi.[ii]

With love
Dalibhunga

To Winnie Mandela,[iii] his wife

[Translated from isiXhosa]

Nelson MANDELA (466/64) A GROUP   1.10.1976

My dearest sister,

The girls have given me the good news that you appear to be in good health. I had been worried by your weight loss ever since I returned from my overseas trip in July 1962.

Exercise will assist you a great deal, try and jog around the yard everyday if you can. Exercise is the best medicine. I start off my day by jogging and I stretch before I go to bed. Exercise helps with a lot of things, insomnia and helps to keep the body fit and healthy

I heard about that you and Ntatho[iv] were attacked, and that you ended up approaching the courts. Had I known you were taking such a step I would have discouraged you, because that is not a sure way of protecting

---

i   The special branch of the police.
ii   Zenani (1959–) and Zindzi (1960–) Mandela, his and Winnie Mandela's daughters – see the glossary.
iii   Nomzamo Winifred Madikizela-Mandela (1936–) – see the glossary.
iv   Nthato Motlana (1925–2008), friend, medical doctor, businessman, and anti-apartheid activist – see the glossary.

yourself. Even though you are the ones that were attacked and suffered damage to property, you may be liable for legal costs. It can amount to thousands of rands. However if you have taken such steps, don't withdraw, I support you wholeheartedly. I am looking forward to seeing you in January, if all goes well. I miss you most on the days when problems overwhelm me. I don't know where you can get money to be able to stay for two days on your next visit. George[i] will try and get permission for Ntatho to follow so we can discuss matters. I suggest that the children should go and study in England if they are able to get study visas. They told me about the widow's mother who is prepared to contribute to the costs of their trip overseas. I supported that, but included certain conditions. It will be a great honour for Sabata[ii] to organise a dinner in honour of Zindzi,[iii] however if you are planning such a big celebration then both girls should be honoured, because Zeni[iv] is the eldest.

I support the suggestion that we buy the house in Orlando, when we have the money, though that might be a challenge as you are unemployed. I heard about the efforts that had been made to find someone to look after our home, please keep me informed of the developments. After your arrest I wrote a letter enquiring about the well-being of the children and that of the property. I have not received a response as yet. The only feedback I received was that I received from the girls. Your letter dated 22 August is the first one to give me a detailed account about family matters. . . .

I notice that you did not receive my letters dated 18 July and 1 August which I sent to our home address. I wrote the first one in English as usual, the second one in isiXhosa, like the postcard of 1 September, in which I wished you good health, success and happiness. It was sent to Pretoria so that it could be passed on to you, just like those of 18 and 19 August. I hope you have received all five by now. . . .

One has a lot of time for self-reflection, and to think about various issues. Right now I am reflecting on all the things I did not do while I was still able to. One of these is not having a home. It brings me joy when I think of great opportunities I have had as well as the happy times I have experienced.

One has a lot of time to reflect on matters, as opposed to the hectic schedule that I had on the outside. There are always activities to keep the mind busy, engaging with comrades, reading different types of books, recreational activities that relax the mind, writing letters to family and

---

i   George Bizos (1927–), defence lawyer in the Rivonia Trial – see the glossary.
ii   King Sabata Jonguhlanga Dalindyebo (1928–86), paramount chief of the Transkei homeland and leader of the Democratic Progressive Party, the opposition party in Transkei which opposed apartheid rule – see the glossary.
iii Zindziswa Mandela (1960–), his and Winnie Mandela's youngest daughter – see the glossary.
iv   Zenani Mandela (1959–), his and Winnie Mandela's eldest daughter – see the glossary.

friends, and repeatedly reading letters that have come from the outside. These thoughts flow over me when I'm lying down, they concern. They surround one person, my lifelong friend [illegible words] I have bared my soul; however, what is left is love and respect. In spite of all of this, I remain rich in spirit.

I am pleased that you are in Johannesburg, nearer home, and especially that family and friends visit you and you get to hear about family matters. I had a good time when the girls came for a visit, but I was however saddened by the fact that they had to go back the same day. Though I wish their planned trip overseas gets finalised quickly, I will miss them. I can only imagine how it will be for you, in your current state of being a widow, since they have now become true friends to you. But their future compels us to be headstrong. I have just read two stories that were published in 1957, hoping that I will be able to tell you about them one day. I can't seem to get these two dates out of my head, they relate [to] our friends: 11 September 1926 and Friday 13. I look forward to your second letter. Other letters are for Kgatho,[i] Xoliswa – Daliwonga's[ii] daughter and a condolence letter for Mr Ngakane, trying to console him. With love, my friend. Dalibhunga.

Mrs Nobandla Mandela c/o Commanding Officer, Women's jail, Johannesburg.

<hr>

To the commanding officer, Robben Island

[In another hand in Afrikaans] 466/64 Nelson Mandela Special Letter[iii] to B/O[iv]

October 7, 1976

The Commanding Officer
Robben Island

Attention: Col. Roelofse

---

i   Makgatho Mandela (1950–2005), Mandela's second-born son – see the glossary.
ii   K. D. Matanzima (1915– 2003), Mandela's nephew, a Thembu chief, and chief minister for the Transkei – see the glossary. His middle name was Daliwonga.
iii   Special letters were not deducted from a prisoner's quota.
iv   Stamped 'Robben Island Officer Commanding 11-10-75'. B/O is Bevelvoerende Offisier in Afrikaans meaning Commanding Officer.

With reference to my letter of July 12, 1976[i] addressed to the Commissioner of Prisons, Gen. Du Preez, I confirm that on September 9 you advised me that you had received a letter from him, dated August 26, in which he states that he is satisfied that the administration on this Island is acting properly, and that he cannot investigate the complaints of individual persons kept in custody in the country's prisons, or words to that effect.

I further confirm that you refused me permission to write down the Commissioner's reply as summarised by you.

I had hoped that the Commissioner would apply his mind to this matter more seriously than he has done, and that we could settle the whole affair satisfactorily within the framework of Departmental channels. But his reply clearly shows that he has given his official blessings to all the abuses detailed in my letter of July 12. In the circumstances, I am compelled to ask you, as I hereby do, to allow me to instruct my attorneys to arrange an urgent consultation for me with Advocate George Bizos[ii] of the Johannesburg Bar for the purpose of instituting legal proceedings against the Prisons Department to restrain them from abusing their authority, persecuting us and from committing other irregularities.

In particular, I intend asking for an order declaring that the Commissioner:

1. has a legal obligation to visit me and other prisoners on this island and, depending upon the nature of the complaint or request, to deal with such complaint or request in person;

2. is obliged to furnish me with the names and addresses, if any, of all the persons who write letters to me or send money, birthday, Christmas and Easter cards and telegrams, and, if such money has for any reason not been credited to my account,[iii] to advise me accordingly;

3. in regard to the censoring of correspondence and telegrams may only object to the contents thereof but not to the person who writes or sends the letter or telegram or card, unless such writer or sender is under some express legal restriction.

I will further ask for an order restraining you and your officials from:

---

i   See his letter on page 293.
ii   George Bizos (1927–), defence lawyer in the Rivonia Trial – see the glossary.
iii   Upon entering prison, a list was made of the belongings a prisoner had with them. Details of the amount of cash a prisoner may have brought with them were recorded in an individual account under the name of the prisoner (this was not a bank account but simply a separate bookkeeping record). Thereafter, any funds reaching the prison in the name of that prisoner were recorded in that account and so too were any disbursements made in the name of the prisoner. When they were discharged from prison, the prisoner was given what remained in the account.

1. preaching racialism to prisoners of different population groups in the Single Cell section where I am kept, and from trying to foment feelings of hostility amongst us;

2. interfering with the preservation of the good relationship between myself and members of my family and friends;

3. entrusting the task of censoring my correspondence to persons who are not proficient in English and the African languages;

4. removing the date and other essential information from telegrams sent to me by members of my family and my relatives and friends;

5. treating me and my fellow prisoners as hostages and ill-treating us whenever South Africa is heavily attacked by one or other from the numerous countries or international organisations that are opposed to her racial policies;

I also intend asking for an order restraining:

1. the Prison Board from conducting political discussions with me and my fellow prisoners at its sittings;

2. the Security Police from interfering with the internal administration of the Prisons Department and, more specifically, with treatment of persons convicted of political offences and incarcerated on this Island.

I must also refer you to my letter of September 7 in which I advised you that this month I proposed using my ordinary monthly letters to write to Mrs Helen Joseph,[i] Mr Alan Paton[ii] and Mr Benjamin Pogrund[iii] to attend to the question of the guardianship, maintenance and education of my children, both of whom are minors, payment of their school fees and allowances, text books, travelling expenses to and from school and to advise them on their problems and to look after their welfare in the absence of their mother in prison.

On October 7 Lt Prins informed me that the Commissioner had refused my request on the ground that my wife received regular visits from an attorney and was consequently in a better position to handle these prob-

---

i   Helen Joseph (1905–92), teacher, social worker, and anti-apartheid and women's rights activist – see the glossary.

ii   Alan Paton (1903–88), author and founder and leader of South Africa's anti-apartheid Liberal Party. He gave evidence in mitigation of sentence for Mandela and his co-accused at the Rivonia Trial – see the glossary.

iii   Benjamin Pogrund (1933–), former editor of the *Rand Daily Mail* and Mandela's friend – see the glossary.

lems. The Commissioner, however, offered me a special letter to the Bantu Administration Board[i] to whom I could put all my problems.

I regret to tell you I am not prepared to accept the Commissioner's decision and do not regard his offer as a genuine attempt to help me solve my domestic problems. On the contrary, I regard it as the typical reaction of an official who is preoccupied with questions of colour and who is essentially indifferent to the hardships now experienced by the children and to our concern for their welfare. The real truth is that the Commissioners finds it revolting and contrary to Government policy, which treats Blacks as inferiors, that African children should be assisted by democratic Whites who treat all human beings as equals.

If your reason for not allowing me to entrust life-long friends with my household affairs is the fact that my wife is in a better position to handle these matters, why should you offer me the opportunity to place the same issues to the Board? Your offer is yet another instance of abuse of authority and is intended to deny me the opportunity of placing the welfare of my children to persons who will certainly give them all the care and love they deserve and who will make them forget that they are orphans.

Moreover, the Commissioner's decision has the effect of depriving me of my legal right as guardian of my children to look after their persons and welfare and to take all the necessary precautions to promote their interests.

Secondly, his decision is calculated to ruin my wife financially by forcing her to instruct an attorney and to incur unnecessary expenses in fees for services I could freely obtain by means of ordinary monthly letters. The Commissioner has taken this startling decision although he knows only too well that my wife is out of work and has no funds to engage an attorney in this particular matter.

Thirdly, the Commissioner also knows that the Bantu Administration Board has nothing to do with the question of the guardianship, maintenance and education of children, payment of their school fees, allowances, text books, travelling expenses to and from school, and cannot undertake the task of looking after their welfare. Even if the Board was in a position to do so, I would certainly not entrust the future of my children to an apartheid institution whose members are part of the machinery of racial oppression and who work closely with the Security Police and this Department in persecuting me and my family.

In 1973 I wrote and asked the Board to allow my wife's brother to live with her at our Orlando home. He had previously stayed in the house

---

i   Under the apartheid regime, government-appointed white officials ran Bantu administration boards which
     controlled black local authorities. They owned all the houses in black areas and collected rent from the occupants.
     They also controlled the electricity and other municipal services.

and after the Security Police had repeatedly harassed him, he was finally ordered to leave the district of Johannesburg. It was immediately after that that my wife was subjected to a series of cowardly night attacks which I have reason to believe were all instigated by the Security Police, no matter whom they actually selected to launch the attack, the last one having taken place 8 days before she was arrested. That Board never even had the courtesy of acknowledging the receipt of my letter. Why would it be prepared now to undertake a family problem which is even more onerous.

The attitude of the Board hardly differs from that of the Commissioner who has simply ignored my letter to him of August 19 in which I asked a series of questions arising out of my wife's arrest. I am not even sure whether the 3 letters I have written her, care of the Commissioner, ever reached her. The only letter I have received from her since her arrest was posted from Johannesburg on Aug. 25 and was only delivered to me on September 18 viciously mutilated and scratched out as usual.

From the way it is censored, it is clear that you wanted to keep me ignorant of what are essentially domestic affairs. My wife was seized on August 13 at about 7.30 am and the children returned from the boarding school the same day finding the house locked. Four lines are then cut out from the letter, but the second line after the incision makes it clear that in the four lines that were taken out she was giving me details of how a friend put them up for the night.

In the same letter she also tells me that she had asked her attorney to give me particulars of her latest application to court arising out [of] petrol bomb attacks on the house on August 5. On October 9 I received a letter from Attorney Ayob[i] enclosing another letter from her apparently meant for me. That letter was approved by the C.O. of the Johannesburg Prison but was not given to me on the spurious ground that it was not "found suitable for release". If that statement were true, why would the C.O. of the Johannesburg jail have released it?

Finally, I note that the Commissioner evaded the whole question of the money sent to me by Mr Pogrund in spite of the fact that I first made a formal enquiry about the amount on or about July 24. I must accordingly ask you to allow me to institute proceedings for an order calling upon the Department to furnish me with a statement of account in respect of that amount.

I expect you to grant me a privileged consultation with Counsel and attorney and will strenuously contest any condition that you may impose and that will arouse the suspicion that the interview is not privileged.

---

i   Ismail Ayob (1942–), Mandela's attorney – see the glossary.

Treat the matter as extremely urgent.

[Signed NRMandela] NELSON MANDELA

To the commanding officer, Robben Island

12 October 1976

The Commanding Officer,
Robben Island.

Attention: Lt. Prins

I should be pleased if you would approve of the attached order to Messrs
Prolux Paints for wood paper which I require for the purpose of covering
my cabinet and the cost of which may be debited against my account.[i]

[Signed NRMandela]
Nelson Mandela 466/64

[In another hand] Approved: To be purchased from either Juta's or Van
Schaick only.
[Signed]
14/10/76

◇◇◇◇◇◇◇◇

*Another blow to Mandela and his family was Winnie Mandela's sudden depor-
tation on 16 May 1977 to the rural town of Brandfort in the Orange Free State
(now Free State). She was wrenched from her family home with her youngest
daughter Zindzi and dumped in a tiny house with a meagre collection of her
possessions, in the African location[ii] of Phathakahle, just outside the town. She
knew no one and did not know the local language.*

---

i   Upon entering prison, a list was made of the belongings a prisoner had with them. Details of the amount of cash a
     prisoner may have brought with them were recorded in an individual account under the name of the prisoner (this
     was not a bank account but simply a separate bookkeeping record). Thereafter, any funds reaching the prison in the
     name of that prisoner were recorded in that account and so too were any disbursements made in the name of the
     prisoner. When they were discharged from prison, the prisoner was given what remained in the account.
ii   A 'location' was an area the government had set aside for blacks that was usually smaller than a township.

To Adelaide Tambo[i] ('Thorobetsane Tshukudu'[ii]), friend, anti-apartheid activist, and the wife of Oliver Tambo, ANC president and Mandela's former law partner

Nelson Mandela 466/64   1.1.77

Our dear Thorobetsane

Last mnth I sent 12 Xmas cards, all to members of the family. I however excluded you hoping that you'll understand that my quota is limited & that those who don't regularly hear from me are very often people who are continually in my thoughts.

Nonetheless, we belong to a closely-knit folk where households, kins & clans are more than blood relations. The sense of guilt that weighs on me when I cannot wish you the compliments of the season will probably ease a bit when I learn that this note has reached you. I say a bit because what my heart longs for really is the resumption of our '61 correspondence[iii] where we freely talked about things closer to our hearts, about our sweet home & the dream of building a bigger & sweeter home right on the Khamhlaba.

From Jeppe[iv] you moved to the E. Rand & in June '62 I bade you fare-well.[v] During the last 14 yrs Zami,[vi] the conscientious girl that she is, has written regularly & tried wherever possible to squeeze in vital family details. You, ROR,[vii] Gcwanini[viii] & others are frequently mentioned, leaving me with the tremendous feeling that, after all, our world is the best of all worlds. Fourteen yrs is a long period in which setbacks & good fortune have gone hand in hand. Beloved ones have aged rapidly as a result of all kinds of physical & spiritual problems too terrible to mention. Bonds of affection tend to weaken whilst the idealist recites the maxim: absence makes the heart grow fonder, chdn grow old & develop outlooks not in line with the wishes of pa & mum. When absent parties eventually return, they find [a] strange

---

i   Adelaide Tambo (1929–2007) – see the glossary.
ii   She was born Adelaide Frances Tshukudu. Thorobetsane was a made-up name.
iii   Oliver Tambo left South Africa on the instructions of the ANC in March 1960. His wife and children followed later that year.
iv   A suburb of Johannesburg.
v   Mandela is referring to when he visited the Tambos in London, in June 1962 while on his clandestine trip out of South Africa.
vi   One of Winnie Mandela's names.
vii   He is referring to Oliver Tambo, often known as OR. Throughout this letter, Mandela has added an 'R' before his name. This may be to avoid alerting the prison authorities to whom he is talking about since Tambo was a known political activist running a banned organisation.
viii   Advocate Duma Nokwe (1927–78), political activist and advocate – see the glossary.

and unfriendly environment. Dreams [and] time schedules prove difficult to fulfil & when misfortune strikes fate hardly ever provides golden bridges.

But significant progress is always possible if we ourselves try to plan every detail of our lives & actions & allow the intervention of fate only on our own terms. I spend much time reading and rereading Zami's wonderful letters & the notes I keep on family matters after each of her visits & the knowledge that the family has managed to keep together, that the chdn are growing up & living up to expectation, that every crisis, domestic or otherwise, leaves us more closer to one another, stronger & more experienced is a source of strength beyond words.

Nevertheless, I miss your frank letters which made us as a family see ourselves as others saw us. But now, after your silence for almost a decade, I'm beginning to feel that no metal, not even gold or diamond, is free from the corroding effects of rust. I wonder what has made you to be as slow-moving & unsystematic with your correspondence as ROR. Even when I make allowances I find it somewhat difficult to appreciate his abnormal and sustained reticence. A family is such because its members keep their mutual obligation of sharing what they know & feel. Unless we strive ceaselessly to do this, there's the likelihood of divergencencies [divergencies]even as regards such simple things as love & marriage, initiation ceremonies & inheritance & the place where relations should be buried. But I must assure you that I fully understand that remarks of this kind can naturally be very irritating if, unknown to me, you've made as much or more fruitless efforts than I've done to reach you.

~~Nevertheless, I miss your frank letters which made us as a family.~~[i] I hope that our petite Ruta still remembers my promise to buy her an overcoat if she increased the family. . . .

For more than 15 yrs now ROR has been an enthusiastic commercial traveller,[ii] a strenuous occupation which takes him away from you & kids for long stretches. His continued absence from home can have damaging emotional shocks for the chdn & I do hope they're all well & making good progress at school. From Zami's letters I gather that you've also become [a] traveller, probably on a fulltime basis. Though it may not be altogether good for the chdn that both of you should be constantly away, it will help the business[iii] to flourish, keep you occupied & stop you from brooding. I love you all and sharp[ly] feel the wretchedness of living away from those whose friendship has been a source of encouragement & hope. A merry Xmas &

---

i   It is not known who drew the line through this sentence.
ii   Oliver Tambo travelled to Europe, Scandinavia, and the United Sates to drum up support for the ANC, and also visited ANC camps in Angola and the ANC headquarters in Zambia.
iii He is referring to the ANC.

Happy New Yr will span the miles that separate us. Sincerely, Nel.

Mrs Thorobetsane Tshukudu, c/o Nkosk. Nobandla Mandela, P.O. Box 2947 JHB. 2000

To Advocate Duma Nokwe (Gcwanini Miya)[i]

Nelson Mandela 466/64   1.1.77

Our dear Gcwanini,

When I was free as an eagle it wasn't easy for me to keep track of developments in the field of music & drama.

I attended a few of the most colourful shows, hurriedly read the reviews in between court sessions & the more serious commitments & thereafter forgot about the matter. Now it's even more difficult to follow cultural events on the mainland & even cautious comment would literally be to rush in where angels fear to tread. But perhaps to you & Radebe I may risk & speak freely about things where my information is dangerously thin, knowing that you'd keep them to yourselves, [and] supply me with the relevant material I need to talk more confidently.

The only aspect which makes me hesitant is your closeness to Ishy & Mohla[ii] &, having once had [the] frightening experience of seeing you & AP flexing your muscles at dawn some yrs back outside Dila's lodge,[iii] I'm not so sure whether after spending a whole night at Ishy's, you may not feel like singing your favourite Ch's song[iv] of the rising star & thereafter loose and reveal things about which you should be silent.

Anyway 3 musicals seem to have attracted a lot of attention recently, namely *Umabatha*,[v] *Ipi-Tombi*[vi] & *Meropa*.[vii] All of them seem tremendous on print, so much so that I was even tempted to wonder whether the claim that Africans are natural actors may not be true after all.

---

i   Advocate Duma Nokwe (1927–78), political activist and advocate – see the glossary. Mandela is addressing Nokwe by two of his clan names so that the officials don't know who he is writing to and will post his letter.

ii   These are the friends Mandela wrote to on 1 February 1971 – see his letter on page 220.

iii   Dr. Diliza Mji, a friend and neighbour of Mandela's from Orlando West, Soweto.

iv   This may be a coded reference to the Communist Party with which Duma Nokwe was affiliated.

v   A Zulu version of *Macbeth* written in 1970 by South African playwright Welcome Msomi and performed by Zulu actors.

vi   A musical written by Bertha Egnos Godfrey and her daughter Gail Lakier in 1974.

vii   A musical produced by Candian producer Clarence Williams in 1974, which toured to Japan and the Far East. It was adapted from a musical called *Isintu* created by Cocky Thlotothlamaje, and after being redeveloped as *Meropa*, its name was changed to *Kwazulu*.

The first is Welcome Msomi's adaptation of Shakespeare's *Macbeth* & is cast in indigenous music, tradition & dancing. This is clearly a promising playwright who has gathered around him a group of talented and versatile players. I believe in England the play impressed a galaxy of stars like Peter Ustinov,[i] Sidney Poitier,[ii] Rex Harrison,[iii] ballerina Margot Fonteyn[iv] & other artist[s] & public figures. *Ipi-Tombi* attempts to portray the social forces that influence the life of the African & again, from the pictures & scattered clues I've seen, the actors seem to be boys & girls of ability. It's said to have broken all records in JHB[v] when it ran for 122 weeks & was seen by about 500,000 people. I also understand that in London it had similar success & that 3 companies are presently performing in several continents.

Meropa is yet another attempt to depict the African background by means of drums, music & dancing. In all these plays the scenes are exciting & arouse feelings I've rarely experienced when attending the more sophisticated functions of the Western type. You must have seen the reviews & probably even spoken to some of the leading actors.

However, all of them have major themes that are disturbing & that dwarf the beautiful play acting on the stage. In addition, it's not clear who the real bosses are & who holds the purse strings. Whilst Msomi was assisted by Prof E. Sneddon,[vi] P. Scholtz[vii] & the Englishman P. Daubeny,[viii] Bertha Egnos, Sheila Wartski & Liz MacLeish worked together on *Ipi-Tombi*. The latter & *Meropa* were quite obviously written by persons who are familiar neither with our life & culture nor who are fully aware of our aspirations.

There's much praise for Bra Gibbs[ix] as a playwright & I believe some of his works have drawn full houses for many wks. Unfortunately, I've not been so lucky to see any of his scripts nor write-ups. I would also like to have seen the productions of the Music, Drama & Literature Institute & those of the other young black artists I believe are now coming forward. I envy you very much. Do you still see Bakwe[x] & Dan[xi]? I hope Mabhomvu[xii],

i   Peter Ustinov (1921–2004), Russian-English actor, writer, filmmaker, and theatre director.
ii   Sidney Poitier (1927–), Bahamian-American actor, film director, author, and diplomat. He played Mandela in the 1997 television film *Mandela and De Klerk*.
iii Rex Harrison (1908–90), English stage and screen actor.
iv   Margot Fonteyn (1919–91), English ballerina who danced with the British ballet company, the Royal Ballet.
v   Johannesburg.
vi   Elizabeth Sneddon, head of the department of speech and drama at the University of Natal and director of the Natal Theatre Workshop Company. She commissioned Welcome Msomi to write *Umabatha*.
vii Pieter Scholtz who directed *Umabatha* at the University of Natal and translated the play from Zulu into English.
viii Peter Daubeny (1921–75), British theatre impresario who brought *Umabatha* to London where it was performed to sell-out audiences as part of his World Theatre Sessions.
ix   Gibson Kente (1932–2004), playwright, composer, and director. Like Mandela, he was from the Madiba clan, so Mandela referred to him as a nephew – see the glossary.
x   Bakwe (Joe) Matthews (1929–2010), political activist and son of Frieda and Z. K. Matthews – see the glossary for these three individuals.
xi   Dan Tloome (1919-92), leader of the ANC and the South African Communist Party who was working for the ANC in Botswana, and who spent many decades in exile in Zambia.
xii A code word for the Communist Party. *Bhomvu* means red in isiXhosa and ANC members attached 'Mabhomvu'

Alfie, Tom, John, Gabula & your colleague, Joe[i], are all keeping well & fit. I've also written to Thorobetsane.[ii]

I think of you all & sincerely wish that today we could be together & as in older dys, sit down & tell stories, tall & otherwise. What a moment that could be! The varied experiences each one of us has had during the past 15 yrs add up to real life. All the same fond memories & warm thoughts have pulled the world with its sunshine into my quarters. That's why you're all so near; with me on this Island. Perhaps one dy I'll hear you singing and dancing, this time not only to the rising star, if you please, but also from songs from the soil[iii], accompanied by the brass band with its trumpets & bugels, drums & all. Merry Xmas & happy new yr to Radebe,[iv] the kids, you & all our friends. Very sincerely, Nel.

Mr Gcwanini Miya, c/o Nkosk Nobandla, P.O. Box 2947, JHB, 2000

◇◇◇◇◇◇◇◇

On 18 January 1977 Mandela complained to a prison guard, Lieutenant Prins, about the non-delivery of letters to his wife. The 45–minute conversation became a quarrel and Mandela was subsequently charged for contravening prison regulations by having 'insulted and threatened'[v] a prison guard.

He prepared two documents for his attorneys as a defence to this charge. One forty-page document comprised correspondence between himself and the commanding officer of Robben Island, commissioner of prisons, and his attorneys. The other was an eight-page document concerning the room at the prison where legal consultations were held. He prepared written documents as he believed the prison authorities might secretly record his meeting with his lawyer. When he attempted to hand the documents to his lawyer, Stanley Kawalsky, at a meeting on 2 February 1977, the prison authorities objected.

On 21 July 1977 the commissioner of prisons wrote to Kawalsky, allowing him to consult with Mandela and to receive documents and statements in connection with the case.

Mandela appeared in the Robben Island court a few times in connection with this case, but on 3 August 1977 all charges against him were withdrawn.

---

when referring to a person regarded as Communist. (Nomvuyo Nokwe in an email to Sahm Venter, 11 December 2017.)

i   Members of the ANC leadership
ii   Made-up name for Adelaide Tambo (1929–2007), friend, anti-apartheid activisit, and wife of Oliver Tambo, Mandela's former law partner and president of the ANC – see the glossary. The Tambos were living in exile in London.
iii   ANC freedom songs
iv   Vuyiswa Nokwe (Radebe is her clan name), Duma Nokwe's wife.
v   NM, *Long Walk to Freedom*, p. 563.

Kawalsky was not present and prison warder Warrant Officer Olchers demanded Mandela hand over the documents to him. He refused but was given no alternative and handed them over. The authorities later refused to return the documents to him.

On 17 November, Olchers informed Mandela that the commanding officer of Robben Island had authorised that the documents be burned. Kawalsky became involved and eventually Mandela took legal action against the minister of prisons.

On 9 January 1980 Mandela launched a Supreme Court appeal against the minister of prisons to have the documents returned to him. Two weeks later, the commanding officer of the prison showed him the documents he had been instructed to return to him but Mandela refused to accept them without first consulting his attorney. On 18 February the prison regulations were amended to allow the authorities to take into safekeeping any article belonging to a prisoner. Mandela's attorneys believed this change was as a result of his legal action, but the authorities denied this.

His application was 'dismissed with costs' on 23 October 1980 and Mandela took the matter on appeal. His appeal was lodged in court on 4 February 1981. The matter was heard on 18 September 1981 and judgment was handed down on 1 December 1981. The appeal was dismissed with costs.[55]

To Frank, Bernadt & Joffe, his attorneys

21 January 1977

Messrs Frank, Bernadt & Joffe
PO Box 252
Cape Town

Dear Sirs,

Attention: Mr Bernadt

I attach herewith a copy of the charge-sheet which was served on me yesterday at about 4.15 pm and which speaks for itself. The case has been set down for hearing in the Officer's Court at Robben Island Prison on 7th February 1977 at 9 am, giving me only four days' notice when one bears in mind that the 23rd is a Sunday.

In this connection, I should be pleased if you would kindly instruct

Advocate George Bizos[i] of the Johannesburg Bar, or any other barrister he may recommend, to appear for me.

The facts surrounding the whole case are slimy and disgusting and my wife, who works for the Johannesburg firm of Frank and Hirsch and whose home telephone number is Orlando 113, and Dr. Fatima Meer,[ii] 148 Burnwood Road, Sydenham, Durban, and Mr Benjamin Pogrund,[iii] 38A Six Avenue, Parktown North, Johannesburg, will be essential witnesses. It is absolutely necessary that I have full consultation with Counsel in the presence of my wife and Dr. Meer before the date of the hearing, so that the relevant facts relating to the intrigues of the officials of the Department of Prisons and, in this particular instance, of Lt. Prins, acting in collaboration with the Security Police, in an attempt to besmirch my wife's good name and to create mutual suspicion between us, may be brought to light and placed before the court.

Both my wife and Dr. Meer have been served with notices under the Internal Security Act, 1950, and will have to apply to the relevant authorities for permission to leave their respective areas. A remand of the case for at least one month seems unavoidable.

Meantime, I would request you to warn the Commanding Officer not to tamper with or remove any material in my possession that may be relevant to the case.

I have sufficient funds to cover fees and disbursements.

Yours faithfully,
N.R. MANDELA

Received the original hereof for transmission to Messrs Frank, Bernadt & Joffe this twenty-first day of January 1977.[iv]

Public Prosecutor

[Signed by another hand][v]
21-1-76

◇◇◇◇◇◇◇◇◇

---

i   George Bizos (1927–), defence lawyer in the Rivonia Trial – see the glossary.
ii Fatima Meer (1928–2010) , friend, professor, author, and anti-apartheid activist – see the glossary.
iii Benjamin Pogrund (1933–), former editor of the *Rand Daily Mail* and Mandela's friend – see the glossary.
iv This sentence is written in Mandela's hand.
v   It is unclear whether this is the signature of the public prosecutor as they did not sign in the space created by Mandela.

On 25 April 1977 the authorities famously brought a selected group of reporters on a tour to the island as a response to rumours of unforgiving conditions. As part of a manufactured spectacle for the media, the guards put the men to work in the 'garden' near the cell block. It was a far cry from their daily grind, by then at the shoreline pulling up seaweed.

Photographs were taken of Mandela and his comrades. His response was a furious written charge against the prison head for the creation of the photo opportunity.

At the end of the year, Mandela and Ahmed Kathrada had their study privileges revoked when it was discovered that Mandela had been secretly writing his autobiography with the help of a handful of trusted comrades.

To the head of prison, Robben Island

[Typed]

19 May 1977

The Head of Prison
ROBBEN ISLAND

We strongly protest against the purpose for and manner in which the visit to this prison of the local and overseas press and television men on the 25th April was organised and conducted by the Department of Prisons. We resent the deliberate violation of our right of privacy by taking our photographs without our permission, and regard this as concrete evidence of the contempt with which the Department continues to treat us.

On the 26th April fellow prisoner Nelson Mandela was informed by Major Zandberg that the Minister of Prisons had finally agreed to the repeated requests by the press over the years to visit Robben Island. We also learnt that the minister had authorised the visit provided no communication whatsoever would take place between pressmen and prisoners.

The Minister planned the visit in the hope that it would whitewash the Prisons Department; pacify public criticism of the Department here and abroad; and counteract any adverse publicity that might arise in the future. To ensure the success of the plan we were not given prior notice of the visit, on that particular day the span[i] from our Section was given the special work

---

i   Afrikaans word for 'team' that was used in prison.

of "gardening" instead of pulling out bamboo from the sca[i] as we normally do when we go to work. Some 30 litres of milk was placed at the entrance to our Section,[ii] quite obviously to give the impression that it was all meant for us, whereas in truth we receive only 6½ litres a day.

Most of us know that a section of the press here and abroad is sympathetic to our cause, and that they would have preferred to handle the operation in a dignified manner. Nevertheless, the Minister's disregard for our feelings has led to the situation where total strangers are now in possession of photographs and films of ourselves. The impropriety of the Minister's action is sharpened by the Department's persistent refusal to allow us to take and send our photographs to our own families.

We stress the fact that the way in which the Minister planned this visit in no way differs from previous ones. In August 1964 reporters from the "Daily Telegraph"[iii] found those of us who were here at the time "mending clothes" instead of our normal work at the time of knapping stones with 5 lb. hammers. As soon as the reporters left we were ordered to crush stones as usual. At the end of August 1965 Mrs Ida Parker from "The Sunday Tribune" found us wearing raincoats on our way back from the lime quarry – raincoats which were hurriedly issued to us at work on the very day of her visit, and which were immediately taken away when she left. The rain coats were not issued to us again until a year or so later.

We emphatically state that under no circumstances are we willing to co-operate with the Department in any manoeuvre on its part to distort the true state of affairs obtaining on this island. With few exceptions our span has been kept inside for several months now, but our normal work is still that of pulling seaweed, and the Department has given no assurance that we will never be sent out to the quarry again.

We also cite the example of the cupboards we have in our cells. Any television viewer is likely to be impressed with this furniture and would naturally give all the credit to the Department. It is unlikely that such television-viewers and newspaper readers would be aware that the cupboards have been painstakingly built with crude tools in a crude "workshop" from cardboard cartons and from driftwood picked up on the beaches by prisoners, that the costs for beautifying them have been borne by the prisoners themselves[iv] and that they have been built by a talented fellow prisoner, Jafta

---

i   This is actually a type of seaweed which had the Afrikaans name of *bambous*. (Christo Brand, *Doing Life with Mandela* (Johannesburg: Jonathan Ball, 2014. p. 38.)

ii   A handwritten note in the margin, presumably from a prison official, reads: 'Not true. I didn't even see the milk (JM)'.

iii   It was actually the *Daily Express*, identified by photographer Cloete Breytenbach (who accompanied writer John Rydon to the Island) in an interview with Sahm Venter, Johannesburg, 30 June 2013.

iv   A handwritten note in the margin reads 'Rubbish!'.

Masemola,[i] working approximately 8 hours a day on weekends at the rate of R1.50 (One Rand fifty Cents) a month.[ii]

At all times we are willing to have press and television interviews, provided that the aim is to present to the public a balanced picture of our living conditions. This means that we would be allowed to express our grievances and demands freely, and to make comments whether such comments are favourable or otherwise to the Department.

We are fully aware that the Department desires to project a favourable image to the world of its policies. We can think of no better way of doing so than by abolishing all forms of racial discrimination in the administration, by keeping abreast of enlightened penal reforms, by granting us the status of political prisoners, and by introducing a non-racial administration throughout the country's prisons. With few or no skeletons to hide the Department will then no longer stand in any need for resorting to stratagems.

The actual execution of the plan was entrusted to Gen Roux[iii] and in his presence, the reporters and cameramen stormed down upon us like excited visitors to an agricultural show.[iv] For all that we have seen of Gen Roux, we are convinced that he has no respect whatsoever for our feelings and dignity. The way he handled the visit is no different from his conduct when he visited this prison on the 15 November 1976. On that occasion he conducted his interviews with us individually in a cloak-and-dagger fashion in the hope of finding us at a complete loss when confronted with the unexpected. That there were no ugly incidents as a result of the provocative action on the 25th April was due solely to our sense of responsibility.

We are fully aware that we cannot prevent the publication of such articles on prison conditions here as the Minister might authorize. But we are equally aware that, whatever the law might be, the taking of our photographs by the press for publication purposes or otherwise without our consent, constitutes an invasion of our privacy. That privacy has been blatantly violated by the very people who, within the framework of the law, are considered to be its guardians. And, having violated that privacy, the Department had the temerity to ask us for permission to make us objects of public scrutiny.

We stress that we are not chattels of the Prisons Department. That we happen to be prisoners in no way detracts from the fact that we are, nevertheless, South African and Namibian citizens, entitled to protections against any abuses by the Department.[v]

---

i   Jafta Kgalabi 'Jeff' Masemola (1929–90), teacher, member of the ANC Youth League, member of the Pan Africanist Congress, and political prisoner – see the glossary.

ii   A handwritten note in the margin reads, 'The same as other prisoners'.

iii   General Jannie Roux was then the commissioner of prisons and accompanied the journalists on the visit.

iv   A handwritten note in the margin reads: 'Very interesting'.

v   A handwritten note in the margin reads: 'I suppose all other SA citizens are also entitled to protections against them!'

Finally, we place on record that we cannot tolerate indefinitely any treatment we consider degrading and provocative and, should the Minister continue to do so, we reserve to ourselves the right to take such action as we deem appropriate.

F. Anthony[i]

J.E. April[ii]

L. Chiba[iii]

T.T. Cholo[iv]

E.J. Daniels[v]

T.L. Daweti[vi]

M.K. Dingake[vii]

M.S. Essop[viii]

J. Fuzile[ix]

K. Hassim[x]

T.H. Ja-Toivo[xi]

A.M. Kathrada[xii]

N.R. Mandela[xiii]

J. Masemola[xiv]

G. Mbeki[xv]

R. Mhlaba[xvi]

K. Mkalipi[xvii]

W.Z. Mkwayi[xviii]

A. Mlangeni[xix]

E. Motsoaledi[xx]

---

i   Frank Anthony, African People's Democratic Union of South Africa prisoner.
ii   James April (1940–), ANC prisoner.
iii Laloo Chiba (1930–2017), ANC prisoner – see the glossary.
iv   Theophilus Cholo (1926–), ANC prisoner.
v   Eddie Daniels (1928–2017), African Resistance Movement prisoner – see the glossary.
vi   Thompson Daweti, ANC prisoner.
vii Michael Dingake (1928–), ANC prisoner.
viii Salim Essop, ANC prisoner.
ix   Jackson Fuzile, ANC prisoner.
x   Kader Hassim (1934–2011), African People's Democratic Union of South Africa prisoner.
xi   Namibian prisoner Andimba Toivo ya Toivo (1924–2017), South West African People's Organisation.
xii Ahmed Kathrada (1929–2017) – Rivonia trialist and ANC and South African Communist Party prisoner – see the glossary.
xiii Nelson Mandela. (1918–2013) – Rivonia trialist and MK prisoner.
xiv Jafta Kgalabi 'Jeff' Masemola (1929–90), teacher, member of the ANC Youth League, member of the Pan Africanist Congress, and political prisoner – see the glossary.
xv   Govan Mbeki (1910–2001), Rivonia trialist prisoner – see the glossary.
xvi Raymond Mhlaba (1920–2005), Rivonia trialist and MK prisoner – see the glossary.
xvii Kwedi Mkalipi, PAC prisoner.
xviii Wilton Mkwayi (1923–2004), Little Rivonia trialist and MK prisoner – see the glossary. The Little Rivonia Trial took place in November 1964, five months after the Rivonia Trial (see the glossary) ended, after Laloo Chiba, Mac Maharaj, Wilton Mkwayi, Dave Kitson and John Matthews were charged with sabotage for their activities on behalf of MK. The former three were sent to Robben Island and the other two, being white, were held in Pretoria.
xix Rivonia trialist Andrew Mlangeni (1925–), Rivonia trialist and MK prisoner – see the glossary.
xx   Elias Motsoaledi (1924–94), Rivonia trialist and ANC prisoner – see the glossary.

J. Mpanza[i]
P. Mthembu[ii]
B. Nair[iii]
J.N. Pokela[iv]
S. Sijake[v]
W.U. Sisulu[vi]
M.M. Siyothula[vii]
J.B. Vusani[viii]
R.C. Wilcox[ix]

========

To Nobulile Thulare, a relative[x]

Nelson Mandela 466/64   19.7.77

Our dear Sisi,

Our families are far larger than those of Whites & it's always pure pleasure to be fully accepted throughout a village, district or even several districts occupied by your clan, as a beloved household member, when you can call at any time, completely relax, sleep at ease & freely take part in the discussion of all problems, where you can even be given livestock & land to build free of charge.

As you know I was barely 10 when our father died[xi] having been deposed as chief & lost all his wealth.[xii] Mother could neither read nor write & had no means to send me to school. [Yet] a member of our clan[xiii] educated me from elementary school right to Fort Hare[xiv] & never expected any refund.

---

i   Justice Mpanza, (1937–2002), ANC prisoner.
ii   Peter Mthembu, ANC prisoner.
iii   Billy Nair (1929–2008), MK prisoner – see the glossary.
iv   John Pokela (1922–85), Pan Africanist Congress prisoner.
v   Sandi Sijake, ANC prisoner.
vi   Walter Sisulu (1912– 2003), Rivonia trialist and MK prisoner – see the glossary.
vii   Mannert Siyothula, Pan Africanist Congress prisoner.
viii   Joseph Bransby Vusani.
ix   Robert Wilcox, African People's Democratic Union of South Africa (APDUSA) prisoner.
x   Nobulile Thulare, most likely one of Mandela's relatives.
xi   It has since been established both through documentation in his own hand and the dates of birth of his siblings, that Mandela's father, Nkosi (chief) Mphakanyiswa Gadla Hendry (d. 1930), died when he was twelve.
xii   Mandela's father was a chief who was deposed by a magistrate after a dispute against him over cattle.
xiii   Chief Jongintaba Dalindyebo (d. 1942), the chief and regent of the Thembu people. He became Mandela's guardian following his father's death – see the glossary.
xiv   University College of Fort Hare, Alice in the Ciskei homeland – see the glossary. Mandela attended Fort Hare from 1939 and was expelled in 1940 for embarking on protest action.

According to our custom I was his child and his responsibility. I have a lot of praise for this institution, not only because it's part of me, but also because of its usefulness. It caters for all those who are descended from one ancestor & holds them together as one family.

It's an institution that arose & developed in the countryside & functions well only in that area. Capitalism & industrialisation have now cut it into pieces & we are now scattered all over the country, making it difficult for clan members to fulfil their obligations to one another. Can you imagine how I must have felt at Xmas & New Yr when I could not send you, of all people, the compliments of the season, you who is not only our sister but a loyal friend whom Zami[i] & I love & admire, even though the 2 of you are always locked up in all sorts of nonsensical rows that you both blow up into mountains? I certainly will not again waste my time by trying to make peace between 2 big women who should know better than they seem to be at present. I had expected that both of you would spare me the countless headaches you have brought on me.

But the real aim of this letter is to let you know that you are still as dear to the same Zami & me as the unforgettable day when you accompanied us across the courtyard at Mbizana almost 20 yrs ago now.[ii] We think of you & pray that you may be blessed with sound health & that you may live even longer than the Old Lady did. It's against this background that, with all my heart, I wish you, the chdn, grandchdn & great grandchdn a Merry Xmas & a bright and happy New Yr.

One of my fondest wishes these last 14 yrs has been to be with you again, listen to your humorous stories, hear you make your many vows & then break them repeatedly. Do you still remember telling us that you'll never eat potatoes again? Also I have attended many services when I knew you would be asked to pray. When divine words come from you they are realistic, simple & inspiring. But there have been times when you reminded me of Nongqawuse [iii] & prophesied that Sekwati would soon rise as Christ did. I still remember clearly how embarrassed you were at Twist St & the Pretoria Temple when Libhebhethe & Vanikeke reminded you of these unfulfilled promises.

Perhaps that had its advantages as it may have sobered you up & made the daily experiences of believer & non-believer the subject of your prayers even more than ever before. I was of course, baptised in the Wesleyan Church & went to its missionary schools. Outside & here I remain a staunch

---

i   One of Winnie Mandela's names.
ii   He is referring to Bizana rather than Mbizana, Winnie Mandela's home village Bizana in the Transkei.
iii Nongqawuse claimed that the spirits had told her that the Xhosa people should destroy their crops and kill their cattle, the source of their wealth as well as food. If they did so, the British settlers would be swept into the sea.

member but one's outlook tends to broaden & to welcome efforts towards denominational unity. I have listened to sermons by priests of several denominations here – Anglicans, Dutch Reformed, Hindus, Presbyterian & Roman Catholics. I almost forgot the Moravians. Most of them are eloquent & experienced men & some of their sermons have been memorable. I'm in favour of a move towards the merger of all S.A. churches, so long as the doctrine of the new church is progressive & moves away from the rigid & backward dogmas of olden times.

Finally, all people throughout the world have at one time or other had clans & some clans were certainly mightier & better known in history than ours. But to you, Zami & me, ours is the whole world, our umbrella & the broad steel blade that removes all obstacles. It's our hope,[i] the navel that links us together as a family, that binds you & me, sisi. I have not seen you for a long time but this letter is a reunion & calls to mind all the lovely moments we spent together in the past. I believe your hands are rheumatic & it's difficult for you to write. Dictate the reply to the chdn. Once again a Merry Xmas & Happy New Yr. Very sincerely, your Bhuti.[ii]

Mrs Nobulile Thulare, c/o Nkosk Nobandla Mandela, 8115 Orlando West, P.O. Phirima, (1848), Johannesburg

---

To Zenani[iii] and Muzi Dlamini,[iv] his middle daughter and her husband

[In other another hand] 466/64 Letters rewritten

Nelson Mandela 466/64   24.7.77

My darling Zeni & Muzi,

The birth of Zaziwe[v] is one of the happiest moments in our lives & Mum & I give you our warmest congratulations.

We would like to have been there to rejoice with both of you directly & to see the baby in [the] flesh. In her telegram Mum said she would try to come over and see the baby & you. Whether or not she succeeded I don't

---

i   It is not known whether it was Mandela or the prison authorities who underlined this.
ii   'Brother' in Afrikaans.
iii Zenani Mandela (1959–) – see the glossary.
iv   Prince Thumbumuzi Dlamini is a son of King Sobhuza of Swaziland and a businessman. He and Zenani Mandela married in 1977.
v   The eldest child of HRH Zenani Dlamini and her husband HRH Thumbumzi Dlamini. As royals they had diplomatic passports which allowed them to easily travel the world to collect various awards for Mandela. They studied in Boston in the United States in the 1980s.

know. But although we are far away from you our pride & love for Zaziwe is just as strong & we hope one of these days we will have the pleasure of seeing your photo & that of the baby.

I hope you will on no account delay your departure for England. At the present moment the most important aim should be your education and both of you should not allow anything to interfere with this object. Without proper qualifications you will not be able to serve your people nor fully appreciate the stupendous developments that are now taking place in various fields of knowledge. Such data & new principles of human relations can best be exploited by those that are properly prepared for these significant challenges.

I miss you Zeni & long to see Muzi. I hope you will come soon. Meantime, give my fondest regards & humble respects to the King and Iindlovukazi[i]. With love.

Affectionately,
Tata[ii]

———————————————

To Zindzi Mandela[iii] & Oupa Seakamela, his youngest daughter and her partner

Nelson Mandela 466/64   24.7.77

My darling Zindzi & Oupa,

It is always pure pleasure to get birthday greetings from Zindzi. It was particularly so to get the message from both of you. There are times when I feel that the best things become better & this is exactly how I feel at the present moment with affectionate messages from our beloved Mum & from you & Oupa.

Zindzi once promised that Mum would tell me all about Oupa, but as you both know, she has always been hard pressed by pressure of work & other problems & up to now she has not been able to give me a full sketch. Perhaps Zindzi will now have to do it.

---

i   King Sobhuza of Swaziland and the queen mother.
ii   'Father' in isiXhosa.
iii   Zindziswa Mandela (1960–), Mandela's youngest daughter – see the glossary.

I hope Mr de Waal[i] has been able to arrange for your registration. I also hope you continue to read & write poetry[ii] concentrating not only on that of Europe but also that of Africa, Asia & Latin America; in fact on poetry of the whole world.

You must try to grasp the rules very well & having mastered them, then develop your own individual style. You can easily keep within the rules but be original & free. Good luck & much love,

Affectionately,

Tata[iii]

<hr>

To the head of prison, Robben Island

[Note in another hand in Afrikaans] Letter to head approved

Robben Island
18th September 1977
The Head of Prison,

I protest in the strongest terms against the unethical conduct of the Department of Prisons in violating my right of privileged communication with my legal representatives.

The persistent infringement of the law and flouting of the principles of justice by officials are some of the factors that have destroyed harmonious prisoner-warder relations throughout the country, and that make it difficult for us to accord to such officials the respect and courtesy we should like to give to those who are entrusted with our welfare as prisoners. The manner in which the Department encroached on this right tends to show that the use of improper methods in dealing with us forms an inseparable part of prison policy.[iv]

On 12th September 1977 I was brought before the Officers' Court on a charge in which Lt. Prins was the complainant, and that had been remanded several times since January this year. The prosecutor, W/O Bierenbroodspot, withdrew the charge in terms, I believe, of Section 6 of the Criminal Procedure Act. As the court adjourned and in the presence of the

---

i   Winnie Mandela befriended a lawyer in Brandfort called Piet de Waal. She also had a friendship with Dr. Chris Hattingh who offered her a job. The day she was due to start he was killed in a car accident.
ii   Zindzi's collection of poetry *Black As I Am* (Los Angeles: Guild of Tutors Press, 1978) was published a year later
iii   'Father' in isiXhosa.
iv   The underlining in this letter doesn't appear to be Mandela's as it is not his usual neat, straight underlining.

prosecutor, W/O Olchers, seized my file which contained privileged papers relating to the case. Amongst those documents was a 7-page statement in which I gave reasons why I believed that the building where consultations between prisoners and lawyers are held had a secret device by means of which officials could listen to consultations. There was also a 40-page document with annexures, in which I set out the issues involved, my defence to the charge and the names of prisoners and non-prisoners I considered material witnesses.

I pointed out to both officials that the right they were violating was permanent and protected privileged communications not only during, but also after the disposal of the proceedings. I further told them that right formed the foundation of the administration of justice throughout the enlightened world, and that I expected any prosecutor, worth the name, to respect it both in theory and practice. I added that nothing would stop the institution of fresh proceedings against me after the complainant had studied my statements, that by taking away my papers they were attacking not only the principles of natural justice, but were acting in contravention of an express provision of their own regulations.

It soon became clear, however, that the 2 officials were carrying out instructions from their superiors and that no amount of persuasion would convince them not to interfere with the right. The prosecutor kept on telling me that, since he had withdrawn the charge, he no longer had jurisdiction because the matter was now purely administrative. W/O Olchers was even more taciturn and all that he could say in reply to my arguments was that he wanted the file. In the course of the discussion I said, for all I knew, the Security Police, who are the real people who run this prison, might be waiting for the papers somewhere in the same building. By way of a compromise, I suggested that I destroy the papers in their presence. They rejected the suggestion and, in spite of my protests, seized the file, promising to return it later during that day. I then asked them to give me an inventory of all the papers in the file. This request was also refused.

My legal representatives could not have been aware of this manoeuvre. I even suspect that when the Department advised me last week that the court would convene on 12th September, and that permission had now been given for me to hand over my statement to my lawyers, prison officials already knew that the case would be withdrawn. I further suspect that the real purpose of giving me this information was to induce me to load the file with illegal messages which, it was hoped, the lawyers would then smuggle out.

My experience during the last 15 years of my imprisonment has taught me that, when dealing with prisoners, the average prison official does not at all consider it improper to transgress the law, to plot secretly and to brush aside the moral code.[i] There have been notable exceptions of officers who have tried in difficult situations to carry out their duties fairly and justly and who tempered the strict letter of the law with a bit of humanism. But such men have been few and far between. Clearly the Department prefers that political prisoners, in particular, should be handled by men who are not strongly committed to any exemplary standard of conduct.

It has been disconcerting for us to see the tragedy of otherwise gifted and friendly young men who, on arrival here, worked quite well with us, but who were later forced to do many things which conflicted with their own feelings and views.

W/O Bierenbroodspot is a case in point. In the early stages of the case, he made a good impression on me and his sense of fairness and impartiality was striking. But within 8 months of his arrival his whole personality has changed, the idealism with which he began his work has disappeared and the role he has played in the case makes it now difficult for him to face me. Like many other young people, he has been forced to pursue a line which clashes with his principles as an individual and as an official. I have known several officers of higher ranks than he who found themselves in a similar predicament.

I regret that in a letter of this nature I should even mention his name and that of his colleague, W/O Olchers. I know that the strategy in regard to the conduct of this case was probably all worked out to its finest details in higher quarters, and that the 2 officials were merely functionaries who had no choice but to carry out instructions from above.

In due course the Department may be asked to justify its conduct in this matter. I hope when that happens Government propagandists will resist the temptation to mislead the public by claiming that subversive documents were found in the file whose contents cannot be published on "security grounds". No illegal material can be produced because there was none in fact.

I further hope the Minister of Prisons, Mr J.T. Kruger, now that my confidential papers are in the possession of his officials will be big enough to acknowledge his mistake and to apologise to my legal representatives, Mr Kawalsky,[ii] Mr Ismail Ayob[iii] and to advocate George Bizos[iv] for questioning their integrity. The privileged papers could only have been taken away on the ground that they contained communications that had nothing to do with the case, and which the lawyers would smuggle out, an act which would make them guilty of unprofessional conduct.

---

i   A vertical line has been made in the margin from here until the end of the paragraph.
ii   Stanley Kawalsky (1946–), attorney at Frank, Bernadt and Joffe.
iii   Ismail Ayob (1942–), Mandela's attorney – see the glossary.
iv   George Bizos (1927–), defence lawyer in the Rivonia Trial – see the glossary.

Finally, I must ask you to return all the papers at once and to allow me to report the whole matter to my legal representatives without further delay.

Meantime, I should like you to acquaint the Commissioner of Prisons, through your Commanding Officer, with the contents of this letter.

[Signed NRMandela]
NELSON MANDELA

To Winnie Mandela,[i] his wife

[Translated from isiXhosa]

NELSON MANDELA (466/64)

1977-12-04

Dear Sister,

At one time there was a certain farmer who specialised in wheat; he had all the material as he was married to a rich farmer's daughter. The family was well-off. They had a nine-year-old daughter. Everybody believed that it was only death that would break their marriage. It so happened that he was elected to take charge of warriors as it was during the time of war.

He asked his wife to prepare food and clothing for him but his wife refused, she told the husband that she would not dare remain alone on the farm but the husband insisted as his word was always final. So he left with the warriors leaving the wife behind. The child noticed that there was a quarrel between his parents and started crying. Although the child was always number one at school she immediately came down after the quarrel.

It so happened that the farmer and his party were captured in the war. At home the workers became hostile and there was no productivity. The wife met her former boyfriend who was also rich. He managed to influence her to resume their love affair and that she must sue her husband for divorce. It so happened that the news of the wife's misbehaviour reached the poor husband who was in prison. He was disappointed because he loved and respected his wife.

You must remember that the above method is the best weapon to destroy one's house. It was then that the wealth changed to poverty.

---

i   Nomzamo Winifred Madikizela-Mandela (1936–) – see the glossary.

The wife wrote to her husband and explained the former boyfriend's intention, as she still has regard for her husband. What she was doing was to make sure whether the husband still loved her.

According to the Bantu Custom a man does not swim in water where boys usually swim, so the husband's reply was 'marry him'. The wife, understanding that her husband no longer loved her, got married to this rich man but her daughter decided to stay not with the new father but with her uncle. It was hardly two years when the news came that the husband was coming back and he was regarded as a true leader in the community. He had all the potential of a leader. This talk was spread by his followers who were released before him.

Preparations were made for the reception of the leaders in the locality. It was during this time that the wife became aware that she loved her former husband more than the present one.

It was a great pity as the rich farmer was now a poor man, his clothes were too big for him, he had no home and no wife. But although it was so, his daughter stood firmly by his side as well as the relatives and all the people.

It is easy to study one's conduct even if he pretends not to be what he actually is. The former wife started crying secretly. One person asked her if she still wanted to return to him. The answer was 'yes but it appears that he doesn't love me.'

The farmer and his daughter emigrated to another area where he hired a farm and stayed in happiness but his former wife was never happy with the new husband although the world was at their fingertips. Shame was on her.

With love, MADIBA

Mrs Nobandla MANDELA
802 Phathakahle Location
PO Brandfort (9400) OFS

◇◇◇◇◇◇◇◇

In 1975 Walter Sisulu and Ahmed Kathrada approached Mandela and suggested that he secretly write his autobiography in prison and smuggle it out for publication in time for his sixtieth birthday in 1978. He agreed and began writing. In Long Walk to Freedom, the book it eventually became, he recalled: 'I would write most of the night and sleep during the day. During the first week or two I would take a nap after dinner, wake at 10 p.m. and then write until it was time for breakfast. After working at the quarry, I would then sleep until *dinner, and the process would begin again. After a few weeks of this, I notified the authorities that I was not fooling well and would not be going to the quarry. They did not seem to care, and from then on I was able to sleep most of the day.*[56] *Each day Mandela would pass what he had written to Kathrada who commented in writing and handed it to Sisulu. After Mandela had made the corrections, the pages were given to fellow prisoners Isu 'Laloo' Chiba and Mac Maharaj to transcribe into tiny handwriting. In an interview in 2010, Chiba described how he and Maharaj transcribed the 600 pages of manuscript into about 60 pages. That manuscript was then divided into cocoa containers and buried in the garden of B Section, Robben Island.*[i] *Their later discovery by prison officials during the construction of a wall resulted in Mandela, Sisulu, and Kathrada – whose handwriting was on the original – in losing their study privileges for four years.*

To the commissioner of prisons

6th December 1977

The Commissioner of Prisons
Pretoria
Attention: Major Van Vuuren

The contents of your letter addressed to the Commanding Officer, and dated 15th November 1977, were conveyed to me on 1st December by the Head of Prison. I was informed that you cancelled my study privilege permanently with effect from 1st January 1978, on the allegation that I abused the said privilege by using study material to write my memoirs.

I must point out that I was appalled to note that in taking such a decision, you violated the fundamental principle of natural justice, and you did not even consider it necessary to inform me beforehand of the case against me.

The principle of natural justice rests on two basic rules which have ben upheld by judges of the highest authority in the country, and which form an essential part of the administrative process. The party to an enquiry must be afforded a full and fair opportunity of presenting his case, and the administrative agency must be free from bias.

The object of these rules is to prevent a miscarriage of justice and to ensure that administrative decisions are taken in the spirit, and with the

---

i   Interviews with Isu Laloo Chiba, Ahmed Kathrada, Rashid Seedat, Shabir Ballim, Prema Naidoo, and Razia Saleh, Johannesburg, 2010.

sense of responsibility of an administrative official whose duty it is to render justice by reaching just decisions for just means. Only in facist states is there no room for the golden rule that "Justice should not only be done, but should manifestly and undoubtedly be seen to be done".

In this regard I regret to tell you that you did not at all act in good faith. Not only did you conceal the fact that you were investigating an allegation against me, but you also denied me the opportunity of contradicting any relevant facts which I might have considered prejudicial to my interests.

It is unlikely that I would have contested my handwriting which appeared in any material in your possession. But there have been occasions in the past when some of us were accused of having abused their study and privilege on the strength of material which was not in their handwriting, and their studies were saved simply because they were able to establish that the accusation was false.

To the best of my knowledge and belief, neither you nor any of your staff members are handwriting experts, and any opinion you may have on the identity of a particular handwriting would be quite valueless. Even if your opinion was based on expert evidence, his views would be equally untrustworthy if they were not tested by me before you made your finding. Such a decision would inevitably cause grave injustice by punishing a man for an offence for which he is not guilty.

For example, if you had given me the opportunity to state my case before you withdrew the privilege, I might have convinced you that last year I had no permission to study and, therefore, could not have abused any study privilege. This is quite apart from the fact that, in any case, in the enlightened world of the Seventies, I see nothing wrong whatsoever in incarcerated freedom fighters writing out their life-stories and preserving them for posterity. Such privileges have been granted freely by all sorts of regimes since Roman times.

I am compelled to tell you that the unusual procedure you followed in dealing with this matter is sadly lacking in that spirit and sense of responsibility that we expect from the Head of a government department which handles the affairs of close to 100,000 prisoners. I sincerely believe that your real aim in taking away our studies is to emasculate us mentally and to detroy our morale which is one of the worst forms of cruelty. The inexplicable departure from the established procedure in handling the whole question confirms this impression. These high-handed methods tend to undermine any desire on my part to respect the law and authority and you cannot expect me to accept such an unjust decision.

But strictly without prejudice and in order to determine what course of action I should take, I should like you supply me with the following particulars:

1) The legal provision or provisions under which you cancelled my study privilege
2) The exact date or period when the alleged memoirs were written
3) If the alleged memoirs were completed before 1st January 1977, is it alleged that I had study permission when I wrote them?
4) Copies of all such memoirs in your possession
   Lastly, I must remind you that I have applied for an aegrotat examination in February 1978 and I am presently preparing to write these examinations.

[Signed NRMandela]
NR MANDELA 466/64

To Amina Cachalia,[i] his friend and comrade

Special letter[ii]   Nelson Mandela 466/64   12.12.77

Vahali Aminaben,[iii]

I've been given special permission to write to you in connection with an album for a photo of 21 x 27 centimetres. The Mother City[iv] cannot supply me with that size & I should like you to enquire from Juta & Co or Van Schaik's Bookstore, Pretoria, whether they have that size in stock; the price & postage. These 2 book firms are the approved stores from which we can order & if they've not got the right size in stock, they can get it from other firms. You in person should not buy & send it as that would be a waste of your fortune. Regulations expressly prohibit the receipt of articles from outside that are not ordered directly by the Prisons Dpt. We will then order it from this end.

Perhaps I could exploit this chance & ask you to send a family photo so that I could have the pleasure of seeing how Kaene & Nomente are maturing & how you & Yusuf are struggling to hide the marks of creeping age. Your letter of 18/7/75, the last I received from you, gave me the hope that I might

---

i   Amina Cachalia (1930–2013), friend and anti-apartheid and women's rights activist – see the glossary.
ii   Special letters were not deducted from a prisoner's quota.
iii *Vehalie* means 'dear' in Gujarati. Mandela probably would have consulted with one of his fellow prisoners who was fluent in Gujarati, such as Laloo Chiba, about how to write it. Mandela spelled it various ways including as *wahalie*. *Ben* means 'sister' in Gujarati.
iv   Cape Town.

see Miss Johannesburg, you Amina, & I said so in so many words in my reply of 1/11 that yr, adding that out of the much sought-after school of snoek[i] fish that milled around F. Square[ii] in Fordsburg those exciting days, you looked the right one to handle such delicate negotiations. I am still convinced that there's no one in S.A. who can rival him in that field & he could only fail in getting you permission to come down if he himself does not wish you to do so. To make sure that you got the message, I wrote to Zami[iii] to let you know that I would never excuse you & Yusuf if you aroused in me expectations you could not fulfil. But the poor girl has been so hard-pressed in my absence that she often overlooks or finds it difficult to attend to matters affecting even those, like you & Yusuf, she loves very much.

In your last letter you remarked that the children were growing, that you intended visiting them that August for a few mnths & rightly complained of loneliness. I fully understand your difficulties. But my friend who can prepare a dove meal so beautifully knows only too well that, apart from Yusuf, few men in this country know her as much as I do. I've no doubt that she'll always welcome the chance to be all alone with her man; that when she says they are lonely the pen is putting words into her mouth. Her heart & the whole of her system feel differently. Do you realise how hard it is to rub off images that friends write into our minds during trying & blissful moments?

Still I must admit that seeing Kaene & Nomente must have been a great moment for all of you. In that environment they must be as bright & resourceful as their Mum & Dad. At 20 & 19 respectively they should be writing interesting letters which bring you much joy. You'll probably be surprised to know that the picture of them that stands out clearly in my mind is when I last saw them in Jeppe in May '61. I still recall how Nomente rushed into the sitting room & asked for your attention, claiming that some object had bumped her smooth forehead. From the way she looked, one would have thought she had collided with a goods train; & for all I know an innocent butterfly might have touched her face. When she got what she wanted she melted at once & romped away beaming & bright like an iris in good soil & in good weather. So are all kids & that's one reason why we love them so much.

Sometimes I come across familiar names in approved publications circulating here. Just the other day I discovered that Effie's husband[iv] was busy doing research on renin, cholesterol & the like & I really wished I could read the results of his investigations. From all that I am able to read,

---

i   A South African name for barracouta.
ii   Freedom Square in the suburb of Fordsburg, Johannesburg, was a popular location for political meetings during the 1940s and 1950s.
iii   One of Winnie Mandela's names.
iv   Effie Schultz's husband, Professor Harry Seftel.

unfortunately in popular & not professional journals, it would appear that heart diseases, from which Blacks were once thought to be immune, are now deadly killers. I used to enjoy reading the British Medical Journal, *The Lancet*. I was wondering whether Effie was also doing research.[i] As student, houseman & practitioner she was non-conformist. Perhaps she still is, or maybe pressure of patients hardly give her time to breathe. I hope sincerely that Yusuf's eye troubles have cleared & that he still spends the greater part of each day praising your face, one of his precious treasures. It will not be easy for you to find parking space at Jutas & trust that your mini legs are still as strong & reliable as they were in the early 60s, & that they'll be able to carry you from Ferreirastown[ii] (or is it Oriental Bazaar?).[iii] I miss both of you & the children. Love & fondest regards, Very sincerely, Nelson

Mrs Amina Cachalia, P.O. Box 3265, Johannesburg

To Marie Naicker, the wife of Dr Monty Naicker

Nelson Mandela 466/64   1.10.78

Dear Marie,

Please accept our deepest condolences on Monty's passing.[iv] All of us loved and respected him & his death shook us. Although news of his illness reached us earlier, we did not think it was so serious that he would succumb to it.

Unfortunately, it was physically impossible for us to be at his bedside, nor tragically were many outside prison able to visit him when he needed them most. One of these is Mota[v] who would have spared nothing to be with Monty, had circumstances permitted. For our part we regret that we did not send him a message of goodwill during his illness in appreciation of the sacrifices he made for the happiness of all of us. The knowledge that his friends thought of him at such a critical moment would have given him a

---

i   Effie Schultz was a medical doctor and activist.
ii   A suburb in inner-city Johannesburg.
iii   Mandela is probably referring to the Oriental Plaza, which was established in the 1970s.
iv   Monty Naicker (1910–78), doctor, politician, and anti-apartheid activist – see the glossary.
v   Yusuf Dadoo (1909–83), medical doctor, anti-apartheid activist, and orator. President of South African Indian Congress, deputy to Oliver Tambo on the Revolutionary Council of MK, and chairman of the South African Communist Party – see the glossary. Yusuf Dadoo was commonly known as Mota, short for *Motabhai*, the Gujurati word for 'elder brother'. He had been living in exile since 1960.

bit of strength as he fought the last & greatest battle of his life. Our sincere apologies for this shortcoming.

In addition to the passing of your two brothers, Monty's death must have been a disastrous blow to you & the family. We are confident that the public response to the bereavement helped you to face the tragedy with courage. Be assured that you, Krissan, Vasugie & other members of the family are constantly in our thoughts.

Circumstances unfortunately prevent me from freely expressing my thoughts on the impact Monty made on the affairs of S.A. & on us as individuals. It suffices to say that he was one of our national heroes whose able leadership & wide experience we highly esteemed. He travelled widely & met many other international figures like Mahatma Gandhi & General Smuts. He made a great impression on me on the very first occasion we met during the hectic days of '46. The 30 yrs that followed justified the confidence the people had in him as a public figure & a professional man. His friendship with Mota, in particular, showed among other things how two strong & prominent personalities with differing outlooks could work together harmoniously for a great cause. This prevented possible friction & paved the way for great understanding.

Monty played an important part in uniting our people. His pact with Dr Xuma & Mota[i] was a significant contribution to this end. This historic development was put to a severe test within 12 months after it was made. The yr '49 was an unforgettable experience for those who had given their lives to the promotion of inter-racial harmony. Monty played an important role in quickly restoring peace & in the further promotion of understanding & goodwill.

We spent about two weeks together in J.H.B.[ii] in Dec '56. During the Treason preparatory examination[iii] that followed we met daily, & I came to know him better. In the solution of the problems that arose during the case, we were able to tap his vast experience. He earned the respect of all of us for his honesty and frankness.

When at the end of the P.M.B.[iv] Conference in March '61 I went to

---

i   'The Doctors' Pact' of 1947 signed by Dr. Yusuf Dadoo, Dr. Alfred Xuma, and Dr Monty Naicker about cooperation between the ANC, the Transvaal Indian Congress, and the Natal Indian Congress and calling for the right of freedom of movement, education, the right to vote, and equal opportunities for all 'non-European' South Africans.

ii   Johannesburg.

iii   Mandela is referring to the Treason Trial (1956–61), which was a result of the apartheid government's attempt to quell the power of the Congress Alliance, a coalition of anti-apartheid organisations. In early-morning raids on 5 December 1956, 156 individuals were arrested and charged with high treason. By the end of the trial in March 1961 all the accused either had the charges withdrawn or, in the case of the last twenty-eight accused (including Mandela), were acquitted.

iv   Pietermartizburg All-in Africa Conference at which Mandela was a surprise guest and delivered an address on 25 March 1961.

report to the Chief[i] at Groutville,[ii] I also paid Monty a courtesy call & outlined to him the conference resolutions. It was a happy meeting after several months. I saw him again two days before I left on the African tour early in Jan 62 & once again briefed him on my mission. On my return in July the same yr we met again. You will remember the occasion very well. We had a lengthy discussion &, like Mota, he was not happy about certain aspects of my report.[iii] Although I tried to allay his concern, Monty, as always, made no bones about how he felt & I got the impression that I had not convinced him. I am, however, confident that subsequent developments proved to him that my report was appropriate & timely.

On Aug. 5[iv] I said goodbye to both of you. I did not know then that I would never have the pleasure of seeing him again. Had I known, I would have perhaps conversed with him a little longer & shook his hand more firmly.

Although we regularly received your festive greeting, I missed Monty during the last 15 yrs & longed to hear about him. I was, therefore, overjoyed when Winnie told me that Monty was one of those who welcomed her in Durban on her return from prison in '75. I regard the moments I spent with him as amongst the most fruitful in my life & I will always think of him with fond memories. Please give our sympathies to your sisters-in-law. Though belated, they are sincerely meant. We also thought of Ansu[v] & Fatima[vi] when Ashwin & Dawood passed away.

Our love & best wishes to you & the children, Nokukhanya,[vii] Ismail & Fatu,[viii] Radi & JN[ix] & to all our friends.

Sincerely,
Nelson

---

i   Chief Albert Luthuli (1898–1967), president-general of the ANC, 1952–67 – see the glossary.
ii   A town in Ilembe District Municipality in the Natal homeland (now KwaZulu-Natal). Chief Albert Luthuli lived there.
iii Mandela is referring to the ANC's decision to form an armed wing.
iv   The day Mandela was arrested.
v   Ansuyah Ratipal Singh (1917–78), doctor, author, and the first Indian woman in South Africa to receive a bursary from the Council for Scientific and Industrial Research. She married lawyer and Natal Indian Congress member Ashwin Choudree in 1948.
vi   Fatima Seedat (1922–2003) was the twin of Rahima Moosa, one of the leaders of the 1956 Women's March. A member of the Natal Indian Congress and ANC, Fatima was jailed for her role in the Passive Resistance Campaign waged by the Transvaal and Natal Indian Congresses from 1946 to 1948 against the Asiatic Land Tenure Act of 1946 which sought to confine Asian ownership of land to particular areas. She was jailed again in 1952 for participating in the Defiance Campaign (for the Defiance Campaign, see the glossary).
vii Nokhukhanya Luthuli, widow of Chief Albert Luthuli.
viii Ismail (1918–2000) and Fatima (1928–2010) Meer, friends. Ismail was a lawyer and anti-apartheid activist and Fatima was a professor, author, and anti-apartheid activist – see the glossary for both these individuals.
ix   Radi and J. N. Singh, friends.

Mrs Marie Naicker, c/o Mr Ismail Meer, 148 Burnwood Road, Sydenham, Durban

P.S. The only birthday message I received from Durban was from Annetta Memeth.[i] I should like to acknowledge it, but do not know her address. Nelson

---

To the head of prison, Robben Island

[A cut-off note in another hand reads] Looks like it is about who Dr Ayesha Ahmed is.

Robben Island
16 January 1978

The Head of Prison,
Robben Island.

I should be pleased if you would be good enough to allow Dr Ayesha Ahmed, a member of the Malay community from Cape Town, to pay me a special visit at your earliest possible convenience in connection with my family affairs. She and her husband, also a medical practitioner, are friends of our family and my wife and children stay with them when they visit me. Although Dr Ahmed is one of the leaders of the women's organisation, Rape Crisis, to the best of my knowledge and belief she is not politically active, as well as her husband.

This year our youngest daughter, Zindzi,[ii] plans to study at the University of Cape Town and will be living with Dr Ahmed. Her health has been affected by the difficulties under which she grew up: the imprisonment of her father, numerous police raids in our home at odd hours, assaults on my wife from various quarters, her arrest and imprisonment, the insecurity that is caused by the imprisonment of both parents, acute longing for parental love and fear of the unknown. All these things have been too much of a strain on her. Dr Ahmed has been observing her for some time now and I should like to get her report directly and to make my suggestions to her also directly.

---

i   This name may be code for a person Mandela does not want to name.
ii   Zindziswa Mandela (1960–) – see the glossary.

I could not write and discuss all these matters with Dr Ahmed, but as you will readily appreciate, it is undesirable for obvious reasons that such confidential matters should be handled through correspondence. In conclusion, I should like to assure you that a meeting with Dr Ahmed will enable me to play my part in the creation of the ideal atmosphere for the restoration of my daughter's health.

[Signed NRMandela]

To Mangosuthu Buthelezi,[i] family friend and Zulu prince

Nelson Mandela 466/64   1.10.78

Shenge![ii]

Your unexpected birthday[iii] message roused fond memories & made me reflect nostalgically on the multitude of things that mutually interested us. Yrs ago you & I met either in Durban or J.H.B.[iv] & pre-occupied ourselves with warm téte-a-tétes. Each of these occasions left us refreshed & created a greater urge to meet again for rejuvenation.

Eighteen yrs have passed since those good old days & the distance between Mahlabatini[v] & Robben Island became even more magnified through our respective silence. Happily a few govt publications here carried your pictures & those of your family. This usually turned my thoughts to you & Mndlunkulu[vi] Irene. The arrival of your telegram naturally helped to bridge the gap between us.

Thoughts from friends, especially from the old ones, are always a source of strength & inspiration. I should like you to know that I set store by your message. Apart from your telegram I received six other birthday messages, three from the family & three from friends. I treasure all of them & they have given me much comfort. I feel like a 30-yr old. As few as they

---

i   Chief Mangosuthu Gatsha Buthelezi (1928–), Zulu prince, member of the ANC until the relationship deteriorated in 1979, chief minister of KwaZulu 1972–94, founder and president of the Inkatha Freedom Party in 1975 – see the glossary.
ii   Chief Buthelezi's praise name.
iii He was writing three months after his birthday most likely because he had used up his quota of letters. We also have no way of knowing if Mandela received the letter in time for his birthday on 18 July.
iv   Johannesburg.
v   A small town in KwaZulu Natal where Buthelezi lived.
vi   A royal reference to Mangosuthu Buthelezi's wife, Irene Buthelezi – see the glossary.

are, they are representative of all the country's population groups. I believe they form part of the shower of good wishes that have come from far & wide. All of them have given me a shot in the arm. Phungashe!![i]

Recently I saw films of King Zwelithini's coronation[ii] & of his wedding to Princess Mantombi.[iii] You led the dancing remarkably well. The scenes reminded me of the beautiful country that straddles iThukela[iv] where part of our history is buried. Unlike the Egyptian pyramids which attract thousands of tourists every yr from all parts of the globe, Dukuza[v] has vanished & perhaps even the land marks of the Royal village have been destroyed by all the debris of the 19th and 20th Cs. But history will record the proud achievements which issued from the capital of that ancient kingdom, the achievements of Dlangezwa[vi] and Ntshingwayo.[vii] These names form part of our heritage & are excellent models on which worthy life patterns may be built. When I looked at those films I wondered, as I have done many times in the past, what was so unique in the waters of the Mfolosi[viii] as to drive those who drank from it to go through life with such frightening fervour.

Apart from the disappearance of the indigenous States of yore, the S.A. of only 16 yrs ago is no longer the same. The toddlers I left behind have become serious-minded adults. They live in the milieu of rapid change & development of science & technology & readily respond to the intricate challenges of life. They move with lightweight speed in almost everything they do. Perhaps education & the influence of the mass media have helped to close the generation gap. We must, therefore, allow for what may appear superficially to be excesses of the youth. Wordsworth succinctly said that the "Child is father of the man ."[ix]

Meantime the stalwarts of the past two decades who pioneered in many fields are no more with us & with their demise has gone part of the world I knew so well. During the past 16 yrs I sent numerous messages of condolence to members of my family, relatives & friends. Today, for instance, I wrote to Marie, the widow of the late Monty in Durban,[x] expressing our

---

i   One of Buthelezi's clan names.
ii   King Goodwill Zwelithini kaBhekuzulu (1948–) is king of the Zulu nation. His coronation was on 3 December 1971.
iii   A daughter of Swaziland's King Sobhuza II, Queen Mantombi Dlamini was King Zwelithini's third wife. They married in 1977.
iv   The largest river in KwaZulu-Natal where Buthelezi lived.
v   Dukuza was the name for the town founded by zulu king Shaka (1787–1828) in 1820. After he was assassinated by his half-brothers in 1828, the town was burnt down. A new town called Stranger was built there by European settlers in 1873, but in 2006 its name was officially changed to KwaDukuza.
vi   A Zulu regiment from the 1800s.
vii   Ntshingwayo kaMahole Khoza (c. 1809–1883) led a victorious 20,000-strong Zulu army against the British.
viii   A river in KwaZulu-Natal, which is also known as the Umfolozi River.
ix   These words appear in English poet William Wordsworth's poem 'My Heart Leaps Up' (also named 'The Rainbow'), written in 1802.
x   See his letter on page 357.

sympathy on the death of her husband. Not so long ago I had to do the same to Nokukhanya,[i] Aunt Freda Matthews,[ii] to Michael's daughter, Barbara[iii] & to the wife of Moses,[iv] to mention but a few. All the deceased were so much a part of the great family that it is tragic that their graves are so widely scattered.

The loss of trusted & respected veterans who played such decisive roles in our lives has been a great blow. What was even more heart breaking is that we were unable to pay homage to them by being present at their graveside. Notwithstanding these great misfortunes, rest assured that there are no feelings of despair or isolation. Currents of goodwill surge forward continually from all points of the compass infusing confidence & hope. I look forward optimistically to the next day, because it may bring me a pleasant surprise in the form of a visit or letter from the family, some message of good wishes & encouragement from an old friend, just as July 18 brought your inspiring felicitations.

From* the few pictures I have seen of Mndlunkulu,[v] she betrays few signs of old age. She still looks very much the young daughter she was of Mzila & uMakoti wa kwa Phungashe.[vi] I hope she will live long & continue to hold fort at Phindangene,[vii] adding flavour to the fish, vegetables & salads & checking the children of Mnyamana[viii] from straying too far from the house. I also hope Mntwana Magogo,[ix] Mndlunkulu's mother & brother are keeping well. To all of them I send my fondest regards.

Halala Sokwalisa!!![x] Sincerely, Nelson.

Chief Gatsha M. Buthelezi, Kwa Phindangene, P.O. Box 1 Mahlabatini, KwaZulu

*I also heard of the sudden death of your sister's son, Hlubi, & it must have been a painful experience to her. Kindly convey my deepest sympathy. Nelson.

---

i	See his letter to Nokukhanya Luthuli from 8 June 1970, page 172.
ii	Frieda (also spelt by Mandela as 'Freda') Matthews (1905–98), one of the first black women to earn a university degree in South Africa – see the glossary.
iii	Michael Harmel (1915–74), South African Communist Party and MK member – and his daughter Barbara.
iv	Moses Mabhida (1923–86), a former secretary-general of the South African Communist Party and ANC member who was born in Natal (now part of KwaZulu-Natal).
v	Irene Buthelezi.
vi	A name in the Buthelezi family that is also a praise name for Buthelezi.
vii	Buthelezi lived at Kwa Phindangene. He is also known as uMntwana ka Phindangene (the child of Phindangene).
viii	Buthelezi's grandfather was Mnyamana Buthelezi, prime minister to the king of the Zulu kingdom, Cetshwayo kaMpande (c.1826–84).
ix	Princess Magogo, Buthelezi's mother.
x	Halala is an isiZulu word used for praising someone. Sokwalisa is one of Mangosuthu Buthelezi's praise names.

To the head of prison, Robben Island

2.10.78

The Head of Prison
Robben Island

<u>Attention: Capt. Harding</u>

I refer to the interview I had with you this afternoon and should be pleased if you would kindly allow me to buy the book "B. J. Vorster"[i] By D'Oliveira (English).[ii]

Although I am not certain of the publishers, Tafelberg Uitgewers or Messrs Juta & Co will certainly have it in stock[iii].

I have already been allowed to purchase "One Eerste Ses Premiers" and "10 Politieke Leiers"[iv] both by Piet Meiring and sincerely hope you will readily approve my application and debit my account[v] with the cost thereof.

[Signed NRMandela]
466/64

To the minister of justice

[Telegram]

23.10.78[vi]

Attention: ABO security

---

i   Balthazar Johannes Vorster, prime minister of South Africa 1966–78.
ii   The book by D'Oliveira is actually called *Vorster: The Man* (Johannesburg: Ernest Stanton, 1977).
iii Mandela did read *Vorster: The Man* in prison. While he regarded Vorster as a racist and a fascist, he said in a conversation with Richard Stengel that he believed he was an 'interesting character': 'He discussed things very objectively, with his limited range, you know, of knowledge, of black politics. Full of a sense of humour about himself.' (NM in conversation with Richard Stengel, 23 December 1992, CD 12, Nelson Mandela Foundation, Johannesburg.)
iv   *10 Politieke Leiers* (10 political leaders) (Cape Town: Tafelberg, 1973).
v   Upon entering prison, a list was made of the belongings a prisoner had with them. Details of the amount of cash a prisoner may have brought with them were recorded in an individual account under the name of the prisoner (this was not a bank account but simply a separate bookkeeping record). Thereafter, any funds reaching the prison in the name of that prisoner were recorded in that account and so too were any disbursements made in the name of the prisoner. When they were discharged from prison, the prisoner was given what remained in the account.
vi   Mandela wrote in his prison calendar that his wife and daughter Zindzi had informed him during a visit on 4 June 1977 that Winnie had been deported to Brandfort in the Orange Free State on 16 May 1977. Winnie was still able to visit while she was in Brandfort, although she had to get permission to leave the town.

Re: Request: Series No 913: Nelson Mandela

[In Afrikaans] 1. Contents of request received from the above named prisoner is given below:

[In English] 'Please allow me to send an urgent telegram to the Minister of Justice in connection with my household affairs x

On May 15 1977 my wife was deported to Brandfort where she is now restricted and where no employment is available for her x

My daughter who visited me yesterday informs me that she has now been offered employment in the neighbouring town of Welkom but which is outside the magisterial district of Brandfort x

In this connection I should like to ask the Minister to release the restriction so that my wife could take the job x

Secondly the treatment my wife is receiving from members of the South African Police borders on outright persecution and I should like to ask the Minister to order the police to confine themselves strictly to the execution of their duties according to the law x

PS: My wife's prospective employer is Dr Chris Hattingh x
     As far as I know he is a medical practitioner
[In Afrikaans] 2. Your decision is awaited x Application not useful

End

Robben Island

———

To Zindzi Mandela,[i] his youngest daughter

Nelson Mandela 466/64   26.11.78
My darling Zindzi,

You don't say whether or not you got my letter of 30/7. Amongst other things. I asked you to send me Oupa's[ii] birth date, so that I could also wish him well on such occasions. Please do confirm and let me have the information.

---

i   Zindziswa Mandela (1960–) – see the glossary.
ii   Zindzi's partner, Oupa Seakamela.

I also got a letter from Zeni,[i] perhaps the best I have received from her for a long time, informative & carefully worded. To anyone who has watched her development from a distance as I have done, her letters, especially since last yr, showed that her vocabulary & ability to express herself had been a bit affected. But the last letter shows that she is picking up again, & that has really delighted me. When you phone her, please add my congrats.

I am happy to learn that you have taken Mum's advice and that you will now go to the convent to prepare for your exams. I have already sent you & Oupa my sincerest good wishes. Again I say: "best of luck". I am confident that you will easily make it.

At Roma there used to be a sister Elizabeth Thys [Sometimes spelt Teyise] from Griquatown. I once asked Mum to find her present address so that I could express our condolences on the death of her sister, Sanna, from the famous Blue Lagoon, Von Wielligh St, J.H.B.[ii] Sanna helped many African students with fees & food;[iii] I was very sorry that neither I nor Mum could be at her graveside. To write to Elizabeth [Tukkie as we called her] will be some consolation. She is well known to Mum.

I was pleased to hear that you met Lady Eleanor[iv] & that you talked about your education. I hope you were able to go to JHB on 13 & 14/11 to see Sir Robert[v] and to finalise matters concerning the family. It will please the Birleys[vi] to know that, at least, they have not lost you; that you will finally land in Britain. Studying in Britain will give you an immense advantage & I hope you will make full use of that opportunity. We can discuss the problem of how to get a passport later. Meantime, please remind Mum about it when she next comes down.

The weird dreams you sometimes have are no strange phenomena. Your childhood has been spent in a harsh home environment. The strain of that type of life has naturally affected you. I never forget that you were barely 3 mths old when I had to leave home, you, Zeni and Mum behind.

Although I saw you often during the 18 months that followed. From Aug. 62 until 3 yrs ago when you started coming down, we longed for each other. The mere thought about what you went through terrifies me. But what is important, darling, is that you have faced the challenge well; you are alive. You stand at that crossroads where visibility is so good that you can clearly see the vast terrain ahead & the distant horizon. In spite of

---

i   Zenani Mandela (1959–), his middle daughter and Zindzi's sister.
ii   Johannesburg.
iii   He talks about this in his letter to Sanna from 1 December 1970 (see page 201).
iv   Lady Elinor Birley (Mandela misspelled her name as 'Eleanor').
v   Sir Robert Birley (1903–82), the former headmaster of Eton College and at the time the visiting professor of education at the University of the Witwatersrand.
vi   Sir Robert and Lady Birley took over funding Zeni and Zindzi's education.

all our difficulties, Mum has produced intelligent, tough, warm & friendly darlings in you & Zeni. That is what should dominate your thoughts & influence,your actions. At present, just as in the past, Mum is going through a rough time. But that wonderful Pondo is a rock & can take care of herself. Please take things easy, my darling. Everything will come right in the end.

You should not at all be worried by the question of premonitions either. In your particular case, all that this means is that you have more than average ability to foresee things. There is nothing magical about this at all. What is certainly incorrect would be the belief that such powers are given to you by some supernatural being; that some events around you have a hidden meaning beyond the reach of science.

To take an example, there is nothing particularly strange in your dream about hidden treasure at Bizana.[i] My absence from home has made you feel insecure in numerous respects, & financially as well. You would like to live in a spacious home, to eat & dress well. Grandpa C.K.,[ii] was a well-to-do man who was fond of you, Zeni & Mum. He left behind a large estate & since his death, there has been much talk about inheritance.

In the home environment in which you have grown, it would be quite natural for you to be deeply involved in the issue, even if unconsciously. Mrs Ngakane was an old family friend, your Granny. It is not strange that in your dream she should be an instrument to fulfil one of your most fervent ambitions in life, i.e. financial security.

The incident of the tortoise & the injured bird are also capable of scientific explanation. The tortoise is a tame animal & makes a good pet. It may have escaped from the owner or was fairly used to human beings. Equally, the bird may have been tame, chased by a hawk or forced by the injury to perch on your arms. You will be safe if you always try to seek a scientific explanation for all that happens, even if you come to a wrong conclusion. Do I make sense or do I sound like any ou toppie from the bundu?[iii]

Please try to push Zeni & Muzi to buzz off at once,[iv] before they rust any further. I miss you badly & long to see you. Tons and tons of love and a million kisses. Affectionately,
Tata[v]

Miss Zindzi Mantu Mandela, 802, Phathakahle Location, P.O. Brandfort

---

i   Winnie Mandela's home village in the Transkei.
ii   Columbus Kokani Madikizela, Winnie Mandela's father – see the glossary.
iii   'An old man from the rural areas' in Afrikaans.
iv   Zenani and her husband Prince Thumbumuzi Dlamini were moving to the United States.
v   'Father' in isiXhosa.

P.S. Give my best wishes to the Mother Superior & members of her staff. Mum & I are very indebted to her for giving you the chance to study quietly. Perhaps one day we will be able to thank her face to face. Tata

---

To Ndileka Mandela,[i] his granddaughter and eldest daughter of his late son, Thembi[ii]

Nelson Mandela 466/64   21.1.79

My darling Zukulu,[iii]

It seems it was only yesterday when, on February 19 last year, I sent you a card on your 13 birthday. Again I say "Many Happy Returns and a wonderful year!"

I hope you and Nandi[iv] got the Xmas cards I sent you and that you enjoyed your Xmas. I also hope you will write and tell me everything about it. Will you?

I am told that you passed your Form I. Aunt Rennie wrote to me from Inanda[v] to say that this year you will be doing Form II there. I don't know whether you have succeeded in doing so. My warmest congratulations!

If you are at Inanda, please tell me about the total amount of fees to be paid so that I can arrange for a scholarship. In your last letter you asked that I send you a leather jacket with a fur neck. I passed on your request to Khulu,[vi] Winnie. She has many problems and easily forgets. But she is a very kind person & loves you & Nandi very much. Although she is out of work, she will struggle and send you the things you want.

I keep on thinking of 1981 which is only 2 years from now, and when you will be able to visit me. I am dying to see you, and I cannot wait at all for that day.

Give my love to Mum Thoko[vii] and Tata Phineas.[viii]

What is his surname and address in Claremont?[ix] I wanted to send them

---

i   Ndileka Mandela (1965–) – see the glossary.
ii   Madiba Thembekile (Thembi) Mandela (1945–69), Mandela's eldest son – see the glossary.
iii   Mzukulu is 'grandchild' in isiXhosa. Zukulu is a diminutive of mzukulu.
iv   Nandi Mandela (1968–), his granddaughter and youngest daughter of his late son, Themi.
v   Inanda Seminary, a prestigious boarding school in Durban, KwaZulu-Natal.
vi   'Grandparent' in isiXhosa.
vii   Thoko Mandela, wife of Thembekile Mandela and mother of their two daughters – see glossary.
viii Thoko's second husband, Phineas Nkosi. *Tata* means 'father' in isiXhosa.
ix   A suburb in Durban.

a Xmas card, but I could not do so because I do not know their Claremont address.

Meantime I wish this year will bring you a lot of joy & good luck. A million kisses and tons and tons of love, darling.

Affectionately, Khulu To Ndindi Mandela. Inanda Seminary

Miss Ndileka Mandela
c/o Mrs Rennie Mandela
Inanda Seminary
Private Bag X54105
DURBAN
4000

—————————————

To Winnie Mandela,[i] his wife

Nelson Mandela 466/64   21. 1. 79

Mntakwethu,[ii]

There are very few occasions in which I have actually feared to write to you as I now do. I cannot excuse myself for my failure to find out about your exam results on 26/12.

My sense of guilt is sharpened by the fact that a few dys before you came, I congratulated several colleagues who had passed the same exam & I sympathised with those who failed; good friends [of] mine they all are, but just friends. That is a relationship that can be valuable & which it pays to cultivate & nurse. But however strong it may be, it lacks the tenderness & intimacy that exist between a man & his mum, dade[iii] & the special friend that you are. This particular relationship carries with it something that cannot be separated from self. It imposes on one certain elementary decencies of which the failure to carry out is well-nigh inexcusable. Are you cursing me for this [?] slip-up? [?], Ngutyana![iv] Is it too late for me to ask? Last yr I collected another harvest of 15 visits and 43 letters. Of these letters 15 came from you. There were 7 birthday cards & the birthday message from

---

i   Nomzamo Winifred Madikizela-Mandela (1936–) – see the glossary.
ii   A term of endearment in isiXhosa.
iii 'Sister' in isiXhosa. In this context it means Winnie Mandela.
iv   One of Winnie Mandela's names.

Helen[i] was in the form of a letter. I had more visits than in '77 but, although the letters were more than the previous year, I have not reached the record number of 50 that I got in '75. Those wonderful visits and lovely letters make the atmosphere around me relatively pleasant and the outlook bright.

Though cheerful on 19/2 you, nonetheless, looked a bit ill, and the tiny pools of water in your eyes drowned the love and tenderness they always radiate; the love and tenderness that always pulls me so close to you. But the knowledge of what I have enjoyed in the last 20 years made me feel the force of that love even though physically dimmed by illness. On 29/10 you were even more queenly and desirable in your deep green dress and I thought you were lucky that I could neither reach [?] nor confide to you how I felt.

Sometimes I feel like one who is on the sidelines, who has missed life itself. Travelling with you to work in the early morning, phoning you during the dy, touching your hand or hugging you as you moved up & down the house, enjoying your delicious dishes, the unforgettable hrs in the bedroom, made life taste like honey. These are things I cannot forget. On 2/12 Zindzi[ii] hinted that she & you planned to be here on her birthday. I looked forward to that dy as if I would be seeing both of you for the first time. But on the morning of that dy I prayed that you might not come.

Unconsciously during the previous dy & night I worked a little harder than I realised. I thought the eyes might betray me again, much to your concern as when Zindzi visited me on 21/10. I was, therefore, much relieved when you did not turn up. I was, however, certain that you would be here in a few dys' time. What a moment that turned out to be, mntakwethu!

The only thing that worried me was to note that you have over-scaled your weight to the extent of endangering your health. In spite of the fact that several people thought you looked like Nobandla's[iii] daughter, which is very encouraging, you frightened me. Frankly I don't want to see you again so starved & bony. Fortunately your elegant outfit & matching headgear saved the occasion. An otherwise enjoyable yr would have ticked off on an anti-climax. By the way, I liked the khaki garments you & Zindzi wore on 27/8. You looked really fresh like isidudu brewing in yeast. Your love & devotion has created a debt which I will never attempt to pay back. So enormous is it that even if I were to continue paying regular instalments for another century, I would not settle it. All I can say Mum is, Nangomso![iv]

---

i   This is most likely his friend Helen Joseph (1905–92), teacher, social worker, and anti-apartheid and women's rights activist – see the glossary.

ii   Zindziswa Mandela (1960), his and Winnie Mandela's youngest daughter.

iii   Nobandla is one of Winnie Mandela's names.

iv   'Nangamso' is an isiXhosa word that expresses deep gratitude to a person who has gone beyond the call of duty. Mandela sometimes spelled it nangomso.

In regard to Zeni's[i] education, I was perhaps very rash with my advice because of anger. We should constantly consult with her as to how the matter should be handled. Everything should be done to get her away even if alone, if Muzi[ii] is not ready to leave. Keep on putting the pressure on Douglas, Ismail[iii] & on Muzi.

I hope Zindzi's health has improved. In regard to her bronchitis I would suggest that she should use no anti-biotics but very hot tea. In addition she should use Mendel's throat paint with throat brush. That is how Mohammed Abdula cured mine. Bronchitis troubled me here for several mnths in '70 but once I used hot water or tea & Mendel's paint it completely disappeared to this dy. Do let me know if Lady Eleanor[iv] has cleared the question of her registration for the exams.

If you can raise the money a car would definitely be a good investment for Zindzi even though fuel is becoming more scarce & dear. I fully approve of your stand in regard to the suggestion or veiled hint that you should shift to Welkom. You were deported to that place & there you should remain. Even though Brandfort is no more than a farming village, you have now found your feet there & paid heavily for doing so. I don't want you to start all over again trying to turn a cave into a habitation. After my arrest you had a difficult time in J.H.B.[v] & later things improved. As your legal representatives have told the court & Brig Coetzee,[vi] your arrival in Brandfort was followed by unusual experiences which made your life difficult. Even in Brandfort conditions are improving. If you go to Welkom the same process will start all over again. I repeat you should stay where you are. Neither Kgatho[vii] nor Maki[viii] has turned up.

With regard to my health I feel fine both physically & spiritually. I keep fit through indoor & outdoor exercises. The B.P.[ix] is under control. You see me often & rumours that I am ill ought not to worry you. Zwangendaba[x] is such a conscientious nephew that I am surprised that up to now he has not helped Zindzi in her attempt to write the family history. You ought to find out what his difficulties are before the child thinks we are indifferent to her

---

i   Zenani Mandela, his and Winnie's eldeset daughter – see the glossary.
ii   Zenani's husband, Prince Thumbumuzi Dlamini, a son of King Sobhuza of Swaziland.
iii   Douglas Lukhele, Harvard-educated Swazi lawyer who did his articles at Mandela and Oliver Tambo's law firm in the 1950s, and Ismail Meer (1918-2000), Fatima's husband and a lawyer and anti-apartheid activist – see the glossary.
iv   Lady Elinor Birley whose husband Sir Robert Birley (1903–82) was the former headmaster of Eton College and at the time the visiting professor of education at the University of the Witwatersrand. Mandela misspelled her name as 'Eleanor'.
v   Johannesburg.
vi   Head of the security police.
vii   Makgatho Mandela (1950–2005), Mandela's second-born son – see the glossary.
viii   Makaziwe Mandela (1954–), Mandela's eldest daughter – see the glossary.
ix   Blood pressure.
x   A nephew.

request. Lack of co-operation from us can discourage her. I still have not got Oupa's[i] birth date. Again a million thanks for your warm love & tender care. I LOVE YOU Devotedly, Dalibhunga

Nkosk. Nobandla Mandela, 802 Phathakhahle Location, P.O. Brandfort 9400

To Makaziwe Mandela,[ii] his eldest daughter

Nelson Mandela 466/64   13.5.79

To my darling Maki
    On your 25th birthday.
    MAY 1st
    Many Happy Returns!

How does it feel to be 25? I still remember that when I was 8 I was in a hurry to get old, to have a grey patch on my head like my father. But now I am battling to keep young & even try to compete with young people in various kinds of indoor & outdoor games. Though not so easy it's a challenge I thoroughly enjoy. All that you need with only ¼ century behind you is to use the amount of energy you possess in such a way as to keep you in good health & to enjoy living almost every day in your life.

    You must be wondering just why I have taken so long to send you a birthday card. For the last 2 months I had a persistent conjunctivitis inflammation of the conjunctiva. I had good treatment & soon I will see an eye specialist. I had a similar problem in '76 and he prescribed then the same treatment that I use now. He thought that for my age my eyesight was quite good. Naturally I always feel good. My worry throughout this period has been you, darling, & your birthday. It's such a relief for me to be able to say at last: Happy Birthday! Ukhule ude Ukhokhobe![iii] Aunt Helen[iv] is now 74 but still fairly active. Perhaps you may live longer than herself. Again: Many Happy Returns! About your school work I was happy to know that you got

---

i   Zindzi's partner, Oupa Seakamela.
ii   Makaziwe Mandela (1954–) – see the glossary.
iii   An isiXhosa saying which means 'Wishing you a long life'.
iv   Helen Joseph (1905–92), teacher, social worker, and anti-apartheid and women's rights activist – see the glossary.

58% in your first Sociology test. I know Prof Hough[i] and Mr. Somhlahlo[ii] well from the Jan Hofmeyr School of Social Work in JHB. But I have not had the pleasure of meeting Miss Mabete.[iii] Please give all of them my best regards. I was also pleased to hear that Aunt Helen & Uncle Steve wrote to you and I hope you have answered both of them punctually. Giving attention to matters which seem to many people small is normally one of the marks of a good sense of responsibility. You should cultivate that habit carefully by having a particular day of the week or month reserved for writing letters. It's always better to draft a letter & then go over it to check its mistakes & to improve your formulations.

I hope you have already written to the secretary of the Memon Bursary Fund[iv] to thank his organisation for helping you to pursue one of your most fervent ambitions in life. Tell him that without their help, it would have been well-nigh impossible for you to further your university studies. Let them know that you intend seeing them in June when you will thank them directly.

You should also thank Aunt Helen for all her efforts. Tell her that you would like to spend your June holidays with a sociologist or sociology student where you can pick up in this subject as well as in your English.

You could perhaps ask her to give the task of getting a suitable person in this regard to ILONA[v] or her (Aunt Helen's) neighbour, Sheila. Dr. Fatima Meer's address is 141 Burnwood Rd, Sydenham (4091) Durban. She would be delighted to hear from you, but my only fear is that she might ask you to go over to the Natal University where she is a lecturer.

You are also quite mistaken in thinking I am the person who got you the bursary. All that I did was to ask Aunt Helen to get in touch with some of my JHB friends. I was certain that they would raise the necessary funds. But by then Mum Winnie had already contacted the Memon Bursary Fund through our attorney Mr. Ismail Ayob,[vi] himself a Memon.[vii] That is the true story. That is the person who, more than any other one, deserves your thanks. Whether or not you will do what every decent beneficiary would do in your circs.[viii] is, of course, entirely your affair.

---

i   Professor Hough taught Winnie Mandela at the Jan Hofmeyr School of Social Work.
ii   A former classmate of Winnie Mandela at the Jan Hofmeyr School of Social Work, who later became a lecturer at the University College of Fort Hare.
iii A friend.
iv   The Memon Association of South Africa was established in 1965 and provides funding to tertiary students.
v   Ilona Kleinschmidt, a friend and the wife of Horst Kleinschmidt, an activist who worked for the South African Christian Institute. The Kleinschmidts provided financial assistance when Winnie Mandela was in prison, and Mandela appointed Kleinschmidt to be the legal guardian of Zenani and Zindzi Mandela when Winnie Mandela was in prison in 1974.
vi   Ismail Ayob (1942–), Mandela's attorney – see the glossary.
vii Mandela's use of the word Memon possibly refers to a subgroup of Muslims who descend from the western part of South Asia.
viii Circumstances.

Concerning Dr. Vilakazi's[i] efforts your sharp reaction equally surprised me. Both Mum Winnie and he are only trying to help you and not to dictate to you. I agree that you should complete your first degree at F.H.[ii] and then go abroad for Honours and Masters. All that you should do is to inform her accordingly, sign the forms & return them to her at once; and ask her to postpone the particular bursary for 1982 when you will be able to take it.

I am also pleased to know that Maureen is your friend. I used to know a grand old man, Mr. Pike, who lived next to the Orlando East Communal Hall. I wonder if Maureen knew him. Perhaps he was her grandfather. Please give her my love.

Zeni's[iii] address is P.O. Box 546 Mbabane, Swaziland. Her official name is Princess La Mandela Dlamini and she and her husband intend leaving for studies in the U.S.A. in this yr. You are right when you say that she is a kind person. Have you read Zindzi's[iv] anthology?[v] It is now being sold by S.A. book firms. Unfortunately I have not seen it and do not know its title. I am looking forward to seeing you this June. Meantime, do study hard and know that we are holding up thumbs for you. Above all, we love you & once again, wish you a very very Happy birthday & the best of luck.

Tons and tons of love and a million kisses
Your loving Tata[vi]

Miss Makaziwe Mandela, Elukhanyisweni, P.O. Alice.

P.S. Send me your latest photo of not more than 15 x 20 centimetres. Treat the matter urgently.

By the way, aunt Helen is herself a well-qualified sociologist with an Honours Degree from the University of London.

[words printed in card:]
However you
May celebrate
Here's hoping
You will find
Your special day
In every way

---

i   Herbert Vilakazi (1943–2016), professor of sociology.
ii   University College of Fort Hare, Alice in the Ciskei homeland – see the glossary.
iii   Zenani Mandela (1959–), Mandela's middle daughter and Makaziwe's half-sister.
iv   Zindziswa Mandela (1960–), Mandela's youngest daughter and Makaziwe's half-sister.
v   Zindzi Mandela's book of poetry, *Black As I Am* (Los Angeles: Guild of Tutors Press, 1978).
vi   'Father' in isiXhosa.

Will be
The perfect kind

To the head of prison, Robben Island

20.5.79

The Head of Prison
Robben Island

Attention: Capt. Hesselman

Yesterday the Censor office advised me that my letter from my daughter, Zindzi,[i] has been withheld on the ground that my quota for this month is full.

My daughter will be sitting for an examination soon & she may be raising things relevant to those exams or some problems that it would be advisable to attend to at once. I should, therefore, be pleased if you would kindly arrange for the letter to be given to me at your earliest convenience in lieu of the June quota.
[Signed NRMandela] 466/64

[Note in another hand in Afrikaans]. His request is recommended. It is good let him have it. [Signed by a captain and dated] 21.5.79

To Peter Wellman,[ii] a friend and journalist

Nelson Mandela 466/64

27-5-79

My dear Peter
I was quite flattered to receive your telegram &, even more, by the knowledge that I am godfather to the chdn.

---

i   Zindziswa Mandela, Mandela's youngest daughter – see the glossary.
ii   Peter Wellman (1941-2001) was a journalist on the *Rand Daily Mail* when he met Mandela. He used to drive Mandela's daughters Zenani and Zindziswa to school in Swaziland.

To be godparent is always an intimate honour.[i] For one thing it makes one virtually a member of the family & the fulfilment of its responsibilities is a challenge that affords plenty of joy & satisfaction in my current circs.[ii] The honour has a wider significance which I hope I deserve. A million thanks, Peter!

My present position will of course make it quite difficult, in certain cases even impossible, for me to do what I would have liked to do. But I will always try to let the chdn know that I love them & always think of them. I sincerely hope that soon you will send me a group photo not more than 10 x 15 cms. If I cannot give them chocolates,[iii] put them on my lap, talk, play & sing with them at least they, Pa & Mom can all appear in the family album. Naturally I expect you to give me their full names & dates of birth & a bit of family history. You & Winnie may have tried in the past to tell me that I am godfather & to give me all the relevant information. But your telegram was the very first hint of the fact. Once more, many thanks!

I like you to know that throughout the many yrs of incarceration numerous messages of good wishes & hope sent by people from different walks of life, have cut through massive iron doors & grim stone walls, bringing into the cell the splendour & warmth of springtime. No two messages are ever the same & each one has struck a special note. Yours was typical. Frankly, there are moments, like now, when I feel as if the whole world, or at least the greater part of it, has been squeezed into my tiny cell. I have comparatively more time to think & dream; obsessed with a sense of involvement & with far more friends than ever before. Your telegram pulled me across these waves towards the Golden City[iv] which, from many photographs I have seen, appears to have in many ways changed from the town I once knew so well.

A few slums have been cleared away & the underlying social problems transported elsewhere.[v] In the process beloved nooks & dens cherished in fond memories have been destroyed, & those who once hoped for the day when shacks would become hallowed monuments must start building new shrines.

On the cleared areas modern buildings & skyscrapers, all glittering in wealth & power dominate the scene, while spacious highways crisscross

---

i   Wellman sent Mandela a telegram asking him to be godfather to his daughter Emily.
ii   Circumstances.
iii When Emily Wellman met Mandela after his release he told her that he was sorry he did not send her the chocolates. (Emily Welman in an email to Sahm Venter, 6 September 2017.)
iv   Johannesburg is called the Golden City due its origins as a gold-mining town in the nineteenth century.
v   In order to separate people according to their race, the apartheid government enacted a range of laws including the Group Areas Act which separated residential areas. From the 1950s and right through until the early 1980s, areas were designated for white occupation and black people were forcibly moved from those areas. One of the most well-known of these moves was of the people of Sophiatown, a mixed suburb close to the CBD of Johannesburg. Thousands of people in Johannesburg were moved to the new township of Soweto.

the City bringing widely separated outskirts closer than ever before. In the field of economics, govt, education, and many arts, new faces, eager to live in unconventional ways, have come to the fore, sharpening the generation gap. Aging pessimists may be looking around constantly lest carrion birds notice that death is about to strike.

Thinking about J.H.B.[i] reminds me of my return in '55 to the country village across the Kei[ii] where I grew up. During our young days there was a thick bush that covered a mountain slope. In the valley below, especially on the river banks, there were several imposing trees I thought would stand for all time. Apart from Zami's[iii] love and affection that bush was to me as a child the nearest thing to paradise I ever experienced. Have you ever been out on a fox hunt, togged out in smart riding breeches, shining boots & spurs, with the ponies at full gallop & the hounds yelling? Then you have an idea of how we felt in that bush. Full of wild fruit, a variety of small game & bird life, wild honey, plenty of fresh water & parlangs, the bush attracted almost all the boys in the village.

We hunted rabbits, polecats, partridges & doves & pulled fish from the water. Even when I was at boarding school I returned to the bush during the holidays & enjoyed the chase even more. My early crowded programme in J.H.B. & its attractions never wiped off the mind the pleasant memories of my youth & I thought often of the bush & veld.[iv] After an absence of 15 yrs I returned home & one of the first places I visited was that bush. It was springtime & the vegetation was green. The bush had lost most of its picturesqueness. The once imposing trees on the river bank had either disappeared or withered away & those that were still healthy no longer looked so swaggering. All over the valley vigorous young bushes were asserting themselves. I recalled the words of an English poet who once said ". . . changeth, yielding place to new, & God fulfils himself in many ways, lest one good custom corrupts the world."[v] I have not seen this poem for almost 40 yrs & may have mixed up the lines.[vi] But that is what went through my mind as I surveyed my boyhood paradise. Similar memories, though not so nostalgic, transport me to a world that once was when I see pictures of J.H.B.

I am looking forward to seeing you & family one day. Meantime, my thoughts are in Main Street[vii] particularly after receipt of your telegram.

---

i   Johannesburg
ii   'River'.
iii   One of Winnie's names.
iv   'Field' in Afrikaans.
v   Alfred Lord Tennyson's poem 'Morte d'Arthur' written in 1838.
vi   His quotation is actually very close. The original lines read: 'The old order changeth, yielding place to new. / And God fulfils himself in many ways. / Lest one good custom should corrupt the world.'
vii   A street in Johannesburg.

Hazel once worked with you. If you still see her & Hymie give them my fondest regards. I shake your hand very firmly. Sincerely Nelson

Mr Peter Wellman, 171 Main St, Johannesburg

To Alan Paton,[i] author and leader of the Liberal Party who gave evidence in mitigation of sentence in the Rivonia Trial

Nelson Mandela 466/64   29.7.79

[Note at the top of the letter in Afrikaans] Rejected. Objections to Alan Paton]

Dear Dr Paton,

This is my third attempt to reach you during the last 15 years. I first wrote to you immediately I could send out more than just two letters a year, and I thanked you for your courageous response of June 1964.[ii] It was not so easy those days to come forward as you did and few people are likely to forget that inspiring gesture.

In the second letter I expressed my sympathies on the passing away of your first wife. I pointed out that the tragedy, coming so soon after the death of your friend, Chief Luthuli, must have been exceptionally difficult to endure. I mentioned the Browns,[iii] Kupers[iv] and the late Dr Edgar Brookes[v] and asked you to give all of them my fondest regards.

I hope the letters reached you and that your long silence is due to pressure of engagements. If they did not, then I will hardly blame you if you think our sense of gratitude is not very high. I have taken the precaution of registering this particular one to make sure that it reaches you.

When I and a friend visited their house, Mrs Brown served us with coffee and buttered scones so fresh and soft that they went down before one could chew. Almost two decades have passed since that day, yet the

---

i   Alan Paton (1903–88) – see the glossary.
ii   A refere to the evidence in mitigation of sentence that Paton gave for Mandela and his co-accused at the Rivonia Trial (for the Rivonia Trial, see the glossary).
iii The Browns were members of the Liberal Party.
iv   Hilda Kuper (1911–92), social anthropologist. Her husband, Leo Kuper (1908–94) was a sociologist. They helped to found the Liberal Party in Natal (now KwaZulu-Natal).
v   Edgar Brookes (1987–79), South African Liberal Party politican, professor of history, and author.

memory of that visit has not faded. I also met the Kupers only once; in their house in Durban. Although I am confident that they will never cease burrowing wherever they may be, I was sorry to hear that they had emigrated. Their contribution in the fields of education and literature has been impressive and their exit must have weakened their school of thought in several directions. As a matter of fact, I first heard of their emigration when I was trying to order their work on the African bourgeoisie.[i] Unfortunately, the book was unknown to the firms approved by this Department.[ii] Though I have never had the honour of meeting Dr Brookes, our generation of students in Native Administration,[iii] as the subject was then known, knew of him quite well. He was widely acknowledged as the leading authority on that topic. I was sorry to learn of his death and would be pleased if you would kindly give my condolences to his family.

In March last year my wife told me that you had visited her in Brandfort. Even at our best moments in Johannesburg, such visits always left us with a tremendous feeling. Today they assume a special significance and I was happy to know that many of our friends could have the courage and time to travel to Brandfort[iv] bringing good wishes to the family. I was also pleased to know that you made it possible for my daughter-in-law, Rayne,[v] to return to college. I saw her only once when she came down in 1974. She struck me as a sweet and ambitious child who is keen on education. I hope she will not disappoint those who love and wish her well. The other day I read your article in *Fair Lady*[vi] of January 31 on your visit to Zindzi[vii] in Brandfort. Unfortunately I could neither keep it nor make notes. Still it struck me as a powerful story and a shot in the arm for the young lady. To be introduced to the readers of *Fair Lady* by a well-known and experienced writer is a flattering compliment to Zindzi. When I reached the last line "joy was great and sorrow small."

A few days before I saw your review I had read an article in this month's issue of the *Readers' Digest*. It attempted to analyse the problems facing amateur writers in the country. To illustrate the point, the writer referred to the number of manuscripts received by various publications and the number accepted by each. Among the magazines mentioned in the article is *Fair Lady* which in 1977 received about 700 fiction manuscripts. According to

---

i   Leo Kuper, *African Bourgeoisie: Race, Class and Politics* (New Haven, Yale University Press, 1965). The book was banned by the apartheid government.
ii   The book was banned in South Africa.
iii   Mandela is referring to a subject that he possibly studied at the University College of Fort Hare, which he attended from 1939 to 1940 until he was expelled for embarking on protest action.
iv   Brandfort is around 350 km from Johannesburg by car.
v   Rose Rayne 'Rennie' Mandela, the wife of his son Makgatho.
vi   *Fair Lady* is a South African women's magazine.
vii   Zindziswa Mandela, Mandela's youngest daughter – see the glossary.

the writer, it published only fifty of these most from overseas. In the light of these, I thought it significant that Zindzi's efforts had attracted the attention of such a selective magazine. I will try to keep my hand clean so that I can give you a firm handshake when we meet.

It is because we have many good friends whose support and encouragement has been a source of tremendous inspiration that Zindzi has been inspired to urge the tomorrow to "increase your speed, I eagerly await you."

The family has experienced a lot of problems, some of which you are aware. In my current position it is difficult to handle even such personal problems. It is much more difficult to intervene when such problems go beyond first degree relatives. But if the road between Hillcrest[i] & Brandfort should cave in on the sides & develop potholes, I would do everything in my power to repair it, to clear any debris that might block the free passage of the love and goodwill that characterises the relations between our respective families. Particularly at this moment, I like you never to forget that.

I do not know what works you published during the last 17 years, and I have no means of knowing. All I can tell you is that I am confident that you have not been idle. In fact, last year I heard that an American university had awarded you an honorary doctorate.[ii] Although I have no other information on the matter, I was happy to receive the news. Such an honour was well-deserved. That award has a personal and wider significance. For one thing it shows that your labours have not been in vain, that in spite of persistent droughts and choking weed, you sowed on good ground, that "the harvest is late; has not failed." My love and fondest regards to you and your wife, and to all the friends mentioned above.

Sincerely,
[Signed NR Mandela]

Dr Alan Paton, P.O. Box 278 Hillcrest 3650, Natal.

To Winnie Mandela,[iii] his wife

Nelson Mandela 466/64   2.9.79

---

i   Paton lived in Hillcrest, Natal (now KwaZulu-Natal).
ii   Paton received twelve honorary doctorates during his life, including from Yale University and the Univeristy of Michigan.
iii Nomzamo Winifred Madikizela-Mandela (1936–) – see the glossary.

My darling Mum,

I have handed in two telegrams for dispatch to Nxeko[i] asking him to visit me on an urgent family matter. One I sent c/o Qunu and the other to the Sithebe address. I should like him to act at once.

I fully support your own stand in regard to Jonguhlanga,[ii] but I have been thinking about the matter since I last saw you. I naturally welcome every opportunity you get to travel around & to escape the confinement into which you are forced to live. But I am not in favour of you travelling to Dbn[iii] for a consultation. Such a trip will be expensive to the family as a whole, even if the costs of this particular trip are paid. . . .

As far as Reggie's[iv] decision that you should do some research work and not worry once about the job with the Oppenheimer Hospital, I am not clear in my own mind, simply because I do not have the proper particulars, especially your financial position. But he makes that suggestion you should examine it most carefully. If the proposal entails special problems, then you should discuss them with him . . . .

It pleased me to know that people as far afield as Pmburg[v] have visited you. Apparently Dr Biggs is a well-known orthopaedic surgeon and his wife & Mrs [Coring?] Hall are all familiar names in that province & beyond. Give them a hug on my behalf when you meet them again. . . .

Did Peter Wellman get my letter of 27/5?[vi] You probably will not be able to check on whether Mr Ngakane, P.O. Box 118 Groot Marico, 2850, got his dated June '78.

For this first time since I came here I won't be sending any birthday card to Kgatho.[vii] I don't think it serves much purpose anymore. You probably know that Maki[viii] is back at F.H.[ix] and that she has written the other subjects except Stat Methods which she regards as difficult. She badly wants a job in J.H.B.[x] Though she's prepared to live with Kgatho, I suggested that she stays with someone in town so as to improve her English[xi] and general knowledge.

You will be quite right to regard '79 as women's yr.[xii] They seem to be

---

i   Nxeko (also known as Bambilanga) is the brother of King Sabata Dalindyebo, paramount chief of the Transkei homeland.
ii   King Sabata Jonguhlanga Dalindyebo (1928–86), paramount chief of the Transkei homeland and leader of the Democratic Progressive Party, the opposition party in Transkei which opposed apartheid rule – see the glossary.
iii   Durban.
iv   Oliver Reginald Tambo (1917–93), Mandela's friend, former law partner, and the president of the ANC – see the glossary. His middle name was Reginald and Mandela referred to him as Reggie.
v   Pietermaritzburg.
vi   See his letter, page 375.
vii   Makgatho Mandela (1950–2005), Mandela's second-born son – see the glossary.
viii Makaziwe Mandela (1954–), Mandela's eldest daughter – see the glossary.
ix   University College of Fort Hare, Alice in the Ciskei homeland – see the glossary.
x   Johannesburg.
xi   Makaziwe's first language was isiXhosa.
xii   The United Nations had named 1975, four years earlier, International Women's Year.

demanding that society lives up to its sermons on sex equality. The French lady Simone Veil has lived through frightful experiences[i] to become President of the European Parliament, while Maria Pintasilgo cracks the whip in Portugal. From reports it is not clear who leads the Carter family. There are times when Carter's Rosalynn[ii] seems to be wearing the trousers. I need hardly mention the name of Margaret Thatcher. Despite the collapse of her world-wide empire & her emergence from the Second World War as a 3rd-rate power, Britain is in many respects still the centre of the world. What happens there attracts attention from far & wide.

Indira[iii] will rightly remind us that in this respect Europe is merely following the example of Asia which in the last 2 decades has produced no less than 2 lady premiers. Indeed she may have added that past centuries have seen many female rulers. Isabella of Spain, Elizabeth I of England, Catherine the Great of Russia (how great she really was, I don't know), the Batlokwa queen, Mantatisi, and many more. But all these became first ladies in spite of themselves – through heredity. Today the spotlight falls on these women who had pulled themselves up by their own bootstraps. For these '79 has yielded quite a harvest.

Matlala's[iv] case is quite touching and emphasises the tragedy of life hardly apparent to many. I think of her every year on 18/7 & I only hope that telepathic waves are able to link us across the miles on such days. Please give her our love and congratulations.

On 16/8 orthopaedic surgeon, Dr Breitenbach examined my right heel which worries me now & again. I will discuss the matter further with Dr Edelstein on his next round to the island. That morning the *Dias* carried me to C.T.[v] the sea was rough & though I occupied a sheltered spot on the deck it seemed rain was falling.[vi] The boat rocked on endlessly taking the waves, on its brows. Midway between the island & C.T. an army of demons seemed to be on the rampage and, as the *Dias* was tossed about, it seemed as if a thousand irons were falling apart. I kept my eyes constantly on a life-belt a few paces away. There were about 5 officials in between me and the belt, 2 young enough to be my grandsons. I said to myself "If something happens and this boat goes under, I will commit my last sin on earth and humbly repent when I reach the Holy City. I will run over them all and be the first on that belt." Fortunately there was no disaster.

---

i   Simone Veil (1927–2017) was a Holocaust survivor.
ii   Rosalynn Carter (1927–), wife of US president Jimmy Carter.
iii Indira Gandhi (1917–84), prime minister of India 1966–99 and 1980–84.
iv   A nickname for Adelaide Tambo (1929–2007), friend, anti-apartheid activisit, and wife of Oliver Tambo, Mandela's former law partner and president of the ANC – see the glossary. The Tambos were living in exile in London.
v   Cape Town.
vi   Robben Island prisoners were occasionally sent to Cape Town to see medical specialists.

But about you, darling Mum, what can I tell you? At 45 you have changed so much from the night we sat alone in the open veld[i] south of the city.

Remember the night after we entertained Gwigwi & others? Yet as the youth drains away from your veins as your once full & smooth face shows signs of erosion and the magnetic complexion that made you so desirable in the 50s continues to fade, the more you become adorable, the more I long to cuddle up to you. You are everything a Mum should be. Happy birthday, darling Mum! I LOVE YOU!

Devotedly, Madiba

Nkosk Nobandla Mandela, 802 Phatakahle Location, P.O. Box Brandfort, 9400

To the minister of prisons and police

NELSON MANDELA 466/64

4th September 1979

The Commanding Officer
Robben Island

Attention: Brig Botha

I should be pleased if you would kindly approve of the attached letter to the Minister of Prisons, which speaks for itself, and forward it to him through the normal channels.

[Signed NRMandela]

4th September 1979

The Honourable Mr L Le Grange,[ii]
Minister of Prisons and Police
Pretoria

---

i   'Field' in Afrikaans.
ii   Louis Le Grange (1928–91), minister of prisons, 1979–80, and minister of police, 1979–82 – see the glossary.

Dear Sir,

On several occasions during the past decade we, the political prisoners on Robben Island, made representations to the Government that we be released from incarceration and that, pending such release, we be treated as political prisoners.

Our first request to this effect was made in a letter dated 22nd April, 1969, addressed to Mr P. Pelser, then Minister of Prisons,[i] in which our arguments were set out. Mr Pelser did not even have the courtesy to reply to our letter, in spite of our written reminder to him in 1971. We again broached the matter with your predecessor, Mr J.T. Kruger, but like Mr Pelser he did not respond.

In 1973 we added to this principal request that of the introduction of a non-racial administration in the Department of Prisons. By this we meant, and still mean, not an administration manned by Blacks, but one in which prison personnel will be appointed on merit, and who will be free from racial prejudice.

We further asked that all members of Umkhonto weSizwe, who are arrested in the course of their operations, be granted the status of prisoners-of-war in terms of the 1977 Geneva Convention which has been accepted by civilised governments in different parts of the world. We also urge your Government to allow political prisoners, Black and White, to be kept together in one prison. In pursuance of this request, we ask for the immediate transfer of White political prisoners from Pretoria Prison to this Island.

Our request for recognition as political prisoners will include, among others, the following rights:

1.   to have contact visits from members of our family, friends and relatives,

2.   to be released on remission, parole or probation,

3.   to mix freely with other political prisoners on the island and, to this end, to terminate the segregation of prisoners from one another,

4.   to be allowed to acquire radios and newspapers,

5.   to write to, and receive from, members of the family, relatives and friends (irrespective of their colour or political association) an unlimited number of letters,

---

i   See his letter on page 82.

6. to study any course or subject with a recognised educational institution local or abroad,

7. to train in some skill or trade,

8. to receive sums of money from any charitable institution or person for our personal use, and to be allowed to use for, or transfer to, those who have none,

9. to have access to all unbanned books and other publications,

10. to write and publish books, memoirs and essays and to keep diaries,

11. to have a non-racial diet and, until the introduction of such a diet, to be allowed to purchase such types and quantities as we may wish,

12. to purchase groceries and toilets according to one's personal means and taste and, to this end, to terminate the practice of classifying political prisoners in groups which debar them from doing so,

13. to move freely on the island,

14. to acquire and wear civilian clothing in accordance with one's personal taste,

15. to have access to our legal representatives and to be able to conduct legal consultations in such a manner as to remove any suspicion that the Department of Prisons is interfering, directly or indirectly, with the right of privileged communication between prisoners and their legal representatives.

It is a well-known fact that common-law prisoners, many of whom were convicted of the most heinous offences, are allowed contact visits, radios and newspapers. They are released on remission, parole or probation. But these privileges are not accorded to political prisoners whose only offence is that they fought against a racial policy and for their inherent right to human freedom and dignity.

Our fight for freedom and equality is not unique in South Africa. Reference was made in our letter of 22nd April 1969 to the struggle of the Afrikaner people against British domination. Political changes were sought through violence, but unlike us, the culprits were treated as political prisoners, although they were convicted of the crime of high treason.

The inconsistency in treatment is obvious and patently racial. Soon after the present Government assumed office, it released Robey Leibrandt[i] and others convicted of high treason for colluding with a foreign power during the war.

Even more glaring is the discriminatory treatment of Black and White political offenders. White students who were convicted of sabotage in the mid-sixties were released from prison before they had completed their respective sentences.[ii] On the other hand, no such indulgence has been shown to the Black students and youth jailed in the course of the 1976 demonstrations. These demonstrations were spontaneous and perfectly justified, sparked off as they were by the 'Government''s enforcement of unjust and unpopular measures in African schools.[iii] That these measures were later withdrawn is a tacit admission by the State that it erred in introducing them in the first place. Paradoxically, the young men who were wronged are still behind bars.

We are convinced that the leniency shown to those who participated in the 1914 Rebellion, and in the treasonable activities of the Second World War were clearly prompted by the fact that they were whites.

Since the early sixties with the exception of about forty Whites, the overwhelming majority of political prisoners were Blacks. Obviously, the Government is reluctant to grant the status of political prisoners to Blacks who challenge White supremacy and the discrimination which flows from it.

We are the victims of a situation which is not of our making, and we place full responsibility for the explosive situation that now prevails in the country in the hands of the Government. They, and they alone, have the power to prevent the coming national catastrophe, and it is our sacred duty to warn you not to drag the country into civil war merely to defend racial oppression.

It is time the Government revised their entire approach to the question of political prisoners, especially in the light of recent statements by senior Government spokesmen and cabinet ministers which condemn racialism and which proclaim the equality of all human beings regardless of their

---

i   Sidney Robey Leibbrandt (1913–66), the South African heavyweight boxing champion, was led by the German military intelligence under the pseudonym 'Robert Leibbrand'. He was a South African Boer of German and Irish descent.

ii   See his letter from 22 April 1969 on page 82.

iii   Students wre protesting against the Afrikaans Medium Decree, which required all black schools to use a fifty-fifty mix of Afrikaans and English in their lessons, and some subjects to be taught solely in Afrikaans.

colour. If our information is correct, and if the Government's intentions are not merely propagandistic, there appears to be a shift in their policy. This makes our case to be treated as political prisoners even stronger.

Moreover, it is incumbent on the State to reopen the case of each and every prisoner convicted in the country's courts for cases which basically spring from the Government's discriminatory policies and denial of basic human rights to Blacks. The penalties imposed on us, ranging from five years to life imprisonment, have been savage, to say the least. It is a travesty of justice to sentence to imprisonment an opponent of racial discrimination. To this end, we urge you to create an independent panel of jurists to review our sentences. Many of us have been in prison for over ten years, some as many as seventeen years. Even a year of a prisoner's lifetime in prison is deprivation enough, let alone seventeen years.

We are once again placing our representations to you in the hope that you will give them urgent and serious attention, and then you will advise us of your decision in due course.

Yours faithfully,
[Signed NRMandela]
NELSON MANDELA

[Signed Raymond Mhlaba]
RAYMOND MHLABA

To the commanding officer, Robben Island

Nelson Mandela 466/64

19th November 1979

The Commanding Officer,
Robben Island.

Attention: Brig Botha

I should be pleased if you would be good enough to approve the attached letter to the Commissioner of Prisons. Both the said letter and annexure speak for themselves.

[Signed NRMandela]
Nelson Mandela 466/64

19th November 1979

The Honourable Mr Louis L. Le Grange,
Minister of Police and Prisons,
Pretoria.

Dear Sir,

1. In terms of the Prison Rules and Regulations I am entitled to two visits
    a month. During the past two years my wife has tried without success
    to take advantage of the privilege. In May 1977 she was deported from
    Johannesburg to Brandfort where she is now restricted under the pro-
    visions of the Internal Security Act, 1950. Although the Department of
    Prisons readily gives her a permit to visit me for two days, the magis-
    trate of Brandfort refuses her permission to leave the district for more
    than one day. For this reason, she is unable to come to the Island for
    two successive days. In the belief that the objection against her seeing
    me for two days had come from the South African Police, I discussed
    the matter with the Head of the Security Police, Brig Coetzee, last
    February. He, however, assured me that the objection did not come
    from the S.A.P.;[i] but that it was a decision which was taken by the
    Department of Justice independently; an assurance which I accepted.*

    Four months ago I placed the matter before the Commissioner
    of Prisons in the hope that he would take it up with the Minister of
    Justice. I further asked that, pending a decision on the issue, each visit
    from my wife should be extended to at least one and a half hours. To
    date the Commissioner has not responded to my request.

    When I became aware that my wife intended visiting me on the
    17th and 18th of this month I gave the Commanding Officer an urgent
    telegram addressed to you, in which I requested you to arrange with
    your colleague, the Minister of Justice, for my wife to be allowed by
    the Magistrate to visit me on the above dates. But the Commanding
    Officer did not forward the telegram for reasons which were explained
    to me. As I expected, the Magistrate permitted my wife to see me on
    the 17th only. However, at my request this Department extended the
    visit to one and a half hours.

    I must add that an extended visit is an extraordinary measure which

_____

i   South African Police.

creates problems for the administration, my wife and for me into which I do not propose to enter. I should, therefore, appreciate it if you would discuss the whole matter with the Minister of Justice at your earliest possible convenience. Meantime, my wife has applied to visit me on the 25th and 26th of next month and I am keen to see her on these days.

2. I must also draw attention to another condition which the magistrate invariably imposes on my wife when she pays me a visit. He insists that she should travel between Bloemfontein and Cape Town by air. He knows quite well that she cannot get employment in Brandfort and that for the past two years she has been unemployed. In the circumstances, the condition has the effect of making it difficult for her to visit me. I should accordingly be pleased if you would also take up the matter with your colleague.

3. The final point I should like you to examine is the manner in which the letters I write to my wife are handled in transit. She informs me that many of them reach her in a mutilated or illegible condition. According-ing to her some of them appear to have been treated with chemicals. I believe this is the result of tests carried out by the Security Police to ascertain whether the letters contain any invisible writing. I have written letters from prison to my wife for the last seventeen years. If the police have never found any secret messages in those letters through-out this period, that means that I do not use my correspondence to take out messages. In the circumstance, it does not appear to me reasonable for the police to continue defacing the letters. This practice is applied indiscriminately to our private correspondence and to privileged communications between clients and their legal representatives. In the letter she wrote to me on the 29th October 1979 she informed me that a letter from a Durban attorney which dealt with a privileged matter was similarly mutilated. I place the matter before you in the belief that you are not aware of this practice; and in the hope that you will give it your immediate attention.

Yours faithfully,
[Signed NRMandela]

*P.S. Representations made to the Minister of Justice by my wife's legal representatives for a relaxation of this restriction have been unsuccessful.

[Signed NRMandela]

◇◇◇◇◇◇◇◇

This letter to Mandela's youngest daughter, Zindziswa, was never sent. It was discovered in the National Archives and Record Service of South Africa with a note from prison officials reading: 'The attached piece that prisoner Mandela included with his Christmas card will not be sent. The card will be sent. The prisoner has not been informed that this piece has been rejected. He does not have permission to include it with the card. I discussed this on 20 December 1979 with Brigadier du Plessis and he agrees with the decision. Keep it in his file.'

===

To Zindzi Mandela,[i] his youngest daughter

Nelson Mandela 466/64   9.12.79

My darling Zindzi,

I sometimes wonder what happened to our boxing gym at what used to be called St Joseph's in Orlando East. The walls of that school and of the D.O.C.C.[ii] are drenched with sweet memories that will delight me for yrs. When we trained at the D.O.C.C. in the early 50s the club included amateur & professional boxers as well as wrestlers. The club was managed by Johannes (Skip Adonis) Molosi, a former champ & a capable trainer who knew the history, theory and practical side of the game.

Unfortunately, in the mid-50s he began neglecting his duties and would stay away from the gym for long periods.

Because of this, the boxers revolted. Twice I settled the matter, but when Skip failed to pay heed to repeated protests from the boxers, things reached breaking point. This time I was totally unable to reconcile the parties. The boxers left the D.O.C.C. & opened their own gym at St Joseph's. Thembi[iii] and I went along with them. Simon Tshabalala, who is now abroad, became the manager, & the star boxer was, of course, still Jerry (Uyinja) Moloi who later became the Tvl[iv] lightweight champ and leading contender for the

---

i   Zindziswa Mandela (1960–) – see the glossary
ii   The Donaldson Orlando Community Centre was a community space in Soweto that hosted dances, concerts, and boxing matches. It was built by the Donaldson Trust, established in 1936 by Lieutenant Colonel James Donaldson D.S.O. to 'advance the status, improve the conditions and remove the disabilities suffered by the black African population of South Africa; and generally to seek their benefit and betterment'. Nelson Mandela used to box there in the 1940s and 1950s and spent many of his evenings training at the gym with his eldest son, Thembi.
iii   Madiba Thembekile (Thembi) Mandela (1945–69), Mandela's eldest son – see the glossary.
iv   Transvaal.

national title. Apart from Jerry we produced 3 other champs: Eric (Black Material) Ntsele who won the national bantamweight from Leslie Tanjee, Freddie (Tomahawk) Ngidi who became Tvl flyweight champ, a title which was later held by one of our gym mates, Johannes Mokotedi. There were other good prospects like Peter, the flyweight, who built our garage at home. He hailed from Bloemfontein & was a student at the Vacation School in Dube. Thembi himself was a good boxer & on occasions I sat until very late at night waiting for him to return from a tournament in Randfontein, Vereeniging[i] or other centres. I and my gym mates were a closely knit family and when Mum came into the picture that family became even more intimate. Jerry & Eric even drove Mum around when I could not do so and the entire gym turned up at our engagement party.

By the way, Freddie worked for our firm as a clerk. He was quiet & reliable and the entire staff was fond of him. But on one Xmas eve I returned to the office & who did I find lying flat & helpless in the passage just outside the general office? Freddie. His appearance so shocked me that I rushed him to a doctor. The quack gave him one quick look & assured me that the champ was O.K. but that he needed more sleep. He had succumbed to the usual Xmas sprees & over-indulged himself. I drove him to his home at OE[ii] quite relieved. Incidentally, I should have told you that during the dispute at the D.O.C.C. Skip accused Jerry of stabbing him in the back just as Mark Antony betrayed his friend Caesar. Thembi asked who Antony & Caesar were. At the time Thembi was only 9. Skip explained, * "Don't tell us about people who are dead." If I had not been there Skip would have pulled out the child's bowels, so furious he was. He bitterly complained to me about what he considered to be discourtesy on the part of the boy. I reminded him that in my house I was the patriarch & ruled over the household. But that I had no such powers in the gym; that Thembi had paid membership fees, we were perfect equals & I could give him no instructions.

We would spend about 1½ hrs in the gym & I was at home about 9 pm. Tired & with hardly a drop of water in my body. Mum would give me a glass of fresh and cold orange juice, supper served with well-prepared sour milk. Mum was gloweth with good health & happiness those dys. The house was like a beehive with the family, old school friends, fellow workers from Bara,[iii] members of the gym & even clients calling at the house to chat with her. For more than 2 yrs she and I literally lived on honey-moon. I quietly resisted any activity that kept me away from home after office hrs. Yet she & I kept warning each other that we were living on borrowed time,

i   Both places are between 50 to 60 km from Johannesburg.
ii   Orlando East.
iii Baragwanath Hospital in Soweto, Johannesburg, where Winnie Mandela worked as a social worker.

that hard times would soon knock at the door. But we were having a great time with good friends & we did not have much time for self-pity. It is more than 2 decades since then, yet I recall those dys so clearly as if everything happened yesterday.

But this letter, darling is not about old boxing mates, school friends and social workers or even about Mum. It is meant for a lovely young lady whose picture is always in my mind, a go getter who makes Mum & me dangerously proud of being parents. As I write this letter, her photo and that of her sister are on the book case on my left with the frames of the 2 photos touching each other & with a simple blue rosary strung on them for ornament. It has a sentimental value as it reminds me of our connection with the Catholic church through "Our Lady of Sorrows".[i] That young lady is none other than our lady Mantu Nobutho Zindzi, you Nkosazana.[ii]

On the 23/12 you will be 19 & I send you my love and congrats. Mum tells me that you will be here on that Sunday & I am looking forward to it with great expectation. Until then, I will keep my fingers crossed. Someone once said that happy couples get happy children & happy children make happy families and happy nations. May you be blessed with all these, Mantu.

Again, Many Happy Returns & the best of health.

Tons and tons of love and a million kisses, darling. Affectionately, Tata.[iii]

Miss Zindzi Mantu Nobutho Mandela
802 Phathakahle, P.O. Brandfort 9400, OFS

[*] your brother hit back

———

To the head of prison, Robben Island

NELSON MANDELA 466/64   23.12.79

Head of Prison
Robben Island

---

i   Our Lady of Sorrows was the Roman Catholic boarding school in Swaziland that Zindziswa was attending.
ii   *Nkosazana* means 'Miss' or 'princess' in isiXhosa.
iii   'Father' in isiXhosa.

Attention: Major Harding

The attached letter to my wife dated 9.12.'79 was returned to me by the Censor Office with instructions to rewrite it and to leave out the entire first page. In this connection I should appreciate it if you would be good enough to arrange for the same letter to be posted to my wife as it is. The page to which they object contains not a single sentence or even a word that can reasonably be interpreted as reflecting against government policy, the Prisons Department or as threatening state security or violating discipline.

The letter discusses a domestic issue relating to our son-in-law. It is a reply to the enclosed letter from my wife, dated 23.9.79, and the relevant passage appears on pages 3 and 4 and is underlined with red ink. That letter, and the paragraph in particular, was approved by the same censors and released to me. As you will readily realise on reading that paragraph, my remarks are intended to persuade my wife to see the problem against a broader perspective and not to judge the parties involved too harshly. I urge her to concentrate mainly on the creative and positive aspect of those involved.

I do not know whether any of the censors on the Island are proficient in the language in which the letter from my wife is written. But in your office there are men who have a thorough understanding of that language and you would be perfectly at liberty to get them to interpret it for you.

I must draw your attention to the fact that to write a letter is, in my present state of health, quite a torture. In spite of the speedy improvement of the heel, I still cannot sit comfortably at a table. Whenever I try to do so, the heel starts swelling up. In the circumstances, I hope you will not force me to rewrite the letter.

I must further draw your attention to the fact that we have repeatedly requested the censors not to mark returned letters with a ballpoint, but instead to use a pencil. The advantage of this procedure is that when a prisoner wins his appeal to superior officers, he will not be put into the trouble and expense of rewriting the same letter. To the best of my knowledge and belief, almost every past Commanding Officer on this Island recognised that this request is reasonable and fair, and approved of it readily. For quite some time that procedure was followed by the censors, but now they have gone back to the earlier practice.

I trust that you will give the matter your earliest and earnest attention. I might add that my wife is a responsible and experienced person, and your problems will not be multiplied if she receives the letter with the line across

Robben Island 7400
South Africa.
8 1 80.

Dear Mr Healey,

I crave your indulgence in a personal matter, and unfortunately this 'Special Letter' is confined to that purpose. I should be grateful if you would be so kind as to arrange a scholarship in England for my grand-niece, Miss Xoliswa Matanzima, whose present address is 19 Nattergasse 21/4, 1170 Wien, Austria. She is the daughter of my nephew, Chief K. D. Matanzima, President of Transkei. Partly to the encouragement of her parents and partly to that of my wife and I, Xoliswa undertook studies abroad. But she is experiencing certain difficulties in Austria.

Her Austrian scholarship for a senior degree in political science will only be tenable in 1981. In the meantime she will have to spend a year to master the German language. Even if she overcomes the language hurdle next February, she is doubtful that she will be sufficiently proficient to undertake a senior degree.

I must stress that she is a talented, industrious and determined person, and has pledged to complete her degree in German if all else fails. Her difficulties will be eased if she studies in the English medium, preferably in England. Attempts are being made to obtain a United Nations Scholarship for her. Even if this is successful, our preference is that the scholarship should be tenable in England. Please contact her for any particulars you may require.

An added problem is that she lives in a flat, the rent of which will be borne by a certain undertaking only up to May 1980, after which she has to meet the rent herself.

If I were free I would have handled these problems myself but, in the circumstances, I am forced to shift my responsibilities to my good friends. You may discuss this matter with my friends, Lord Astor and Mrs Barbara Castle. To whom please convey my fond regards.

I recall with nostalgic memories my meetings with you, Lord Astor, the late Mr Hugh Gaitskill and again with you on Robben Island in September 1970. Our lengthy discussions with Mrs Castle in Johannesburg in the fifties are also unforgettable.

Good health and cheer to you, your family and to all friends, my family and I are well.

Sincerely Yours
NRMandela

Mr Denis Healey,
The House of Commons
London, England.

A letter to Denis Healey, 8 January 1980, see opposite and overleaf.

the front page. All that I need tell her is that the page was crossed out in good faith and through no fault of any particular person.

[Signed NRMandela]

To Denis Healey, Labour Party member of Parliament, UK[i]

8.1.80

Dear Mr Healey,

I crave your indulgence in a personal matter and unfortunately this 'special letter' is confined to that purpose.

I should be grateful if you would be so kind as to arrange a scholarship in England for my grand-niece, Miss Xoliswa Matanzima, whose present address is 17 Nattergasse 21/4, 1170 Wien, Austria. She is the daughter of my nephew, Chief K.D. Matanzima, President of Transkei.[ii] Partly to the encouragement of her parents and partly to that of my wife and I, Xoliswa undertook studies abroad. But she is experiencing certain difficulties in Austria.

Her Austrian scholarship for a senior degree in Political Science will only be tenable in 1981. In the meantime she will have to spend a year to master the German language. Even if she overcomes the language hurdle next February, she is doubtful that she will be sufficiently proficient to undertake a senior degree.

I must stress that she is a talented, industrious and determined person, and has pledged to complete her degree in German if all else fails. Her difficulties will be eased if she studies in the English medium, preferably in England. Attempts are being made to obtain a United Nations scholarship for her. Even if this is successful, our preference is that the scholarship should be tenable in England. Please contact her for any particulars you may require.

An added problem is that she lives in a flat, the rent of which will be borne by a certain undertaking only up to May 1980, after which she has to meet the rent herself.

If I were free I would have handled these problems myself but, in the circumstances, I am forced to shift my responsibilities to my good friends.

---

i   Mandela first met Healey (1917–2015) on a short visit to London in 1962. Later Healey visited him in prison.
ii   K. D. Matanzima (1915– 2003), Mandela's nephew, a Thembu chief, and chief minister for the Transkei – see the glossary. He was Xoliswa Matanzima's father.

You may discuss the matter with my friends, Lord Astor[i] and Mrs Barbara Castle,[ii] to whom please convey my fond regards.

I recall with nostalgic memories my meetings with you, Lord Astor, the late Mr Hugh Gaitskell[iii] and again with you on Robben Island in September 1970. Our lengthy discussions with Mrs Castle in Johannesburg in the fifties are also unforgettable.

Good health and cheer to you, your family and to all friends. My family and I are well.

Sincerely yours,
[Signed NRMandela]

Mr Denis Healey,
The House of Commons
London, England

To Zindzi Mandela,[iv] his youngest daughter

Nelson Mandela 466/64   27.1.80

My darling,

Seventy-nine was a good yr for me. The pressures that Mum has endured for so long continued to ease.[v] At the worst of time, she has always been able to give me a seductive smile. But that smile flickered through a lifeless skin stretched out over bone & cartilage. This time there was blood in her cheeks, fire in her eyes & she became an inch taller after getting the Unisa exam results. Seeing her in that healthy & gay mood makes me feel really good.

During the yr you were here 6 times & I got 9 letters from you, each one bringing much love & good wishes. Apart from the several telegrams you sent I also received from you, birthday & Xmas cards. All these help to

---

i   During his incarceration, Mandela received financial support from people such as the British newspaper publisher David Astor (1912–2001).
ii   British Labour Party MP Barbara Castle.
iii   Politican and leader of the British Labour Party 1955–63.
iv   Zindziswa Mandela – see the glossary
v   Winnie Mandela was still living in the rural township of Brandfort in the Orange Free State (now Free State), where she had been banished in 1977. She lived there until 1985.

iron out the wrinkles of advancing age, makes all limbs flexible & the blood to flow smoothly.

I still remember when I saw you on 20 & 21/10, you were really striking in your pantaloons & every fabric in your garments seemed to be crying out for attention, urging all around to take note that "this young lady across the partition is Mantu".[i] The impact of your visit on 23/12[ii] is still fresh in my mind. It was a significant gesture for a young lady to spend her 19th birthday crossing & recrossing the polluted waters of the Atlantic. Your visits calm the nostalgic feeling that immediately wells up when I think of how you & me used to play at home & in the other dens in which I used to live. As usual you left me in a tremendous mood. I will always treasure the memory of that visit.

On 14/1 I sent you a telegram of good wishes in your exams & I hope that you received it. Did you get my letter of 9/12[iii] & the Xmas card? Again I wish you the best of luck, darling. I sincerely hope that the eccentric young man who embarrassed you as you walked into the exam room last June was trapped by hurricanes & floods & that he did not turn up this time.

Do tell Grandpa Mdingi[iv] that in response to my enquiries, the G.P.O.[v] informed me that the condolence telegram I sent him on 17/9 could not be delivered "on technical grounds". The strange thing is that a relative of the Mdingis also sent a similar telegram on the same day to the same person at the same address. His telegram crashed through the web of "technical problems" & reached. I have made further enquiries about the one that did not reach you.

I am also sending you Maki's[vi] F.H.[vii] exam results from which you will see that she did rather well. Please show them to Granny Amina[viii] as soon as you can & then leave them with Ismail[ix] probably for the Memon Bursary Fund. Rennie[x] is worried about the results, especially Biology. I wish her well. After all that she has gone through, she deserves a pass.

Black As I Am[xi] turned out to be something quite different from what I had imagined. I don't know to what extent you and Mum were in actual

---

i   One of Zindziswa Mandela's names.
ii   Zindziswa Mandela's birthday.
iii   See his letter on page 390.
iv   This is most likely Chief Mndingi, a relative of Mandela's and the Thembu chief who named Mandela's two younger daughters. The eldest he named Zenani, meaning 'What have you brought?', and the Madikizelas (Winnie Mandela's family) named her Nomadabi Nosizwe, meaning 'battlefield of the nation'. Chief Mndingi named the youngest daughter Mantu Nobutho Zindziswa.
v   General Post Office.
vi   Makaziwe Mandela (1954–), Mandela's eldest daughter – see the glossary.
vii   University College of Fort Hare, Alice in the Ciskei homeland – see the glossary..
viii Amina Cachalia (1930–2013), friend and anti-apartheid and women's rights activist – see the glossary.
ix   Ismail Ayob (1942–), Mandela's attorney – see the glossary.
x   Mandela's daughter-in-law and mother of his grandson Thembi.
xi   Zindzi Mandela's book of poetry *Black As I Am* (Los Angeles: Guild of Tutors Press, 1978).

control of the joint project. The arrangement of the outside cover, the precedence of biographical notes and the contents of each note gave the impression that you were both on the sidelines. I was also not aware that the same firm that published *Black As I Am* was given the right to bring out *Black and Fourteen*. I wish you had consulted me first and fully about the matter, because I would have discussed the matter with you and Mum and advised differently.

You will no doubt realise the permanent impact good literature can make. Remember that Homer wrote about 1200 B.C. and yet his works still appeal to this dy. But this is an aspect which need not at all worry you. All things considered, you have done more than I expected. What Kenneth Rexroth has said about your poetry, sums up my own views remarkably well.[i] I would have thought that the excellent photography in the book[ii] would overshadow the poetry, leaving it only to Mum and Tata[iii] to appreciate it. Thinking about the matter now after seeing the book, I felt that it was just as well that it was a joint venture and that in its actual planning for publication you may have played second fiddle.

It is even more remarkable that the poetry has actually stolen the thunder and towered above the photography.[iv] Your pen is as talkative as our darling Mantu. But the ideas reveal a depth and maturity that should be reserved for older hands.

Good verse and photography can give even poverty, with all its rags, filth and vermin a measure of divineness rarely noticeable in real life. The old man at page 29 looks really strong and majestic. I find it difficult to forget his calm and confident bearing. The weeping lady at page 48 looks like our neighbour, Mrs Mtimkulu. The only difference is that she looks younger than our neighbours should now be.

Our darling Mum was here this morning and yesterday and she tells me that you were happy about the papers that you have so far written, may everything go well, Mantu. Is Nomfundo[v] working now? I no longer know which of my old friends are still at Bara.[vi] They have probably retired by now or moved to other areas. Do let me know more about her in your next letter.

---

i   In his endorsement for the book American poet and essayist Kenneth Rexroth (1905–83) wrote: 'The poems of Zindzi Mandela are astonishing. They are not only deeply moving and poetically wrought with great skill – an astonishing accomplishment for a young woman of sixteen years – but they are completely self-confident and completely devoid of self-pity.' (*Black As I Am*, Los Angeles: Guild of Tutors Press, 1978.) Zindzi was actually eighteen when the book was published.
ii   The photographs were by award-winning photographer Peter Magubane (1932–).
iii   IsiXhosa for 'father'.
iv   The photographs in *Black As I Am* portrayed images of township life for black South Africans.
v   He is most likely referring to Olive Nomfundo Mandela, daughter of Mandela's sister Notancu.
vi   Baragwanath Hospital in Soweto, Johannesburg.

Give Nkosazana Mdingi, Mfundo, Violet[i], Kgomotso and husband[ii] my love and fondest regards. Tons and tons of love and a million kisses to you.

Affectionately, Tata.

Miss Zindzi Mantu Mandela, 8115 Orlando West, PO Phirima, 1848

════════════

To the minister of education c/o head of prison

Nelson Mandela 466/64   Robben Island
                                                       1st February 1980
The Honourable Mr J.N.H. Jansen,
Minister of National Education

Dear Sir,

My daughter, Zindziswa,[iii] has this year applied for admission to the University of the Witwatersrand for the Degree of Bachelor of Arts. The University has accepted her application subject to your approval.

In requesting your approval, I should like to draw your attention to the fact that in May 1977 my wife was banished to the district of Brandfort where she is now restricted. When my wife was deported, my daughter was on school holiday at our Orlando home and she was then removed together with her mother to Brandfort. She was thus compelled to give up school in Swaziland, where she was doing her A Levels for the General Certificate of Education, in order to keep her mother company in Brandfort.

Since the deportation of my wife, we have experienced considerable difficulties in getting a caretaker for the house. Finally, my daughter had to return home to look after it. If you approve of her application to study at the above university, she will be able to look after the house and at the same time to further her studies.

I should like to add that my daughter is only 19 and still needs the care and guidance of her mother. For this reason, she travels to Brandfort every weekend and returns to Orlando on Mondays.[57] For these reasons the University of the Witwatersrand is the most convenient institution in which

---

i   *Nkosazana* means 'Miss' or 'princess' in isiXhosa.
ii   These are most likely to be family members.
iii Zindziswa Mandela (1960), Mandela's youngest daughter – see the glossary

to study. No other university in this country is as suitable as this one.

I am placing the matter before you in the hope that you will consider it purely on merit and grant my daughter the required permission.

Yours faithfully,
[Signed NRMandela]
N R MANDELA

To Zindzi Mandela,[i] his youngest daughter[ii]

Nelson Mandela 466/64   10.2.80

My darling Mantu,

The other day I was going through the notes I took from *Black As I Am*.[iii] Unfortunately, the actual book is no longer in my possession, & although I can now read the collection a little more carefully, I do not have the advantage of studying each poem with the help of the accompanying photography.[iv] Nevertheless, when I first saw the anthology, I took the necessary precaution that may help me to remember the associated picture whenever I dealt with a particular poem.

Reading a tree was chopped down[v] with the picture of the dry tree above it clear in my mind, & with the shanties & mountain range in the background, I was immediately fascinated by the symbolism of contradictions that clearly looms from the lines. It is this type of contradiction that is inherent in almost every aspect of life. In nature & society these contradictions are in the centre of every phenomenon & can stimulate the urge for serious thinking & real progress.

Without the lines below, the tree would look less than ordinary. Hardly anybody would even notice it. It seems to have been struck by lightning during the Stone Age & its sap to have been drained by a thousand vam-

---

i   Zindziswa Mandela (1960–), Mandela's youngest daughter – see the glossary
ii   There are various versions of this letter in Mandela's prison file, including one written on 20 March 1980.
iii   Zindzi Mandela's book of poetry, *Black As I Am* (Los Angeles: Guild of Tutors Press, 1978).
iv   The photographs were by award-winning South African photographer Peter Magubane (1932–).
v   One of the poems in the book, 'A Tree is Chopped Down', refers to Zindzi's family being separated. 'A tree was chopped down / and the fruit was scattered / I cried / because I had lost a family / the trunk, my father / the branches, his support / so much / the fruit, the wife and children / who meant so much to him / tasty / loving as they should be / all on the ground / the roots, happiness / cut off from him.' (Zindzi Mandela, *Black As I Am*, Los Angeles: Guild of Tutors Press, 1978.)

pires. If inanimate objects could ever become ghosts, that tree would easily have been one.

Age or disease have destroyed it. It can no longer trap the energy of sunlight nor draw the vital water supplies from the soil below. Its branches & its leaves, its beauty & dignity that once caught the eye of nature lovers & game of all kinds have disappeared. The tree is no more than firewood on roots. It is as barren as an iron-stone & few people will easily believe that at some stage in the course of its history it could bear fruit.

Yet the metaphor has turned that same dead spectacle into a living object of tremendous meaning, more significant than a young & healthy tree in a fertile & well-watered valley; with a range as wide as that of David's sling of Biblical fame. There must be few things in nature that are so dead & deadly at one & the same time as that wretched looking tree. But in verse it ceases to be an insignificant object in a local area & becomes a household possession, part of world art that helps to cater for the spiritual needs of readers in many countries. The skilful use of the metaphor makes the tree the centre of a conflict that is as old as society itself; the point where two worlds meet: The one that was & the other that is; the symbol of a dream house raised to the ground, of hopes shattered by the actual reality in which we live out our lives.

Good art is invariably universal & timeless & those who read your anthology may see in those lines their own aspirations & experiences. I wonder what conflicts in Mum's thoughts & feelings must have been aroused by the anthology. Happiness & pride must have been galore. But there must be moments when your pen scratches the most tender parts of her body, leaving it quivering with sheer pain & anxiety, all of which would turn her bile ever more bitter.

The chopping down of the tree & the scattering of the fruit will remind her of the loving peach tree that stood next to our bedroom window & its harvest of tasty peaches. Her dreams must have been haunted by the picture of a merciless wood-cutter whose trade is to demolish what nature has created & whose heart is never touched by the lament of a falling tree, the breaking of its branches & the scattering of its fruits.

Chldn on the ground & out of reach! I immediately think of the late Thembi & the baby Makaziwe I[i] who succeeded him & who has slept at Croesus[ii] for the last 3 decades. I think of you all in the wretchedness in which you have grown & in which you now have to live. But I wonder

---

i   Thembekile , his eldest son who was born in 1945 and died in 1969 and his first-born daughter, Makaziwe, who was born in 1947 and died at nine months old. He and his first wife, Evelyn, gave their second-born daughter the same name.

ii   Croesus Cemetery in Newlands, Johannesburg.

whether Mum has ever told you of your brother who died before he was born. He was as tiny as your fist when I left you. He nearly killed her.

I still remember one Sunday as the sun was setting. I helped Mum out of bed to the toilet. She was barely 25 then & looked loving & tasty in her young & smooth body that was covered by a pink silk gown. But as we returned to the bedroom she suddenly swayed & almost went down. I noticed that she was also sweating heavily & I discovered that she was more ill than she had revealed. I rushed her to the family doctor & he sent her to Coronation Hospital[i] where she remained for several dys. It was her first dreadful experience as a wife; the result of the acute tensions brought on us by the Treason Trial[ii] which lasted more than 4 yrs. 'A tree was chopped down' reminds me of all these harsh experiences.

But a good pen can also remind us of the happiest moments in our lives, bring noble ideas into our dens, our blood & our souls. It can turn tragedy into hope & victory. This is how I felt as I reached the last page of your anthology. Your first effort, darling, arouses the hope that you will produce enduring literary works. May it be so! Tons & tons of love & a million kisses. Affectionately, Tata[iii]

Miss Zindzi Nobutho Mantu Mandela, 8115 Orlando West, PO Orlando [1804] Johannesburg.

To Dullah Omar,[iv] lawyer & comrade

466/64: Nelson Mandela   1.6.80

My dear Abdullah,

We were deeply disturbed when we heard of your illness. I had seen you barely a month before the depressing news reached us & it was not so easy for us to believe that sickness could break down so suddenly a middle-aged

---

i   In Coronationville in Johannesburg. The hospital is now called Rahima Moosa Mother and Child Hospital and is named after activist Rahima Moosa (1922–93), one of the leaders of the Women's March in Pretoria in 1956 to protest the extension of pass laws to women.
ii   The Treason Trial (1956–61) was a result of the apartheid government's attempt to quell the power of the Congress Alliance, a coalition of anti-apartheid organisations. In early-morning raids on 5 December 1956, 156 individuals were arrested and charged with high treason. By the end of the trial in March 1961 all the accused either had the charges withdrawn or, in the case of the last twenty-eight accused (including Mandela), were acquitted.
iii   'Father' in isiXhosa.
iv   Dullah Omar (1934–2004), anti-apartheid activist and advocate – see the glossary.

man who looked so fresh & strong. Fortunately for us, we got the news a few days after you had been discharged from hospital & the shock was immediately tempered by a feeling of relief & rejoicing. We join Farida, the children[i] & the many friends & clients who congratulated you on your recovery.

The hospital & your family doctor must have given you the best advice on how to look after yourself during & after recuperation. All that I can add here is the common sense advice which almost all those who are concerned with your welfare must have already given you, that is, to hamba kahle[ii] & let your colleagues in the firm handle the more exacting duties. Perhaps an extended overseas holiday would benefit you immensely. Meantime we wish you a speedy & complete recovery & many years of prosperity & happiness.

With regard to the passing away of Bennie,[iii] our daughter, Zindzi,[iv] visited his home to express the sympathies of my family directly. Unfortunately Helen[v] was not in, but we hope she got the message. At the time of his death Bennie was working together with Advocate Dison on a Notice of Motion in which I was the Petitioner. I looked forward to seeing him at last. But that was not to be & I was very sorry when we heard of the tragedy. Please give her our condolences. We think of her & hope that similar messages from numerous friends & well-wishers have given her the courage to bear the cruel blow.

Turning to the question of Sabata Dalindyebo,[vi] the case against him was still pending when I last saw you & I hope that your Durban correspondents have already advised you of its outcome. He was found not guilty & discharged on the first count but fined R700 on the second. I am informed that his Counsel advised him not to appeal against the conviction & sentence. But I have now received a letter from Sabata in which he informs me that he has nevertheless seen the Registrar of the Supreme Court at Umtata[vii] & personally noted the appeal. He has also applied to see me &, if the Department of Prisons give the required permit, I will discuss the whole matter with him when he comes.

But this is not all. I am informed that, in the meantime, Chief Matanzima[viii] is taking steps to depose Sabata as Paramount Chief[ix] & that Sabata

---

i   Dullah Omar's wife and children.
ii   *Hamba kahle* means 'go well' in isiXhosa and isiZulu.
iii   Benjamin 'Bennie' Kies (1917–79), a professor, anti-apartheid activist, and member of the New Unity Movement, who in 1957 was banned from teaching for life because of his political activity.
iv   Zindziswa Mandela (1960–), Mandela's youngest daughter – see the glossary
v   Helen Kies (1926–), teacher and member of the Teachers' League of South Africa and the Non-European Unity Movement. She was married to professor and anti-apartheid activist, Benjamin (Bennie) Kies.
vi   King Sabata Jonguhlanga Dalindyebo (1928–86), paramount chief of the Transkei homeland and leader of the Democratic Progressive Party, the opposition party in Transkei which opposed apartheid rule – see the glossary. He fled to Zambia in 1980 after being convicted of violating the dignity of the Transkei's president K. D. Matanzima.
vii   Umtata (now called Mthatha) was the capital of the Transkei homeland.
viii K. D. Matanzima (1915–2003), Thembu chief, and chief minister for the Transkei – see the glossary.
ix   In his 14 June 1989 letter to Fatima Meer, Mandela wrote that Sabata 'had bravely and honourably rejected the

intends to seek a court order restraining the former from deposing him. I hope your Durban correspondents will keep me informed about these developments; more specifically that they will send me a copy of the Petition plus Respondent's Replying affidavit.

I must confess that this case worries me. Sabata's health is not so good & I fear that the strain that he has endured for so long may worsen his condition. What encourages me is that he has lived up to expectations in every sense of the word & has carried himself quite well. We are much indebted to you & your correspondents for the services you rendered.[i]

I should like Advocate Mohammed to know this.

Once more, we wish you the best of luck.

Love & fondest regards to Farida & the children, to Fatima,[ii] Rahima[iii] and Ike & to all their children. Very sincerely, Nelson

Abdullah Omar, P.O. Box 187, Salt River, 7925

======

To Winnie Mandela,[iv] his wife

466/64: Nelson Mandela   30.7.80

My darling Mum.

How dare you send me a mere telegram on the occasion of my 62nd birthday! I was tempted to let it go up in flames, if only I could destroy the paper on which it is written without doing so to the message, & if only I could make you feel the pain there in Brandfort. You have now forgotten that I always want to feed my vanity for displaying the affectionate messages on the bookcase long enough to attract my inmates without any formal invitation from me.

---

conversion of Transkei into a homeland. KD Matanzima whose great-grandfather had refused to sell out to the British, and thus became a famous man in Thembuland, collaborated with the Government, deposed a people's hero, Sabata, and forced him into exile where he died.'

i   Dullah Omar was providing legal services.

ii   Fatima Seedat (1922–2003) was the twin of Rahima Moosa, one of the leaders of the 1956 Women's March. A member of the Natal Indian Congress and ANC, Fatima was jailed for her role in the Passive Resistance Campaign waged by the Transvaal and Natal Indian Congresses from 1946 to 1948 against the Asiatic Land Tenure Act of 1946 which sought to confine Asian ownership of land to particular areas. She was jailed again in 1952 for participating in the Defiance Campaign (for the Defiance Campaign, see the glossary).

iii Rahima Moosa (1922–93), anti-apartheid activist and one of the leaders of the Women's March in Pretoria in 1956 to protest the extension of pass laws to women. Twin sister of Fatima Seedat.

iv   Nomzamo Winifred Madikizela-Mandela (1936–) – see the glossary.

Do you relaise that this yr I did not even get the wedding anniversary card you occasionally send? Of course both cards would, like all your letters & telegrams, be subjected to the usual censorship; but unlike the type of telegram I receive this end, they can be preserved so as to remind our chdn of these hectic dys, especially your harrowing problems in that backveld.[i]

Never mind, darling Mum, your love & affectionate messages always lift me in whatever form they come. I was delighted to get the telegrams after spending the 19/7 with Mantu.[ii] Coming at the same time with the visits on 13 & 19/7 it made me feel ever more certain that the springs in you that have flown so strong all these yrs & whose waters are so cool & sweet, will never dry. This is the case even though you did not look so well. The fire that usually glows so brilliantly in you was missing. May be the pains on your back had not eased much & that the rough seas may have unconsciously affected you. I hope you will continue to do your regular exercises, darling. The only answer is to develop the back muscles & make them strong enough to hold the backbones in position. Take it easy, however, especially while the pain still lingers.

Apart from your telegram I received 2 cards both from Zeni & Muzi[iii] and from Zazi & Swati.[iv] I believe that those of Mantu are in the pipeline. There were 3 other telegrams, one from J.H.B.'s[v] Ismail, Kentane's Kepu[vi] and Mangosuthu.[vii] So far I have received not a single one of the multitude that friends have sent from all over the world. Nevertheless, it is very comforting to know that so many friends still think of us after so many yrs.

As far as the illness of Nali[viii] is concerned, I sincerely hope nothing will happen to her. Such a tragedy would open up a wound that would be difficult to heal. We love her & the chdn so much. I would have preferred her to remain in J.H.B. & get some work. There she would at least be sure of the best medical care in the country & would also be nearer the chdn. Were it not for the scarcity of doctors & work in Brandfort, I would have strongly advised that she should stay with you. Life in Pondoland[ix] would be as tough & depressing as it has been for Lungile[x] &, if possible, we should

---

i   Winnie Mandela was still living in the rural township of Brandfort in the Orange Free State (now Free State), where she had been banished in 1977. She lived there until 1985. Veld means 'field' in Afrikaans.

ii   Their younger daughter, Zindzi.

iii   Their older daughter, Zenani, and her husband, Prince Thumbumuzi Dlamini, a son of King Sobhuza of Swaziland. They married in 1977.

iv   Zenani Mandela's children, Zaziwe (1977–) and Zamaswazi (1979–).

v   Johannesburg.

vi   Kepu Mkentane, the wife of Lincoln Mkentane, a former university classmate of Mandela's who became a lawyer.

vii   Chief Mangosuthu Gatsha Buthelezi (1928–), Zulu prince, member of the ANC until the relationship deteriorated in 1979, chief minister of KwaZulu 1972–94, founder and president of the Inkatha Freedom Party in 1975 – see the glossary.

viii Winnie Mandela's sister.

ix   The district in the Transkei where Winnie Mandela grew up.

x   Winnie Mandela's brother.

466/64 Nelson Mandela   30. 7. 80

My darling Mum,

How dare you send me a mere telegram on the occasion of my 62nd birthday! I was tempted to let it go up in flames, if only I could destroy the paper on which it is written without doing so to the message, & if I could make you feel the pain out there in Brandfort. You have now forgotten that I always want to feed my vanity by displaying your affectionate messages on the bookcase long enough to attract to ~~attract~~ my inmates without any formal invitation from me.

Do you realise that this yr I did not even get the wedding anniversary card you occasionally send? Of course both cards would, like all your letters & telegrams, be subjected to the usual censorship; but unlike the type of telegram I receive this end, they can be preserved so as to remind our chdn of these hectic days, especially your harrowing problems in that backveld.

Never mind, darling Mum, your love & affectionate messages always lift me in whatever form they come. I was delighted to get the telegrams after spending the 19/7 with Manila. Coming at the same time with the visits on 13 & 19/7 it made me feel ever more certain that the springs in you that have flown so strong all these yrs & whose waters are so cool & sweet, will never dry. This is the case even though you did not look so well. The fire that usually glows so brilliantly in you was missing. May be the pains on your back had not eased much & that the rough seas may have unconsciously affected you. I hope you will continue to do your regular exercises, darling. The only answer is to develop the back muscles & make them strong enough to hold the backbones in position. Take it easy, however, especially while the pain still lingers.

Apart from your telegram I received 2 cards both from Zeni & Muzi & from Zazi & Swati. I believe that those of Manila are in the pipeline. There were 3 other telegrams, one from JHB's Ismail, Nkentane's Kepu & Mangosuthu. So far I have received not a single one of the multitude that friends have sent from all over the world. Nevertheless, it is very comforting to know that so many friends still think of us after so many yrs.

As far as the illness of Nali is concerned, I sincerely hope nothing will happen to her. Such a tragedy would open up a ~~would~~ wound that would be difficult to heal. We love her & the chdn so much. I would have preferred her to remain in JHB & get some work. There she would at least be sure of the best medical care in the country & would also be nearer the chdn. Were it not for the scarcity of doctors & work in Brandfort, I would have strongly advised that she should stay with you. Life in Phuthaditjhaba would be as tough & depressing as it has been for Kungile &, if possible, we should try to help her. Niki & Marsh may find it very difficult to assist in view of the distress

----

our darling Matlala, I miss you, Reggie & the chdn very badly & hope you are all well. Both you & Reggie do need a holiday & a complete rest for a couple of mths. That's absolutely necessary. Zami tells me that you are very angry with her for using part of the money you sent me. In actual fact she consulted me before hand & I authorised her to use it. You are of course aware that circs. have reversed the roles in this

A letter to Winnie Mandela, 30 July 1980, see previous and following pages.

ing report you gave me on what they recently went through. I would certainly have no objection to the 2 of them going over to Zeni. It would mean a great deal to her to have them nearby.

It pleased me to hear that Kunele is now in JHB for treatment, though Mandla thinks that he is a bit violent. Staying a while with his niece may alone benefit his health. But I think he probably would have been more happy with you & Nyanya. If you still have some of my clothing I wouldn't mind giving them to him as a present provided that you have no objection.

I would suggest that you do not worry yourself much about the effect our Mother's genes & those of Sobhuza or the elders. Medical science is advancing & conditions that were incurable yesterday can easily be controlled today & even healed altogether tomorrow.

You heard about the sudden death of Sanjay in a private plane accident & I do hope that you sent a message of condolence to his mother. Nothing could ever excuse our failure to do so. If you have not yet done so, Mum, I would suggest that you dispatch a message immediately. It will also be proper for the elders to lay a wreath on his "grave" when they go over for the presentation ceremony. I hope there will be coordination between you & Reggie about the proposed trip.

You will not believe me when I tell you that apart from the long letter I received from Suzy, he also followed with a beautiful post card sent from Mombasa. He says his return has been postponed by 1½ wks. I am writing to him c/o Mbabane but I should miss him if I direct it to Kenya. I am also writing to Zeni.

I forgot to tell you during the last visit that Mr. Phathudi visited the island last month & asked to see me. I wrote him a short note in which I pointed out that I could not accede to his request. But I added that my refusal to see him should not be regarded as a discourtesy to him.

I came out empty-handed with Mandla. She suggested bringing Oupa along so that the 3 of us could put our heads together. But she added that it will not be so easy to discuss the problem with me in my present circumstances. I am, nevertheless, keen to see them & hope that they have applied.

The family is growing fast, Mum, & in spite of our present position, it is of some importance that we try to acquire a proper home. It is far better that we work on the idea of buying a house in Soweto & abandon the plan of extending the present one. The entire stand is too small for our purposes. Here Mandla cannot get the privacy needed for his studies & writing. My suggestion is that the R10,000 should be invested in such a project. I would have liked to exchange views on the matter with someone like Marsh or Ntatho if they could come down.

The other matter that worries me presently is the fact that you are now staying alone. I am racking my brains for a solution. It is something for which we should find a way out without delay. We both know how your being alone will be adversely exploited. Meantime, I miss you a lot & hope you will look far better when I see you again. I Love You! Devotedly, Madiba ‖ Nkosk Nobandla Mandela. 802 Phathakahle.

family & Zami has established herself as the undisputed final-head, so much so that I doubt if on my return I will be able to dislodge her from that position. She is generally a frugal person & I depend entirely on her in matters of this kind. Again I miss you & even this form that I am using is full of nostalgic memories. We all love you, Malala. Very sincerely, Bhuti. P.s. A million thanks for the fish & for everything else. Bhuti.

try to help her. Niki & Marsh[i] may find it difficult to assist in view of the disturbing report you have given me on what they recently went through. I would certainly have no objection to the 2 of them going over to Zeni. It would mean a great deal to her to have them nearby.

It pleased me to hear that Lungile is now in J.H.B. for treatment. Staying a while with his niece may alone benefit his health. But I think he probably would have been more happy with you & Nyanya.[ii] If you still have some of my clothing I wouldn't mind giving them to him as a present, provided that you have no objection. . . .

You heard about the sudden death of Sanjay[iii] in a private plane accident & I do hope that you sent a message of condolence to his mother.[iv] Nothing could ever excuse our failure to do so. If you have not yet done so, Mum, I would suggest that you dispatch a message immediately. It will also be proper for the chdn to leave a wreath on his "grave" when they go over for the ceremony.[v] I hope there will be coordination between you and Reggie[vi] about the proposed trip.

You will not believe me when I tell you that apart from the long letter I received from Muzi,[vii] he also followed with a beautiful postcard sent from Mombasa.[viii] He says his return has been postponed by 1½ wks. I am writing to him via Mbabane[ix] lest I should miss him if I direct it to Kenya. I am also writing to Zeni. I forgot to tell you during the last visit that Dr. Phatudi[x] visited the Island last mnth & asked to see me. I wrote him a short note in which I pointed out that I could not acede to his request. But I added that my refusal to see him should not be regarded as a discourtesy to him.[xi]

I came out empty-handed with Mantu. She suggested bringing Oupa[xii] along so that the 3 of us could put our heads together. But she added that

---

i   Winnie Mandela's eldest sister Niki and her husband Marshall Xaba (for Niki Xaba, see the glossary).
ii   Nonyaniso (Nyanya) Madikizela, Winnie Mandela's youngest sister.
iii Sanjay Gandhi (1946–80), a son of India's prime minister Indira Gandhi, was killed in an airplane accident on 23 June 1980.
iv   Mandela did not meet Indira Gandhi but he had been impressed by India's stand against apartheid since 1946.
v   Fatima Meer wrote to Indira Gandhi in 1979 suggesting she put Mandela forward for the Jawaharlal Nehru Award for International Understanding. He was awarded the prize in 1979 and when Winnie Mandela was denied a passport to attend the ceremony on 14 November 1980, he was represented by Oliver Tambo. Mandela's middle daughter, Princess Zenani Dlamini, also attended the ceremony.
vi   Oliver Reginald Tambo (1917–93), Mandela's friend, former law partner, and the president of the ANC – see the glossary. His middle name was Reginald and Mandela referred to him as Reggie.
vii Prince Thumbumuzi Dlamini, a son of King Sobhuza of Swaziland and Zenani Mandela's husband.
viii A city on the coast of Kenya.
ix   The largest city in Swaziland.
x   Cedric Phatudi, chief minister of the Lebowa homeland, Transvaal. An article in the *Citizen* newspaper dated 28 June 1980 reports that he was to ask Prime Minister P. W. Botha to release Mandela and that he had visited Robben Island that week but that he did not meet Mandela. ('Phatudi to Ask PM to Free Nelson Mandela', *The Citizen*, 28 June 1980.)
xi   Just as Mandela had refused to be released to the Transkei homeland, he also refused to recognise the Lebowa homeland.
xii Zindzi's partner, Oupa Seakamela.

it will not be so easy to discuss the problem with me in my present circs.[i] I am, nevertheless, keen to see them & hope they have applied.

The family is growing fast, Mum, & in spite of our present position, it is of some importance that we try to acquire a proper home. It is far better that we work on the idea of buying a house in Soweto & abandon the plan of extending the present one. The entire stand is too small for our purpose. There Mantu can never get the privacy needed for her studies & writing. My suggestion is that the R10,000 should be invested in such a project. I would have liked to exchange views on the matter with someone like Marsh or Ntatho[ii] if they could come down. The other matter that worries me presently is the fact that you are now staying alone. I am wracking my brains for a solution. It is something for which we should find a way out without delay. We both know how your being alone will be adversely exploited. Meantime, I miss you a lot & hope you will look far better when I see you again. I LOVE You! Devotedly, Madiba.

Nkosk. Nobandla Mandela, 802 Phathakahle.

[At the bottom of each page of this letter there is a note to Adelaide Tambo.[iii] It could be that he tried to sneak it into this letter to his wife.] 'Our darling Matlala,[iv] I miss you, Reggie & the chn very badly & hope you are all well. Both you & Reggie do need a holiday & a complete rest for a couple of mths. That's absolutely necessary. Zami[v] tells me that you are very angry with her for using part of the money you sent me. In actual fact she consulted me beforehand & I authorised her to use it. You are of course aware that circs. have reversed the roles in this family & that Zami has established herself as the undisputed kraal-hand,[vi] so much so that I doubt it if, on my return, I will be able to dislodge her from that position. She is generally a frugal person & I depend entirely on her in matters of this kind. Again I miss you & even this pen that I am using is full of nostalgic memories. We all love you, Matlala. Very sincerely, Bhuti.[vii] P.S. A million thanks for the cash & for everything else. Bhuti.

---

i   Circumstances.
ii   Nthato Motlana (1925–2008), friend, medical doctor, businessman, and anti-apartheid activist – see the glossary.
iii   Adelaide Tambo (1929–2007), friend, anti-apartheid activist, and wife of Oliver Tambo, Mandela's former law partner and president of the ANC – see the glossary for both these individuals. The Tambos were living in exile in London.
iv   A nickname for Adelaide Tambo.
v   One of Winnie Mandela's names.
vi   A *kraal* is an Afrikaans word for a traditional collection of huts surrounded by a fence for enclosing cattle. A *kraal*-hand would be a worker who provided assistance.
vii   'Brother' in Afrikaans.

To Amina Cachalia,[i] friend and comrade

466/64 : Nelson Mandela   26.10.80

My dear Amina,

Eid Mubarak, ben![ii] How are you getting on? Have you reached the stage where you experience strange lumbar pains or where you have to use spectacles? I suppose it is the case with all men in my position, it is difficult for me to imagine you to be anything different in physical appearance than how I last saw you. I always get a shock when I see some of my friends in publications that are available here. Some seem to be feeding themselves 24 hours a day, so bloated they have become, while others look like sucked oranges. As I told you in my last letter, among the people who look surprisingly well are Fatima & Ismail.[iii] They make the cell really glitter.

But it is about you that I am thinking about [*sic*] at the present moment & repeat: Eid Mubarak! I can literally smell the biryani, pilau & samoosa[s] that you prepared for the occasion, with Yusuf's[iv] waistline expanding daily.

I hope you are able to travel to India, that you saw not only the shrines in which the Asvats[v] rest, but also the famous places in that country, including the Taj Mahal. But I hope that Yusuf will not invest his hard won fortune in a similar project just to immortalise you, or as a momument to the wonderful moments you spent together. After all, your memory will be perpetuated not only by those who have had the honour & pleasure of knowing you, but by the patforms & squares in which you appeared, the streets on which you walked & the records that will pass to posterity. All I wish to say at this moment is not to be so possessive about your experiences & impressions of the country & people. Share them with us! Did you meet Indiraben?[vi]

I have literally pestered Zami[vii] about the India trip & I have now suggested that if she & the chdn are finding it difficult to obtain the necessary travelling documents, they should give us the trip & let OR[viii] make the

---

i   Amina Cachalia (1930–2013), friend and anti-apartheid and women's rights activist – see the glossary.
ii   'Blessed Eid' in Gujarati, referring to one of the two official Muslim holidays. *Ben* means sister in Gujarati.
iii Fatima (1928–2010) and Ismail Meer (1918–2000), friends. Fatima was a professor, author, and anti-apartheid activist. Imail was a lawyer and anti-apartheid activist – see the glossary for both these individuals.
iv   Yusuf Cachalia (1915–95), Amina Cachalia's husband, political activist and secretary of the South African Indian Congress – see the glossary.
v   A family name for ancestors of Amina Cachalia.
vi   Indira Gandhi (1917–84), prime minister of India.
vii One of Winnie Mandela's names.
viii Oliver Reginald Tambo (1917–93), Mandela's friend, former law partner, and the president of the ANC – see the glossary.

necessary arrangements for someone to attend the ceremony.[i] Despite our special problems it would not be proper for us to hold them up for so long.

Zindzi[ii] told me during the July visit that Zainub[iii] was back to see your brother who was very ill. I took it for granted that it was Solly[iv] who was affected, & it was only when I was reporting here that I discovered that you have several brothers. How scandalous that I should know so little about your family after being with you for a lifetime. Which one is it? Is Zainub still in the country or is she back in England? I hope she & Aziz[v] are still well. Do you still see Esackjee & family, & Farid[vi] & his? I hardly hear about Mota,[vii] Winnie,[viii] Shireen & the youngest child[ix] & wonder whether you received the letter I once wrote to him several years ago c/o you.[x] Please be patient with me & don't be cross even though I may repeat questions you may have already attempted to answer. You write beautifully & I never miss even a punctuation in your letters. If I had received your comments on any points I would certainly not pester you again.

About my daughter Maki[xi] I wonder whether you received my registered letter of 27/4 in which I informed you that she had now received a scholarship, but that as a student in social work she still required a lot more funds. I expressed the hope that you & the other Ismail[xii] would be able to sort out the problem. I also wrote & told her to expect to hear from you.

But on 11/10 I got a letter from her in which she had not heard from you. She adds that she told Helen[xiii] not to worry anymore because she understood that she (Helen) might be having certain difficulties. Even before you reply I am quite certain that you have a perfectly valid explanation. It may well be that the closure of Fort Hare, her admission to hospital as a result of the injuries she sustained during the F.H.[xiv] demonstrations, or your absence in India, may have upset your plans. But I thought you should know that up

---

i   Fatima Meer wrote to Indira Gandhi in 1979 suggesting she put Mandela forward for the Jawaharlal Nehru Award for International Understanding. He was awarded the prize in 1979 and when Winnie Mandela was denied a passport to attend the ceremony on 14 November 1980, he was represented by Oliver Tambo. Mandela's middle daughter, Zenani, also attended the ceremony.
ii   Zindziswa Mandela (1960–), Mandela's youngest daughter – see the glossary.
iii   Amina Cachalia's sister, Zainub Kazi.
iv   Amina Cachalia's brother.
v   Zainub Kazi's husband, Dr. Aziz Kazi.
vi   Former Treason trialists (for the Treason Trial, see the glossary).
vii   Yusuf Dadoo (1909–83), medical doctor, anti-apartheid activist, and orator. President of South African Indian Congress, deputy to Oliver Tambo on the Revolutionary Council of MK, and chairman of the South African Communist Party – see the glossary. Yusuf Dadoo was commonly known as Mota, short for *Motabhai*, the Gujarati word for 'elder brother'. He had been living in exile since 1960.
viii   Yusuf Dadoo's wife.
ix   Yusuf Dadoo's children.
x   See his letter to Yusuf Dadoo from 1 November 1975, page 282.
xi   Makaziwe Mandela (1954–), Mandela's eldest daughter – see the glossary.
xii   Ismail Ayob (1942–), Mandela's attorney – see the glossary.
xiii   This is likely to be Helen Joseph (1905–92), teacher, social worker, and anti-apartheid and women's rights activist – see the glossary.
xiv   University College of Fort Hare, Alice in the Ciskei homeland – see the glossary.

to the time of writing to me she had not heard from you.

I was sorry to hear from you that Ismail[i] had not been well. Such people should never allow themselves to be ill. When they sneeze all of us contract a cold. I hope he is better now & that Jamilla & the chdn are also fine. Tell him that I have asked Zami to raise R400 for me for my studies, even though I did not know just whom she will have to swindle. I did not have the nerve to tell her that I spent the funds she sent me early this year towards the yearly subscription for the *Rand Daily Mail* & *Rapport*. I propose registering for five subjects next yr & the Unisa[ii] fees have become prohibitive. Few can afford them at R70 tuition fees per subject + R40 for registration. I was not allowed to complete the remaining four subjects I owe for the law course in London University.[iii] Instead I was allowed to study with Unisa. I don't even know just how I shall manage with the prescribed text books.

My fondest regards to all our friends & love to you and Yusuf. Sincerely, Nelson.

Mrs Amina Cachalia, P.O. 3625, Johannesburg

4th January 1981
P.S. Amina,

This letter was returned to me by the P.O. Johannesburg marked "Unclaimed". I am re-addressing it to you and hope that this time you will have the courage to claim it. I have been thinking that it reached Johannesburg in your absence. I love you as always, Sincerely, Nelson

━━━━━━━━━━━

To Zindzi Mandela,[iv] his youngest daughter

[Note in another hand] Censored original letter 10.2.81

466/64: Nelson Mandela   1.3.81

My darling,

---

i   Maulvi Cachalia (1908–2003), Amina's brother-in-law and anti-apartheid activist – see the glossary.
ii   University of South Africa.
iii   The prison authorities had not allowed Mandela to continue studying for his LLB with the University of London.
iv   Zindziswa Mandela (1960–) – see the glossary.

Prison, <u>especially for those who stay in single cells,</u>[i] provides many moments of reflection on problems too numerous to be listed down on paper. Often as I walk up & down the tiny cell, or as I lie on my bed, the mind wanders far & wide, recalling this episode & that mistake. Among these is the thought whether in my best days outside prison I showed sufficient appreciation for the love & kindness of many of those who befriended & even helped me when I was poor & struggling.

The other day I was thinking of the Xhomas in 46 – 7th Avenue, Alexandra Township, where I lived on my arrival in JHB.[ii] At that time I was earning the mthly wage of £2 (R4.00)[iii] & out of this amount I had to pay the mthly rent of 13/-4d plus bus fare of 8d a day to town & back. It was hard-going & I often found it quite difficult to pay the rent & bus fare. But my landlord & his wife were kind. Not only did they give me an extension when I could not raise the rent, but on Sundays they gave me a lovely lunch free of charge.

I also stayed with Rev Mabuto of the Anglican Church in 46 8th Avenue in the same township & he & Gogo,[iv] as we fondly called his wife, were also very kind, even though she was rather strict, insisting that I should take out only Xhosa girls. Despite the fact that my political outlook was still formative, Healdtown & Fort Hare[v] had brought me into contact with students from other sections of our people, & at least I had already developed beyond thinking along ethnic lines. I was determined not to follow her advice on this particular matter. But she & husband played the role of parents to me rather admirably.

Mr Schreiner Baduza,[vi] originally from Sterkspruit,[vii] lived as tenant with his wife in 46 7th Avenue. He & Mr J.P. Mngoma,[viii] although much older than myself, especially the latter, were among some of my best friends of those days. Mr Mngoma was a property owner & father to Aunt Virginia, one of Mum's friends.[ix] Later I was introduced to Mr P. Joyana, father-in-law to the brother of the late Chief Jongintaba Mdingi.[x] He (Mr Joyana) was a

---

i   This underlining has mostly probably been done by a prison censor.
ii   Mandela fled an arranged marriage in 1941 after his expulsion from the University College of Fort Hare and went to Johannesburg where he lodged with the Xhoma family in Alexandra.
iii   He was an articled clerk at the law firm Witkin, Sidelksy & Eidelman.
iv   'Granny' in isiZulu and isiXhosa.
v   Mandela attended the Wesleyan College Healdtown in Fort Beaufort in 1937 and then the University College of Fort Hare, in Alice, in 1939 – see the glossary.
vi   One of Mandela's best friends who, with his wife, lodged in the same house as him in Alexandra. After he moved to Soweto he became a prominent figure in civic affairs.
vii   A town in the Transkei homeland.
viii   Mandela's friend in Alexandra. A property owner and the father of Aunt Virginia, a friend of Winnie Mandela's.
ix   Winnie Mandela.
x   This is most likely Chief Mdingi, a relative of Mandela's and the Thembu Chief who named Mandela's two younger daughters. The eldest he named Zenani, meaning 'What have you brought?', and the Madikizelas (Winnie Mandela's family) named her Nomadabi Nosizwe, meaning 'battlefield of the nation'. Chief Mdingi named the youngest daughter Mantu Nobutho Zindziswa.

clerk at the Rand Leases Mine. I used to travel there on Saturdays to collect his rations – samp,[i] rice, mealie meal,[ii] meat, peanuts & other items.

Much later my financial position slightly improved, but I hardly thought of those who had stood on my side during difficult times, nor did I ever visit them except once or twice only. Both the Mabutos[iii] & the Baduzas subsequently came to live in Soweto & I visited the Mabutos on a few occasions. I met both Messrs Joyana & Baduza on many occasions, but not once did I even think of returning their kindness. Both in the late forties & early fifties Mr Baduza became a very prominent figure in the civic affairs of Soweto & our association was limited to that level.

I was deeply upset when one day early in 1953 the Old Lady, Mrs Xhoma, once a lively & beautiful person, shuffled into my office at Chancellor House looking quite aged & broken. The old man had passed away & she wanted me to wind up his estate. I had hardly known about his illness, to say nothing of his death & funeral, an occasion I had no right not to know.

Even to my beloved Old Lady[iv] I was not as attentive as I should have been. I rarely wrote to her, except to try to persuade her to come up to live with me in J.H.B.[v] There are many other examples I could give & these are but a few which I give by way of illustration.

My arrest for treason on 5/12/56[vi] & the lengthy proceedings that followed, worsened the position. The world around me literally crumbled, income disappeared & many obligations could not be honoured. Only the coming of Mum[vii] into the picture helped to bring about a bit of order in my personal affairs. But the chaos had gone too far even for herself to bring back the stability & easy life I had only just begun to taste when misfortune struck.

It is all these things which keep turning up as the mind strays over my days in the Golden City.[viii] But this soul-searching melts away altogether when I think of Mum & all the chdn, of the pride & joy you all give me. Among us is Nobutho,[ix] the beautiful Mantu whose love & loyalty, visits, letters, birthday & Xmas cards are an essential part in the efforts of the family to help me endure many of the challenges of the past two decades.

---

i   A porridge made of coarsely ground corn.
ii   An ingredient made from ground maize, also known as maize meal, which is combined with boiling water to make a porridge.
iii   A friend of Mandela's.
iv   His mother, Nosekeni Mandela.
v   Johannesburg.
vi   Mandela is referring to the Treason Trial (1956–61), which was a result of the apartheid government's attempt to quell the power of the Congress Alliance, a coalition of anti-apartheid organisations. In early-morning raids on 5 December 1956, 156 individuals were arrested and charged with high treason. By the end of the trial in March 1961 all the accused either had the charges withdrawn or, in the case of the last twenty-eight accused (including Mandela), were acquitted.
vii   Winnie Madikizela whom he married in 1958.
viii   Johannesburg is called the Golden City due its origins as a gold-mining town in the nineteenth century.
ix   One of Zindzi's names.

Nobutho is a Capricorn & according to astrologers the stars last mth fore-
told a period of pleasure & excitement that awaited the Capricorns, that
you are likely to have many visitors, many invitations & that health should
be excellent. It is a carefully worked out superstition & which is attractively
presented. It has fascinated mankind from the dawn of history & has even
inspired many people, who believe in it, to excel themselves in many fields.
Indeed many Capricorns may have felt flattered when they read these fantastic predictions. But let us leave superstitions & close this note with an
observation that is based on facts. It is my real message to you, darling
– your ability to appreciate the love & kindness of others. It is a precious
virtue to try to make others happy & to forget their worries. It is a quality
which you & Zeni[i] seem to have inherited from Mum. My wish is that it
may deepen as you grow so that more & more people may benefit from it.
Love to you, Oupa[ii] & Zobuhle.[iii]

Affectionately, Tata.[iv]

Miss Zindzi Mandela, 8115 Orlando West, JHB [1804]
What is the address of Nozizwe Mvembe?

To Winnie Mandela,[v] his wife

466/64   26.4.81

My darling Mum.

I continue to dream, some pleasant, others not. On the eve of Good Friday
you & I were in a cottage on the top of a hill overlooking a deep valley &
with a big river coursing the edge of a forest. I saw you walk down the
slope of the hill, not as erect in your bearing as you usually are & with
your footsteps less confident. All the time your head was down, apparently
searching for something a few paces from your feet. You crossed the river
& carried away all my love, leaving me rather empty & uneasy. I watched
closely as you wandered aimlessly in that forest keeping close to the river

i   His middle daughter.
ii   Zindzi's partner, Oupa Seakamela.
iii   One of Zindzi's names.
iv   'Father' in isiXhosa.
v   Nomzamo Winifred Madikizela-Mandela (1936–) – see the glossary.

bank. Immediately above you there was a couple which presented a striking contrast. They were obviously in love & concentrating on themselves. The whole universe seemed to be on that spot.

My concern for your safety & pure longing for you drove me down the hill to welcome you back as you recrossed the river on your way back to the cottage. The prospect of joining you in the open air & in such beautiful surroundings evoked fond memories & I looked forward to holding your hand & to a passionate kiss. To my disappointment I lost you in the ravines that cut deep into the valley & I only met you again when I returned to the cottage. This time the place was full of colleagues who deprived us of the privacy I so wanted to sort out so many things.

In the last scene you were stretched out on the floor in a corner, sleeping out depression, boredom & fatigue. I knelt down to cover the exposed parts of your body with a blanket. Whenever I have such dreams I often wake up feeling anxious & much concerned, but I immediately become relieved when I discover that it was all but a dream. However, this time my reaction was a mixed one.

On 23/4 I was called by the Head of the Prison, something quite routine in this set-up & to which I am used. Suddenly I felt he had unpleasant news for me. When I reached the interview room, I saw him talking to some staff members in the reception office across the passage with a telegram in his hand. This deepened my anxiety. He could not have remained there for more than a minute when he walked towards me, but the tension from anxiety was so distressing that it seemed I had waited for a whole hr. "I have bad news for you" he said as he gave me the telegram. It was from Ismail[i] & reported the death of Samela. I was shocked because I always think of her as a young, strong & healthy girl. To the best of my memory I last saw her on the day we were convicted 17 yrs ago & she was then working at NEH. I was immediately in difficulties & did not know to whom I should send a message of sympathy. Her father, Mehthafa, during his lifetime chief of Sithebe, died in the late thirties already & buried her mother NoFrance. Her brother Zwelizolile, is also late. Her eldest sister, who did Std VI with me at Qokolweni[ii] in the mid-thirties, got married, but I have now forgotten her address & even her husband's surname. Equally regrettable, is the fact that I don't even know whether Samela was now married. In the circumstances I thought it better to wait in the hope that I will get the necessary details in due course. Sometimes I pause to reflect on the countless relatives & friends we have lost over the last 18 yrs of my imprisonment, the tragedy of

---

i   He may be referring to Ismail Ayob (1942–), one of his attorneys while he was in prison – see the glossary.
ii   The primary school Mandela attended in Qokolweni in the Transkei.

being unable to nurse those who mean so much to us & of being unable to pay our last respects when they die. Feelings of shock & grief for the death of a relative or close friend are perfectly understandable – CK,[i] the Old Lady,[ii] Thembi,[iii] Nali,[iv] NoEngland,[v] Nqonqi,[vi] Connie & several others too numerous to mention. But there are many other acquaintances who never did anything particularly significant for us other than a warm handshake or pleasant smile when we met, but whose death touched us all the same. But when it is close relatives like Samela, & when you receive the tragic news in the circumstances in which they reached me, without the slightest clue as to the cause of death, then the blow becomes particularly brutal. I sincerely hope that when the fatal hr struck she was at least surrounded by those who could give her love & whose deep concern could assure her efforts were fully appreciated. May be that I will get further details some day.

. . . Yesterday, I also received an equally beautiful letter from Amina[vii] with two lovely photos. She & her Yusuf have kept their ages very well & they both look very impressive indeed. She has all the reason to claim, as she does, that "Yusuf [viii] doesn't look like a sucked orange, but he does not look like an overfed puppy either.". . .

Perhaps one day I will be able to know whether Zindzi[ix] got my telegram rc the Durban boarding school which Fatima[x] undertook to arrange. I am thinking of sending another telegram to her (Fatima) to find out whether Zindzi is now there. Age seems to have affected Zindzi's capacity for writing letters, not even about such essential matters as her education. But she is a good & responsible girl & I am always prepared to give her the benefit of the doubt.

It would appear that a friend has made a press statement that your husband may be suffering from cancer. I have assumed that the statement was made in good faith by one who believes the allegation. But I must at once allay your fears, for I have no reason whatsoever to suspect that any part of my body is cancerous. I can only think the rumour was sparked off by the operation on the right heel in Nov. 79. It has healed beautifully & no longer gives me trouble. I have, however, a lingering pain on the inside part

i   Columbus Kokani Madikizela, Winnie Mandela's father – see the glossary.
ii   This is likely to be his mother, Nosekeni Fanny Mandela, who died in 1968.
iii   Madiba Thembekile (Thembi) Mandela (1945–69), Mandela's eldest son – see the glossary.
iv   Nali Nancy Vutela, Winnie Mandela's sister.
v   Wife of the regent Chief Jongintaba Dalindyebo who was Mandela's guardian after his father died when he was twelve (see the glossary).
vi   Nqonqi Mtirara, a cousin of Mandela's.
vii   Amina Cachalia (1930–2013), friend and anti-apartheid and women's rights activist – see the glossary.
viii   Yusuf Cachalia (1915–95), Amina Cachalia's husband, political activist and secretary of the South African Indian Congress – see the glossary.
ix   Zindziswa Mandela (1960–), his and Winnie Mandela's youngest daughter – see the glossary.
x   Fatima Meer (1928–2010), friend, professor , author, and anti-apartheid activist – see the glossary.

of the left knee. But I feel it only when I climb or go down some steps & on some nights it has rather been painful; not so much though as to induce me to take any pain tablets. Up to now I have successfully resisted using any of that junk. Earlier in the year I took the precaution of having a blood test & the medical report was negative. The present pain is receiving attention & apart from distance running, it has not affected my exercises very much. I still do quite a lot of leg exercises including station [sic] running. Please tell the chdn & all those who may inquire that I feel tremendous. Devotedly, Madiba. I LOVE YOU!

Nkosk. Nobandla Mandela, 802 Phatakahle, P.O. Brandfort, 9400

To Petronella Ferus, widow of ex political prisoner Hennie Ferus[i]

466/64: Nelson Mandela   3.5.81

Dearest Sussie,[ii]

The sudden death of your beloved husband, Hennie,[iii] deeply shocked me and my family and I send our deepest sympathy to you, Henshil, Wilna, Peter and Aunt Stienie.

I live in the hope that one day I may be privileged to meet you and family in order to speak more freely and fully on those aspects of Hennie's life which impressed me most. All I can say here is that I spent three years with him on this Island & I look back to that period with fond memories.

I still clearly remember the day when he was released from here on January 22nd, a departure I accepted with mixed feelings. I was sorry to part with such a good and loyal comrade, but I shared the happiness which freedom and reunion with his family would bring him.

During those three years Hennie was highly active in sports, music and other activities which looked after the welfare of his fellow prisoners. One year he became the table-tennis champion of the single cell section, and was a dangerous opponent in chess. He was a key member of both the quartet and the bigger choir we formed in this Section. Both music groups played an important role in the entertainment of his fellow-prisoners.

---

i   Hennie Ferus (1940–81), anti-apartheid activist who had been a political prisoner on Robben Island.
ii   'Sister' in Afrikaans.
iii   He died in a car accident on 20 April 1981.

His entire life was that of a man who lived in a world of reality, who could think clearly and act correctly. In this regard he was largely influenced by Aunt Stienie, herself a person of strong character and equally clear vision, who will always be remembered for her love of and loyalty to the family and community at large.

It is never easy to close the gap left by a man like Hennie, but I sincerely hope that it was a source of real comfort to you that he was accompanied to his resting place by a crowd of more than 4 000 mourners, four television crews and several press men.[i] That demonstration was but a small measure of the high esteem in which he was regarded by the people.

Again, my family and I send you our deepest sympathy and love, Sussie. We hope that time will in due course heal your painful wounds, and that the children will follow on the father's footsteps and bring a lot of pride and joy to you and Aunt Stienie. Josephine and her elder sister, Susan, are included in this message of sympathy. Very sincerely, [Signed NR Mandela]

Mrs Petronella Ferus, c/o Mrs Hadjie, 45 Le Seur Street, Worcester, 6850

To Camagwini Madikizela,[ii] daughter of his nephew K. D. Matanzima[iii]

466/64: Nelson Mandela   15.11.81

My darling Mzukulu,[iv]

I hope you enjoyed your trip to C.T.,[v] especially the 90 minutes or so you spent on this Island.

As you know, I have now been here for more than 19 yrs, during which I have had numerous visits from the family & friends. Mum Nobandla[vi] from Brandfort & the children naturally come over here more often than others, & practically every one of their visits has brought me joy in a very special way, making my stay here far more tolerable than it would otherwise have been.

---

i   Mourners at Hennie Ferus's funeral in Worcester wore ANC colours and khakis and raised the illegal ANC flag.
       It is widely perceived as being a 'political funeral' that motivated activists to become more defiant (Pippa Green,
       Choice Not Fate: The Life and Times of Trevor Manuel (Johannesburg:Penguin Books, 2008). p. 166.
ii   Daughter of KD Matanzima. She married Winnie Mandela's first cousin Prince Madikizela.
iii   K. D. Matanzima (1915–2003), Thembu chief, and chief minister for the Transkei – see the glossary.
iv   'Granddaughter' in isiXhosa.
v   Cape Town.
vi   One of Winnie Mandela's names.

Your visit always meant very much to me & I want to assure you and Prince[i] that I fully grasped its timing & significance. It brought me up to date on several important issues, giving me as it did, a better understanding of some family problems which have greatly disturbed me for the greater part of my imprisonment, especially during the last 3 yrs.

I was even more pleased to note just how devoted you & Prince are to each other & those 90 minutes or so that you spent here gave me a good impression of Prince, & fully confirmed the positive reports Mum Nobandla has given me from time to time. My only regret is that I could not see the children, but I hope that you gave them my love, at least. I look forward to seeing you again, whenever it is convenient to you & Mum Nobandla. Meantime, I think of Oct 24 & 25 with fondest memories.

As I told you during the visit, I spent a lot of time with Zwelithambile during my 3 mnths stay in the Mother City in '48 and we developed a strong friendship indeed. Although I never actually wrote to him after leaving C.T., I kept thinking of him & the lovely moments we spent together. I was therefore particularly disturbed when I heard that he was late. The death of Mthetho[ii] also took me by surprise and I knew exactly what it meant to you & your parents. Death is always a tragic event when it affects an elderly person. It is even more so when it strikes down a young person like the late Mthetho. I was happy to hear about his son and hope that he will be blessed with good health & lots of luck.

It pleased me to note that you & Prince are expecting an addition to the family. He/she will be able to boast to the other children that he/she visited the Island long before they could do so, even if at the time of the visit she was not aware of the fact. Perhaps you will bring him/her along when you next come. As you may know, you are permitted to bring along children under 2 yrs of age. Meantime, we wait for his arrival and I hope you will let us know when that wonderful day comes.

It also pleased me to hear that Mum Nobandla[iii] from Port St Johns is now working, that she even drives to Durban & that she is generally happy with her present work. During the visit I outlined to you how I introduced Daliwonga[iv] to her as well as some bare details about the marriage at Qamata.[v] As you will remember she came up to JHB[vi] about '58 and started nursing at Baragwanath,[vii] returning to Qamata soon thereafter. She was at our Orlando

---

i   Camagwini Madikizela was married to a relative of Winnie Mandela's called Prince Madikizela.
ii   Chief Mthetho Matanzima (d. 1972), Mandela's nephew K. D. Matanzima's son and chief of the Noqayti region – see the glossary. He died in a car accident.
iii   Another of K. D. Matanzima's wives.
iv   K. D. Matanzima. His middle name was Daliwonga.
v   A small town in what is now the Eastern Cape province.
vi   'Johannesburg'.
vii   Baragwanath Hospital in Soweto, Johannesburg.

home very often those days. I last saw her in Dec '60 when I came down to fetch Kgatho.[i] I think of her very often and will be writing to her soon.

It was rather an unusual coincidence for me to receive a letter from Mum Nosango[ii] from Deckerts Hill[iii] while I was busy writing you this letter. Unlike Mum Nobandla from Port St Johns, she is a good correspondent & usually writes letters that are ever full of information. Such letters are very valuable to one in my present position & I always look forward to them. She promises to be here early next yr & also confirms that Xoli[iv] is now at the University of York in England and that she plans to holiday in SA for 3 wks from Dec. 20. She probably would like to come over to the Island & I hope you will advise her as to how to arrange it.

I forgot to ask you about my nephew, Chief Luvuyo Mtirara, from Mpheko. He visited me several times until '73. Please check on him, if you can, and tell him that I always think of him.

I trust that Prince is attending to all the other problems I placed in his able hands & that I will soon get a report from him. Meantime, I am thinking of you with the fondest regards.

Tons & tons of love, a million kisses and a Merry Xmas & Happy New yr, Mzukulu. Affectionately, Tatomkhulu.[v]

Nkosazana Camagwini Madikizela,[vi] c/o Madikizela, Madala and Mdlulwa, P.O. Box 721, Umtata

---

To Ayesha Arnold[vii]

466/64: Nelson Mandela   15.11.81

Our dearest Ayesha,

You will certainly be able to smell the feeling of guilt & shame that has seized me since I received your invitation to attend your 50th natal Day,

---

i   Makgatho (Kgatho) Mandela (1950–2005), Mandela's second-born son – see the glossary.
ii   One of K. D. Matanzima's wives.
iii   A town in Transkei.
iv   Xoliswa Jozana, K. D. Matanzima's daughter.
v   'Granddad' in isiXhosa.
vi   *Nkosazana* means 'Miss' or 'princess' in isiXhosa.
vii   Dr. Ayesha Arnold was a medical doctor in Cape Town whom Mandela's wife and children would stay with when they visited him in prison. She was a friend of Fatima Meer's (see the glossary).

plus the flattering, if amusing, birthday card you sent me.

Although I received your letter long after 6/8 & should have brushed aside everything & written this letter on the spot, so that you could get my best wishes before the heady effects of champagne & halal had cleared away. Perhaps you are aware that over the last 3 or 4 months I endured an ever-growing pressure which made it difficult for me to write even to you & Zami[i] – two women whose love & affection has been such a source of strength to me, & who I would never like to disappoint.

The moment the pressure eased I reached out for pen & paper & here is your letter, Ayeshaben. It brings to you my warmest love & congratulations on hitting the half-century. My sincere wish is that you should live to be a centurion spanning 2 centuries, & continue to be a source of strength & hope to Ameen,[ii] Shukri & Mymoena[iii] & to your multitude of friends. I have included the 6/8 in the growing list of family birthdays & will not forget it. By the way, the date is so remarkably close to the 5/8 – the day on which I was arrested – that I regard the two dates as one & the same. Once again my warmest congratulations, Ben.[iv]

The birthday card was so smart that I even thought that it was designed & its message drawn up by Muhammad Ali, so full of punch & wit it was. The affectionate sentiments you added made me feel as strong as a tank & full of expectation as a bridegroom on the eve of [his] wedding day. You certainly will be able to congratulate me personally one day & I look forward to it very eagerly.

Zami had earlier told me about the beautiful present from you. Despite the fact that she described it rather elaborately, I had no idea of just how beautiful it actually was until I tried it on. It fitted well & I immediately felt twice as tall & half my age. I hug you. Zami also told me that Ameen had given up General Practice & gone back to hospital for paediatrics. Although his patients will certainly miss him, & despite the disparity in salaries, I think his decision has much to commend itself. With his background, training & experience he should be an exceptionally valuable medical guru. The treatment of children's diseases is an essential part of the medical profession. One eventually learns to endure disease, pain & suffering on the part of adults, but it is, to say the least, very disturbing to see an innocent child in any form of physical or mental disability or distress. Although I am not conversant with the complex problems in this field, I assume that as a hospital doctor &, apart from his actual studies in paediatrics, he will relatively

---

i   One of Winnie Mandela's names.
ii   Ameen Arnold, her husband, was also a medical doctor.
iii   The Arnolds' children.
iv   'Ben' means sister in Gujarati.

speaking, have more time for theory than was the case as a busy doctor in General Practice.

The other dy I was paging through the family album & particularly looked at the photo where you appear with Ameen & the chdn. He looks sharp & professional. Written across his face is the expression of a man who has been steeled by the tough sport of karate & who knows how to enjoy success in life without ostentation. I wish him well in his new venture & his decision should bring a lot of joy to both the patients & staff of the Red Cross Hospital.[i] There he will probably work together with Mrs Monica Kobas, an old friend from Fort Hare.[ii] If so, please ask him to give her & family our fondest regards.

Thinking about you hitting a century, I was listening to a radio tape on longevity a few dys ago, particularly on people who had reached 100 yrs of age. The speaker dealt with the position in England & stressed that the number of these people had increased substantially, especially after the introduction of the National Health Scheme in that country. I was somewhat surprised, even though pleasantly, to hear from the speaker that senility is a problem that can be medically controlled even at such an advanced age in a man's life. I had all along equated it with old age & assumed that one's mental faculties must inevitably deteriorate as he ages. But apparently it is not necessarily so.

But to come back to Mother Earth, it pleases me to hear that Mymoena & Shukri are making good progress at school. From the photo, they seem to be growing very fast & the difference between their pictures taken at Burnwood Rd & the one you sent me is quite remarkable. I wish I could see them face to face & chat to them at their present age. It would be such a pleasure to do so & this is an aspect I miss very badly. Kindly give them my love.

I thought I had written sometime this yr to assure you that, contrary to press reports during the April General Election to the effect that I was ill, in fact I felt quite well. But on checking through my letter-book, I could find no evidence that I had actually written to you.

Even as I read the press statements that sparked off the speculation & disturbed Zami & the children, I was almost overwhelmed by a feeling of well-being, nevertheless, Dr Coetzee, the District Surgeon, gave me what I, as a layman, considered a thorough examination. Shortly thereafter, Dr Le Roux, who also lectures to medical students at Tygerberg,[iii] gave me an even more exhaustive check-up. Both of them cleared me. On [?]/8, the day after

---

i   Red Cross Children's Hospital in Cape Town.
ii   University College of Fort Hare, which Mandela attended in 1939 until 1940 when he was expelled for embarking on protest action.
iii   Tygerberg Hospital in Cape Town.

I received your invitation & birthday card, their finding was confirmed by Dr Jorg Nagel of the I.R.C.[i] I believe that such illness can be treacherous & eat you away without betraying its presence to both victim & quack. Subject to that I feel quite well & in high spirits.

Many thanks for the beautiful photos you sent me; they were all well-taken & I loved each & every one of them. But why should a generous person be so stingy this time? I thought you would send me quite a batch. Except for the one in which you appear with Ameen & the chdn, they have all disappeared. I couldn't even save the one in which you appeared with Zami.

Finally, Ayeshaben, I like you to know that it is always a pleasure to think of you, Ameen & the chdn. It gives me even more pleasure & joy to write to you. Tons & tons of love & a million kisses.

Very sincerely, Nelson

Dr Ayesha Ahmed, Cor. 39th Avenue & Connaught Rd, Elsies River, 7460

∞∞∞∞∞∞

Throughout much of Mandela's time in prison he was forced to write to various government bodies from the police to the minister of justice in a desperate attempt to protect his wife. From the time he was imprisoned right up until he was released, Winnie Mandela was the subject of a sustained campaign of abuse by the apartheid state. Her husband could only learn of attacks on his wife through some of the letters from her that reached him, from lawyers and later through the media. His sense of powerlessness must have been overwhelming at times when he could do little to assist her and could only imagine what she had to endure. To add to his anxiety was the question of the safety of their children.

═══════════

To Major-General Coetzee, South African Police

NELSON MANDELA: 466/64   Robben Island,
                                                        27 November 1981

Major-General Coetzee,
South African Police Headquarters,
Pretoria.

---

i   Possibly this stands for 'International Red Cross'.

Dear Sir,

My wife has been the subject of continuous harassment, and even persecution, by members of the Security Police for the past 12 years and, on no less than three occasions, she was even assaulted by the same police.

As a result of this treatment, and on the assumption that no senior official of the Department of Justice or of Police could have known about it, to say nothing of sanctioning or conniving at it, I wrote to Mr Pelser,[i] then Minister of Justice, and later to his successor, Mr Kruger,[ii] and drew their attention to the matter. I also requested them to order the police not to transgress the law in the execution of their duties relating to her. In neither case did I even receive the courtesy of an acknowledgement and the harassment continued unabated. Despite the fact that I have already placed the matter before two Cabinet Ministers, and notwithstanding the representations which were made from time to time to your department by the family's legal representatives, as well as my wife's independent efforts to the same effect, I have all along assumed that you may not be personally aware of the misconduct of the police in this regard.

But it is the harassment of my wife by the police in Brandfort[iii] – especially by Sgts Prinsloo, De Kock and Ramolohloane – that is my immediate concern and to which I particularly wish to draw your attention. It would seem that police hostility to her and family grows as her restriction orders in terms of the Internal Security Act of 1950 are about to expire. The implication is clear. In this connection I attach herewith a copy of a statement sent to me by my wife on the 26th September 1981 and which speaks for itself.

The application referred to in paragraph (3) of the attached statements is the urgent application I [lodged] in the Supreme Court, Bloemfontein, for an order restraining the police from preventing my daughter from receiving visitors in the house occupied by my family in Brandfort.

With regard to paragraph (II) of the same statement I must advise you that on the 29th September 1981 Mr Malefane[iv] was found not guilty and discharged by the court.

On the 2nd October 1981 I received the following telegram from my wife:

> "Ramolohloane, Mbanyane and De Kock removed car parts and deflated tyres. Malefane case dismissed. Contemplating action against administration and police."

---

i   See his letters from 14 September 1970 and 19 November 1970, pages 195 and 199.

ii   See his letters from 13 May and 25 May 1974, and 12 February 1975 on pages 251, 264, and 279.

iii Winnie Mandela was still living in the rural township of Brandfort in the Orange Free State (now Free State), where she had been banished in 1977. She lived there until 1985.

iv M. K. Malefane, a family friend.

The police are naturally at liberty to remove car parts and to deflate tyres if they reasonably believe that such measures are necessary from the point of view of security. But they are in law bound to leave the car in the same condition in which they found it. To leave it dismantled and with its tyres deflated goes beyond the execution of their duties according to law.

I must add that the Brandfort police, especially Sgt Prinsloo, have brought a variety of charges against my wife, all of which were dismissed by the courts. From what my wife tells me, it is clear that his failure to secure a conviction against her has made him bitter and vindictive. Over the past four years my wife has given me accounts on the conduct of Sgt Prinsloo, all of which indicate that he is given to offensive behaviour and violent language. In this regard I refer you to paragraph (1) of the statement in which he was described in the course of judicial proceedings as having been paralytic drunk when he raided my family.

I must further add that when my wife visited me on the 21st November 1981, she told me that on the last occasion Sgt Prinsloo searched the house, he made remarks which indicated that he was aware that we were making moves to report his conduct to his superiors and about which he made further threats against her in his usually aggressive manner. It is not clear to my wife and me just how he obtained this information; although I had already written and requested the Commissioner of Prisons for permission to communicate with you, Sgt Prinsloo apparently became aware of my correspondence on the matter before I was told that I could write to you.

Be that as it may, I am placing the whole matter before you in the hope that you will regard it as extremely undesirable that vindictive police officials, who have no respect for the law and whose conduct is so repugnant, should be entrusted with the duty of maintaining law and order in a small and isolated farming community where there is hardly any sanction whatsoever to restrain a disorderly police force.

There is another aspect to which I must also draw your attention. My wife may in terms of Prison Regulations visit me twice a month. It sometimes happens, however, the Island boat does not operate on certain days due to unfavourable weather conditions. Although other visitors may then stay over until the weather clears, she must nevertheless return to Brandfort on the day stipulated by the magistrate of that district whether or not she has been able to visit me.

In this connection I must add that she intends paying me a visit over the Christmas period and she has also applied to return on the 2nd and 3rd January 1982. As the two periods are separated by six days and she would like to spend the week after Christmas in Cape Town so as to avoid the incurring of unnecessary expenses. I hope you will be able to arrange with the Department of Justice for her to remain in Cape Town as requested.

Yours faithfully.
[Signed NRMandela]
NELSON MANDELA

[Below his letter is the following statement attached in NRM's handwriting.] Statement with regard to certain problematic areas in our household as requested by my husband on 26th September 1981 during a visit on Robben Island.

1. After the case heard on 24th August 1981, which the state lost, and in which in my evidence I explained to the court that Sgt Gert Prinsloo was paralytic drunk when he conducted the raid in my house, and harassment of myself and members of my household has been renewed with utmost zeal. The court confirmed that Matthews Mabitsela is part of my household.

2. Since then I have been raided in the early hours of the morning and once more told to identify his visitors and threatened with their detention by one Sgt De Kock who also raided the people who were fixing up my car and whom he had personally found doing so in my premises.

3. During my last visit in August Sgt de Kock and Sgt Ramolohloane, who was named in the application made by my husband for our daughter Zindzi,[i] were seen dismantling some part of the car as a result of which it was stuck [for hours] at the airport. Again on the above date during my next visit the same thing has happened.

4. The area that is causing me grave source of anxiety concerns our daughter, Zindzi. Several Bloemfontein students who have been detained and interrogated have advised me that they were questioned about her, told that it was known that they are "poisoned" by her and that she would be "removed".

5. At home Zindzi has been receiving most vulgar anonymous Afrikaans speaking telephone calls one of which said, "How about a bullet between your eyeballs."

6. Because I have been refused permission to fix up her documents I have solicited the aid of numerous friends who went with her to several offices with some of our relatives to enable her to go back to school. These people succeeded in fixing up her "pass" and obtained a travel document. She then left for university in Swaziland.

---

i   Zindziswa Mandela (1960), their youngest daughter – see the glossary.

7. My family in Orlando reports that they are harassed almost daily, questioned about Zindzi's legal travel document, how she got it, what she is doing in Swaziland, what weekend she will be visiting home, where she plans spending her holidays. Only a Mr Claasen [was] reported to be polite about these enquiries.

8. The telephone calls home pursued our daughter in Swaziland where she gets called from the middle of a lecture to be insulted on the phone.

9. Lt General Johan Coetzee personally told me how he resents communication by attorneys on family matters, because of this I have made numerous applications and requests through both Mr de Waal[i] and Mr Ismail Ayob[ii] and through the local magistrate to see Lt General Coetzee to resolve these matters. I have not even had the courtesy of a reply.

10. I have made numerous appeals to my husband as well to try and intervene in his position as head of the family. I learn he himself has grave problems with the present head of the Prisons Department, not even his correspondence is acknowledged timeously, he has no problems with the Robben Island staff.

11. Matthews Malefane[iii] is now facing trumped-up charges all instigated by the Security Branch which are allegedly:
    a) Traffic offence
    b) Reading a message to me in [L]efty Smith's[iv] funeral in Bloemfontein
    c) Being in Brandfort Location without a permit
    d) Fraud for giving 802 New Location as his address when he has no legal right to be there.

    The first matter will be heard on the 29th September 1981

12. Afrikaans speaking officers have telephoned the local shopkeeper's wife, Mrs Phehlane, and asked to call me to the phone. The voices say, "I am Mandela, call her to the phone. I have been released from the Island," then they insult her.

13. Numerous reports of friends and people unknown to me throughout the country who are detained, tortured and interrogated about me continue.

(Signed NOMZAMO Z W MANDELA)

---

i   Piet de Waal in Brandfort whose wife, Adele, had befriended Winnie Mandela.
ii   Ismail Ayob (1942–), Mandela's attorney – see the glossary.
iii M. K. Malefane.
iv   It is unclear from Mandela's handwriting whether he is referring to 'Lefty' or 'Jefty' Smith.

POLLSMOOR
MAXIMUM SECURITY
PRISON

||||||||||||

MARCH 1982–AUGUST 1988

Nelson Mandela, Walter Sisulu, Raymond Mhlaba, and Andrew Mlangeni[i] were transferred on 31 March 1982 from Robben Island to Pollsmoor Maximum Security Prison on the mainland, where they were held in a large communal cell. Shortly after their arrival, Mandela wrote to the 'kitchen department' to inform the staff of his dietary requirements[ii] and then to his lawyers in case they were not aware that he was now in another prison. They were joined in Pollsmoor Prison by Ahmed Kathrada on 21 October 1982. Mandela said he was never told why they were all transferred. He asked the commanding officer who replied that he could not say.

'I was disturbed and unsettled. What did it mean? Where were we going? In prison, one can only question and resist an order to a certain point, then one must succumb. We had no warning, no preparation. I had been on the island for over eighteen years, and to leave so abruptly?

'We were each given several large cardboard boxes in which to pack our things. Everything that I had accumulated in nearly two decades could fit into these few boxes. We packed in little more than half an hour.'[58]

A large face-brick prison complex nestling at the foot of the mountains outside Cape Town, with beds and better food, Pollsmoor was in a way a tougher existence for the men. Gone was the open space they had walked in from the cell block to the lime quarry; or down to the seashore to harvest seaweed. Separated from the rest of the prison population, they were held in a rooftop cell and could only see the sky from their yard.

---

i   For notes on these individuals, see the glossary.
ii   Mandela was strict about his diet and asked for it to be salt-free.

To the head of prison, Pollsmoor Maximum Security Prison

D220/82[i]: NELSON MANDELA

The Head of Prison,
Pollsmoor Maximum Prison
Attention: Kitchen Department

Kindly note that for health reasons I am on a salt free diet. I am also not on eggs.
[Signed NRMandela]
[not dated but the date handwritten by a prison official is 82/04/20]

[In another hand in Afrikaans] Dealt with
[Signed] W/O[ii] Venter

To the head of prison, Pollsmoor Maximum Security Prison

D220/82: N MANDELA

21.1.83

The Head of Prison,
Pollsmoor Maximum Prison.
Attention: Captain Zaayman

I must ask you to investigate, once again, the question of the letter which Prof. Carter[iii] wrote to me, the censoring of the letter from Mrs Mgabela,[iv] as well as the three other issues mentioned below. I repeat this request in the hope and confidence that you will re-examine these questions with the detachment and understanding they deserve.

I must stress that the reply I received in response to my representations to you suggests that despite the care and patience with which I explained the whole matter, in fact you did not understand me and accordingly misdirected your enquiries.

---

i   He was issued with a new prison number at Pollsmoor Prison (see page xvii for more information about his prison numbers).
ii   Warrant Officer.
iii   Professor Gwendolen M. Carter (1906–91), Canadian–American political scientist and scholar of African affairs. She was a benefactor.
iv   Wife of Patrick Magubela (d. 2009), an MK cadre who was released from Robben Island in 1990.

1. Letter from Prof. Carter

   On the two previous occasions I raised this particular matter with you, I pointed out that Prof. Carter had written to me in May last year after she had read press reports that I had been transferred to this prison. I further pointed out to you that the letter was probably lying in some office in this establishment and that you might be able to trace it in the course of a proper search.

   But then the other day the warder in charge in this section read me a written note, purporting to come from you, to the effect that Robben Island Prison had informed you that no letter from Prof. Carter had been received. In view of the fact I expressly explained to you that the letter had been addressed to this prison, I could not understand why Robben Island was ever brought in. I must, therefore, request you to look into this matter again and to advise me of the results of your enquiry in due course.

2. Letter from Mrs Mgabela

   You did not respond at all to my request relating to this question. But in the notes which were read out to me by the warder in charge there was a message to Mr Magubela which appeared to be your response to the request I had earlier made to you on the same issue.

   You will readily appreciate that it is not easy for one to comment with regard to the actual words which were deemed by the censors to be objectionable. But what is perfectly clear is that either your failure to respond to me or the error you made is certainly no evidence you gave the matter the attention it deserves.

3. Letter from Mrs Njongwe[i]

   About a week or so before Christmas I received a Christmas card from Mrs Njongwe in which she said I should expect a letter from her. In this connection, I will appreciate it if you will be good enough to advise me whether the letter has been received.

4. Heads of Argument in the case of myself v. the Minister of Prisons[ii]

   Again, you have not responded in this matter. As you are aware this is a different question from the one you referred to Pretoria.

---

i   Connie Njongwe, wife of Jimmy Njongwe (1919–76), medical doctor, ANC leader, and organiser of the Defiance Campaign (for the Defiance Campaign, see the glossary) in the Eastern Cape – for Jimmy Njongwe, see the glossary.
ii   Mandela brought a case against the Minister of Prisons when documents he handed to his attorney were confiscated.

5. Letter from Mrs Mandela

When my wife visited me on Christmas Day she brought me a letter addressed to her from an organisation of women from the U.S.A. When she was refused permission to show it to me, she promised to post it from Cape Town. Please advise me whether the letter has been received.

I wish to indicate in conclusion that I would really like to settle these and other matters falling within your jurisdiction directly with you, and not to burden the Commanding Officer about issues which you can easily and satisfactorily dispose of. It is in this spirit that I request you to go into these matters, and it is to be hoped that you will handle them in this spirit.

[Signed NRMandela]

[Handwritten note in another hand] Warrant Officer Gregory. Refer this matter to Captain Zaayman.
[Signed]
83/02/25

———————

To the head of prison, Pollsmoor Maximum Security Prison

D220/82: N MANDELA

25.2.83

The Head of Prison,
Pollsmoor Maximum Prison.

Attention: Major Van Sittert

The warder in charge of this section advises me that you have instructed that no woollen head-cover should be bought for me, and that I will be allowed to select a suitable hat from several kinds supplied by the Prisons Department.

I trust that you will be able to reconsider your decision and that you will not refuse a recommendation made by a specialist physician and from a medical practitioner attached to this prison; recommendations which are based on medical and humanitarian considerations and on grounds of convenience.

The plaster and stitches were removed from the wound[i] on 14th February and I have been battling to get a head cover since that day. It is, to say the least, indifference on the part of this Department to withhold from me, for so long, an article which will facilitate recovery.

I have already tried to wear a prison hat and it has proved totally unsuitable. Its effect has only been to make a sensitive wound even more sensitive, apart from the fact that I cannot sleep wearing a hat.

I have the confidence that you will be good enough not to use your authority as to make me a caricature of myself by compelling me to see my family and legal representatives without a suitable head cover.

[Signed NRMandela]

To Russel Piliso, his brother-in-law and husband of his sister Leabie[ii]

[Translated from isiXhosa]

D220/82: N MANDELA,

29.6.83

Dear brother-in-law,

I received the response from Miss Leabie giving me feedback on the role you played during the burial of my sister Baliwe. I received the news of her death in a telegram from Bambilanga,[iii] which I quickly responded to. Miss Leabie's letter came after I had sent my letter of gratitude to Bambilanga. There is only one thing I would like to say to you, and that is to echo the words of our elders, 'I thank you'.[iv] As you are aware, my present circumstances do not allow me to say anything further; however receive my heartfelt condolences.

Again, I thank you.

Please pass my sincerest regards to Miss Leabie, Phathiswa[v] and the rest of the family. Yours truly, Madiba

---

i   Mandela wrote on 2 February 1983 in his prison desk calendar that he was admitted to Woodstock Hospital for surgery on his toe and the back of his head. He does not provide other details.
ii   Leabie Makhutswana Piliso (1930–97), Mandela's sister.
iii   Bambilanga (also known as Nxeko) is the brother of King Sabata Jonguhlanga Dalindyebo, paramount chief of the Transkei homeland.
iv   In the original letter Mandela uses the isiXhosa word *nangamso*, which expresses deep gratitude to a person who has gone beyond the call of duty.
v   Possibly Leabie Piliso's daughter.

9.3.84. This letter was written on 29.693

[envelope]
Mr Russel S. Piliso
S.A.P.
Tsolo
P.O. Tsolo, TRANSKEI

─────────────

To Adele de Waal, a friend of his wife, Winnie Mandela

D220/82: NELSON MANDELA

29.8.83

Dear Adele,

[Written in Afrikaans] My knowledge of Afrikaans is very bad and my vocabulary leaves a lot to be desired. At my age I am struggling to learn grammar and to improve my syntax. It would certainly be disastrous if I wrote this letter in Afrikaans. I sincerely hope you will understand if I change to English.

[Written in English] Zami[i] has told me several times of the interest you and Piet[ii] have shown in her problems over the past 6 years. Although I have on each occasion requested her to convey my appreciation to you, the beautiful and valuable present of books you sent me has given me the opportunity of writing to thank you directly for your efforts.

It was certainly not so easy for her at middle-age to leave her home and to start life in a new and strange environment and where she has no means of earning a livelihood. In this regard, the response of friends has, on the whole, been magnificent, and it made it possible for her to generate the inner strength to endure what she cannot avoid. We were particularly fortunate to be able to count on the friendship of a family that is right on the spot and to whom she can turn when faced with immediate problems. [Written in Afrikaans] You and Piet have contributed significantly to her relative safety and happiness. [Written in English] I sincerely hope that one

---

i   One of Winnie Mandela's names.
ii   Petrus Johannes de Waal (1932–2001), a lawyer, had a legal practice in Brandfort where he met Winnie Mandela who had been banished to the town. They became friends. He was a friend of justice minister Kobie Coetsee. The couple's friendship with Winnie Mandela is said to have made an impact on Coetsee who later visited Mandela in hospital in late 1985. Mandela then contacted him about talks with the government which began the following year.

day I will be able to join you in your village and shake your hands very warmly as we chat along.

[Written in Afrikaans] Schalk Pienaar's book *Witness to Great Times* is one of the books on the shelf. On page 13 there is a reference to a farmer,[i] Pieter de Waal, who participated in the 1938 oxwagon trek to Monument Hill. According to the story he succeeded to calm a group of restive trekkers in Oggies in the Free State. Perhaps he was Piet's father or grandfather.

[Written in English] Whenever Piet's name is mentioned, especially when I receive a letter from him, I instinctively think of a friend, Mr Combrink, from that world who probably is now running a flourishing legal firm. I last saw him about 30 years ago when he used to work in a dairy during the night and as an articled clerk during the day. Perhaps Piet will be able to give him my regards if and when he meets him.

Meantime, I send you, Piet and the children my fondest regards, and hope that your daughter is doing well in England.

Sincerely,
Nelson.

Mrs Adele de Waal, Duke Street, P.O. Brandfort, 9400.

To the commissioner of prisons

[This letter is in Ahmed Kathrada's handwriting but signed by Mandela]

6th October 1983

The Commissioner of Prisons
Pretoria

Sir,

We have been informed by the local authorities that in accordance with an instruction from Prison Headquarters, prisoners who are taken to doctors, hospitals, courts etc. will in future be handcuffed and put in leg irons. We are told that this is to be applied to all prisoners, i.e. security

---

i   The Afrikaans word Mandela used is *uitsaaiman*, which can mean farmer or broadcaster.

prisoners[i] as well as common law prisoners.

We wish to make an earnest appeal to you to reconsider your decision relating to security prisoners, and allow the present position to continue.

During the 20 years that we have spent in prison there have been numerous changes in our treatment. Previously we had been handcuffed when we were taken from Robben Island to Cape Town, but for a number of years this had been discontinued. We welcomed and appreciated the discontinuance, as we welcomed all changes that were designed to alleviate the hardships of prison life and make our stay more tolerable. Of special concern to us was the removal of practices which were not only outdated but which were unnecessarily burdensome and humiliating.

While we do not wish to comment on the general security arrangements of the Prisons Department, we nevertheless wish to make some observations in support of our present appeal.

1) To the best of our knowledge, during the entire period of our incarceration there has not been a single instance where a security prisoner has escaped, or even attempted to do so, while being escorted to Cape Town for medical reasons.

2) For the year and a half that we have been at Pollsmoor our experience has been that each time any of us was taken out, he was invariably accompanied by four or more warders, some armed. Often the warders were accompanied by a member of the Security Police.

3) This elaborate arrangement has been strictly applied in spite of our advanced ages and physical condition.

4) In our opinion such arrangements were, and still remain, quite adequate and the additional restraints are totally unwarranted, burdensome and humiliating. This is aggravated by the great deal of attention and curiosity that is aroused among the public at the sight of handcuffed prisoners.

5) We are certain that Robben Island and Pollsmoor authorities will be able to bear out our contention that security prisoners could not be accused of having abused the "medical outings".

6) It has been pointed out to us – and recently with greater emphasis –

---

i   A security prisoner is the same thing as a political prisoner.

that there is no distinction in the treatment of prisoners irrespective of whether they are common law or security prisoners.

7) With respect, Sir, may we remind you that this is not strictly in accordance with the factual position. For example, security prisoners are denied the privilege of contact visits, and, generally even though they may be classified as "A Groups" they suffer from restrictions in their day to day stay. Perhaps more important; security prisoners on the whole are being denied the facilities for remission and parole enjoyed by other prisoners. We believe that the few to whom this dispensation was extended were given remission ranging from a couple of weeks to a few months.

8) We submit that since differential treatment does in fact exist, there should be no reason why security prisoners should not be exempted from the instructions regarding handcuffs and leg irons.

9) Lastly, from the point of view of health we consider these new arrangements to be a decided disadvantage. A number of us are suffering from high blood pressure, and it is important that when we are taken to specialists we should be relaxed and completely free of tension. It is likely that the humiliation and resentment caused by handcuffs will adversely affect our blood pressure. To an extent, therefore, this would be defeating the purpose [of] our consulting the specialists.

We respectfully state that we cannot think of a single valid reason why this new restriction should be applied to us, and we once again appeal to you to abandon them.

Thank you,
Yours faithfully
[Signed NRMandela]
N.R. Mandela

To Fatima Meer,[i] a friend

[Stamp dated 30.1.84]

---

i　Fatima Meer (1928–2010), writer, academic, and anti-apartheid and women's rights activist – see the glossary.

Our dear Fatimaben,[i]
Arthur & Louise Glickman c/o Glickman farm R.F.D. 2, Clinton, Maine, 04927, U.S., have twice sent me a cheque but without a covering note. Although I asked Zami[ii] to write & thank them on my behalf, it is proper for me to add to what she has said to them. But my main difficulty is that I have not information on them other than the particulars that appear on their cheques. You will be the best person to contact them & thereafter send me the particulars at your earliest convenience.

Our niece, LWAZI VUTELA, a teenage daughter of Zami's late elder sister, is also over there. She is a second yr student at Wellesly College, Box 128, McAfee Hall, Wellesley M.A., 02181, U.S.A. I don't know just how far her college is from Swarthmore,[iii] but I will be happy if you can see her & perhaps introduce her to some of your friends there.[iv]

She tells me that she has written me several letters from the States, all of which I never received. She adds that most of the time she is lonely & homesick, which is quite understandable for a person of her age. She will find your advice on both academic & personal matters valuable.

Talking of people in the U.S.A., I was very disturbed when I read in the *Time* Magazine that our friend, Senator Paul Tsongas, from Massachusetts, is suffering from some form of cancer & that, as a result, he will not seek election for a second term in Nov. As you know, he has visited Zami in Brandfort & has, in the process, become a good family friend. I was sorry to learn of his illness & sincerely hope that the illness was detected in time & that he will recover completely in due course. As you know, I cannot write to him & all that I can do is to ask you to give him our good wishes & fondest regards. Do you hope to see professors Gwen Carter[v] & Karis?[vi]

I trust that it will be possible for you to visit the holy city of Mecca & Tehran & New Delhi. I would have written to Indira[vii] long ago but, as you know, she is among those who are beyond my reach in terms of my current circumstances.[viii] From this distance she seems to be doing exceptional[ly] well & I always read news about her with great interest.

My fondest regards to her.

What is Rashid[ix] doing now & where? You have kept me informed about the girls but given away very little on the heir.

---

i   *Ben* means 'sister' in Gujarati.
ii   One of Winnie Mandela's names.
iii   Swarthmore College, Pennsylvania, United States.
iv   Fatima Meer was a visiting lecturer at Swarthmore College.
v   Professor Gwendolen M. Carter (1906–91), Canadian–American political scientist and scholar of African affairs. She was a benefactor.
vi   Thomas Karis (1919–2017), American academic and author who wrote about South Africa's political history.
vii   Indira Gandhi (1917–84), prime minister of India.
viii Mandela was not allowed to write to heads of state.
ix   Fatima and Ismail Meer's son.

Needless to say, in my current circumstances it is not easy to appreciate precisely what game Bansi[i] is now playing. Whatever it may be it seems to me that he has chosen a pitch more likely to favour batsmen George,[ii] Archie,[iii] Farouk[iv] & others rather than him, Pat,[v] J,[vi] B & YS.[vii]

The Chancellorship![viii] I had already exhausted my 1983 quota of outgoing letters when your telegram came, & my response was limited to the special brief note of acceptance that I sent to you and the principal. This is the very first opportunity I have to thank you & all those who supported our candidature for the office. I am, however confident that everybody was from the outset well aware of the real issues involved, & that it is unrealistic, at this stage in the country's history, to expect an incarcerated black candidate to be elected Chancellor of a white university, especially of Natal where apparently the Senate, & not members of Convocation, has the final say on the matter. Maybe that on your return, it will be possible for you to investigate, if that is possible, exactly what measure of support we enjoyed. Meantime do give everybody our sincere appreciation & thanks.

I have not heard from Maki[ix] for quite some time now. But she promised to start this mnth & I hope you fully briefed Ismail[x] on her before your departure.

Coming back to you, it seems that I must congratulate you in every letter that I write to you. In my last letter I congratulated you on your appointment as Prof; press reports indicate that Swarthmore will honour you with a doctorate, an honour, which in my view, you rightly deserve. This is more than a triumph of Women's Lib & I fear that poor Ismail had joined those husbands who are known more through their wives. There must be many who now refer to him as "Fatima's husband". I miss him very much & I was very happy when press reports indicated that he was one of the speakers in Mota's[xi] commemoration service. This is a very long

---

i   Amichand Rajbansi (1942–2001), known as the 'Bengal Tiger'. He formed the National People's Party in 1981, and was appointed to the tricameral parliament as head of the House of Delegates, a body for South African Indians, by prime minister P. W. Botha in 1984. Prisoners were not allowed to write about political events which is probably why he is using a cricket metaphor.

ii   George Sewpersadh (1936–2007), former president of the Natal Indian Congress and a United Democratic Front activist who campaigned against the tricameral parliament.

iii   Archie Gumede (1914–98), son of Josiah Gumede, a president of the South African Native National Congress (which later became the ANC), was a lawyer and activist in the ANC and the United Democratic Front of which he was a joint president with Oscar Mpetha and Albertina Sisulu – see the glossary.

iv   Dr Farouk Meer, brother of Fatima Meer (for Fatima Meer, see the glossary) and a Natal Indian Congress and United Democratic Front activist.

v   Pat Poovalingam (d. 2009), who also accepted appointment to the South Africa Indian Council.

vi   J is possibly J. N. Reddy, chair of the South African Indian Council initiated by the apartheid regime. Rajbansi later took over chairmanship from Reddy.

vii   Y. S. Chinsamy also joined the South African Indian Council.

viii   Mandela was nominated for the position of chancellor of Natal University.

ix   Makaziwe Mandela (1954–), Mandela's eldest daughter – see the glossary.

x   Ismail Meer (1918–2000), Fatima's husband and a lawyer and anti-apartheid activist – see the glossary.

xi   Yusuf Dadoo (1909–83), medical doctor, anti-apartheid activist, and orator. President of South African Indian Congress, deputy to Oliver Tambo on the Revolutionary Council of MK, and chairman of the South African

letter & I must now stop so that you can rest a bit. Tons & tons of love
Fatimaben.

Very sincerely, Nelson.

Kindly register all your letters to me.

───────────

To Trevor Tutu, son of Desmond & Leah Tutu[i]

[This letter was retyped in a telex[ii] to the Commissioner of Prisons]
[Note in Afrikaans] Confidential
913

Commissioner of Prisons
AK Security

For immediate delivery to Brig Venster please

1. The prisoner is still trying to make contact with Bishop Desmond
   Tutu. He is now writing to the Bishop's son, Trevor Tutu, and is in this
   way attempting to contact the Bishop.
2. Below find the contents of the letter

D220/82: NELSON MANDELA   Pollsmoor Maximum Prison
                                 P/B X 4
                                 TOKAI
                                 7966
                                 84.08.06

My dear Trevor,

It was shocking to learn that your home was attacked and damaged, and I
sincerely hope that the knowledge that you and your parents are constantly
in our thoughts, particularly since we saw the disturbing report, will give
you more strength and courage.

───────────

Communist Party – see the glossary. Yusuf Dadoo was commonly known as Mota, short for *Motabhai*, the Gujarati
word for 'elder brother'. He had been living in exile since 1960.

i   Desmond Tutu (1931–), first black archbishop of Cape Town, and his wife Leah Tutu (1933–) – see the glossary for
      notes on both these individuals.
ii   A telex is a method of communication where teletypewriters are connected to a telephonic network to send
      messages via radio signals or electricity.

We love and respect your parents; they are never very far from the ramparts, and they carry a lamp which throws up a strong and bright flame which tends to shine far beyond the family circle. Any danger or threat of danger to them immediately becomes a matter of real concern to us all. Please assure them that they enjoy our admiration and that we wish them good fortune and the best of luck. That is one reason why the cruel attack on the house disturbed us so much.

During the last ten years, and more particularly since 1979, there is virtually nothing I have not tried to contact your father, but all my efforts were in vain. If this brief note reaches you, he must know that this is the nearest I can come to him.

But this is your letter and I want to tell you that a few years back, I read an article under your name in the *Sunday Express*, I think, which I found interesting. I thought it then, as I still do, that you have something to say. I accordingly hoped that you would write regularly in that paper and I was disappointed when your articles did not appear.

There is a wide and eager audience for fresh ideas, from young people who can think correctly and express themselves well. This is why I still look forward to seeing your articles some day. Meantime, I send my fondest regards and best wishes to you, Zanele[i] & the baby; your sisters, Thandeka and Naomi and their husbands and, of course, to your parents.

Very sincerely,
Uncle Nelson

Mr Trevor Tutu, P.O. Box 31190, Braamfontein, 2017

PS. Any response to this note must be registered

[Another note in Afrikaans]
3. The recipient [Trevor Tutu] is being encouraged to go ahead with propaganda in the newspapers. And he [Mandela] is also encouraging and supporting Bishop Tutu's action on various fronts
4. This letter must not be released
   Commanding Officer
   Commander of Pollsmoor Prison
   Brigadier F C Munro

---

i   Trevor Tutu's wife.

◇◇◇◇◇◇◇◇◇

The first offer to release Mandela from prison came in 1974, on condition that he agreed to move to the region of his birth, the rural Transkei. His rejection of the proposal was not enough to kill the idea. Ten years later, his nephew Kaiser Matanzima[i] approached him with the same offer. Matanzima, known by his initials, KD, or by his initiation name, Daliwonga, had been with his freedom fighter relative at Fort Hare University. Mandela was angry to discover years later that Matanzima had involved himself in the apartheid regime's 'Bantustan' programme whereby nominal independence was given to so-called African homelands. The apartheid regime aimed to rid South Africa of all black people and so created ten homelands set aside for the occupation of Africans, which were organised by ethnic group. Four of them – Transkei, Ciskei, Bophuthatswana, and Venda – were declared 'independent states' but were not recognised by other countries. Others had partial autonomy. The government carried out forced removals and literally dumped millions of people in these territories. They were generally poverty-stricken and provided few opportunities. Bophuthatswana, for instance, consisted of scattered and separate pieces of land and one had to cross through South African territory to get from one part of it to the other.

Within months of Mandela's refusal of Matanzima's offer, South Africa's president, P. W. Botha, used his State of the Nation Address at the opening of Parliament to suggest that all political prisoners would be freed on condition that they denounced violence as a method to achieving democracy. Mandela's responses were withering in their rage. Both the letter written to Botha directly and a message written for a political rally, where it was read out by his daughter Zindzi,[ii] showed to the world a man who was not about to be manipulated.

Black South Africans were once more on the rise and virtually on a daily basis protests emerged from almost every corner of the country. The United Democratic Front, a huge umbrella body of anti-apartheid organisations, was unveiled in late 1983 and became the de facto internal ANC.

Botha's declaration of a series of states of emergency from 1985 did not quell the anger of the people but increased their determination. South Africa was subject to martial law, leaving tens of thousands, including children, detained without trial, many for years. Each protest resulted in death at the barrel of the state's weaponry. And every funeral resulted in further death.

The potent combination of the ANC in exile and the anti-apartheid movement in general had succeeded in bringing the inhumanity of apartheid into the world's psyche. Economic and other sanctions were beginning to bite against the apartheid regime.

---

i   K. D. Matanzima (1915– 2003), Thembu chief, and chief minister for the Transkei – see the glossary.
ii   Zindziswa Mandela (1960–), Mandela's youngest daughter – see the glossary.

To Winnie Mandela,[i] his wife

D220/82: NELSON MANDELA   27.12.84

Darling Mum,

[Sections of] the letter to Daliwonga,[ii] which I handed in this morning for dispatch to Umtata,[iii] were summarised in the front page of today's *Die Burger*[iv] with the following headline: Matanzima doen aanbod (Matanzima makes an offer) Mandela verwerp vrylating (Mandela rejects release). This is the letter.

"Ngubengcuka,[v]

Nobandla[vi] has informed me that you have pardoned my nephews,[vii] and I am grateful for the gesture. I am more particularly touched when I think of my sister's feeling about the matter and I thank you once more for your kind consideration.

Nobandla also informs me that you have now been able to persuade the Government to release political prisoners, and that you have also consulted with the other "homeland" leaders who have given you their full support in the matter. It appears from what she tells me that you and the Government intend that I and some of my colleagues should be released to Umtata.

I perhaps need to remind you that when you first wanted to visit us in 1977 my colleagues and I decided that, because of your position in the implementation of the Bantustan system, we could not accede to your request.

Again in February this year when you wanted to come and discuss the question of our release, we reiterated our stand and your request was not acceded to. In particular, we pointed out that the idea of our release being linked to a Bantustan was totally and utterly unacceptable to us.

While we appreciate your concern over the incarceration of political

---

i   Nomzamo Winifred Madikizela-Mandela (1936–) – see the glossary.

ii   K. D. Matanzima (1915– 2003), Mandela's nephew, a Thembu chief, and chief minister for the Transkei – see the glossary.

iii   Umtata (now called Mthatha) was the capital of the Transkei homeland.

iv   Daily Afrikaans-language newspaper.

v   A reference to him being a descendant of King Ngubengcuka who was also Mandela's great-great-grandfather.

vi   His wife, Winnie Mandela.

vii Mandela wrote 'nephews' plural but he is referring to King Sabata Jonguhlanga Dalindyebo (1928–86), paramount chief of the Transkei homeland and leader of the Democratic Progressive Party, the opposition party in Transkei which opposed apartheid rule – see the glossary. He fled to Zambia in 1980 after being convicted of violating the dignity of the Transkei's president K. D. Matanzima.

prisoners, we must point out that your persistence in linking our release with the Bantustans, despite our strong and clearly expressed opposition to the scheme, is highly disturbing, if not provocative, and we urge you to not continue pursuing a course which will inevitably result in an unpleasant confrontation between you and ourselves.

We will, under no circumstances, accept being released to the Transkei or any other Bantustan. You know fully well that we have spent the better part of our lives in prison exactly because we are opposed to the very idea of separate development which makes us foreigners in our own country and which enables the Government to perpetuate our oppression up to this very day.

We accordingly request you to desist from this explosive plan and we sincerely hope that this is the last time we will ever be pestered with it.

Ozithobileyo,[i]
Dalibunga.''

Purely as a matter of courtesy, I would have preferred that the contents of the letter should be published only after Daliwonga had received it. But publication was made without our consent and even knowledge.
I hope you will be able to make it on the 5th & 6th of next month. Our time was very short and we had so much to talk about.

About the Charman's, I can see no objection whatsoever in you accepting an unconditional offer which will enable you to feed those hungry mouths around you. But as I said, you must consult very fully but quickly on the matter. You now need a nightwatchman to look after the house and the complex; a reliable watchman, and you should be able to sort out the matter with the church leaders there.

With regard to the forthcoming clinic I suggest that you also include Dr Rachid Saloojee[ii] from Lenasia. He is a good fellow and Amina[iii] should be able to contact him on your behalf.

Thanks a lot for the visit, the nice things you said and for your love, darling Mum. Looking forward to seeing you soon. I LOVE YOU!
Affectionately, Madiba.
Nkosk Nobandla Mandela, 802 Phathakahle, P.O. Brandfort.

---

i   'Yours obediently' in isiXhosa.
ii   Dr. Rashid Ahmed Mahmood Salojee (1933–) Transvaal Indian Congress vice president and later ANC member of Parliament and Gauteng Provincial Legislature.
iii   Amina Cachalia (1930–2013), friend and anti-apartheid and women's rights activist – see the glossary.

NELSON MANDELA.   27 · 12 · 84

Mum,

...s of the letter to Dalwonga, which I handed in this morning for dispatch
to Umtata, were summarised in the front page of today's _Die Burger_ with the
following headline; Matanzima doen aanbod (Matanzima makes an offer)
Mandela verwerp vrylating (Mandela rejects release). This is the letter
cc Ngubengcuka,

Nobandla has informed me that you have pardoned my nephews, and I am
grateful for the gesture. I am more particularly touched when I think of my sister's
feeling about the matter and I thank you once more for your kind consideration.

Nobandla also informs me that you have now been able to persuade the
Government to release political prisoners, and that you have also consulted with
the other "homeland" leaders who have given you their full support in the
matter. It appears from what she tells me that you and the Government intend
that I and some of my colleagues should be released to Umtata.

I perhaps need to remind you that when you first wanted to visit us in 1977
my colleagues and I decided that, because of your position in the implementation
of the Bantustan scheme, we could not accede to your request.

Again in February this year when you wanted to come and discuss the question
of our release, we reiterated our stand and your request was not acceded to.
In particular, we pointed out that the idea of our release being linked to a
Bantustan was totally and utterly unacceptable to us.

While we appreciate your concern over the incarceration of political prisoners, we
must point out that your persistence in linking our release with the
Bantustans, despite our strong and clearly-expressed opposition to the
scheme, is highly disturbing, if not provocative, and we urge you not to
continue pursuing a course which will inevitably result in an unpleasant
confrontation between you and ourselves.

We will, under no circumstances, accept being released to the Transkei
or any other Bantustan. You know very well fully well that we have spent the
better part of our lives in prison exactly because we are opposed to the
very idea of separate development, which makes us foreigners in our

A letter to Winnie Mandela, 27 December 1984, see previous pages.

2

47

own country, and which enables the Government to perpetuate our oppression to this very day.

We accordingly request you to desist from this explosive plan, and we sincerely hope that this is the last time we will ever be pestered with it.

Ozithokileyo,
Dalibunga.   "

Purely as a matter of courtesy, I would have preferred that the contents of the letter should be published only after Dalibunga had received it. But publication was made without our consent and even knowledge.

I hope you will be able to make it on the 5th & 6th of next month. Our time was very short and we had so much to talk about.

About the Chairman's £. I can see no objection whatsoever in you accepting an unconditional offer which will enable you to feed those hungry mouths around you. But as I said, you must consult very fully but quickly on the matter. You now need a night watchman to look after the house and the complex; a reliable watchman, and you should be able to sort out the matter with the church leaders there.

With regard to the forthcoming clinic I suggest that you also include Dr Rachid Saloojee from Lenasia. He is a good fellow and Amina should be able to contact him on your behalf.

Thanks a lot for the visit, the nice things you said and for your hot, darling mum. Looking forward to seeing you soon. I love you!

Affectionately, Madiba.

Nkosk Nobandla Mandela, 802 Phathakahle, P.O. Brandfort.

To Ismail Meer,[i] friend and comrade

D220/82: NELSON MANDELA   29.1.85

Dear Ismail,

I have missed you so much these 22 yrs that there are occasions when I even entertain the wild hope that one good morning I will be told that you are waiting for me in the consultation room downstairs.

As I watch the world ageing, scenes from our younger days in Kholvad House[ii] & Umngeni Rd[iii] come back so vividly as if they occurred only the other day – plodding endlessly on our text books, travelling to & from Milner Park,[iv] indulging in a bit of agitation, now on opposite sides & now together, some fruitless polemic with Boola[v] & Essack,[vi] & kept going throughout those lean yrs by a litany of dreams & expectations, some of which have been realised, while the fulfilment of others still eludes us to this day.

Nevertheless, few people will deny that the harvest has merely been delayed but far from destroyed. It is out there on rich & well-watered fields, even though the actual task of gathering it has proved far more testing than we once thought. For the moment, however, all that I want to tell you is that I miss you & that thinking of you affords me a lot of pleasure, & makes life rich & pleasant even under these grim conditions.

But it is about that tragic 31 October[vii] that I want to talk to you. You will, of course, appreciate that my present position does not allow me to express my feelings & thoughts fully & freely as I would have liked. It is sufficient to say that when reports reach us that Indiraben[viii] had passed away, I had already exhausted my 1984 quota of outgoing letters. This is the only reason why it took me so long to respond.

Even though Zami[ix] may have already conveyed our condolences (please

---

i   Ismail Meer (1918–2000), a lawyer and anti-apartheid activist – see the glossary.
ii   Kholvad House, an apartment block in downtown Johannesburg where Ismail Meer had an apartment. Mandela writes in *Long Walk to Freedom*, 'At Wits I met and became friends with Ismail Meer, J.N. Singh, Ahmed Bhoola, and Ramlal Bhoolia. The centre of this tight-knit community was Ismail's apartment, Flat 13, Kholvad House, four rooms in a residential building in the centre of the city. There we studied, talked and even danced until the early hours of the morning, and it became a kind of headquarters for young freedom fighters. I sometimes slept there when it was too late to catch the last train back to Orlando.' (NM, *Long Walk to Freedom*, p. 105.)
iii   Where Ismail and Fatima Meer lived in the 1950s.
iv   Location of the University of the Witwatersrand where Mandela and Ismail Meer met.
v   Ahmed Bhoola, a Durban lawyer who wrote for the *Leader* newspaper.
vi   Abdul Karrim Essack, African People's Democratic Union of Southern Africa and Natal Unity Movement leader who went into exile in the 1950s and died in Tanzania in 1997.
vii   Indian prime minister Indira Gandhi (1917–84) was assassinated on 31 October 1984.
viii   Indira Gandhi.
ix   His wife, Winnie Mandela.

check) I would like Rajiv[i] to know that he & family are in our thoughts in their bereavement, that on occasions of this nature it is appropriate to recall the immortal words which have been said over & over again: When you are alone, you are not alone, there is always a haven of friends nearby. For Rajiv now to feel all alone is but natural. But in actual fact he is not alone. We are his friends, we are close to him & we fully [Share] the deep sorrow that has hit the family.

Indira was a brick of pure gold & her death is a painful blow which [we] find difficult to endure. She lived up to expectations & measured remarkably well to the countless challenges which confronted her during the last 18 yrs.

[There] must be few world leaders who are so revered but who are lovingly [referred] to by their first name by thousands of South Africans as Indira. [People] from different walks of life seemed to have accepted her as one of [them] &, to them, she could have come from Cato Manor,[ii] Soweto,[iii] or District [Six].[iv] That explains why her death has been so shattering.

[I] had hoped that one day Zami and I would travel all the way to India to meet Indira in person. That hope became a resolution especially after 1979. Although the yrs keep on rolling away & old age is beginning to threaten, hope [never] fades & that journey remains one of my fondest dreams.

[We] wish Rajiv well in his new office[v] & we sincerely hope that his youth & good health, his training & the support of friends from far & wide will enable him to bear the heavy work load with the same strength & assurance as was displayed by his famous mother over the past 18yrs. Again, our sincerest sympathies to Rajiv, Sonia[vi] & Maneka.[vii]

I must repeat that I miss you badly & I hope you are keeping well. I do look forward to seeing you some day. Until then our love & fondest regards to you, Fatima,[viii] the children & everybody. Please do tell me about Nokhukhanya[ix] & her children.

Very Sincerely,
Nelson

Mr Ismail Meer, 148 Burnwood Rd, Sydenham, 4091

---

i   Rajiv Gandhi (1944–91), one of Indira Gandhi's sons.
ii   A working-class are outside of Durban, Natal (now KwaZulu-Natal).
iii Township in Johannesburg.
iv   Working-class area in Johannesburg.
v   He succeeded his mother as prime minister of India.
vi   Rajiv Gandhi's wife Sonia.
vii The widow of Sanjay Gandhi, Rajiv's brother who died in a plane crash in 1980.
viii Fatima Meer, Ismail Meer's wife.
ix   Nokhukhanya Luthuli, widow of Chief Albert Luthuli.

To P. W. Botha, president of South Africa

13 February 1985

The Commissioner of Prisons,
Pretoria.

The subjoined letter is for the attention of the State President,
Mr P. W. Botha :

"The State President,
Cape Town

Sir,

Copies of the *Hansard* parliamentary record to 25 January to 1 February
were delivered to us on 8 February.

We note that during the debate in the House of Assembly you indicated that you were prepared to release prisoners in our particular category
provided that we unconditionally renounce violence as a means of furthering our political objectives.

We have given earnest consideration to your offer but we regret to
inform you that it is not acceptable in its present form. We hesitate to associate you with a move which, on a proper analysis, appears to be no more
than a shrewd and calculated attempt to mislead the world into the belief
that you have magnanimously offered us release from prison which we
ourselves have rejected. Coming in the face of such unprecedented and
widespread demand for our release, your remarks can only be seen as the
height of cynical politicking.

We refuse to be party to anything which is really intended to create
division, confusion and uncertainty within the African National Congress
at a time when the unity of the organisation has become a matter of crucial
importance to the whole country. The refusal by the Department of Prisons to allow us to consult fellow prisoners in other prisons has confirmed
our view.

Just as some of us refused the humiliating condition that we should be
released to the Transkei,[i] we also reject your offer on the same ground. No
self-respecting human being will demean and humiliate himself by making

---

i   A homeland which was absorbed back into the Eastern Cape province in 1994.

GEHEIM
SECRET   13 February 1985

The Commissioner of Prisons
PRETORIA

THE SUBJOINED LETTER IS FOR THE ATTENTION OF THE STATE PRESIDENT,
MR P W BOTHA :

"The State President,
CAPE TOWN

Sir,

Copies of the Hansard parliamentary record of
25 January to 1 February 1985 were delivered to us on
8 February.

We note that during the debate in the House of Assembly you
indicated that you were prepared to release prisoners in our
particular category provided that we unconditionally renounce
violence as a means of furthering our political objectives.
We have given earnest consideration to your offer but we
regret to inform you that it is not acceptable in its present
form. We hesitate to associate you with a move which, on a
proper analysis, appears to be no more than a shrewed and
calculated attempt to mislead the world into the belief
that you have magnanimously offered us release from prison
which we ourselves have rejected. Coming in the face of such
unprecedented and widespread demand for our release, your
remarks can only be seen as the height of cynical politicking.
We refuse to be party to anything which is really intended to
create division, confusion and uncertain ty within the

GEHEIM
SECRET

Page from a letter to the commissioner of prisons, 13 February 1985, see opposite.

a commitment of the nature you demand. You ought not to perpetuate our imprisonment by the simple expedient of setting conditions which, to your own knowledge, we will never under any circumstances accept.

Our political beliefs are largely influenced by the Freedom Charter,[i] a programme of principles whose basic premise is the equality of all human beings. It is not only the clearest repudiation of all forms of racial discrimination, but also the country's most advanced statement of political principles. It calls for universal franchise in a united South Africa and for the equitable distribution of the wealth of the country.

The intensification of apartheid, the banning of political organisations and the closing of all channels of peaceful protest conflicted sharply with these principles and forced the ANC to turn to violence. Consequently, until apartheid is completely uprooted, our people will continue to kill one another and South Africa will be subjected to all the pressures of an escalating civil war.

Yet the ANC has for almost 50 years since its establishment faithfully followed peaceful and non-violent forms of struggle. During the period 1952 to 1961 alone[ii] it appealed, in vain, to no less than three South African premiers to call a round-table conference of all population groups where the country's problems could be thrashed out, and it only resorted to violence when all other options had been blocked.

The peaceful and non-violent nature of our struggle never made any impression to your government. Innocent and defenceless people were pitilessly massacred in the course of peaceful demonstrations. You will remember the shootings in Johannesburg on 1 May 1950[iii] and in Sharpeville in 1960.[iv] On both occasions, as in every other instance of police brutality, the victims had invariably been unarmed and defenceless men, women and even children. At that time the ANC had not even mooted the idea of resorting to armed struggle. You were the country's Defence Minister when no less than 600 people, mostly children, were shot down in Soweto in 1976. You were the country's premier when the police beat up people, again in the course of orderly demonstrations against the 1984 coloured

---

i   A statement of the principles of the Congress Alliance (see the glossary), adopted at the Congress of the People in Kliptown, Soweto, on 26 June 1955. The Congress Alliance rallied thousands of volunteers across South Africa to record the demands of the people. The Freedom Charter espoused equal rights for all South Africans regardless of race, along with land reform, improved working and living conditions, the fair distribution of wealth, compulsory education, and fairer laws. It was a powerful tool used in the fight against apartheid.

ii   Mandela wrote twice to Prime Minister H. F. Verwoerd, calling on him to set up a national convention on a non-racial and democratic constitution for South Africa. His letters were ignored.

iii   On 1 May 1950, eighteen people were shot dead by police during a strike over the apartheid regime's plans to ban the Communist Party.

iv   On 21 March 1961 in Sharpeville, police shot and killed sixty-nine unarmed people protesting against having to carry identity documents which controlled where they could live and work.

and Indian elections,[i] and 7000 heavily armed troopers invaded the Vaal Triangle to put down an essentially peaceful protest by the residents.[ii]

Apartheid, which is condemned not only by blacks but also by a substantial section of the whites, is the greatest single source of violence against our people. As leader of the National Party, which seeks to uphold apartheid through force and violence, we expect you to be the first to renounce violence.

But it would seem that you have no intention whatsoever of using democratic and peaceful forms of dealing with black grievances, that the real purpose of attaching conditions to your offer is to ensure that the NP should enjoy the monopoly of committing violence against defenceless people. The founding of Umkhonto weSizwe was designed to end that monopoly and forcefully bring home to the rulers that the oppressed people were prepared to stand up and defend themselves and to fight back if necessary, with force.

We note that on page 312 of *Hansard* you say that you are personally prepared to go a long way to relax the tensions in inter-group relations in this country but that you are not prepared to lead the whites to abdication. By making this statement you have again categorically reaffirmed that you remain obsessed with the preservation of domination by the white minority. You should not be surprised, therefore, if, in spite of the supposed good intentions of the government, the vast masses of the oppressed people continue to regard you as a mere broker of the interests of the white tribe, and consequently unfit to handle national affairs.

Again on pages 318–319 you state that you cannot talk with people who do not want to cooperate, that you hold talks with every possible leader who is prepared to renounce violence.

Coming from the leader of the NP this statement is a shocking revelation as it shows more than anything else, that there is not a single figure in that party today who is advanced enough to understand the basic problems of our country, who has profited from the bitter experiences of the 37 years of NP rule, and who is prepared to take a bold lead towards the building of a truly democratic South Africa.

It is clear from this statement that you would prefer to talk only to people who accept apartheid even though they are emphatically repudiated by

---

i   In 1984 Prime Minister P. W. Botha established a tricameral parliament with separate chambers for Indians, coloureds, and whites. The United Democratic Front, which was formed in 1983, mounted nationwide protests against this parliament and its elections. All the protests were met with a violent response by police.

ii   In September 1984 the townships of Boipatong, Bophelong, Evaton, Sebokeng, and Sharpeville in the area known as the Vaal Triangle exploded in protests again rent increases proposed by the black-run town councils. Three township councillors, including the deputy mayor of the Vaal Triangle, Kuzwayo Jacob Dlamini, were killed in mob violence on this day. Five men and one woman who become internationally known as the 'Sharpeville Six' were tried, convicted, and sentenced to hang for the killings.

the very community on whom you want to impose them, through violence, if necessary.

We would have thought that the ongoing and increasing resistance in black townships, despite the massive deployment of the Defence Force, would have brought home to you the utter futility of unacceptable apartheid structures, manned by servile and self-seeking individuals of dubious credentials. But your government seems bent on continuing to move along this costly path and, instead of heeding the voice of the true leaders of the communities, in many cases they have been flung into prison. If your government seriously wants to halt the escalating violence, the only method open is to declare your commitment to end the evil of apartheid, and show your willingness to negotiate with the true leaders at local and national levels.

At no time have the oppressed people, especially the youth, displayed such unity in action, such resistance to racial oppression and such prolonged demonstrations in the face of brutal military and police action. Students in secondary schools and the universities are clamouring for the end of apartheid now and for equal opportunities for all. Black and white churchmen and intellectuals, civic associations and workers' and women's organisations demand genuine political changes. Those who "co-operate" with you, who have served with you so loyally throughout these troubled years have not at all helped you to stem the rapidly rising tide. The coming confrontation will only be averted if the following steps are taken without delay.

1. The government must renounce violence first;
2. It must dismantle apartheid;
3. It must unban the ANC;
4. It must free all who have been imprisoned, banished or exiled for their opposition to apartheid;
5. It must guarantee free political activity.

On page 309 you refer to allegations which have regularly been made at the United Nations and throughout the world that Mr Mandela's health has deteriorated in prison and that he is detained under inhuman conditions.

There is no need for you to be sanctimonious in this regard. The United Nations is an important and responsible organ of world peace and is, in many respects, the hope of the international community. Its affairs are handled by the finest brains on earth, by men whose integrity is flawless. If they made such allegations, they do so in the honest belief that they were true.

If we continue to enjoy good health, and if our spirits remain high it has not necessarily been due to any special consideration or care taken by the Department of Prisons. Indeed it is common knowledge that in the course of our long imprisonment, especially during the first years, the prison authorities had implemented a deliberate policy of doing everything to break our morale. We were subjected to harsh, if not brutal, treatment and permanent physical and spiritual harm was caused to many prisoners.

Although conditions have since improved in relation to the Sixties and Seventies, life in prison is not so rosy as you may suppose and we still face serious problems in many respects. There is still racial discrimination in our treatment; we have not yet won the right to be treated as political prisoners. We are no longer visited by the Minister of Prisons, the Commissioner of Prisons and other officials from the headquarters, and by judges and magistrates. These conditions are cause for concern to the United Nations, Organisation of African Unity,[i] Anti-apartheid Movement[ii] and to our numerous friends.

Taking into account the actual practice of the Department of Prisons, we must reject the view that a life sentence means that one should die in prison. By applying to security prisoners the principle that "life is life" you are using double standards, since common law prisoners with clean prison records serve about 15 years of a life sentence. We must also remind you that it was the NP whose very first act on coming to power was to release the traitor Robey Leibrandt[iii] (and others) after he had served only a couple of years of his life sentence. These were men who had betrayed their own country to Nazi Germany during the last World War in which South Africa was involved.

As far as we are concerned we have long ago completed our life sentences. We're now being actually kept in preventative detention without enjoying the rights attached to that category of prisoners. The outdated and universally rejected philosophy of retribution is being meted out to us, and every day we spend in prison is simply an act of revenge against us.

Despite your commitment to the maintenance of white supremacy,

i   Formed in 1963 in Addis Ababa, Ethiopia, with thirty-two signatory governments and eventually including all of Africa's fifty-three states excluding Morocco, which withdrew in 1984. It aimed to eradicate all forms of colonialism and white minority rule on the African continent. It also aimed to coordinate and intensify the cooperation of African states to achieve a better life for the people of Africa and to defend the sovereignty, territorial integrity, and independence of African states. It was disbanded on 9 July 2002 by its last chairperson, South African President Thabo Mbeki, and replaced by the African Union.

ii   Originally called the Boycott Movement, the British Anti-Apartheid Movement (AAM) was established in London in 1959 and opposed South Africa's system of apartheid. It demanded international sanctions against apartheid South Africa and called for its total isolation. In 1988 the AAM organised a pop concert, known as the Free Nelson Mandela Concert, at Wembley Stadium, London, to celebrate Mandela's seventieth birthday. A second concert, Nelson Mandela: An International Tribute for a Free South Africa, took place there in 1990, two months after Mandela's release from prison, and was attended by him.

iii Sidney Robey Leibbrandt (1913–66), the South African heavyweight boxing champion, was led by the German military intelligence under the pseudonym 'Robert Leibbrand'. He was a South African Boer of German and Irish descent.

however, your attempt to create new apartheid structures, and your hostility to a non-racial system of government in this country, and despite our determination to resist this policy to the bitter end, the simple fact is that you are South Africa's head of government, you enjoy the support of the majority of the white population and you can help change the course of South African history. A beginning can be made if you accept and agree to implement the five-point programme on pages 4–5 of this document. If you accept the programme our people would readily cooperate with you to sort out whatever problems arise as far as the implementation thereof is concerned.

In this regard, we have taken note of the fact that you no longer insist on some of us being released to the Transkei. We have also noted the restrained tone which you adopted when you made the offer in Parliament. We hope you will show the same flexibility and examine these proposals objectively. That flexibility and objectivity may help to create a better climate for a fruitful national debate.

Yours faithfully,

NELSON MANDELA

WALTER SISULU

RAYMOND MHLABA

AHMED KATHRADA

ANDREW MLANGENI[i]

[Each one signed above their name]

◇◇◇◇◇◇◇◇◇

From time to time in the latter years of his imprisonment, Mandela received letters from people he had never met – ordinary members of the public who knew of him and wrote to show that he had support outside of his normal circle of friends and family. Mrs Ray Carter, a British-born nurse married to an Anglican bishop, John Carter, was one such supporter. This letter was provided by her family who said that she and Mandela had struck up a pen-pal relationship

---

i   Rivonia trialists imprisoned with Mandela. See the glossary for notes on the individuals other than Mandela. Each prisoner signed their name twice.

after she telephoned the head of Pollsmoor Prison saying she wanted to bring a birthday gift to Nelson Mandela. She promptly dropped off a paperback, called Daily Light, *containing Biblical texts, two readings a day. Some months later a registered letter arrived from Mandela.*

To Ray Carter, a supporter

4.3.85

D220/82: NELSON MANDELA

Our dear Ray,

The picture on the outside cover of *Daily Light* has upset me beyond words. Although I spent no less than two decades on the Rand[i] before I was arrested, I am still essentially a peasant in outlook. I am intrigued by the wilds, the bush, a blade of grass and by all the things which are associated with the veld.[ii]

Every time I look at the book – and I try to do so every morning and evening – I invariably start from the cover, and the mind immediately lights up. Long-forgotten scenes come back as fresh as dew. The thick bush, the ten fat sheep on a green field remind me of my childhood days in the countryside when everything I saw looked golden, a real place of bliss, an extension of heaven itself. That romantic world is engraved permanently in the memory and never fades, even though I now know as a fact that it is gone never to return.

Fourteen years after I had settled in Johannesburg I went back home[iii] and reached my village in early evening. At sunrise I left the car behind and walked out into the veld in search of the world of my youth, but it was no more.

The bush, where I used to pick wild fruits, dig up edible roots and trap small game, was now an unimpressive grove of scattered and stunted shrubs. The river, in which I swam on hot days and caught fat eels, was choking in mud and sand. I could no longer see the blazing flowers that beautified the veld and sweetened the air.

---

i   An abbreviated name for the Witwatersrand, a 56-kilometre-long ridge in the Gauteng province of South Africa where Johannesburg is based.

ii   'Field' in Afrikaans.

iii   Mandela is referring to Qunu, Transkei, where he grew up.

Although the sweet rains had recently washed the area, and the rising sun was throwing its warmth over the entire veld, no honey bird or sky-lark greeted me. Overpopulation, overgrazing and soil erosion had done irreparable havoc, and everything seemed to be crumbling. Even the huge ironstones which had stood out defiantly for eternity appeared to be suc-cumbing to the total desolation which enveloped the area. The cattle and sheep tended to be skinny and listless. Life itself seemed to be dying away slowly. This was the sad picture that confronted me on my return home almost 30 yrs ago. It contrasted very sharply with the place where I was born. I have never been home again, yet the romantic years of my youth remain printed clearly in the mind. The cover picture in *Daily Light* calls forth those wonderful times.

Where does this picture come from? It looks so familiar.

How long it has taken for a parcel or message from you to come through! It was some time in 1982, I think, that Zami (Winnie) asked whether I had received a postcard from you. My enquiries from the Commanding Officer drew a blank. You have to be a prisoner serving a life sentence to appreciate just how frustrating and painful it can be when the efforts of friends to reach and encourage you are blocked somewhere along the line.

But as I look back now, that frustration was not without value. You have turned it into triumph. Your determination to break through the bar-riers is a measure of the depth of your love and concern. The three-word inscription in the book makes it a precious possession indeed. I sincerely hope that Zami and I will prove to be worthy of that love and support. I look forward to seeing you and John[i] one day. Meantime, I send you my love and best wishes.

Sincerely,
Nelson

Mrs Ray Carter, 51 Dalene Rd, Bramley, 2192

---

i   Her husband, the Anglican bishop John Carter.

To Lionel Ngakane,[i] a friend and filmmaker

1.4.85

D220/82: NELSON MANDELA

Dear Lionel,

The world we knew so well seems to be crumbling down very fast, and the men and women who once moved scores of people are disappearing from the scene just as quickly. Lutuli,[ii] Dadoo,[iii] Matthews,[iv] Kotane,[v] Harmel,[vi] Gomas, the Naickers,[vii] Marks,[viii] Molema,[ix] Letele,[x] Ruth First,[xi] Njongwe,[xii] Calata,[xiii] Ngoyi,[xiv] Peake,[xv] Hodgson,[xvi] Nokwe[xvii] and many others now sleep in eternal peace; and all this happens in less than two decades.

We will never see them again, exchange views with them when problems arise, or exploit their immense influence in the struggle for the South Africa of our dreams. But few people will deny that in their lifetime they made a magnificent achievement and, in the process created a rich tradition which serves as a source of pride and strength to those who have now stepped into their shoes.

We were so busy outside prison that we hardly had time to think seri-

---

i	Lionel Ngakane (1928–2003), filmmaker, actor. He went into exile in the 1950s and returned to South Africa in 1994.
ii	Chief Albert Luthuli (1898–1967), president-general of the ANC, 1952–67 – see the glossary. Mandela also spelt his name 'Lutuli'.
iii	Dr Yusuf Dadoo (1909–83), medical doctor, anti-apartheid activist, and orator. President of South African Indian Congress, deputy to Oliver Tambo on the Revolutionary Council of MK, and chairman of the South African Communist Party – see the glossary.
iv	Professor Z. K. Matthews (1901–68), academic, politician, anti-apartheid activist, and ANC member – see the glossary.
v	Moses Kotane (1905–78), ANC member and secretary-general of the South African Communist Party.
vi	Michael Harmel (1915–74), a leading member of the Communist Party. He died in exile in Prague.
vii	Monty Naicker (1910–78), doctor, politician, and anti-apartheid activist – see the glossary. M. P. Naicker (1920–77), anti-apartheid activist, journalist, leader, and organiser for the Natal Indian Congress, South African Communist Party, and the Congress Alliance. The Naickers were not brothers, but comrades.
viii	J. B. Marks (1903–72), ANC member and a leader in the 1952 Defiance Campaign (for the Defiance Campaign, see the glossary).
ix	Dr Silas Modiri Molema (1891–1965), medical doctor and ANC activist.
x	Dr Arthur Elias Letele (1916–65), medical doctor and ANC activist. An accused in the 1956 Treason Trial (for the Treason Trial, see the glossary).
xi	Ruth First (1925–82), journalist and Communist Party and ANC activist. An accused in the 1956 Treason Trial (for the Treason Trial, see the glossary). She went into exile in 1964 and was killed by a parcel bomb sent by apartheid agents while she was living in Mozambique.
xii	Dr. James Jimmy Njongwe (1919–76), medical doctor, ANC leader, and organiser of the Defiance Campaign (for the Defiance Campaign, see the glossary) in the Eastern Cape – for Jimmy Njongwe, see the glossary.
xiii	Rev. James Arthur Calata (1895–1983), a teacher and a priest in the Anglican Church, he was a leading member of the ANC.
xiv	Lilian Ngoyi (1911–80), politician, and anti-apartheid and women's rights activist – see the glossary.
xv	George Edward Peake (1922–), founding member of the South African Coloured People's Organisation. Was an accused in the 1956 Treason Trial (for the Treason Trial, see the glossary). He was jailed for two years in 1962 for his involvement in a sabotage plot. He was forced into exile in 1968, where he died.
xvi	Percy John 'Jack' Hodgson (1910–77), an accused in the 1956 Treason Trial and a founding member of the ANC's armed wing, Umkhonto weSizwe. He died in exile.
xvii	Advocate Duma Nokwe (1927–78), political activist and advocate – see the glossary.

ously about death. But you have to be locked up in a prison cell for life to appreciate the paralysing grief which seizes you when death strikes close to you. To lose a leading public figure can be a painful blow; but to lose a lifelong friend and neighbour is a devastating experience, and sharpens the sense of shock beyond words.

This is how I felt when Zami[i] gave me the sad news of the death of your beloved mother, adding that at that time your father was under detention and had to attend the funeral under police escort. I thought of you, Pascal,[ii] Lindi, Seleke, Mpho, Thabo[iii] and, of course, your father. I sent him a letter of condolence which I hope he also conveyed to you all.

The death of your father was equally devastating, and particularly so because I learnt about it from press reports as I was about to reply to his last letter which I had received on 31 December 1984. That shock unlocked a corner of my mind and I literally re-lived the almost 40 years of our friendship.

I particularly recalled an occasion at the Bantu Men's Social Centre[iv] when we were addressed by Dr Yergan[v] towards the end of the Defiance Campaign.[vi] Attendance was by invitation only and the City's top brass was all there – Xuma,[vii] Mosaka, Rathebe, Denelane, Madibane, Ntloana, Xorile, Twala, Rezant, Mali, Nobanda, Magagane, Mophiring and so on. The audience had been made specially receptive by the D.C.[viii] and Yergan, who gave an outstanding review of the national movements on our continent, was in terrific form. You could hear a pin drop. He closed that brilliant speech with a concerted attack on Communism – and drew prolonged ovation from that elitist audience.

There followed a chorus of praises for Yergan until your father took the floor. He could not match Yergan in eloquence and in the vast amount of scientific knowledge the American commanded. But he spoke in the simple language we all understood and drew attention to issues we deeply cher-

---

i   One of Winnie Mandela's names.
ii   Pascal Shaudi Ngakane (1930–2015), one of Lionel Ngakane's siblings who was in prison with Mandela.
iii   William Barmey (1902-88), ANC activist and Monzondeki Ngakane's children. Siblings of Lionel Ngakane.
iv   The Bantu Men's Social Centre (BMSC), founded in Sophiatown, Johannesburg, in 1924, was an important cultural, social, and political meeting place for black South Africans. Its facilities included a gym and a library, and it hosted boxing matches, political meetings, and dances. Mandela and four others founded the ANC Youth League there in 1944.
v   Dr Max Yergan (1892–1975), the grandson of a slave in the United States, he was stationed in South Africa for eighteen years after World War II as senior secretary of the International Committee of the YCMA.
vi   Initiated by the ANC in December 1951, and launched with the South African Indian Congress on 26 June 1952 against six apartheid laws, the Defiance Campaign Against Unjust Laws (known as the Defiance Campaign for short) involved individuals breaking racist laws such as entering premises reserved for 'whites only', breaking curfews, and courting arrest. Mandela was appointed national volunteer-in-chief and Maulvi Cachalia as his deputy. Over 8,500 volunteers were imprisoned for their participation in the Defiance Campaign.
vii   Dr Alfred Bitini Xuma (1893–1962) was the first black South African to become a medical doctor and president-general of the ANC (1940–49).
viii   Defiance Campaign.

ished. He made pertinent observations on Yergan's deafening silence on our struggle generally and on the current D.C. in particular. Pressing his attack he challenged our guest speaker to speak about the giant American cartels, trusts and multi-national corporations that were causing so much misery and hardship throughout the world, and he foiled Yergan's attempt to drag us into the cold war. The same people who had given the speaker such a prolonged ovation now applauded your father just as enthusiastically. I must confess that I was more than impressed.

During the 1960 state of emergency,[i] we spent several months with him in the Pretoria local prison. Again he showed special qualities of leadership and was of considerable help in the maintenance of morale and discipline. There are many aspects of his life that flashed across the mind on that unforgettable day when I learnt of his death. But a restricted prison letter is not a suitable channel to express my views frankly and fully on such matters. It is sufficient for me to say that Zami and I will always treasure the memory of our friendship with your parents. Please convey these sentiments to Pascal, Lindi, Seleke, Mpho and Thabo. The attached cutting from the *Sowetan* is hopelessly inadequate and inaccurate and I sincerely hope that you or Lindi will in due course record the story of his life and make it available to a wider audience. That is a challenge to you all, but especially to Lindi,[ii] who has special qualifications, both academically and from her actual role in the struggle, to undertake such an important task.

Turning now to more lighter matters, I must confess that I am keen to hear more about your personal affairs. I know a direct question will not ruffle you. Are you married? If so, who is the fortunate young lady? How strong is your manpower? I must add that I never forget the day we spent together in London, and it pleased me tremendously to know that around O.R.[iii] there were talented young men of your calibre. You may not be aware that that discovery made me even more attached to your parents.

Pascal and I spent a lot of time together at home, and when I visited Durban in 1955 I made a special point to see him. But it was the three years that we spent together somewhere that made an even greater mark on me. I have not heard of him for some time now and would like to have his address. It was a pleasant surprise to me to learn that Clifford[iv] is now Lesotho's ambassador in Rome.[v] Until I saw press reports to that effect, I had

---

i   Declared on 30 March 1960 as a response to the Sharpeville Massacre, the 1960 State of Emergency was characterised by mass arrests and the imprisonment of most African leaders. On 8 April 1960 the ANC and Pan Africanist Congress were banned under the Unlawful Organisations Act.

ii   One of Lionel Ngakane's sisters.

iii   Oliver Reginald Tambo (1917–93), Mandela's friend, former law partner, and the president of the ANC – see the glossary. His middle name was Reginald and Mandela referred to him as Reggie.

iv   Clifford Morojele was married to Lindi, Lionel Ngakane's sister.

v   Clifford Morojele worked for the United Nations in Addis Ababa and in Rome, but was not an ambassador. That

been under the impression that he was a UNO. I will be quite happy if these reports are correct. I have a lot of admiration for Chief Leabua and, from this distance, he seems to be playing the trump cards exceptionally well.

Seleke[i] was a mere teenager when I last saw her, but I was later told that she was happily married to a medical practitioner in Maseru. I look forward to seeing all of you some day. Meantime I send you my fondest regards and best wishes.

Sincerely,
Madiba

Mr Lionel Ngakane, c/o Mr Paul Joseph, London

P.S. If you find time to reply to this note, please register your letter.

———————————

To Sheena Duncan,[ii] president of Black Sash

D220/82: NELSON MANDELA   1.4.85

Dear Mrs Duncan,

In my current position it is by no means easy to keep abreast of the course of events outside prison. It may well be that the membership of the B-Sash has not grown significantly over the last 30 years and that, in this respect, this pattern of development is not likely to be different in the immediate future at least.

But few people will deny that, in spite of its relatively small numbers, the impact of the Sash is quite formidable, and that it has emerged as one of the forces which help to focus attention on those social issues which are shattering the lives of so many people. It is giving a bold lead on how these problems can be concretely tackled and, in this way, it helps to bring a measure of relief and hope to many victims of a degrading social order.

The ideals we cherish, our fondest dreams and fervent hopes may not

---

fact was incorrectly reported in the newspapers at the time. (Sahm Venter in conversation with his son, Morabo Morojele, 14 October 2017.)

i   One of Lionel Ngakane's sisters.

ii   Sheena Duncan (1932–2010), member of Black Sash, an organisation of white middle-class women who protested against apartheid laws and assisted its victims. Sheena's mother, Jean Sinclair, had been one of its founding members in 1955.

be realised in our lifetime. But that is besides the point. The knowledge that in your day you did your duty, and lived up to the expectations of your fellowmen is in itself a rewarding experience and magnificent achievement. The good image which the Sash is projecting may be largely due to the wider realisation that it is fulfilling these expectations.

To speak with a firm and clear voice on major national questions, unprotected by the shield of immunity enjoyed by members of the country's organs of government, and unruffled by the countless repurcussions of being ostracised by a privileged minority, is a measure of your deep concern for human rights and commitment to the principle of justice for all. In this regard, your recent comments in Port Elizabeth,[i] articulating as they did, the convictions of those who strive for real progress and a new South Africa were indeed significant.

In spite of the immense difficulties against which you have to operate, your voice is heard right across the country. Even though [it is] frowned upon by some, it pricks the conscience of others and is warmly welcomed by all good men and women. Those who are prepared to face problems at eyeball range, and who embrace universal beliefs which have changed the course of history in many societies must, in due course, command solid support and admiration far beyond their own ranks.

In congratulating you on your 30th birthday,[ii] I must add that I fully share the view that you "can look back with pride on three decades of endeavour which now, at least, is beginning to bear fruit."

In conclusion, I must point out that I know so many of your colleagues that if I were to name each and every one in this letter, the list would be too long. All I can do is to assure you of my fondest regards and best wishes.

Sincerely,
[Signed NRMandela]

◇◇◇◇◇◇◇◇◇

These two letters to anti-apartheid activist and lawyer Archie Gumede demonstrate the difficulties and frustrations with writing and receiving letters in prison and the lack of information about what happened to the letters.

Suspecting that the letter he wrote to Gumede in 1975 never reached him, Mandela rewrites it, from the copy he jotted down at the time, and resends it to him nearly ten years later.

---

i   City in Eastern Cape province.
ii   Black Sash's thirtieth anniversary.

To Archie Gumede,[i] comrade & friend

D220/82: NELSON MANDELA

8.7.85

Phakathwayo! Qwabe![ii]

The other day I was going through the notebook in which I keep the record of my outgoing letters, and I came across the copy of the attached letter, which I wrote to you on Jan 1, 1975.[iii] As you have never responded, and in view of the peculiar problems we were experiencing with our post at the time, I have assumed that it never reached you.

Although more than 10 years have passed since it was written, and although some of its contents are now hopelessly outdated I, nonetheless, thought you should get it. The letter was written when Mphephethe,[iv] Siba-lukhulu, Danapathy[v] and Georgina's husband from Hammarsdale were all with you over there[vi] and fairly active. One of the aims of the letter was to make them aware that there was deep appreciation for their work.

You will also bear in mind that, at that time, the relations between Khongolose[vii] and Shenge[viii] were good, and there was cooperation in many areas. In addition, he and I had been in contact since the late 60's, and he still sends me goodwill messages on specific occasions. On the Island we fully discussed the matter in a special meeting of reps from all sections, and it was felt that it would be a mistake to ignore his gestures. I accordingly continued to respond.

Last year he sent me another telegram on a personal matter and my colleagues and I exchanged views. Again it was felt that, subject to what you might advise, I should write and thank him. But by the time the note reached the family you could no longer be reached. The note was ultimately forwarded to him.

At this stage I would like to digress a bit and tell you about a young lady, Ms Nomsa Khanyeza, 3156, Nkwaz Rd, Imbali, whose letter I received in

---

i   Archibald Jacob Gumede (1914–98) – see the glossary.
ii   Archie Gumede's clan names.
iii   See his letter on page 468.
iv   Bakwe (Joe) Matthews (1929–2010), political activist and son of Frieda and Z. K. Matthews – see the glossary for these three individuals.
v   The middle name of M. D. Naidoo who was in prison with Mandela on Robben Island.
vi   Mandela is most likely referring to Natal.
vii   Mandela is referring to the African National Congress – *khongolose* for 'congress'.
viii   Chief Mangosuthu Buthelezi (1928–), Zulu prince, chief minister of KwaZulu 1972–94, and founder and president of the Inkatha Freedom Party in 1975 – see the glossary. His clan name is Shenge. Mandela is talking about relations with the ANC and Inkatha.

Nov '82 and to which I immediately replied. I never heard from her again. I would like you to visit her home when you are in the area. In particular I would like to know whether she is still at school, and whether her parents have the funds for her education. From her letter she appears to be a child of ability.

Perhaps Thozamile and Sisa are aware that Between the Lines: Conversations in SA[i] by Harriet Sergeant has been published. She has some interesting observations to make on a wide variety of interviews. But a young lady of 26 can often be outspoken, and she seems to have recorded intimate sentiments and reactions which were not meant for public consumption. Although she is forthright in her manner, in my opinion, she has said nothing really damaging about the trade unionists she met. I am keen to know who Connaugh is. This is apparently the cover name of the bearded white man with jeans, earphones on his head, microphone in hand and a recording machine at the EL[ii] trade union meeting. Please get me this information if they already have the book.

In conclusion, I would like to draw your attention to a letter in a JHB[iii] daily which dealt with the case of 9 men who were condemned to death by Queen Victoria for treason. As a result of protests from all over the world the men were banished. Many years thereafter, the Queen learned that one of these men had been elected PM[iv] of Australia,[v] the second was appointed Brigadier-General in the U.S.A. Army,[vi] the third became Attorney-General for Australia,[vii] the fourth succeeded the third as A.G.,[viii] the fifth became Minister of Agriculture for Canada,[ix] the sixth also became Brigadier-General in the U.S.A.,[x] the seventh was appointed Governor-General of Montana,[xi] the eighth became a prominent New York politician,[xii] and the last was appointed Governor-General of Newfoundland.[xiii]

It is a relevant story which, although you are probably aware of it, I

---

i   Harriet Sergeant's *Between the Lines: Conversations in South Africa* (London: J. Cape, 1984) was a book that explored the effect of apartheid on South Africans in the 1980s.

ii   This most likely stands for 'East London', a city in the Eastern Cape province.

iii 'Johannesburg.'

iv   'Prime minister'.

v   Charles Duffy (1816–1903) was not the prime minister of Australia but the eighth premier of the Australian state of Victoria. Historical information about Duffy doesn't suggest that he was sent into exile, and the article Mandela is referring to may be incorrect.

vi   Patrick Donahue.

vii Morris Leyne.

viii Michael Ireland succeeded Morris Leyne as attorney-general of Australia.

ix   Thomas Darcy McGee (1825–68) became the minister of agriculture, immigration, and statistics.

x   Thomas McManus.

xi   Thomas Francis Meagher (1823–67) became a cattle baron and the governor of Montana following the American Civil War.

xii John Mitchel (1815–75), Irish nationalist, author, and journalist who supported the Confederate States of America during the American Civil War. His son, John Purroy Mitchell (1879–1918), later served as mayor of New York City

xiii Richard O'Gorman.

think it proper to remind you of it. Fondest regards and best wishes to you and all your colleagues. Remember that you are all in our thoughts.

Sincerely, Madiba.

P.S. Nomsa was at the time of writing the letter a pupil at the Georgetown High School.

[The attached letter]
To Archie Gumede,[i] friend and comrade

D220/82: NELSON MANDELA

P/B X4, TOKAI, 7966

January 1, 1975 [resent on 7 July 1985]

Phakathwayo Qwabe![ii]

I have been thinking of writing to you since the death of A.J.[iii] You were so close to him that, though I immediately wrote to the Old Lady,[iv] I felt I should also send my condolences to you, M.B.,[v] Zanu [or Zami],[vi] Sibalukhulu and Siphithiphithi. You have been together for a long time, handled important problems jointly, and moved forward in tight formation as Nodunehlezi did many years ago. It is difficult to think of the chief without at the same time thinking of the five of you.

I still well remember the Drill Hall[vii] when you would come together almost instinctively, talk about soil and sand and, at times, relax over a dish of amadumbe,[viii] punctuating the conversation with repeated "ha-a-a-wu! ha- a-a-a-wu!"[ix]

In due course you were admitted as an attorney and only now do I write to say: well done! People who hardly hear from us may be those we trust and respect most. We may keep quiet because we are certain that they

---

i   Archibald Jacob Gumede (1914–98) – see the glossary.
ii   Archie Gumede's clan names.
iii   AJ is Chief Albert Luthuli (1898–1967), president-general of the ANC, 1952–67 – see the glossary – who was killed by a train in July 1967.
iv   Nokhukhanya Luthuli, widow of Chief Albert Luthuli.
v   M. B. Yengwa (1923), ANC member, trade unionist, and Treason trialist (for the Treason Trial, see the glossary).
vi   This is not Winnie Mandela.
vii   The venue for the 1956 Treason Trial (for the Treason Trial, see the glossary).
viii   Dumplings.
ix   *Hawu* is an isiXhosa and isiZulu expression of disbelief or condemnation. It is pronounced 'How'. It's part of conversation so if people were telling stories, it would be natural to respond in that way.

will understand that pressure of other commitments makes it difficult to reach them.

I have thought of you often these twelve years, equally felt the grimness that gripped you, especially in '63,[i] and rejoiced with you when the sun shone again. I was at Mgungundlovu[ii] in March '61[iii] and have been wondering whether I actually met you on that occasion. I stayed with Mandla's parents. In '55 I had spent a whole night at Boom St.[iv] chatting with Moses,[v] Chota,[vi] Omar[vii] and others. The next day Mungal[viii] and I travelled to Groutville[ix] where I spent a whole day with AJ. By the way, I was returning from him in Aug '62 when I met your homeboys in Howick.[x]

I also think a lot about Mphephethe, Sibalukhulu, Georgina's hubby, MB, RM and Mutwana wa kwa Phindangene with fond memories. When New Age[xi] was strong enough to do her weekly rounds, Mphephethe had a powerful horse he could ride to reach us all, and we knew what he thought. Old and famous horses keel over like many that went before, some to be forgotten forever and others to be remembered as mere objects of history, and of interest to academicians only. But the disappearance of this one has left a void that will be felt alike by stable owners, jockeys, punters and the public at large.[xii] There still will be many race meetings here, but for some time we will miss the tension and sharpness of competition which NA[xiii] brought into every such race.

In his short stories Mphephethe always had something new and meaningful to say, and his theme, style and simplicity always absorbed me. I hope that with age and all the experience of eight full years away from Mgungundlovu, he has returned in earnest to his parchment and quill, more prepared than ever before.

About two years ago I had the pleasure of reading a thesis he had prepared. I would have liked to discuss some aspects discreetly with him, and one of my regrets is that this opportunity never came. The feeling of regret

i   Archie Gumede was banned for five years in 1963.
ii   A place in Natal.
iii   Mandela is referring to the All in Africa Conference he spoke at in March 1961 and which Archie Gumede attended.
iv   Activists Chota and Choti Motala's home was in Boom Street, Pietermaritzburg.
v   Moses Mbheki Mncane Mabhida (1923-86), a leader of the South African Congress of Trade Unions and the ANC. He joined the armed struggle and worked for MK in exile.
vi   Dr. Mahomed 'Chota' Motala (1921-2005), Natal Indian Congress activist, accused in the 1956 Treason Trial (for the Treason Trial, see the glossary) and friend of Mandela and Walter Sisulu. After democracy he became South Africa's ambassador to the Kingdom of Morocco.
vii   Dr. Omar Essack, a member of the Natal Indian Congress who practised medicine with Dr. Motala.
viii   S. B. Mugal who travelled with Mandela to see Chief Luthuli.
ix   A town in Ilembe District Municipality in the Natal homeland. Chief Albert Luthuli lived there.
x   He is referring to his arrest in 1962 by police of the homeland of Natal (now where Gumede comes from).
xi   The New Age was an anti-apartheid newspaper which was banned due to its close ties with the ANC. Each time it was banned, the publication would come out under a new title.
xii   He is referring to the New Age.
xiii   New Age.

is all the more painful because his handling of the theoretical issues made a powerful impact on me. Thereafter I read another essay by him on more topical isses, and I was very happy to learn that our thoughts were substantially similar. I hope he keeps fit by now and again donning ibhetshu,[i] letting every one of his bones swing to the beat of the ox-hide drum and indlamu.[ii]

I have met Sibalukhulu far more often than Mphephethe. We have been together several times in Durban and for a stretch in J.H.B.[iii] I last had a chat with him in Aug '62. He will remember the occasion very well. Milner, Selbourne, MB, Mduduzi and Elias were there. The uncompromising champion of Impabanga was, as usual, neat in dress and his hair was cola black and glossy. Little did I suspect that it was as white as mine, and that Sibalukhulu kept it fresh with Nugget. On that occasion, he revealed surprising flexibility as we chatted along, and I came away feeling much closer than I have ever been to him. This is the impression of him that I have carried during the last 12 years; that is why I miss him so much and really look forward to seeing him one day.

Time was when Georgina's hubby, Danapathy and I were like triplets, and I am still inclined to feel somewhat lonely when I think of the immense mileage that separates us. But it is the fact of being triplets that still dominates my thoughts and feelings.

Many threads bind us together. Centuries ago your forefathers and mine scratched the fertile valleys of the Tukela[iv] for a living and drank from its sweet waters. Mafukuzela,[v] Lentanka,[vi] Rubusana[vii] and others were there in 1912 to extend and deepen those ties, a development with which your Pa's name is closely associated.

You have added yet another thread, and we belong to that tribe which exploits advocates, magistrates and judges. Again, well done Mnguni. I am looking forward to seeing your family some day, as well as Sukthi, Sha, Sahdham[viii] and their mum.

---

i   A traditional skin worn by Zulu men.
ii   A traditional Zulu dance.
iii   Johannesburg.
iv   Mandela probably is referring to the Tugela River, the largest in the KwaZulu-Natal province.
v   John Langalibale Dube (1871–1946), educator, publisher, editor, writer, and political activist. First president general of the South African Native National Congress (renamed as the ANC in 1923) established in 1912. Established the Zulu Christian Industrial School at Ohlange. Established the first Zulu/English newspaper *Ilanga lase Natal (Sun of Natal)* in 1904. Opponent of the 1913 Land Act. Member of the executive of the All-African Convention, 1935. Mandela voted at the Ohlange school in 1994 for the first time in his life, and then visited Dube's grave to report that South Africa was now free.
vi   Mandela is possibly referring to Daniel Simon Lentanka, a journalist and early leader of the ANC.
vii   Walter Rubusana (1958–36), co-founder of the isiXhosa newspaper publication *Izwi Labantu*, the first black person to be elected to the Cape Council in 1909, and a founding member of the South African Native National Congress in 1912.
viii   The children of Phyllis and M. D. Naidoo, a member of the South African Communist Party and the South African Indian Congress who was imprisoned on Robben Island for five years and was in B Section with Mandela.

Fatima[i] has already been here and we maintain regular contact. Alzena, Tryfina, Mabhala, Magoba and Gladys have sent Xmas cards every year since '64 and, in the last three years or so they have been joined by Sukdii and family. All these are ladies who love and friendship I highly value and will ask you to give them my fondest regards. Some day I may be able to shake their hands very warmly.

Once again, my deepest sympathy to you, MB, Zanu [or Zami], Sibalukhulu and Phithiphithi.

Sincerely,
Nel

Mr Archie Gumede, 30 Moodie St, Pinetown [3600]

———

To Victoria Nonyamezelo Mxenge,[ii] lawyer and political activist

8.7.85

8.7.85D220/82: NELSON MANDELA

Our dear Nonyamezelo,

I believe that one of you has already visited Ntobeko at Mgungundlovu,[iii] and I sincerely hope that his preparations are proceeding smoothly. Far more is involved in his case than the simple legal issues set out in the pleadings, and I felt that once you, Pius,[iv] Louis, Boyce, Yunus and others become consciously aware of its wider implications, you would immediately rally to his assistance. In this connection, I trust that you will be good enough to

---

i   Fatima Meer (1928–2010), friend, professor, author, and anti-apartheid activist – see the glossary.

ii   Victoria Nonyamezelo Mxenge (1942–85), lawyer and anti-apartheid activist. Her husband and law partner Griffiths Mxenge was assassinated in 1981 and days after speaking at the funeral of four United Democratic Front activists killed by the police, she was murdered outside her home. The Truth and Reconciliation Commission (TRC) report on the assassination of Victoria Mxenge documents that one Marvin Sefako (alias Bongi Raymond Malinga) was allegedly recruited by the security branch and that Brigadier Peter Swanepoel was his handler. Malinga confessed that he had killed Mxenge, claiming that he shot her five times in the chest, but she never fell and that he followed her with an axe and chopped her next to her dining room door. The TRC report contains no indication whether any person had applied for or had been granted amnesty in relation to her murder. (TRC Final Report, volume 2, chapter 3, subsection 28, p. 227.)

iii   A place in Natal.

iv   Pius Nkonzo Langa (1939– 2013), lawyer who was a founding member of the National Association of Democratic Lawyers. In 1994 Mandela appointed him as chief justice of the Constitutional Court of South Africa. He became deputy chief justice in 2001 and was elevated to chief justice in 2005 by President Thabo Mbeki. He retired in October 2009.

285·07·85

Pollsmoor Maximum Prison,
P/Bag X 4, Tokai, 7966 **51**

JJ220/82 NELSON MANDELA.

8 7 85

Our dear Nonyamezelo,

I believe that one of you has already visited Ntobeko at Ngqungundlovu, and I sincerely hope that his preparations are proceeding smoothly. Far more is involved in his case than the simple legal issues set out in the pleadings, and I felt that once you, Pius, Louis, Bryce, Yunus and others become consciously aware of its wider implications, you would immediately rally to his assistance. In this connection, I trust that you will be good enough to remind attorneys Ismail Meer, Virulam, and J N Singh, Durban, of my message in which I outlined how they could team up on an important aspect of this matter. It will be a splendid victory if Ntobeko will still be on the roll after Aug. 9. But if friends rise to the occasion, as I expect they will, it can still be a resounding triumph even when we lose the actual court battle. Do you meet Tswa and Kali? Do give my fondest regards and best wishes to all of them for the excellent work they are doing all over the country.

Turning now to you, I must tell you that when an inmate discovered that I intended writing to you, he remarked that I was wasting ~~saliva and~~ energy and time, as you are reputed to be a bad correspondent. I brushed him aside by pointing out that those who failed to get your response obviously had nothing worthwhile to say, that even if the rumour were true, this time you would put everything aside and reply.

First, I would like to know just how you have managed over these last three years. I believe that the firm had already grown immensely. I accordingly imagined that you were stretched out almost to the limit when you suddenly found yourself all alone, without the skill and vast experience Gm commanded. Having spent a few years with him on Robben Island, I have a fairly good idea of the precious talents which he so richly possessed. But from all the accounts I have received, it seems that you are a tough and determined girl, a go-getter. I am confident that you are not only equal to the task of running a big firm, but that you have by now succeeded in expanding it to a legal giant.

The news of your Cape Town adventure with Allan and others will have caught many people unawares. It is the last place where I expected you to become involved, and I was happy indeed when I heard that you did not have to travel down again. Nevertheless, the incident beautifully confirmed the image you have projected in my mind

A letter to Victoria Nonyamezelo Mxenge, dated 8 July 1985, see previous page and following pages. Various names mentioned in the letter have been highlighted in yellow highlighter by another hand.

2.   52

over these years.

Are the children well, and how are they faring with their school work? Where and when did you spend your last holiday? An overseas vacation, if you have a passport, would certainly be a refreshing experience both from the point of view of your own health and that of the firm. The batteries that keep you going require to be constantly charged and re-charged, if you are going to maintain a high standard of performance on professional and wider issues. It would also be an unforgettable experience for you to visit some of the big USA legal firms, some of which have no less than 100 partners each, with computers and well-stocked libraries. Do consider that.

I note that we now have several lawyers' organisations: Lawyers for Human Rights, Black Lawyers Association and the Democratic Lawyers' Association. To which do you belong? Can you give me some information on the DLA?

Now I would like you to put a few telephone calls on my behalf to some friends over there: my sympathy to Chief Lutuli's son, Sebusiso, and his wife, Wilhelmina, who were attacked at their Blanheim Store recently. We wish them a speedy and complete recovery. Last year I wrote to the old lady, Nokukhanya; I don't know whether she ever received the letter as she never responded. Fondest regards to Bliza Nyi, Sono, whose impressive contribution in the late 40s and early 50s can never be forgotten. The same sentiments to Bliza Nyi, junior, in regard to his current efforts. We are particularly proud of him. Assure attorney Vahed that, although I have not seen him for 30 yrs, I think of him and his wife. To Billy Nair just say "Madiba sends warmest greetings to Thambi and Elsie." and to attorney Bhengu I say "Hatala Adabazana!".

In conclusion, I want to tell you that Zami and I love you, and we often talk about you when she visits me. We sincerely look forward to seeing you one day. Hope and the future are always before us, mainly because SA has produced many men and women of your calibre, who will never allow the flames to die down. Our love and best wishes to you and the children. Kindly register your reply. Sincerely, Madiba.

Mrs Nonyamezelo Victoria Mxenge, 303 Lanyee Centre, 138 Victoria St, Durban, 4001

remind attorneys Ismail Meer, Verulam,[i] and JN Singh, Durban, of my message in which I outlined how they could team up on an important aspect of this matter. It will be a splendid victory if Ntobeko will still be on the roll after Aug 9. But if friends rise to the occasion, as I expect they will, it can still be a resounding triumph even when we lose the actual court battle. Do you meet Poswa[ii] and Kall? Do give my fondest regards and best wishes to all of them for the excellent work they are doing all over the country.

Turning now to you, I must tell you that when an inmate discovered that I intended writing to you, he remarked that I was wasting energy and time, as you are reputed to be a bad correspondent, I brushed him aside by pointing out that those who failed to get your response obviously had nothing worthwhile to say, that even if the rumour were true, this time you would put everything aside and reply.

First, I would like to know just how you have managed over these last three years. I believe that the firm had already grown immensely. I accordingly imagined that you were stretched out almost to the limit when you suddenly found yourself all alone; without the skill and vast experience GM[iii] commanded. Having spent a few years with him on Robben Island, I have a fairly good idea of the precious talents which he so richly possessed. But – from all the accounts I have received, it seems that you are a tough and determined girl, a go-getter. I am confident that you are not only equal to the task of running a big firm, but that you have by now succeeded in expanding it to a legal giant.

The news of your Cape Town adventure with Allan and others will have caught many people unawares. It is the last place where I expected you to become involved, and I was happy indeed when I heard that you did not have to travel down again. Nevertheless, the incident beautifully confirmed the image you have projected in my mind all these years.

Are the children well, and how are they faring with their school work? Where and when did you spend your last holiday? An overseas vacation, if you have a passport, would certainly be a refreshing experience both from the point of view of your own health, and that of the firm. The batteries that keep you going require to be constantly charged and recharged, if you are going to maintain a high standard of performance on professional and wider issues. It would also be an unforgettable experience for you to visit some of the big USA legal firms, some of which have not less than 100 partners each, with computers and well-stocked libraries. Do consider that.

I notice that we now have several lawyers' organisations: Lawyers for

---

i   Town in KwaZulu-Natal where Mandela's friend Ismail Meer lived.
ii   Mandela is most likely referring to Ntsikelelo Poswa, who was a lawyer and is now a judge.
iii   Nonyamezelo's husband, Griffiths Mxenge.

Human Rights,[i] Black Lawyers Association[ii] and the Democratic Lawyers Association.[iii] To which do you belong? Can you give me some information on the DLA?[iv]

Now I would like you to put a few telephone calls on my behalf to some friends over there: my sympathy to Chief Lutuli's[v] son, Sibusiso, and his wife, Wilhelmina, who were attacked at their Gledhow store recently. We wish them a speedy and complete recovery. Last year I wrote to the Old lady, Nokhukhanya;[vi] I don't know whether she ever received the letter as she never responded. Fondest regards to Diliza Mji, Senior,[vii] whose impressive contribution in the late 40s and early 50s can never be forgotten. The same sentiments to Diliza Mji, Junior[viii] in regard to his current efforts. We are particularly proud of him, Assure attorney Vahed that although I have not seen him for 30 yrs, I think of him and his wife. To Billy Nair[ix] just say, "Madiba sends warmest greetings to Thambi and Elsie" and to attorney Bhengu I say "Halala Dlabazana!"[x]

In conclusion I want to tell you that Zami[xi] and I love you, and we often talk about you when she visits me. We sincerely look forward to seeing you one day. Hope and the future are always before us, mainly because S.A. has produced many men and women of your calibre, who will never allow the flames to die down. Our love and best wishes to you and the children.

Kindly register your reply.

Sincerely, 'Madiba'

Mrs Nonyamezelo Victoria Mxenge, 503 Damjee Centre, 158 Victoria St, Durban, 4001

---

i   A non-government, non-profit organisation established in 1979.
ii   Established in 1976 to oppose the Group Areas permit system.
iii   The National Association of Democratic Lawyers was established in 1987 (note that Mandela's letter to Victoria Mxenge was written in 1985) and was established by the Black Lawyers Association.
iv   Democratic Lawyers Association.
v   Chief Albert Luthuli (1898–1967), president-general of the ANC, 1952–67 – see the glossary – who was killed by a train in July 1967. Mandela also spelt his name 'Lutuli'.
vi   Nokhukhanya Luthuli, Chief Luthuli's widow.
vii   Dilizantaba Mji, physician and president of the Transvaal ANC Youth League in the early 1950s.
viii Son of Diliza Mji, also a medical doctor and one-time president of the South African Students' Organisation.
ix   Billy Nair (1929–2008), comrade and MK member who was charged with sabotage in 1963. He was imprisoned in B Section with Mandela on Robben Island and was released in 1984 – see the glossary.
x   'Halala' is a greeting and Dlabazana is probably Bhengu's clan name.
xi   One of Winnie Mandela's names.

To Nolinda Mgabela

D220/82: NELSON MANDELA

                                                              8.7.85

My dear Nolinda,

Your letter and beautiful photograph, for which I thank you, came when I was thinking of writing to Nongaye. Early last year, I wrote to Khayalethu enquiring, amongst others, about the funeral of your late Mum, your father's health, and about a few friends. I received no reply from him, and I was quite surprised because I have never heard of a coward in Khwalo's family. I still want that information and, if he cannot send it to me, then I am confident that you or Nongaye will gladly do so.

With regard to your schooling, I suggest that you immediately apply to a boarding school, like Lovedale[i] or Clarkebury,[ii] where you can continue your studies with less interference. For this purpose, I suggest that you approach some influential person, such as Dr Gilimamba Mahlati,[iii] to help you with the application for admission.

As far as your school fees and pocket money are concerned, I want you to write without delay, to Dr Beyers Naude, Secretary of the South African Council of Churches, P.O. Box 31190, Braamfontein, 2017. Tell him that you had written to me and that I would like them to help you with your matric and university fees.

Your letter should state that your mother, who was detained several times, died last year shortly after your father, Malcomess Mgabela, had returned after serving 18 years on Robben Island for a political offence. Because of his long imprisonment, and present harassment, he has been unable to save funds for the education of the children. At his age and with his views, it is almost impossible for him to get employment. It is for these reasons that you have no other way but to ask the SACC[iv] for help. You must indicate the standard you are doing at present and the school in which you are a pupil. Let Khayalethu and Nongaye help you in writing the letter and make sure that you include all the points mentioned above.

How is Mkhozi Khwalo? I sincerely hope that he is back home and that his blood pressure is under control. Give him my best regards.

Once more I would like you to know that I am grateful to you for your lovely letter and beautiful photo. I hope to hear from you again. From the

---

i   Lovedale Missionary Institute in the Ciskei homeland.
ii   Clarkebury Boarding Insitute in the town of Engcobo, Transkei, which Mandela attended as a teenager.
iii   Gilimamba Mahlati, medical doctor and businessman.
iv   South African Council of Churches.

photo you appear to be an attractive young lady, and I suspect that the boys are going to worry you. What is important, at the present moment, is your education. It would be advisable for you not to have any serious affair until you complete your legal studies.

Meantime, I send my love and fondest regards to you, Nongaye, Khayaletu, Nosizwe and Ntomboyise.

Sincerely,
Tata[i]

Miss Nolinda Mgabela, 8235, Mdantsane, 5219

Do register all your letters to me, as well as that to Dr Naude

∞∞∞∞∞

Nelson Mandela's health became the subject of widespread public discussion and concern in late 1985 when it became known that he had been admitted to a Cape Town hospital for prostate surgery.

During the preceding twenty years he had been admitted to hospital for minor and short procedures, but this was different. He was sixty-seven years old and the idea that he could die in prison was as alarming to the regime as to his family and supporters.

He was admitted to the Volks Hospital in a leafy suburb close to the city centre on Sunday 3 November. He and his family had assembled an impressive array of trusted medical practitioners to watch over him and the procedure.

Significantly, he had 'a surprising and unexpected visitor,[59] *the then minister of justice, Kobie Coetsee. Although Mandela had written to Coetsee asking for a meeting to discuss potential talks between the government and the ANC, he had not expected to see him in the hospital. Their first conversation was confined to pleasantries but Mandela did broach the subject of his wife whose home of banishment in Brandfort had been firebombed when she was away in Johannesburg for medical treatment. The house was repaired and the police were making attempts to have her return there, to a dangerous situation. He asked Coetsee to allow her to remain in Johannesburg.*[60]

Coetsee became a crucial connection in talks Mandela began with a government team the following year. These exploratory talks were planned to investigate whether the government could enter into formal negotiations with the ANC about the end of white minority rule.

---

i   'Father' in isiXhosa.

The meeting with Coetsee could also have been the catalyst for his sepa-
ration from his comrades when he returned to Pollsmoor on 23 November. From
that time, they had to make official requests to see each other after having spent
almost every day of the last almost twenty-two years together. Mandela suspected
that it was so that the meetings with government could begin.[61] *Finally, in May*
1986, he began what became a long series of meetings with Coetsee and other
government officials – the precursor to eventually full-blown talks between the
apartheid regime and the ANC after his release from prison in 1990.

To the University of South Africa

Student no. 240-094-4

15.10.85

The Registrar (Academic),
University of South Africa,
PO Box 392, Pretoria 0001

Dear Sir,

I am compelled to request you to allow me to write the October/November examinations in five subjects in January 1986.

I had intended having an operation[i] immediately after I had written the examinations. But I was advised on medical grounds to do so without further delay, an advice which I accepted.

As a general rule, and probably for security reasons, the Department of Prisons does not advise a prisoner of the actual date when an operation will be made. But on 29 September, and after consultation with the medical team which will conduct the operation, it was indicated that this would be done during the week commencing on 7 October. I then suspended my preparations for the examinations in the hope that I would apply for a special aegrotat in due course.

Later I was informed that the operation had been postponed to the end of this month or beginning of November. I then resumed preparations for the examinations but I was, at the same time, subjected to a series of medi-

---

i   Mandela was admitted to the Volks Hospital in Cape Town on 3 November 1985 for prostate surgery and returned
     to prison on 23 November 1985.

cal tests and consultations which affected my concentration and disrupted my preparations. [For] these reasons, I must request you to permit me to write the examinations next January.

Enclosed please find [a] medical certificate issued by Dr. Stoch, District Surgeon of Wynberg, in support of the application.

Yours faithfully,
[Signed NRMandela]

To Winnie Mandela,[i] his wife

D220/82: NELSON MANDELA   5.12.85

My darling Mum,

You have been in my thoughts ever since your last visit to Volks Hospital.[ii] Even then, I could easily notice the ravages of growing pressures & strains right across your beautiful face. In normal times I would have been at your bedside, holding your warm hand & caressing your pains. I sincerely hope that you will be able to rest for some time now. You have done remarkably well & nobody can justly blame you if you take things easy for some time. Remember, we all love you & wish you a speedy recovery.

Tons & tons of love & a million kisses. Affectionately, Madiba

[Greeting card with the printed words:]
Hope that each day
brings something happy . . .
sunshine through your window,
friendly smiles,
some pleasant news,
whatever will make
the time pass quickly
until you feel better again!

---

i   Nomzamo Winifred Madikizela-Mandela (1936–) – see the glossary.
ii   Mandela was admitted to the Volks Hospital in Cape Town on 3 November 1985 for prostate surgery and returned to prison on 23 November 1985.

To Dr. Dumisani Mzamane, medical doctor and friend

D220/82: NELSON MANDELA

17.12.85

Dear Dumisani,

I was discharged from Volkshospital on 23rd November, and I am still undergoing post-operative treatment. I am on

Folic Acid	1 three times a day
Brewer's Yeast	1 three times a day
Ferrus Sulphate	2 three times a day
Bactrim	1 two times a day

Plus

40ml Isoptin	twice a day

The cut has completely healed and the scar is hardly noticeable. Last week the blood unit of the Conradie State Hospital examined my blood sample and the results were as follows.

Haemoglobin	13,0
White cells blood count	4,7

Throughout the entire period of my hospitalisation the urologist, Dr Loubscher, visited me twice a day, and the specialist physician, Dr Shapiro, once a day. They are presently coordinating arrangements for a further check-up and, should there be any unexpected developments (which I much doubt), I will keep you informed.

Your friend and District Surgeon, Dr Stoch, is away on three months' holiday. I had a long consultation with him on the day before he left, in the course of which he explained patiently, and as fully as was possible, the purpose of the present treatment. Dr Brand, who retired from the District Surgeon's office a few months ago, will act in Dr Stoch's absence. He also spent quite some time with me and we are in daily contact. For the moment that is the score.

I must add that I was more than delighted to discover only recently that Woody was the Chairman of the Hospital Board, and his stand on a matter that concerned us all was indeed magnificent. My congratulations to him and fondest regards to his family, as well as to your matron-in-chief (African) even though I have not had the pleasure of meeting her. But I must conclude this note by hoping that hardly anyone of us remains unmoved when she/he thinks of Lesedi.[i] That institution represents far more than the buildings, installations and equipment that bear its name. It is a symbol and a very fond dream, and Ntatho[ii] must be warmly complimented for the excellent pioneering work. It was also a source of pride and joy to know that you are closely associated with so significant an experiment. My congratulations to you, your matron-in-chief and the entire nursing, administrative staff and the labour force.

Love and fondest regards to Sally[iii] & Ntatho, Dr Gecelter[iv] and family and, of course to you and your family.

Sincerely,
Madiba

P.S. Kindly remind Winnie that there are many visitors on Xmas Day and I would urge her to be here not later than 8.45 am to make it fairly easy for the official in charge. Regards to Dr Matseke and family.

Madiba

[Envelope]
Dr Dumisani Mzamane,
Nephrological Unit,
Baragwanath Hospital,
Potchefstroom Road,
JOHANNESBURG.
2001

To the commissioner of prisons

[Translated from Afrikaans]

[telex stamp dated 1986-02-04]

Confidential
Commissioner of Prisons

---

i   Lesedi Clinic in Soweto, Johannesburg, founded by Dr. Nthato Motlana.
ii   Nthato Motlana (1925–2008), friend, medical doctor, businessman, and anti-apartheid activist – see the glossary.
iii Dr Motlana's wife, Sally.
iv   Mandela's urologist from Johannesburg.

[AK?] Security Services

Thank-you letters 913[i]

913 has permission to write thank-you letters to the doctors who took care of him before and after his hospitalization.

He would like to write to the following people.

Dr Jack Baron: The doctor who did the "scan"

Dr Nthato Motlana[ii] one of the designated doctors

Dr L Gecelter urologist from Johannesburg who acted as an observer during the operation

Dr Dumisani Mzamane, one of the doctors designated by the family

Dr C J Dekenah the anaesthetist

Prof A B Bull anaesthetist

Prof G Chisholm and Dr van Edenburgh from Scotland who also acted as an observer

Dr WM Laubscher the urologist who conducted the surgery

Dr P Turner the Medical Superintendent of the Volks Hospital

Dr Norman Shapiro the internist who, according to him, looked after him before and after the operation

Dr SW Stoch Head District Surgeon of Wynberg

Dr R Schapera the State Pathologist of Conradie Hospital

The content of the letters reads as follows:

Dear ....

I delayed in the writing of this note in the hope that it would be accompanied by a suitable present coming direct from me, in appreciation of your attendance during my operation at Volks Hospital in Cape Town on November 3, 1985.

Unfortunately I encountered insurmountable problems in this regard and, much as I tried, this hope simply could not be realised.

But I must assure you that my sense of gratitude is deep and complete, and I will always think of you in this spirit.

Meantime, please accept my fondest regards to you and your family.

Sincerely,

Mr Mandela

---

i   Mandela's prison file number was 913. Prison officials often referred to him as 913 in correspondence with each other.

ii   Nthato Motlana (1925–2008), friend, medical doctor, businessman, and anti-apartheid activist – see the glossary.

Vrystelling van die brief word aanbevele[i]

Bevelvoerende Offisier[ii]
Brig FC Munro

◇◇◇◇◇◇◇◇◇◇

The first two paragraphs in this, one of Mandela's most seminal prison letters, signals his absolute faith in his chosen path of political activism and becoming a freedom fighter to win change in the country of his birth. He would have been writing this letter to Joy Motsieloa in his small single cell at Pollsmoor Prison, aware that outside its walls the country was in many parts literally burning.

Since September 1980 he and his comrades had been allowed access to newspapers and radio news, and by the mid-1980s they would have been fully informed of the events unfolding in South Africa. An upsurge in anti-apartheid activity in response to President P. W. Botha's establishment of a tricameral parliament with separate chambers for whites, coloureds and Indians – and nothing for Africans – in 1983 had given birth to a powerful new organisation, the United Democratic Front.

In 1985 the ANC in exile called upon South Africans to make black neighbourhoods 'ungovernable'. In July the same year the 'Pollsmoor March' was planned for activists to march on the prison and to 'free' Nelson Mandela. Although thousands of protesters set off from Cape Town on the march to Pollsmoor Prison on 28 August 1985, the iron fist of the apartheid regime crushed this march before it got anywhere near the prison and that day nine activists were killed, with a further nineteen people dead by the end of the week. This led to widespread protests throughout Cape Town for the rest of the year.

As Mandela was writing this letter activists were being detained en masse, kidnapped, and murdered. Six months earlier, Victoria Mxenge, one of the friends he wrote to from prison (see his letter from 8 July 1985, page 471) was assassinated by a man paid by apartheid security forces. The country was under a State of Emergency, in effect martial law. Severe restrictions were in place to prevent the media from reporting on the action of the security police.

---

i   'The letter may be released' in Afrikaans.
ii   'Officer Commanding' in Afrikaans.

To Joy Motsieloa, his friend

D220/82: NELSON MANDELA

17. 2. 86

Dear Joy,

When a man commits himself to the type of life he has lived for 45 years, even though he may well have been aware from the outset of all the attendant hazards, the actual course of events and the precise manner in which they would influence his life could never have been clearly foreseeable in every respect.

If I had been able to foresee all that has since happened, I would certainly have made the same decision, so I believe at least. But that decision would certainly have been far more daunting, and some of the tragedies which subsequently followed would have melted whatever traces of steel were inside me. The death of your beloveds and your intimate friends to whom you are linked by countless ties, some going back for several decades; the wide variety of problems to which your family would be exposed in your absence, are personal disasters which are often difficult to endure and, on most occasions, leaving you wondering whether in this kind of life one should have a family, raise children and make firm friendships.

There have been many occasions on which such thoughts have crossed the mind. The death of your brother, Gabula,[i] was one of those painful moments. The report literally paralysed me; I could write neither to you or to Zozo, I was not certain whether the old people were still alive or not and, if so, what their address was. All that I could do in my circumstances was to retire to the privacy of the cell, heavily stunned by the knowledge that I would never see him again. I, however, felt relieved when I thought of the happy days we spent together and his wonderful sense of humour.

Later as the turmoil inside me slowly began clearing away, I succeeded in rationalising the situation, and consoled myself with the belief that a man of his positive outlook would like to be remembered through his constructive efforts, which were fairly substantial, and for the joy and laughter he brought to those around him. I have missed him ever since.

Kepu,[ii] who has been corresponding with me since our Robben Island days, informed me by telegram about the death of Thandi,[iii] and I sent a message of sympathy to the family.

---

i   Gabula Mahlasela, Joy Motsieloa's brother, who visited Mandela at the Fort Prison in Johannesburg while he was awaiting trial in 1962.

ii   Kepu Mkentane, the wife of Lincoln Mkentane, a friend and former university classmate of Mandela's who became a lawyer.

iii   One of Joy Motsieloa's relatives.

Last year Vuyiswa[i] sent me a birthday telegram and, in response to my letter of thanks, she wrote me a [?] letter which I value very much. She wrote on a piece of paper she probably retrieved from a waste paper basket. On the reverse side it was criss-crossed by untidy roneoed[ii] particulars. But the actual letter was, notwithstanding, warm and sweet, and its total lack of formality made it somewhat unique. She seems to be a tremendous person and I look forward to seeing her in the flesh one day.

When I visited London in June 1962 I thought of you and Jimmy,[iii] but the visit was a secret and highly packed one and I was unfortunately unable to contact many people I would have liked to see. Until I got Vuyiswa's letter I did not know that you were in Mogadishu[iv] and Jimmy in Scandinavia. I hope you find a lot of pleasure and satisfaction in your respective occupations, although I imagine that you probably do a lot of travelling. How many children have you got and what are they doing? When last did you come home? Remember that we think of you and your Jimmy. Meantime, we send you our fondest regards and best wishes.

Sincerely,
Madiba

P.S. Should you ever forget the above address or wish not to use it, send the letters by registered post to P.O. Box 728 Johannesburg, 2000

[Envelope]
Mrs Joy Motsieloa,
United Nations High Commissioner for Refugees,
P.O. Box 2925.
MOGADISHU
Somalia

---

i   Duma Nokwe's wife Vuyiswa died in South Africa in 2008.
ii   Copies made on a Roneo duplicating machine.
iii   Jimmy Njongwe (1919–76), medical doctor, ANC leader, and organiser of the Defiance Campaign (for the Defiance Campaign, see the glossary) in the Eastern Cape – for Jimmy Njongwe, see the glossary. He was a relative of Joy Motsieloa's.
iv   The capital of Somalia.

Tukwini, Dumani, and Kweku, his grandchildren and children of his eldest daughter Makaziwe Mandela[i]

D220/82: NELSON MANDELA

To Tukwini, Dumani and Kweku,

I miss you very much and think of you always. Tons and tons of love and a million kisses.

From Khulu,

Pollsmoor Maximum
P/B X4, Tokai, 7966

Envelope:

Tukwini, Dumani and Kweku
429 North Pleasant St.,
Appt # 108
Amherst, MA 01002
U.S.A

To Michael Dingake,[ii] friend, comrade and former fellow prisoner

D220/82

24.4.86

Dear Tlou,[iii]

This letter to Rakgadi[iv] was returned by the Post Office in Gaborone[v] marked

---

i   Makaziwe Mandela (1954–), Mandela's eldest daughter – see the glossary.
ii   Michael Dingake (1928), ANC member who was convicted for sabotage and imprisoned on Robben Island – see the glossary.
iii Tlou is Michael Dingake's clan name.
iv   'Sister' in Setswana. He is referring to Frieda Matthews (1905–98), friend and wife of his university professor Z. K. Matthews – see the glossary for both individuals.
v   Capital of Botswana where the Matthewses lived.

"Box Closed". Please ensure that it reaches her, and thereafter kindly inform me by registered letter of the results of your efforts.

This is a special letter strictly confined to the above message. But I must, at least, tell you that you, Edna[i] and the young lady[ii] are always in my thoughts. When Ntatho[iii] came last year I literally interrogated him on you. I sincerely hope that your health is sound and that you still find some time for jogging. Do let me know about the university and the young lady in your reply.

Fondest regards and best wishes to Quett,[iv] Gaositwe,[v] Sefton,[vi] Tloome,[vii] Martha, Ishy,[viii] Nana & hubby,[ix] Dan, Edna & last, but not least, to you.

Very sincerely,
Madiba

To K. D. Matanzima,[x] his nephew, a Thembu chief, and chief minister of the Transkei

D220/82: NELSON MANDELA

19.5.86

Ngubengcuka,[xi]

The Department of Prisons informs me that you will in no circumstances come to Cape Town to see me, because I grossly insulted you when I refused your request to visit me last year.

I have on several occasions in the past expressly warned you against using our relationship to involve me and my organisation in Bantustan politics, and I will not allow you to do so.

---

i   Edna Dingake, (d. 2009) Michael Dingake's wife.
ii   The Dingakes' daughter Goseo Dingake.
iii   Nthato Motlana (1925–2008), friend, medical doctor, businessman, and anti-apartheid activist – see the glossary. He was Edna Dingake's brother-in-law.
iv   Sir Quett Ketumile Joni Masire (1925–2017), second president of Botswana 1980–98.
v   Dr. Gaositwe Chiepe (1922–), former Botswana cabinet minister.
vi   Mandela's brother-in-law Sefton Vutela, who was working for the Botswana Book Centre in Gaborone.
vii   Dan Tloome (1919-92), leader of the ANC and the South African Communist Party who was working for the ANC in Botswana, and who spent many decades in exile in Zambia.
viii   Ishmael and Martha Matlhaku, political activists and friends. They went into exile in Botswana.
ix   ANC activists Euphenia and Solly Hlapane, who were refugees in Botswana.
x   K. D. Mantanzima (1915–2003) – see the glossary.
xi   A reference to him being a descendant of King Ngubengcuka who was also Mandela's great-great-grandfather.

But I am disturbed by recent press reports which indicate the existence of a tragic turmoil in family affairs.[i] It has distressed me even more to discover from your reaction that this state of affairs no longer moves you. I sincerely hope that wiser counsels will ultimately prevail, and that you will in due course reconsider your decision, so that we can at least contain the simmering anger and bitterness. Had it not been for my current circumstances I would long have come down, as I did in 1955, to discuss these problems with you. When conditions change for the better I will certainly arrange to see you, and I only hope that an attempt to resolve the matter will then still be timely and fruitful.

I need hardly remind you that our political beliefs differ most radically, and it is my duty to remind you of this fact whenever you tend to ignore it. But I still regard you as an important member of the family whose friendship and co-operation is essential for the preservation of family unity and peace. I will not consciously insult or belittle you, or any other person for that matter. But I must stress with all the emphasis at my command that a public figure, whether – as you would put it – he is a "dangerous revolutionary", or a mere Bantustan leader, who allows his image to be so severely dented by recrimination, touchiness and intemperate language is no model for my own approach to people and problems.

Fondest regards and best wishes to you, Bambilanga,[ii] Mzimvubu,[iii] Ngangomhlaba,[iv] Zwelidumile and Wonga. I miss you all. Ngubengcuka!

Very sincerely,
Dalibunga

◇◇◇◇◇◇◇◇

It is suspected that the dampness of Mandela's single cell away from the sunshine of the roof of Pollsmoor Prison contributed to the illness that permanently removed him from that prison. Almost a year before he fell ill with tuberculosis, he petitioned the authorities about what he saw as a threat to his health.

---

i   Mandela could be referring to K. D. Matanzima's actions regarding King Sabata Jonguhlanga Dalindyebo
      (1928–86), paramount chief of the Transkei homeland and leader of the Democratic Progressive Party, who fled to
      Zambia after he was convicted of violating Matanzima's dignity in 1980 and died there in 1986.
ii   Nxeko (also known as Bambilanga) is the brother of King Sabata Jonguhlanga Dalindyebo, paramount chief of the
      Transkei homeland.
iii   George Matanzima (1918–2000), K. D. Matanzima's brother, Transkei leader and chief. While Mandela was at
      University College of Fort Hare with KD, George studied at nearby Lovedale College.
iv   Chief Ngangomhlaba Matanzima, a relative.

To the head of Prison, Pollsmoor Maximum Security Prison

D220/82: NELSON MANDELA

6.10.86

Head of Prison
Pollsmoor Maximum Security Prison

Attention: Major Van Sittert

I would like to be transferred, at the earliest possible convenience, from my present cell to the opposite and empty cell across the passage primarily on health grounds.

My present cell has proved to be quite unhealthy and, if I continue staying in it, my health will eventually be impaired. At no time of day does the cell get the natural light, and I am accordingly compelled to keep the electric lights burning throughout the day.

The interior window panes are opaque and thick and the exterior fittings are made of louvre boards, all of which make the cell dark and depressing. Six panes have been removed and the cell becomes unbearable on cold and windy days.

Part of the wall and floor are perpetually damp and, during the ten months of my stay here, I have had to endure this inconvenience. You will readily appreciate, I trust, that it is not desirable that I should be compelled to live under such unwholesome conditions when there is a far better cell right in the same unit in which I could stay with relative comfort.

I must add that the dampness, as well as the metal fittings on the walls, also affect the reception in both the wireless and television set, resulting in uncontrollable flickering on the screen.[i] I believe that I would get a better performance in a dry and properly ventilated cell which is not cluttered with metal material. I accordingly suggest that you allow me to move to the opposite cell.

You will recall that on 26 September 1986 I requested an urgent interview with the Commanding Officer, and I would urge you to remind him again about the request. In conclusion, I would like to point out that no

---

i   The Rivonia prisoners at Pollsmoor were allowed to have television sets in 1986. Mandela received one in his cell at Pollsmoor Prison on 1 October 1986.

explanation has been made to me as to the conditions under which the television set has been made available to

P.T.O. [The letter ends abruptly. We are unsure if the second page was not copied or if it is not held by the National Archives and Records Service of South Africa.]

=====

To Mabel Nontancu Timakwe,[i] his sister

[Translated from isiXhosa]

18.2.87

My Beloved Princess,

The years are rolling by. It is difficult to believe that two years have passed since I've been here.[ii]

I've been meaning to write to you for a while to thank you for kindly visiting me to bring me great news about home. The population has grown in here; some people are from this country, others from Swaziland and America. The responsibility they bestow upon me (in bringing their problems to me) makes it difficult for me to write to you all as often as my heart desires. I am limited to a few letters a year and am monitored not to exceed the maximum. Since this is the case, I should tell you in just two lines that I am still healthy. I hope you are the same.

I have written to Kholeka[iii] and Leabie[iv] and sent the letter to c/o Langa High School, Butterworth.[v] I don't know if the letter will make it to that address. I ask that you and Notsatsumbana visit Mrs Nobandla[vi] at House no. 8115, Orlando West, 1804, for a few weeks so you can get "some fresh air".

Nobandla[vii] is a very kind person with lots of love for the family. Here is her telephone number 936-5402. I should be the one asking her for permission for you to visit and am upset I am not able to. I would have also liked for you to go along with my older sister.

---

i   Mabel Nontancu Timakwe (1924–2002) – see the glossary.
ii   He'd been at Pollsmoor Prison for almost five years so he is possibly referring to the two years he had been in a single cell there, separate from his comrades.
iii   Mandela's niece, the daughter of his sister Mabel's daughter.
iv   His youngest sister.
v   A town in what is now the Eastern Cape province.
vi   His wife, Winnie Mandela.
vii   One of Winnie Mandela's names.

Greet brother-in-law Daniel and the rest of the family.

Your brother,
Madiba

To Frieda Matthews,[i] friend & wife of his university professor Z. K. Matthews

D220/82: NELSON MANDELA   25.2.87

Our dear Rakgadi,[ii]

You have no idea just what your visit to Pollsmoor has meant to all of us here. A visit to a prisoner always has significance difficult to put into words. Routine is the supreme law of a prison in almost every country in the world, and every day is for all practical purposes like the day before: the same surroundings, same faces, same dialogue, same odour, walls rising to the skies, and the ever-present feeling that outside the prison gates there is an exciting world to which you have no access. A visit from your beloved ones, from friends and even from strangers is always an unforgettable occasion, when that frustrating monotony is broken & the entire world is literally ushered into the cell.

Your visit was typical and it made one feel that, after all, he is still part of the world to which we were born and grew up. It lighted a corner in me and a whole panorama of pleasant memories going as far back as 1939, flashed across the mind. Under different conditions we would have urged you to visit Robben Island, Pretoria, Diepkloof and Kroonstad[iii] to take to them directly the same sentiments you expressed to me. But of course that is not possible. . . .

It pleased us to learn that Kgosie, together with J.J. and company, visited you. That is the field to which a Matthews should be active, and we were happy indeed to know that he is keeping the family tradition alive. I hope he has inherited Bakwe's[iv] excellent gift of wide and disciplined

---

i   Frieda Matthews (1905–98) – see the glossary.
ii   'Sister' in Setswana.
iii   Prisons where other political activists were incarcerated.
iv   Bakwe (Joe) Matthews (1929–2010), political activist and son of Frieda and Z. K. Matthews – see the glossary for these three individuals.

reading. During the Treason Trial[i] Bakwe had a set pattern from which he rarely deviated. On returning from the case he would chat with the family for some time, have his supper, retire to the bedroom and get stuck to his reading for hours on end. Equally important was the fact that he knew how to absorb what he read and to apply it to his political work. I have missed him and Fiki over the years.

As far as the other grandchildren are concerned, you are mistaken to think that talking about them may bore me. On the contrary, the progress made by children can be very fascinating, even when they are your grand-children. Admittedly, and having regard to your family background, there is nothing particularly astonishing in your grandchildren reaching out for the stars. The very achievements of their parents and grandparents are in themselves a challenge and an inspiration. But even when making allow-ance for that, what they have achieved gives a person in prison a fairly clear picture of the far-reaching changes which are taking place in Southern Africa today, and put the social turmoil in this region in perspective.

It would seem that some kind of diaspora is in full swing and children from urban townships and simple country villages alike are scattered all over the world and, in the process, horizons are widened beyond recog-nition, and new ideas acquired; with this background they return home to an environment not yet ready to accommodate them. This phenomenon is evident in many of the letters we receive and I am happy to note that your grandchildren are right in the centre of this process. I congratulate all of them and send them my fondest regards and best wishes.

I see Walter and others[ii] now and again and we had a pleasant get together on Boxing Day. We are like a family and share almost everything we have. Naturally, we miss you all and literally crave for the open veld, some fresh air and plenty of sunshine.

Much love, Rakgadi,

Very sincerely,
Nelson

---

i   The Treason Trial (1956–61) was a result of the apartheid government's attempt to quell the power of the Congress Alliance, a coalition of anti-apartheid organisations. In early-morning raids on 5 December 1956, 156 individuals were arrested and charged with high treason. By the end of the trial in March 1961 all the accused either had the charges withdrawn or, in the case of the last twenty-eight accused (including Mandela), were acquitted.

ii   Walter Sisulu and the other Rivonia trialists imprisoned at Pollsmoor (for Walter Sisulu, see the glossary).

To Kepu Mkentane,[i] friend

D220/82: NELSON MANDELA   25.2.87

Dear Kepu,

My last letter to you was on 17 February last year. On the same day I wrote to your niece, Joy,[ii] to express the sympathy of the family on the death of Gabula[iii] and Thandi. The letter took a long time to reach her; I had addressed it care of Mogadishu[iv] only to find [that] she had moved to Sweden. . . . Although she may now work elsewhere, her base will remain in Stockholm and I propose writing to her some time towards the end of the year.

As usual you promptly replied to my letter and supplied me with information I badly needed and for which I thank you. When it comes to correspondence you get some idea just what has happened to our people in South Africa during the past 25 years. There are hardly any men to correspond with. Life-long friends are either dead or out of the country. Many of those who are still in the country cannot be reached and, with perhaps a few notable exceptions, the few that can still be contacted seem to be totally unaware of the fact that letters are meant to be answered. By comparison, women have proved to be far better correspondents, more aware of the needs of prisoners.

Down there, and quite apart from you, I receive regular letters and encouraging sentiments from my sisters, grandchildren, Florence (Nosango) Matanzima,[v] and Connie Njongwe.[vi] Chiefs Bambilanga[vii] and Luvuyo Mtirara from Mpheko[viii] have visited me several times. Chief Zwelidumile Joyi from Baziya twice, George Matanzima,[ix] his nephew Ngangomhlaba, Mtutuzeli Lujabe once each. There are several others who have been here and who reminded me of old times, but all of them know very little about the value of a simple and informative letter to a friend.

Sobhini Mgudlwa from Qumanco, married to a Mesatywa nurse, lived

---

i   A friend of Mandela's.
ii   See his letter on page 484.
iii   Gabula Mahlasela, Joy Motsieloa's brother, who visited Mandela at the Fort Prison in Johannesburg while he was awaiting trial in 1962.
iv   The capital of Somalia.
v   One of KD Matanzima's five wives.
vi   Connie Njongwe, wife of Jimmy Njongwe (1919–76), medical doctor, ANC leader, and organiser of the Defiance Campaign (for the Defiance Campaign, see the glossary) in the Eastern Cape – for Jimmy Njongwe, see the glossary.
vii   Nxeko (also known as Bambilanga) is the brother of King Sabata Jonguhlanga Dalindyebo, paramount chief of the Transkei homeland.
viii   A village outside Umtata (now Mthatha) in the Transkei.
ix   George Matanzima (1918–2000) , K. D. Matanzima's brother, Transkei leader and chief. While Mandela was at University College of Fort Hare with KD, George studied at nearby Lovedale College.

with us in Orlando West in the late forty's and early fifties. Have you ever met them and do you know where they are at present? Mr Mvambo, who is now in Pretoria, is he the same man who was once inspector of schools in the Ciskei and who was with us at Fort Hare?[i] Am I correct in thinking that he is also your brother? If so, please give him and his wife my regards. Incidentally, Winnie's telephone number is 936-5402 and you may contact her whenever you feel bored.

Aunt Frieda Matthews[ii] from Botswana visited me on 22 November and literally brought an entire library for which I am very grateful. Although over 80 years she still looks fresh, strong and with an alert mind. The forty minutes we spent together were most enjoyable.

Many thanks for the beautiful Christmas cards in which you complain that I am quiet. Twelve months' silence justifies such a complaint, but I must assure you that, in spite of the rapid growth of the family and the host of problems that entails, you and the children are always in my thoughts. You and Kent looked after us during the most difficult period of our imprisonment when many good friends did not consider it safe to remember us. My conscience would torture me even in my grave if, in better days, I chose to forget about you. Do keep well, Kepu; my fondest regards and very best wishes to you and the children.

Very sincerely,
Nelson

To Helen Joseph,[iii] his friend

1.4.87

Our dear Helen,

Please do not tell me that last yr I forgot to send you birthday greetings. I invariably keep copies of my outgoing correspondence, whether in the form of letters, birthday cards or telegrams. I have just gone through my letter book & despite my firm belief that I sent you the message, I found no record to that effect. But I want to assure you that this time last yr

---

i   University College of Fort Hare, which he attended in 1939 until 1940 when he was expelled for embarking on protest action.
ii Frieda Matthews (1905–98), friend and wife of his university professor Z. K. Matthews – see the glossary for both individuals.
iii Helen Joseph (1905–92), teacher, social worker, and anti-apartheid and women's rights activist – see the glossary.

you were constantly in my thoughts, especially because it was your 80th birthday.

After all, a card is of secondary importance; it is no more than a mere expression of how a person feels towards a friend. That love & loyalty to you will always be there whether the card reaches you or not. It was all there in April last yr & it is in this spirit that I send you my warmest congratulations on your 81st birthday. I hope the girls will all be there to rejoice with you. In my last letter to Amina[i] I suggested that she should arrange a tea party and invite Muriel,[ii] Virginia, Catherine, Rahima,[iii] Bertha,[iv] Greta, Onica[v] & co. to commemorate praiseworthy efforts and precious contributions – the deathless yrs. Perhaps you can take up the matter with her & Ntsiki? The response may far exceed your expectations. How about it, Helen? By the way, do you still remember my reply when you told me that the late Dr Moroka[vi] had celebrated his 92nd birthday? You abhorred the prospect of living till that age. It would seem that the gods want you to drink that cup. Now it is my turn to say that I hope I will not live as long as Helen. How do you like that?

Caroline Mashaba[vii] disappointed me very much. When I sent her a letter of sympathy on the death of Andrew, I asked her to give me certain information on him which I needed urgently. Andrew did more than we expected both outside & especially on the Island, & we had a duty to acknowledge that contribution. That was not possible without that information. I cannot understand why she had to be so flat-footed in a matter of this nature. In May last yr, I also wrote to Esther Maleka;[viii] until then she was as good a correspondent as you, but I never heard from her again. There was also no response from Onica to my letter of sympathy on the occasion of her mother's death. I would not want you to actually travel in order to ascertain what happened. But if & when you bump against them do find out if they received the letters. How is Ruth,[ix] Sheila[x] and others? I trust that they still look after you. Ruth & Sheila are very good children & I am always happy to hear about them. It is, however, not so easy to reconcile

i   Amina Cachalia (1930–2013), friend and anti-apartheid and women's rights activist – see the glossary.
ii   Muriel Sodinda, anti-apartheid activist and singer.
iii   Rahima Moosa (1922–93), anti-apartheid activist and one of the leaders of the Women's March in Pretoria in 1956 to protest the extension of pass laws to women.
iv   Bertha Mashaba (1934–2010), anti-apartheid activist, feminist, and trade unionist. Alternatively he could be referring to Bertha Mkhize (1889–1981), an ANC Women's Leaguer and a vice-president of the Federation of South African Women.
v   Onica Mashohlane Mashigo from Alexandra township was an ANC activist who participated in many of its important campaigns and boycotts.
vi   James Moroka (1892–1985), medical doctor, politician and anti-apartheid activist, president of the ANC, 1949–52.
vii   The wife of former Robben Island prisoner, Andrew Mashaba.
viii   Sister of ANC activist Tito Maleka, who played a role in taking letters from him to his family during his Africa trip.
ix   Ruth Fischer (1941–) is the eldest of Advocate Bram Fischer's two daughters.
x   Sheila Weinberg (1945–2004) was the daughter of activists Violet and Eli Weinberg. An activist in her own right, she was detained as a teenager. At the time of her death she was a member of the Gauteng Provincial Legislature.

myself with the fact that I will never see their parents again – Braam, Molly, Violet & Eli.[i] When you see Nadine[ii] do give her my fondest regards & best wishes. She has turned out to be a formidable communicator whose message reaches far beyond the visible horizons. How such girls have become so precious today!

By now you probably know that Aunt Frieda Matthews[iii] from Botswana paid me a special visit last November & brought along a whole library. Except that she has become shorter, she is in many respects like you. She carries her 81 yrs with much grace & charm & is very strong & alert. I enjoyed the visit very much. I have, however, no hope of seeing you, Amina & Fatima.[iv] All my efforts from this side to make such a visit possible have been unsuccessful. But we will always be in touch through correspondence & you will constantly be in my thoughts.

Lastly, I must tell you that I saved a piece of fruit cake which I hope to enjoy as you celebrate in a few days time. Although I have tea leaves & condensed milk I don't think I will be able to prepare it as well as you make yours. Nevertheless, it will be a very enjoyable moment for me. Have a wonderful time! Love & best wishes.

Very sincerely,
Nelson

◇◇◇◇◇◇◇◇

When Nelson Mandela was first sent to serve a prison sentence he was the father of five children aged from nearly two years old to seventeen. By the late 1980s he was a grandfather of twelve, with some of his grandchildren living abroad. His relationships with them were stitched together by birthday cards, simple notes, and in the cases of the older ones, extraordinary efforts to help them in their own endeavours at school and university. In this letter to his oldest grandson Mandla, he speaks of assisting his mother and his stepfather. Throughout, Mandela continued his long-distance parenting of his children and their spouses, cajoling and encouraging and in some cases admonishing them, even though they were grown and had children of their own.

---

i   Violet and Eli Weinberg. Violet Weinberg was a member of the Communist Party and the ANC. She left South Africa in 1977 to join her husband in exile.
ii   Nadine Gordimer, the South African author.
iii   Frieda Matthews (1905–98), friend and wife of his university professor Z. K. Matthews – see the glossary for both individuals.
iv   Fatima (1928–2010) and Ismail Meer (1918–2000), friends. Fatima was a professor, author, and anti-apartheid activist. Imail was a lawyer and anti-apartheid activist – see the glossary for both these individuals.

To Mandla Mandela,[i] his grandson and the son of his son Makgatho[ii]

D220/82: NELSON MANDELA

9.7.87

My dear Mzukulu,[iii]

Why do you not write to me? Did you get the birthday card I sent you?

How are you getting on with your studies? We are trying to get you a scholarship to go to Waterford,[iv] and I sincerely hope that you will pass the test for admission.

I am keen to see you and I have told Grandma[v] to bring you down so that we can talk about your school work.

Our friends in London have met Mum Rennie[vi] and they are helping her to get glasses for her eyes. Uncle Adrian[vii] has already got work with a building firm in London.

[I] am sending you R50,00 for pocket money.[viii] Please look after it.

Love and fondest regards. Affectionately,
Tatomkhulu[ix]

[Envelope]
Mandla Mandela,
c/o Prince Kuzulwandle Dlamini,
Ministry of Education,
MBABANE, Swaziland

---

i   Mandla Zwelivelile Mandela (1974–) – see the glossary.
ii   Makgatho Mandela (1950–2005), Mandela's second-born son – see the glossary.
iii   'Grandchild' in isiXhosa.
iv   Waterford Kamhlaba school in neighbouring Swaziland.
v   Winnie Mandela.
vi   Rose Rayne Mandela-Perry, known as Rennie, Mandla's mother. After her marriage to Makgatho Mandela ended, she married Adrian Perry.
vii   Mandla's stepfather, Adrian Perry.
viii   Mandela received money from family, friends, and supporters.
ix   'Grandad' in isiXhosa.

To Nandi Mandela,[i] granddaughter & eldest daughter of his late son Thembi[ii]

D220/82: NELSON MANDELA

17.8.87

My darling Mzukulu,[iii]

I enjoyed the last visit very much and it is a great pity that one visit is no more than a mere 40 minutes. Even more regrettable is the fact that we may not be able to see each other until early next year, because of the limited number of the remaining visits. But it is just possible that there may be one spare visit towards the end of the year which we could use. I would accordingly suggest that you telephone again, say, during the last week in October to find out whether you and Thumeka[iv] could come round. Remember that I love you and it is always a great day when you walk into the visiting room.

As I pointed out during the last visit, 43% and 44% in Economics and Accounting respectively, and bearing in mind the whole background, and that this is your first year, is by no means a bad performance. I am confident that, if you work harder during the next two months, you may be able to overcome, at least, some of your difficulties and improve your over-all performance.

Zindzi[v] ought to have been here on 5 August but she never turned up. I sincerely hope that she will be here one of these days. Have you written to Mandla?[vi] Tell Mamphela[vii] that I fully reciprocate the sentiments she expressed and keenly look forward to seeing her one day. Meantime, I send her my fondest regards and best wishes.

You must tell me a little more about your boyfriend. I never knew until the last visit that he was also at UCT.[viii] All you told me a year or two ago was that he was working at Umtata[ix] and studying through Unisa.[x]

---

i   Nandi Mandela (1968–) – see the glossary.
ii   Madiba Thembekile (Thembi) Mandela (1945–69), Mandela's eldest son – see the glossary.
iii   'Granddaughter' in isiXhosa.
iv   K.D. Matanzima's daughter Tumeka Matanzima.
v   Zinziswa Mandela (1960–), his middle daughter.
vi   Mandla Mandela (1974), son of Mandela's youngest son Makgatho Mandela and Rose Rayne Mandela, known as Rennie.
vii   Mamphela Ramphele (1947–), anti-apartheid activist and a founding member of the Black Consciousness Movement, medical doctor, academic, and businesswoman – see the glossary.
viii   University of Cape Town.
ix   Umtata (now called Mthatha) was the capital of the Transkei homeland.
x   University of South Africa.

Fondest regards to Herbert[i] & Nono[ii] and to your room-mate Pearl Ralei.

Tons and tons of love and a million kisses, darling!

Affectionately,
Khulu[iii]

Miss Nandi Mandela, 718 Tugwell Hall, UCT, Rondebosch, 7700

To Zindzi Mandela,[iv] his youngest daughter

D220/82: NELSON MANDELA   31.8.87

My darling Mantu,[v]

Somebody I have not seen for the last 25 yrs or so, & whose views I have come to respect a great deal, remarked: "Zindzi is like a rock; nothing seems ever to upset her!" That is just the kind of remark a father would like to hear about his beloved child. I literally swelled with pride & satisfaction.

That remark reached me at the right time, shortly after you had just gone through a rather harrowing experience. As you would suspect, it is not always so easy in my present position to assess the impact of events outside prison. That observation reassured me beyond words. Indeed, when I later met you after that incident, I could notice no visible spiritual scars or disturbance in you.

Please pull yourself together, darling, & be the solid rock you are known to be. The most tragic mistake you could make in this situation is to remain paralysed, waiting for disaster to overwhelm you. The correct attitude is to continue with your set programme – in this case your studies – until conditions beyond your control make it absolutely impossible for you to do so. From all that I hear from you, Mum & the mass media you will certainly not be able to get into stride with your work until you move to a new environment. That is why I hope, even at this late hr, that you

---

i   Herbert Vilakazi (1943–2016), professor of sociology.
ii   Noni Vilakazi. It seems that Mandela may have spelt her name incorrectly.
iii   'Granddad' in isiXhosa.
iv   Zindziswa Mandela (1960–) – see the glossary.
v   One of Zindzi Mandela's names.

may get some accommodation at campus and prepare for the exams on 18 September from there.

Finally, I wish to let you know that I am keeping my fingers crossed, hoping that nothing will happen to you. But if something does happen and you find that you will not be able to pursue your studies, I will risk everything & give full support to a wonderful girl.

Tons and tons of love, darling, & a million kisses.

Affectionately,
Tata[i]

To Mamphela Ramphele,[ii] academic and friend

D220: NELSON MANDELA

1.3.88

Dear Mamphela,

The Prisons Department has turned down your application to visit me. No grounds are ever given for such decisions.

Although I was never over-hopeful, I did not rule out the possibility that the impossible might happen, so much so that the refusal disappointed and even shocked me. I will, nevertheless, continue to urge the approval of the visit. But you must be patient; the wheels of government grind very slowly, and it may take several months, and even a year or more, before we get a favourable answer.

Regarding your academic work,[iii] I informed Nandi[iv] that I am definitely interested. But in terms of prison policy I may not receive such material. I will, however, also take up the matter.

The camera has the ability to give one and the same person different faces. Way back in the fifties, I brought up a grand-nephew.[v] He left Johannesburg at the age [of] 6, giving the impression that he would be tall and powerful in build. He later occupied a prominent position in the structures which have since the seventies, in particular, mushroomed around us. I saw

---

i   'Father' in isiXhosa.
ii   Mamphela Ramphele (1947–), anti-apartheid activist and a founding member of the Black Consciousness Movement, medical doctor, academic, and businesswoman – see the glossary.
iii   Ramphele was an academic at the University of Cape Town where Mandela's granddaughter Nandi was studying.
iv   Nandi Mandela (1968–), granddaughter and the second daughter of his late son Thembi.
v   This is likely to be N. Mtirara.

several of his pictures in the press and now and again he even appeared on television – all of which seemd to confirm my earlier impression. Then last December he walked into the visitors' room, and I was amazed to discover that he was short and slender, a real flyweight. Had I met him in the street I probably would not have recognised him.

I wonder just how many people are able to make you out at first sight, as you also have been given different faces by the media. The Woman of the Year picture published by *The Star* differs markedly from the one where the cameraman caught you chatting with Sally[i] during the 1986 National Assembly of Women. Those two pictures are, in turn, quite different from the one on the outer cover of the *Leadership* magazine. The pensive mood in which the picture is cast would make one think that you are not even a distant relative of the first two ladies. However, the portrait seems to be a highly professional work.

The reviews on Cry Tokoloho[ii] are, from this distance, disturbingly confusing. Unfortunately, in my current circumstances, I do not have access to reliable literary publications whose judgment I can trust. It has, therefore, not been possible for me to make any independent assessment. Your own assessment?

Fondest regards and best wishes!

Very sincerely,
Ntate[iii]

P.S. Please forgive me for the mistake in spelling your first name. Your worth remains constant whether the "h" is added or omitted.

Ntate

Dr Mamphela Ramphele
c/o Department of Anthropology
University of Cape Town
Private Bag, Rondebosch
7700

---

i   This is likely to be Sally Motlana, the wife of Dr. Ntatho Motlana (for Ntatho Motlana, see the glossary).
ii   Mandela is possibly referring to the film *Cry Freedom*, which came out in 1987 and was about activist Steve Biko (1946–77) who was Mamphela Ramphele's partner before he was killed. *Tokoloho* is seSetho for 'freedom'.
iii   'Uncle' in Setswana, Mamphela Ramphele's language.

TYGERBERG HOSPITAL & CONSTANTIABERG MEDICLINIC

||||||||||||

AUGUST–DECEMBER 1988

On 12 August 1988, at the age of seventy, Mandela was taken to Tygerberg Hospital where he was diagnosed with tuberculosis. While he was being treated in hospital he remained a prisoner of Pollsmoor Prison in Cape Town, which remained his address and point of contact for official requests and correspondence. He arrived at night on Friday 12 August 1988 at the government hospital in Bellville, known as Tygerberg Hospital, which serves as a teaching institution for Stellenbosch University. He had last been there fifteen months previously for surgey to repair a 'torn retina' of his right eye. That admission was not public knowledge and only became known through his personal calendar after his release.

The first doctor he saw in August 1988 announced that there was 'nothing wrong' with him.[62] The next morning he was examined by a Professor de Kock, head of internal medicine, who sent him straight to theatre where 2 litres of fluid were drained from his lung. Tuberculosis was found.[63] This time, news of his hospitalisation went global. The world's most famous prisoner was being treated for a serious illness while South Africa staggered through constant protests and continued repression. It was as if the universe held its breath.

Almost three weeks later, on 31 August 1988, after nineteen nights in hospital, he was transferred to the comfortable private hospital Constantiaberg MediClinic, close to Pollsmoor Prison, where he continued to be treated for tuberculosis. While there he received a string of visitors, including his wife and other family members as well as the minister of justice Kobie Coetsee, Reverend Anthony Simons, his lawyer, and the anti-apartheid activist and MP Helen Suzman.

Coetsee arrived on Mandela's first morning at the clinic just as Mandela was about to tuck into bacon and eggs instead of his prescribed cholesterol-free diet. 'They brought two eggs and a lot of bacon and then cereal, and then the Major . . . said, "No, Mandela, you can't eat this food – it's against the instruction of the doctor." I say, "Today I am prepared to die; I am going to eat it." Yes, I hadn't had eggs and bacon for a long time,' he laughed.[64]

He also befriended several of his nurses, delighting in their tales of life outside prison and hospital walls.

At the clinic, Mandela continued to meet with Coetsee and the 'secret committee' of government officials. It was during those talks that Coetsee told him that he would like to see him 'in a situation halfway between freedom and confinement' without explaining what he meant.[65]

He discovered what Coetsee was referring to on 7 December 1988 when unusual movement and tense conversations began between prison officials in his ward. 'I could see something was afoot but I didn't know what it was. Eventually in the evening, then the Major came in and said, "Mandela, prepare yourself, we are taking you to Paarl."[i] And I said, "What for?" He says, "Well, that is where you are going to be now." And at nine o'clock we left with a big escort.'[66]

To the head of prison, Pollsmoor Maximum Security Prison

Tygerberg Hospital

29 August 1988

Head of Prison
Pollsmoor Maximum Prison

Please purchase, at my own cost, the following articles of clothing: -
1 woolen long underpant and vest
1 warm jersey
1 small suitcase to convey clothing for washing.

[Signed NRMandela]

[In another hand] Approved by Maj van Sittert op 88.08.29. Seen by G365
No 254/88
[Signed] W/O
88.08.29

◇◇◇◇◇◇◇◇◇

Throughout his illness and hospitalisation, Mandela continued to study for his law degree and spent some considerable effort in the last months of his imprisonment pressuring the University of South Africa to recognise some of the credits he had already obtained. He wanted not to have to complete the courses in practical Afrikaans and practical isiXhosa, his home language, but to be credited with a course he had already passed in another South African language, Sesotho, in order that he may complete the degree.

---

i   A city in the Cape province (now the Western Cape province).

To Professor W. J. Hosten

Student no: 240-094-4

25.11.88

[Stamped] censored 88.11.26
Prof WJ Hosten,
Dean of the Faculty of Law,
Unisa,
P.O. Box 392,
Pretoria.
0001

Dear Sir,

I hope it will be possible for me to get an exemption from Practical Afrikaans (PAF100-A) and Xhosa I (XHA100-F), both of which I am expected
to write in January 1989.

I had intended to write the four remaining subjects for the LL.B
Degree during the October/November 1988 examinations, but I became
indisposed at a crucial stage in the preparation for the examinations.

I fell ill on 28 July 1988, was admitted into Tygerberg Hospital on 12
August, and I was compelled to suspend studying until 15 September when
I was able to resume preparations. However, I had by then already completed all the assignments set for the four subjects, and obtained passing
marks in all of them.

I am presently being treated with a combination of drugs which will
probably be maintained until early in February 1989. Dr. Stoch, the District
Surgeon of Wynberg,[i] whose letter is attached here, has since 1 September
visited me daily for the various examinations indicated in the management
of my illness. I also receive regular visits from three consultants from Tygerberg who are the heads of their respective departments at the hospital.

Although I am now feeling far better compared with the beginning of
the treatment, the possibility that drugs may induce side-effects which may
affect stamina and concentration, as well as the standard of performance in
the examinations, continues to worry me.

I must point out with regard to Practical Afrikaans that, if I complete
the degree I do not intend to practice either as an attorney or advocate. I

---

i   Wynberg is a suburb of Cape Town.

must further point out that in 1963, I passed the London University examination on the history of English Law, and I hope you will be able to take this fact into account when considering the application for exemption from Xhosa I. The University of London will readily send me written confirmation in this regard, should you require such confirmation,

It would have been proper for me to make this application after the publication of the examination results in December. But as it is more than likely that you may be away on vacation by then, I thought it advisable to submit it now.

Yours faithfully,
[Signed NRMandela]
NELSON MANDELA

To Nandi Mandela,[i] his granddaughter and youngest daughter of his late son Thembi[ii]

D220/82: NELSON MANDELA   5.12.88

To Nandi,

I miss you very much and think of you always.

Tons and tons of love and a million kisses!
From Khulu[iii]

[Envelope]
Ms Nandi Mandela,
Woolsack Residence,
Court 4, Room 111, U.C.T.
RONDEBOSCH

---

i   Nandi Mandela (1968–) – see the glossary.
ii   Madiba Thembekile (Thembi) Mandela (1945–69), Mandela's eldest son – see the glossary.
iii 'Grandfather' in isiXhosa.

To Zoleka & Zondwa Mandela,[i] his granddaughter and grandson and children of his youngest daughter, Zindzi[ii]

D220/82: NELSON MANDELA   [Looks like 5.12.88]

To Zozo and Zondwa,

I miss you very much and think of you always. Tons and tons of love and a million kisses.

From Khulu[iii]

To Zaziwe, Zamaswazi and Zinhle,[iv] his granddaughters & grandson to his middle daughter Zenani[v]

D220/82: NELSON MANDELA   5.12.88

To Zaziwe, Zamaswazi and Zinhle,

I miss you very much and think of you always.

Tons and tons of love and a million kisses.
From Khulu,[vi]

---

i   Zoleka (1980-) and Zondwa (1985–) Mandela – see the glossary.
ii   Zindziswa Mandela (1960–) – see the glossary.
iii   'Grandfather' in isiXhosa.
iv   Zaziwe (1977–), Zamaswazi (1979–), and Zinhle (1980–) Mandela.
v   Zenani Mandela (1959–) – see the glossary.
vi   'Grandfather' in isiXhosa.

To the head of prison, Pollsmoor Maximum Security Prison

D220/82: NELSON MANDELA   5.12.88

Head of Prison
Pollsmoor Maximum Prison

I would appreciate it if you would authorise a telephone call to the Dean of the Law Faculty, Professor WJ Hosten, Unisa, and inform him that the following telegram is on the way to him. The cost of both the telephone call and the telegram should be debited to my account.[i]
PROFESSOR WJ HOSTEN, LAW FACULTY, UNISA, P.O. Box 392 PRETORIA

Student No 240-094-4 concerning application exemption from Xhosa I I add that in Seventies I passed with distinction Unisa special course in Sotho.
NELSON MANDELA
POLLSMOOR PRISON

[Signed NRMandela]
5.12.88

---

[i]   Upon entering prison, a list was made of the belongings a prisoner had with them. Details of the amount of cash a prisoner may have brought with them were recorded in an individual account under the name of the prisoner (this was not a bank account but simply a separate bookkeeping record). Thereafter, any funds reaching the prison in the name of that prisoner were recorded in that account and so too were any disbursements made in the name of the prisoner. When they were discharged from prison, the prisoner was given what remained in the account.

VICTOR VERSTER
PRISON

||||||||||

DECEMBER 1988–FEBRUARY 1990

On the evening of 7 December 1988 Nelson Mandela was taken from his hospital ward at Constantiaberg MediClinic and driven to Victor Verster Prison, about an hour away. The destination was the bungalow of a former prison warder and it had modern furnishings, a large garden, and a swimming pool. Warrant Officer Jack Swart, who had first encountered Mandela in the early days on Robben Island, was instructed to cook for him and run the house.

Swart recalls that Mandela was not restricted in the number of letters he could write while he was at Victor Verster Prison but he remembers three boxes containing 'hundreds of letters' that were not given to him.[67]

The next morning Mandela was visited by the minister of justice, Kobie Coetsee, armed with a housewarming gift – a case of wine. He told Mandela that it had been decided that he would be held in the house so that he could continue the discussions he had begun with government officials in 1986.

The talks with the 'working group' continued apace. The schedule depended on a request to meet from either the government team or from Mandela, who would communicate through the commanding officer of the prison.[68] The meetings were not negotiations, but rather an attempt by Mandela to get to a point where the ANC and the government could eventually negotiate about the end of apartheid. They were later described technically, as 'talks about talks'. He used these discussions with the officials to arrange the release of the remaining six Rivonia Trial colleagues still in prison. The oldest, Govan Mbeki, had been freed in November 1987 and Denis Goldberg was released in 1985.

While prospective visitors still had to apply to see him, and their applications were still sometimes rejected by the authorities, Mandela had many visits from his wife, Winnie Mandela, their children, and grandchildren and other family members as well as friends and comrades. His letters were similarly less controlled and they assumed the role of an instrument for him to reach back into the world he seemed increasingly likely to inhabit again.

In 1988 Mac Maharaj, his comrade from Robben Island, had been infiltrated back into South Africa as part of an underground strategy, called Operation Vula, to smuggle MK operatives into South Africa in case the government did not negotiate in good faith. Maharaj devised a method for Mandela to communicate from the prison to Oliver Tambo and other ANC leaders in exile. He informed Mandela's attorney Ismail Ayob of a nickname they had arranged before Maharaj's release from prison and told him to refer to it on one of his visits. This signalled to Mandela that Ayob was conveying a message from Maharaj. The first one was a tiny rolled-up note the size of a matchstick. It asked him to participate in a secret exchange of messages that would be hidden inside a book cover. Mandela agreed. In this way, Mandela and the organisation were able to share information on the discussions he was having with the government team.[69]

∞∞∞∞∞∞∞∞

A mark of Nelson Mandela's character was his determination to stick at his law studies. Forty-five years after he first enrolled at the University of the Witwatersrand as a twenty-four-year-old, he received notification that he had passed his LLB. As the years dragged on in prison and after weathering obstacles designed to grind down his will to continue with his studies, continue he did. Finally, at the age of seventy, knowing that it was highly unlikely that he would ever practise as a lawyer again, Mandela learned that he would indeed graduate with a law degree.

To Professor W. J. Hosten, University of South Africa

Student no: 240-094-4

                                               23 December 1988

Prof W.J. Hosten,
Dean of the Law Faculty,
Unisa,
P.O. Box 392.
Pretoria
0001

Dear Prof Hosten,

I thank you for your letter of 5 December 1988 in which you advise that I have completed the LL.B degree.

It was fitting that you should be the first to congratulate me on this achievement. I firmly believe that, without your support, my request for exemption from the languages would probably not have succeeded. The accomplishment will certainly strengthen my ties with Unisa,[i] and will enable me to join the scores of men and women, inside and outside South

---

i   University of South Africa.

Africa, whose ability to serve their respective communities has been considerably enhanced by obtaining this degree.

Kindly convey my thanks to the Faculty Board and to the Registrar (Academic and Student Affairs), to Prof Wiechers for his complimentary press comments, to Prof P.A.K le Roux, who provided me with prescribed literature, and all the lecturers who guided me so well in my studies.

Yours sincerely,
[Signed NRMandela]

To Archie Gumede,[i] friend and comrade

1335/88: NELSON MANDELA

10 January 1989

Dear Qwabe,[ii]

The wish to join family and friends outside prison burns ever so strongly every hour of the day. But release from incarceration does not appear to be round the corner. There is, however, the remote possibility that, from my present quarters, I may see you and others. Meantime, I send fondest regards and best wishes to you, your family, to George,[iii] Diliza (Senior),[iv] Curnick,[v] Thabekhulu and everybody.

Yours sincerely,
Madiba

Phakathwayo Archie Gumede,
c/o Louis Bar & Restaurant.
P.O. Box 96,
CLERNERVILLE
3602

---

i   Archie Gumede (1914–98), son of Josiah Gumede, a president of the South African Native National Congress, lawyer and activist in the ANC and the United Democratic Front of which he was a joint president with Oscar Mpetha and Albertina Sisulu – see the glossary.
ii   Archie Gumede's clan name.
iii   Possibly George Sewpersadh (1936), political activist who was a member of the Natal Indian Congress.
iv   Diliza Mji, medical doctor and political activist.
v   Curnick Ndlovu (1932–2000), trade unionist and MK member. He was sentenced to 20 years in prison for sabotage and served it on Robben Island.

To Archbishop Desmond Tutu and his wife, Leah Tutu[i]

1335/88: NELSON MANDELA   17.1.89

Leah & Mpilo[ii]

I was not at all surprised to receive your get-well card when I was a patient at the Tygerberg Hospital.[iii] You are widely known as a couple who care for others, and who have served our people and country with remarkable courage and humility. My speedy and complete recovery has been due to the excellent treatment I received from my medical team, nurses and friends. For very obvious reasons your message played a special role in that recovery.

Fondest regards and best wishes to you, Trevor[iv] and family, and to his sisters.

Sincerely,
[Signed NRMandela]

To Rev Austen Massey, general secretary, Methodist Church of South Africa

1335/88: NELSON MANDELA   17.1.89

Rev Austen Massey,
General Secretary, Methodist Church of South Africa
114 Rissik St,
Braamfontein,
Johannesburg.
2001.

---

i   Desmond Tutu (1931–), first black archbishop of Cape Town, and his wife Leah Tutu (1933–) – see the glossary.
ii   Archbishop Tutu's African name.
iii   Mandela was treated for tuberculosis at Tygerberg Hospital in August 1988.
iv   The Tutus' son, Trevor.

Dear Moruti,[i]

The six thousand rands I received from you enabled me to meet pressing financial commitments. My family responsibilities extend beyond my wife, children and grandchildren.

During the 26 years of my incarceration the inability to respond meaningfully to deserving appeals for financial help has indeed been a harrowing experience for me. The grant by the church made it possible for me to provide this help.

Please give my sincere thanks and best wishes to the church.

Sincerely,
[Signed NRMandela]

Victor Verster Prison, Private Bag X6005, Paarl South, 7624

<><><><><><>

Mangosuthu Buthelezi, a long-time friend of Nelson Mandela and former member of the ANC Youth League, founded the Inkatha National Cultural Liberation Movement in 1975. Initially close, the two organisations drifted apart over Buthelezi's embrace of the homeland system which the ANC was opposed to. Inkatha was in favour of non-violent change while the ANC had its own armed wing. Thousands of South Africans were killed in violence between the two groups which was later found to have been fomented by the apartheid regime.

To Mangosuthu Buthelezi,[ii] president of Inkatha

1335/88: NELSON MANDELA   3 February 1989

Dear Shenge,[iii]

I thank you for the warm and well-considered telex message you sent me on behalf of King Zwelithini[iv] and Inkatha on the occasion of my seventieth

---

i   'Priest' or 'pastor' in Sesotho and Setswana.
ii   Mangosuthu Buthelezi (1928–) – see the glossary.
iii   Mangosuthu Buthelezi's clan name.
iv   King Goodwill Zwelithini kaBhekuzulu (1948–) is king of the Zulu nation. His coronation was on 3 December 1971.

birthday. I also received your letter of 26 August 1988 in which you wished me a speedy recovery from illness, and in which you outlined your efforts both locally and abroad to secure the release of political prisoners in South Africa.

Apart from your telex and a telegram from Mrs Helen Suzman,[i] hundreds of similar messages came from well-wishers in the country and from different parts of the world. Although none of these actually reached me, I requested O.R[ii] to thank these friends on my behalf. It is partly the unswerving support of such men and women, and partly the progress and achievements made by our organisation within and outside the country which has given political prisoners so much strength and hope.

I hope you will readily accept that it is not easy from my present quarters to comment freely and fully on the sentiments you so eloquently expressed in the abovementioned correspondence. It is sufficient to state that your persistent demand for the unconditional release of political prisoners, and your refusal to negotiate with the government until that demand is fully met, is a stand which I have always welcomed as a positive contribution to the liberation struggle in this country.

Obviously, my fervent hope is to see, in due course, the restoration of the cordial relations which existed between you and O.R.,[iii] and between the two organisations in the seventies. One of the most challenging tasks facing the leadership today is that of national unity. At no other time in the history of the liberation movement has it been so crucial for our people to speak with one voice, and for freedom fighters to pool their efforts. Any act or statement, from whatever source, which tends to create or worsen divisions is, in the existing practical situation, a fatal error which ought to be avoided at all costs.

Far more information than I possess at the moment is required before I can blame any of the parties involved in the deplorable conflicts now taking place in certain parts of Natal.[iv] All the same, I consider it a serious indictment against all of us that we are still unable to combine forces to stop the slaughter of so many innocent lives.

The struggle is our life and, even though the moment of victory may not be at hand, we can nevertheless make the freedom fight either immensely enriching or absolutely disastrous. In my entire political career

---

i   Helen Suzman (1917–2009), academic, politician, anti-apartheid activist, and MP for the opposition party – see the glossary. Suzman continuously raised the issue of political prisoners in Parliament and first met Mandela and his comrades on Robben Island in 1967.

ii   Oliver Reginald Tambo (1917–93), Mandela's friend, former law partner, and the president of the ANC – see the glossary.

iii   Tambo was the president of the ANC.

iv   Conflict in KwaZulu-Natal between supporters of Inkatha and the ANC had reached virtual civil war proportions by the late 1980s.

few things have distressed me as to see our people killing one another as is now happening. The entire fabric of community life in some of the affected areas has been seriously disrupted, leaving behind a legacy of hatred and bitterness which may haunt us for years to come. It is a matter which requires the urgent attention of all freedom fighters regardless of political affiliation. Nothing will please me more than to know that my concern and appeal has not fallen on deaf ears.

Once again, I thank you and the King and Inkatha for the inspiring message.

My best wishes to you and Mdlunkulu.[i]

Yours sincerely,
Madiba

———————

To Elaine Kearns, a matron who took care of him in Tygerberg Hospital

1335/88: NELSON MANDELA

                                                                14.2.89

Dear Elaine,

My transfer from the Tygerberg Hospital to Constantiaberg MediClinic,[ii] and from there to this place, interfered with the smooth flow of correspondence. As a result, your letter of 8 November only reached me last week. I never received the post card you sent from London.

I know just how disappointing it will be for you to learn that your efforts and message were fruitless. But I must assure you that I am equally sorry to have missed it. Your letter has, however, made up for all that. I also got your lovely Christmas card for which I thank you.

With regard to health, you are entitled to know that last month I was visited by your Chief Medical Superintendent, Dr Strauss, and Prof De Kock. After they had examined me and other medical data, they felt that the infection had completely cleared and the lung fully expanded. They accordingly stopped the treatment. You will probably recall that after drain-

———————

i   Chief Mangosuthu Buthelezi's wife Irene Buthelezi – see the glossary.
ii   Mandela was admitted to Tygerberg Hospital in August 1988 with tuberculosis.

ing the liquid from the affected lung my weight dropped to 68 kg. Now it fluctuates between 75 and 76 kg. I feel so well that I could challenge for the heavyweight boxing championship of the world.

It pleases me to know that you enjoyed your overseas trip, and that you learnt a lot from the Burns Conference. That knowledge will benefit not only you but your patients as well. You are, however, silent on your Katmandu [*sic*] friend. I hope the disaster affected neither herself nor any of her relations.

I am also pleased to note that you still remember the legend, and that you wish for better luck next time. I ought to remind you that you are one of those who need no luck to lean on, since good fortune is written all over your person. What make[S it] so frugal in putting into practice the vital lessons entailed in that legend? Thrift, especially on the part of a young lady, is a virtue; taken to extremes, however, many people may equate it with self-denial and misery as dangerous as anorexia. What you require is not only to remember the moral of the legend, but to put it into practice.

Under normal conditions I would reprimand you severely [and] insist that you normalise your situation. But it would be highly improper, to say the least, to thrash out such matters on this piece of paper. It may well be that there will be time enough for that.

Meantime do assure Matrons Jansen and Orphen and Sister de Waal, as well as the young ladies who helped in looking after me, that I also think of them. Did Sister De Waal write her examinations?

Fondest regards and best wishes to you and your Mum.

Sincerely,
[Signed NRMandela]

[Envelope]
Matron Elaine Kearns, 38 Fourie Str.,
BELLVILLE
7530

To Dumani Mandela, his grandson and his eldest daughter Makaziwe's[i] son

1335/88: NELSON MANDELA   28.2.89

My dear Mzukulu,[ii]

I am told that you are doing well at school, and that you are particularly good in Mathematics. This subject is very difficult but very important. If you always get the best marks and pass well in the end, you will always have a good job wherever you may be.

I believe that you are also doing well with the trumpet. Perhaps in your letter you will tell me who teaches you music, and whether you have any music book to guide you. Exercise is also very good. Taking part in sport like running, swimming and tennis will keep you healthy, strong and bright. But swimming is also a very dangerous sport. You must have a good coach and never swim in the absence of the coach until you have mastered the hobby.

Please tell your Mum that I got her letter and that I spent years trying to persuade Uncle Kgatho[iii] to go back to school. There is absolutely nothing more I can now do. Books, clothing and videos will not be allowed. Buying and sending them will be a waste of money, as they will not be given to me.

I have recovered from illness and I now feel well and strong. The other matters mentioned in Mum's letter will be discussed when she visits the country next June.[iv] I miss you, Tukwini and Kweku[v] very much and look forward to seeing you one day.

My love and best wishes to you all.

Affectionately,
Khulu[vi]

[Envelope]
Mr Dumani Mandela,
108 University Apartments,
Amherst,
Massachusetts,
01002
U.S.A.

---

i   Makaziwe Mandela (1954–)– see the glossary.
ii   'Grandchild' in isiXhosa.
iii   Makgatho (Kgatho) Mandela (1950–2005), Mandela's second-born son – see the glossary.
iv   Makaziwe Mandela was living in Boston, United States.
v   Dumani Mandela's sister and brother.
vi   'Grandfather' in isiXhosa.

To Kwedi Mkalipi, friend and former Robben Island prisoner

1335/88: NELSON MANDELA

28.2.89

Dear Dlamini,[i]

I was more than relieved to hear that you and the two Nyawuzas,[ii] cousin Grace Matsha and Inspector Ndamase, were of great help to my niece, Zukiswa, for which I am very grateful. She was a complete stranger to C.T.[iii] and, without that assistance, it would have been impossible for her to get to Tygerberg Hospital. To all of you I say Nangomso![iv]

We were all happy to learn that Zeph,[v] Harry[vi] and Zwelakhe[vii] had been released. I managed to send all of them welcome cards. Harry and Zwelakhe received theirs, but I have no feedback as far as Zeph's card is concerned.

Progress is disturbingly slow on the question of the installation of Buyelekhaya[viii] in his father's position. I invited my grand nephew, General Zondwa Mtirara, to visit me and on 31 December 1987 I discussed the matter with him in Pollsmoor Prison. Like his late father, Bambilanga,[ix] he was cooperative, pointing out during the discussion, that he was merely acting for Buyelekhaya. I then requested him to bring Chief Mveleli[x] along so that we could finalise the matter. He never returned.

Last December I was visited by Brig. T. Matanzima,[xi] who fully supported Buyelekhaya's claim; we worked out a strategy. He is, however, encountering formidable problems and it would appear that if the present court action – which I have been trying to prevent – fails, nothing concrete will emerge until we are over there in [the] flesh. Contrary to what many people think, that moment is, in my view, far, far away.

---

i   Kwedi Mkalipi's clan name.

ii   Nyawuza or Mnayawuza refers to members of the Nyawuza clan Mandela knew from his childhood.

iii   Cape Town.

iv   'Nangomso' is an isiXhosa word that expresses deep gratitude to a person who has gone beyond the call of duty. Mandela sometimes spelled it nangomso.

v   Zephania Mothopeng (1913–90), Pan Africanist Congress leader.

vi   Harry Gwala (1920–95), ANC activist who was charged with sabotage for recruiting members to MK and sentenced to eight years in prison on Robben Island. Continued his activism on his release in 1972 and in 1977 he was sentenced to life imprisonment and returned to Robben Island – see the glossary.

vii   Zwelakhe Sisulu (1950–2012), South African journalist and editor who was imprisoned for his journalism.

viii Buyelekhaya Dalindyebo (1964–), Sabata Jonguhlanga Dalindyebo's son – see the glossary. He returned from exile in 1989 and was restored to the throne.

ix   Nxeko (also known as Bambilanga) is the brother of King Sabata Jonguhlanga Dalindyebo, paramount chief of the Transkei homeland.

x   Mandela's cousin and a Thembu chief.

xi   This is probably a relation of K. D. Matanzima, the chief minister of the Transkei (see the glossary).

But let me conclude by expressing the hope that you are now happily married and that you and your beloved are contributing generously towards the country's manpower. Fondest regards and best wishes.

Sincerely,
Madiba

[Envelope]
Mr Kwedi Mkalipi, c/o Mrs Grace Matsha,
5 Sandile St.,
LANGA.
7455

To Eddie Daniels,[i] friend and former Robben Island prisoner

<u>1335/88: NELSON MANDELA</u>   28.2.89

Dear Danie,

I have received several unforgettable messages from you, the latest on 24 February 1989. My difficulty has always been the fact that none of your cards bore your address, a difficulty which I ultimately resolved by addressing this note care of Dullah.[ii] Rest assured that you and Eleanor[iii] will always be in my thoughts, hoping that one day Winnie and I will be able to picnic together with you. Fondest regards and best wishes.

Sincerely,
Dalibhunga

Mr Eddie Daniels,
c/o Advocate Dullah Omar,
31 Mabel Rd.,
Rylands Estate, ATHLONE.
7764.

---

i   Eddie Daniels (1928–2017), member of the African Resistance Movement who spent fifteen years on Robben Island – see the glossary.
ii   Dullah Omar, Mandela's advocate.
iii Eddie Daniels's wife.

To Rev Allan Boesak,[i] anti-apartheid leader

1355/88: NELSON MANDELA   28.2.89

Dear Alan [*sic*],

The solid support I have received from you and Dorothy[ii] generally, and particularly during my illness, gave me the strength and confidence required for complete recovery. The medical treatment was stopped towards the end of last month, and I again feel on top of the world. I am sincerely grateful to both of you, and you will always be in my thoughts. Meantime I send you my love and best wishes.

    Sincerely,
Uncle Nelson

To Amina Cachalia,[iii] friend and comrade

1335/88: Nelson Mandela

                                     28.2.89

Dear Aminaben,[iv]

You and Yusuf[v] must apply without delay for a visiting permit. Both of you visited me last July, and I do not anticipate problems from the Department of Prisons. We must sort out a problem which will be very demanding on your love and on Yusuf's experience. If you cannot both undertake the journey, I will be happy to spend an hour or two with one of you.

    You will be happy to know that according to the doctors attending to me, I have completely recovered from the illness, and the medical treatment was stopped towards the end of last month. Fortunately, the bacteria was

---

i   Allan Aubrey Boesak (1946–), South African Dutch Reformed Church cleric and a politician and anti-apartheid activist. He was sentenced to prison for fraud in 1999 but was subsequently granted an official pardon and reinstated as a cleric in late 2004.
ii   Boesak's then wife.
iii Amina Cachalia (1930–2013), friend and anti-apartheid and women's rights activist – see the glossary.
iv *Ben* means 'sister' in Gujarati.
v   Yusuf Cachalia (1915–95), Amina Cachalia's husband, political activist and secretary of the South African Indian Congress – see the glossary.

detected at an early stage before there were any spots or lesion in the lung, and before the condition had become infectious. The lung has now fully expanded, and breathing clean air far from the pollution of the cities has considerably benefited my health.

Zami[i] and family visit me often, and I hope she will be able to spend a few days here when certain problems will hopefully have been resolved.

Meantime, while I miss you two very much and look forward to seeing you soon. Love and best wishes.

Sincerely,
Nelson.

Victor Verster Prison, P/B X6005, Paarl South, 7624

[Envelope]
Mrs Amina Cachalia,
P.O. Box 3265.
JOHANNESBURG.
2000

———————————

To Sipho Sepamla,[ii] South African poet and novelist

1335/88: NELSON MANDELA

4.4.89

Dear Sipho,

A few years ago the radio relayed some striking verses from your pen, and I was indeed very sorry that my current circumstances do not allow me to acquire any of your publications.

Some time last year you briefly appeared on television and I was happy to see you in [the] flesh at last. Of course, your poetry has cut deep into the hearts of many people, known and unknown to you, inside and outside the country. You will readily appreciate it when I say I envy them for the privilege of being able to read your works.[iii]

---

i   One of Winnie Mandela's names.
ii   Sipho Sepamla (1932–2007), a cultural activist influenced by the Black Consciousness Movement and protested against the apartheid regime through his novels and poetry.
iii   Several of Sepamla's books were banned in South Africa incuding his book of poems dealing with the student uprising of 1976, *The Soweto I Love*, published in 1977.

You, Don Mattera,[i] Oswald Mtshali,[ii] Mongane Serote,[iii] Mziwakhe[iv] and Nomsa Mbuli,[v] and the constellation of budding muses across the country are in my thoughts. I look forward eagerly to meeting you someday when I will be able to thank you face to face for your impressive contribution on the occasion of the Seventieth birthday.

Meantime, I send you and your family my fondest regards and best wishes.

Yours sincerely,
Madiba

[Envelope]
Mr Sipho Sepamla,
c/o Zamila Ayob,
P.O. Box 728,
JOHANNESBURG
2000

To Candie Lawless, a nurse who took care of him at Constatiaberg MediClinic

1335/88: NELSON MANDELA

4.4.89

Dear Candie,

I have been expecting your letter ever since my discharge from the Constantiaberg MediClinic.[vi] I am indeed very happy that it has come at last.

I am even more pleased to hear that you and Trevor are engaged. My warmest congratulations! I am sure he will make a fine husband; a source of lasting happiness and security to you. If he had not proposed by now, I would have urged you to seize the bull by its horns and propose to him.

---

i   Don Mattera (1935–), South African writer.
ii   Oswald Mtshali (1940–), South African poet.
iii   Mongane Serote (1944–), South African poet and writer.
iv   Mzwakhe Mbuli (1959–), South African poet, deacon, and Mbaqanga singer.
v   Nomsa Mbuli was Mzwakhe Mbuli's wife. All the poets listed here are from the South Afircan literary movement referred to as the New Black Poetry of the 1970s.
vi   He was admitted to Constantiaberg MediClinic while he was recovering from tuberculosis in late August 1988.

After all, the acceptance of the principle of the equality of the sexes gives you that right when the young man drags his feet.

From your sketch it would seem that the engagement ring will be very special, and Trevor's salary increase should be able to cover the price without difficulty. Again, my warmest congratulations!

I am very sorry to hear about Kitty's death. But that is the way of life, and it is far better to be realistic and to accept what has happened. My deepest sympathy to you and Trevor.

The clinic will miss you very much, as they regarded you as one of their best sisters. But I will rejoice with you if you find your new job rewarding. I will be holding thumbs for you.

Meantime, I send my fondest regards and best wishes to you, Trevor, Dara, Tami (whose success in the exams delighted me), Kim and your parents.

Sincerely,
[Signed NRMandela]

To Sir Robin Renwick, British Ambassador c/o commissioner of prisons

1335/88: NELSON MANDELA

10 April 1989

Commissioner of Prisons
Cape Town

I would appreciate it if you would be good enough to pass the attached copy of the letter addressed to the British Ambassador to the Minister of Justice for publication.

[Signed NRMandela]

The Ambassador
British Embassy
Pretoria

NELSON MANDELA

10 April 1989

Sir Robin Renwick
British Ambassador
Cape Town

Dear Sir Renwick,

Press reports on 10 April 1989 indicate that I wrote a letter to Prime Minister Margaret Thatcher to thank her for the positive work she was doing on the South African issue.

I must point out in this regard that I neither wrote such a letter nor dictated it to any attorney as alleged in the reports. If I had wanted to express my views on Mrs Thatcher's work, or on the policy of the British Government on any specific matter, I would have preferred to do so in the course of a face-to-face discussion with you in person.

Meanwhile I am happy to request you to pass my very best wishes to the Prime Minister.[i]

Yours sincerely,
[Signed NRMandela]

To Mike Tyson,[ii] American heavyweight boxing champion

1335/88: NELSON MANDELA

10.5.89

Dear Champ,

It pleased me and my family very much to learn that the Central State University[iii] has awarded you an honorary doctorate, an honour which is rightly deserved. Please accept our warmest congratulations.

We must also thank you for the pair of boxing gloves which you sent to mark my 70th birthday.

It is such messages of solidarity which has enabled me and scores of others to remain so strong and full of hope throughout these trying times.

Fondest regards and best wishes,

---

i   Margaret Thatcher (1925–2013), prime minister of the United Kingdom.
ii   Mandela met Mike Tyson and other American boxers in the United States on 22 June 1990.
iii   University in Wilberforce, Ohio, United States.

Sincerely,
[Signed NRMandela]

[Envelope]
Dr Mike Tyson
Heavyweight Boxing Champion of [the] World
c/o President Arthur E Thomas
Central State University
WILBERFORCE, OHIO 45384
USA

======

To Rev Frank Chikane, secretary-general of the South African Council of Churches

1355/88: NELSON MANDELA   10.5.89

Moruti wa sechaba,[i]

My grandson, Mandla,[ii] has asked me to raise a scholarship for his maternal cousin, Grace Foolo (15 years), 1373 B Mfolo Villages, P.O. Iketlo, 1805. She is presently in Form III at the Holy Cross High School, Diepkloof.[iii] Her mother, who was a single parent, died under very tragic circumstances a few years ago. She now lives with her granny at the above address. She (granny) is struggling to educate a daughter who is now in Form IV at the same school. I would appreciate it if the South African Council of Churches could be good enough to provide the scholarship.

It is possible that the granny has already paid Grace's school fees for this year. If that is the case and you are, nonetheless, in a position to assist, I would suggest that you consider reimbursing her for that amount.

. . . Meanwhile I send you fondest regards and best wishes.

Sincerely,
Ntate[iv]

---

i   'Priest of the nation' in Setswana and Sesotho.
ii   Mandla Mandela (1974–), son of Mandela's youngest son Makgatho Mandela and Rose Rayne Mandela, known as Rennie – see the glossary for notes on these individuals.
iii   An area in Soweto, Johannesburg.
iv   'Uncle' in Setswana.

To Mrs E. N. Mbekeni, a cousin

1335/88: NELSON MANDELA

10.5.89

Bayethe![i]

Recently I had a series of interesting coincidences. On 27 April 1989 I received letters from three different nurses, all of whom are doctors' wives. Telly[ii] was not one of them. About a week later a young lady I call "granddaughter" wrote and told me that her friend, Noelene, with whom she was sharing a flat, had decided to move to Plettenberg Bay.[iii] It was only the second time I had heard that name. That very day I read in the press about the wife of a well-known diplomat whose name is also Noelene. On 4 May 1989 I was visited by a prominent leader and friend from Natal, Mr Harry Gwala,[iv] with two companions, one of whose first name is Linda.[v] A few hours before their arrival, the radio in two separate bulletins mentioned the name Linda twice, one a South African and the other an American. In your letter you told me that you and inkosi[vi] will soon be in Cape Town, you to attend a girl's [sic] guide meeting, he to see cardiologist Dr. le Roux. Dr. le Roux is also my cardiologist, and has been attending to me since 1979. I need hardly explain that I attach no significance whatsoever to coincidences of this nature, but they are nevertheless, rather interesting.

In dealing with purely family matters, I must let you know that my late sister left three daughters, Nomfundo, who is nursing at the Umtata Hospital and the breadwinner of the family; Ntonto ($\pm$ 40 years) and Zukiswa ($\pm$ 32). The last two left school after passing Std VI. At the beginning of last year they informed me that they wanted to go back to school and asked me to raise funds for this purpose, which I managed to do. This year they are in Std X,[vii] but in view of their poor academic background, I doubt if they will be able to make it in the November examinations. But I am, nevertheless, encouraging them in their desire to improve their education.

They want me to get them part-time employment in Cape Town,

---

i An isiXhosa salute to royalty.
ii Telia (Telli or Tellie) Mtirara, a relative of Mandela's.
iii A town in the Western Cape province.
iv Harry Gwala (1920–95), ANC activist who was charged with sabotage for recruiting members to MK and sentenced to eight years in prison on Robben Island. Continued his activism on his release in 1972 and in 1977 he was sentenced to life imprisonment and returned to Robben Island – see the glossary.
v Harry Gwala's lawyer, Linda Zama.
vi 'Chief' in isiZulu and isiXhosa.
vii Standard ten, the last year of high school

which I can do without much difficulty. But I have advised them against doing so. The travelling expenses from Umtata[i] to Cape Town, shuttling between their residence and work place, and the high cost-of-living in the Mother City will swallow up a large portion of whatever wages they earn. I will accordingly be happy if u-Mhlekazi[ii] Wonga[iii] could get them part-time work in Umtata or surrounding areas for the June and December holidays.

With regard to your visit to this place, it will take me quite some time to cool down. It was easily one of the happiest moments in my life as a prisoner. I had not seen Umhlekazi for more than 30 years,[iv] and it was unbelievable that we were again together at last. He has always been a very kind and warm person, and I was not surprised when he left me literally swimming in wealth on prison standards. It was equally pleasing to know that all the good things I have heard about you over the years were no exaggeration. You complement him fully both in nature and charm.

Although you outlined your background we, however, did not go deep into your family affairs. I am interested to know about the late Wabana Makawula's house. At Healdtown[v] he was very popular as a sportsman, an all-rounder who played in the institution's first soccer and cricket teams. Would it be one of his sons who is now Paramount Chief? If so, do advise him that if he ever visits C.T.[vi] I would be happy to see him. Please give him my best wishes and provide me with his full names.

By the way, you will be happy to know that immediately after seeing you off at the end of the visit, I walked into the bathroom and picked up a fat five rand note. I sealed it in an envelope and locked it up in my suitcase for luck.

Lastly, I have written this note to you despite your request that I should reply directly to Umhlekazi. As you well know, he is a man who takes things easily and who hardly ever rushes unnecessarily. I feared that if I carried out your request, it may take quite some weeks, and even months, before he showed you the note. Love and best wishes to you, Mhlekazi and the children.

Sincerely,
Madiba

PS. It was fortunate that Mhlekazi never got involved in the Bantustan pol-

---

i   Umtata (now called Mthatha) was the capital of the Transkei homeland.
ii   An isiXhosa honorific which has a similar meaning to 'sir'.
iii   This is possibly Wonga Mbekeni, E. N. Mbekeni's husband.
iv   Dr. Dotwana and Dr. Mbekeni and his wife visited Mandela in March 1989.
v   The Wesleyan college in Fort Beaufort that Mandela attended as a young man – see the glossary.
vi   Cape Town.

itics. This is one reason why his name and reputation is still as clean and respected as when I last saw him.

I am happy to learn that you are attending to the writing of the history of Thembuland, and that Mr Kuse[i] will also be involved. An influential and knowledgeable person from each of the Thembu lines should be brought in.

I never got your get-well cards. It is always safer to send all letters addressed to me by registered position [*sic*].

Madiba

[Envelope]
Nkosikazi E.N. Mbekeni
Emampondweni Store,
P.O. Box 111
TSOLO
UMTATA

To Helen Suzman,[ii] opposition member of Parliament

1335/88: NELSON MANDELA

22 May 1989
Dear Helen,

The consistency with which you defended the basic values of freedom and the rule of law over the last three decades has earned you the admiration of many South Africans.

A wide gap still exists between the mass democratic movement[iii] and your party[iv] with regard to the method of attaining those values. But your commitment to a non-racial democracy in a united South Africa has won you many friends in the extra-parliamentary movement.

Allow me to hope that you will continue to enjoy good health for years

---

i   Wandile Kuse, professor who from 1983 was director of the Bureau for African Research and Documentation at the University of Transkei.

ii   Helen Suzman (1917–2009), academic, politician, anti-apartheid activist, and MP for the opposition party – see the glossary. Suzman continuously raised the issue of political prisoners in Parliament and first met Mandela and his comrades on Robben Island in 1967.

iii   The Mass Democratic Movement was the 1988–90 formation of anti-apartheid forces encompassing the umbrella body the United Democratic Front and the Congress of South African Trade Unions.

iv   The Progressive Federal Party.

to come, that in the days that lie ahead your voice will be heard throughout the country, free from the constraints which parliamentary convention imposes.

Fondest regards and best wishes to you and your family.

Sincerely,
Nelson

[Envelope]
Mrs. Helen Suzman M.P.,
Parliament.
Cape Town.

◇◇◇◇◇◇◇◇

Nelson Mandela's name was read out on Wednesday 17 May, 1989 at a graduation ceremony of the University of South Africa, the world's largest correspondence university. He could not stand and be capped for his achievement. He was still incarcerated at Victor Verster Prison outside the city. But the fact that his name was read out at all signalled a South Africa that was changing, as a country that would soon welcome him back.

To Richard Maponya,[i] businessman and friend

1335/88: NELSON MANDELA

Victor Verster Prison,
P/B X6005,
Paarl South,
7620.
3 February 1989

28 6 89

---

i   Richard John Pelwana Maponya (1926–) is a South African entrepreneur and property developer best known for building a business empire despite the restrictions of apartheid, and his determination to see the Soweto township develop economically. He hosted a celebration after Mandela and the last twenty-seven accused in the Treason Trial were acquitted on 29 March 1961. (For the Treason Trial, see the glossary.)

Dear Richard,

It is almost 30 years since the day when you held a roaring party for us at the end of the 1960 state of emergency.[i] Be assured that that gesture, and others that followed it, will not easily be forgotten. In fact, you and Marina[ii] have often been in my thoughts during the 27 years of my imprisonment. I look forward to seeing you in Soweto one day when I will be able to shake your hand very warmly. Meanwhile I send you my very best wishes. Regards to Dr. Sam Motsuenyane[iii] and family.

     Sincerely,
Nelson

Mr Richard Maponya
Soweto

To Acting Paramount Chief Mdayelwa Mtirara, his cousin

[Translated from isiXhosa]

1335/88: Nelson Mandela

                     Victor Verster Prison,
                     P/B X6005,
                     Paarl South,
                     7620.
                              4.7.89

Ngubengenka,[iv]

I am delighted to hear that the Thembu clan have concluded the long drawn out issue of the installation of Buyelekhaya[v] as the rightful heir to the throne.

---

i   Declared on 30 March 1960 as a response to the Sharpeville Massacre, the 1960 State of Emergency was characterised by mass arrests and the imprisonment of most African leaders. On 8 April 1960 the ANC and Pan Africanist Congress were banned under the Unlawful Organisations Act.
ii   Maponya's wife.
iii   Businessman.
iv   A reference to him being a descendant of King Ngubencuka who was Mandela's great-great-grandfather.
v   Buyelekhaya Dalindyebo (1964–), Sabata Jonguhlanga Dalindyebo's son – see the glossary. He returned from exile in 1989 and was restored to the throne.

The repatriation of exiled Buyelekhaya should be handled with care and sensitivity. He must be allowed the time to learn the ways of his people while at the Royal Homestead.[i] We urgently need to discuss this matter in detail. I hope you will make all the necessary arrangments to come and visit me so that we can discuss this matter further.

Best regards,
Sincerely,
Dalibunga

Acting Paramount Chief Mdayelwa Mtirara
The Royal Place
Sithebe
Bityi, Umtata[ii]
TRANSKEI

◇◇◇◇◇◇◇◇◇

On 5 July 1989 Mandela was taken from prison to meet President P. W. Botha. It was a cordial visit with the man preceded by his fearsome reputation, even amongst his government colleagues, as the 'Great Crocodile'.

He was the third head of state of South Africa since Mandela had been arrested. H. F. Verwoerd who was assassinated in 1966 had been replaced by B. J. Vorster who was in turn replaced by P. W. Botha. By the time Mandela was released there was a new president, F. W. de Klerk.

While in prison on Robben Island, Mandela and his comrades had learned of Botha's assent to power in the National Party. When they were in Pollsmoor, Botha announced a tricameral parliament to include Indians and so-called coloureds – a move Mandela saw through: 'This was an effort to lure Indians and Coloureds into the system, and divide them from Africans. But the offer was merely a "toy telephone", as all parliamentary action by Indians and Coloureds was subject to a white veto. It was also a way of fooling the outside world into thinking that the government was reforming apartheid.'[70]

Mandela noted in his prison calendar on 5 July 1989 that he had a meeting with a 'Very Important Person. No politics discussed.' While they did not discuss politics, Mandela impressed Botha with his knowledge of Afrikaner history. His years of studying Afrikaner history, culture, and language had paid off.

---

i   He had been living in exile in Zambia since 1980 after his father, Sabata Jonguhlanga Dalindyebo, was convicted of violating K. D. Matanzima's dignity in 1980.
ii   Umtata (now called Mthatha) was the capital of the Transkei homeland.

To the commissioner of prisons

1335/88: NELSON MANDELA

17.7.89

<u>Personal and Confidential</u>

Commissioner of Prisons,
Pretoria.

I trust that the photographs taken on July 5, 1989 will not be published or distributed without consulting the parties involved.[i] I hope to have a further discussion with you on this matter in due course.

I am also happy to advise you that on July 14 I had the opportunity of briefing my colleagues from Pollsmoor and Robben Island on the latest developments. Unfortunately, and because the occasion was also a birthday, we did not have enough time to complete our discussion. I would accordingly appreciate it if you would allow us further meetings at your convenience.

I also wish to be advised whether I should now acccpt that my colleague, Mr Walter Sisulu,[ii] will not be released before September 6.

On July 4 the Minister of Justice touched on the question of Mr Oscar Mpetha,[iii] another colleague of mine. He is now very busy with the elections and is unlikely to give attention to matters of this kind. I would appreciate it if you would remind him.

[Signed NRMandela]

---

i   These must be photographs taken during his meeting with P. W. Botha in Cape Town. Mandela was first given a suit in prison in early 1986 to wear when he met Nigerian leader and head of the Commonwealth Eminent Persons Group General Olusegun Obasanjo in Pollsmoor Prison.

ii   Walter Sisulu (1912– 2003), ANC and MK activisit and fellow Rivonia trialist who was imprisoned with Mandela – see the glossary.

iii Oscar Mpetha (1909–94), trade unionist and ANC member who was sentenced to five years' imprisonment at Pollsmoor Prison and was released in 1989 – see the glossary.

To Tim Wilson, son-in-law of Advocate Bram Fischer[i]

1335/88: NELSON MANDELA

> Victor Verster Prison,
> P/B X6005,
> Paarl South,
> 7620.
>
> 23.7.89

Dear Tim,

The significance of an institution lies not merely in the size of its buildings, staff or budget, but mainly in the quality of its service to the community. On this standard the Alexandra Health Centre[ii] is a unique project in more senses than one.

For one thing, it brings hope where there was despair, and even life where death would have triumphed. Its independence from government control, the diversity of its benefactors, its goals and range of activities all make it an effort of far-reaching potential; an example of what would happen in the new South Africa we are all striving to build.

Sixty years of community service is an appropriate occasion for celebration, and I send the Centre my congratulations and best wishes.

***

I spent some exciting years in Alex in the early forties,[iii] and the mere mention of that famous township makes me more nostalgic. I intend visiting the place at the earliest opportunity when better times return.

Meantime, I think of you, Ilse[iv] and Ruth[v] with warm regards,

Sincerely,
Uncle Nelson

---

i   Bram Fischer (1908–75), lawyer and political and anti-apartheid activist – see the glossary.
ii   The Alexandra Health Centre and University Clinic in Alexandra, Johannesburg, was initially established in 1929 as a maternal and child health centre before evolving into a primary health care centre.
iii   Soon after Mandela arrived in Johannesburg in 1941 he moved into the township of Alexandra, where he boarded with the Reverend J. Mabutho of the Anglican Church at his home in Eighth Avenue. He later moved into a room in the yard of the Xhoma family in 46 Seventh Avenue.
iv   Ilse Wilson, Tim Wilson's wife and daughter of Bram Fischer.
v   Ruth Fischer, Tim Wilson's sister-in-law and daughter of Bram Fischer.

To Adelaide Tambo,[i] friend, anti-apartheid activist, and the wife of Oliver Tambo, ANC president and Mandela's former law partner

14.8.89

Proposed telegram to Mrs Tambo –
Winnie and I deeply shocked by Oliver's illness. Wish him a speedy and complete recovery. You and children much in our thoughts.

Love

To Makhi Jomo Dalasile

1335/88: NELSON MANDELA   14.8.89

Dear Makhi,

I had a pleasant discussion with Chief Zanengqele[ii] on 8 August and I found him warm and wise.

Seeing him reminded me of the late Chief Sakhela,[iii] who was good to me even after my arrest in 1962. Sakhela was a worthy descendant of the great Dalasile, who became a people's hero when some traditional leaders of his time chose to crawl on their bellies. Perhaps one day I may be able to give you interesting details in this regard. For the present it is sufficient to say that Dalasile is a martyr on whom the country's youth can fruitfully model their own lives.

From what is said above you will readily agree, I hope, that the world is full of people with natural leadership qualities. The traditional leaders, who led the independence struggle from the 17th century, were such men.

But times have changed and education has become a very powerful weapon in the struggle to produce a well-developed person. That is why I was so happy when I heard that you were doing your B. Juris[iv] this year. I wish you the best of luck.

Fondest regards to you and all your fellow students.

---

i   Adelaide Tambo (1929–2007) – see the glossary.
ii   A Thembu chief who visited him in prison.
iii   A Thembu chief.
iv   Bachelor of Laws.

Sincerely,
Tata[i] Madiba

[Envelope]
Mr Makhi Jomo Dalasile,
University of Transkei,
Private Bag
UMTATA[ii]

To Rev Abel Hendricks, former president of the South African Methodist Church, and his wife, Frieda

1355/88: NELSON MANDELA

Victor Verster Prison,
P/B X6005,
Paarl South,
7620.

15.8.89

Dear Abel & Frieda,

I learnt with deep shock of the tragic death of your beloved son, Andrew, and I send you my deepest sympathy. Winnie and I would have preferred to be at your side to give you support as Andrew's remains are laid to rest. But, as you know, this cannot be. I must, however, assure you that you are much in our thoughts. Once again, our sincere condolences!

Sincerely,
Nelson

---

i   'Father' in isiXhosa.
ii   Umtata (now called Mthatha) was the capital of the Transkei homeland.

To Archbishop Desmond Tutu and his wife, Leah Tutu[i]

1335/88: NELSON MANDELA

21. 8. 89

Dear Desmond & Leah,

You are so busy travelling in and out of the country that few people would expect you to find time for other people's hopes and despairs, dreams and frustrations, joys and celebrations; yet this is one of the roles you play so well. Many thanks for the flowers and good wishes.

Religion has throughout the centuries and in all countries been one of society's most powerful forces, and it may well be that it will always be so. But there are men and women who have the capacity to make it more relevant than ever before.

Achievements, great and small, will always be acknowledged whether by means of prizes or simple awards. Some people decline such honours, while others accept and then use them selfishly. But there are still others who get them as a result of selfless service to the community, and who tend to use them as an effective instrument in our striving for justice and human dignity. Trevor and sisters[ii] will know very well who we have in mind.

The South African churches have made a substantial contribution to the struggle for real change in this country, and the Church of the Province[iii] has pride of place in that historic line-up. Its consistency and forthrightness on national issues inspires us all. The Durban Resolution of 31 May to 7 June 1989[iv] has given me strength and hope beyond words.

I also felt much honoured to be invited to become a patron of the William Wilberforce Council and to receive their coveted tie. I hope you will thank the Council on my behalf.

Lastly, I must inform you that on several occasions in the past, I requested the Department of Prisons to allow you to visit me, all without success. But now I have the hope that such a visit is a definite possibility. Its exact timing will, however, be a subject of very special consideration.

We will keep our fingers crossed.

Fondest regards and best wishes.

---

i   Desmond Tutu (1931–), first black archbishop of Cape Town, and his wife Leah Tutu (1933–) – see the glossary.
ii   The Tutus' children.
iii The Anglican Church of Southern Africa was known until 2006 as the Church of the Province. While some prominent priests, including Archbishop Desmond Tutu, took a stand against apartheid, the church apologised in 1997 to the people of South Africa for contributing to the oppression of blacks during apartheid.
iv   The Anglican Church's ruling provincial synod had called on Anglican bishops to investigate a range of sanctions against apartheid, including a halt to the rescheduling of foreign debt, a denial of overseas landing rights to South African Airways, and a ban on all foreign airline flights to South Africa.

Sincerely,
Madiba.

P.S. Stanley's death deeply shocked me and I hope you will be able to pass my condolences to his family.

[Envelope]
The Most Reverend Desmond M. Tutu
Bishopscourt,
CLAREMONT, CAPE
700

To Adelaide Tambo,[i] friend, anti-apartheid activist, and the wife of Oliver Tambo, ANC president and Mandela's former law partner

1355/88: NELSON MANDELA   21.8.89

Kgaitsedi,[ii]

The telegram I sent on 15 Aug., care of Mary,[iii] must have reached you by now. It was a relief to learn from the media, as well as from Ismail,[iv] that O.R.'s[v] illness[vi] was not so serious as was first reported, and I hope he will soon be back at his desk.

But it seems to me that certain precautions should immediately be taken to ensure that his daily workload is made manageable, and with adequate midday rest every day.

It will be absolutely useless for anybody, yourself included, merely to urge O.R. to take things easy. He is totally incapable of doing so on his own. As you know, I have repeatedly urged him in the past to be careful, an appeal, I am sure you and Thembi[vii] have also made.

Unless the National Executive[viii] advises differently I would suggest that,

---

i   Adelaide Tambo (1929–2007) – see the glossary.
ii   'My sister' in both Sesotho and Setswana.
iii   Mary Benson (1919–2000), friend, author, journalist, and anti-apartheid activist – see the glossary. She lived in London.
iv   Ismail Ayob (1942–), Mandela's attorney – see the glossary.
v   Oliver Reginald Tambo (1917–93), Mandela's friend, former law partner, and the president of the ANC – see the glossary.
vi   He had a stroke in August 1989.
vii   One of the Tambos' daughters.
viii National Executive Committee of the ANC.

from now on, you stay and travel around with him to ensure that these precautions are strictly observed. This will naturally be an expensive exercise, but it is the only way to ensure that the doctor's instructions are carried out. Whatever you and O.R. think about this suggestion, I would appeal to you to inform the N.E.[i] of my views.

Lastly, I want you to know that I badly miss you, O.R., the children and other comrades, to whom I send my best wishes.

Love,

Sincerely,
Nelson.

To J. N. & Radhi Singh, friends[ii]

1334/88: NELSON MANDELA

21.8.89

Dear J.N. and Radhi,

Many thanks for the birthday telegram. Spending the day with almost the whole family was a momentous occasion in more senses than one. The numerous messages from friends gave the occasion a special dimension.

You talk of imminent freedom? I am no prophet, but it is my prerogative to express serious doubts. You will be wise to try to visit me here as others are doing.[iii]

Meantime I send you my love and best wishes.

Sincerely,
Nelson

[Envelope]
Mr. J.N. Singh,
23 Elwork Rd.
Durban

---

i   National Executive.
ii   J. N. Singh (d. 1996), member of the Transvaal Indian Congress and the Natal Indian Congress. He studied towards his LLB degree with Nelson Mandela at the University of Witwatersrand. His wife was Radhi Singh (d. 2013), anti-apartheid activist, teacher, and attorney.
iii   They visited him on 1 January 1990 and gave him a diary.

To Mary Benson,[i] friend, author, journalist, and anti-apartheid activist

1335/88: NELSON MANDELA   21.8.89

Dear Mary,

It was very, very difficult, if not altogether impossible, for me to write to you from Pollsmoor. The more I failed to reach you, the more I missed you. But now there is some hope that this letter will reach you, and that the correspondence which fizzled out during the last few years will start flowing again. May I say the ball is now in your court?

Many thanks for the beautiful birthday card with its warm message. It was nice to have the family around – the children, a daughter-in-law, 9 grandchildren, 1 great grandson and Zami,[ii] of course. Maki's[iii] husband, Isaac, Zeni[iv] and family, and a great grandson were unable to attend. Nevertheless it was a memorable occasion, I wished you were here to add some touch to the get together.

I expect that the longer Mandla[v] remains at boarding school the more he will develop the aptitude for vivid description. It may well be that even the mere fact of visiting this area will stimulate that talent. It is, as you rightly say, a place of beautiful scenery. Some of the surrounding areas are beyond words.

Lord Anthony Barber[vi] of the famous Eminent Persons Group,[vii] promised me a book – the story of his escape from a German prison camp during the last war. The turn of events before they left South Africa may have compelled him to change his mind. Do remind him and also tell him that I still think of him.

It is rather ironic that you should tell me about the heatwave over there when we are freezing in the Boland. Indeed "God fulfils himself in many ways".

Frances[viii] is apparently just like you; she has touch and I like her painting. A painter is undoubtedly good if he can convey to a layman like myself

---

i   Mary Benson (1919–2000) – see the glossary. Mandela hadn't seen her since his vist to London in 1962.
ii   His wife, Winnie Mandela.
iii   Makaziwe Mandela (1954–), Mandela's eldest daughter – see the glossary.
iv   His middle daughter, Zenani Mandela (1959–) – see the glossary.
v   Mandla Mandela (1974), son of Mandela's youngest son Makgatho Mandela and Rose Rayne Mandela, known as Rennie.
vi   Lord Anthony Barber (1920–2005), British Conservative Party politican.
vii   The Commonwealth established an Eminent Persons Group to investigate apartheid in 1985. They visited Mandela in Pollsmoor Prison on 16 May 1985.
viii   Mary Benson's daughter.

so clearly. Please give her my congratulations and David my warm regards. With love.

Sincerely,
Nelson

To Helen Joseph,[i] his friend

1335/88: NELSON MANDELA   21.8.89

Our dear Helen,

I was sorry to hear that your application to visit me and two other friends has been turned down for the umpteenth time. What an unforgettable moment it would have been to welcome you here. And to lunch together as in the olden days. I will again make representations from this side for a special visit from you. It may well be that by spending some hours with you your longevity will rub off on me. Meantime, I thank you for the wonderful birthday telegram. Love and best wishes.

Sincerely,
Nelson

To Cyril Ramaphosa,[ii] trade union leader and activist

21.8.89

Dear Cyril,

You wear the mantle of labour leader exceedingly well. Your skill and caution in handling complicated and delicate problems have earned you the respect of friend and foe alike.

Comrade James Motlatsi[iii] and other leaders of the National Union of

---

i   Helen Joseph (1905–92), teacher, social worker, and anti-apartheid and women's rights activist – see the glossary.
ii   First general secretary of the National Union of Mineworkers.
iii   First president of the National Union of Mineworkers.

Mineworkers complement your leadership very well.

It is indeed a source of both pride and humility to be associated with a trade union whose roots are firmly planted in our soil, but whose outlook is global.

July 18[i] is an important day in the family album. Your impressive card and magnificent message add a new dimension to it, for which I thank you.

Please accept my very best wishes.

Sincerely,
Madiba

Cyril Ramaphosa
c/o Attorney Ayob and Associates
P.O. Box 728
JOHANNESBURG
2000

———————————

To Amina & Peter Frense[ii]

1335/88: NELSON MANDELA

21.8.89

Dear Amina & Peter,

You have brought Mqhekezweni and all the sweet memories of my child-hood right into Victor Verster.[iii] I can literally cut the feeling of nostalgia with a knife. Few things convince me that the universe is fast ageing more than the dilapidated condition of the once stately buildings of the Mqekezweni of my childhood. A lot of history lies locked up in those silent walls. Perhaps one day we will be able to drive down to Umtata[iv] together; it will then be comparatively easy for me to tell you from where I really come. Meanwhile I send you my love and best wishes. Many thanks for the birthday greetings.

Sincerely,
Nelson

———————————

i   Mandela's birthday.
ii   Amina Frense was a television journalist and anti-apartheid activist. Her husband, Peter, was a journalist. They did not know Mandela.
iii They had sent Mandela a photograph of Mqhekezweni, the Great Place, where he grew up in the Transkei homeland.
iv   Umtata (now called Mthatha) was the capital of the Transkei homeland.

To the commissioner of prisons

1335/88: NELSON MANDELA

11.9.89

Commissioner of Prisons
Pretoria

The release of the following prisoners, all of whom are serving sentences of life imprisonment, will be widely appreciated:[i]

1. Kathrada, Ahmed,
2. Mhlaba, Raymond,
3. Mlangeni, Andrew,
4. Motsoaledi, Elias,
5. Sisulu, Walter.[ii]

All of them were sentenced in June 1964, and all of them are now more than 60 years of age, Mr Sisulu having turned 77 last May and Mr Mhlaba 70 last February.

6. Mr Wilton Mkwayi[iii] was sentenced in December 1964. Although he was arrested after the above persons had already been convicted, he is for all practical purposes a co-accused, the only difference being that he escaped the police net when the others were arrested in July 1963.

7. *Messrs Meyiwa and Mdlalose, both of whom are held in Robben Island, were released in the Seventies after each had served eight years. They were again arrested and this time sentenced to life imprisonment together with Mr Harry Gwala,[iv] who was released last year on medical grounds.

---

i   This was part of Mandela's secret negotiations with the government. He later wrote: 'I pressed the government to display evidence of its good intentions, urging the state to show its bona fides by releasing my fellow political prisoners at Pollsmoor and Robben Island.' (NM, *Long Walk to Freedom*, p. 661.)
ii   For more on these Rivonia Trialists, see the glossary.
iii   Mkwayi was serving a life sentence for his role in the Little Rivonia Trial. The Little Rivonia Trial took place in November 1964, five months after the Rivonia Trial (see the glossary) ended, after Laloo Chiba, Mac Maharaj, Wilton Mkwayi, Dave Kitson and John Matthews were charged with sabotage for their activities on behalf of MK. The former three were sent to Robben Island and the other two, being white, were held in Pretoria.
iv   Harry Gwala (1920–95), ANC activist who was charged with sabotage for recruiting members to MK and sentenced to eight years in prison on Robben Island. Continued his activism on his release in 1972 and in 1977 he was sentenced to life imprisonment and returned to Robben Island – see the glossary.

8.   Mr Jeff Masemola,[i] presently held in Diepkloof,[ii] was sentenced to life imprisonment in 1963. All his co-accused have been released, some of them as far back as four years ago. But the Department of Prisons continues to hold him in spite of his poor state of health and age.

I should add that the release of one or a couple of these men only will no longer have any significance.

If you grant this request, as I hope you will, then I would like to see them before they are released. I can see Mr Masemola immediately after he is released.

[Signed NRMandela]

*The full names are

Matthews Meyiwa
Zakhele Mdlalose

[In another hand]: Oscar Mpetha – added on request of Mr Mandela[iii]

————————

To Frieda Matthews,[iv] friend and widow of his university professor Z. K. Matthews

1335/88: NELSON MANDELA   18.9.89

Dear Rakgadi,[v]

Although you have not heard from me for several months you are always in my thoughts, hoping that you are keeping well and that the children and grandchildren are progressing. If my silence has surprised and even shocked you, I will ask you to bear in mind that I have missed you and your informative letters very much. It may well be that by the time you get this

i   Jafta Kgalabi 'Jeff' Masemola (1929–90), teacher, member of the ANC Youth League, member of the Pan Africanist Congress, and political prisoner – see the glossary. After being arrested in 1962 and charged with sabotage for blowing up power lines and smuggling freedom fighters out of South Africa he was sentenced to life imprisonment in July 1963. He was released from prison on 15 October 1989, and on 17 April 1990 he was killed in a mysterious car accident.
ii   A prison in Johannesburg.
iii   All except Meyiwa and Mdlalose were released on 15 October 1989.
iv   Frieda Matthews (1905–98) – see the glossary.
v   'Sister' in Setswana.

letter your birthday will have passed, that the sweetness of the cake and taste of the champagne will have been forgotten. Nevertheless, I hope it will be the happiest birthday in you life. Love and best wishes!

Sincerely,
Nelson

To Kepu Mkentane,[i] friend

1335/88: NELSON MANDELA   18.9.89

Dear Kepu,

Last month I received a telegram from Kini[ii] reporting the death of Leo Sihlali.[iii] I immediately sent a condolence telegram followed by a letter. I hope these were received. I assume that Kini was either his wife or child.

As you know, a large number of people have visited me during the last eight months. From your area came the Joyi brothers, Xobololo, Fadana, Advocate Phathekile Holomisa, Chief Ngangomhlala Matanzima and his brother, the brigadier who frightened you when he knocked on your door earlier this year, Stella Sigcau, my sisters, nieces, and of course, the children and grandchildren.[iv]

I also spent a whole day with Chief Zanengqele Dalasile of AmaQwati, and he impressed me very much. He is smart and well-informed and he briefed me well on a variety of important matters. He is your neighbour and the visit made me think of you and the children, and to wonder just how you spend your time these days.

Do you know Connie Njongwe[v] at Matatiele? You share common virtues. Both of you are dependable, good correspondents, quick to respond with sentiments which leave one with much hope. I have corresponded with Connie and her late husband, Jimmy, since the Sixties, just as I have done

---

i   A friend of Mandela's.
ii Kini Sihlali.
iii Leo Sihlali was one-time president of the Non-European Unity Movement (NEUM), a Trotskyist organisation formed in South Africa in 1943. It was committed to non-racialism and its primary tactic was one of non-collaboration with the apartheid regime. The movement split in 1957.
iv Relatives of Mandela's.
v   Connie Njongwe, wife of Dr. James 'Jimmy' Njongwe (1919–76), medical doctor, ANC leader, and organiser of the Defiance Campaign (for the Defiance Campaign, see the glossary) in the Eastern Cape – for Jimmy Njongwe, see the glossary.

with you and Kent, and I am always happy to hear from all of you.
    Fondest regards and best wishes!

    Sincerely,
Nelson

[Envelope]
Mrs Kepu Mkentane,
P. O. Box 13,
ENGCOBO.
TRANSKEI

To Connie Njongwe,[i] friend

1335/88: NELSON MANDELA

> Victor Verster Prison,
> P/B X6005,
> Paarl South,
> 7620.
>   18.9.89

Our dear Connie,

A heavy work load during the last eight months forced me to delay writing
to you. As you know I have since the sixties written to you at least every year
in May to let you know that you and the children are often in my thoughts.
    The workload is being heavier every day, but this time I simply decided
to push aside everything and attend to you. I hope you and the children are
in good health and that the business is really flourishing.
    You are probably well aware that many people from all over the coun-
try are visiting Victor Verster, and should you also wish to come over, you
would be more than welcome. Your visit would be a memorable event giving
me, as it would, the opportunity to see whether age has made any impression on you. I doubt it, and it may well be that you still look so strong and

---

i   Connie Njongwe, wife of Dr. James 'Jimmy' Njongwe (1919–76), medical doctor, ANC leader, and organiser of the
     Defiance Campaign (for the Defiance Campaign, see the glossary) in the Eastern Cape – for Jimmy Njongwe, see
     the glossary.

well that people who see you for the first time may think that you are the eldest sister of Zweli and Phathi.[i]

You would be free to come together with Kepu Mkentane from Engcobo, if you so wish. She and her late husband, Lincoln,[ii] are like you and Jimmy[iii] to me, and I have received Christmas cards from them since the sixties, a practice which Kepu has maintained to the present day. My nephew, Brigadier Themba Matanzima, of the Transkei Defence Force will arrange the visit for you. Please do not hesitate to approach him; he is a good young man. His home telephone number is 24523 and office 25946.

Fondest regards and best wishes!

Sincerely,
Nel
[Envelope]
Mrs Constance Njongwe
P.O. 122
Matatiele
4730

To Mamphela Ramphele,[iv] friend and academic

1335:/88: NELSON MANDELA   18.9.89

Dear Mamphela,

A train of staggering coincidences hit Victor Verster after your visit, so much so that I have since wondered whether coincidences are coincidences.

You were here on 10 September. That same evening there was a television programme on successful women – Marina Maponya,[v] Lindi Myeza,[vi] Ronel Erwee,[vii] Mafuna, Tshabalala and, believe it or not, the down-to-earth Mamphela.

---

i   Connie Njongwe's daughter Patiswa (Phati) and her son Zwelinzima (Zweli).
ii   Lincoln Mkentane was a classmate of Mandela's at University College of Fort Hare. They were both in the drama society and while at university Mkentane adapted a play about Abraham Lincoln and played Lincoln himself. Mandela played the role of his assassin, John Wilkes Booth. Like Mandela, Mkentane became an attorney.
iii   Connie Njongwe's husband Dr. James 'Jimmy' Njongwe (1919–76) – see the glossary.
iv   Mamphela Ramphele (1947–), anti-apartheid activist and a founding member of the Black Consciousness Movement, medical doctor, academic, and businesswoman – see the glossary.
v   Marina Maponya (1934–92), South African businesswoman and community leader who gave to the poor.
vi   Lindi Myeza, social worker and prominent Methodist Church member.
vii   Ronel Erewe, professor.

Among the issues you raised in the course of our conversation was that of sexism. In that TV programme, men's prejudice against women became the central issue.

That should have been enough to illustrate the fact of undesigned occurrences, but that was not to be. Soon after your departure I browsed through the draft on the ethnography of the children when the *Star Nation Weekly* was delivered. There on the centre page was an article on the education of children in South Africa. Sue Valentine commented on the remarks of Anglo-America's Michael O'Dowd at a C.S.I.R.[i] conference in Pretoria. He touched on aspects raised in the draft, and the similarity of approach was quite striking.

Then Nandi[ii] brought me your message containing sentiments I was on the point of conveying to you. Here telepathy may have been at work. But it is indeed reassuring that the world has crawled or is crawling out of the superstitions of previous centuries. Otherwise many gurus would accept purely fortuitous occurrences for causal connections.

Your sense of modesty ought not to be compromised by the observation that the draft is a scholarly work. It is made even more impressive by the skill and experience of a perceptive researcher who speaks as an insider.

I had occasion to reflect on the paper in bed, and I was not at all flattered when I recalled that during the two decades I spent on the Rand before my arrest, the only hostel I ever visited was the Denver Men's Hostel twice; on both occasions for political meetings.

The paper on the challenges of transformation is equally impressive in its relevance and fresh thinking. It is a pleasure to read it. The remarks on page eight are likely to upset some vested interests. Nevertheless, these are observations worth making.

I would have liked you, Professors Herbert Vilakazi[iii] and Frances Wilson,[iv] as well as others, to advise me on a matter which may assume some importance soon. But from experience I am convinced that Frances and Herbert will not be allowed.

Perhaps when you want a bit of rest from your academic work, another visit may be arranged.

Meantime I think of you and the boys.

Love and best wishes,

---

i   Council for Scientific and Industrial Research.
ii   Nandi Mandela (1968), daughter of Mandela's late son Thembi (for Thembi Mandela, see the glossary).
iii Herbert Vilakazi (1943–2016), professor of sociology.
iv   Frances Wilson, a fellow academic of Mamphela Ramphele's at the University of Cape Town. They wrote a book together, *Uprooting Poverty – The South African Challenge* (Cape Town: David Philip, 1989).

Sincerely,
Ntate[i]

[Envelope]
Dr. Mamphela Ramphele,
Department of Social Anthropology,
University of Cape Town,
Rondebosch.
7700

To Rashid & Ayesha Kola, friends[ii]

Dear Rashid & Ayesha,

You may have forgotten me by now, but during the last 27 years I have often thought of you and your tidy apartment in Jeppe.[iii]

When I last saw Ayesha she was carrying life in her body and she looked radiant and lovely. She had to. After all she was, and still is, Rashid's wife, one of the most impressive young men in that city those days.

I hope he still plays cricket and that the tasty breyani and roti, which Ayesha can prepare so well, have not given him a paunch as yet, at least. I look forward to seeing you one day, although that may not be so near as many people think. Meanwhile, I would like you to know that you are in my thoughts, and that I have forgotten none of your hospitality. May you be blessed with the best in life.

Fondest regards,

Sincerely,
Nelson

Rashid & Ayesha Kola,
c/o Attorney Ismail Ayob,
P.O. Box 728
Johannesburg.
2000

---

i   Uncle' in Setswana, Mamphela Ramphele's language.
ii   This letter is undated but the registration slip with this letter is dated 25.9.89.
iii   A suburb of Johannesburg.

To the secretary, Post and Telecommunications Workers Association (POTWA),[i] trade union

25.9.89

Secretary
P.O.T.W.A.

Dear Qabane,[ii]

Your terrific birthday message considerably strengthened feelings of optimism and hope, and forcefully highlighted your concern for the well-being of those who think and act like Potwa.
　　Fondest regards and best wishes.

　　Sincerely,
Madiba

Secretary, P.O.T.W.A,
c/o/ Attorney Ismail Ayob,
P.O. Box 728,
Johannesburg
2000

To Fatima Meer,[iii] friend and comrade

1335/88: NELSON MANDELA

28.9.89

Dear Fathu,[iv]

Your letters of 7 and 14 September were delivered to me only yesterday, and the nature of the issues you raise in the correspondence demands a prompt reply.

---

i　　An affiliate of the Congress of South African Trade Unions.
ii　　'Comrade' in isiXhosa and isiZulu.
iii　　Fatima Meer (1928–2010), writer, academic, and anti-apartheid and women's rights activist – see the glossary.
iv　　A nickname for Fatima Meer.

I fully agree with Iqbal's[i] suggestion that the services of Mr Geoffrey Bindman[ii] should be retained.

With regard to the publication of the local edition, I enclose for your attention authority empowering you to choose the publisher. Unfortunately, my information on the Madiba Trust is very scanty, but I will respect your decision if you nonetheless consider it wise to publish under it. Would IBR[iii] not be better able to undertake it? In my opinion distribution by the CNA[iv] would be a good arrangement.

I suspect, ben,[v] that you easily forget that you are still fairly young and wide awake. You have no reason whatsoever to behave like a sexagenarian. We discussed Anant's[vi] offer to make the film and I expressly assured you that I accept the offer.[vii] Iqbal can draw up a formal acceptance document if one is required.

Sidney Potier[viii] is a super-star and it would be a shot in the arm for him to act in the film. But he is probably very rich now to accept our offer. I am making an application to the Department of Prisons for you and Iqbal to visit me. But, as you know, it may take quite some time before we get a reply.

The new cover for the South African edition looks impressive and I am happy with it. I would have preferred that we renew the contract with Skotaville.[ix] But bearing in mind your views on the matter I would suggest that either the Institute for Black Research or the Madiba Trust or any other agency of your choice should handle publication.

As far as legal representation is concerned, Krish[x] has already done a lot of good work and I suggest that he should represent us in this matter.

Unfortunately, I have no information on the significance of the words "authorised version". But if this will contribute to the success of the project then I sanction the suggestion both for the overseas and local editions.

Love and best wishes.

---

i   Fatima's nephew, Iqbal Meer.

ii   A London attorney who was assisting with the publication of Fatima Meer's book about Mandela, *Higher Than Hope: The Authorized Biography* (New York: Harper & Row, 1988).

iii   The Institute for Black Research.

iv   A book retailer called Central News Agency.

v   'Sister' in Gujarati.

vi   Anant Singh, South African filmmaker.

vii   Anant Singh and Fatima Meer had discussed making a film version of *Higher than Hope*, which Mandela agreed to. Singh met him at Meer's house two weeks after he was released and Mandela indicated that he had written his autobiography and was going to publish it. 'We both then agreed that we should wait until that is published to get the movie made.' (Anant Singh, email to Sahm Venter, 7 September 2017.) Singh eventually produced the feature film based on Mandela's autobiography, *Long Walk to Freedom*, and it was released in 2013.

viii   Sidney Poitier (1927–), Bahamian-American actor, film director, author, and diplomat. *Higher Than Hope* was never adapted into a film but Poitier later played Mandela in the 1997 television film *Mandela and De Klerk*.

ix   The first South African publisher of *Higher Than Hope*.

x   Krish Naidoo, a lawyer.

Sincerely,
Nelson

To Madanjit & Marjorie Kapitan, proprietors of Kapitan's Indian restaurant, Johannesburg

[Registered letter dated 89.9.28]

Madanjit & Marjorie Kapitan,
c/o Attorney Ismail Ayob.
P.O. Box 728
Johannesburg.
2000

Dear Madanjit & Marjorie,

I learn with sorrow that your famous Oriental Restaurant in Kort Street is closing down.

During the last 27 years we have lost so many dear friends and so many noted buildings, that I sometimes fear that by the time I return, the world itself will have disappeared. There are many palates and tummies inside and outside the country which will justifiably be outraged by the disastrous news.

But I will always think of the Restaurant, and particularly of you, with fond memories. My best wishes.

Sincerely,
Nelson

To Winnie Mandela,[i] his wife

1335/88: NELSON MANDELA   9.10.89

Darling Mum,

---

i   Nomzamo Winifred Madikizela-Mandela (1936–) – see the glossary.

Thanks very much for the smart suit. I will certainly wear it on the occasion you mentioned.[i] Again, many thanks! I would, however, appeal that no further articles of clothing should be sent. I have more than you would find in the best retailers in your city.

Daluxolo gave me the report on the funeral. I worked hard on this and surrounding matters, and I am sometimes tempted to believe that if I had not literally pestered every key figure in that part of the country, that historic day would never have come.

With regard to the building of the house at Qunu,[ii] I hope Mdayelwa has been informed that I do not want any financial contribution from any person, no matter who he may be, towards the house. All I want from them is their co-operation in securing the ground for the building.

Makgatho[iii] underwent an operation at Tygerberg on 6 October and will probably be discharged today.

We are busy with Zindzi's[iv] passport which will also include the three children.[v] I have also asked for one for Fathu[vi] and I am keeping my fingers crossed. Although I am presently handling a number of very sensitive issues, I will also make enquiries about yours. I would be very happy if you could travel abroad, provided the trip is properly sanctioned by the family here at home. . . . Love.

Affectionately,
Madiba

To the commanding officer, Victor Verster

1335/88: NELSON MANDELA

9.10.89

The Commanding Officer
Victor Verster Prison

Attention: Brig Keulder

---

i   The suit was probably for him to wear on the day of his release.
ii   The village where Mandela grew up in the Transkei.
iii   Makgatho (Kgatho) Mandela (1950–2005), Mandela's second-born son – see the glossary.
iv   Zindziswa Mandela (1960–), his and Winnie Mandela's youngest daughter.
v   Zindzi's children and Mandela's grandchildren.
vi   A nickname for Fatima Meer.

A rapidly increasing weight has induced me to cut out lunch and the afternoon snack. I have explained the matter to the medical staff, who are monitoring various aspects of my health on a regular basis.

In addition, I have opted for white sugar, for purposes of variety, which is bought out of my own funds.[i]

[Signed NRMandela]

∞∞∞∞∞∞

During his talks with government in prison, which he hoped would lead to eventual negotiations with the ANC, Mandela had repeatedly called for the release of other prisoners. In particular he wanted the remaining five of his Rivonia Trial colleagues out of prison before he could be freed, along with ANC prisoners Oscar Mpetha, Wilton Mkwayi and Jafta Masemola of the PAC. (See his letter from 11 September 1989, page 545.)

De Klerk made an announcement on television on 10 October 1989. Mandela had been visited by his imprisoned comrades, Walter Sisulu, Ahmed Kathrada, Andrew Mlangeni, and Raymond Mhlaba,[ii] that day, at the end of which he said, 'Chaps, this is goodbye.' Then, instead of being returned to prison, the four of them were given dinner at Victor Verster Prison while a television set was brought in. There they watched the announcement of their impending freedom. Five days later they were free.

To the commissioner of prisons

[Typed]

COMMISSIONER OF PRISONS

In my letter dated 11 September 1989 I have made representations for the release of certain of my colleagues. I have today been informed that the Government has decided to approve the release of the following eight colleagues:

---

i   Mandela received brown sugar as his ration at Victor Verster Prison. When Jack Swart cooked for him he bought white sugar. Mandela paid for groceries for feeding guests from a monthly allowance he received from his attorney Ismail Ayob.

ii   They were held at Pollsmoor Prison. The other remaining Rivonia trialist, Elias Motsoaledi, was still on Robben Island.

Ahmed Kathrada
Raymond Mhlaba
Andrew Mlangeni
Elias Motsoaledi
Walter Sisulu
Wilton Mkwayi
Jeff Masemola
Oscar Mpetha[i]

It is my hope that their release will contribute to the creation of a climate that will be conducive to peaceful development and to normalising the situation in our country. As previously stated I have not raised the question of my release.

[Signed NRMandela]

10.10.89

To the commissioner of prisons

<u>1335/88: NELSON MANDELA</u>

16.10.89

The Commissioner of Prisons
Pretoria

Dear General Willemse,

The fruitful meeting between some leaders of the Mass Democratic Movement and the writer hereof on 10 October 1989 has highlighted the urgency of similar meetings with leaders from other regions.[ii]

The meeting on 10 October will most certainly be followed by intensive countrywide discussions, and similar meetings with the writer, provided they are held soon, may facilitate a common approach to some of the problems discussed with the officials on the same date.

---

i   For notes on these individuals, see the glossary.
ii   In the last months of his imprisonment Mandela requested meetings with activists from various organisations to brief them on his talks with the government.

Your early response will be appreciated.

With kind regards,
[Signed NRMandela]

To Sheikh Nazeem Mohamed,[i] leader of the Muslim Judicial Council

1335/88: NELSON MANDELA

21.8.89

Dear Shaikh Nazeem,

The Muslim Judicial Council[ii] is one of South Africa's most powerful organisations, and which is committed to the winning of human rights for all our people. During the 27 years of our imprisonment, we have been considerably inspired by its material and spiritual support. Your warm birthday message has given me and my family much strength and comfort. Please accept my warm regards and best wishes,

Sincerely,
Nelson

[Envelope]
Sheikh Nazeem Mohamed,
P.O. Box 4118,
Cape Town.
8000

---

i   Sheikh Nazeem Mohamed, president of the Muslim Judicial Council and active in the anti-apartheid movement.
ii   In the mid-1980s the Muslim Judicial Council aligned itself with the United Democratic Front, effectively declaring apartheid forbidden and aligning millions of South African Muslims in the struggle against apartheid.

To Rev T. S. N. Gqubule,[i] friend, clergyman, and scholar

1335/88: NELSON MANDELA

23.10.89

Ngubengcuka,[ii]

You have been in my thoughts all along, especially after Nobandla[iii] informed me a few years back of your visit to Brandfort[iv] together with EKM[v] and others.

I am aware of the delegation you led to the former State President[vi] to demand the release of political prisoners.

You must be as pleased, as are all of us, with the release of my eight colleagues. The event is undoubtedly an important move which, I hope, will in due course be followed by even more significant developments.

I am also aware of your application to visit me and I was indeed very disappointed when it was turned down. I also made efforts from this side to see you, without success. But the climate for such a visit has improved somewhat, and I would suggest that you apply again.

I hope the young man overseas,[vii] as well as Thandeka,[viii] are keeping well.

Fondest regards and best wishes to the family, E.K.M., L.D. and D.H.

Yours very sincerely,

Madiba

[Envelope]
Rev. T.S.N. Gqubule,
John Wesley College,
P.O. Box 2283,
Pietermaritzburg.
3200

---

i　Theocritus Simon Ndziweni Gqubule (1928–2016), teacher, Methodist priest, and the first African student to graduate with a doctorate from Rhodes University. Also an anti-apartheid activist and a member of the United Democratic Front, in 2016 the South African government awarded him the Order of Luthuli for his contribution to the liberation struggle.

ii　A reference to him being a descendant of King Ngubengcuka who was also Mandela's great-great-grandfather.

iii　One of Winnie Mandela's names.

iv　Winnie Mandela was still living in the rural township of Brandfort in the Orange Free State (now Free State), where she had been banished in 1977. She lived there until 1985.

v　Elliot Khoza Mgojo (1932–), former leader of the Methodist Church.

vi　P. W. Botha (1916–2006) – see the glossary.

vii　T. S. N. Gqubule's son, Duma, who was studying economics at Aberdeen University in Scotland.

viii　T. S. N. Gqubule's daughter.

To Ntiski Sisulu, granddaughter of Walter Sisulu, his friend, comrade, and a former fellow prisoner, and his wife Albertina[i]

1335/88: NELSON MANDELA   23.10.89

Dear Ntsiki,

I told your Grandma when she visited me recently that I had answered your letter. After she left I decided to check, and found that I had made a mistake. In fact I had not written to you. Please excuse me for the delay.

In your letter you wrote: "You've too many things on your mind . . ." Perhaps that is the reason why I forgot. Next time I will try to reply soon.

Your Grandpa, Walter, receives treatment for blood pressure. You must remind him to have it tested regularly. He should also continue his exercises on the bicycle at least about four times a week, and your Grandma ought to join him. Will you telephone and give them that message?

In conclusion, I want you to know that I was very happy to get your letter. I know just how busy you are with your school work, and it was good for you to find time to write to me. I hope I will see you when I also return.

Meantime I think of you.

Love and best wishes!

Sincerely,
Uncle Nelson

[Envelope]
Ntsiki Sisulu
Saint Mark's College,
P.O. Box 373,
JANE FURSE
1085

---

i   For Walter (1912–2003) and Albertina Sisulu (1918–2011), see the glossary.

To Len & Beryl Simelane,[i] daughter and son-in-law of Walter Sisulu, his friend, comrade, and a former prisoner, and his wife Albertina[ii]

1335/88: NELSON MANDELA

2.11.89

Dear Len & Beryl,

You have often been in my thoughts during these past years, but I have thought of you and the children almost daily since 10 October 1989, when the announcement was made that your Uncle,[iii] Walter, and seven others would be released. It is to be hoped that this important development has brought joy and relief to all of you. Love and best wishes.

Sincerely,
Uncle Nelson

Len & Beryl Simelane,
P.O. Box 308
CLERNAVILLE
3602

To Chief Zonwabile Sandile Mtirara, a relative

6.11.89

Ngubengcuka,[iv]

My sister, Mabel,[v] informs me that you have unlawfully impounded her cows, and you are refusing to return them. You dismiss her pleas by saying that the matter has been handed over to lawyers. I am pleading with you to return her property immediately, and settle the lawyers' fees.

I do not expect you to act like a shameless coward, worse still by taking pleasure in my current situation. More painful, grandson of Jongintaba,[vi] is that my family suffers under your watch.

---

i   Len Simelane married Beryl Lockman.
ii   For Walter (1912–2003) and Albertina Sisulu (1918–2011), see the glossary.
iii Possibly Ahmed Kathrada (see the glossary), who was known as Uncle Kathy.
iv   A reference to him being a descendant of King Ngubengcuka who was also Mandela's great-great-grandfather.
v   Mabel Nontancu Timakwe (1924–2002), Mandela's sister.
vi   Chief Jongintaba Dalindyebo (d. 1942), the chief and regent of the Thembu people. He became Mandela's guardian following his father's death – see the glossary.

1335/88: NELSON MANDELA.

3/1/89

Victor Verster Prison,
P/B X 6003,
Paarl South. 7624.
2   11   89

Dear Len & Beryl,

You have often been in my thoughts during these
past years, but I have thought of you and the
children almost daily since 10 October 1989, when
the announcement was made that your uncle,
Walter, and seven others would be released. It is
to be hoped that this important development has
brought joy and relief to all of you. Love and
best wishes.

Sincerely,

Sylvia

Len & Beryl Simelane,
P.O. Box 308
CLERNAVILLE
3602

A letter to Len and Beryl Simelane, 2 November 1989, see previous page.

I hope that my request will be well received and that the matter will be resolved in a just and amicable manner. I was delighted by the recent visit by the abaThembu chiefs and council. However, I was disappointed by your conspicuous absence.

Regards and greetings to Queen Nozozile, Princess Ntombizodwa and to your wife.

Yours sincerely,
Dalibunga

[Envelope]
Chief Zonwabele Sandile Mtirara
The Royal Place,
Mqhekezweni.
P.O. Bityi
UMTATA[i]
Transkei

To Fatima Meer,[ii] friend and comrade

1335/88: NELSON MANDELA

6.11.89

Dear Fatu,

I wish to confirm that your biography *Higher than Hope* is the only biography with which I have collaborated and that I am unaware of any other published biography relating to me.[iii]

I further confirm that I wrote an autobiography in prison in the 70s, but I do not know the whereabouts of the manuscript.[iv]

---

i   Umtata (now called Mthatha) was the capital of the Transkei homeland.
ii   Fatima Meer (1928–2010), writer, academic, and anti-apartheid and women's rights activist – see the glossary.
iii Mandela might have been unaware of, or was avoiding drawing the attention of the authorities to, his friend Mary Benson's book, published in 1986, *Nelson Mandela: The Man and the Movement* (New York: W. W. Norton).
iv   Mandela is referring to the autobiography he secretly wrote in prison with the help of his comrades, which formed the basis of *Long Walk to Freedom*, published in 1994 after Mandela collaborated on it with American writer Richard Stengel.

Love and best regards,

Sincerely,
Nelson

=======

To the commissioner of prisons

[Typed]

1335/88: NELSON MANDELA

22-01-90

General WH Willemse
Commissioner of Prisons
PRETORIA

Dear General Willemse

Please find attached a photostat of an article from the newspaper UMAF-RIKA[i] of 11 November 1989, together with an English translation.

The article fully confirms the concern expressed to Ministers Kobie Coetsee[ii] and Dr Gerrit Viljoen[iii] on 10 October 1989.[iv] It is to be hoped that everything will be done to ensure the release of the four fellow prisoners at earliest possible convenience. As in previous cases, it would be appreciated if arrangements are made for them to visit these premises before they are released.

With kind regards,
NELSON MANDELA

UMAFRIKA
Nov 11, 1989

---

i   An isiZulu newspaper. The letter was a loose translation of the isiZulu article into English, and was presumably done for the purpose of this letter to the commissioner of prisons.

ii   Kobie Coetsee (1931–2000), South African minister of justice.

iii Gerrit Viljoen (1926–2009), minister of constitutional development.

iv   On Tuesday, 10 October 1989, Mandela met with the commissioner of prisons, Minister Gerrit Viljoen, Minister Kobie Coetsee, and S. S. Van der Merwe and was informed that his request had been granted for the release of eight prisoners: Ahmed Kathrada, Raymond Mhlaba, Andrew Mlangeni, Elias Motsoaledi, Walter Sisulu, Wilton Mkwayi, Oscar Mpetha, and Jafta Masemola (see the glossary for notes on these individuals).

IT IS ABSOLUTELY QUIET ABOUT THOSE (PRISONERS) FROM
NATAL WHO WERE LEFT BEHIND WHEN THE SISULUS WERE
RELEASED

By Fred Khumalo

At a time when the country rejoices at the release of six ANC leaders, who
were freed two weeks ago, one of the most prominent families of Mpumalanga, Hammarsdale,[i] did not fully rejoice because its head was not released.
He is still serving a sentence of life imprisonment in Robben Island.

The family, which is still under a dark cloud is that of Matthews Mak-
holeka Meyiwa, who was born at Hammarsdale, and who is a veteran of the
ANC and the South African Congress of Trade Unions. He has already
served 23 years at the famous island, and he was also a member of the Natal
Region of Umkhonto weSizwe, on which Mr Harry Gwala and Joseph
Masobiya Mdluli also served.

"The release of the leaders of the ANC has pleased us, as it has done
to the country as a whole, but that event reminded us that our own father is
still incarcerated. This development has saddened us a great deal," said Mrs
Sylvia Hlalelani, a Mazondi.

"The release of Mr Sisulu reminded me of the poor state of health of
my husband when I last visited him in June this year." Continues Mrs Meyiwa, who is born at Nadi. According to her when she last saw her husband
he was experiencing such severe stomach pains that he could hardly move.
Pains were written clearly across his face.

Mr Meyiwa was first arrested in July 1963 for terrorism. He was sentenced to eight years on 28 February 1964. He did most of his sentence in
Robben Island before he was released in 1972.

He was arrested again in 1975 with Mr Harry Gwala of Pietermaritzburg, Mr Joseph Masobiya Mdluli of Lamontville, Mr Zakhele Mdlalose of
Hammarsdale and six others from different parts of Natal. All of them were
sentenced to life imprisonment.[ii]

The trial of Mr Meyiwa and co-accused was a very different one,
because of them complaining of persecution by the police. The authorities continued to deny this allegation, but the truth became plain when
Mr Masobiya Mdluli died at the hands of the police in March 1976. Mrs
Meyiwa spoke about her husband with whom they have six children.

---

i   A township in Natal.
ii   They were all sentenced to life imprisonment for sabotage.

(There follows several paragraphs which deal mainly with Meyiwa's background prior to the arrest.)

Mr Humphrey Meyiwa (31) who is completing his teachers course at the Primary Teacher's Diploma at Mpumalanga College of Education says "to grow without a father was indeed an extremely heavy burden on my mother and to us all her children. My mother had the difficult responsibility of bringing us up – she was both our mother and father, an almost impossible task in the case of a family which is as big as ours."

Mrs Meyiwa says that hope had always been there that her husband would be released, but it died away when there was not even mention of him when Mr Harry Gwala, a co-accused, was freed.

Real joy will come to the Meyiwa family the day the head of the family is released without restrictions, concluded Mr Meyiwa who spoke with a dignified but worried tone.

Other persons who were sentenced to life imprisonment and who are still held in Robben Island are Anthony Mfene Xaba (56),[i] Zakhele Elphas Mdlalose (65),[ii] Vusumzi John Nene.[iii]

But the longest serving life imprisonment prisoner who was sentenced 27 years ago, is Dr Nelson Mandela.

◇◇◇◇◇◇◇◇

As 1989 rolled to an end, rumours of Mandela's release from prison began to grow daily. They had already reached a new height on 5 July 1989 when he was taken from prison before dawn to meet with President F. W. de Klerk who had assumed leadership of the National Party and the country after P. W. Botha suffered a stroke.

The new president made it clear during his first state of the nation address at the opening of Parliament in 1990 that he would be different. On Friday 2 February 1990 protests demanding the release of Nelson Mandela dissolved into street celebrations when De Klerk announced that he would at long last be freed. He also immediately legalised the ANC, the Pan Africanist Congress and all other banned political organisations – other steps Mandela had called for to level the playing fields.

---

i   David Anton Ndoda 'Mfenendala' Xaba (1933–2009). ANC activist and MK member. He served ten years on Robben Island from 1963 to 1973. He was sentenced to life imprisonment in 1977 with Harry Gwala, Matthews Meyiwa, Elphas Mdlalose, John Nene and Zakhele Mdlalose for trying to revive the trade union movement in Natal. Mandela also appealed to President De Klerk for their release. They were released in 1990.

ii   Elphas Mdlalose was arrested for his political activities with Meyiwa and others in 1975.

iii Vusumuzi John Nene, vice-chairperson of the Transport and General Workers' Union in Natal. He was sentenced to life imprisonment with nine others on 25 July 1977 for membership of the ANC, recruiting members for Umkhonto weSizwe, and attempting to overthrow the apartheid regime. He had previously spent seven years on Robben Island for a political offence. He was released in 1990.

The following letter was written on the day that President F. W. de Klerk announced that he had legalised the ANC and other political organisations. It concerns a report of a meeting of the ANC in exile, which Mandela wanted to be sent to Minister Gerrit Viljoen, who at the time had been part of the government team talking with Mandela. With all his Rivonia Trial colleagues now out of prison, Mandela's release was imminent. The letter also reveals that he had had a telephone conversation with a leading figure of the exiled ANC, Thabo Mbeki, eleven days before De Klerk's historic speech.

<hr>

To the commissioner of prisons

1335/88: NELSON MANDELA

2.2.90

General WH Willemse
Commissioner of Prisons
Cape Town

Dear Gen Willemse,

Please ensure that the attached statement reaches Dr Gerrit Viljoen[i] at the earliest possible convenience.

With kind regards,
[Signed NRMandela]

[This whole resolution is in Mandela's hand.]

Resolution adopted at a meeting of the National Executive Committee of the African National Congress attended by the internal leaders released from prison.[ii]

The meeting reaffirmed the significance of the Harare and United Nations declarations,[iii] the latter unanimously adopted by the General

---

i   Gerrit Viljoen (1926–2009), minister of constitutional development.
ii   The meeting was held in Lusaka, Zambia.
iii   At a meeting in Harare, Zimbabwe, on 21 August 1989, the Organisation of African Unity endorsed a statement
      by the ANC's which outlined five preconditions in order for negotiations with the South African government to
      begin. These included the release of all political prisoners, the unbanning of political parties, removing troops
      from townships, an end to political executions, and the end of the State of Emergency. This became known as the
      Harare Commonwealth Declaration. On 14 December 1989 the United Nations General Assembly adopted the
      'Declaration on Apartheid and its Destructive Consequences in South Africa', which called for an end to apartheid

Assembly for the political settlement in our country. It emphasised the importance of the fact that these documents are supported by the overwhelming majority of the people of South Africa, the rest of Africa and the international community.

It reiterated that in keeping with the provisions of these declarations, no negotiations can take place until the necessary climate for such negotiations has been created. The refusal of the Pretoria regime[i] to take the appropriate action in this regard is yet another element confirming its unwillingness to see the apartheid system ended with as little bloodshed and destructions as possible.

In this regard the meeting reaffirmed the importance of the immediate and unconditional release of Nelson Mandela and other political prisoners. It paid tribute to our dear comrade and fellow leader, Nelson Mandela, and expresses its full support for his continuing action even from within prison, which are fully in keeping with the policies and objectives of our movement, to take [forward] the struggle to end apartheid.

The meeting further reaffirmed the preference of the A.N.C. for a settlement arrived at by political means. The A.N.C. has held this position from its very foundation. Throughout the 78 years of its existence it has done everything it could to prevail on successive white minority regimes to adopt the same position to no avail. The meeting reaffirmed that our commitment to these positions is not in doubt. It is fundamental to the nature of the A.N.C. as a movement which seeks democracy, peace and justice for all. At the same time the process of ending apartheid through negotiations requires that the Pretoria regime should itself demonstrate its commitment to a political solution by taking the necessary action which would make such a solution possible.

The meeting warned that no solution can be arrived at while the apartheid regime seeks to impose its will on the majority of our people and their representatives. A negotiated settlement must address the fundamental aspirations of all the people of our country, with those aspirations having been expressed by the people themselves in open political activity and debate.

The National party and its Government, therefore, needs to take a decisive step forward by meeting the conditions for the creation of a climate conducive to negotiation, and recognise the central importance of the genuine representatives of the people of our country.

---

and the establishment of a non-racial democracy.

i   A reference to the government-led apartheid regime. Pretoria is the South African government's administrative capital.

The above statement was read over to me by Mr Thabo Mbeki[i] on 22 January 1990,[ii] and contains no reference whatsoever to violence.

[Signed NRMandela]
2.2.90

[A note in Afrikaans by General Willemse]
Min. G Viljoen
Here is the requested information following yesterday's conversation.

[Signed]
WH WILLEMSE
09/02/02

◇◇◇◇◇◇◇◇◇

At a press conference on 10 February 1990, De Klerk advised the media that Mandela would walk free from Victor Verster Prison the next day at 3 p.m. He actually walked through the gates some ninety minutes later, when he was released the following day, bringing to an end his 10,052 days in prison. He had entered custody a forty-four-year-old father of five children and left it as a seventy-one-year-old grandfather.

It is likely that this is Nelson Mandela's last letter from prison. On Sunday, 11 February 1990, before he walked through the gates of the prison, the future president wrote to the commissioner of prisons referring to a photograph taken with officials the night before. He is either confusing that occasion with photographs taken with De Klerk two nights before or else there remains a photograph of which the world is so far unaware.

---

i   Thabo Mbeki (1942–), head of the ANC's department of internal affairs who was living in exile at the time. He was deputy president of South Africa, with former president F. W. de Klerk, from 1994 to 1999, then succeeded Mandela as the second president of a democratic South Africa, serving from 1999 until 2008.

ii   Mandela didn't have a phone in the house at Victor Verster, and would have had to have gone to a next-door office to take any calls (Sahm Venter in conversation with Jack Swart, 28 June 2017).

To the commissioner of prisons

1335/88: NELSON MANDELA   11 February 1990

General W.H. Willemse
Commissioner of Prisons
Cape Town

Dear General,

I acknowledge receipt of your letter of 10 February 1990, contents of which have been noted and for which I thank you.

Last night a series of photographs of me[i] and some officials was taken. The identity of some of these officials was disclosed to me by Brigadier Gillingham only after the photo session. I then requested him to inform Dr Roux[ii] that I would prefer that these photos should under no circumstances be published without first consulting me. I hope steps will be taken to ensure that this request is respected. I must add that I had hoped that I would by now have got some of the photos we took in July and this year's[iii] [meeting].

Yours sincerely,
[Signed NRMandela][iv]

---

i   Jack Swart (1947–), Mandela's prison guard and his chef at Victor Verster Prison cannot recall any meeting with officials on the night before Mandela's release or any pictures being taken. Mandela only met with his lawyer, Dullah Omar, and his colleagues. Pictures taken with President F. W. de Klerk on the night of 9 February were published. Swart and Mandela had a good relationship and Mandela invited him and his wife, Marietha, to his inauguration on 10 May 1994 and his first State of the Nation address at the opening of Parliament on 24 May 1994. He also invited him and his wife to tea on more than one occasion after his retirement.

ii   Possibly General Jannie Roux, a prison official and psychiatrist who was involved in the media's visits to Robben Island in 1975. Later he served as director-general in the presidency under Mandela.

iii Mandela may have been referring to the meetings he had with P. W. Botha in July 1989 and FW de Klerk on 9 February 1990.

iv   On the same day the Commissioner of Prisons, W.H. Willemse replied and said: "Thank you for your letter dated 1990/02/11. The photos that you are concerned about have not yet been processed and are in good hands. They will be dealt with in such a fashion as to accommodate your request. Some of the other photos that you refer to will first have to be cleared with the parties involved. Thereafter I will contact you again."

SUPPLEMENTARY INFORMATION

GLOSSARY

Alexander, Dr Neville

(1936–2012). Academic, and political and anti-apartheid activist. Founder of the National Liberation Front against the apartheid government. Convicted of sabotage in 1962 and imprisoned on Robben Island for ten years. Awarded the Lingua Pax Prize for his contribution to the promotion of multilingualism in post-apartheid South Africa, 2008.

ANC

Established as the South African Native National Congress (SANNC) in 1912. Renamed African National Congress (ANC) in 1923. Following the Sharpeville Massacre in March 1960, the ANC was banned by the South African government and went underground until the ban was lifted in 1990. Its military wing, Umkhonto weSizwe (MK), was established in 1961, with Mandela as commander-in-chief. The ANC became South Africa's governing party after the nation's first democratic elections on 27 April 1994.

Aucamp, Brigadier

Based in Pretoria, he was in charge of security in all prisons that had political inmates. He would visit Robben Island Maximum Security Prison several times a year. He was also a member of the Prison Board which had the task of monitoring prisoners and to recommend them for a higher grade. In Mandela's autobiography written in prison, he wrote: 'Brig. Aucamp: (a) Did well as officer commanding (b) position of Security Officer difficult – changes man's personality (c) had direct access to Minister (d) became quite unpopular (e) allowed correspondence between self and Zami [Winnie Mandela]'.

Ayob, Ismail

(1942–). Qualified as a barrister in London and returned to South Africa where he practised law from 1969, acting mainly for opponents of the apartheid regime. He served as an attorney for Mandela while he was in prison and for some years after his release. The pair split acrimoniously in 2004.

Benson, Mary

(1919–2000). A friend of Mandela's, Benson was a journalist, author, and anti-apartheid activist. After serving as an aide to various generals in World War II she settled in England. She returned to South Africa in 1957 and worked to raise funds for the defence of Mandela and 155 other accused in the Treason Trial. Mandela visited her in London on his clandestine trip out of South Africa in 1962. Among her books is *Mandela: The Man and the Movement* (New York: W. W. Norton, 1986).

Bernstein, Lionel (Rusty)

(1920–2002). Architect and anti-apartheid activist. Leading member of the Communist Party of South Africa. Founding member and leader of the Congress of Democrats, one of the participating organisations in the 1955 Congress of the People at which the Freedom Charter was adopted. Defendant in the 1956 Treason Trial. After being acquitted in the Rivonia Trial, he and his wife, Hilda, went into exile (they crossed into neighbouring Botswana on foot). He remained a leading member of the ANC, whilst practising as an architect.

Bizos, George
(1927–). Greek-born human rights lawyer. Member and co-founder of the National Council of Lawyers for Human Rights. Committee member of the ANC's Legal and Constitutional Committee. Legal advisor for the Convention for a Democratic South Africa. Defence lawyer in the Rivonia Trial. Also acted for high-profile anti-apartheid activists, including the families of Steve Biko, Chris Hani, and the Cradock Four during the trials of the Truth and Reconciliation Commission. Appointed by Mandela to South Africa's Judicial Services Commission.

Botha, P. W.
(1916–2006). Prime minister of South Africa, 1978–84. First executive state president, 1984–89. Advocate of the apartheid system. In 1985 Mandela rejected Botha's offer to release him on the condition that he rejected violence. Botha refused to testify at the Truth and Reconciliation Commission in 1998 about apartheid crimes.

Brandfort
A small town in the Free State province that was established in the mid-1800s in honour of President Brand of the then Orange Free State (now Free State) after he visited a church on a farm. It housed a British concentration camp for Boer women and children during the Second Boer War (1899–1902). Prime Minister H. F. Verwoerd completed his high school education in the town. Winnie Mandela was banished there by the apartheid regime in 1977 and lived there until 1985.

Buthelezi (née Mzila), Irene
A family friend and also the wife of Chief Mangosuthu Buthelezi. Mandela also refers to her as Mndhlunkulu and Umdlunkulu, a royal term. When Mandela worked in the mines in 1942 and 1943 he stayed at the Witwatersrand Native Labour Association Compound. It was here that he met Irene Mzila, the daughter of the compound manager.

Buthelezi, Mangosuthu Gatsha (also called by his clan name Shenge; Mandela sometimes spelled his surname Butelezi and sometimes spelled his first name as Mangosutu)
(1928–). South African politician and Zulu prince. Founder and president of the Inkatha Freedom Party in 1975. Chief minister of the KwaZulu Bantustan. Appointed South African minister of home affairs 1994–2004, and acted as president several times during Mandela's presidency.

Cachalia (née Asvat), Amina (also referred to as Aminabehn or Aminaben – *ben* is the Gujarati word for 'sister')
(1930–2013). Anti-apartheid and women's rights activist. Member of the ANC and Transvaal Indian Congress. Co-founder and treasurer of the Federation of South African Women. Founder of the Women's Progressive Union. Married Yusuf Cachalia. Banning orders from 1963 to 1978 prevented her from attending social gatherings or political meetings, entering any place of education or publishing house, and leaving the magisterial district of Johannesburg.

Cachalia, Ismail Ahmad (Maulvi)
(1908–2003). Anti-apartheid activist. Leading member of the South African Indian Congress, Transvaal Indian Congress and ANC. Key participant in the 1946 Passive Resistance Campaign. Deputy volunteer-in-chief to Mandela in the 1952 Defiance Campaign, and amongst the twenty accused in the Defiance Campaign Trial. With Moses Kotane, he attended the Bandung Conference, a meeting of African-Asian states focused on peace, decolonisation, and African-Asian economic development, in Bandung, Indonesia, in 1955. Fled to Botswana

in 1964 and set up ANC offices in New Delhi. His father, Ahmad Mohamed Cachalia, was a close associate of Gandhi's and was chairperson of the Transvaal British Indian Association, 1908–18.

Cachalia, Yusuf
(1915–95). Political activist. Secretary of the South African Indian Congress. Brother of Maulvi Cachalia. Husband of Amina Cachalia. Co-accused with Mandela and eighteen others in the 1952 Defiance Campaign Trial. They were convicted and sentenced to nine months imprisonment, suspended for two years. Banned continuously from 1953.

Carlson, Joel
(1926–2001). One of Mandela's attorneys who began representing opponents of apartheid after his 1957 exposé of the brutal working conditions of farmworkers. He presented nearly 100 cases of torture to the courts. Several attempts were made on his life and he left South Africa in 1971 and lived in the United States of America.

Chiba, Isu (Laloo)
(1930–2017). Anti-apartheid activist. Member of the South African Communist Party and Transvaal Indian Congress. Platoon commander of MK. Tortured by the South African security police causing him to lose the hearing in one of his ears. Member of MK's Second National High Command, for which he was sentenced to eighteen years' imprisonment, which he served on Robben Island. Assisted in transcribing Mandela's autobiographical manuscript in prison. Released in 1982. Member of the United Democratic Front. MP, 1994–2004. Received the Order of Luthuli in Silver in 2004 for his lifetime contribution to the struggle for a non-racial, non-sexist, just, and democratic South Africa.

Coetsee, Hendrik (Kobie)
(1931–2000). South African politician, lawyer, administrator, and negotiator. Deputy minister for defence and national intelligence, 1978. Minister of justice, 1980. Held meetings with Mandela from 1985 about creating the conditions for talks between the National Party and the ANC. Elected president of the Senate following South Africa's first democratic elections in 1994.

Communist Party South Africa (Communist Party of South Africa)
(*See* South African Communist Party.)

Congress Alliance
Established in the 1950s and made up of the ANC, South African Indian Congress, Congress of Democrats and the South African Coloured People's Organisation. When the South African Congress of Trade Unions was established in 1955, it became the fifth member of the Alliance. It was instrumental in organising the Congress of the People and mobilising clauses for inclusion in the Freedom Charter.

Congress of the People
The Congress of the People was the culmination of a year-long campaign where members of the Congress Alliance visited homes across the length and breadth of South Africa recording people's demands for a free South Africa, which were included in the Freedom Charter. Held 25–26 June 1955 in Kliptown, Johannesburg, it was attended by 3,000 delegates. The Freedom Charter was adopted on the second day of the Congress.

Cyprian, King Bhekuzulu Nyangayezizwe kaSolomon

(1924–68). King of the Zulu nation from 1948 until his death in 1968. He succeeded his father, King Solomon kaDinizulu. He was the father of the current king of the Zulus, Goodwill Zwelithini.

Dadoo, Dr Yusuf

(1909–83). Medical doctor, anti-apartheid activist and orator. President of South African Indian Congress. Deputy to Oliver Tambo on the Revolutionary Council of MK. Chairman of the South African Communist Party, 1972–83. Leading member of the ANC. First jailed in 1940 for anti-war activities, and then for six months during the 1946 Passive Resistance Campaign. Was among the twenty accused with Mandela in the 1952 Defiance Campaign Trial. He went underground during the 1960 State of Emergency, and into exile to escape arrest. Awarded the ANC's highest honour, Isitwalandwe Seaparankoe, in 1955 at the Congress of the People.

Dalindyebo, Buyelekhaya Zwelibanzi a Sabata

(1964–). The son of Sabata Jonguhlanga Dalindyebo, he reigned as Thembu king from 1989 until December 2015 when he was imprisoned for offences including culpable homicide, kidnapping, arson, and assault. He was customarily dethroned as a result.

Dalindyebo, Chief Jongintaba

(d. 1942). Chief and regent of the Thembu people. Became Mandela's guardian following his father's death. Mandela went to live with him at the Great Place at Mqhekezweni when he was twelve years old.

Dalindyebo, King Sabata Jonguhlanga

(1928–86). Paramount chief of the Transkei, 1954–80. Leader of the Democratic Progressive Party. Nephew of Chief Jongintaba Dalindyebo. Fled to Zambia in 1980 after being convicted of violating the dignity of President Matanzima of the Transkei. Sabata was the great-grandson of King Ngangelizwe.

Daniels, Edward (Eddie; Mandela sometimes refers to him as Danie)

(1928–2017). Political activist. Member of the Liberal Party of South Africa. Member of the African Resistance Movement which sabotaged non-human targets as a statement against the government. Served a fifteen-year sentence in Robben Island Prison where he was held in B Section with Mandela. He was banned immediately after his release in 1979. Received the Order of Luthuli in Silver from the South African government in 2005.

de Klerk, Frederik Willem (F. W.)

(1936–). Lawyer. President of South Africa, 1989–94. Leader of the National Party, 1989–97. In February 1990 he unbanned the ANC and other organisations and released Mandela from prison. Deputy president with Thabo Mbeki under Mandela from 1994 to 1996. Leader of New National Party, 1997. Awarded the Prince of Asturias Award in 1992 and the Nobel Peace Prize in 1993 with Nelson Mandela, for his role in the peaceful end to apartheid.

Defiance Campaign Against Unjust Laws (Mandela also refers to it as the Defiance Campaign)

Initiated by the ANC in December 1951, and launched with the South African Indian Congress on 26 June 1952, against six apartheid laws. The campaign involved individuals breaking racist laws such as entering premises reserved for 'whites only', breaking curfews, and courting arrest. Mandela was appointed national volunteer-in-chief and Maulvi Cachalia as his deputy. Over 8,500 volunteers were imprisoned for their participation in the Defiance Campaign.

Dingake, Michael Kitso

(1928–). Joined the African National Congress in 1952 and went into hiding after the Rivonia arrests in 1963. He left South Africa to work underground. As he was born in the British protectorate of Bechuanaland (Botswana) he had the protection of the British government. Nevertheless, in 1965 he was taken off a train in Southern Rhodesia and unlawfully handed over to South African police. He was driven to South Africa where he was tortured, charged, and convicted for sabotage. He was sentenced to fifteen years' imprisonment which he served in the same section on Robben Island as Mandela. In late 1967 he was transferred from the island to Pretoria where he was again tortured for information. A few weeks later he was returned to Robben Island. On his release in 1981 he was repatriated to Botswana.

Eprile, Cecil L.

(1914–93). Journalist and editor. Wrote and edited for *Arthur Barlow's Weekly*, the *Sunday Times*, and *Sunday Express*. Editor-in-chief of *Golden City Post* (*Drum* magazine's sister paper), 1955–67, where he trained many prominent black South African journalists.

Fischer, Abram (Bram)

(1908–75). Lawyer and political and anti-apartheid activist. Leader of the Communist Party of South Africa. Member of the Congress of Democrats. Charged with incitement for his involvement in the African Mine Workers' Strike for better wages in 1946. Successfully defended Mandela and other leading ANC members in the Treason Trial. Led the defence in the Rivonia Trial, 1963–64. Continually subjected to banning orders, and in 1966 he was sentenced to life imprisonment for violating the Suppression of Communism Act and conspiring to commit sabotage. Awarded the Lenin Peace Prize in 1967.

Freedom Charter

A statement of the principles of the Congress Alliance, adopted at the Congress of the People in Kliptown, Soweto, on 26 June 1955. The Congress Alliance rallied thousands of volunteers across South Africa to record the demands of the people. The Freedom Charter espoused equal rights for all South Africans regardless of race, as well as land reform, improved working and living conditions, the fair distribution of wealth, compulsory education, and fairer laws. The Freedom Charter was a powerful tool used in the fight against apartheid.

Goldberg, Denis

(1933–). Anti-apartheid and political activist. Member of the South African Communist Party. Co-founder and leader of the Congress of Democrats. Technical officer in MK. Arrested at Rivonia in 1963 and subsequently served a life sentence in Pretoria Local Prison. On his release in 1985 he went into exile in the UK and represented the ANC at the Anti-Apartheid Committee of the United Nations. Founded Community HEART in 1995 to help poor black South Africans. Returned to South Africa in 2002 and was appointed special advisor to Minister of Water Affairs and Forestry Ronnie Kasrils, who was named as a co-conspriator in the Rivonia Trial.

Gumede, Archibald Jacob

(1914–98). The son of Josiah Tshangana Gumede a founder of the South African Native National Conference (SANNC), a precursor to the ANC, Gumede, an anti-apartheid activist and lawyer, joined the ANC in 1949. He was an accused with Nelson Mandela and 154 others in the infamous 1956 Treason Trial which went on for four and a half years and resulted in all the accused being acquitted. In 1983 he was elected as a joint president with Albertina Sisulu and Oscar Mpetha of the United Democratic Front. He and a group of activists famously sought refuge in the British consulate in Durban in 1984 when the security police threatened to detain them, which they did when they left the building after ninety days. They were charged with high treason. Charges against Gumede and eleven others were withdrawn in December 1985 and also for the four remaining accused in June 1986.

Guzana, Knowledge (Mandela refers to him as Dambisa)

(1916–). A fellow student at University College of Fort Hare with Mandela, he went on to a political career in the Transkei after qualifying as an attorney. He was the leader of the New Democratic Party in the Transkei which rejected 'independence' of black homelands or Bantustans. He led the party until 1976 when he was replaced by Hector Ncokazi.

Gwala, Harry (also called by his clan name Mphephetwa) Themba

(1920–95). Known as 'The Lion of the Midlands', he was a school teacher and activist in the South African Communist Party and the ANC Youth League. In 1964 he was arrested and charged with sabotage for recruiting people to MK. He was sentenced to eight years in prison and served his sentence on Robben Island until 1972. He was arrested again in 1975 and sentenced to life imprisonment and sent again to Robben Island. He contracted motor neuron disease, which led to the loss of the use of his arms. As a consequence of his illness he was released in 1988. In 1992 he was awarded the ANC's highest honour, Isitwalandwe Seaparankoe.

Healdtown

Healdtown was a boarding school in Fort Beaufort, run by the Methodist Church. Nelson Mandela enrolled there in 1937 and completed his matric there in 1938. He took up long-distance running there and in his second year became a prefect.

Hepple, Bob

(1934–2015). Lawyer, academic, and anti-apartheid activist. Member of the Congress of Democrats and South African Congress of Trade Unions. Assisted Mandela to represent himself in 1962 following his arrest for leaving the country illegally and for inciting workers to strike. Arrested at Liliesleaf Farm in 1963, but the charges were dropped on the condition that he appeared as a state witness. Named as a co-conspirator in the Rivonia Trial. He subsequently fled South Africa. Knighted in 2004.

Joseph (née Fennell), Helen

(1905–92). Teacher, social worker, and anti-apartheid and women's rights activist. Founding member of the Congress of Democrats. National secretary of Federation of South African Women. Leading organiser of the 1956 Women's March of 20,000 women to Pretoria's Union Buildings. An accused in the 1956 Treason Trial. Placed under house arrest in 1962. Helped care for Zindziswa and Zenani Mandela when their parents were both imprisoned. Awarded the ANC's highest honour, Isitwalandwe Seaparankoe, in 1992.

Jozana, Xoliswa

(1952–). A daughter of K. D. Matanzima's by Princess Nosango. In 2017 she retired from the Department of Rural Development and Land Reform in South Africa where she was the chief director responsible for co-operation and development.

Kantor, James

(1927–75). Lawyer. Despite not being a member of the ANC or MK, he was put on trial at Rivonia, possibly due to the fact that his brother-in-law and business partner was Harold Wolpe who had been arrested at Liliesleaf Farm and named as a co-conspirator in the Rivonia Trial. Was later acquitted and fled South Africa.

Kathrada, Ahmed
(1929–2017). Anti-apartheid activist, politician, political prisoner, and MP. Leading member of the ANC and of the South African Communist Party. Founding member of the Transvaal Indian Volunteer Corps and its successor, the Transvaal Indian Youth Congress. Co-accused with Mandela in the Defiance Campaign Trial of 1952, and one of the last twenty-eight accused in the Treason Trial who were acquitted in 1961. Placed under house arrest in 1962. Arrested at Liliesleaf Farm in July 1963 and charged with sabotage in the Rivonia Trial. Imprisoned on Robben Island, 1964–82, then Pollsmoor Prison until his release on 15 October 1989. MP from 1994, after South Africa's first democratic elections, and served as political advisor to President Mandela. Chairperson of the Robben Island Council, 1994–2006. Awarded Isitwalandwe Seaparankoe, the ANC's highest honour, in 1992; the Pravasi Bharatiya Samman Award from the President of India; and several honorary doctorates.

Kente, Gibson
(1932–2004). Considered by many to be the father of black theatre in South Africa, between 1960 and 1990 he produced more than twenty plays in the genre of what became known as the 'township musical'. He wrote music for Miriam Makeba in the 1950s. Mandela refers to him as 'nephew' in his letter to him as they were both from the Madiba clan.

Kruger, James (Jimmy)
(1917–87). Politician. Minister of justice and police, 1974–79. President of the Senate, 1979–80. Member of the National Party. Infamously remarked that Steve Biko's death in detention in 1977 left him 'cold'.

Le Grange, Louis L.
(1928–91). Joined the cabinet of the ruling National Party in 1975. In 1979 to 1980 he served as minister of prisons and from 1979 to 1982 as minister of police. From 1982 to 1986 he was minister of law and order.

Lukhele, Douglas (Duggie)
Former legal colleague. Moved to Swaziland and became the attorney-general there. He did his articles at the firm Mandela and Tambo in the 1950s.

Luthuli, Chief Albert John Mvumbi
(1898–1967). Teacher, anti-apartheid activist, and minister of religion. Chief of Groutville Reserve. President-general of the ANC, 1952–67. From 1953 he was confined to his home by government bans. Defendant in the 1956 Treason Trial. Sentenced to six months (suspended) in 1960 after publicly burning his passbook and calling for a national day of mourning following the Sharpeville Massacre. Awarded the Nobel Peace Prize in 1960 for his non-violent role in the struggle against apartheid. Awarded the ANC's highest honour, Isitwalandwe Seaparankoe, in 1955 at the Congress of the People.

Luthuli, Nokhukhanya
The wife of Chief Albert Luthuli. When Mandela writes Nkosikazi Luthuli, it means Mrs. Luthuli.

Madikizela, Columbus Kokani
Also known as C. K., he was Winnie Mandela's father. In letters to his wife, Mandela referred respectfully to him as Bawo. A history teacher, he later became the minister of forestry and agriculture in the Transkei government under K. D. Matanzima.

Madikizela-Mandela, Nomzamo Winifred (Winnie, Nobandla, Nomzamo, Mhlope, Zami and Ngutyana)

(1936–). Social worker and anti-apartheid and women's rights activist. Member of the ANC. Married to Nelson Mandela, 1958–96 (separated 1992). Mother of Zenani and Zindziswa Mandela. First qualified black medical social worker at the Baragwanath Hospital in Johannesburg. Held in solitary confinement for seventeen months in 1969. Placed under house arrest from 1970 and subjected to a series of banning orders from 1962 to 1987. Established the Black Women's Federation, 1975, and the Black Parents' Association, 1976, in response to the Soweto Uprising. President of the ANC Women's League, 1993–2003. ANC MP.

Maharaj, Satyandranath (Mac)

(1935–). Academic, politician, political and anti-apartheid activist, political prisoner, and MP. Leading member of the ANC, South African Communist Party, and MK. Convicted of sabotage in 1964 and sentenced to twelve years' imprisonment which he served on Robben Island. Helped to secretly transcribe Mandela's autobiography, *Long Walk to Freedom*, and smuggled it out of prison when he was released in 1976. Commanded Operation Vulindlela (Vula), an ANC underground operation to establish an internal underground leadership. Maharaj served on the secretariat of the Convention for a Democratic South Africa. Minister of transport, 1994–99. Envoy to President Jacob Zuma.

Maki

(*See* Mandela, Makaziwe.)

Mandela (née Mase), Evelyn Ntoko (also referred to as Mqwati or Ntoko)

(1922–2004). Nurse. Married to Nelson Mandela, 1944–57. Mother to Madiba Thembekile (1945–69), Makaziwe (1947) who died at nine months old, Makgatho (1950–2005) and Makaziwe (1954–). Cousin of Walter Sisulu who first introduced her to Mandela. Married a retired Sowetan businessman, Simon Rakeepile, in 1998.

Mandela, Madiba Thembekile (Thembi; Mandela also spells it Tembi sometimes)

(1945–69). Mandela's eldest son to his first wife, Evelyn. Died in a car accident.

Mandela, Makaziwe

(1947). Mandela's first-born daughter to his first wife, Evelyn. Died at nine months old.

Mandela, Makaziwe (Maki)

(1954–). Mandela's eldest daughter to his first wife, Evelyn.

Mandela, Makgatho (Kgatho)

(1950–2005). Mandela's second-born son to his first wife, Evelyn. Lawyer. Died of AIDS complications on 6 January 2005 in Johannesburg following the death of his second wife, Zondi Mandela, who died from pneumonia as a complication of AIDS in July 2003.

Mandela, Mandla Zwelivelile

(1974–). Mandela's oldest grandson and first-born child of Makgatho Mandela. He is now Chief of the Mvezo Traditional Council.

Mandela, Nandi

(1968–). Mandela's second grandchild and youngest daughter of Thembekile and Thoko Mandela. She was a year old when her father was killed in a car accident.

Mandela, Ndileka

(1965–). Mandela's first grandchild and eldest daughter of Thembekile and Thoko Mandela. She was four years old when her father was killed in a car accident.

Mandela, Nkosi Mphakanyiswa Gadla

(d. 1930). Chief, counsellor, and advisor. Descendant of the Ixhiba house. Mandela's father. Deprived of his chieftainship following a dispute with a local white magistrate.

Mandela, Nolusapho Rose Rayne (referred to as 'Rennie')

The mother of Mandela's grandson Mandela Mandela. She was married to Mandela's second son Makgatho.

Mandela, Nosekeni Fanny

(d. 1968). Mandela's mother. Third wife of Nkosi Mphakanyiswa Gadla Mandela.

Mandela, Thoko (aka Molly de Jager)

The wife of Thembekile Mandela and the mother of their two daughters. She was in the car accident which killed her husband and her sister Irene Simelane. Her brother was injured in the same accident. Newspaper articles on the accident refer to her as Molly de Jager which is a name she adopted from a relative which meant she could be classified under apartheid laws as coloured and live in a better area. Mandela also refers to her as *molokazana* which means daughter-in-law. After her husband's death she went back to her maiden surname of Mhlanga.

Mandela, Winnie

(*See* Madikizela-Mandela, Nomzamo Winifred.)

Mandela, Zenani (Zeni) Nomadabi Nosizwe

(1959–). Mandela's first-born daughter to his second wife, Winnie. Her names mean 'What have you brought?' and Battle of the Nation. She is South Africa's ambassador to Mauritius.

Mandela, Zindziswa (Zindzi)

(1960–). Mandela's second-born daughter to his second wife, Winnie. Her first name means 'well-established'; she is named after the daughter of the Xhosa poet, Mqhayi. She is South Africa's ambassador to Denmark.

Mandela, Zoleka (1980–)

Mandela's granddaughter and only daughter of Zindziswa Mandela.

Mandela, Zondwa (1985–)

Mandela's grandson and oldest son of Zindziswa Mandela.

Masemola, Jafta Kgalabi ('Jeff')

(1929–90). Known as the 'Tiger of Azania', he was a member of the ANC Youth League and a founder of the armed wing of the Pan Africanist Congress. After being arrested in 1962 and charged with sabotage for blowing up power lines and smuggling freedom fighters out of South Africa, he was sentenced to life imprisonment on July 1963. On 13 October 1989, while still in prison, he met with Nelson Mandela at Victor Verster Prison. It was rumoured that they discussed unity between the ANC and the PAC. He was released from prison on 15 October 1989, and on 17 April 1990 he was killed in a mysterious car accident.

Matanzima, Kaiser Daliwonga (K. D.) (also referred to as Wonga)

(1915–2003). Thembu chief and politician. Mandela's nephew. Member of the United Transkei Territorial Council, 1955, and an executive member of the Transkei Territorial Authority, 1956. Chief minister of the Transkei, 1963. Established and led the Transkeian National Independence Party with his brother George Matanzima. First prime minister of the Transkei Bantustan when it gained nominal independence in 1976. State president of the Transkei, 1979–86. He was the great-grandson of King Matanzima.

Matanzima, Mthetho

(d. 1972). A son of K. D. Matanzima's by Princess Dade. He was educated at University College of Fort Hare, passing his law examination in 1968. Chief of the Noqayti region. He died in 1972.

Matthews, Frieda Deborah Bokwe

(1905–98). The daughter of Reverend John Knox Bokwe, a leading Xhosa intellectual and hymn writer of the 1880s. She was one of the first black women to earn a university degree in South Africa. A teacher herself, she married educationalist Z. K. Matthews. She published *Remembrances* in 1984.

Matthews, Vincent Joseph Gaobakwe (Bakwe)

(1929–2010). Matthews was the son of Professor Z. K. Matthews and Frieda Matthews. Both he and his father were charged with treason in 1956 along with 154 other anti-apartheid activists. He qualified as an attorney and while in exile became assistant attorney-general of Botswana. He returned to South Africa in 1992 and that year left the ANC. He was a member of Parliament for the Inkatha Freedom Party from 1994 and deputy minister of safety and security from 1994 to 1999.

Matthews, Professor Zachariah Keodirelang (Z. K.)

(1901–68). Academic, politician, and anti-apartheid activist. Member of the ANC. First black South African to obtain a BA degree at a South African institution, 1923. First black South African to obtain an LLB degree in South Africa, 1930. Conceptualised the Congress of the People and the Freedom Charter. Following the Sharpeville Massacre, with Chief Albert Luthuli he organised a 'stay-away', a national day of mourning, which took place on 28 March 1960. In 1965 he retired to Botswana, and became its ambassador to the USA.

Mbeki, Archibald Mvuyelwa Govan (clan name, Zizi)

(1910–2001). Historian and anti-apartheid activist. Leading member of the ANC and the South African Communist Party. Served on the High Command of MK. Father of Thabo Mbeki (president of South Africa, 1999–2008). Convicted in the Rivonia Trial and sentenced to life imprisonment. Released from Robben Island Prison, 1987. Served in South Africa's post-apartheid Senate, 1994–1997, as deputy president of the Senate, and its successor, the National Council of Provinces, 1997–99. Awarded the ANC's highest honour, Isitwalandwe Seaparankoe, in 1980.

Meer, Professor Fatima (also referred to as Fatimabehn and Fatimaben – *ben* means sister in Gujarati)

(1928–2010). Writer, academic, and anti-apartheid and women's rights activist. Married Ismail Meer, 1950. Established Student Passive Resistance Committee in support of the 1946 Passive Resistance Campaign against apartheid. Founding member of Federation of South African Women. First black woman to be appointed as a lecturer at a white South African university (University of Natal), 1956. Banned from 1953 and escaped an assassination attempt.

She embraced the Black Consciousness ideology. Founded the Institute of Black Research, 1975. First president of the Black Women's Federation, established in 1975. Author of *Higher Than Hope* (published 1988), the first authorised biography of Mandela.

Meer, Ismail Chota I. C.

(1918–2000). Lawyer and anti-apartheid activist. He met and befriended Nelson Mandela in 1946 when they were studying law at the University of the Witwatersrand in Johannesburg. He joined the Communist Party of South Africa while at university and played pivotal roles in the 1946 Passive Resistance Campaign and the 1952 Defiance Campaign as well as participated in the drawing up of the Freedom Charter. He was married to Professor Fatima Meer.

Mhlaba, Raymond (clan name, Ndobe)

(1920–2005). Anti-apartheid activist, politician, diplomat, and political prisoner. Leading member of ANC and South African Communist Party. Commander-in-chief of MK. Arrested in 1963 at Rivonia and sentenced to life imprisonment at the Rivonia Trial. Imprisoned on Robben Island until he was transferred to Pollsmoor Prison in 1982. Released in 1989. He was involved in the negotiations with the National Party government leading to the democratisation of South Africa. Member of the ANC National Executive Committee, 1991. Premier of the Eastern Cape, 1994. South African high commissioner to Uganda, 1997. Awarded the ANC's highest honour, Isitwalandwe Seaparankoe, in 1992.

MK

(*See* Umkhonto weSizwe.)

Mkwayi, Wilton Zimasile (clan name, Mbona; nickname, Bri Bri)

(1923–2004). Trade unionist, political activist, and political prisoner. Member of the ANC and South African Congress of Trade Unions. Union organiser for African Textile Workers in Port Elizabeth. Volunteer in the 1952 Defiance Campaign, and later active in the campaign for the Congress of the People. Escaped during the 1956 Treason Trial and went to Lesotho. Joined MK and had military training in the People's Republic of China. Became MK's commander-in-chief after the arrests at Liliesleaf Farm. Convicted and sentenced to life in what became known as the Little Rivonia Trial. He served his sentence on Robben Island. Released October 1989. Elected to the Senate in the National Assembly in 1994, then deployed to the Eastern Cape Provincial Legislature, where he served until his retirement from public life in 1999. Awarded the ANC's highest honour, Isitwalandwe Seaparankoe, in 1992.

Mlangeni, Andrew Mokete (clan name, Motlokwa; nickname, Mpandla)

(1926–). Anti-apartheid activist, political prisoner, and MP. Member of the ANC Youth League, ANC and MK. Convicted at the Rivonia Trial in 1963 and sentenced to life imprisonment. Served eighteen years on Robben Island and was transferred to Pollsmoor Prison in 1982. Awarded the ANC's highest honour, Isitwalandwe Seaparankoe, in 1992.

Motlana, Ntatho Harrison

(1925–2008). Dr Ntatho Motlana, a medical doctor, community leader, political campaigner, businessman, and close friend of Nelson and Winnie Mandela. He entered extra-parliamentary politics in the 1940s and was appointed secretary of the ANC Youth League in 1949. Chargted with Mandela eighteen others in the Defiance Campaign Trial of 1952. He served two banning orders and one period of detention. In the 1970s he helped to establish the Black Parents' Association to help those affected by the 1976 student uprising. He also founded the Committee of Ten, an influential organisation of Soweto residents. In the 1980s he led the Soweto Civic Association, a body affiliated to the broad-based United Democratic Front.

Motsoaledi, Elias (clan name, Mokoni)

(1924–94). Trade unionist, anti-apartheid activist, and political prisoner. Member of the ANC, South African Communist Party, and Council of Non-European Trade Unions. Banned after the 1952 Defiance Campaign. Helped to establish the South African Congress of Trade Unions in 1955. Imprisoned for four months during the 1960 State of Emergency and detained again under the ninety-day detention laws of 1963. Sentenced to life imprisonment at the Rivonia Trial and imprisoned on Robben Island from 1964 to 1989. Elected to the ANC's National Executive Committee following his release. Awarded the ANC's highest honour, Isitwalandwe Seaparankoe, in 1992.

Mpetha, Oscar

(1909–94). A trade unionist and political activist from the Transkei, he joined the ANC in 1951 and in 1958 became president of the Cape ANC. In 1983 he was sentenced to five years in prison for inciting a riot in which two white people were killed. In the same year, he was elected as one of three co-presidents of the newly formed United Democratic Front. He served most of his prison sentence wheelchair-bound in hospital after both legs had been amputated due to diabetes. He was released on 15 October 1989 with a group of prisoners including the last remaining Rivonia trialists.

Naicker, Dr Gangathura Mohambry (Monty)

(1910–78). Medical doctor, politician, and anti-apartheid activist. Co-founder and first chairperson of the Anti-Segregation Council. President of the Natal Indian Congress, 1945–63. Signatory of the 'Doctor's Pact' of March 1947, a statement of cooperation between the ANC, Transvaal Indian Congress, and Natal Indian Congress, which was also signed by Dr Albert Xuma (president of the ANC) and Dr Yusuf Dadoo (president of the TIC).

Naidoo, Indres Elatchininatha

(1936–2016). A member of the South African Communist Party and the Transvaal Indian Congress, he spent ten years on Robben Island for his activities on behalf of MK. On his release he published the book *Island in Chains: Prisoner 885/63*. A son of Ama and Thambi 'Naran' Naidoo and brother to Shanti Naidoo.

Naidoo, 'Shanti' Shanthivathie

(1935–). The eldest of five children of Ama and Thambi 'Naran' Naidoo, she became a political activist while still at school. She was a member of the Transvaal Indian Congress and the Federation of South African Women. Banned from the 1960s, she was detained in 1969. When she refused to testify against Winnie Mandela she was convicted and sentenced to two months in prison. Her banning orders meant that she could not visit her brother Indres Naidoo who was imprisoned on Robben Island from 1963 for ten years. She was refused permission to leave the country until 1972 and visited him in prison for the first time before she left South Africa. She lived in England and at the ANC's school in Tanzania. She returned to South Africa with her husband Dominic Tweedie in 1991.

Nair, Billy

(1929–2008). Politician, anti-apartheid activist, political prisoner, and MP. Member of the ANC, Natal Indian Congress, South African Communist Party, South African Congress of Trade Unions, and MK. Named as co-conspirator in the Rivonia Trial, he was charged with sabotage in 1963 and imprisoned on Robben Island for twenty years. Joined the United Democratic Front on his release. Arrested in 1990 and accused of being part of Operation Vula, an underground operation to smuggle freedom fighters into South Africa and keep the lines of communication open with ANC leaders in prison, at home, or in exile. MP in the new democratic South Africa.

National Party
Conservative South African political party established in Bloemfontein in 1914 by Afrikaner nationalists. Governing party of South Africa, June 1948 to May 1994. Enforced apartheid, a system of legal racial segregation that favoured minority rule by the white population. Disbanded in 2004.

Ngoyi, Lilian Masediba
(1911–80). Politician, anti-apartheid and women's rights activist, and orator. Leading member of the ANC. First woman elected to the ANC Executive Committee, 1956. President of the ANC Women's League. President of Federation of South African Women, 1956. Led the Women's March against pass laws, 1956. Charged and acquitted in the Treason Trial. Detained in the 1960 State of Emergency. Detained and held in solitary confinement for seventy-one days in 1963 under the ninety-day detention law. Continuously subjected to banning orders. Awarded the ANC's highest honour, Isitwalandwe Seaparankoe, in 1982.

Njongwe, James 'Jimmy' Lowell Zwelinzima
(1919–76). One of the first two black male graduates of the University of the Witwatersrand medical school in 1946, he was the first black medical doctor to open a practice in Port Elizabeth in the Eastern Cape. He was on the executive of the ANC Youth League and later president of the ANC in the Cape. He was banned and forced to resign from his position. He left Port Elizabeth and established his practice in Matatiele in the Transkei. He was detained in the 1960 State of Emergency.

Nokwe, Philemon Pearce Dumasile Nokwe (Duma)
(1927–78). Political activist and advocate. Taught by O.R. Tambo at St. Peter's High School, Johannesburg and was elected to the executive of the ANC Youth League while a student. He was, with Mandela, in the last group of accused in the 1956 Treason Trial. He attended Mandela's marriage to Winnie Madikizela. Nokwe served as the secretary-general of the ANC from 1958 to 1969. Named as co-consprirator in the Rivonia Trial. He went into exile in 1963 and died in Zambia.

Omar, Abdulla 'Dullah'
(1934–2004). Anti-apartheid activist and an advocate who attended to some of Mandela's legal work while he was in prison. He was a member of the Unity Movement before he joined and became a leading member of the United Democratic Front from 1983. He was banned and detained by the apartheid regime which also tried to assassinate him. He served as democratic South Africa's first minister of justice under Nelson Mandela from 1994. In 1999, under President Thabo Mbeki, he became minister of transport.

OR
(See Tambo, Oliver.)

Pan Africanist Congress
Breakaway organisation of the ANC founded in 1959 by Robert Sobukwe, who championed the philosophy of 'Africa for Africans'. The PAC's campaigns included a nationwide protest against pass laws, ten days before the ANC was to start its own campaign. It culminated in the Sharpeville Massacre on 21 March 1960, in which police shot dead sixty-nine unarmed protesters. Banned, along with the ANC, in April 1960. Unbanned on 2 February 1990.

Paton, Alan

(1903–88). Teacher and author of the famous South African novel *Cry, the Beloved Country* (published 1948). Principal of the Diepkloof Reformatory, 1935–49. In 1953 he founded the Liberal Party of South Africa which fought against the apartheid legislation of the ruling National Party. He gave evidence in mitigation of sentence at the Rivonia Trial for Nelson Mandela and his colleagues.

Pogrund, Benjamin

(1933–). A journalist and friend of Mandela's, he worked for the *Rand Daily Mail* from 1958 and covered the Sharpeville Massacre on 21 March 1960. Mandela soon told him of his belief that the days of non-violent protest were over. Pogrund moved to London in 1986.

Pollsmoor Maximum Security Prison

Prison in the suburb of Tokai, Cape Town. Mandela was moved there along with Walter Sisulu, Raymond Mhlaba, Andrew Mlangeni, and, later, Ahmed Kathrada in 1982.

Qunu

Rural village in South Africa's Eastern Cape province where Mandela lived after his family moved from his birthplace of Mvezo.

Ramphele, Mamphela Aletta

(1947–). Anti-apartheid activist and a founding member of the Black Consciousness Movement, medical doctor, academic, and businesswoman. When she was the partner of Steve Biko she was banished in 1977 by the apartheid regime to Tzaneen in the then Northern Transvaal (now Limpopo province) where she remained until 1984. She joined the University of Cape Town as a research fellow in 1986 and one of its vice-chancellors in 1991. In 2000 she was appointed one of the four managing directors of the World Bank.

Rivonia Trial

Trial between 1963 and 1964 in which eleven leading members of the Congress Alliance were initially charged with sabotage and faced the death penalty. Named after the suburb of Rivonia, Johannesburg, where six members of the MK High Command were arrested at their hideout, Liliesleaf Farm, on 11 July 1963. Incriminating documents, including a proposal for a guerrilla insurgency named Operation Mayibuye, were seized. Mandela, who was already serving a sentence for incitement and leaving South Africa illegally, was implicated, and his notes on guerrilla warfare and his diary from his trip through Africa in 1962 were also seized. Rather than being cross-examined as a witness, Mandela made a statement from the dock on 20 April 1964. This became his famous 'I am prepared to die' speech. On 11 June 1964, eight of the accused were convicted by Justice Qartus de Wet at the Palace of Justice in Pretoria, and the next day were sentenced to life imprisonment.

Robben Island

Island situated in Table Bay, 7 kilometres off the coast of Cape Town, measuring approximately 3.3 kilometres long and 1.9 kilometres wide. Has predominantly been used as a place of banishment and imprisonment, particularly for political prisoners, since Dutch settlement in the seventeenth century. Three men who later became South African presidents have been imprisoned there: Nelson Mandela (1964–82), Kgalema Motlanthe (1977–87) and Jacob Zuma (1963–73). It is now a World Heritage Site and museum.

Sikhakhane, Joyce Nomafa

(1943–). Journalist and anti-apartheid activist. Wrote about the families of political prisoners, including Albertina Sisulu and Winnie Mandela, which resulted in her being arrested under the Protection Against Communism Act, then re-detained under the Terrorism Act and forced to spend eighteen months in solitary confinement. Banned on her release. She fled South Africa in 1973. Employed by the Department of Intelligence in the democratic South Africa. In his letter to her, Mandela calls her Nomvula as she was engaged to a relative of his, John Fadana. They never married, as after they registered the marriage at the Magistrates Court the security police accused her of having broken her banning and restriction orders by going to the court without permission and that therefore the marriage was invalid. John Fadana was banished to the Ciskei where he married another woman and later died.

Sisulu (née Thethiwe), Nontsikelelo (Ntsiki) Albertina

(1918–2011). Nurse, midwife, anti-apartheid and women's rights activist, and MP. Leading ANC member. Married Walter Sisulu, whom she met through her nursing friend, Evelyn Mase (Mandela's first wife), 1944. Member of the ANC Women's League and Federation of South African Women. Played a leading role in the 1956 women's anti-pass protest. The first woman to be arrested under the General Law Amendment Act, 1963, during which time she was held in solitary confinement for ninety days. Continually subjected to banning orders and police harassment from 1963. She was elected as one of the three presidents of the United Democratic Front at its formation in August 1983. In 1985 she was charged with fifteen other United Democratic Front and trade union leaders for treason in what became known as the Pietermaritzburg Treason Trial. MP from 1994 until she retired in 1999. President of the World Peace Council, 1993–96. Recipient of the South African Women for Women Woman of Distinction Award 2003, in recognition of her courageous lifelong struggle for human rights and dignity.

Sisulu, Walter Ulyate Max (clan names, Xhamela – sometimes spelt by Mandela as Xamela and Tyhopho)

(1912–2003). Anti-apartheid activist and political prisoner. Husband of Albertina Sisulu. Met Mandela in 1941 and introduced him to Lazer Sidelsky who employed him as an articled clerk. Leader of the ANC, and generally considered to be the 'father of the struggle'. Co-founder of the ANC Youth League in 1944. Charged with Mandela and eighteen others under the Suppression of Communism Act for playing a leading role in the 1952 Defiance Campaign. Arrested and later acquitted in the 1956 Treason Trial. Continually served with banning orders and placed under house arrest following the banning of the ANC and Pan Africanist Congress. Helped establish MK, and served on its High Command. Went underground in 1963 and hid at Liliesleaf Farm, in Rivonia, where he was arrested on 11 July 1963. Found guilty of sabotage at the Rivonia Trial, and sentenced to life imprisonment on 12 June 1964. He served his sentence on Robben Island and at Pollsmoor Prison. Released on 15 October 1989. One of the ANC negotiating team with the apartheid government to end white rule. Awarded the ANC's highest honour, Isitwalandwe Seaparankoe, in 1992.

Sobukwe, Robert Mangaliso

(1924–78). Lawyer, anti-apartheid activist, and political prisoner. Member of the ANC Youth League and the ANC until he formed the Pan Africanist Congress based on the vision of 'Africa for Africans'. Editor of the *Africanist* newspaper. Arrested and detained following the Sharpeville Massacre in 1960. Convicted of incitement and sentenced to three years' imprisonment. Before he was released, the General Law Amendment Act No. 37 of 1963 was passed, which allowed for people already convicted of political offences to have their imprisonment renewed – this later became known as the 'Sobukwe Clause' – which resulted in him spending another six years on Robben Island. He was released in 1969 and joined his family in Kimberley, where he remained under twelve-hour house arrest and was restricted from participating in any political activity as a result of a banning order that had been imposed on the PAC. While in prison he studied law, and he established his own law firm in 1975.

South African Communist Party (also referred to as the Communist Party of South Africa)

Established in 1921 as the Communist Party of South Africa, to oppose imperialism and racist domination. Changed its name to the South African Communist Party in 1953 following its banning in 1950. The South African Communist Party was only legalised in 1990. The South African Communist Party forms one-third of the Tripartite Alliance with the ANC and Congress of South African Trade Unions.

South African Indian Congress

Founded in 1923 to oppose discriminatory laws. It comprised the Cape, Natal, and Transvaal Indian Congresses. Initially a conservative organisation whose actions were limited to petitions and deputations to authorities, a more radical leadership that favoured militant non-violent resistance came to power in the 1940s under the leadership of Yusuf Dadoo and Monty Naicker.

State of Emergency, 1960

Declared on 30 March 1960 as a response to the Sharpeville Massacre. Characterised by mass arrests and the imprisonment of most African leaders. On 8 April 1960 the ANC and PAC were banned under the Unlawful Organisations Act.

Suppression of Communism Act, No. 44, 1950

Act passed 26 June 1950, in which the state banned the South African Communist Party and any activities it deemed communist, defining 'communism' in such broad terms that anyone protesting against apartheid would be in breach of the Act.

Suzman, Helen

(1917–2009). Academic, politician, anti-apartheid activist, and MP. Professor of economic history, University of Witwatersrand. Founded a branch of the United Party at University of Witwatersrand in response to the apartheid state's racist policies. MP for the United Party, 1953–59, then later the anti-apartheid Progressive Federal Party (1961–74). The only opposition political leader who was permitted to visit Robben Island. She continuously raised the issue of political prisoners in Parliament and first met Mandela and his comrades on Robben Island in 1967.

Tambo (née Tshukudu), Matlala Adelaide Frances (also referred to as Matlala and sometimes spells it Matlale)

(1929–2007). Nurse, community worker, and anti-apartheid and women's rights activist. Married Oliver Tambo, 1956. Member of the ANC Youth League. Participated in the Women's March, 1956. Lived in exile in London, UK, until 1990. Recipient of numerous awards including the Order of Simon of Cyrene, July 1997, the highest order given by the Anglican Church for distinguished service by lay people; and the Order of the Baobab in Gold, 2002.

Tambo, Oliver Reginald (OR) (Also referred to as Reggie, Reginald)

(1917–93). Lawyer, politician, and anti-apartheid activist. Leading member of the ANC and founder member of the ANC Youth League. Co-founder, with Mandela, one of South Africa's first African legal practices. Became secretary-general of the ANC after Walter Sisulu was banned, and deputy president of the ANC, 1958. Served with a five-year banning order, 1959. Named as a co-conspirator in the Rivonia Trial. Left South Africa in 1960 to manage the external activities of the ANC and to mobilise opposition against apartheid. Established military training camps outside South Africa. Initiated the Free Mandela Campaign in the 1980s. Lived in exile in London, UK, until 1990. Acting president of the ANC, 1967, after the death of Chief Albert Luthuli. Was elected president in 1969 at the Morogoro Conference in Tanzania, a post he held until 1991 when he became the ANC's national chairperson. Awarded the ANC's highest honour, Isitwalandwe Seaparankoe, in 1992.

Thembu royal house
Nelson Mandela was a member of the Thembu royal house, descended from King Ngubengcuka (c.1790–1830) who united the Thembu nation before it was subjected to British colonial rule.

Timakwe, Nontancu Mabel
(1924-2002). Nelson Mandela's sister.

Transkei
Transkei is a region of South Africa in what is now the Eastern Cape province. During the apartheid era, under Mandela's nephew K. D. Matanzima it accepted nominal independence with the neighbouring Ciskei as a homeland or Bantustan set aside for people of Xhosa origin.

Treason Trial
(1956–61). The Treason Trial was the apartheid government's attempt to quell the power of the Congress Alliance. From 5 December 1956, 156 individuals were arrested and charged with high treason. By the end of the trial in March 1961 all the accused either had the charges withdrawn or, in the case of the last twenty-eight accused including Mandela, were acquitted.

Tutu, Archbishop Desmond
(1931–). Archbishop Emeritus and anti-apartheid and human rights activist. Bishop of Lesotho, 1976–78. First black general secretary of the South African Council of Churches, 1978. Following the 1994 election, he chaired the Truth and Reconciliation Commission to investigate apartheid-era crimes. Recipient of the 1984 Nobel Peace Prize for seeking a non-violent end to apartheid; the Albert Schweitzer Prize for Humanitarianism, 1986; and the Gandhi Peace Prize, 2005.

Tutu (née Shenxane), Nomalizo Leah
(1933–). The wife of Archbishop Desmond Tutu. They began dating while both were at St Thomas's Teacher Training College in Johannesburg. They married on 2 July 1955. The daughter of a domestic worker, she became an activist for the rights of South African domestic workers. The Desmond and Leah Tutu Legacy Foundation was established in 2007 to support initiatives that promote peace, reconciliation and Ubuntu.

Umkhonto weSizwe (MK)
Umkhonto weSizwe, meaning 'spear of the nation', was founded in 1961 and is commonly known by the abbreviation MK. Nelson Mandela was its first commander-in-chief. It became the military wing of the ANC. After the 1994 elections, MK was disbanded and its soldiers incorporated into the newly formed South African National Defence Force with soldiers from the apartheid South African Defence Force, Bantustan defence forces, Inkatha Freedom Party's self-protection units, and Azanian People's Liberation Army, the military wing of the Pan Africanist Congress.

University College of Fort Hare (UFH)

Originally the South African Native College, the University College of Fort Hare was founded on the site of an old fort through the initiative of the United Free Church of Scotland. Until 1960 it was the only university for blacks in the country. It offered training to students from all over Southern Africa and from as far afield as Kenya and Uganda. The National Party government took over control of the university from 1959 and turned it into an ethnic college for Xhosa speakers. Leaders such as Nelson Mandela, Robert Mugabe, Robert Sobukwe, Mangosuthu Buthelezi, and Oliver Tambo studied there.

University of South Africa (UNISA)

UNISA is one of the largest distance education institutions in the world, and the university through which Nelson Mandela achieved his LLB degree. After he was forced to end his studies through the University of London, he continued through UNISA and graduated, in absentia, in 1989. He was able to practise as a lawyer before he was imprisoned as, in those days, only a diploma in law was necessary.

Victor Verster Prison

Low-security prison located between Paarl and Franschhoek in the Western Cape. Mandela was transferred there in 1988, and lived in a private house inside the prison compound. There is a statue of Mandela just outside the prison gates. Now named Drakenstein Correctional Centre.

Wolsey Hall

Situated in Oxford, United Kingdom, and established in 1894, Wolsey Hall is a distance education provider which caters for students at various levels and through the University of London. Mandela began his correspondence LLB studies through the University of London.

Xaba, Niki Iris Jane Nondyebo

(1932–1985). Winnie Mandela's eldest sister who was detained at the same time as her in 1969. Then unmarried and called Iris Madikizela, she brought a case against the government to stop her and her fellow accused being assaulted.

Zami

(*See* Madikizela-Mandela, Nomzamo Winifred.)

Zeni

(*See* Mandela, Zenani.)

Zindzi

(*See* Mandela, Zindziswa.)

8115 Orlando West

In 1944 when Mandela married his first wife, Evelyn Mase, they were allocated a two-roomed house in Orlando East, Soweto, and early in 1947 they moved to a red-brick three-roomed matchbox house at number 8115 Orlando West. He also lived there with his second wife, Winnie Mandela. The South African government declared it a national heritage site in 1999 and it is now a museum.

PRISON TIMELINE

5 August 1962: Nelson Mandela, wearing a coat, cap, and dark glasses, is arrested along with his friend, Cecil Williams, at a roadblock at Cedara, a town outside Howick in KwaZulu-Natal. His twenty-seven and a half years in custody begins.

6 August 1962: Appears in court in the nearby town of Pietermaritzburg and is remanded to Johannesburg.

8 August 1962: Appears in the Johannesburg Magistrates Court in handcuffs. He is defended by attorney James Kantor. No evidence is led. He only admits his identity and is remanded until 16 August.

16 August 1962: Appears in the Johannesburg Magistrates Court wearing a jackal-skin kaross and is remanded for trial in the Johannesburg Regional Court.

15 October 1962: Transferred to Pretoria Local Prison. He appears in the Old Synagogue, Pretoria, which has been transformed into a 'Special Regional Court' for his trial. Mandela wears a jackal-skin kaross, shirt, khaki trousers, sandals, and a necklace in the yellow and green colours of the ANC. He complained that the last minute change of venue from Johannesburg to Pretoria was a deliberate attempt by the government to deprive him of his attorney Joe Slovo, who was restricted to Johannesburg.

22 October 1962: Makes an hour-long speech from the dock for the recusal of the magistrate, saying that as a 'black man in a white man's court' he would not get a fair trial. He pleads not guilty to incitement in connection with calling a national strike on 29, 30 and 31 May 1961, and leaving the country without a passport. Mandela conducted his own defence, and was assisted by advocate Bob Hepple.

7 November 1962: He is convicted of inciting workers to stay at home and on leaving the country without a passport, and is sentenced to five years in prison. He begins serving his sentence in Pretoria Local Prison.

27 May 1963: After being transferred without reason or warning, he arrives at Robben Island Maximum Security Prison.

12 June 1963: Transferred back to Pretoria Local Prison.

11 July 1963: Police raid his former hideout at Liliesleaf in the Johannesburg suburb of Rivonia. Many of his comrades are arrested and held in solitary-confinement detention.

9 October 1963: Mandela appears in the Palace of Justice in Pretoria for the first time with ten other accused in connection with 222 charges of sabotage committed between 1961 and 1965, in what becomes known as the Rivonia Trial. The case is remanded to 29 October.

29 October 1963: He and ten others are charged with 199 acts of sabotage in the Rivonia Trial. The defence applies for the indictment to be quashed.

30 October 1963: It is announced that one of the accused, Bob Hepple, will be called as a state witness. Charges against him are withdrawn and he is released. He did not testify and fled the country. The indictment against the remaining ten is quashed, but they are immediately rearrested in court and charged with 199 acts of sabotage.

12 November 1963: A new indictment splitting the sabotage charges into two parts is presented in the Rivonia Trial by prosecutor Percy Yutar to Mr. Justice Galgut. The case is remanded to 25 November.

26 November 1963: The 199 acts of sabotage are reduced to 193 and the defence applies to have the new indictment quashed. Justice de Wet dismisses the application.

3 December 1963: Mandela and nine fellow accused plead not guilty to sabotage and the first evidence is heard. The indictment lists 24 co-conspirators, 23 of which left the country, and one of whom died in police detention.

2 March 1964: The State's case comes to an end.

4 March 1964: Fellow accused James Kantor is acquitted.

20 April 1964: The defence case begins. Wearing a blue suit, Mandela makes a speech that lasts almost four hours, and famously ends it by saying that he is prepared to die for a non-racial, democratic South Africa.

11 June 1964: In a brief judgment, Judge Quartus de Wet convicts Nelson Mandela, Walter Sisulu, Govan Mbeki, Ahmed Kathrada, Denis Goldberg, Raymond Mhlaba, Elias Motsoaledi, and Andrew Mlangeni of sabotage. Rusty Bernstein is acquitted but is immediately rearrested on another charge.

12 June 1964: Alan Paton, president of the Liberal Party, gives evidence in mitigation of sentence for the accused. Judge Quartus de Wet sentences Mandela and seven others to life imprisonment. He says the offences were essentially 'treasonous' but that they have not been charged with treason.

13 June 1964: Nelson Mandela, Walter Sisulu, Govan Mbeki, Ahmed Kathrada, Raymond Mhlaba, Elias Motsoaledi, and Andrew Mlangeni arrive on Robben Island. (Denis Goldberg, because he is white, is sent to Pretoria Central Prison.)

24 September 1968:	His mother dies. His request to attend her funeral is refused.
13 July 1969:	His eldest son, Madiba Thembekile, is killed in a car accident. Mandela's letter to the prison authorities requesting permission to attend his funeral is ignored.
31 March 1982:	After almost eighteen years at Robben Island Maximum Security Prison, Mandela is transferred with Walter Sisulu, Raymond Mhlaba, and Andrew Mlangeni to Pollsmoor Maximum Security Prison at the foot of the mountains outside Cape Town. They held together in one large cell. On 21 October, Ahmed Kathrada joins them.
3 November 1985:	Mandela is admitted to the Volks Hospital in Cape Town for prostate surgery.
10 February 1985:	After rejecting an offer from President P. W. Botha to release him if he renounces violence as a political strategy, his statement of rejection is read out to a rally in Soweto by his daughter, Zindziswa.
17 November 1985:	Visited in hospital by South Africa's minister of justice, Kobie Coetsee, and the commissioner of prisons.
23 November 1985:	Discharged from the Volks Hospital and returned to Pollsmoor Prison, but held separately from his comrades. During this period he begins exploratory talks with members of the government over the creation of conditions for negotiations with the ANC.
11 June 1988:	A twelve-hour pop concert to celebrate Mandela's seventieth birthday, held at Wembley Stadium, London, UK, is broadcast to sixty-seven countries.
12 August 1988:	Admitted to Tygerberg Hospital in Bellville, Cape Town.
13 August 1988:	Diagnosed with tuberculosis and pleural effusion.
31 August 1988:	Transferred from Tygerberg Hospital to Constantiaberg Medi-Clinic, Cape Town, where his tuberculosis treatment continues.
7 December 1988:	Discharged from Constantiaberg MediClinic and transferred to Victor Verster Prison near Paarl where he is housed in a bungalow belonging to a former prison warder.
8 December 1988:	He is visited by Minister of Justice Kobie Coetsee who tells Mandela that it has been decided that he will be held in the house so that he can continue the discussions he began with government officials in 1986.
17 May 1989:	Graduates with an LLB degree in absentia at the University of South Africa.
5 July 1989:	Meets President P. W. Botha in his office in Cape Town.
15 October 1989:	The remaining Rivonia Trialists, apart from Mandela, are released from prison.

13 December 1989:	He is driven before dawn from prison to meet President F. W. de Klerk at his office in Cape Town.
9 February 1990:	He is taken to Tuynhuys in Cape Town to meet President F. W. de Klerk.
11 February 1990:	He is released from Victor Verster Prison at 4:22 p.m. He addresses a crowd from the balcony of the City Hall in Cape Town and spends the night at Archbishop Desmond Tutu's official residence in Bishopscourt.

MAP OF SOUTH AFRICA, *c.1996*

Pretoria
Monument Hill

East Rand
Benoni
Germiston
Kempton Park

Johannesburg
Bantu Men's
Social Centre
Braamfontein
Coronation
Hospital
Ferreirastown
Killarney
Milner Park
Moila
Nasrec

Soweto
Baragwanathan Hospital
Donaldson Orlando
Community Centre
Jabavu
Moroka

• Gazankulu

LIMPOPO

• Lebowa

• Nylstroom

Zeerust •

• Wolfsanschal
Mmabatho •
Mafikeng
NORTH WEST

PRETORIA
GAUTENG
• Wilbank

• Ogies   • Evaton
• Bethal
• Brakpan
• Boipatong

MPUMALANGA

MBABANE
• Manzini
SWAZILAND

Nelspruit •

• Hlati

Vryburg •
Klerksdorp •
• Potchefstroom

Standerton •

Kuruman •

• Kroonstad

Vryheid •

FREE STATE
Bethlehem •

Upington •

Griekwastad •
• Kimberley

Welkom •
Brandfort •
Phatakahle •

SOUTH
AFRICA

Bloemfontein •
Botshabelo •

MASERU
LESOTHO

Trust Feeds •
Greutville Reserve •
Huwick • Dhlanga •
Pietermaritzburg •

Kwazulu-Natal
Nongoma
Mahlabatini
Groutville
KwaDukuza
(formerly Stranger)
Umfolozi River
Mahlabatini
Inanda
uMgungundlovu
Imbali

• De Aar

NORTHERN CAPE

Port Shepstone •

Calvinia •
Victoria West •

Middelburg •

Euycobo •   Qutu •
Mghekezweni •
Mvezo • Tsolo •
Bityi
Mthatha
Baziya

Durban
Claremont
Cato Manor
Hammarsdale
Hillcrest
Sydenham
Umgeni Rd
Westville

Vanrhynsdorp •

Queenstown •

Beaufort West •

Craddock •
Fort Beaufort •
• Alice   • Bisho

Qumbu
Shawbury College

Grahamstown •

Cofimvaba
Decker's Hill
Qamata

WESTERN CAPE

Robben Island
Table Bay
Cape Town
Bellville
Constantiaberg
MediClinic
Mowbray
Retreat
Rondebosch
Tokai
Tygerberg
Hospital

• Worcester

Paarl •

• Oudtshoorn

• Swellendam

Simonstown •

Port Elizabeth •

East London •

Eastern Cape
Mbongweni
Ezibeleni
Bizana
Great Kei River
Butterworth
Matatiele
Sterkspruit
Qumanco
Mqanduli
Peddie

PROVINCE	CITY/TOWN/VILLAGE	DESCRIPTION
Eastern Cape	Mvezo	Mandela's birthplace.
	Qunu	Village where Mandela lived as a child and built a home after his release from prison.
	Mqhekezweni	The Great Place where Mandela moved to when he was around the age of nine.
	Engcobo	Clarkebury Boarding Institute where Mandela obtained his junior certificate.
	Fort Beaufort	Attended college at Healdtown.
	Alice	Attended University College of Fort Hare.
Gauteng	Johannesburg	Moved to Johannesburg in April 1941.
		Lived in Alexandra and Soweto before his imprisonment.
		Lived in Soweto and Houghton upon his release.
	Pretoria	Pretoria Central Prison, 1962–63, 1963–64.
		Location of his trial in 1962 and the Rivonia Trial.
	Sharpeville	Sharpeville Massacre, 21 March 1960.
	Rivonia	Liliesleaf Farm, the underground safe house.
KwaZulu-Natal	Pietermaritzburg	All-In African Conference, 22 March 1961.
	Howick	Arrested, 5 August 1962.
Western Cape	Robben Island	Imprisoned on Robben Island for two weeks from May 1963, and for eighteen years from 13 June 1964 to 30 March 1982.
	Cape Town	Imprisoned at Pollsmoor Prison, March 1982 to August 1988.
		Treated at Tygerberg Hospital, 1988.
		Treated at Constantiaberg MediClinic, 1988.
	Paarl	Held at Victor Verster Prison, December 1988 to 11 February 1990.

When South Africa's first democratically elected government came to power in 1994, the government reorganised the ten existing Bantustans, or homelands, and the four existing provinces into nine smaller fully integrated provinces as shown on this map. The four provinces that existed from 1910–94 were reorganised into the new provinces as follows:

OLD PROVINCES	NEW PROVINCES
Cape Province	Eastern Cape
	Northern Cape
	Western Cape
Natal	KwaZulu-Natal
Orange Free State	Free State
Transvaal	North West
	Limpopo
	Mpumalanga
	Gauteng

ENDNOTES

1   Mac Maharaj (ed.), *Reflections in Prison*, (Cape Town: Robben Island Museum and Zebra Press, 2001), p. xi.
2   Nelson Mandela, summarised statement minuted at Robben Island Prison, Robben Island, 11 December 1978.
3   Robert Vassen, 'Life as a Political Prisoner', South Africa: Overcoming Apartheid, Building Democracy, a project of MATRIX: The Center for Humane Arts, Letters, and Social Sciences; the African Studies Center; and the Department of History, Michigan State University, http://overcomingapartheid. msu.edu/sidebar.php?id=65-258-8&page=3.
4   Walter Sisulu, introduction to *Letters from Robben Island*, Ahmed Kathrada (ed. Robert D. Vassen) (Cape Town: Mayibuye Books and East Lansing: Michigan State University Press, 1999), p. xvi.
5   Eddie Daniels, *There and Back: Robben Island 1964-1979* (Cape Town: CTP Book Printers, third edition, 2002), p. 160.
6   NM in conversation with Richard Stengel, Johannesburg, 14 December 1992, CD 6, Nelson Mandela Foundation, Johannesburg.
7   Eddie Daniels, *There and Back: Robben Island 1964-1979*, p. 160.
8   Elinor Sisulu, *In Our Lifetime: Walter & Albertina Sisulu* (Cape Town: David Philip Publishers, 2002), p. 200.
9   NM, summarised statement minuted at Robben Island Prison, Robben Island, 11 December 1978.
10 See his letter to the commissioner of prisons dated 12 July 1976 on page 288, reference page 293.
11 Michael Dingake, 'Comrade Madiba' in *Nelson Mandela: The Struggle is My Life*, (London: Idaf, 1986), p. 224.
12 Ibid.
13 Ibid.
14 Ibid., pp. 224–5.
15 Ibid., p. 225.
16 Ibid.
17 NM, speech at the 46664 Concert, Cape Town, 29 November 2003, http://db.nelson-mandela.org/speeches/pub_view.asp?p-g=item&ItemID=NMS950&txtstr=46664.
18 NM in conversation with Richard Stengel, Johannesburg, 16 April 1993, CD 51, Nelson Mandela Foundation, Johannesburg.
19 'Mandela Wins Week's Adjournment', *Cape Times*, 16 October 1962.
20 NM, speech to the court, Old Synagogue, Pretoria, 22 October 1962, http://db.nelson-mandela.org/speeches/pub_view.asp?p-g=item&ItemID=NMS011&txtstr=recusal.
21 NM in conversation with Richard Stengel, 16 and 17 April 1993, CD 52, Nelson Mandela Foundation, Johannesburg.
22 Bob Hepple, *Young Man With a Red Tie: A Memoir of Mandela and the Failed Revolution, 1960–1963* (Johannesburg: Jacana, 2013), p. 48.
23 'Mandela Gets 5 Years: Described as Master-mind', *The Argus*, 7 November 1962.
24 'Shouts, Clenched Fists, Songs, as Mandela is Gaoled, *Cape Times*, 8 November 1962.
25 Ibid.
26 For the Pan Africanist Congress (PAC) see the glossary.
27 'Mandela is Asked Not to Become "Difficult"', *Rand Daily Mail*, 25 October 1962.
28 NM in conversation with Richard Stengel, Johannesburg, 16 April 1993, CD 51, Nelson Mandela Foundation, Johannesburg.
29 NM in conversation with Richard Stengel, Johannesburg, 3 December 1992, CD 2,

Nelson Mandela Foundation, Johannesburg.

30 NM in conversation with Richard Stengel, Johannesburg, 16 and 17 April 1993, CD 52, Nelson Mandela Foundation, Johannesburg.

31 NM, *Long Walk to Freedom* (London: Abacus, 2013), p. 414.

32 Ibid.

33 Joel Joffe, *The State vs. Nelson Mandela: The Trial that Changed South Africa* (London: One World Publications, 2007) p. 41.

34 Ibid., p. 42.

35 Ibid., p. 42.

36 'Sir Bob Hepple Obituary', *The Guardian*, 26 August 2015, https://www.theguardian.com/law/2015/aug/26/sir-bob-hepple.

37 NM, *Long Walk to Freedom*, p. 33.

38 Ibid., p. 444.

39 Ibid., p. 447.

40 NM in conversation with Richard Stengel, Johannesburg, 3 December 1992, CD 2, Nelson Mandela Foundation, Johannesburg.

41 Christo Brand, *Doing Life with Mandela* (Johannesburg: Jonathan Ball, 2014), p. 46.

42 Indres Naidoo, as told to Albie Sachs, *Island in Chains: Ten Years on Robben Island by Prisoner 885/63* (Harmondsworth: Penguin Books, 1982), p. 87.

43 Mac Maharaj, 'Interview with Mac Maharaj', 1978, in *The Struggle is My Life*, p. 208.

44 Ibid.

45 NM, *Long Walk to Freedom*, p. 458.

46 NM in conversation with Richard Stengel, Johannesburg, c. March 1993, CD 21, Nelson Mandela Foundation, Johannesburg.

47 Ibid.

48 Ibid.

49 Mac Maharaj, telephone conversation with Sahm Venter, 27 June 2017.

50 Winnie Madikizela Mandela (eds. Sahm Venter and Zamawazi Dlamini Mandela), *491 Days: Prisoner Number 1323/69* (Johannesburg: Picador Africa, 2013), p. 25.

51 Joel Carlson, *No Neutral Ground* (London: Davis-Poynter Ltd, 1973), p. 291.

52 NM, *Long Walk to Freedom*, p. 682.

53 Ibid, p. 120.

54 Ahmed Kathrada and Sahm Venter, *Conversations with a Gentle Soul* (Johannesburg: Picador Africa, 2017), p. 87.

55 *Mandela v Minister of Prisons* [1981] 3 All SA 449 (A) in the Cape of Good Hope Provincial Division.

56 NM, *Long Walk to Freedom*, p. 568.

57 Ibid, p. 624.

58 Ibid., p. 608.

59 Ibid., pp. 624–25.

60 Ibid., p. 625.

61 NM in conversation with Richard Stengel, Johannesburg, 8 February 1993, CD 19, Nelson Mandela Foundation, Johannesburg.

62 NM, *Long Walk to Freedom*, p. 646.

63 NM in conversation with Richard Stengel, 8 February 1993, CD 19, Nelson Mandela Foundation, Johannesburg.

64 NM, *Long Walk to Freedom*, p. 647.

65 NM in conversation with Richard Stengel, c. 2 and 3 February 1993, CD 17, Nelson Mandela Foundation, Johannesburg.

66 Ibid.

67 Jack Swart, telephone conversation with Sahm Venter, 7 September 2017.

68 Padraig O'Malley, *Shades of Difference: Mac Maharaj and the Struggle for South Africa* (New York: Viking, 2007), p. 312.

69 Ibid., p. 313.

70 NM, *Long Walk to Freedom*, p. 618.

LETTERS AND COLLECTIONS

The letters in this book come from various collections, including the notebooks Mandela transcribed his letters into and the Himan Bernadt Collection, as follows:

Nelson Mandela Prison Archive, National Archives and Records Service of South Africa:
commanding officer, Pretoria Local – 23 Sept 1963; commanding officer, Pretoria Local – 8 October 1963; commanding officer, Pretoria Local – 25 October 1963; Frank, Bernadt & Joffe – 15 June 1964; Bram Fischer – 2 August 1964; commanding officer Robben Island – 30 November 1964; Major Visser – 25 August 1965; commissioner of prisons – 10 October 1965; Winnie Mandela – 17 February 1966; University of South Africa – 22 August 1966; American Society of International Law – 31 August 1966; commanding officer, Robben Island – 8 September 1966; Cecil Eprile – 11 February 1967; commanding officer – 27 February 1967; Frank, Bernadt & Joffe – 21 March 1967; Joel Carlson [1967]; registrar of the Supreme Court – 6 December 1967; Adelaide Tambo – 5 March 1968; commanding officer – 29 April 1967; British Embassy – 29 April 1968; commanding officer, Robben Island –16 September 1968; K. D. Matanzima – 14 October 1968; Knowledge Guzana – 14 October 1968; Mangosuthu Buthelezi – 4 November 1968; commanding officer, Robben Island – 28 February 1969; minister of justice – 22 April 1969; Brigadier Aucamp – 5 August 1969; London University – 1 October 1969; commanding officer, Robben Island – 9 October 1969; London University – 18 November 1969; commanding officer, Robben Island – 2 April 1970; commanding officer, Robben Island – 20 April 1970; commanding officer, Robben Island – 29 May 1970; commanding officer, Robben Island – 2 June 1970; Nkosikazi Nokukhanya Luthuli – 8 June 1970; Winnie Mandela – 20 June 1970; commanding officer, Robben Island – 24 December 1970; medical officer, Robben Island – 24 December 1970; commanding officer – 31 March 1971; commanding officer, Robben Island – 4 April 1971; commanding officer, Robben Island – 14 June 1971; Vanguard Booksellers – 26 September 1971; commanding officer, Robben Island – 27 March 1972; Winnie Mandela – 1 June 1972; commanding officer, Robben Island – 7 March 1973; commanding officer, Robben Island – 7 March 1973; Helen Suzman – 1 March 1974; minister of justice – 13 May 1974; minister of justice – 25 May 1974; West Rand Board – 18 June 1974; commanding officer, Robben Island – 26 June 1974; commanding officer, Robben Island – 1 December 1974; Winnie Mandela – 1 February 1975; minister of justice – 12 February 1975; Yusuf Dadoo – 1 November 1975; commanding officer, Robben Island – 15 December 1975; commissioner of prisons – 23 January 1976; D. B. Alexander – 1 March 1976; Felicity Kentridge – 9 May 1976; commanding officer, Robben Island – 12 July 1976; commissioner of prisons – 12 July 1976; commanding officer, Robben Island – 18 August 1976; Winnie Mandela – 18 August 1976; Winnie Mandela – 19 August 1976; Winnie Mandela – 1 September 1976; Winnie Mandela – 1 October 1976; commanding officer, Robben Island – 7 October 1976; commanding officer, Robben Island – 12 October 1976; Thorobetsane Tshukudu (Adelaide Tambo) – 1 January 1977; head of prison – 19 May 1977; Nobulile Thulare – 19 July 1977; Duma Nokwe (Gcwanini Miya) – 1 July 1977; Zenani and Muzi Dlamini – 24 July 1977; Zindzi Mandela and Oupa Seakamela – 24 July 1977; head of prison, Robben Island – 18 September 1977; Winnie Mandela – 4 December 1977; commissioner of prisons – 6 December 1977; head of prison – 16 January 1978; Marie Naicker – 1 October 1978; Mangosuthu Buthelezi – 1 October 1978; head of prison – 2 October 1978; minister of justice – 23 October 1978; Zindzi Mandela – 26 November 1978; Ndileka Mandela – 21 January 1979; Winnie Mandela – 21 January 1979; Makaziwe Mandela – 13 May 1979; head of prison, Robben Island – 20 May 1979; Alan Paton – 29 July 1979; Winnie Mandela – 2 September 1979; minister of police and prisons – 4 September 1979; commanding officer, Robben Island – 19 November 1979; Zindzi Mandela – 9 December 1979; head of prison, Robben Island – 23 December 1979; Denis Healey – 8 January 1980; Zindzi Mandela – 27 January 1980; minister of education – 1 February 1980; Zindzi Mandela – 10 February 1980; Dullah Omar – 1 June 1980; Winnie Mandela – 30 July 1980; Zindzi Mandela – 1 March 1981; Winnie Mandela – 26 April 1981; Petronella Ferus – 3 May 1981; Camagwini Madikizela – 15 November 1981; Dr. Ayesha Arnold – 15 November 1981; Major-General Coetzee –

27 November 1981; head of prison, Pollsmoor – 20 April 1982; head of prison, Pollsmoor – 21 January 1983; head of prison, Pollsmoor – 25 February 1983; Russel Piliso – 29 June 1983; commissioner of prisons – 6 October 1983; Trevor Tutu – 6 August 1984 ; Winnie Mandela – 29 December 1984; Ismail Meer – 29 January 1985; P. W. Botha – 13 February 1985; Sheena Duncan – 1 April 1985; Archie Gumede – 1 July 1985 (from 1975); Archie Gumede – 8 July 1975; Victoria Mxenge – 8 July 1985; Nolinda Mgabela – 8 July 1985; University of South Africa – 15 October 1985; Winnie Mandela – 5 December 1985; Dr. Dumisane Mzamane – 17 December 1985; commissioner of prisons – 4 February 1986; Joy Motsieloa – 17 February 1986; Tukwini, Dumani and Kweku – date unknown; K. D. Matanzima – 19 May 1986; head of prison, Pollsmoor – 6 October 1986; Nontancu Mabel Timakwe – 18 February 1987; Frieda Matthews – 25 February 1987; Kepu Mkentane – 25 February 1987; Mandla Mandela – 9 July 1987; Nandi Mandela – 17 August 1987; Zindzi Mandela – 31 August 1987; Mamphela Ramphele – 1 March 1988; head of prison, Pollsmoor – 29 August 1988; Prof. W. J. Hosten – 25 November 1988; Nandi Mandela – 5 December 1988; Zoleka and Zondwa Mandela – 5 December 1988; Zaziwe, Zamaswazi and Zinhle – 5 December 1988; head of prison – 5 December 1988; Prof. W. J. Hosten – 23 December 1988; Archie Gumede – 10 January 1989; Archbishop and Mrs. Tutu – 17 January 1989; Rev. Austen Massey – 17 January 1989; Mangosuthu Buthelezi – 3 February 1989; Elaine Kearns – 14 February 1989; Dumani Mandela – 28 February 1989; Kwedi Mkalipi – 28 February 1989; Eddie Daniels – 28 February 1989; Alan Boesak – 28 February 1989; Amina Cachalia – 28 February 1989; Sipho Sepamla – 28 February 1989; Candie Lawless – 4 April 1989; Sir Robin Renwick – 10 April 1989; Mike Tyson – 10 May 1989; Rev. Frank Chikane – 10 May 1989; Mrs E. N. Mbekeni – 10 May 1989; Helen Suzman – 22 May 1989; Richard Maponya – 28 June 1989; acting paramount chief; Mdayelwa Mtirara – 4 July 1989; commissioner of prisons – 17 July 1989; Tim Wilson – 23 July 1989; Adelaide Tambo – 14 August 1989; Makhi Dalasile – 14 August 1989; Rev. Abel & Freda Hendricks – 15 August 1989; Desmond and Leah Tutu – 21 August 1989; Adelaide Tambo – 21 August 1989; J. N. and Radhi Singh – 21 August 1989; Mary Benson – 21 August 1989; Helen Joseph – 21 August 1989; Cyril Ramaphosa – 21 August 1989; Amina and Peter Frense – 21 August 1989; commissioner of prisons – 11 September 1989; Connie Njongwe – 18 September 1989; Frieda Matthews – 18 September 1989; Kepu Mkentane – 18 September 1989; Mamphela Ramphele – 18 September 1989; Rashid and Ayesha Kola – 25 September 1989; The secretary POTWA – 25 September 1989; Fatima Meer – 28 September 1989; Madanjit and Marjorie Kapitan – 28 September 1989; Winnie Mandela – 9 October 1980; commanding officer, Victor Verster – 9 October 1989; commissioner of prisons – 10 October 1989; commissioner of prisons – 16 October 1989; Sheikh Nazeem Mohamed – 23 October 1989; Rev. T. S. N. Gqubule – 23 October 1989; Ntsiki Sisulu – 23 October 1989; Len and Beryl Simelane – 21 November 1989; chief Zonwabile Sandile Mtirara – 6 November 1989; Fatima Meer – 6 November 1989; commissioner of prisons – 22 January 1990; commissioner of prisons – 2 February 1990; commissioner of prisons – 11 February 1990.

The books into which Mandela transcribed his letters (the Donald Card Collection housed at the Nelson Mandela Foundation): Zenani and Zindzi Mandela – 4 February 1969; Makaziwe Mandela – 16 February 1969; Lilian Ngoyi – 3 March 1969; Gibson Kente – 3 March 1969; Chief Mthetho Matanzima – 17 March 1969; Winnie Mandela – 2 April 1969; P. K. Madikizela – 4 May 1969; Zenani and Zindzi Mandela – 23 June 1969; Winnie Mandela – 23 June 1969; Niki Xaba – 15 July 1969; Tellie Mtirara – 15 July 1969; Winnie Mandela – 16 July 1969; Evelyn Mandela – 16 July 1969; Col. Van Aarde – 22 July 1969; Makgatho Mandela – 28 July 1969; Sefton Vutela – 28 July 1969; Zenani and Zindzi Mandela – 3 August 1969; Irene Buthelezi – 3 August 1969; Nomfundo Mandela – 8 September 1969; Nolusapho Irene Mkwayi – 29 September 1969; Adelaide Sam Mase – 3 November 1969; Winnie Mandela – 16 November 1969; Paul Mzaidume – 19 November 1969; Thoko Mandela – 29 November 1969; Chief Nkosiyane – 1 January 1970; Winnie Mandela – 21 January 1970; Adelaide Tambo – 31 January 1970; Marshall Xaba – 3 February 1970; Tellie Mandela – 6 March 1970; Makgatho Mandela – 31 March 1970; Makaziwe Mandela – 1 May 1970; Leabie Piliso – 1 May 1970; Winnie Mandela – 20 June 1970; Winnie Mandela 1 August 1970; Senator Douglas Lukhele – 1 August 1970; Winnie Mandela – 31 August 1970; Makgatho Mandela – 31 August 1970; minister of justice – 14 September 1970; Winnie Mandela – 1 October 1970; minister of justice 19 November 1970; Sanna Teyise – 1 December 1970; Winnie Mandela – 28 December 1970; Joyce Sikhakhane – 1 January 1971;

Nomabutho Bhala – 1 January 1971; commanding officer, Robben Island – 2 January 1971; Tim Maharaj – 1 February 1971; Ishmael and Mohla Matlakhu – 1 February 1971; Zenani Mandela – 1 March 1971; Christine Scholtz – 1 March 1971, Thoko Mandela 1 April 1971; 'Sisi' – 1 April 1971.

The Himan Bernadt Collection housed at the Nelson Mandela Foundation: The Liquidator – 23 October 1967; Frank, Bernadt & Joffe – 20 May 1969; Frank, Bernadt & Joffe – 21 January 1977.

The private collections of: Amnesty International: The Secretary Amnesty – 6 November 1962; Amina Cachalia: Amina Cachalia – 12 December 1977, Amina Cachalia – 26 October 1980; Nick Carter: Ray Carter – 4 March 1985; Meyer de Waal: Adele de Waal – 29 August 1983; Michael Dingake: Michael Dingake – 24 April 1986; Fatima Meer: Fatima Meer – 1 March 1971, Fatima Meer – 1 November 1974, Fatima Meer – 1 January 1976, Fatima Meer – 30 January 1984; Morabo Morojele: Lionel Ngakane – 1 April 1985; Coen Stork: Coen Stork – 11 June 1964; Emily Wellman: Peter Wellman – 27 May 1979.

ACKNOWLEDGEMENTS

We are grateful to Zamaswazi Dlamini-Mandela for her invaluable assistance on this book and for her beautiful foreword. As she says, *The Prison Letters of Nelson Mandela* helps us understand how people like her grandfather who were 'caught opposing the apartheid government's system to oppress an entire race of people, endured terrible punishments'.

This is so much more than the collected words of an imprisoned freedom fighter and world icon, and greater than the work of an editor and an associate editor. It is the result of a sustained collective effort over many years.

The long journey to publication began in 2006 when Verne Harris, Nelson Mandela Foundation director of archive and dialogue, approached Nelson Mandela for permission to access the letters written during his twenty-seven years in prison with a view to publishing them some day. He assigned Anthea Josias the task of cataloguing everything in the scores of boxes that comprise Mandela's prison record at the National Archives and Records Service of South Africa. In the next stage, I went through the correspondence to identify all his letters to family and friends. During this research, I discovered a range of compelling official letters to and from prison officials and various institutions, many of which appear in this collection. Gerrit Wagenaar, Natalie Skomolo, and Zahira Adam worked tirelessly to assist in the copying of the letters.

The task of collating and transcribing the letters took years, and in the process other letters were unearthed, both in the archive of Mandela's personal papers at the Nelson Mandela Foundation and in private collections. Our thanks go particularly to Nicholas Carter, Meyer de Waal, Michael and Sithembile Dingake, Emily Wellman, and Morabo Morojele for offering us letters we had previously not seen. Amnesty International gave us a copy of a letter we were unaware of, which Mandela wrote in 1962 and which is housed in its London archive. The late Coen Stork gave us the letter Mandela wrote to him in 1964. The late Himan Bernadt, who was one of Mandela's lawyers while he was in prison, donated his papers to the Nelson Mandela Foundation. In 2004, a former security policeman, Donald Card, handed back to Mandela the two hardcover books containing copies of his letters which he had kept for decades after they had been confiscated from his prison cell. They are now housed at the Nelson Mandela Foundation.

We also deeply appreciate the assistance from Vanessa van Copenhagen and the executors of Madiba's estate, Archbishop Emeritus Desmond Tutu, Chief Mangosuthu Buthelezi, the Rev. Frank Chikane, Dr Richard Maponya, Tumeka Matanzima, Xoliswa Matanzima Jozana, Nqaba Ngoyi, Vicky Kente, Duma and Thandeka Gqubule, Trevor Tutu, Anant Singh, Shamim Meer, Her Excellency Nomvuyo Nokwe, Joyce Sikhakhane Rabkin, Ilse Wilson, Tim Wilson, Nosizwe Macamo, Nina Jones and Sanja Gohre.

Mandela did not write only in English, some of the letters included in this collection were written in his mother tongue of isiXhosa and some in Afrikaans. We are grateful to the following people for their translation skills: Pumeza Gwija, Luzuko Koti, Diketso Mufamadi, Vukile Pokwana, Benjamin Harris, Nosisa Tiso, and Jeannie Adams. Thanks also to those who translated various terms in other languages as well as identifying individuals and explaining cultural practices and historical events: Zanele Riba, Florence Garishe, Razia Saleh, Ramni Dinath, Fred Khumalo, Zubeida Jaffer, Siraj Desai, Jimi Matthews, and Zohra Kathrada Areington.

It was a mammoth task to identify individuals and other details in the letters, and without the assistance of many people the supplementary information would not have been as rich as it is. Mac Maharaj never refused one request for information and spent considerable time providing much detail of prison life and of individuals.

Others who did not hesitate to pitch in when we requested their help were John Allen, Edwin Arrison, Christo Brand, Belinda Bozzoli, Laloo Chiba, Tony Eprile, Dali Tambo, Andile Xaba and Sino Xaba, the family of Dr. Gordon Handelsman, Sharon Gelman, Bobby Heaney, Carmen Heydenreich, Willie Hofmeyr, Stanley Kawalsky, Libby Lloyd, Sam Mabale, Mosie Moolla, Saleem Mowzer, Nthabiseng Msomi, Bruce Murray, Prema Naidoo, Shirona Patel, Greta Soggot, Faiza Sujee, Jack Swart, Luli Callinicos and Lyndith Waller. We are also indebted to Zodwa Zwane, Lucia Raadschelders, Claude Colart, Zandile Myeka, Lerato Tshabalala, Khalil Goga, Joe Ditabo, Mongezi Njaju, Sophia Molelekoa, Kerileng Marumo, Tshwarelo Mphatudi, Mark Seftel, Ntsiki Sisulu, Beryl Lockman and Effie Seftel.

Robert Weil of W. W. Norton & Company waited patiently for years after he first expressed a desire to publish the letters and provided wonderful support. Ruth Hobday and Geoff Blackwell of Blackwell & Ruth joined the partnership to publish this book and gave it wings. We are indebted to Rachel Clare's exceptional and thorough editing and dedication to this book, Cameron Gibb for his handsome design and Elizabeth Blackwell for her assistance.

Sello Hatang, the chief executive of the Nelson Mandela Foundation, encouraged this book from the beginning and continues to use every opportunity to promote it. We would be remiss in not thanking the rest of the Nelson Mandela Foundation team who have all contributed in different ways to this publication. They are Ethel Arends, Victoria Collis-Buthelezi, Lee Davies, Maeline Engelbrecht, Fikile Gama, Yase Godlo, Heather Henriques, Sumaya Hendricks, Lungelo Khanyile, Gregory Katsoras, Lesego Maforah, Ann-Young Maharaj, Aletta Makgaleng, Clive Maluleke, Palesa Manare, Namile Mchunu, Koketso Mdawo, Limpho Monyamane, Kholofelo Monyela, Kealeboga Morembe, Lunga Nene, Eric Nhlengetwa, Patronella Nqaba, Buyi Sishuba, Lindiwe Skhosana, Morongoa Thobakgale, Given Tuck, Noreen Wahome, and Louisa Zondo.

Members of the Mandela family generously helped with identifying people mentioned in the letters. Winnie Madikizela-Mandela was exceptional and spent many hours assisting us. HRH Princess Zenani Dlamini-Mandela, Her Excellency Ms. Zindziswa Mandela, and Ndileka Mandela also gave us essential information. We would also like to thank other members of the Mandela family, Nandi Mandela, Makaziwe Mandela, Tukwini Mandela, Kweku Mandela, Dumani Mandela, Zinhle Dlamini, Zaziwe Manaway, Zoleka Mandela, Chief Zwelivelile Mandela, and Nolusapho Rayne Rose Mandela.

Nelson Mandela's pain at being separated from his family runs prominently through this valuable chronicle, as does his recognition of their own suffering during those twenty-seven years. We owe them all our deep gratitude.

Sahm Venter
Editor

PERMISSIONS ACKNOWLEDGEMENTS

We are grateful for permission to reproduce the following items.

Extract from 'Interview with Mac Maharaj', *Nelson Mandela: The Struggle is My Life* (London: International Defence and Aid Fund for Southern Africa, 1978), used by permission of Mac Maharaj. Extract from 'Comrade Madiba', *Nelson Mandela: The Struggle is My Life* (London: International Defence and Aid Fund for Southern Africa, 1978), used by permission of Michael Dingake. Extract from *Young Man With a Red Tie: A Memoir of Mandela and the Failed Revolution*, 1960–1963 by Bob Hepple (Johannesburg: Jacana Media, 2013), used with permission. Extracts from 'Shouts, Clenched Fists, Songs, as Mandela is Gaoled' *Cape Times*, 8 November 1962, used with permission. Extracts from *The State Vs. Nelson Mandela: The Trial that Changed South Africa* by Joel Joffe (London: OneWorld Publications, 2007), used with permission. Extract from *Island in Chains: Ten Years on Robben Island by Prisoner 885/63* by Indres Naidoo (Joahnnesburg, Penguin Books, 2012), used with permission. Extracts from *Saving Nelson Mandela: The Rivonia Trial and the Fate of South Africa* by Kenneth S Braun (USA: Oxford University Press, 2012), used with permission. Extract from *Black As I Am* by Zindzi Mandela (Los Angeles: Guild of Tutors Press, 1978), used by permission of Zindzi Mandela. Extracts from recordings of Nelson Mandela in conversation with Richard Stengel (Johannesburg: Nelson Mandela Foundation, 1992–3), copyright © Nelson R. Mandela, used by permission of Nelson Mandela Foundation. Extracts from *Long Walk to Freedom* by Nelson Mandela (Abacus: London, 2013), copyright © Nelson R. Mandela, used by permission of Nelson Mandela Foundation, Johannesburg. Extract from *491 Days: Prisoner Number 1323/69* by Winnie Madikizela-Mandela (eds. Sahm Venter and Zamawazi Dlamini Mandela) (Johannesburg: Picador Africa, 2013), used by permission of Winnie Madikizela-Mandela.

Front endpaper, pages 8–9, 18–19 and back endpaper Matthew Willman; pages xviii–1: Nelson Mandela Prison Archive, National Archives and Records Service of South Africa; pages 430–1 Mikhael Subotzky, Installation view: 'Die Vier Hoeke' exhibition, in the Nelson Mandela Cell, Pollsmoor Prison, South Africa, 2005, courtesy of the artist and Goodman Gallery; pages 502–3 Getty Images/TSJ MERLYN LICENSING BV/Gallo Images; pages 510–1 Getty Images/Matthew Willman; pages 572–3 Nelson Mandela Foundation.

Photographs of letters: pages ii–iii, 78, 108–9, 135–8 and 194 Donald Card Collection housed at the Nelson Mandela Foundation, photographs by Ardon Bar-Hama; pages 36–7, 252–3, 256–7, 260–1, 263, 313, 320–1, 394, 406–7, 448–9, 453, 472–3 and 562 Nelson Mandela Prison Archive, National Archives and Records Service of South Africa; page 92 Himan Bernadt Collection housed at the Nelson Mandela Foundation, photograph by Ardon Bar-Hama; page 7 Amnesty International, courtesy Nelson Mandela Foundation; and page 17 Coen Stork, courtesy Nelson Mandela Foundation.

Colour plates: plate 1: Herbert Shore, courtesy Ahmed Kathrada Foundation (top); Eli Weinberg, University of Western Cape – Robben Island Museum Mayibuye Archives (bottom); plate 2: Matthew Willman – Robben Island Museum Mayibuye (top); Nelson Mandela Prison Archive, National Archives and Records Service of South Africa (bottom); plate 3: Nelson Mandela Prison Archive, National Archives and Records Service of South Africa; plates 4–5: Donald Card Collection housed at the Nelson Mandela Foundation, photograph by Ardon Bar-Hama; 6–7: Nelson Mandela Prison Archive, National Archives and Records Service of South Africa; and plate 8: Cloete Breytenbach/*Daily Express* (top), Nelson Mandela Prison Archive, National Archives and Records Service of South Africa (bottom).

INDEX

Page numbers beginning with 574 refer to glossary.